D1483537

environmentalism

T O'Riordan

Research in Planning and Design

Series editor Allen J Scott

1 **Place and placelessness** E Relph
2 **Environmentalism** T O'Riordan
3 **The 'new' urban economics** H W Richardson
4 **The automated architect** N Cross

Pion Limited, 207 Brondesbury Park, London NW2 5JN

environmentalism

T O'Riordan

Pion Limited, 207 Brondesbury Park, London NW2 5JN

© 1976 Pion Limited

All rights reserved. No part of this book may be reproduced in any form by photostat microfilm or any other means without written permission from the publishers.

ISBN 0 85086 056 3

Printed in Great Britain

They tell a story of a man who asked a socially conscious friend: "If you had two houses, what would you do with them?"

"Keep one and give the other to the State", the friend replied.

"If you had two cows what would you do with them?", the first man asked.

"Keep one and give the other to the State", the friend replied.

"If you had two chickens, what would you do with them?", the first man persisted.

"Keep them both", the friend replied.

"Why?", the first man asked.

"Because I *have* two chickens", the friend replied.

Varindra Tarzie Vittachi
Executive Secretary
World Population Year, 1974

Contents

Preface

When the publishers of my previous book *Perspectives on Resource Management* (O'Riordan, 1971a) informed me that the first printing had all but sold out, I readily took up their suggestion for a complete revision. For I was acutely conscious of the failings of that work, particularly its backward looking philosophy and the narrowness of its scope. In part, I suppose, this criticism reflects my own intellectual immaturity at the time, but it also indicates the speed and direction of events that have revolutionised the field of environmentalism during the past five years. The ripples have expanded far and wide, penetrating the reaches of political and social philosophy, moral and ethical ideology, politics, planning, education, and the law. With the acuity of hindsight I know now that these modulations in environmental philosophy and practice were emerging as I wrote *Perspectives* in the summer of 1969, but the message was not really driven home until I had read and discussed with Robert Kates his review of the book. "The theory of the sixties", he observed (Kates, 1972, p.519), "is primarily economic theory, and the theory to explain the environmental crisis relies upon the concept of externalities in the productive process. And despite the current heroic effort to weld thermodynamics and economics into a general equilibrium model of material flows, all existing economic theory, capitalist or otherwise, presupposes the existence of scarcity, the rightness of growth and the conquest of nature. One seeks in vain for a theory to explain adequately the existence of hunger and gluttony, to rechannelize growth and redistribution, and to define the limits, not of the earth, but of human dominance."

As this was being written the western world was entering the final spurt of a whole generation of virtually uninterrupted growth. Between 1950 and 1973 the industrial output of western nations more than quadrupled—a rate four times as fast as the doubling in real economic activity during the period 1900–1950—and growth in real personal wealth improved the demonstrable affluence of some 25% of the world's peoples by between two and four percent every year (*Economist*, December 28, 1974, p.41). Throughout this boom period raw material prices (including energy) declined both in relative and in real terms (Landsberg, 1974a, p.35; Nordhaus, 1974b, p.24) to the point where market prices were clearly depressed below their true worth. This was a bonanza period for the wealthy nations which were obtaining their raw materials 'on the cheap', while selling their high value added products dearly to the third world through discriminatory trading arrangements (World Development Movement, 1972; Elliott, 1973; Müller, 1973; Commonwealth Secretariat, 1975).

If proof was ever required, this situation demonstrated that market forces do not determine commodity prices; these are subject to political intervention by governments, to unfair trading agreements and to the carefully prepared plans of oligopolies (Galbraith, 1973, pp.164–174; Barnet and Müller, 1974). The consequence was a massive surge in the demand for all types of raw materials plus a general disregard for careful conservation in use, because cheap commodity inputs encouraged the substitution of nonreusable energy and machines for labour. Continuous improvements in economic well-being unleashed a consumer demand of considerable proportions in all areas of the economy, a demand that was constantly being fed by product innovations, changes of fashion, social mobility, and increasingly effective advertising.

All this resulted in unusually rapid rates of resource consumption in the western world during the late sixties and early seventies. To take the United States as an example, protein consumption rose at between 1% and 3% *per capita* per year (Brown, 1973, p.28), timber demand at 3% *per capita* per year (US, President's Advisory Panel on Timber and the Environment, 1973, pp.58–59), mineral requirements at between 2% and 6% *per capita* per year (Malenbaum, 1973, p.36), and total energy consumption at around 3·5% *per capita* per year (petrol at 3·9%; Landsberg, 1974a, pp.32–33). High resource removal rates were matched by growing waste generation and a proliferation of residuals (for a good summary see Commoner, 1972a, p.36; Marx, 1972; Simmons, 1974, pp.275–319). The affluent generation which had become accustomed to cheaply provided comfort was most reluctant to give up anything when raw material (especially energy) prices began to rise early in 1973. In fact, buying actually increased as fears of shortages grew rapidly and supply inelasticities became evident. When it became clear that wealthy nations were apparently prepared to pay the prices rather than sacrifice growth, the resource-rich nations and commodity organisations began to realise their (now) extraordinary economic and political powers.

Today the western world is confronted with a very real challenge to its accustomed modes of living and policy making, for the politics of resource scarcity have forced all nations to reassess their social priorities, and to seek indigenous resource supplies (particularly energy supplies) which are both very costly and environmentally damaging to produce. International diplomacy has taken on an unexpectedly more important role as the geopolitics of resource availability throw strange international bedfellows together. In the meantime, western nations must pay up to commodity cartels if they wish to sustain their cherished standards of living.

Certainly this is the case for oil where, by the end of 1974, some 1·5% of total world wealth was diverted to the unprepared economies of only thirteen nations (though by mid-1975 this figure had been drastically reduced as a world economic slump and the mixed success of efforts to conserve oil slowed world trade dramatically). It is by no means clear whether either the oil cartel or other commodity cartels can be sustained for long (Bergsten, 1973, 1974; Adelman, 1974; Krasner, 1974; Landsberg, 1974b). This will depend a lot upon the effectiveness of the new international diplomacy and the determination of all nations to pursue economic progress (Westlake, 1975). Already Britain has been forced to consider new trading agreements which favour the resource producing commonwealth nations over the resource consuming countries, while the recently formed International Energy Agency has been compelled to consider price, buffer stocks, and distributional questions relating to commodities before any world-wide energy trading arrangements are signed.

The short-run effect for many developed nations is a stagnation of economic output plus a stabilisation or even decline in real personal wealth, while medium-term consequences will be massive improvements in efficiency of resource use, recycling, and hence some reductions in residuals discharges; but the long-range influence is far less certain. It obviously depends on how individuals will react singly and collectively to the changing expectations and realities of the next few years. In the western world we do not really have a theory of the economic steady state (though intellectual antecedents will be described in chapter 2, pp.39–50, and alternative models discussed in chapter 3, pp.101–104), and certainly not a theory of improved distribution of wealth and social well-being within a steady-state condition. Nor do we have an adequate theory of man which relates the understandable demands of the individual to the necessities of collective living (chapter 1, pp.27–36). So, while there may not be an answer to Kates' plea for a new resource theory, at least the turbulent events of the past two years have demanded a more widespread recognition of the need for such a theory, for the issues he raised must now be confronted without evasion.

But this is not another doom book about the predicament of man nor a treatise on the current economic depression. I am happy to leave these topics to bolder and more informed individuals. My purpose here is to extend the framework of environmental management philosophies and techniques tentatively offered in *Perspectives* to the present and beyond in the light of the radical changes that are currently sweeping the world. As was the case with *Perspectives* the aim is not so much to write a textbook as to provide a comprehensible and workable structure within which the reader can assess recent writings and research in the general area of environmental philosophy and its application. One cannot, however, substitute 'theory' for 'structure' as I doubt that there is a workable theory of environmental management in vogue at this time. Perhaps this is one reason why environmental policies are so tantalisingly difficult to formulate and to implement, though I suspect that another reason for this derives from the inherent contradictions that environmentalism reveals in all of us—contradictions over what we believe and *should* believe and how we act and *ought* to act as individuals and as social beings.

So the modest aim of this book is to provide a perspective based upon critical analysis of what I feel are key writings in the area of environmental philosophy and design, and especially to link the intellectual antecedents of the various ideologies discussed to the political and administrative institutions responsible for putting ideas into practice in the real world of uncertainty and compromise.

Some definitions

But first some definitions, for already I have used a number of words that could be interpreted in different ways. By *environmental philosophy* I mean the pattern and content of intellectual thought together with its evaluative and moralistic connotations as applied to three relationships: (a) between man and his biophysical surroundings, (b) between man and his fellow human beings as these relationships affect his thoughts and actions with respect to his biophysical surroundings, and (c) within each of us as individual beings, again as these notions influence our cognitions and behaviour. Philosophy, of course, can only be interpreted in a cultural context; it is conditioned by the legacy of collective beliefs and framed by modes of production and commonly accepted means of making a living. Our philosophy, then, is partly a product of our capitalistic consciousness.

Given this context, the fusion of environmentalism with philosophy is an important landmark in the maturity of environmentalist thought, for philosophy provides an essential contemplative perspective to a mode of thinking that has been mostly interested in the application of management techniques and political activism. The recent writings of Schumacher (1973), Galbraith (1973), Pirages and Ehrlich (1974), Watt (1974) and Brown (1972, 1974a) are some diverse examples of full-length discussions of the social and moral implications of the current economic and environmental dilemma by 'recognised environmentalists', although a number of prominent social historians and philosophers have also embraced the 'environmental imperative' in proposing their solutions for utopian reform. Examples include Theobald (1970, 1972), Leiss (1972), W. I. Thompson (1972, 1973), Land (1974), Dumont (1974), Heilbroner (1974a, 1976), Mumford (1974), and Ferkiss (1974). Much of their writing is controversial and some downright utopian, but they all make a valuable contribution to the ever recurring debate about what kind of existence man should be seeking, why there are real biophysical and sociopolitical limits to the present courses of action we persist in pursuing, and why national leaders give too little thought to the precipice (or at least the slippery slope) that lies somewhere ahead in the murky mists.

Environmental ideologies relate to a systematic and logical structure of thinking as applied by various writers and practitioners devoted to the formulation of environmental policy. Because ideologies usually have long and powerful antecedents deeply embedded in intellectual thought, crucial premises can be transmitted across whole generations with little scrutiny or distortion. Nevertheless ideologies will always persist. "A society cannot exist", observes Robinson (1964, p.9), "unless its members have common feelings about what is the proper way of conducting its affairs, and these common feelings are expressed in ideology." Though she cautions (p.28) that "the leading characteristic that dominates our society today is its extreme confusion. To understand it means only to reveal its contradictions".

Much of this book is devoted to appraisals of the differing ideologies relating to population and resource consumption (chapter 2), to economic growth and nongrowth (chapter 3), to environmental attitudes and behaviour (chapter 6), and the policy making process itself (chapter 7), to the roles of law (chapter 8) and education (chapter 9), though these themes are not confined entirely to the chapters indicated. Because all environmental issues involve what Schumacher (1973, p.90) calls 'divergent patterns of thought'—irreconcilable dilemmas that force man to seek higher and more fundamental modes of thought so as to find accommodation and reconciliation—the clash of opposing ideologies is all the more potent in elucidating the environmental perspective.

The notion of *environmental design* is quite a different matter. By design I mean the practical application of environmental philosophies, though not by means of plans, blueprints, or didactic policies thrust upon the populace by an administrative or technical elite. Design involves the much softer concept of creative participatory effort based upon the existence of cooperative trust between the executor and the client, utilising the lessons learned by experience and experiment. The objective of the design process is practical policy and creative application, but whereas in planning much of the aim of participation is the completion of a document for subsequent action by professionals, in design the educative and political 'consciousness raising' value of the experience of participation is just as meaningful as the final outcome. Indeed the 'final outcome' may merely be regarded as an intermediate step, a pause in the continuing collective search for a better existence.

There are enormous barriers to the development and application of creative environmental design, not the least of which is the fact that present political and educational arrangements are poorly prepared for unfettered participatory experimentation. Owing to the understandable hesitation and suspicious caution with which most inexperienced people view such proposals, empirical trials in environmental design are all too readily emasculated before they demonstrate their full value. A review of environmental design techniques appears in chapters 4 (pp.150–153), 5 (pp.186–189), and 7 (pp.261–263) though the design notion also permeates the discussions in chapters 6 (pp.222–227) and 9 (pp.311–315).

Mode of presentation

A second major weakness of *Perspectives* was its rather confusing presentation. This was pointed out in reviews by both Kates (1972) and Hanke (1972a), the latter especially commenting on the obscurity of the major lines of argument. To meet this criticism, I attempt here to relate the contextual themes of major environmentalist writings to the principal strands of modern environmentalist thought. So what follows is hopefully less of a review and more of an analysis. While I devote much attention to the philosophical and ideological characteristics of some of the major disputes in environmentalism, I also seek to outline the political and practical implications of these controversies in promoting or impeding policy execution as the case may warrant. Sometimes the key actors in such disputes fail to provide clear guidance to policy makers at critical times, exposing the executive elites (politicians and their principal administrators) to the full force of public criticism or rendering them vulnerable to the various axes being ground by vested interests. The fault is rarely one-sided so I hope that this style of presentation will help to elucidate some of the dilemmas which face policymakers in the real world.

But because one of the aims of this book is to outline and refer to differing ideological perspectives on various environmental matters, it is not my purpose to produce either conclusions or solutions. I hope that each reader will attempt to work out conclusions appropriate to his/her own view of the world, for I would like the text to be regarded as a participatory document for the active-minded. As for simple solutions, I do not believe there are any. Solutions can only emerge from struggle and the personal conviction that a better collective existence is possible for all the world's population, living and yet to be born. The answers cannot be 'handed down' by academics (heaven forbid!) or politicians; they must be sought from within the polity and acted upon in a spirit of realistic optimism.

Some initial reflections

As we shall see in chapter 1 (pp.19–27), the 'environmental perspective' is deeply embedded in the social and political fabric of our existence. It has become a penetrating and pervasive feature of our daily lives, influencing our judgements, our moral positions, our systems of belief, and our everyday conduct. But, as with all fundamental social issues, the environmental perspective offers neither reconciliation nor peaceful resolution, but rather a set of tantalising contradictions or divergent patterns of belief and action which constantly defy solution yet persisently invite a striving for mediation. Tuan (1970, p.249) concludes that environmental malpractice simply reflects contradictions between our ideal of nature or the environment and the necessities of our day-to-day actions.

> "Such conflicts are embarrassing to observe for they expose our intellectual failure to make the connection and perhaps also our hypocrisy; moreover they cannot always be resolved. Contradictions of a certain kind may be inherent in the human condition, and not even stable or simple cultures are exempt."

There is a constant tension between what we believe we should do and what reality appears to compel us to do. Many people feel that this tension is inevitable and desirable, for it constantly jolts us back to the principal messages of environmentalism—the reconciliation between self-seeking beliefs and actions and the necessity for some self-denial in the community interest, and the resolution of the arrogance of a man-orientated view of the world with the humility of accepting man's dependence upon the offerings of nature.

These contradictory elements are well-known to students of literature on environmentalism. In more detail they include (i) the curtailment of individual freedoms in order to ensure greater flexibility of communal choice when managing common property resources (chapter 1, pp.27–36), (ii) the protection of national sovereignty while recognising the existence of global or multinational responsibilities (chapter 8, pp.292–295), (iii) guarantees of the rights of racial and other cultural minorities to enjoy diverse lifeways while ensuring that the interests of the majority are not thereby jeopardised (a classic debate when minority cultures are threatened by resource development proposals, and an important feature in the ideology of participation), (iv) the protection of options for future generations (including protecting the option of continued existence for certain biotic communities and natural landscapes of intrinsic natural value) while not unreasonably limiting the pleasures of the present generation (a matter of particular interest when making decisions with possibly irreversible consequences), and (v) the controversies over how much affluence or austerity, what degree of materialism or spirituality, and the extent of redistribution of wealth and social and political opportunity that regularly dominate the growth–nongrowth debate (chapter 3, pp.85–100).

So the challenge of modern environmentalism is essentially the search for mediation—an outcome that for many can only be found by consciously applying one's whole being to the ultimate meaning of existence. Tuan (1968, p.181) observes that knowledge of the earth elucidates the world of man, for to know the world is to know oneself. But to know the world requires a resolution of antipodal images among which two predominate: the garden of innocence (a symbol of the dominance of nature) which provides nurture and security, and the cosmos (a symbol of the dominance of man) which embodies artifact, artificially determined harmony, and grandeur. According to Tuan (1974, p.248), the most satisfying environments are those which harmonise these two images at all scales, such as the home and the garden, the cluster of dwelling units and the incorporated open space, the town and its adjacent countryside, the metropolis and the wilderness. The creation of this paradoxical harmony, the essence of environmental design, parallels the notion of ecological harmony long advanced by environmentalists. And where it is found, it is deeply cherished and fiercely protected.

For Schumacher (1973, pp.72–94) the fusion of emotion, intellect, self-purpose, and deep conviction is the true purpose of living and the quintessence of education. "Divergent problems", he argues (p.90), "force man to strain himself to a level above himself; they demand and thus provoke the supply of forces from a higher level, thus bringing love, beauty, truth and goodness into our lives. It is only with the help of these higher forces that opposites can be reconciled in the living situation." The mediating forces are the four great virtues of prudence, justice, fortitude, and temperance, redefined by Schumacher (1973, p.281) as love, truth, goodness, and beauty. So environmentalism becomes a moral code of conduct, a set of mediating values. For example, Schumacher (1973, pp.280–281) defines prudence as "the opposite of a small, mean calculating attitude to life which refuses to see and value anything that fails to promise an immediate utilitarian advantage".

Schumacher is talking about total awareness, a regulated system of ideas about self and existence which is reflected in speculations about the meaning of good and of progress. The same theme of total environmental awareness is developed by Teilhard de Chardin (1959) in his concept of 'point Omega'. Huxley (1964, p.213) interprets Teilhard's notion as the culmination of two major evolutionary trends—the development of the individual and the recognition of conscious participation—where the self is integrated with the outer world of men and nature, and the separate elements of the self are likewise integrated one with another. The Omega point is a triumph of evolutionary positivism, the conscious awareness of the cosmos and the role of man (not just the self) in shaping the future.

'Wholeness', 'total awareness', and 'point Omega' are not mere philosophical semantics. They refer to an utterly central philosophical tenet of modern environmentalism—the understanding of man's purpose on this earth, his obligations to all other living and inanimate things, and his proper code of conduct given a choice between conflicting and equally tempting courses of action. This search is a familiar philosophical burden for environmentalists. It dominated much of the writings of the mid-19th century romantic transcendentalists (see chapter 1, pp.3–11) who saw the ideal community as composed of self-reliant individuals, freely acting from inner drives, never conscious of class or caste, striving to improve their communal well-being. The conflicting virtues of equality and freedom are fused in the triumph of cooperation over exploitation, for men are free precisely because they recognise necessity. This utopian image was derived from the transcendentalists' close observation of nature, by contacts so intimate that some claim even to have passed beyond the corporeal into the ethereal. Consider this passage from Emerson (1836, reprinted in Opie, 1971, p.5):

> "Into the woods, we return to reason and faith. There I feel that nothing can befall me in life—no disgrace, no calamity ... which nature

> cannot repair. Standing on the bare ground ... I become a transparent eyeball; I am nothing; I see all; the currents of the universal Being circulate through me; I am part and parcel of God."

The fusion of the self with the natural surroundings provides new ways of contemplating the nature and purpose of human existence. How it can be attained is open to debate. The transcendentalists and their later disciples such as Muir and Leopold believed passionately that large areas of unmodified wilderness were necessary to produce such excited cerebral states, a point argued on more mundane psychological grounds by N. R. Scott (1974). Others such as Schumacher (1973) and Taylor (1973) talk more of *human* settings that are intimate, nurturing, and enlivening, such as can be found in congenial working conditions and harmonious family situations.

Environmentalism is as much a state of being as a mode of conduct or a set of policies. Certainly it can no longer be identified simply with the desire to protect ecosystems or conserve resources these are merely superficial manifestations of much more deeply-rooted values. At its heart environmentalism preaches a philosophy of human conduct that many still find difficult to understand, and those who are aware seemingly find unattainable. As we face the final quarter of the 20th century with growing uncertainty and increasing fears about the permanence of our institutions and the threat of violence and strife, the search for the environmentalist perspective may well come to dominate our total consciousness.

Acknowledgements

This book is the result of many years of field experience, teaching, reading and conversation with friends, professional colleagues, and policymakers. So many people have helped me, knowingly or inadvertently. Janet Williams typed the final draft with speed and accuracy. My father struggled nobly to improve my style. My wife, Ann, helped me throughout, typing my early manuscripts, editing, and proofreading. She is a wonderful source of strength.

I also wish to express my gratitude for the permissions received to reproduce the following material:

George Allen and Unwin Ltd, Hemel Hempstead, Hertfordshire. Table 7.1 from L. Allison, 1975, *Environmental Planning: A Political and Philosophical Analysis.*

American Association for the Advancement of Science. Figures 2.7 and 3.2 from D. Chapman *et al.*, 1972, *Science,* **178**, 705–707, © 1972 by the American Association for the Advancement of Science.

American Geophysical Union, Washington, DC. Table 5.1 from C. W. Howe, 1971, *Benefit Cost Analysis for Water System Planning,* © 1971 by American Geophysical Union.

Bulletin of the Atomic Scientists, Chicago, Illinois, and Bruce C. Netschert. Table 3.6 from B. C. Netschert, 1972, in *The Energy Crisis.*

Ian Burton, Department of Geography, University of Toronto. Table 6.1 from A. Auliciems, I. Burton, J. Hewings, M. Schiff, C. Taylor, 1972, internal paper, Department of Geography.

The Christian Science Monitor, Boston, Massachusetts. Table 4.4 from W. Marlin, 1974, *The Christian Science Monitor,* June 17, page F1.

Daedalus, Journal of the American Academy of Arts and Sciences, Boston, Massachusetts. Table 3.1 from W. R. Johnson, 1973, *Daedalus,* **102**, 165–190.

A. H. J. Dorcey. Figures 3.7 and 3.11 from A. H. J. Dorcey, 1973, *Natural Resources Journal,* **13**, 118–133.

The Economist. Figure 3.13 from *The Economist*, June 14, 1975, page 49.

Ian E. Efford. Figure 2.9 from M. Goldberg, 1973, in *Energy and the Environment,* Eds I. Efford, B. M. Smith, University of British Columbia Press, Vancouver.

Ford Foundation Energy Policy Project, New York, NY. Figure 2.11 from *Exploring Energy Choices,* 1974, page 40.

The Gallup Organization. Table 3.5 from G. Gallup, Jr., 1973, "What do Americans think about limiting growth?", Gallup, Princeton, NJ.

C. S. Holling. Figure 4.1 from C. S. Holling, 1971, internal paper, Department of Resource Ecology, University of British Columbia.

Information Canada, Ottawa, Ontario. Figure 2.5b from Canada, Department of Energy, Mines and Resources, 1973, *An Energy Policy for Canada.*

The Johns Hopkins University Press, Baltimore, Maryland. Poem on page 33 from K. E. Boulding, in *Energy, Economic Growth and the Environment,* Ed. S. Schurr, © 1972 by the Johns Hopkins University Press. Table 2.1 from H. J. Barnett, C. Morse, *Scarcity and Growth,* © 1963 by the Johns Hopkins University Press.

William Kaufmann, Inc., Los Altos, California. Figure 4.5 adapted from A. Heller (Ed.), 1972, *The California Tomorrow Plan.*

H. Kunreuther. Figure 6.8 from H. C. Kunreuther, 1974, "Protection against natural hazards: a lexicographic approach", Fels Institute for State and Local Government, University of Pennsylvania.

National Bureau of Economic Research, Inc., New York, NY. Figure 3.4 adapted from W. D. Nordhaus, J. Tobin, 1972, "Is growth obsolete", which appeared in *Fiftieth Anniversary Colloquium V.*

National Petroleum Council, Washington, DC. Figure 2.5a from *U. S. Energy Outlook: An Initial Appraisal 1971–1985*, volume 2, p.35, 1971.

William D. Nordhaus. Table 2.1c from W. D. Nordhaus, 1974, "Resources as a constraint on growth", *American Economic Review,* **64**, 22–26.

Pacific Northwest River Basins Commission, Vancouver, Washington. Figure 4.7 and table 4.6 from *Ecology and The Economy: A Concept for Balancing Long Range Goals,* 1973.

David Pearce. Figure 3.9 from D. W. Pearce, 1974, "Economic and ecological approaches to the optimal level of pollution", *International Journal of Social Economics,* **1**, 146–159.

Prentice-Hall, Inc., Englewood Cliffs, NJ. Figures 4.3d and 6.8 redrawn from B. J. L. Berry, F. E. Horton, 1974, *Urban Environmental Management: Planning for Pollution Control.*

Public Opinion Quarterly, New York, NY. Figure 6.6b from H. Erskine, 1971, "The polls: pollution and its costs", *Public Opinion Quarterly,* **35**, 120–135.

The Rand Corporation, Santa Monica, California. Information in figure 3.12 and in table 2.4 from R. D. Doctor, K. P. Anderson, 1972, *California's Electricity Quandary: III. Slowing the Growth Rate.*

Random House, Inc., New York, NY. Tables 3.2 and 3.3 from L. R. Brown, 1972, *World Without Borders,* © 1972 by Random House.

Resources for the Future, Inc., Washington, DC. Figure 2.3 from H. H. Landsberg, 1974, in *Resources for the Future Annual Report,* pages 27–49.

Sage Publications, Beverly Hills, California. Figure 5.13 from G. L. Peterson, 1974, "Evaluating the quality of the wilderness environment: congruence between perception and aspiration", *Environment and Behavior,* **6**, 169–193.

Scottish Academic Press Limited, Edinburgh. Figures 5.5, 5.6, and 5.7 from R. A. Waller, 1974, in J. T. Coppock, C. B. Wilson (Eds), *Environmental Quality.*

Stanford Environmental Law Society, Stanford, California. Table 4.5 from *Handbook for Controlling Local Growth,* © 1973 by the Board of Trustees of the Leland Stanford Junior University.

John S. Steinhart. Figure 2.12 from C. E. Steinhart, J. S. Steinhart, 1974, *Energy: Sources, Use and Role in Human Affairs,* Appendix D, Duxbury Press, North Scituate, Massachusetts.

Unesco Courier. Table 2.5 from *Unesco Courier,* number 27, May 1974, page 15.

Urban Studies. Table 4.1 from L. Wingo, 1972, table 4.2 from Hoch, 1972, in *Urban Studies,* **9** (1), 3–28 and 229–328.

T. O'Riordan
Colney, Norwich; June 1975

B*

1

The evolution of modern environmentalism

The contradictions that beset modern environmentalism reflect the divergent evolution of two ideological themes which arose at the birth of the conservation movement (McConnell, 1971), although their intellectual antecedents lie deeper in history. One line of thought can be identified as the *ecocentric mode*, described by McConnell (1965, p.190) as "resting upon the supposition of a natural order in which all things moved according to natural law, in which the most delicate and perfect balance was maintained up to the point at which man entered with all his ignorance and presumption". Thereafter the 'web of life' was broken by a degenerative succession of 'disturbed harmonies' leading ultimately to the destruction of man himself. The other viewpoint is the *technocentric mode* characterised by Hays (1959, p.2) as the application of rational and 'value-free' scientific and managerial techniques by a professional elite, who regarded the natural environment as 'neutral stuff' from which man could profitably shape his destiny.

The two perspectives differ not just in their attitudes to nature but also in their morality that tempers action. Ecocentrism preaches the virtues of reverence, humility, responsibility, and care; it argues for low impact technology (but is not antitechnological); it decries bigness and impersonality in all forms (but especially in the city); and demands a code of behaviour that seeks permanence and stability based upon ecological principles of diversity and homeostasis. Until recently ecocentrism was more of a moral or spiritual crusade, its proponents generally preferring to shun the political arena in favour of the world of rhetoric and contemplation. The technocentric ideology, by way of contrast, is almost arrogant in its assumption that man is supremely able to understand and control events to suit his purposes. This assurance extends even to the application of theories and models to manipulate and predict changes in value systems and behaviour, while the exercise of science to 'manage' nature has been assumed for some time.

Ecocentrism is concerned with *ends* and the proper kind of means, whereas technocentrism focuses more on *means per se*, particularly the utilisation of managerial principles, since its optimism about the continued improvement of the human condition allows it to be rather less troubled about the evaluative significance of its achievements. The technocentrist admires the comforting power of technology and is usually found among an urban-dwelling elite who thrive on the sophisticated communications of the electronic global village and the jet age invisible college. Technocentrists tend to be politically influential for they usually move in the same circles as the politically and economically powerful, who are soothed by the confidence of technocentric ideology and impressed by its presumption of knowledge.

But we should avoid the temptation to divide the world neatly into an ecocentric camp of environmentalists and a technocentric camp of manipulative professionals and administrators. In real life the boundaries are much more blurred. There is every reason to believe that each one of us favours certain elements of both modes, depending upon the institutional setting, the issue at hand, and our changing socioeconomic status. The engineer, the planner, the administrator, and the technician are not insensitive to the beauties of nature, nor are they unaware of the consequences of 'tampering' with ecosystems. They differ from the ecocentric environmentalist largely in the degree of responsibility their job demands of them and in the extent to which a 'natural morality' guides their actions. Sometimes the very nature of the roles they play may channel them into decision paths from which they have little escape. For example, Sax (1970a, pp.34–35) describes how the noted conservationist Stanley Cain (when an Assistant Secretary in the US Department of the Interior) signed an order permitting the destruction of a small area of wildfowl habitat, a decision he later admitted was 'based first on political considerations and second on the feeling that the values [that were lost] were not great in the area [i.e. the wildfowl nesting area] to be filled'. Sax's (1970a, p.56) commentary on this act illustrates the dilemma:

> "The greatest problems are often the outcome of the smallest-scale decisions precisely because the ultimate, aggregate impacts of these decisions are so difficult to see and the pressures so difficult to cope with from the perspective of the insider. It is much easier to tell a developer that he cannot dam up the Grand Canyon than to tell each real estate investor, one by one over time that he cannot fill an acre or two of marshy 'waste' land."

The ecocentrist is not immune from this duality. Henry Thoreau, probably the best known ascetic to shun the 'comforts' of civilised life for a more 'natural' existence in the New England woodland, depended upon Bostonian society to publish and proselytise his views and eventually returned to that society which had given him the education and status he so very much enjoyed. The British naturalist Fraser-Darling (1971, pp.79–80, 97) is quick to defend his Scottish Highlands home even though he admits that he can only continue to live there and be effective because of the technologically sophisticated and energy-intensive life-support systems which he criticises.

The duality of the technocentric and ecocentric modes is probably evident to most of us and need not be further elaborated. Suffice it to conclude that coexistence does not necessarily produce compromise, though in thoughtful people it should lead to better understanding. The reader is urged to peruse the delightfully readable account by McPhee (1972) of the conflict between the two ideologies in which he describes the confrontation between David Brower, former executive director of the

Sierra Club, and various developers. The fascinating feature of McPhee's account is the apparent irreconcilability of the two viewpoints. The developers accept population pressure and economic growth as inevitable forces that can and must be accommodated by proper multiple-purpose management and the application of sensitive planning controls. They claim that the result is a better habitat for man—more rewarding, no less beautiful, yet more accessible to more people. To the environmentalist, however, growth is not a deterministic force but a process that can and must be controlled to save man from his damaging excesses. To leave the natural landscape alone is an act of faith, worship, and moral justice, for the beauty that is lost can never be replaced. In McPhee's account the arguments are never concluded, though beneath the baying and the trumpeting there is much mutual respect between the protagonists for their sincerity and commitment.

1.1 The ecocentric mode

The ecocentric root of modern environmentalism is nourished by the philosophies of the romantic transcendentalists of mid-nineteenth century America. Burch (1971, pp.67–108) contends that their philosophies provided a powerfully credible account of the relationship between nature and society, an interpretation that straddled the fierce individualism (freedom without equality) of the frontier and the bland homogeneity (equality without freedom) of the agrarian landscape and the suburb. The frontiersman was less concerned with obligation and more interested in self-centred freedom, while the rural or suburban 'yeoman' was willing to lose some of his individualism in order to conform to the comforting and law-abiding values of his neighbours. The transcendentalists sought to blend these two images through the symbol of nature. Nature, they claimed, enjoyed its own morality which, when understood, could lead the sympathetic and responsive human being to a new spiritual awareness of his own potential, his obligations to others, and his responsibilities to the life-supporting processes of his natural surroundings.

The power of transcendentalism lay not so much in its naturalism as in its intense social morality about democracy, truth, beauty, and a respect for nature. Their rudimentary understanding of the ecosystem led the transcendentalists to believe that democracy could only be attained by imitating what they understood as the lesson of nature—the pursuit of self-actualisation and creative diversity within mutually sustaining communities. "I can conceive of no flourishing and heroic elements of Democracy maintaining itself at all", wrote Whitman (1955, p.692), "without the Nature element forming the main part—to be its health element and beauty element—to really underlie the whole politics, sanity, religion and art of the New World." The nature metaphor carried with it reformist connotations, for the symbiotic relationships among organisms symbolised attempts by minorities to gain political recognition.

The transcendentalists regarded the city as the antithesis of Nature, for it bred the values of individualism, competition, snobbery, and social rigidity that they despised. No kind of freedom would ever be found under such conditions, only an increasing autocratic control and a deadening conformity to rules and restrictions.

The transcendentalist philosophies sired two subsequent lines of thought which have influenced modern environmental policies. One is the case for a 'bioethic' advocated by 'nature moralists' such as Muir (see Wolfe, 1945), Leopold (1949), P. Anderson (1971), Brooks (1971, 1972), J. Olson (1971), Sauer (1971), Dasmann (1972), Ehrenfeld (1972), Shepard and Shepard (1973), and Goetham (1974) in the United States; Brinkhurst and Chant (1971), Littlejohn and Pimlott (1971), and Livingston (1972) in Canada; and Nicholson (1970, 1973), Fraser-Darling (1971), and Allsop (1972) in Britain. The other is the theme of self-reliance within the context of a small, recognizably interdependent community, a theme which has stimulated the imagination of many a utopianist ever since.

1.1.1 Bioethics

Supporters of the bioethic line of reasoning seek to protect the integrity of natural ecosystems, not simply for the pleasure of man but as a *biotic right*. Nature, they contend, contains its own 'purpose' which should be respected as a matter of ethical principle. Natural architecture has a grandeur which both humbles and enobles man, and stimulates him to emulate it. Wild nature is not to be regarded merely as a convenient respite from the stresses of 'civilised living', but as an integral companion to man. "Thousands of tired, nerve-shaken, overcivilized people", observed Muir (1971, p.32), "are beginning to find out that going to the mountains is going home; that wildness is a necessity; and that mountain parks and reservations are useful not only as fountains of timber and irrigating rivers, but as fountains of life."

There are a number of political, legal, and moral ramifications of the philosophy of bioethics. Morally, it forces man to be more conscious of his rights and responsibilities toward nature. As Fleischman (1969) correctly observes, nature is not 'in balance', nor is it 'wounded', by man's misdeeds. Man differs from all other members of the global ecosystem in two significant respects, a code of morality and the power of conscious reason. "There is no biological justification for conservation", he concludes (Fleischman, 1969, p.26), "Nature will not miss whooping cranes or condors or redwoods any more than it misses the millions of other vanished species. Conservation is based on human value systems. Its validation lies in the human situation and the human heart."

The moral implications of the bioethic principle are beginning to be recognised in environmental policy making. Although the early conservation period was noted for its battles to designate national parks and wilderness areas, the political motivations at the time were based less on bioethical notions than on commercial considerations of tourism and the promotion of national prestige (Runte, 1976). Before being dedicated, the first national parks in North America were carefully scrutinised for their forestry and mineral wealth and found wanting. But in modern times bioethical rhetoric is employed to protect wilderness areas, national parks, and wildlife habitats from the pressures of exploitation. The International Union for the Conservation of Nature and the World Wildlife Fund argue persuasively on this basis, and one political outcome has been the agreement to establish a World Heritage Trust, an internationally funded programme of habitat preservation to protect endangered flora and fauna (Council on Environmental Quality, 1973a, pp.347–348; 1974, pp.446–449). International aid is also now available to help less economically advanced nations set aside natural areas of great ecological significance. Sullivan and Shaffer (1975) provide a convincing ecological argument why such a policy should be followed and advocate the setting aside of a system of wild areas to protect a variety of habitats.

Bioethical principles are also evident in modern policies toward managing national parks and wilderness areas. The American Conservation Foundation (1972) has urged the US National Park Service to adopt a 'parks first' philosophy in its future planning for National Parks, to the point of restricting public access, controlling 'anti-nature' behaviour and promoting much more extensive nature education programmes in schools and the parks (see also Houston, 1971). A recent report by the British National Parks Policy Review Committee (Sanford, 1974) recommended that where the conflict between 'landscape preservation' and 'public use and enjoyment of the countryside' became irreconcilable, then the former should *always* take precedence. A bioethical approach to the management of wilderness areas is also recommended by two Forest Service social scientists, Hendee and Stankey (1973). They feel that natural ecological processes should be left undisturbed even to the point of allowing destruction by wildfire. The old management philosophy of 'rearranging' natural processes to protect culturally preferred artificial habitats, they feel, should be abandoned.

An extension of this bioethical development in the area of economics is the introduction of a new theory of discounting, using specially weighted interest rates to reflect the uniqueness and irreplaceability of natural areas (Krutilla, 1973; Smith, 1974) (see chapter 5, pp.174–178). The cost-benefit calculus is thus loaded to favour the long-term protection of special ecosystems whose values should increase as technical options widen. In fact, this is a good example of the overlap between the rationalist scientific and the ecocentric ideologies in environmental management, for Krutilla and his colleagues are manipulating one of the more controversial technocentric tools to justify biocentric principles.

The legal ramifications of the bioethic argument could also be quite profound. Some environmental lawyers (e.g., J. Stone, 1972) have suggested a common law of biotic rights, a doctrine first proposed by US Supreme Court Justice Douglas in his dissenting opinion over the Mineral King case (see Sax, 1973). Referring to Aldo Leopold's well known plea for a land ethic, Justice Douglas commented that "contemporary public concern for protecting nature's ecological equilibrium should lead to a conferral of standing upon environmental objects to sue for their own preservation" (Environmental Reporter Cases, 1972, p.2044). Currently this doctrine is being tested through attempts by American and Canadian environmentalists to alter the definition of legal standing (see chapter 8, pp.271–282).

The political implications of the bioethic argument are significant in that the normal rules of compromise which usually guide political bargaining may not be followed. Wandesforde-Smith (1971, p.481) describes the problem:

> "Treating the environmentalists like any other interest group does not seem to work .... The environmentalists appear intransigent, extremely difficult to bargain with, and unwilling to accept a compromise. To them it is an all-or-nothing proposition because wilderness values are irreplaceable and priceless; not the kind of values that can be traded-off under the rubric of multiple use or according to the principles of professional forestry."

Combined with new legal tools, this approach could open up a pattern of political conciliation and decisionmaking quite different from that which has been the case heretofore.

The bioethic motif is of importance to modern environmentalism in that it stresses the essential humility of man in the face of natural forces. Nature produces 'resistances' which man ignores at his cost or peril, but which he can accept and understand to his inestimable benefit. Thus, bioethics incorporate the notion of *limits*, or nonnegotiable barriers to certain uses of natural areas. There is of course a long-standing controversy over just where and how demanding these limits are, an issue which permeates the growth–nongrowth debate (see chapters 2 and 3). The bioethical viewpoint is that 'limits' establish their own kind of morality upon man, a challenge to his ingenuity and 'humanness' which constantly demands recognition and response. In the planning field Ian McHarg (1969) initiated one kind of response in his colourful (if not always ecologically authentic) philosophy of ecological planning in which he stresses that man is not the creator of his own values but must bow to values set by nature.

Taken to its extreme the bioethics argument proposes that man's actions are 'determined' by ecological boundaries. Odum (1971) and some of his students have carried this principle into the political arena. They have prepared sophisticated computer models of the ecological 'carrying capacities' of cities and regions which they feel should serve as a basis for immigration policies, regional development programmes, and the determination of housing needs. These studies have influenced the state governments of Florida and Oregon to consider 'ceilings' on population and to guide the timing and pattern of regional growth to accord with ecological limitations (see chapter 4, pp.163–167). The temptation is strong to use such calculations to protect the environmental wellbeing of existing residents thereby denying those who already suffer deprivations in environmental quality any chance to improve their conditions (see Godwin and Shepard, 1974). Carrying-capacity planning is another example of the mixing of the ecocentric and technocentric modes with a very significant bearing on modern environmental policymaking.

1.1.2 The self-reliant community

To many utopian writers the method of linking self-actualisation to a sense of collective responsibility lay in the establishment of small, self-sustaining communities where nature still was very much in evidence. Although the transcendentalists talked of this ideal, it was left to others, for example Peter Kropotkin, Ebenezer Howard, Patrick Geddes, Patrick Abercrombie, Lewis Mumford, Paul Goodman, Theodore Roszak, and Murray Bookchin to develop the idea.

All of these writers (and their intellectual colleagues) were profoundly disturbed by the dehumanising and desocialising effects of rapid industrialisation and urbanisation, especially the impersonal and alienating atmosphere of the megalopolis, the intellectually deadening aspects of occupational specialisation, and the increasingly wasteful diversion of scarce resources (energy, skilled manpower, time and organisational talent) into the maintenance and administration of excessively large industrial, social, and governmental organisations. The result, they concluded, was socially counterproductive; the 'conventional wisdom' of economies of scale—proximity, jointly supplied services, variety of jobs, housing and entertainment opportunities, diminishing marginal costs—simply does not apply beyond a certain size. In fact size creates its own disadvantages—low productivity because of job dissatisfaction, delinquency due to alienation and frustration, family disruption caused by boredom and lack of communication—all of which occur before the more conventional diseconomies become evident. The problem, of course, is to devise a measurement that compares economic effects with social consequences. Until this is done modern society will continue to drift in the direction of bigness in many areas, including trading and military blocs, regionalisation of local services and governments, and the expansion and concentration of corporate influence.

A writer whose ideas are now most apposite to environmentalism is the anarchist Peter Kropotkin (Gould, 1974; Ward, 1974; Woodcock, 1974). Kropotkin developed his views at a time when the social effects of the industrial revolution were becoming a matter of political concern, triggering the reports of the Poor Law Commission and the writings of Karl Marx.

Kropotkin was convinced that both economic security and human happiness could be assured through a regional pattern of decentralised communities where agriculture (partly in the form of communal allotments) flourished beside small industrial enterprises, and where the inhabitants enjoyed a breadth of education and a mix of occupations that combined manual labour with creative intellectual activity. Kropotkin followed Marx in bemoaning the consequences of the division of labour, for he believed that it demeaned the value of work, dampened the ardour of labourers, and separated worker from worker to the point where participatory pride in collective toil lost all its significance.

To counter these distressing tendencies, Kropotkin sought to encourage local crafts and the arts, and the option of voluntary retirement at the age of forty when every man and woman "ought to be relieved from the moral obligation of taking a direct part in the performance of necessary work, so as to be able entirely to devote himself or herself to whatever he or she chooses in the domain of art or science or any kind of work" (Ward, 1974, p.187). Only in the small community could the full potential of human endeavour be attained, for:

> "... such a community would not know misery amidst wealth. It would not know the duality of conscience which permeates our life and stifles every noble effort. It would freely take its flight toward the highest regions of progress compatible with human nature" (*ibid*).

The Kropotkin utopia consisted of a simple life based upon limited expectations where there was little demand (and little need) for constant material progress. But Kropotkin was not concerned about economic stability so much as about the advantages of decentralised self-sufficiency and conditions for promoting the enormous reservoirs of human knowledge and creativity. He was well aware of the benefits of science and technology in releasing man from the soul-destroying burdens of monotonous toil:

> "In the spade culture, on isolated small plots, by isolated men or families, too much human labour is wasted, even though crops are heavy; so that the real economy—of both space and labour—requires different methods representing a combination of machinery work with hand work" (Ward, 1974, p.105).

Kropotkin was a hundred years ahead of his time. His vision embraced the notions of the 'economics of permanence' advocated by Schumacher (1973) (small scale organisation, economy of energy use, intermediate technology, and creative communal labour), the 'convivial community' of Pirages and Ehrlich (1974), the 'visionary commonwealth' of Roszak (1973), and the 'monastic commune' of Heilbroner (1974a). These are all appeals for a new social order based upon empathy and participatory cooperation at the level of the neighbourhood, commune, or village.

These notions are also environmentally important because they claim to provide a basis for social improvement with little or no increase in energy use. [Even Kropotkin regarded energy as the limiting factor, in fact he defined economics as "a science devoted to a study of the needs of men and of the means of satisfying them with the least possible waste of energy" (Ward, 1974, p.43).]

A fine example of this 'communal' philosophy is provided by Schumacher (1973, pp.50–58) in his delightful essay entitled 'Buddhist Economics'. For the Buddhist work gives man the opportunity to utilise and develop his faculties while accepting limits to his egocentricity by joining with others in a communal task. "The Buddhist sees the essence of civilization not in the manipulation of wants, but in the purification of the human character" observes Schumacher (1973, p.52). "Character, at the same time, is formed primarily by a man's work. And work, properly conducted in conditions of human dignity and freedom, blesses those who do it and equally their products". Given these circumstances the worker regards his labour as a matter of pride and utility, not as dreary occupational time that must be suffered in order to have the necessary income to buy happiness elsewhere. And to the employer, the worker becomes an indispensible part of the creative process, rather than a human tool to watch dials and press buttons.

To the ecocentric mind this kind of morality can never be found in the city, the result, according to Roszak (1973, p.384) of a "freakish historical departure" which has produced "a passion for megatechnics and artificiality". Salvation can only lie in the reemergence of the 'tribe' and the 'personalised collectivity': damnation is the way of the city, the bureaucracy, and the multinational corporation. With the transformation of scale comes the transformation of ethos, and the transmutation of the technocentric to the ecocentric.

The self-reliant community theme has traditionally been apolitical. Santmire (1973, p.67) claims that this in part accounts for its lack of effectiveness in stopping the drift towards centralisation since, with its preoccupation with new forms of social morality, the ecocentric community had "little psychic energy left for sustained intellectual and moral involvement in the practical political arena, whether that be with a view to upholding, transforming, or overthrowing the inherited order".

But Santmire goes much further in his critique of the modern ecocentric fad for returning to nature, which he terms the "cult of the simple rustic life". He regards it as a political 'cop out', a selfish response on the part of the wealthy who can afford to buy their own private natural amenity, and alienated modern youth, the offspring of the wealthy, who seek to reject totally the materialistic values and the psychological stresses of the 'rat race' by retreating to nature-orientated communes. Both responses are socially reprehensible according to Santmire (1973, p.78) who remarks that

> "... the cult of the simple rustic life, like the nineteenth century religion of nature, brings with it an implicit—sometimes explicit—social irresponsibility. It would be too much to say that the contemporary cult has been consciously developed in order to divert public attention from the pressing urban problems of the day ... [but] there can be little doubt that [it] does reinforce a prior commitment to the *status quo*, especially in the ranks of the small town, suburban and affluent urban citizenry".

Hence the nature image can function as an *escape* from an uncertain future and a *refuge* from a decadent, unjust society, purposes it has served since the days of ancient Israel. Insofar as the rustic movement remains peripheral to the forces of social change, it will never provide a credible alternative to the powerful forces of centralisation. So despite its faddish popularity the tiny, isolated commune is not the answer to our present problems even though many individuals may choose to adopt this form of lifestyle (see Borsodi, 1933/1972; Nearing and Nearing, 1954; Hedgepeth and Stock, 1970; Reich, 1970; Roberts, 1971; Terselle, 1971; Cobb and Cobb, 1973; Fairfield, 1973). Why might the commune fail? According to Leo Marx (1973) the pastoral retreat is little more than an interlude for most people, a period of self-analysis inspired by a natural setting, placed between a period of disillusionment with 'urban' values and a yearning to enjoy the intellectual stimulation of 'civilisation'. For the vast majority, nature 'in the raw' does not provide nurture; the political significance of the self-reliant community theme arises from active social participation, not retreat.

The call for participatory democracy is not new though it has taken on a new urgency in recent years (see chapter 7, pp.255-263). This is particularly evident with respect to community issues at the neighbourhood level. Participation here is regarded as a necessary mechanism in the design of a better community, for the participatory experience reflects the basic themes of environmentalism—the development of human potential within a communal existence, the commitment to a mutually acceptable set of values and a sense of belonging, and the willingness to devise appropriate institutions to allow these needs to blossom into full flower. 'Consciousness raising', self-education, and the political responsibility of collective living have become the clarion calls of the modern activist (see Goodman, 1972, and Kasperson and Breitbart, 1974, pp.49-53) who seeks to undermine what are regarded as the more unpleasant qualities of the technocrat, namely, the assumption and presumption of public values in planning and policymaking.

To summarise, ecocentrism has influenced modern environmentalism in a number of ways. First, it provides a *natural morality*—a set of rules for man's behaviour based upon the limits and obligations imposed by natural ecosystems. Taken to its extreme, this natural morality displaces the humanistic morality that is intrinsically derived through man's cultural institutions. The implications of this line of reasoning will be discussed later in this chapter (pp.27–36). But even in more moderate form, ecocentrism provides checks to the headlong pursuit of 'progress' which, by and large, is the objective of the technocentric mode. Second, it talks of *limits* (blurred perhaps but recognisable) of energy flows or productive capacity, and of the costs of organisation and system maintenance. These limits impose restrictions upon man's activities and hence influence the compass (if not the direction) of 'progress'. Third, it talks in ecosystem metaphors of *permanence and stability*, diversity, creativity, homeostasis, and the protection of options. These have important policy ramifications for the preservation of unique ecological and/or cultural habitats and 'lifestyles'. Fourth, it raises questions about *ends and means*, particularly the nature of democracy, participation, communication among groups holding conflicting yet legitimate convictions, the distribution of political power and economic wealth, and the importance of personal responsibility. These questions have profound political overtones, few of which are fully understood even by the politicians themselves. Finally, ecocentrism preaches the virtues of *self-reliance and self-sufficiency*. Here again the political ramifications of this trend are not properly understood. Anarchist environmentalists aim to develop decentralised institutional arrangements to facilitate flexible and adaptable responses to changing circumstances by individuals and communities alike, and to avoid the vulnerability of dependence upon trade, food supplies, large corporations, or key occupational groups.

1.2 The technocentric mode

Man's conscious actions are anthropocentric by definition. Whether he seeks to establish a system of biotic rights or to transform a forest into a residential suburb, the act is conceived by man in the context of his social and political culture. The distinction between technocentrism and ecocentrism relates to the *values* that are brought to bear on those acts and the estimation of the likely consequences. The technocentric mode is identified by *rationality*, the 'objective' appraisal of means to achieve given goals, by *managerial efficiency*, the application of organisational and productive techniques that produce the most for the least effort, and by a sense of *optimism and faith* in the ability of man to understand and control physical, biological, and social processes for the benefit of present and future generations. Progress, efficiency, rationality, and control—these form the ideology of technocentrism that downplays the sense of wonder, reverence, and moral obligation that are the hallmarks of the ecocentric mode. Many commentators believe that these ideological roots can be traced to the biblical exhortation to "be fruitful and multiply and replenish the earth and subdue it: and have dominion over the fish of the sea, and over the fowl of the air and over every living thing that moveth upon the earth" (*Genesis*, chapter 1, v.28). This is a controversial issue which will be further discussed in chapter 6 (pp.203–208). Others (e.g. Hays, 1959; Weisberg, 1971; Leiss, 1972), contend that technocentrism is a function of a particular kind of economic and political existence, and therefore has emerged most forcefully with the concentration of economic and political power that took place, ironically, during the first American conservation movement at the turn of this century.

1.2.1 Technocentrism and conservation

The early conservationists preached a managerial ethic and created particular resource development institutions that many today regard as serious impediments to harmonious environmental management. The first American conservation movement was promoted by a group of professional resource managers who enjoyed the attention of their political masters but who were neither accountable nor responsible to 'lay' public opinion. These men were proud of their scientific knowledge and their technical mastery. So conservation became a utilitarian notion, the orderly exploitation of resources for the greatest good to the greatest number over the longest time, the prevention of waste and the control of the earth for the good of man. Because rational management required order and control, governments quickly established regulatory mechanisms to stabilise prices and apportion supplies, since it was believed that the improvement of social welfare could best be achieved through the promotion of private interests regulated by public 'scrutiny'. In their passion to achieve rational means, the early conservationists lost sight of the political and ecological consequences of their actions. Weisberg (1971, pp.23–24) comments that

> "... the legislation issued in the Progressive Era was not motivated by a questioning of the distribution or ownership of wealth or resources, but by a question of method: the problem of finding the most reasonable technique to promote efficient growth on the part of those who already controlled land and resource patterns. The conservation movement in fact was built around the difficulties of management, rather than ecological diversity and stability".

1.2.2 Professional ideologies and public participation

The growing specialisation and sophistication of resource management techniques soon separated the policy adviser and the policymaker from the public at large by a gulf of ignorance and jargon. Inevitably even the policymakers (the politicians and senior administrators) became increasingly dependent upon the advice of the professional elite and consultation with special interest groups for guidance in resource matters (see E. Brooks, 1974). So by degrees the professional resource managers became the invisible generals who lacked accountability, except to the ethics of their profession and their special interest constituents (see chapter 7, pp.241–251 for analysis of case studies).

Professionalism implies specialisation and is often accompanied by a reluctance to accept the opinions of people who are regarded as uninformed. This reluctance is shared by all the 'old guard' in resource decisionmaking. Drew (1970, p.58) quotes a professional lobbyist for the US canal building interests as saying

> "The problem a lot of us have ... is that we're not dealing with the knowledgeable and experienced people in ecology, but the bird watchers and butterfly net people who don't want anything changed anywhere, and you can't deal with them."

The technocrat tends to shun the political spotlight and the public forum, and seeks from public opinion only an indication of the *strength* of feeling about an issue, not free advice on techniques (O'Riordan, 1971b).

When the Massachusetts State Public Health Department instructed a technical advisory commission to recommend suitable air quality standards for sulphur dioxide and particulate emissions for Boston, the chairman of the commission ignored the call, made during public hearings on the matter, to tighten up the recommended standards. Noting that he did not regard the public as "competent" to testify about standards since "they didn't understand what the numbers meant", he went on to say that all the commission wanted was some expression of public opinion about "pure air", then the technical people would decide how to achieve it (Lockeretz, 1970, pp.651–652).

Perl (1971) observes that the US administration is interested purely in technical 'facts' from its science advisory committees, not any discussion of the political consequences of different policy options. Indeed, scientific review bodies are noted for their political 'amicability' rather than their scientific competence (see Wade, 1971). Hamilton (1972) and Lewis (1972) discuss this in relation to the setting of radiation standards for nuclear generating stations; Egler (1969), Beatty (1973), and Adler (1975) show much the same thing with respect to the banning of DDT; and Fox and Wible (1973) and Blair (1974) provide similar evidence for the setting of water and air quality standards.

Influence is a difficult attribute to share, so both policymakers and their advisers tend to prefer the sheltered atmosphere of the committee room and bureaucracy to the public forum when determining policy. Politicians, too, dislike too much 'interference' from public discussion. They are far happier with clean-cut advice from the experts for the kinds of reasons spelled out by a British municipal official in this quotation from Davies (1972, p.90):

> "The value of more members [i.e. local councillors] being drawn from business and the professions lies ... in exploiting their general acumen rather than in seeking to use directly their individual professional or vocational knowhow ... . A part-time member [even] with specialist knowledge cannot always (*or perhaps should not*) be expected to have the same full detailed background in local projects or schemes as the responsible specialist officer and his staff who are employed for the purpose". (Italics added.)

Professionalism is not simply specialised competence but a tribal ideology. "A profession", notes Davies (1972, p.93) "is a ... collective memory of the struggles, defeats and victories of an incipient movement and of its drives for recognition and professional status ... . It constitutes the values into which the trainee is *socialised* ... [it] defines and elaborates his [i.e. the professional's] self conception and teaches him the appropriate social difference between himself (as a professional) and other professionals and non-professionals."

The professional is trained as to what to expect, who will be supportive and who will be antagonistic, and how to deal with any situation that arises. The engineer expects to produce artifacts of grandeur which are a tribute to his professional expertise. Drew (1970, pp.51, 61–62) quotes a Chief of the US Corps of Engineers as commenting that "with our country growing the way it is, we cannot simply sit back and let nature take its course ... . [As to] this business of ecology, we're concerned, but, people don't know enough about it to give good advice. You have to stand still and study life cycles and we don't have time ... [W]e have to develop before 1980 as much water resource development as has taken place in the whole history of the nation". Davies (1972, pp.89–104) points out that planners *expect* opposition to their views, opposition from what they regard as selfish, shortsighted property owners who have no interest in the general public good. But they persist, despite frequent controversy, because of an 'evangelical' faith in their abilities to design a better environment for generations yet unborn. Faced with this almost quixotic zeal, any protests from what they regard as 'merely' parochial interests are quickly brushed aside (see also Wilson, 1973).

1.2.3 Regulatory intervention

As with the rationalisation of economic power, the emergence of the regulatory agency was also associated with the first American conservation movement and has blossomed ever since. Hays notes that the regulatory body with its corps of professional administrators was encouraged by big business and by big government both of whom sought advantage from centralised direction based on technical rationality.

"The conservation movement did not involve a reaction against large scale corporate business, but, in fact shared its views in mutual revulsion against unrestrained competition and undirected economic growth. Both groups placed a premium on large scale capital organisation, technology and industrywide cooperation and planning to abolish the uncertainties and waste of competitive resource use" (Hays, 1959, p.266).

The regulatory official is a powerful figure for he is usually to be found in the centre of the political bargaining forum where policies are thrashed out between special interest lobbies and policymakers. His advice is frequently crucial in determining the final outcome which purports to reflect 'the public interest'. Legally he is granted considerable powers of discretion, even to the point of assessing whether 'the public interest' is involved and what information should be revealed at a public inquiry (Lucas and Moore, 1973; Lucas, 1976).

The regulatory body has grown in stature because it suits certain powerful interests that *administrative* decisionmaking is more effective than *political* decisionmaking. While the regulatory official is a professional, he cannot help but be influenced by the values and the specialised information provided by the representatives of the interests he is supposed to monitor (Hardin, 1972a, pp.133–142). Indeed he may be *dependent* upon that information to do his job, with the result that the regulated interests are frequently granted special favours. What was regarded as the necessary regulation of monopoly seventy years ago has largely become the very costly and unnecessary regulation of competition today (McAvoy, 1970; US President's Council of Economic Advisers, 1975). The impartiality of the regulator is constantly challenged in the cause of his job with the result that, over time, the regulated and the regulator identify a common interest, the guarantee of stability and long term mutual influence in the workings of resource allocation. Kolko (1963) described this union as 'political capitalism', while Galbraith (1973) called it the 'planning system'—the massive concentration of capital, investment potential, research, and development into the hands of a minority who become powerful enough to influence the pace of technological change and the scope of resource utilisation. Again the ironic outcome of the technocentric face of conservation has been the creation of a set of circumstances quite unacceptable to modern environmentalists.

1.2.4 The power of objective analysis

Whereas the ecocentric mode likes to discuss questions of morality, values, and limits (albeit inconclusively), the technocentric perspective tends to shun such debate. Resource-allocation techniques such as cost–benefit, systems dynamics, and programme budgeting were created and are popular precisely because they are supposed to be 'value free' and 'rational'. Jay Forrester (1971), the mastermind behind the *Limits to Growth* computer models, argues that only the computer can 'objectively' work through the maze of interconnected loops and relationships to arrive at 'rational' conclusions; the human mind simplifies and distorts 'reality' to suit its prejudices. According to Forrester, the results of computer runs are 'counterintuitive', i.e. rationally 'correct' but subjectively 'wrong'.

The British government established a prestigious Royal Commission (the Roskill Commission) with a mandate to provide a 'politically unbiased' analysis of four alternative sites for a controversial third London airport. The commission was to be the symbol of apolitical objective evaluation. Its chairman, Mr. Justice Roskill was well aware of this role: "not the least of the tasks facing the Commission upon its appointment", he noted in his Final Report (Roskill, 1971), "was the need to establish public confidence that its work would be impartial, unbiassed and entirely uninfluenced by anything that had gone on before". How 'objective' was the Commission's expensive study? The Commission was given the four sites, chosen by political infighting (Kimber and Richardson, 1974, pp.165–211), but its terms of reference never allowed it to investigate whether an additional airport was required in the first place. After an extensive and much criticised appraisal, the Commission recommended one of the four sites, only to see the British government first choose another and subsequently abandon the proposal entirely. The trouble is that 'objectivity' is excellent fodder for political manipulation; the authority of one of the most exhaustive cost-benefit analyses ever attempted was denied before it began. A managerial technique so loudly proclaimed for its powers of independent appraisal was reduced to a voiceless *prima donna*, beautiful and elegant but silent.

Many scientists still struggle to maintain the charade of objectivity. Alvin Weinberg (1970) considers that the axiology of science (the theory of values) now deals with aesthetics (the 'elegance' of theory and research techniques) rather than with ethics. The scientist, he claims, is trained to eschew value judgements about the 'rightness' of research or the ultimate objectivity of inquiry. Roszak (1969) claims that the 'impersonality' of science is part of its mythology and permits the scientist (including the social scientist) to manipulate and harrass without recourse to ethical scrutiny.

The myth of objectivity dies hard; the appeal of quantification is an appeal to 'rational' calculation because numbers have a sometimes spurious, but undeniable, aura of respectability and credibility. For example, the US Atomic Energy Commission (1972) announced that nuclear generating stations were so safe that Americans enjoyed less than a 1 in 10 million chance of being killed or maimed by the radiation from a technical failure or from low level residual emissions (a probability less than that of being killed by a meteorite). However, subsequent checks by the Environmental Protection Agency (Gillette, 1975a) demonstrated that the AEC calculations underestimated these critical probabilities of the human danger from radiation by between two and sixteen times. In early 1975 most nuclear stations in the USA were 'temporarily' closed because of evidence of a serious design failure. Even so, the suitability of quantitative techniques regardless of their statistical limitations is seldom seriously questioned. Schumacher (1973, pp.43–44) observes:

> "All this can do is lead to self-deception or the deception of others; for to undertake to measure the immeasurable is absurd and constitutes but an elaborate method of moving from preconceived ideas to foregone conclusions; all one has to do to obtain the desired results is to impute suitable values to the immeasurable costs and benefits."

The myth of objectivity also emerges when professionals advise decision-makers on policy matters. Beckerman (1974, pp.26–28) argues that the economist cannot tell governments or people whether growth is 'good' or 'bad' or whether resources are man-made or god-given; the job of the economist is to devise techniques for allocating people's preferences amongst conflicting needs. This kind of observation has encouraged writers like Schumacher (1973, p.44) to quip: "economics is primarily concerned with theorising on the bargain hunting activities of the purchaser." That some economists persist in avoiding 'value judgements' is evident in this comment by Harry Johnson (1973, p.116):

> " 'How do we tell when society is better off?' The simplest comment I can think of on these issues paraphrases a pithy remark by Sir W. Arthur Lewis: 'Of course we don't know whether being rich makes you more happy or less happy: therefore you might as well be rich'."

Slowly, however, the myth of objectivity is being eroded. A growing number of scientists are showing a disgust over the ethics of their activities by forming 'public interest' associations, intent on providing contrary scientific evidence to establishment views on many different issues of social relevance (such as nuclear energy, genetic engineering, the composition and use of pesticides, etc.) (C. Brown, 1971; M. Holden, 1971; Union of Concerned Scientists, 1973). In the area of social science, Myrdal (1969) exploded the myth most effectively by demonstrating how economists, sociologists, and political scientists fit every phase of their analyses into preconceived value systems, while Buttimer (1974) has provided much the same evidence in the field of geography.

1.2.5 The faith in optimism

Another characteristic of the technocentric mode is optimism, especially a faith in the technology of intervention and manipulation. The application of scientific knowledge to improving the condition of man is automatically accepted as a fundamental and laudable objective, even though there are no commonly accepted yardsticks (without recourse to a discussion of values and morality) by which to measure 'improvement'.

To the technically-minded scientist, the issue of the energy crisis is not a matter of how we live or why we wastefully allocate depletable resources, but largely a matter of supply: unlock the storehouse of unlimited energy and the problem of 'limits' all but disappears. Naturally, they believe that no obstacles to the generation of plentiful power should deter us. Weinberg and Hammond (1970, pp.415–416) would have half the New England mountains mined for the tiny concentrations of uranium in the Conway granites. While making only passing reference to the new mountains of waste that would be produced, they provide no discussion at all of the loss of the considerable amenities in the area. With the advent of breeder reactors or fusion power, a mere fifteen million tons of the rock daily would meet all the world's energy needs for aeons. And what of the problem of storing the highly toxic and corrosive spent fuels? "There are 500000 square miles of salt in the United States alone", they observe; "although not all of this is suitable for waste disposal, one cannot escape the impression that there is enough salt to sequester wastes from catalytic nuclear burners for a very long time". But what the authors perhaps do not anticipate is (a) that salt mines may not be so suitable as waste disposal sites, (b) that politicians and the public may prefer always that someone else's salt mines (or disposal areas) should be used, (c) that some New Englanders may actually prefer to keep the northern Appalachians intact, and (d) that both net capital and net energy budgets must remain positive. In connection with the last point, P. Chapman (1975, p.102) demonstrates that with conventional nuclear power sources the energy budget 'break even' grade for mining uranium is 0·002% (or 20 ppm). At grades below this level more energy would be required to mine and prepare the nuclear fuel than would be produced by the plant consuming it. In a growing energy economy the dependence upon fusion power becomes critical.

Optimism over man's endeavours is not confined to the physical scientist and technologist; it is an important ideological variable in discussions among social scientists too. Having demolished the Forrester–Meadows *Limits* ideology as elitist and doomsday-Malthusianist, Simmons (1973, p.215) concludes that "it makes no sense to talk of exponential growth in a finite world. Man's inventiveness in changing social arrangements is without limits, even if not without hazards".

The bedfellow of optimism is complacency, an uncritical smugness regarding the favourable outcome of manipulation and intervention. Pro-establishment nuclear scientists demonstrate this in their complete faith in nuclear engineering; they simply cannot believe that 'fail safe' mechanisms could actually fail. But again, this technocentric tendency is not confined to the physical scientist: the noted economist Harry Johnson (1973, p.116) defends his pro-growth argument with the comment that though "the issues are complex, the message is fairly simple: 'Let's have the growth and spend the proceeds as wisely as we can; after all we have not done too badly so far'. If that is not intolerable complacency, I am prepared not to be tolerated". The trouble is that because optimism and complacency are fed by a confidence in competence, they are difficult to counter with speculative argument or by recourse to hypothetical prediction.

To summarise, the technocentric mode has left its legacy in environmental policymaking in a number of ways. First, its *optimism* over the successful manipulation of techniques to extract and allocate resources—an optimism shared by most policymakers who bask in the reflected glory of technological success. Second, its determination to be '*value free*' in advice and analysis, leaving the 'tough' judgements to a political arena that is already shaped by their advice. Third, its *disavowal of widespread public participation*, especially the input of lay opinion, a philosophy much admired by politicians equally intent on preserving their rightful role in acting authoritatively on behalf of the public. This makes it difficult to ensure that minority views, or 'nonquantifiable' factors such as preferences for particular kinds of lifestyles, are adequately represented or properly taken into account. Finally, its disquieting *fallibility*, the constant evidence of error and misinterpretation and of hunches that do not quite pay off. Fallibility is tolerable when it is accepted and accounted for, but it is dangerous indeed when those in important positions ignore its existence. While the Achilles heel of fallibility is now the target of informed scientific opinion, the result can be endless technical debate, fruitless attempts at reconciliation of motives, prevarication and exasperation, all adding to the uncertainties ever present in environmental policymaking. As the credibility of the technocrat is increasingly questioned, more expensive and more careful scrutiny strips off the veils of optimism, revealing a hesitancy that opens up wide avenues for political intervention and public participation. Whether the net effect is better or worse is difficult to determine, though one can be sure that technocentrism is undergoing the critical analysis that many environmentalists feel is long overdue.

1.3 The political framework of modern environmentalism

As nations mature, they modulate their political priorities. Broadly speaking the trend is toward improving the general social welfare and increasing the equality of social opportunity. This evolution is diagrammatically portrayed in figure 1.1 which reveals a hierarchy of national goals. Naturally these blend and overlap, but for the sake of clarity it can be postulated that, if threatened, those goals found higher and to the left in the diagram displace those lower and to the right, in the sense that resources would be removed from the latter to protect the former.

The diagram illustrates national priorities as determined politically by those who influence the allocation of power. To give an example, it is generally accepted that 'public health' is a major collective goal, and there is no doubt that considerable efforts are made to protect the public at large from the dangers of serious contagious diseases. But the concern is for the *general* public health, not necessarily for the medical fitness of (political) minorities. Even the interest in the general public health may be stimulated by mixed motives. When completing his report to the British Poor Law Commission in 1842 urging an improvement in the sanitary conditions of the poor, Lord Chadwick noted that a healthy labouring class was likely to be more productive and politically more contented. In other words, he viewed the upgrading of public health as a matter of economic expediency as much as a question of moral concern. He also chose to ignore the fact that the dreadful state of public hygiene was very much a result of appalling social inequalities of privilege, nutrition, income, and education prevalent at the time (Ridgeway, 1971, pp.18–38). Today infant mortality, malnutrition, and debilitating disease remain more serious among the poor and politically impotent minorities in all nations than among the population at large. Likewise, occupational health hazards remain selectively dangerous for certain groups (e.g. pneumoconiosis among coal miners, asbestosis among asbestos manufacturing workers, lead poisoning among smelter workers) until either the affected groups become politically organised and militant, or the general level of public health

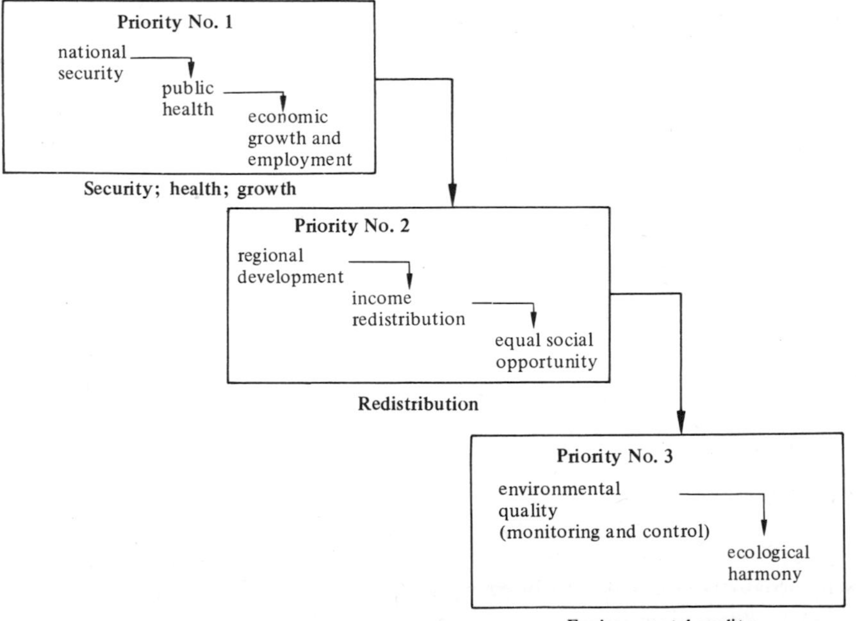

Figure 1.1. The hierarchy of national goals. Broadly speaking, the higher to the left in both the overall diagram and in each box, the more important the goal/objective.

and economic development reaches a sufficient standard to push such 'esoteric' ailments into the political and social spotlight (see for example Brodine, 1973, pp.112–149; Bugler, 1972, pp.86–110).

Returning to the diagram, the first priority of all nations is a goal cluster that embraces national security, public health, and economic growth and employment. A nation that is militarily vulnerable cannot afford the luxury of investing extensively in egalitarian social reform, for nowadays political diplomacy, trading agreements, resource prices and availability (all of which are vital for continued economic growth and employment) are influenced by military muscle. Hence the considerable investment by all nations (even so-called neutral or nonaligned nations) in munitions spending, arms trading, and national defence. Tables 1.1 and 1.2 indicate that most nations spend between a fifth and a third of their national budgets directly on defence. Emerging nations are especially prone to invest precious resources in costly military programmes and prestigious arms buying (missiles, supersonic fighter aircraft, and sophisticated electronic equipment) despite the existence of widespread malnutrition and social suffering. Current estimates of world arms spending run at between \$200 and \$250 billion annually (about £125000 million), a figure that is rising at about 10% per year in real terms and currently represents some 6·5% of total world wealth (Pirages and Ehrlich, 1974, pp.218–222). This is more than twice the total world yearly

Table 1.1. Percentage of national budgets spent on defence and social services (drawn from *UN Yearbooks of National Accounts Statistics*).

Country	Defence		Education		Health		Social services	
	1960	1971	1960	1971	1960	1971	1960	1971
United States	50·3	36·4	20·5	27·2	5·9	1·3	1·4	5·9
United Kingdom	38·1	27·2	16·2	20·2	19·2	20·4	3·5	4·8
Italy	20·8	16·4	23·7	30·6	7·9	7·8	15·6	15·4
New Zealand	21·3	16·0	23·9	36·9	21·7	15·3	0·7	0·1
Singapore	3·0	34·7	30·8	20·2	15·6	8·7	1·5	2·8

Table 1.2. A comparison between defence expenditures and various social services (adapted from Paxton, 1974).

Country	Defence	Social services	Education	Health	Environmental protection
United States	100	←	120	→	10
Canada	100	←	146	→	12
Soviet Union	100	← 351	→	54	
West Germany	100	122	23		
Israel	100		12	8	
India	100	35	53		

investment in education, eight times the annual sum required to guarantee an adequate diet for all the world's peoples (including the necessary agricultural reform) and forty times the current annual foreign aid granted to the lesser developed nations (Benson and Wolman, 1971; H. Jackson, 1974). But when a nation's security is actually threatened, there is no real limit to the diversion of resources to ensure survival. The Middle Eastern countries (such as Israel and Jordan) currently invest about three-fifths of their national budgets (some 25% of total national wealth) in military expenditures even though this leads to high inflation and economic depression.

The scale of military expenditures is emphasised here not simply because it is the target of all peace-loving peoples, but because it exemplifies the willingness to waste valuable resources and to destroy large areas of ecological value in the interest of 'security'. In this era of electronic warfare, enormous capital investment can be totally eradicated in a matter of hours: in the ten days of the Yom Kippur War (October, 1973) the belligerent nations lost over £2500 million in military hardware. Yet despite the profound human suffering and ecological devastation that are caused even by relatively small-scale wars, most nations persist in maintaining a credible military posture. Military exigencies may even outweigh peaceful reasons for research. Gillette (1975c) reports that the US nuclear fusion programme is geared primarily to military needs, not to the peaceful use of abundant energy.

The provision of health facilities to achieve adequate levels of public health is second only to national security in importance, for a work force crippled by disease or anaemia is economically unproductive and susceptible to infiltration by political dissidents. In most western countries any serious threat to the general public health is met by prompt medical action. Consequently medical officers command a credible popular reputation and can exert influence at all levels of policymaking. It is no accident that most legislative initiatives in environmental policy-making were activated by fears about public health. Early water-pollution control legislation was associated with public health acts and administered by public health authorities. The London smog of 1952 and the Los Angeles smog episodes of the early sixties did much to alert public opinion to the dangers of air pollution. The Canadian government banned DDT largely because of evidence that it was dangerous to human health, not because animal predators were dying by the thousand from its effects (Chant, 1970, p.140). Powerful lobbies campaigning for the need to preserve jobs weaken in the face of a demonstrable public health issue, as can be seen in the history of US automobile emission control legislation (Esposito, 1970, pp.26–47; Angeletti, 1973), and progress can be delayed if the technology of emission control fails to remove all health-endangering substances. For example, the requirement of installing catalytic converters on all US cars built after 1975 has been postponed until the device has been adjusted to remove the sulphuric acid 'mist' that it now produces (O'Connor, 1975).

Economic growth is the driving force of the whole mechanism of national priorities, for growth generates the wealth for investment, employment, research and development, and organisation that produce economic health. Increases in the collective wealth are generally regarded as vital for improved personal and social well-being, to provide a range of employment possibilities, to make available sufficient funds for the control of residuals, and to enable research and development to flourish so that growth can be more efficient and equitable. (For a review of the arguments, see Daly, 1973a, 1973b; Olson, 1973; Beckerman, 1974.) Economic growth is a *sine qua non* for all political parties who know that policies to protect jobs and maintain standards of living are essential if they wish to hold power. Despite the rhetoric no political party of any effectiveness has yet been formed under a sincerely expressed no-growth philosophy.

The threat to economic growth is a favourite theme of interests who discount the threat of environmentalism. US energy corporation executives were quick to blame the activities of those who delayed power stations, refineries, superports, and energy development schemes, even though subsequent analyses revealed that more serious delays were caused by shortsighted management, manipulative pricing policies, and insufficient technological safeguards (Landsberg, 1974a). Nevertheless, under the threat of an energy 'crisis', US, Canadian, and British governments have been quick to aid corporate investment in domestic energy supplies, even at the expense of adequate environmental analysis and proper public consultation. For example, President Ford has twice successfully vetoed a congressional bill which demands adequate protection and restoration of open-cast coal-mine sites, noting that it was an 'anti-energy' bill and a 'step backwards'. The Canadian government failed to persuade the Province of Quebec to furnish a comprehensive environmental impact assessment of the controversial James Bay hydroelectric scheme before construction began (Rosenberg, 1974). In January 1975 the British government pushed through the Offshore Petroleum Development (Scotland) Act which allows the Secretary of State for Scotland to acquire by agreement or compulsorily any land in Scotland for any purpose connected with the exploration and exploitation of North Sea oil, and allows a public inquiry to be dispensed with where acquisition is regarded as a matter of urgency.

The redistribution goal cluster generally becomes prominent once a nation has achieved a certain level of performance in the security–health-growth group of goals. In other words, as a wealthy nation can afford to be generous, so efficiency gives way to equity. This is so because growth *qua* growth tends, in capitalist economies at least, to create and to be accompanied by a maldistribution of wealth, occupational opportunity, social equality, and environmental impact—a distributive unfairness that can only be remedied by conscious public recognition and political intervention. The judgement as to whether economic growth actually causes such a maldistribution depends upon one's political ideology. A growing number of development economists now take the view that political elites conspire to suppress policies which might improve the economic well-being of the masses so that they (the elites) can remain powerful and wealthy (e.g. Frank, 1972; Goulet, 1974; Griffin, 1974). Another group of economists contends that the annoying disamenities that we all increasingly suffer today (e.g. jet plane noise, crowded beaches, congested roadways) are brought about by economic growth (Mishan, 1967, 1969, 1971b; Schelling, 1971; Daly, 1973a). Others, especially Beckerman (1974) and the Resources for the Future economists (Freeman *et al.*, 1973), believe this to be more a question of misallocation of resources that effective intervention through the price system can rectify (see generally chapter 3, pp.85–100).

Whatever the relationship between growth and equity, policies to distribute social welfare more fairly are becoming politically more acceptable in economically advanced nations, as indicated in table 1.3. Redistribution takes three forms: regional economic development (to create jobs and boost confidence in economically depressed areas), efforts to equalise economic opportunity (minimum wage legislation, unemployment assistance, social security, and subsidies for necessities), and policies to equalise social opportunity (education, health, equal rights legislation, and better access to social services). Generally speaking, redistributive policies began first in the sphere of regional development and planning (in the mid-thirties in North America and postwar in Europe), to be followed by reform in equalising economic conditions (mostly in the welfare legislation of the mid-sixties), while efforts to achieve better social opportunities for minority groups have faced much stiffer opposition. Although some progress has been made in the field of civil rights, deep-seated prejudices die hard and progress remains slow. In less-developed

Table 1.3. Trends in social expenditures (as percentage of GNP) in EEC countries (adapted from OECD, 1972, p.5).

Country	1960–1962	1969–1970
Germany	17·9	18·8
France	15·4	20·7
Luxembourg	14·9	17·1
Belgium	14·6	16·3
Italy	13·2	17·0
Netherlands	13·2	19·9
United Kingdom	8·4	12·3
(United States)		(9·0)

nations the redistributive goal cluster is not so far advanced, especially with regard to civil rights, though conditions vary widely from nation to nation depending upon the political philosophies of the ruling groups.

The goal cluster around the theme of environmental quality tends to be the last to be politically recognised and remains the most vulnerable if other, higher-priority objectives are threatened. The reasons for its delay are well known: the better-off could always escape environmental distress by buying amenity, public health hazards were gradually taken care of, and in any case environmental quality has always been regarded as a many-sided public good to which no particular individual or group attached special importance and from which no one derived any special benefits (the 'freerider problem'—see Barkley and Seckler, 1972, pp.129–134). Consequently inadequate legal and economic institutions have been, and still remain, unable to cope with increasing environmental damage. One must not forget that much of what we call 'disamenity' results from the fact that people individually (though not necessarily society collectively) are willing to suffer some 'discomforts' (which they happily pass onto society generally) in order to enjoy their preferred goals of improved individual wealth, greater personal comfort, and wider recreational and leisure opportunities.

As we have noted, efforts to improve environmental quality began with perceived dangers to public health, to be followed by 'cosmetic' activities such as data collection, cleaning up pollutants that are manifestly disagreeable to the senses, and legislating treaties of mutual cooperation and noble intent. Even today, most environmental agencies are only able to set standards and nominally enforce performance; few environmental ministries are armed with really punitive sanctions or with the powers of planning controls, and fewer still can influence the nature of industrial production processes or legally control environmentally-damaging public behaviour unless there is a demonstrable danger to the public good (which is often very difficult to prove except *post facto*). (For a good discussion of enforcement problems facing pollution-control agencies, see Angeletti, 1973; Lucas and Moore, 1973; Ayres, 1975; Chernow, 1975; English, 1975; Kneese and Schultze, 1975).

At the international level the effectiveness of environmental quality management is even more limited because of powerful sovereignty arguments which preclude international investigation of matters of national interest (see chapter 8, pp.292–295). After a heated debate, the delegates at the UN Conference on the Human Environment agreed to 26 Declarations of Principle and 109 Recommendations for Action, all of which are significant more for their moral exhortation than as political imperatives (*The Ecologist*, July 1972; Artin, 1973; Stone, 1973). The Conference also established a UN Environment Programme that is confined largely to reviews of policies, monitoring of international pollutants, information exchange and some assistance in research (Hardy, 1973; Mattes, 1975). Although the efforts of the UN programme should not be dismissed, the political ineffectiveness of much of its activity demonstrates that environmental quality has not yet 'arrived' as a major goal: political realities dictate that other priorities take precedence. Ecocentrism as a moral crusade remains peripheral to the political scene.

Environmentalists seek to reorder the hierarchical arrangement of national priorities depicted in figure 1.1. They feel that these 'goal clusters' should not be regarded as irreconcilable and only to be accommodated by 'sacrificing' objectives of a lower order for those of a higher order, but that each objective is equally legitimate and essential for attaining a better society on a more habitable planet. The search for ecological harmony, therefore, must take into account considerations such as the proper composition and rate of economic activity, reform in the functioning of social and political democracy, and the application of technology that guarantees the stability and permanence of natural processes. So the modern environmentalist is as much concerned with land reform in Ethiopia and the organisation of neighbourhood cooperatives, as in protecting the remaining sperm whales or wild waterways. Clean air or pure water in an economically stagnant or politically repressive and unjust state is not the aim of the environmental crusaders of today. They seek novel mechanisms for reappraising social priorities such that a new mood of environmentalism permeates all political priorities, as sketched in figure 1.2.

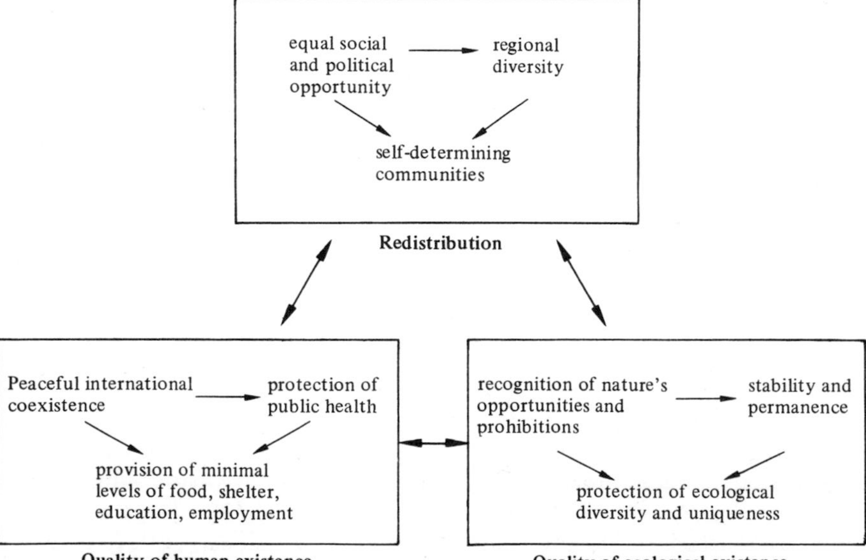

Figure 1.2. Reordered national goals in an environmentalist framework.

The modern environmentalist philosophy is very broad in scope and leftward in political orientation. The focal point of the movement is the redistributive goal cluster, a demand for better economic and social security for the entire global population, linked to an improved level of environmental amenity. Disamenity in all its forms is associated with poverty and hopelessness. The distribution of air and water pollution, of noise and ugliness, of disease and squalour, of malnutrition and unemployment is closely allied to social injustice and political ineffectiveness. Furthermore, it is now generally believed that one of the major menaces to world survival, population growth, is linked to poverty, malnutrition, and despair, and that all people who can genuinely envisage a better and more healthy life for themselves and their children gratefully and voluntarily reduce their fertility (see Neher, 1971; Espinshade, 1972; Cochrane, 1973; Boot, 1974; L. R. Brown, 1974a; Demeny, 1974; J. L. Simon, 1974). It is also accepted that as people enjoy greater economic and social security, so they will support efforts to improve amenity and seek an existence more harmonious with biological imperatives. In this context, it is now recognised that many 'hard line' solutions to environmental problems (especially such allocative devices as depletion taxes, residuals taxes, throughput taxes, and the like) are economically and socially regressive and will only be effective if accompanied by sensible attempts to guarantee fairer distribution (see chapter 3, pp.121–125). In the same vein, it is reasoned that a reduction in consumption and/or economic growth in developed nations will not necessarily help the world's poorer peoples unless this well-intentioned saving releases sufficient resources and funds, and is combined with the international political will to ensure that everyone alive has an adequate minimum standard of living.

Throughout the rest of this book, the implications of current environmentalist philosophies for economic, political, and social policies will be outlined and discussed in the context of particular issues. Environmentalism is emerging as a social movement of considerable depth and scope that has given a powerful new impetus to traditional liberal socialist rhetoric because of its persuasive talk of limits and the growing evidence that current lifeways cannot be continued in an unchanged form.

1.4 The 'tragedy of the commons' doctrine

Probably one of the most powerful essays in current environmental literature is a redrafted version of a presidential address given to the Pacific Division of the American Association for the Advancement of Science in December 1967. The essay is "The tragedy of the commons" by the American biologist Garrett Hardin (1968), a challenging article which should be read in the context of his subsequent book on the same theme (Hardin, 1972a) and two polemics (Hardin, 1972b, 1974) which have stirred up much controversy among the scientific community. The intriguing feature of the essay is not its originality (Hardin clearly acknowledges the antiquity of the 'commons' theme) but the moral implications of its conclusions, for Hardin believes that the inevitability of global destruction predetermines the choices that humanity must make to ensure its survival.

This kind of reasoning is excellent fodder for erudite scientific discussion of a kind similar to the debate that followed the publications of the controversial psychologist B. F. Skinner (1953, 1971). It is obvious that Hardin himself found his own conclusions disturbing, for in the preface to his book he remarks (Hardin, 1972a, p.ix):

> "Never have I found anything so difficult to work into shape. I wrote at least seven significantly different versions before resting content with this one ... . It was obvious that the internal resistance to what I found myself saying was terrific. As a scientist I wanted to find a scientific solution, but reason inevitably led me to conclude that the population problem could not possibly be solved without repudiating certain ethical beliefs and altering some of the political and economic arrangements of contemporary society. As I became used to living with unaccustomed conclusions, a restructuring of my psyche took place and I found I could accept them. I appreciated as never before the wisdom of Hegel's aphorism 'Freedom is the recognition of necessity'. In the end I felt free again, but in a different way."

Let us look at the 'tragedy' argument and its implications in some detail.

1.4.1 The original essay

Hardin devotes most of his discussion to the problem of controlling population growth which he assumes is detrimental to the future of humanity. He begins by defining a class of social problems (of which overpopulation is but one example) for which there are no 'scientific' solutions—in other words, we must seek answers in moral reason and codes of conduct which fall within the domains of the humanities and politics. The 'commons' theme is exemplified by the dilemma facing a mediaeval cattle herder who, along with all his neighbours, has free access and equal rights to graze his cattle on commonly owned pasture. If we assume that a certain number of cattle at a given point in time eat the grass at the same rate as it grows (i.e. there is a steady state in the consumption and production of grass), then the addition of *just one* extra cow will inevitably produce diminishing marginal returns. The herder reasons that if he adds his cow most of the benefits will accrue to him personally while most of the costs will be spread over all the other herders (but in such a manner that no individual is noticeably or unfairly injured). He also knows that if he does not add his cow (and there is no law to stop him), other herders might still add theirs. So the only rational solution is to add the cow. Of course every other herder comes to precisely the same conclusion through a process of similar logic, so the commons becomes hopelessly overgrazed.

The dilemma facing each herder encompasses the classic issues of selfishness versus enlightened public spiritedness, shortsightedness versus an interest in the longer perspective, and the relationship between knowledge of consequences, acceptance of blame, and awareness of alternative courses of action—issues which lie at the heart of environmental behaviour (Heberlein, 1972, 1973a). The 'tragedy' is the *inevitability* of the destruction of communally owned resources, or as Hardin puts it (1972a, p.255):

> "Each man is locked into a system that compels him to increase his [use of the commons] without limit—in a world that is limited. Ruin is the destination to which all men rush, each pursuing his own best interest in a society that believes in the freedom of the commons. Freedom in a commons brings ruin to all."

The key to the 'tragedy' theme is the nature of ownership (and the associated bundles of rights and duties), the scale of management responsibility, and the degree of collective trust existing in the polity. For although the commons are 'scarce' to the community, in the absence of authoritative management they are 'free' to each participating individual as long as they last. To the individual user the commons (now we can widen this term to include all common property resources) offer unrestricted and apparently unlimited opportunities; and because he has the same rights of use as any other he is not constrained by any legal obligations to his fellow users. On the other hand, the manager who is responsible for looking after the collective commons (e.g. the pollution control official, the fisheries commissioner) knows the resource is finite and that additional users will cause diminishing marginal returns. But unless there is someone in authority who can demonstrate limits, who knows when capacity (or assimilability) is attained, and who can exercise his managerial powers, then everyone must lose in the end. This conclusion is all the more likely if people accept a mode of political and economic organisation that encourages selfishness, exploitation and greed at the expense of cooperative trust and a sense of collective well-being. Hardin contends that to avoid the 'tragedy' there must be mutual coercion to limit individual freedom, a compulsion that must be agreed to by *every* participating individual.

Hardin is quite Malthusian in his reasoning for he is sure not only that the commons are finite, but also that everyone will inevitably pursue his own self-interest without concession, right up to the point of collapse. In his view a sense of mutual responsibility must be enforced for it can never be achieved by voluntary means. The survival of the earth therefore depends upon the emergence of an elitist managerial minority armed with powers to regulate human behaviour in the collective interest. Freedom must be tempered by necessity. Thus he believes that the decision to have children cannot be determined purely on personal considerations, despite the pious sentiments of the UN Declaration of Universal Human Rights, because the new morality of the commons dictates otherwise. "To couple the concept of freedom to breed with a belief that everyone born has an equal right to the commons", he states (Hardin, 1972a, p.258), "is to lock the world into a tragic course of action."

1.4.2 The morality of the commons

The morality of the commons is the new morality of limits (or scarcity) which has profound implications for critical policy questions facing the world today. Let Hardin speak for himself (as quoted by Neuhaus, 1971, p.186):

> "... we should go lightly in encouraging rising expectations among the poor ... for if everyone in the world had the same standard of living as we do, we would increase pollution by a factor of 20 ... . Therefore it is questionable morality to increase the food supply. We should hesitate to make sacrifices locally for the betterment of the rest of the world."

Here Hardin's conclusions contrast sharply with the social-justice theme developed in the preceding section of this chapter. To aid the poor and the hopeless will not only fail to improve their condition in the longer term but will diminish the existing freedoms of the 'better-off'.

Hardin develops this theme in an essay entitled "The ethics of a lifeboat" (Hardin, 1974), in which allegorical lifeboats filled with the world's rich people are surrounded by the struggling poor who are desperately trying to clamber aboard. His 'ethics' pertain to how the rich behave. They cannot let everyone in because the lifeboats have a limited capacity; if they allow some people on board they remove the lifeboats' safety margin, and anyway they still have to choose by some means the fortunate few who are to be saved. To Hardin the only realistic solution is to ignore the pleas for aid and retain the spare capacity:

> "We cannot safely divide the wealth equitably among all present peoples, so long as people reproduce at different rates, because to do so would guarantee that our grandchildren—everyone's grandchildren—would only have a ruined world to inhabit" (Hardin, 1974, p.18).

Thus, according to the commons morality, to provide a world food bank or fertiliser fund is to guarantee an escape valve for the poorly managed nations. "If a poor country can always draw on a world bank in a time of need", says Hardin (1974, p.16), "its population can continue to grow, and likewise its 'need'. In the short run, a world food bank diminishes unsatisfied 'need'; in the long run it increases the 'need' without limit." In the absence of a world government controlling reproduction, the ethics of a lifeboat must govern, for someone has to be sacrificed in the interests of 'humanity'.

The lifeboat metaphor is the extreme logical extension of the commons thesis and is subject to three kinds of criticism. Firstly, in postulating that the rich nations (the occupants of the lifeboats) enjoy unilateral power to determine the future of mankind it does not faithfully reproduce the real world situation. In fact, the rich nations are already substantially dependent on some resource-rich, poor countries whose political influence is already quite impressive and still growing (Walsh, 1974). A more realistic version of the lifeboat analogy would be to give some of the swimmers a limpet mine (though they realise that its explosion would probably destroy everybody). Secondly, in accepting the Malthusian belief that people are unable to control their own fertility even when given adequate incentives and means, the premises of the lifeboat metaphor fly in the face of recent research by demographers. For example, Revelle (1974b) stresses that if aid were channelled to the people who really need it (i.e. the very poor) fertility rates would decline markedly and immediately. Withholding aid will only worsen the situation by further widening the gulf between the rich and the poor in rapidly populating nations. Revelle argues the case for a quite different morality—a scarcity morality:

> "In future aid programs, the rich nations would be morally justified in insisting that the major part of capital and technical assistance be directed toward improving the living conditions and raising the aspirations of poor people, through bringing about higher levels of literacy and employment opportunities for women, improved health of both children and adults, better communications, greater opportunities for socio-economic mobility, rational urbanization, agricultural modernisation that benefits small farmers and landless laborers, and family planning services that give poor families freedom to choose the numbers of their children."

Thirdly, the lifeboat metaphor fails because of its own internal inconsistencies. The care of the commons, by definition, requires a communal effort and the mutual respect of all participating members. Indeed the use of the grazing, woodland, and turbary rights of the original English common lands predates feudalism to the era of Germanic laws when the concept of private ownership barely existed and communal rights and obligations governed the use of land (Juergensmeyer and Wadley, 1974, pp.362–365). Yet Hardin advocates the deliberate jettisoning of an undetermined number of the present earthly community for the good of 'humanity' (defined, implicitly, as the affluent minority). The ethics of a lifeboat denies the existence of a community and guarantees the persistence of discrimination. Neuhaus (1971, p.188) puts the case well:

> "The dispassionate observer of the present ecology movement cannot help but be struck by the ironies and contradictions coexisting under one banner. Compassion and callousness, altruism and greed, world vision and nationalistic *hubris*, all join in what some presume to call the ultimate revolution ... the reordering of man's place in nature ... .

The literature of the movement is marked by a moving reverence for the 'seamless web of life', accompanied by a shocking indifference to the weaker and less convenient forms of human life and by an almost cavalier readiness to disrupt the carefully woven web of civility and humane values."

1.4.3 The emergence of an elite minority

The commons argument puts the case for a managerial elite who control individual freedoms in the interest of the social good. In the logic of the lifeboat metaphor the rich and powerful are granted the supreme authority to protect their privileged positions. This of course is nothing new, for the powerful, by definition, have always been in a position to influence and to shape institutions in their favour. The original grazing 'commons' were eventually enclosed and allocated to wealthy private landowners, thereby creating a new exploited class of landless tenants who were forced to find work wherever it was available in circumstances for which they were not prepared. Thus feudalism became replaced by capitalism. Fife (1971) points out that the most successful exploiters of the commons do not suffer from the destruction they help to create, for once they recognise that *their* marginal returns are diminishing the invest elsewhere to maintain their exploitative economic hegemony. Whaling magnates, timber barons, and oil corporation lords have all fallen into this category at one time or another in economic history.

1.4.4 Weighing the incommensurables

Elitism also emerges in Hardin's proposal for a regulatory executive to determine the allocation of use in the commons and to weigh the incommensurable side effects that result. He is well aware (Hardin, 1972a, pp.133–142) of the failings of the regulatory agencies including the lack of public accountability. But someone has to weigh those incommensurables, and in doing so command the respect of the citizenry, so that collective rights and obligations are recognised by everybody. Hardin takes an ecocentric line on the matter of yardsticks for balancing incommensurables. "In nature", he notes (1972a, p.253), "the criterion is survival ... natural selection commensurates the incommensurables. The compromise achieved depends upon a natural weighting of the values of the variables. Man must imitate this process." A milder view of the same ecocentric principle is stated by Leopold (1949, p.223):

"Examine each question in terms of what is ethically and aesthetically right, as well as economically expedient. A thing is right when it tends to preserve the integrity, stability and beauty of the biotic community. It is wrong when it tends otherwise."

Although Hardin would prefer a 'natural' morality by which to judge the intervention of elites, this is viewed as naive presumption by the social scientist who feels that man must work out his own measuring devices based upon mutually agreeable values. Crowe (1969, p.1105), however, doubts that this is possible today, for, as a political scientist, she believes that modern society has fragmented into a pluralistic mix of tribes whose divergent values and expectations make them very reluctant to bow to the authority of a self-styled elite:

> "The critical change in this instance is not the rise of new groups; this is expected within the pluralistic mode of politics. What is new are value positions assumed by these groups which lead them to make demands, not as points for bargaining and compromise with the opposition, but rather as points which are 'not negotiable'. Hence they consciously set the stage for either confrontation or surrender, but not for rendering incommensurables commensurable."

1.4.5 The absence of community

A major underlying theme of the commons argument is the absence of a sense of community, a failure amongst individuals to consider what they may be doing to injure the earth they inhabit or to reduce their neighbours' welfare. Boulding's (1972b, p.139) quip is a serious environmental issue:

> "Economists argue that all the world lacks is
> A suitable system of effluent taxes.
> They forget that if people pollute with impunity
> This must be a symptom of lack of community."

Crowe (1969) shares this pessimistic view, for she contends that in modern society a universally acceptable set of values does not and cannot exist. She thinks that governments may become increasingly ineffectual as their electorates become less and less willing to recognise the acceptability of mutual coercion. The more the community is divided, the more difficult it will be to find a conciliatory mechanism that will work. Frustrated minorities might then turn to extremism to achieve their objectives, and perhaps indulge in violent tactics that could undermine the whole fabric of democracy. Certainly there is evidence that the politics of confrontation (values) is overtaking the politics of conciliation (interests) in almost every sphere of human activity, though it is extremely difficult to forecast with any confidence how individuals, groups, or nations will react when confronted with very real boundaries to their expectations.

Crowe's pessimism is not shared by Schelling (1971) who feels that the divergence of individual concern and the collective interest is more a result of inappropriate social organisation than perverse human nature. Quite elaborate institutional arrangements already exist to overcome this divergence —for example private ownership, contracts, and copyrights in the private sector, and various common laws and statutory legislation in the public domain. These mechanisms serve to give each participant the comforting feeling that everyone else is playing by the same rules. Unfortunately, day-to-day living provides a plethora of commons situations in which people are not legally obliged to play ball and, if there is any suspicion that someone is defaulting, the fragile bonds of participatory cooperation are easily broken. Examples abound and Schelling produces many. Here is one (Schelling, 1971, p.74):

> "People using an overloaded switchboard not only complete fewer calls than they would like but spend time dialing busy signals or waiting for calls that cannot come in; and urgent calls often await the leisurely completion of idle conversations by callers who, once they get on the line, have it as long as they choose to keep it but know that they cannot readily get back."

It is not that people wish to be malicious, argues Schelling, it is simply that we have not yet devised appropriate institutions to deal with an abundance of bads in the way that we have successfully created mechanisms to cope with a scarcity of goods. The commons argument emphasises the need to devise enforceable contracts to cope with the bads we produce. "Medicines are proprietary, but germs are free", observes Schelling (1971, p.78). "I own the tobacco I plant in my field, but you may have the smoke free of charge. I can have you arrested if you steal my electric amplifier, but help yourself to the noise."

The search for enforceable contracts has been initiated by people like Goldie (1971) and Mishan (1974b), who favour a system of amenity rights by which everyone would automatically have legal protection against disamenity. Any proven usurpation of these rights would be subject to legal intervention and compensation. Lawyers (e.g. Sax, 1970b; Sax and Connor, 1972; Scarman, 1974, p.55) have advocated the idea of 'citizen's rights' which would grant citizens standing in court should they suffer adversely as a result of environmental damage (see chapter 8, pp.277–280). Economists have also responded to this general notion by suggesting that emission of all residuals be subject to a tax which, in effect, grants polluters 'rights' to discharge effluent up to socially acceptable levels and eliminates the idea that air, water, and land are 'free goods' (see chapter 3, pp.110–121).

1.4.6 The self-selection of the conscienceless

In a 'commons' situation it takes but one defaulter to test the conscience of the public-spirited. The man who shatters the peace of a Sunday morning by starting up his motor mower weakens the resistance of those who have denied themselves the use of this prime grass-cutting time. The person who ignores the 'no trespassing' sign enjoys his lunch in blissful solitude while the rest may have to suffer the congestion of a crowded picnic area.

Hardin views this matter seriously. He believes that social conscience is self-eliminating, with the result that society will eventually be composed of selfish people who care little for the welfare of others. In the original essay he takes a Darwinian perspective on this question: since couples without consciences will bear plenty of children, while those with consciences produce none or few, 'restraint' will be bred out of the population.

> "The argument ... applies ... to any instance in which society appeals to an individual exploiting a commons to restrain himself for the general good—by means of his conscience. To make such an appeal is to set up a selective system that works towards the elimination of conscience from the race" (Hardin, 1972a, p.259).

In the lifeboat metaphor, the rich with a conscience (i.e. those already on the boat who wish to assist the struggling swimmers) must either give up their own places on the boat (i.e. destroy themselves) or be silenced by the conscienceless majority who are solely intent on maintaining their superiority.

> "This may solve the problem of the guilt-ridden person's conscience, but it does not change the ethics of the lifeboat. The needy person to whom the guilt-ridden person yields his place will not himself feel guilty about his sudden good luck. (If he did he would not climb aboard.) The net result of conscience-stricken people giving up their unjustly held positions is the elimination of that sort of conscience from the lifeboat. Conscience eliminates itself, leaving the ethics of a lifeboat unchanged" (Hardin, 1974, p.4).

This line of reasoning appears to justify the selfish retention of privilege, because otherwise 'goodness' is extinguished from the population. It all fits in with the Hardin ideology but is profoundly abhorrent to many modern environmentalists. Nevertheless Hardin's rhetoric is persuasive, despite its lack of Christianity, because even more liberal thinkers accept that some form of compulsive restraint is necessary. Schelling (1971, p.74) puts the dilemma rather well:

> "With less [use of the commons] the value could have been substantial for those who got to use it. Making it freely available means that anyone who might have been excluded under a scheme to limit use becomes privileged to share a useless asset rather than envy the few who share a valuable one."

1.4.7 Growth and the management of the commons

There is good reason to believe that low-density societies existing in a steady state with little pressure on their resources do not experience the need to regulate individual behaviour (Juergensmeyer and Wadley, 1974). In fact Krier and Montgomery (1973, p.91) believe that, in such societies, potentially disruptive externalities are so unimportant that it would be socially more costly to devise means of collective control than simply to retain a system of private transactions among offending parties when damage does occur. Regulatory intervention is necessary only when the scale of side effects creates transaction costs (negotiation costs) which exceed the gains of negotiation among dispersed two-party agreements. This occurs either when population densities increase, or when scarce and highly valued resources are threatened, or when the nature of economic activity becomes more varied and sophisticated. These conditions are associated with urbanisation and economic growth and provide a powerful argument for members of the nongrowth school who feel that increasing transaction costs of regulation will soon outweigh the gains of further growth. Even economists who favour growth also recognise this problem (McKean, 1973; Olson *et al.*, 1973) so it is likely to become an important issue in the growth–nongrowth debate.

1.4.8 Some concluding observations

The commons parable is powerful because it drives right at the heart of environmentalism—the moral relationship between short-term selfishness and enlightened longer-term community interest. Its fascination is its insolubility, for, as Stillman (1975) correctly observes, the premises of the parable cannot produce a logical solution. For 'tragedy' to occur we must have (a) a finite commons, (b) a consumption pattern that removes more than it puts in, and (c) selfishly motivated users who feel no community spirit. If these three conditions exist then no amount of coercion, no matter how mutually acceptable can be sustained long enough to avoid disaster. Thus the 'tragedy' thesis is challenging because it forces us to seek beyond these premises for an answer. Either we must relate our activities to ecological imperatives (so that input and output are more or less balanced), or we must develop an acceptable code of altruism and longsightedness to regulate our actions willingly in the wider community interest—or both, as many ecocentrists believe. Whether these changes can be achieved by enlightened reason or whether they will be thrust upon the world with the compulsion of catastrophe remains in dispute. The dice could roll either way: Schumacher (1973) provides the views of the optimist, while Martin (1975) presents the pessimist's case. These and other views will be discussed in chapter 9 (pp.302–311).

2

Growth and adequacy of resources

Conservationists and economists may differ on many fronts but they unite in their common interest in scarcity and the proper allocation of resources between present and future generations. When Gifford Pinchot, following his friend McGee (1909/10, p.379), proclaimed that conservation was a matter of furnishing "the greatest good to the greatest number for the longest time", he may have allowed his Benthamite idealism to overcome his practical realism, but he was very much aware that resource wastage could lead to future scarcities and a slowdown of economic growth.

Conservation movements have tended to emerge during periods of economic anxiety and attendant social change (O'Riordan, 1971c), though, far from attempting to slow down economic growth, conservationists have generally been eager to reorganise economic activity so as to ensure continued progress in economic well-being and a reasonable spread of the benefits of growth across the population at large. "The first principle of conservation is development", remarked Pinchot (1910, p.47), "the use of natural resources now existing for the benefit of the people who live here now ... natural resources must be developed and preserved for the benefit of the many and not merely for the profit of the few." Pinchot's views were expressed at a time when some Americans finally realised that their 'frontier' was finite, that indeed there could be a limit to the resource abundance they had taken for granted for so long. The American conservation period of the mid-thirties was dominated by the threat of economic stagnation and by falling birth rates which heralded the possibility of zero population growth. Conservation, mid-thirties style, was really organised natural resource exploitation and regional economic planning; demographers even urged the populace to breed, such was the fear of economic and national decline.

So, far from talking about an economic 'steady state', conservationist philosophy has long been interested in promoting growth and improving social welfare. Why so? Possibly because the spectre of 'limits' with its attendant threat of curtailed social progress has always lurked in the popular imagination.

The current talk of 'limits' and of global Armageddon is really nothing new. Doomsdayers have existed since antiquity and economic Cassandras were propounding their dismal forecasts long before Malthus embraced their cause. We have already noted how the early conservation movements in the United States used the 'politics of scarcity' to arouse popular awareness of limits, and to justify economic hegemony and large scale governmental intervention into the workings of the private sector. Maybe the threat of scarcity is necessary to remind a greedy population enjoying the hedonism of affluence of the need for efficiency and frugality, so that it will accede to the kind of political and economic manipulation that in more plentiful times would be regarded as unacceptable. Certainly there is evidence that, as the demonstrable fear of shortage recedes, conservationist policies weaken (O'Riordan, 1971c). The blissful euphoria of apocryphal abundance may well contain the seeds of its own destruction.

2.1 What is growth?

It is probably true to say that persistent economic growth as we know it has existed for a very brief period in comparison with man's time span on this planet (figure 2.1). Prior to the industrial revolution the vast majority of the world population experienced no demonstrable improvement in either spiritual or economic conditions in their lifetimes. For most living today this situation has not altered, though many are aware that their national leaders are telling them how their standard of living should improve in the foreseeable future. So perhaps the only major difference between today's poor and the poor of two centuries ago is the *expectation* of being better-off. The fact remains, however, that persistent real growth in economic well-being is a very short-lived and recent phenomenon, so we should consider how much longer this somewhat unusual condition can continue.

What exactly is growth? This subject is covered extensively in many standard economic texts (e.g., Solow, 1970), but, put simply, growth is characterised by increases in four aspects of consumption and production:

(i) Increases in goods and services produced and consumed. For many this is nominally the essence of growth—the proliferation of consumer products and social services through the profitable application of labour and capital, which in turn creates the wealth necessary to purchase such commodities.

(ii) Increases in human capital through education, training, and the widening of experience. This is what is known as the knowledge and information component, regarded by many as crucial to human progress.

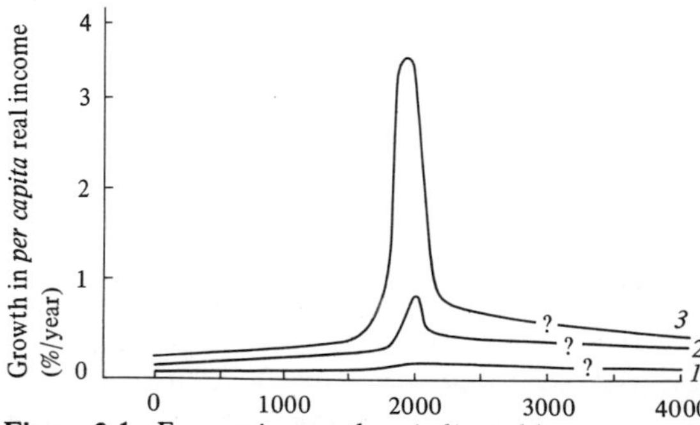

Figure 2.1. Economic growth as indicated by percentage rise in real personal incomes in the perspective of human history: *1*, majority of the population of the less developed nations; *2*, the 15%-25% poor in the developed nations; *3*, the 15%-25% rich in the developed nations.

Human capital is an essential ingredient for increasing productivity, encouraging the mobility of labour, and sustaining political democracy as we know it. A well-informed, suitably trained, and widely educated public is viewed as a prime prerequisite for social progress and peaceful social change.

(iii) Increases in nonhuman capital through investment and the application of science and technology. Investment can only be generated from surplus wealth. Economists, entrepreneurs, and academics differ over what proportion of profit constitutes 'surplus' and hence what should be a 'reasonable' rate of return on investment, but few deny that some degree of investment is vital to sustain economic growth and enhance productivity.

(iv) Improvements in economic organisation and management through the application of organisational theory and techniques. To many modern economists and businessmen effective management is of crucial importance in sustaining economic power and influence. This is a controversial topic, for followers of Marx believe that the organisation of production creates a division of wealth, power, and social class and influences attitudes to growth, while more moderate but still liberal economists believe that modern management techniques serve to maintain economic dominance among a corporate elite.

Depending on one's viewpoint, growth can be defined by a variety of parameters and can result in greater or lesser advances in social welfare. But while there is much talk today about the relative advantages and disadvantages of growth, it should be stressed that, generally speaking, economists have always believed that growth cannot continue indefinitely, and that eventually (though the actual timing is highly debatable) increases in wealth must give way to improvements in spiritual and other aspects of non-monetary well-being. However, throughout history, views about growth have been tremendously influenced by prevailing political ideologies and social attitudes. It is in this context that we shall consider how economic philosophers have regarded growth and the attainment of some kind of economic steady state.

2.1.1 The classical economists

The era of classical economics is generally assumed to have begun with the publication of Adam Smith's *Wealth of Nations* in 1776. Smith was angered by the self-interested views of the mercantile pamphleteers of the late seventeenth century, who pleaded for strong government control of the economy to regulate imports and stimulate protected domestic production. Many of these polemicists were associated with brokers and traders who sought to monopolise much of British trade, depress import prices, and suppress domestic wage rates. But while Smith abhorred monopolistic practice he was by no means in favour of unregulated business enterprise, for he was well aware that the 'corporate ethic' (as the term would be used today), if left to itself, would not work to promote the public good. A properly functioning competitive free market was essential to guarantee that private business would be responsive to the public interest. [Nearly two hundred years later Galbraith (1973) reaches the same conclusion, though he is anxious to see much more public sector spending than Smith would probably have advocated.]

Smith is also well known for his views on the division of labour such that each worker would maximise his productive potential according to his talents and training. Although this is now a hotly contested issue among environmentalists (see Schumacher, 1973, pp.69–82) who feel that occupational specialisation is dehumanising and alienating, to be fair to Smith, he did not visualise industrial technology, or the mass production line, or the mindlessness of much of modern bureaucracy when he wrote. He was simply interested in linking increases in productivity to an enlarged economic market, so that appropriately trained workers could be more contented and better-off. After all, Smith talked not of economic growth but of "the progress of improvement", which presumably referred to better social and psychological conditions as well as monetary wealth (see Pavitt, 1973, p.138).

Smith viewed the possibility of an economic steady state as extremely remote but nevertheless inevitable, since increases in productivity could not be sustained indefinitely and could only result in falling rates of profit and a reduction in investment. In his actual words (Smith, 1961, p.375):

> "As capitals increase in any one country, the profits which can be made by employing them necessarily diminish. It becomes gradually more and more difficult to find within the country a profitable method of employing any new capital."

He also thought that falling rates of profit would be caused by increasing wage demands from a growing labour force and that more aggressive competition would force entrepreneurs to bid down rates of return on investment. Smith also foresaw the possibility of cartel-like practices by owners of agricultural land and other primary commodities, who would accumulate profits as growth created scarcity and drove up prices. But Smith did not follow these premises to their logical conclusions, partly because they were very speculative and partly because he was optimistic that, in the short-run, economic growth would lead to improvements in social conditions that would change the long-term political outlook. For example, he did not regard the likelihood of population growth with any misgivings. "The liberal reward of labour", he stated (Smith 1961, p.90), "as it is the effect of increasing wealth, so it is the cause of increasing population. To complain of this is to lament over the necessary effect and cause of the greatest prosperity." Smith was a humanitarian who believed that economic growth guided by healthy competition and free trade would lead to widespread human happiness; growth therefore was an acceptable means to a laudable end.

Smith's successors were not so sanguine about the social benefits of growth and competition. The key to Smith's argument was the availability of resources and the conversion of surplus profits into improved productivity, pleasanter working conditions, and redistributed wealth. But two events took place around the turn of the eighteenth century to change the face of economic philosophy. The first was the French Revolution in 1789, the second the publication of the first British census in 1801. The French Revolution was manna for social philosophers who yearned for a utopia on earth, and who saw in the Age of Enlightenment the liberation of man through the application of science and reason. Godwin wrote of a world where there would be "no war, no crimes, no administration of justice and no government". Besides this there would be "neither disease, anguish, melancholy nor resentment. Every man will seek, with ineffable ardour, the good of all" (quoted in Maddox, 1972, p.37). In France Condorcet echoed these sentiments, but he admitted that these dreams could be shattered by continued population growth. "Might there not come a time", he asked, "when, because the number of people in the world finally exceeds the means of subsistence, there ensues a continual diminution of happiness, a true regression or at least an oscillation between good and bad?" (*ibid.*). Being a utopian socialist, Condorcet believed that the solution lay in egalitarian policies, which, by improving the general contentment, would induce social responsibility and an interest in family well-being and so reduce fertility.

But contemporary events presented a picture quite opposite to these visions. The overlapping of the agricultural and industrial revolutions stimulated a massive rural–urban migration as landless tenants, dispossessed by landlords profiting from increasing agricultural productivity and rising food prices, were enticed away by empty promises of jobs and higher wages in the towns. The immediate consequence was widespread misery in the form of backbreaking toil for subsistence wages, utterly inadequate housing and sanitary conditions, and only rudimentary social services. In short, there was little evidence of Smith's 'trickle down' theory or of the enlightened egalitarianism of the utopians.

Nevertheless there was some political recognition of this distress, for in 1796 the British government passed the Poor Laws, a piece of quasi-socialist legislation designed to relieve the plight of the poor by granting financial relief to large families on the grounds that "those having enriched their country with a number of children, have claim upon its assistance for their support". Soon afterwards, the (first) British census of 1801 revealed an alarmingly higher population than was anticipated, though, as Huxley (1964, p.233) points out, this should not really have been so unexpected, as successive British governments had consistently encouraged population growth so that they could open up their colonies, man their armies, combat the population explosion in France, and have an abundant reservoir of low-cost labour.

It was during this period that Malthus wrote his famous essays—seven in all, between 1798 and 1823—on the "Principle of population". Although Malthus was the son of a prominent liberal reformist, his first essay was little more than a polemical critique of the views of Godwin and Condorcet. Malthus (1969, p.7) is well known for his 'iron law':

> "Population, when unchecked, increases in a geometric ratio. Subsistence only increases in an arithmetic ratio. A slight acquaintance with numbers will shew the immensity of the first power in comparison with the second."

The postulates underlying this thesis were (a) that resources (particularly food supplies) were limited, (b) that food is necessary to the survival of man, and (c) that certain classes (especially the lower classes) would always bear plenty of children because "passion between the sexes was necessary and constant". Malthus believed that in order to limit his fertility man was faced with two clear alternatives, one voluntary, the other compulsory. Either he could reduce his sexual activity by self-restraint, or his numbers would be reduced through the punitive controls of starvation, misery, and disease.

Perhaps less well known is the fact that Malthus used this thesis to prove that man was not such an enlightened being as the utopians liked to believe and hence that the kind of egalitarian social reform envisaged in the Poor Laws would be a failure. He commented (Malthus, 1969, p.8):

> "This natural inequality of the two powers of population and of production in the earth and that great law of our nature which must constantly keep their effects equal form the great difficulty that to me appears insurmountable in the way to perfectability of society ... . No fancied equality, no agrarian regulations in their utmost extent, could remove the pressure [from the iron law] even for a single century."

Malthus opposed the charity of the Poor Laws, for he was convinced that the granting of aid to the poor would mollify the exigencies of misery sufficiently only to encourage them to have more children. These, in turn, would consume more resources and return the population to the margin of subsistence. This well known 'Malthusian trap' is depicted diagrammatically in figure 2.2. Malthus was quite unconcerned as to the cause of this persistent misery; the dismal result would occur regardless of whether poverty was caused by social injustice ('a bad structure of society') or by insufficiency of food (or unacceptably high food prices), a viewpoint that was furiously criticised by Marx a quarter of a century later. This is an important ideological issue, for Malthus was convinced that reform was futile, regardless of what political ideology was adopted. He thus provided ideological grist for the right-wing mill of social conservatives who feared the revolutionary idealism of the times and felt threatened by contemporary policies of social reform (Pavitt, 1973, pp.142–143).

In effect, Malthus was not simply writing about limits but about the 'politics of squeeze'. Because he felt that the poor could never experience affluence, he supported a policy of 'benign neglect', thinking it the only way the poor could be made to 'learn their lesson' and seek to improve their lot by hard work. Malthus was also of the opinion that sexual continence would be achieved only when the poor knew they could not survive through charity. There is no doubt that in these views there was a fair amount of the class snobbery that most of the intellectual English gentry of the period held toward the poor. But there was also a sincere (albeit misplaced) humanitarianism in this argument, for the middle and upper classes genuinely believed that hard work and rising expectations would bestow self-esteem and improve productivity, and hence generally better the lot of the poor and rich alike. Joseph Townsend (1969, p.24) expressed both these feelings when he wrote:

> "The poor know little of the motives which stimulate the higher ranks to action—pride, honour and ambition. In general it is only hunger which can spur and goad them on to labour; yet our Poor Laws have said, they shall never hunger ... . He who statedly employs the poor in useful labour is their only friend: he, who only feeds them, is their greatest enemy."

Townsend developed this class-centred view into what he regarded as a noble natural law. "It seems to be a law of nature that the poor should be to a certain degree improvident", he commented (quoted in Meek and Weissman, 1971, p.114), "so that there may always be some to fulfil the most servile, the most sordid, the most ignoble offices in the country.

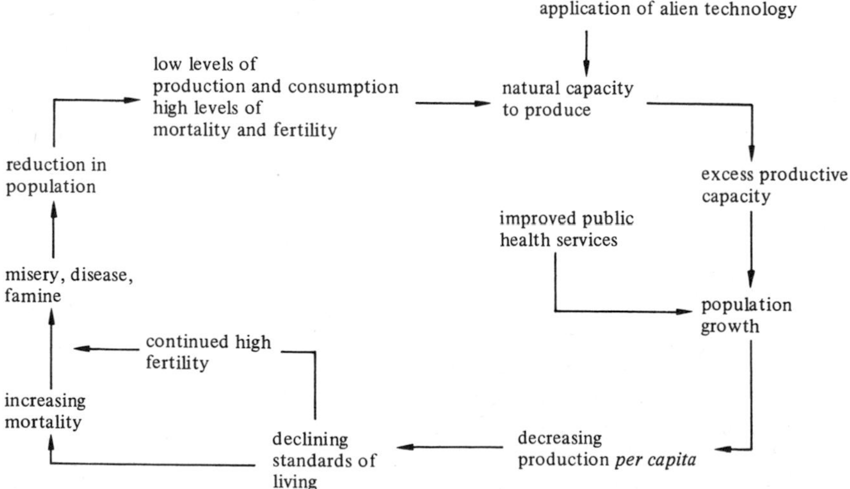

Figure 2.2. The Malthusian trap of population growth and resource scarcity.

The stock of human happiness is thereby much increased, while the more delicate are not only relieved from drudgery ... but are left at liberty without interruption to pursue these callings which are to their various dispositions. [The Poor Law] tends to destroy the harmony and beauty, the symmetry and order of that system which God and Nature have established in the world." Gans (1972) develops the same theme of the positive functions of poverty in the modern context, and hints that only when the poor become a real threat to established order will their grievances be better recognised.

Harvey (1973) thinks that Malthus was not talking just about limits, but also the need to protect the interests of the privileged minority in a world of shortage. He contends that Malthus was not interested in an economic steady state; far from it. He was anxious to encourage economic growth through the stimulation of 'effective demand' (a radical notion that lay dormant for over a century until Keynes realised its tremendous significance), which would assure the accumulation of profits by the capitalist classes. Malthus identified two categories of effective demand (a) conspicuous consumption by the 'unproductive' classes (landlords, the gentry, and the owners of production—people later described by Marx as 'parasites and gluttonous drones'), and (b) the creation of wants amongst the poor, who, enticed by these economic carrots, would be inspired "to excite their exertions in the production of wants". He wrote (quoted in Harvey, 1973, p.8):

> "One of the greatest benefits which foreign commerce confers, and the reason why it has always appeared as an almost necessary ingredient in the progress of wealth, is its tendency to inspire new wants, to form new tastes and to furnish fresh motives for industry. Even civilised and improved countries cannot afford to lose any of these motives."

The logic of 'effective demand' does not accommodate itself easily to the logic of 'limits', a contradiction which has not passed unnoticed by students of nongrowth. One is tempted to conclude that Malthus used the limits thesis largely to suffocate a policy of what he saw as unearned egalitarianism, for he clearly was an apologist for the owners of property who were not only important consumers but who also patronised the arts and sciences and who 'confer upon society a most signal benefit'. Thus Malthus supported the *status quo*—the protection of private property rights, the division of the classes, the dominance of a capitalist and intellectual elite who were vital for investment and managerial expertise—through the mechanism of a contrived threat of scarcity, for scarcity kept prices up and wages down (given a disorganised labouring poor) and stimulated man's creative ingenuity.

Ricardo was more sanguine than Malthus in his views of food shortages, for he believed that the threat of scarcity would encourage more efficient management practices, with the result that poorer quality land could successfully be put into production. Nevertheless, like Adam Smith, he did envisage economic decline, brought about by rising agricultural rents and falling profits, as food became less available and more costly to produce. However, he believed that the evil day could be put off through the vigorous application of labour-saving technology (though he felt that this should be introduced slowly and with caution), the opening up of international trade (whereby primary products could be imported and higher value manufactured goods exported) and plenty of encouragement to the entrepreneur (through a reduced tax on profits to promote investment). While Malthus championed the holders of wealth, Ricardo supported the bourgeoisie, or what we would today call the meritocracy, the people who create wealth by sound business practice and clearheaded investment.

Although neither Smith, nor Malthus, nor Ricardo wanted to see a steady state economy, they regarded it as more or less inevitable, although the timing of its onset was vague. They were all convinced of the merits of increasing economic growth, though they differed as to how it could be attained, who should provide the leadership, and how far the benefits should be spread around. But as the industrial revolution changed the face of the countryside and seemingly failed to alleviate misery, writers began to question the moral values of growth, or at least the means of achieving and distributing wealth.

John Stuart Mill in his *Principles of Political Economy* (1848, with six revisions to 1871) took the former, the more moralistic line; Karl Marx (in various writings between 1845 and 1883) followed with the latter viewpoint. Barber (1967, p.94) notes that Mill rejected many of the cruder formulations of the Benthamite philosophy that attempted to quantify utility, and insisted that qualitative considerations should count as forcefully as quantitative factors. He became convinced that the 'quality of life' was not improving for the majority of the population despite demonstrable increases in the national wealth. But Mill had ambivalent opinions on the steady state, even though he is widely quoted amongst the advocates of nongrowth as favoring its onset. Here he is in Daly (1973a, pp.12–13):

> "I cannot ... regard the stationary state of capital and wealth with the unaffected aversion so generally manifested toward it by political economists of the old school. I am inclined to believe that it would be, on the whole, a very considerable improvement on our present condition. I confess I am not charmed by the ideal of life held out by those who think that the normal state of human beings is that of struggling to get on; that the trampling, crushing, elbowing and treading on each other's heels, which form the existing type of social life, are the most desirable lot of human kind, or anything but the disagreeable symptoms of one of the phases of industrial progress."

Mill's views on the matter were coloured by his aristocratic disdain of vulgar materialism and his genteel preference for loftier pleasures such as cultivation of the arts, intelligent discourse, and the peacefulness of solitude.

> "Solitude, in the sense of being often alone, is essential to any depth of meditation or of character; and solitude in the presence of natural beauty and grandeur, is the cradle of thoughts and aspirations which are not only good for the individual but which society could ill do without" (Mill, 1970, pp.115–116).

It is not clear whether he hoped that the proletariat would come to seek these latter values as a steady state was reached, or whether what he vaguely called 'the progress of civilisation' would grant the masses sufficient income so that they could afford to turn away from the consumption of necessities toward the cultivation and satisfaction of more spiritual needs. It seems that he trusted the course of economic growth to open up the latter route as the threat of scarcity stimulated technological and intellectual endeavour and broadened nonmaterial awareness (see Barnett and Morse, 1963, pp.64–71). So he saw economic growth as distasteful but necessary for the improvement of men's minds and their sets of values, a period of transition before the attainment of a 'stationary state' of capital in which man would be liberated from the anguish of always trying to 'get on' and be free to indulge in "all kinds of mental culture and moral and social progress".

Nevertheless Mill regarded growth as a necessary evil, for he recognised the importance of investment, of research and development, and of managerial expertise in creating the labour-saving technology to release the labouring classes from drudgery and boredom, and for continuously offsetting the dangers of diminishing marginal returns. In this matter he was by no means an ecocentric. While he acknowledged the 'law' of nature's 'limits', he believed (1970, pp.55–56) that "this law may be suspended, or temporarily controlled, by whatever adds to the general power of mankind over nature; and especially by any extension of their knowledge, and their consequent demand, over the properties and powers of natural agents". Mill regarded the economic steady state as a utopian vision, a blissful state where man was free to cultivate his intellect and morals (though one can well argue that these qualities would be needed just as much in attempting to attain the steady state); it was not an ecologically harmonious notion thrust upon man by biological imperatives.

2.1.2 Marx on overpopulation and scarcity

Marx was not particularly interested in a steady state, but in a socialist mode of economic production that distributed wealth according to effort. He was impressed by the technological ingenuity of man and visualised no reasonable bounds to economic or social progress provided that the benefits were properly shared. One of Marx's main concerns was to show that the dreadful state of subsistence and misery afflicting the labouring poor (and which he himself suffered) was not due to overpopulation and a propensity to procreate, but to the capitalistic exploitation of the working classes (for a good discussion see Meek and Weissman, 1971). Since the basic unit of wealth was labour, Marx believed that the 'price' of a commodity should equal the labour units invested in manufacturing it (plus a reasonable surplus for reinvestment). Marx contended that under the guise of competition the capitalist entrepreneur 'overpriced' his goods (i.e. by charging a price higher than the real value of the labour input thus 'underpricing' or 'exploiting' his work force) so that his workers toiled extra hours simply to provide a 'surplus' profit which he accumulated. Thus surplus labour became 'surplus value', the source of rent, interest, and profit. Capitalists, he believed, were therefore interested in population growth, for a static labour force in a growing economy would result in a demand for labour, a consequent rise in wage rates and falling profits. To offset this, the capitalists introduced labour-saving technology at a rate slow enough to avoid excessive costs of investment, yet fast enough to suppress any tendency for wages to rise in relative terms. At the same time, they improved productivity and thus accumulated more surpluses.

Marx, therefore, did not believe in a 'natural' law of overpopulation at all, but in the existence of a deliberately created 'relative surplus population', an oversupply of labour made redundant by the fruits of industrial progress, itself a product of labour.

> "If a surplus labouring population is a necessary product of accumulation or of the development of wealth on a capitalist basis, this surplus population becomes ... a condition of existence of the capitalist mode of production. It forms a disposable industrial reserve army, that belongs to capital quite as absolutely as if the latter had bred it at its own cost" (quoted in Harvey, 1973, p.14).

Hence, in Marx's view capitalism, not sexual passion, determined population growth, and capitalism, not the limits to agricultural productivity, was the cause of poverty. Marx did not talk of a 'population problem' but of a 'poverty problem'. He rejected the *inevitability* of subsistence that Malthus propounded in his 'iron law', replacing it with a theory of capitalist manipulation of the rate of economic progress and control over the social conditions of the working classes. The threat of scarcity was as chimerical as the threat of overpopulation, for scarcity was simply a highly successful capitalist device to control totally the rate and nature of resource exploitation, the level of prices, and the cost of labour. Harvey (1973, p.19) sums up the Marxist view of scarcity as follows:

> "Scarcity, like a relative surplus population, is necessary to the survival of the capitalist mode of production ... capitalism undoubtedly rests upon a structured form of scarcity which means that scarcity is as much created as it is induced by certain natural lacks to meet certain social ends."

Marx certainly challenged the smug optimism regarding the beneficial consequences of economic progress that was prevalent at the time. But he did foresee a possible end to economic growth, as technological advance increased the 'organic composition of capital' (the ratio between investment and wages) to the point where profits began to decline. In any case the growing inequality of wealth would reduce effective demand if the incomes of the masses were to remain at subsistence levels while productive capacity expanded. Economic collapse, though not desirable, was a necessary condition for the takeover of capitalist enterprise by the working classes. A great champion of the proletariat, Marx admired the creative ingenuity of the craftsman and the small agriculturalist whose skills and pride he felt were threatened. Marx was also a humanitarian, with an unbounded faith in the nobility of labour and the magnificence of human imagination. Given appropriate management of the means of production and the distribution of wealth, he felt the steady state need not be contemplated with any misgivings.

2.1.3 The neoclassicists and Keynes

For the most part, Marx's dire predictions of an eventual collapse of capitalist accumulation and a takeover by the proletariat did not occur as the nineteenth century wore on. In fact, owing largely to colonial expansionism, unprecedented economic prosperity continued through the Victorian era, without the checks feared by the classicists, while some of the wealth generated by tremendous increases in productivity began to be shared by the working classes. As Barber (1967, p.103) comments, "continued economic expansion, though not important, appeared to be taking care of itself". The neoclassicists therefore turned to microeconomics, the theory of the firm, of supply and demand, and of the proper allocation of resources, assuming what Daly (1973a) has termed "a paradigm of growth". The classical fears of falling rates of profit were replaced by a theory of interest rates controlling the level of money supply, by a belief in continuous technological innovation, and by a conviction that the working classes would become ever more industrious to maintain their improved standards of living. The notion of an economic steady state all but disappeared. This period saw advances in the scientific understanding of marginality, utility, and welfare, of rational economic man, and of the nature of price. Neoclassical economists sought to avoid the normative implications of materialistic versus nonmaterialistic consumption by simply talking about the production of satisfactions [a point later developed by Beckerman (1974, pp.20–23)]. Value judgements about the rightness or wrongness of growth or the effects of growth were simply not considered: as Robinson (1964, p.25) puts it, "it is the business of the economists, not to tell us what to do, but to show what we are doing anyway is in accord with proper principles".

In the early 1930s the euphoria about economic growth was rudely shattered as a massive and somewhat unexpected economic slump afflicted all western nations. The focus of economic concern was not the threat of overpopulation or resource scarcity—far from it, because fertility was declining and commodities were cheap and abundant—but the threat of demand falling short of production, an imbalance between what the economic system was capable of producing and what the underemployed populace was able to consume. Political attention was riveted on means of stimulating economic activity even if it meant borrowing on the expectation of growth, for there were fears that the persistence of poverty could lead to political and social unrest. Hence the enormous success of Keynes' theory of effective demand and deficit financing in promoting economic growth. Keynes made it clear that governments would have to intervene in the economy to stabilise the *rate* of growth by various fiscal devices, and more than his neoclassical predecessors he realised the tremendous psychological significance of the *promise* of economic progress in influencing capital accumulation, investment, and consumption. This is a vitally important point, for it created the myth of the 'cult of growth' so strongly objected to by nongrowth economists (see especially Hodson, 1972, pp.30–50), who see it as an empty promise that feeds the flames of inflation. According to Hodson (1972, pp.43–44):

> "... we can diagnose the growth cult as the syndrome of rising expectations. Every economic decision, whether by businessmen or investors or trade unions or governments, comes to be coloured by reference to a growth standard ... . A new fantasy world is created in public, private and business imaginations ... heightened by the ... popularly recommended drug [of] monetary inflation, under the cosy brand name of reflation."

Keynes, like other economists, was well aware of the distinction between absolute needs ("we feel them whatever the situation of our fellow human beings may be") and relative needs ("we feel them only if their satisfaction lifts us above, makes us feel superior to, our fellow human beings"). He agreed with Smith and Ricardo that "the desire for food is limited in every man by the narrow capacity of his stomach, but the desire for the conveniences and ornaments of building, dress, equipage, and household furniture, seems to have no limit or certain boundary" (quoted in Pavitt, 1973, p.146). Like his famous predecessors, he recognised and hoped that somehow growth would cease or slow down substantially, once man had the leisure and wealth to enjoy higher and less materialistic satisfactions. In a remarkable essay written during the dark years of the second world war (1943) he noted (Keynes, 1971, p.192) that at that time:

> "The love of money as a possession—as distinguished from the love of money as a means to the enjoyments and realities of life—will be

recognised for what it is, a somewhat disgusting morbidity ... . I see us free, therefore, to return to some of the sure and certain principles of religion and traditional virtue—that avarice is a vice, that the extraction of usury is a misdemeanour, and that the love of money is detestable ..."

Keynes admitted that before this blissful state could be attained (he forecast soberly that it might take a hundred years) a quite opposing morality would hold sway:

"For at least another 100 years we must pretend to ourselves and to everyone that *fair is foul and foul is fair; for foul is useful and fair is not.* Avarice and usury and precaution must be our gods for a little longer still. For only they can lead us out of the tunnel of economic necessity into daylight" (Keynes, 1971, pp.192–193, italics added).

Like Mill, Keynes saw the steady state as a logical outcome of economic development and scientific technological advance, when man would be liberated from the immorality of acquisition to enable him to indulge in the cultivation of his intellect and social mores. There was no question in Keynes' mind of such a condition being forced upon man either by his arrogance or by his avarice or by the reality of limits; it would peacefully evolve as man's baser needs were satisfied and he realised that the qualitative attributes of living were rather important and worth preserving.

2.1.4 Some observations

This brief review of ideologies of scarcity and the stationary state during the period from the emergence of classical economics to Keynes indicates that beliefs about scarcity were very much influenced by prevailing social conditions and the political outlook of the writers concerned. The current growth–nongrowth debate continues this tradition, for it is as much influenced by the political and disciplinary ideologies of the writers as it is by current economic circumstances. But the fact remains that, given predictable economic fluctuations, resource shortage has not tempered economic growth nor has there ever been any evidence of shortages of commodities retarding economic production. Barnett and Morse (1963, p.8) and Nordhaus (1974b, p.23) agree that, if anything, the cost of resource inputs has *fallen* over the past hundred years or so relative to the cost of other factors of production (table 2.1). In other words the costs of resource extraction and refinement have continually declined with the application of improved technology and with the production of goods with higher end-values. The picture appears to be one of increasing, not diminishing, marginal returns. Landsberg (1974a, p.35) produces similar evidence with respect to oil and natural gas: as a result of government regulation, oligopolistic competition, and the enormous production value of all forms of energy, oil and gas have become progressively cheaper in real terms as the American economy has grown over the past thirty years (figure 2.3).

Table 2.1. The relative prices of resources as a factor in economic production.

Indices of labour-capital input per unit of extractive output (1929 = 100). (Source: Barnett and Morse, 1963, p.8.)

Years	Total extractive	Agriculture	Minerals	Forestry
1870-1900	134	132	210	59
1919	122	114	164	106
1957	60	61	47	90

Indices of labour-capital input per unit of output comparing extractive with nonextractive goods (1929 = 100). (Source: Barnett and Morse, 1963, p.9.)

Years	Total extractive to nonextractive	Agriculture to nonextractive	Minerals to nonextractive	Forestry to nonextractive
1870-1900	99	97	154	37
1919	103	97	139	84
1957	87	89	68	130

Relative cost of resource inputs to wages (ratio of resource price to labour price). (Source: Nordhaus, 1974b, p.23.)

Resource	1900	1920	1960	1970
Coal	459	451	111	100
Petroleum	1034	726	135	100
Copper	785	226	82	100
Iron	620	287	120	100
Lead	788	388	114	100
Zinc	794	400	126	100
Aluminium	3150	859	134	100

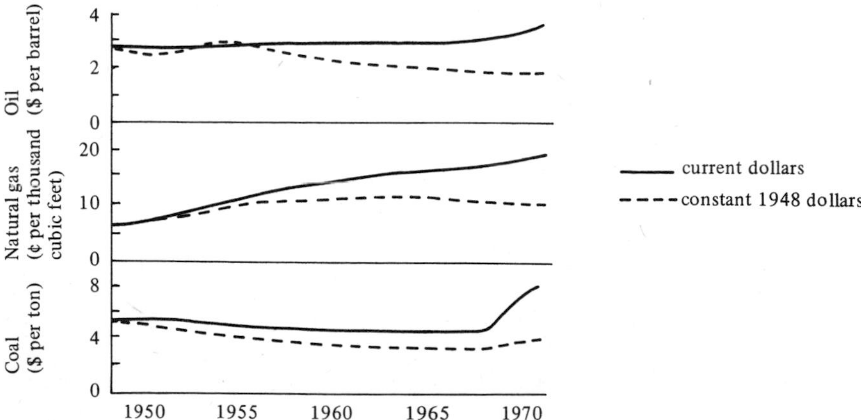

Figure 2.3. Average prices of coal, natural gas, and oil in the US in current and constant dollars. (Source: Landsberg, 1974a, p.32.)

So until 1972 at least there was apparently no evidence of a resource 'drag' upon economic productivity. But these data are highly misleading as for the most part they indicate only the direct costs of resource extraction and transport, ignoring any associated social–environmental costs. They also reflect the vitally important issue that the price mechanism as it is operated today is not capable of doing the job it ought—namely to signal, with adequate warning, impending resource scarcity (Ridker, 1972b, p.24).

Until recently economists have not really concerned themselves with the question of whether net marginal social–environmental economic costs of primary commodity extraction are rising with continued economic growth, with the 'advance warning' inadequacies of the pricing system, or with nonmonetary methods of accounting which could indicate diminishing marginal returns in other aspects of production inputs (for example energy). These are serious omissions, but it must be remembered that many of these effects are difficult and/or costly to measure, few reliable trend statistics are available, and in any case the prevailing paradigm of growth has inhibited such investigations. All this changed with the publication of two important documents and the subsequent controversy that they caused in both scientific and political circles. These publications are the British *Blueprint for Survival* prepared by the *Ecologist* magazine in January 1972 (Goldsmith *et al.*, 1972) and the American *Limits to Growth* published a few months later (Meadows *et al.*, 1972).

2.2 The modern Malthusianists

Both *Blueprint* and *Limits* shook the western world out of its complacency over affluence and resource availability and resurrected the Malthusian spectre of enforced economic collapse and widespread starvation due to overpopulation, falls in agricultural production, depletion of raw materials, and rising pollution. In point of fact, neither document 'proves' its case by standards acceptable to the scientific community. *Blueprint* draws heavily on the MIT study of critical environmental problems (Wilson, 1970) plus some of the findings of a preparatory draft of *Limits*, and like *Limits* attempts to project short-term, rather disparate, historical evidence quite far into the future. Nevertheless both publications were tremendously influential because they appeared during the heyday of environmental scare publicity and popular interest in environmentalism generally (see Munton and Brady, 1970; Erskine, 1971), so were eagerly devoured by an affluent generation who secretly feared it was all too good to last. In any case people tend to be fascinated by (and rather too credulous of) doomsday predictions, especially when they are the subject of heated controversy which contains all the elements of good drama—a suspense-filled plot, environmentalist Davids challenging scientific and corporate establishment Goliaths, and lots of computer printout to show graphically (and in colour) how and when the 'denouement' will come.

It is not the purpose of this book either to discuss in detail the contents of these two publications or to survey the very large body of critical response that they initiated. The *Ecologist* itself produced a number of rebuttals to *Blueprint* (Vol.2, 1972), while perhaps the most comprehensive indictment of *Limits* was prepared by Sussex University's Science Policy Research Unit (Cole *et al.*, 1973). A searing critique of both documents is given in a book by Maddox (1972), while a selection of the many scores of reviews of *Limits* can be found in *Bulletin of Atomic Scientists* (November, 1972, pp.23–25); *Community* (1972, **53**, 37), *The Futurist* (April, 1972, p.62), *Guardian Weekly* (10 June, 1972), *International Development Review* (1972, **19**, 10), *New York Times Book Review* (2 April, 1972), *Psychology Today* (September, 1972), *Saturday Review of Books* (22 April, 1972), *Science* (10 March, 14 April, 23 June, 11 August, 27 October, 1972), and *Teilhard Review* (1972, **7**). (See also Kaysen, 1972; Klein, 1972; Hutchison, 1972; Ruff, 1972; D. B. Brooks, 1973; Chase, 1973; Stahl, 1973; Ulph, 1973; Du Boff, 1974; Hudson and Sullivan, 1974; Nordhaus, 1974a; Day and Koenig, 1975; Hueckel, 1975.) The aim here is to discuss the ideology of these publications in the context of the growth–nongrowth debate and available facts.

2.2.1 Blueprint for Survival

The events leading up to the publication of *Blueprint* are discussed by Schwab (1972) and in articles by *Blueprint's* own intellectual progenitor, Edward Goldsmith (1972a, 1972b, 1974). It emerged as a radical response to what was regarded as the rather wishy-washy, establishment-orientated and middle class views of the British countryside amenity movement which dominated conservationist philosophy in the 1960s (see Nicholson, 1970, pp.163–187; Allison, 1975, pp.109–123; Lowe, 1975). By the early seventies the radicals had 'connected the exponentials' and realised their implications. In August 1971 Gerald Leach, the environmental reporter for the *Observer*, wrote:

> "Most people who have thought hard about the true spaceship economy we have to move towards—or go bust—agree that it will involve the most radical changes in almost every industrial, economic, social and political assumption that we hold dear. *No-one has sketched its details yet*, but the main lines are becoming clear" (italics added, quoted by Schwab, 1972, p.6).

Stimulated by Forrester's (1970) model of world economic collapse Goldsmith (1972a) answered Leach's challenge by organising a conference around the theme 'Can Britain Survive?'. The meeting agreed to construct a flexible, multidisciplinary model of Britain for assessing the economic and ecological impacts of various government policies, together with some quite revolutionary alternative proposals. The latter became a descriptive scenario of how an ecologically harmonious utopia could be attained politically. *Blueprint* describes this effort: its authors make it clear that this was a draft for discussion which put bold ideas into a tentative plan of action (figure 2.4). Its broad principles were endorsed by 33 prominent scientists and supported in principle by a further 180 scientists who felt unable to subscribe to its views completely "because it contained scientifically questionable statements of fact and highly debatable short- and long-term policy proposals" (*The Times*, 25 January 1972).

Blueprint is a very ecocentric document preaching biotic rights, a shift to low-impact technologies and environmentally acceptable production processes. It envisages a steady state economic system compatible with the maximal amount of resource self-sufficiency, the conservation of energy and recycling of materials, and the decentralisation of society into autonomous tribal units, where an interest in the quality of existence and social well-being, not growth and materialistic acquisition, becomes the cultural norm. In true ecocentric fashion *Blueprint* demands these changes because of ecological and thermodynamic imperatives. Population growth must be stopped, the discharge of all toxic substances must cease, the never-ending appetite for energy must be curtailed, and the concentration of population into dense urban areas must end.

Goldsmith's writings provide the ideological background to *Blueprint*. He is convinced that economic growth is a cultural aberration (1972a, pp.21–23), and that man is really genetically and psychologically suited to the steady state. Growth is due to a few capitalistically-minded people who induce the rest of society to try to emulate them. Goldsmith is equally convinced (1975) of the inability of science (a) to organise information objectively, (b) to break out of its narrow-mindedness, and hence (c) to understand what man is doing to himself and to his environment. The consequence of all this, according to Goldsmith, is that science urges us to follow increasingly maladaptive patterns of behaviour from which we cannot extricate ourselves without recourse to radical solutions, imposed morally and politically, which lie beyond the realm of science.

Goldsmith (1972b) is also fascinated by the ecologically harmonious concept of the preindustrial tribe which he believes is happy because it is biologically and culturally adapted to its ecological and social environment. These tribes, he claims, do not suffer from psychosomatic and stress-related diseases or from social delinquency, and hence do not require the elaborate controls and costly social services of the modern metropolis. They are well educated in the sense that education is basically a process "whereby information is communicated via the family and community to a growing child so that it becomes capable of fulfilling its essential functions as a member of its family, community and ecosystem" (1972b, p.57). He also believes that there is no poverty in a tribal society because

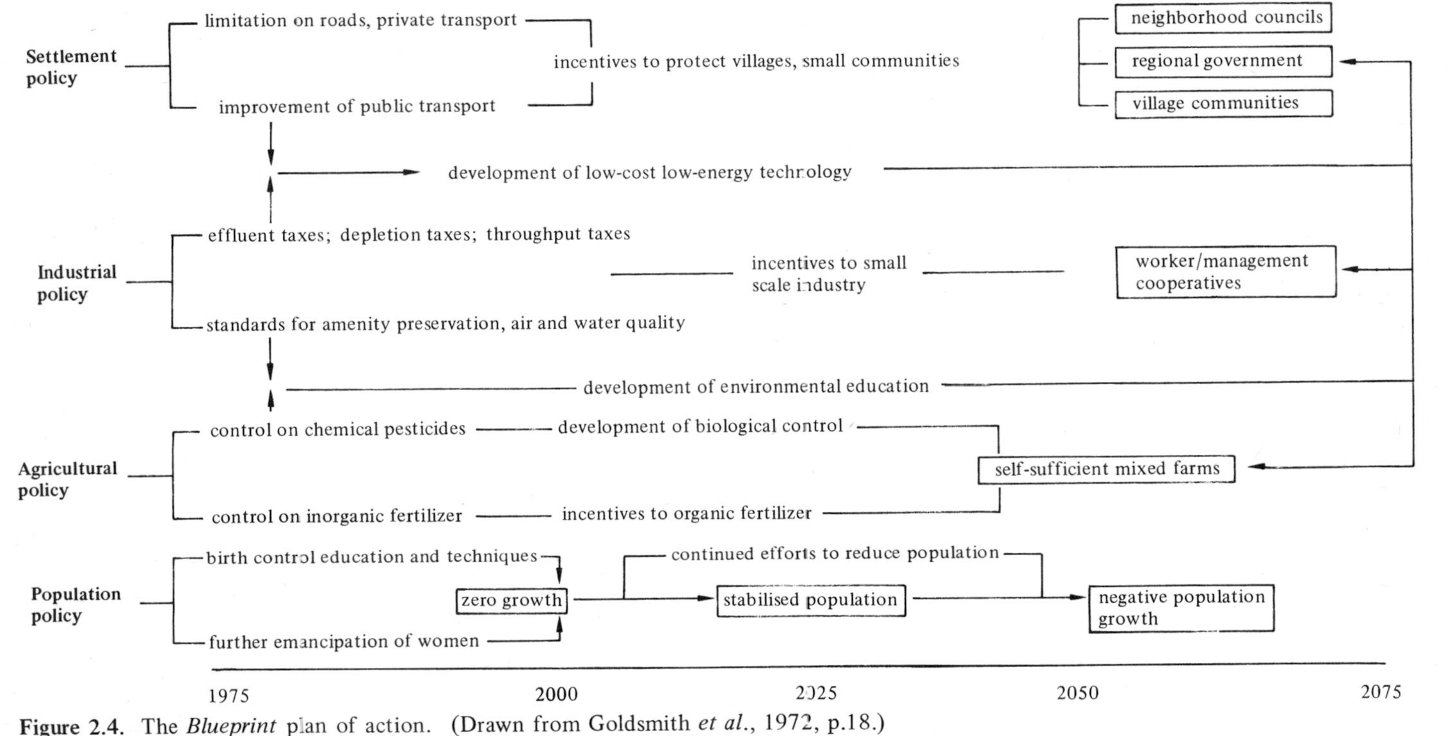

Figure 2.4. The *Blueprint* plan of action. (Drawn from Goldsmith *et al.*, 1972, p.18.)

'poverty is something that occurs when the population expands to a level that can no longer be supported by the land'.

> "The only way to combat poverty is to decentralise society—to create smaller, more viable social units, to give people once more a feeling of belonging somewhere, to give them new loyalties and a new goal in life" (Goldsmith, 1972b, p.61).

To implement its ideas *Blueprint* proposed a 'Movement for Survival', a grassroots coalition of organisations aimed at persuading governments and politicians to recognise its proposed plan of action. The *Ecologist* is organising the 'Movement', but to date there is little indication of its political penetration. However, some of *Blueprint's* ideas (particularly in the areas of materials recycling, energy conservation, and ecologically sensitive agricultural practices) are slowly gaining popular recognition and political respect as Britain's economic predicament worsens. In 1972, at the height of Britain's last economic boom, a government-sponsored working party on natural resources collating public opinion for the British contribution to the UN Conference on the Human Environment commented (Verney, 1972, p.6):

> "We need a better way of defining the kinds of growth we need. And, in the longer term, just as we need to plan to bring our population into balance with what the environment can support, so we need to plan for economic stability at a level that provides the environmental conditions and the quality of life that we would wish for ourselves and our children."

These views were echoed by the majority of a companion working party on pollution (Ashby, 1972a, p.9):

> "The growth we have come to accept as normal cannot go on for ever. Unless we end it in a deliberate and controlled manner, it will simply be halted by a confrontation with environmental limits."

Since then, the British government has been actively considering ways in which to conserve energy, so far with only moderate success (UK Central Policy Review Staff, 1974; UK National Economic Development Office, 1974, 1975). At the same time environmentalists have begun a vigorous campaign urging the government to support a policy of agricultural self-sufficiency and encouraging the British public to replace some of the meat in their diets with vegetable protein (Allaby and Allen, 1974; Allaby *et al.*, 1975; Mellanby, 1975). In March 1975 *New Scientist* sponsored a conference on Britain's capability for resource self-sufficiency, though no consensus was attained because of the many political and economic considerations involved.

2.2.2 Limits to Growth

The ideological background to *Limits* is discussed by Simmons (1973). In the 1930s a small group of systems analysts called the Technocracy Group established itself at MIT, one of the great centres of technocentrism (see Thompson, 1972). The aim of the conclave was to produce a theory of rational control by means of a technique that is now known as cybernetics, for they saw the world in terms of complicated social systems, each composed of many modes or subsidiary states, and each of these full of a mass of interconnecting relationships. Only through simulation of these systems via computerised analogue models, they believed, could the behaviour of a real system be completely understood and predicted. The advantage of the computer model was that it could be repeatedly refined to approximate reality and widely adapted to account for any explicit assumption about the behaviour of the system that the managers cared to make.

A man particularly interested in this technique was Jay Forrester, who became fascinated by the analytical power of the models he was producing. Time and again he discovered that the remedies suggested by corporate executives (whose company difficulties he was trying to resolve) or by politicians (he made his first foray into the analysis of social problems with a study of urban processes—Forrester, 1969), when simulated in his models, either had no effect at all, worsened the problem, or led to other difficulties. What appeared intuitively to be the obvious solution rarely in fact did the job. From these observations Forrester (1971) drew four important conclusions about the behaviour of social systems:

(i) They behave *counterintuitively*; in other words the 'correct' answer is often that which appears at first sight to be 'wrong'. Forrester believes that the human mind is simply not equipped to understand, predict, or control the activities of very complex patterns, because it has not been part of man's evolutionary experience to have had to cope with the monstrosities of organisation (and what he terms 'multi-loop nonlinear feedback systems') that modern urbanised human beings have created for themselves.

Forrester's findings are not new. Wright (1947), Lowenthal (1961), and Tuan (1974) amongst others have demonstrated how man, in order to cope with his world, has to organise his seemingly chaotic sensory and cultural experiences into selectively perceived and 'rationally' reasoned semblances of reality. These are unavoidably distorted by wishful thinking and delusion, and because man can construct and visualise only these highly imperfect models, he is usually unable to anticipate system failure (the collapse mode); in the event of having to make some response his action often exacerbates matters (the 'overshoot' mode). For these reasons, both Forrester (1971) and Goldsmith (1975) were convinced that computer simulation was vital to enable man to cope with modern macropolicy questions. (Goldsmith would argue that once decentralisation is completed the need for such models would disappear; Forrester is more reluctant to relinquish this tool.)

(ii) Social systems are characterised by conflict between the short-term and long-term consequences of policy changes, since short-term improvements nearly always produce long-term degradation of the system. This reasoning leads in turn to Forrester's important claim that remedies which are unpleasant and apparently having the wrong effect in the short term frequently prove to be the most sensible long term courses of action.

(iii) Social systems are often inherently contradictory in the sense that the goals of some of their subsystems may conflict with the welfare of the system as a whole. So a policy to maximise the goal of one subsystem may reduce or eliminate the possibility of achieving the objectives of other subsystems. Again, only recourse to the whole model will permit analysis of the effects of a variety of subsystem policy measures.

(iv) Forrester (1971, p.67) states that 'social systems are inherently insensitive to most policy changes that people select in an effort to influence behaviour. In fact a social system draws attention to the very points at which an attempt to intervene will fail'. In other words only by infinite reiteration will the computer model reveal where to apply political leverage for maximum effect.

Forrester (1969) put these ideas into practice in his model of the urban system, where he proposed a number of 'counterintuitive' remedies. For example, he recommended a moratorium on low-income housing after his models showed that rather than helping to alleviate poverty, additional public housing and slum-clearance schemes were worsening social distress by attracting more low-income families and putting a greater strain on jobs, schools, and other public services. Cities would thrive only by replacing the slums with new industry. In essence, Forrester advocated the tough-minded politics of squeeze favoured by Malthus a century or more earlier. Here are his views on urban planning policies (Forrester, 1971, p.75):

> "Population grows until stresses rise far enough to stop further increase. Everything we do to reduce these pressures causes the population to rise further and faster and hastens the day when expediencies will no longer suffice ... . What does this mean? Instead of automatically accepting the need for new towns and the desirability of locating new industry in urban areas, we should consider confining our cities. If it were possible to prohibit the encroachment by housing and industry into a single additional acre of farm and forest, the resulting social pressures would hasten the day when we stabilize population."

Forrester's reasoning is the very antithesis of traditional political thinking, which usually responds to crises by pragmatic and popularly acceptable short-term remedies that as far as possible minimise interference with day-to-day activities. Thus Forrester is challenging the very principles of political democracy and social adaptation, by recommending rostra which are exogenous to the political framework in which policy prescriptions must be enacted. He is basically rejecting the key sociological tenet that man is a purpose-seeking and adaptive organism, and that his institutions are malleable in the light of the changing circumstances which he helps to create.

Although Forrester's 'counterintuitive' thesis is not original (social scientists have long shown that simplistic manipulation of complicated social systems can produce adverse results), it caught the eye of hard-line conservative politicians, who, like their predecessors in Malthus' time, sought a politically respectable rationale for blocking what they regarded as exceptionally progressive social reform. [The Marxists have been quick to seize upon this point. They regard the *Limits* ideology as a capitalist plot to "break working class resistance to austerity measures", and to justify wage controls so as to freeze consumption at inequitable levels (see National Caucus of Labour Committees, 1972; Hall, 1972).]

Forrester's views also fascinated an Italian management consultant, Aurelio Peccei, who was sure that global problems could not be solved by national policies alone and who felt that "sustained development of the industrial countries (was) a prerequisite to attack the array of future problems" (Simmons, 1973, p.205). With the help of industrial money, Peccei founded an elite 'invisible college' of executives, civil servants, and management specialists, called the Club of Rome, to study the nature of what he called the 'problematique'—the nature and interaction of all the problem elements in the global system. The Club, under Peccei's guidance, soon became convinced that there was too much complacency among scientists and politicians who believed that somehow man would always extricate himself from the mess he was inexorably creating, and decided that only shock treatment would bring the world to its senses.

> "[The Club of Rome's] immediate purpose was thus temporarily shifted from a search for answers to basic questions to the search for a device capable of opening a breach in the hearts and minds of people, of arousing their awareness to the complexity and seriousness of the world problematique. After long consideration, a commando operation was decided upon, in the hope that its rapid tactical success might have strategic consequences" (Siebker and Kaya, 1974, p.233).

First into the breach came Forrester with his computer model World I, followed by his protegé Meadows with World II and World III (for a review of the World models, see Meadows and Meadows, 1973; Day and Koenig, 1975). *Limits to Growth* appeared first in March 1972 and since then has appeared in over twenty languages and sold more than two million copies.

One important feature of all the World models is the fact that they are programmed to catastrophe by Malthusian reasoning. They all begin with the premises of exponential growth in population, pollution, industrial production, and the demand for food and raw materials in a world that is unalterably finite. This is the recipe of doom, and one can only assume that this enormously complicated computer program was produced to estimate the timing of the cataclysmic result that was so predetermined. One may also hypothesise that Peccei's evangelical passion for an earth-awakening 'commando operation' threw a certain amount of scientific caution to the winds.

A second aspect of the three models is the politically explosive counterintuition of their remedies—a massive dose of nongrowth by means of a reduction in industrial investment (by about 40%), a disinvestment in agricultural activity (by about 20%), a fall in the birthrate (by about 40%) and a stabilisation of resource consumption. Although the authors of *Limits* never actually spell this out, one assumes that they expect the world's affluent peoples to redistribute a substantial proportion of their wealth to the less well off while simultaneously undergoing an industrial slump of unprecedented proportions. [This is hinted at in the concluding commentary by the Club of Rome (Meadows *et al.*, 1972, pp.191–192).]

A third attribute of the models is their appeal to 'value free' reasoning. Meadows *et al.* (1972, p.22) state that "once the assumptions have been scrutinised, discussed, and revised to agree with our best current knowledge, their implications for the future behaviour of the world system can be traced *without error* by a computer no matter how complicated they become" (italics added). With its ideology programmed the computer has a logic which is quite independent of the vagaries of human reflection.

Fourthly, the models all stress the urgency of political response. According to their calculations, mankind has at best four generations to revolutionise its cultural perspectives, its institutions, and its values. Indeed there appears to be little time even for debate, for only immediate action across a wide front can bring about salvation.

2.2.3 Criticisms of *Blueprint* and *Limits*

Reaction to these publications is bound to vary according to prejudice. If one is predisposed to the belief that western civilisation is doomed to inevitable collapse, then their arguments and their conclusions are acceptable; but if one has faith in man's capacity for reason and enlightenment and believes that his powerful instinct for survival will drive him to adjust his patterns of living to suit changing circumstances, then their thesis will largely be dismissed. For the most part these two viewpoints dominate critical reaction to the two reports and, because of their opposing nature, leave the matter unresolved. However, to be fair to both sets of authors, this kind of discussion is exactly what they hoped their work would stimulate:

> "The implications of these accelerating trends raise issues that go far beyond the proper domain of a purely scientific document. They must be debated by a wider community than that of scientists alone. Our purpose here is to open that debate" (Meadows *et al.*, 1972, p.23).

Let us look briefly at the major criticisms in turn.
(i) *Loss of faith.* Many critics (e.g. Martin, 1975) have commented that doom books are counterproductive because they demonstrate the hopelessness of taking reasoned action. "For civilisation to continue", writes Clark (1969, p.4), "it requires confidence—confidence in the society in which one lives, belief in its philosophy, belief in its laws and confidence in one's own mental powers." The greatest threat to mankind's survival comes from within, not from without. Maddox (1972, p.vi) stresses this point:

> "The most serious, insidious danger in the environmental movement is that it may sap the will of advanced communities to face the problems which no doubt lie ahead. Throughout history, hope for the future has been a powerful incentive for constructive change."

The danger, of course, is that, in the agony of fatalism, people will embark on courses of action that will fulfil the prophesies of doom. Alternatively, people may simply become numbed by the notion of 'crisis', a grossly overused term nowadays whose real meaning is seldom appreciated. For example, Americans quickly returned to their pre-'energy crisis' gasoline usage following the resumption of Middle East oil imports to the United States (Murray *et al.*, 1974).

The question of faith in human response is vitally important. The authors of both documents reject the charges of mass public demoralisation, claiming that they are optimistic about the ability of man to take appropriate action, given that the issues are clearly outlined and the implications of continuing present behaviour made apparent. They state that their publications were designed to encourage this responsiveness, not to suppress or deaden it. Despair is a function of ignorance, hope of enlightened understanding.
(ii) *Programming social choice.* No prognostication can adequately do justice to the manifold possibilities that humans can fulfil for themselves. A major criticism of both books (but especially of *Limits*) is that the Malthusian model is deterministic and cannot incorporate social and political adaptation based upon human perception and choice (Kaje, 1973). Political goals are *purposive*, capable of redirection and redefinition while *functioning*; while molecules can exhibit only probabilistic behaviour, human beings can exhibit choice based upon expectations and dreams. Thus to this group of critics the *Blueprint* scenario is at best a sketch of possible political response, at worst a facile and beguiling piece of nonsense.

The Club of Rome has taken much of this criticism to heart and is now actively encouraging policy studies of the "value systems, motivational structure and behavioural limitation of the human species" (Siebker and Kaya, 1974, pp.251–252), though one wonders how much these very soft data can be 'objectified and computerised', as currently the Battelle Institute's DEMATEL (Decision Making Trial and Evaluation Laboratory) is attempting. With the help of the Delphi technique (see Linstone and Turoff, 1975), the Battelle scheme hopes to obtain a cross section of views of eighty leading figures in politics, finance, industry, science, the arts, religion, and other fields throughout the globe, and to use this 'college of informed minds' as a basis for refining the policy premises that sculpt the feedback loops. (The Delphi methodology is somewhat controversial for it replaces face-to-face discussion with anonymous 'correspondence', so may not eliminate ambiguity.)

In a parallel effort a Japanese group aims to calculate 'satisfaction indices' (a combination of consumption patterns, lifestyle preferences and values) for various social groups and to trace how these indices will change under differing growth and demographic conditions (see also Koelle, 1974; Lui, 1975). Eventually these indices are to be linked to 'desirable' patterns of consumption and investment, though, inevitably, discontinuities in value responses will have to be postulated. Despite the conceptual complexities, the Japanese study aims to identify the causal link between value modification and social change. Certainly these models should be of help to policymakers in discussing political options for economic and social transformation, though the technocentric nature of some of this work is rather disturbing. Programming values and political response into the computer somehow denigrates the spontaneous nature of the human mind and its democratic ideals.

(iii) *The nature of technological response.* The Malthusian premise of diminishing marginal returns assumes that there must be a slowdown in man's technological abilities to gather resources from the earth in the face of continuously exponential demands for food and raw materials. The measurement of technological maturity is obviously very tricky, but many critics feel that the rate of technological innovation has certainly kept up with all the other exponentials, and indeed that major upward discontinuities (the discovery and use of fossil fuels and nuclear power are often cited) indicate that, given appropriate incentives, man's technological ingenuity has no foreseeable bounds (for a good review, see Hueckel, 1975). Much of this argument is inconclusive because the debaters differ over what constitutes the 'net social benefits' of technology. Moreover, some optimistic statements are embarrassing. For example Maddox (1972, p.5) may now regret his rashness in stating that "there is a good chance that the problems of the 1970s and 1980s will not be famine and starvation but, ironically, the problems of how best to dispose of food surpluses in countries where famine has until recently been endemic"; or (*ibid.* p.274) "the threat of scarcity in energy, real enough in the 1950s, has already been dispelled".

The degree of faith in technological responsiveness is a major area of controversy, for it highlights the differing ecocentric and technocentric environmental philosophies outlined in chapter 1, and exposes different ideologies about the merits and purposes of growth. Technological optimists regard growth and technological improvement as interdependent, while those who doubt the efficacy of much of modern technology believe that a complete change in its form and function is possible outside sustained economic growth. On the face of it, the two ideologies collide and diverge as this phillippic by Goldsmith (1974, p.83) indicates:

> "Technology cannot provide a solution to the pollution generated by our ever increasing industrial activities. Technology can only solve technological problems. It has nothing to offer against the logistic, the economic, the biological, the social and the political aspects of the problem *which our 'experts' are quite incapable of even taking into account*" (italics in original).

(iv) *Criticisms of method.* Although the authors of both publications stress the crudeness and pioneering nature of their models, critics have been quick to expose faults in the mathematics and the underlying assumptions (see Boyd, 1973; Cole *et al.*, 1973). The very nature of dynamic systems renders them highly vulnerable to minute changes in input assumptions and variables, and as many of the input parameters were drawn from discontinuous and aggregated data it is inevitable that the models still err. But by how much? Meadows *et al.* (1973) acknowledge many of their mistakes but state that these simply delay the *timing* of the collapse, not its likelihood.

To analyse this vital matter further a whole new breed of World models are in preparation, many with disaggregated data suitable for nations at different levels of economic development (Siebker and Kaya, 1974, pp.252–256). Many of these strive to pinpoint political and economic policy issues with respect to particular resource subsystems (especially energy) over medium-length time scales which are long enough to break clear of electoral myopia. These 'second generation' regional models aim to overcome a major criticism of *Limits*, namely that *global* solutions cannot be derived solely from western industrial experience and capitalist ideologies. Strategies must be tailored to indigenous social and cultural circumstances with due regard to the local resource base. These models also recognise that political forces, more than market factors, determine commodity prices and influence technological progress, an important acknowledgement of modern global *realpolitik*.

(v) *Criticisms of solutions.* While *Blueprint* addressed itself more to solutions than to analysis of the problems, *Limits* reversed the emphasis, avoiding any real discussion of the new equilibrium state. But a recent book endorsed by the Club of Rome (Mesarovic and Pestel, 1975), and supported by the work of Kaya and Suzuki (1974), has strikingly departed from much of the *Blueprint* philosophy, appealing for global political reconciliation, a minimum adequacy of subsistence for all mankind, a world resource management plan, and cooperative action by the multinationals to spur industrialisation and agricultural development in the third world. This study specifically rejects the notion of self-sufficiency, advocating much freer global trade and resource distribution in its stead. Who is right? Neither approach is regarded as acceptable or practicable by informed commentators.

For example, both McFarlane (1973, p.40) and Burch (1971, pp.30–50) have criticised *Blueprint's* adulation of small, decentralised, semiautonomous tribal societies as failing to recognise cultural and economic realities and misinterpreting the findings of social anthropologists. Preindustrial tribes are not necessarily stable (they frequently experience marked fluctuations in the man–land relationship), nor are they always socially cohesive (a number are ridden with internecine and intertribal strife and suspicion), and in many cases the tendency towards social disruption is tempered only by the recognition of ecological limits and by resort to animism and superstition (Guthrie, 1971). Burch (1971, pp.30–50) suggests that there may be no simple formula for self-regulation, for the social organisation of a tribal culture is tremendously influenced by the way it interacts with its habitat. Nomadic tribes tend to be associated with decentralised and egalitarian social systems, while sedentary groups appear to exhibit more centralised and hierarchical social patterns. He also speculates (*ibid.* pp.49–50) that ruthless exploitation of nature (and of other humans) is more likely during periods of social or ecological stress when traditional social norms are weakened.

On the other hand, although Goldsmith and his colleagues do not specifically refer to it, they may be aware of a controversial thesis in the anthropological literature known as the 'image of limited good' (Foster, 1965, p.296), which implies that many peasant societies deliberately restrain their economic and social expectations because they recognise that many goods (including such things as wealth, health, friendship, influence, virility, and status) "exist in finite quantity and are always in short supply" and that "there is no way directly within peasant power to increase the available quantities". If the 'limited good' thesis is to be believed then it may be conceded that nonindustrial societies living in closed systems have developed cognitive limits to growth. Though he does not entirely accept Foster's viewpoint, Gregory (1975) feels that many societies do accept fairly well defined 'limits' and develop quite complicated patterns of egalitarian behaviour on the expectation of what he calls "circumstantially balanced reciprocity". In other words, the richer members of the group agree to share some of their wealth in return for respect and status recognition by the poor, and by those of equivalent social standing who must eventually reciprocate to preserve their status. Thus affluence and power are harmoniously distributed in a community of restricted economic expectations.

But the 'limited-good' idea is coming under fire in situations either where growth expectations are excited (for example when exogenous technology and organisation are introduced) or where images of a 'better life' are induced by improved communications. Wolf (1966, p.80) believes that traditional collectivist structures are easily disturbed during periods of scientific and technological innovation in a manner that tends to undermine the stabilising influence of reciprocity behaviour. Once this fragmentation begins, it is difficult to see where it might stop.

These criticisms cast some doubt on whether modern western capitalist culture with its ingrained mores of competition and individualism, its interest in 'getting on', and its apparent love of material comforts can peacefully undergo the revolution in values and behaviour necessary to sustain a postindustrial 'tribal' state. They also raise the question of whether the decentralised tribal collectivity is an ecologically pertinent model and therefore worth attaining. The alternative proposition, that of a global resource plan, endorsed by people like Falk (1972) and Brown (1972), also seems sensible in outline but is equally impracticable, again because cultural and political ideals vary so widely.

Neither *Limits* nor *Blueprint* claimed to be a prediction or anything other than a necessary catalyst for reasoned debate and a thought provoking stimulus for sharpened analysis of the age-old issue of growth and resource adequacy. In both respects their authors have achieved their purposes, and in the process have been willing to adjust their original formulations. Probably the most important outcome of the whole controversy surrounding the two publications is the general agreement that there are indeed limits (acknowledged by even the more ardent growth advocates), and therefore that mankind must change his ways and his values, though there is no consensus about when and how these dramatic transformations should take place and what form of altered social organisation should prove the most suitable. Both documents fail to provide even a glimmer of how this formidable and fundamental revolution can actually be achieved. The enormity of the task ahead becomes evident when it is realised how few suggestions of a truly practical nature have been offered so far. Surely to devise a peaceful and orderly pathway toward worldwide social and ecological justice is the real predicament of man.

2.3 Growth, pollution, and resource availability

During the heyday of popular interest in environmentalism (1970–1972) a curious and somewhat ludicrous controversy raged between two of America's most prominent 'environmentalists', Paul Ehrlich and Barry Commoner. The dispute boiled around what precisely caused environmental deterioration—the result according to Ehrlich and Holdern (1971) of multiplying three factors: population size, *per capita* consumption, and the environmental impact of productive technology. Thus:

$$\text{Environmental impact} = \text{Population} \times \frac{\text{Economic good}}{\text{Population}} \times \frac{\text{Pollutant}}{\text{Economic good}} .$$

The Ehrlich–Holdern article opened the debate by stating that the real culprit was population growth, exacerbated by urban concentrations of large numbers of affluent people making *disproportionate* demands upon both local and nonlocal resources, and the assimilative capacity of the surrounding environmental media. They contended that environmental disruption could be curtailed by a sharp turn toward zero population growth, decentralisation of urban areas, and decreased *per capita* consumption. Not surprisingly these are the cornerstone principles of the environmentalist organisation Zero Population Growth Inc., of which both authors were prominent executive members. In the original article Ehrlich and Holdern used little data to support their case which was based largely on the Ricardian argument that as less accessible materials were more extensively exploited there would be an increasing *per capita* environmental demand upon energy and mineral resources. They also claimed that population growth exaggerated the costs of transportation, communication, and organisational maintenance, and in time (but with little or no advance warning) could push environmental impact beyond the buffering capabilities of natural systems. Eventually, they believed, it would become prohibitively expensive to protect existing levels of environmental quality because of the persistent concentrations of environmental insults in relatively confined regions.

Commoner responded to this analysis with a contrary view, first published in the journal *Environment* (Commoner *et al.*, 1971), but subsequently revised (Commoner, 1972a, 1972b). Commoner's major thesis was that certain elements of technological change provided the main source of blame, especially a shift to energy-intensive productive processes, and the substitution of synthetic products with their toxic residuals for natural substances with organic residuals. He largely dismissed the 'affluence' variable, on the dubious assumption that many of our present-day consumer goods (e.g. shirts, beer) are scarcely superior in use to their prewar counterparts. In other words, he claimed that people were still consuming similar amounts of goods; it was just that these goods were now environmentally more costly both to produce and to discard.

He therefore rejected the population-growth hypothesis (which he said was never 'scientifically' proven) in favour of a thesis of technological impact, and implied that national environmental policies should be concerned more with the improvement of process efficiencies (and institutional devices to control residuals) than with population control.

For over a year neither group would give much ground, though they agreed to modify the original equation to reflect more accurately the marginal nature of the three interacting factors: thus,

$$1+\frac{\Delta I}{I}=\left(1+\frac{\Delta P}{P}\right)\times\left(1+\frac{\Delta A}{A}\right)\times\left(1+\frac{\Delta T}{T}\right)$$

(where I is environmental impact, P population, A *per capita* consumption, and T technological effect).

Though this changed the results it did not significantly affect their ideological positions. Then during early 1972 the debate became more heated and the contestants more vituperative. The struggle between the two men reached its climax in a tempestuous exchange in *Environment* (April 1972) where each side tried to demolish the views of the other by recourse to selective examples, aggregated data, and quite unscholarly accusations over methodology. The reader can judge for him or herself the merits of the debate which finally resolved itself with both sides agreeing that all three factors (affluence, population, and technology) interacted in complicated and nonlinear ways to produce environmental damage, though the antagonists continued to differ on appropriate policy options to grapple with the problem.

To some extent, as Holden (1972) points out, this whole battle was as much a struggle for popular recognition and ego satisfaction as it was an attempt to uncover the causes of our serious environmental predicament. Both men have strong personalities and an evangelical sense of mission which appeared to cloud their scientific 'objectivity' and erode their scientific ethics. Inadequately informed readers can be dangerously misled by the results of such malpractice, though perhaps more serious is the confusion created in the minds of policymakers.

The Ehrlich–Commoner affray reveals the influence of ideology on environmental philosophy and policy. Ehrlich has long been committed to the view that the 'population bomb' is the most serious threat facing mankind. In his initial exposé (Ehrlich, 1970) he viewed population limitation as essential—at any cost. "We must have population control at home, hopefully through a system of incentives or penalties, but by compulsion if voluntary methods fail", he wrote. "We (i.e. the United States) must use our political power to push other countries into programs which continue agricultural development and population control" (quoted in Neuhaus, 1971, p.164). In a later work (Ehrlich and Harriman, 1971) he goes even as far as to advocate the use of the economic and military power of the United States to divide and rearrange underdeveloped nations.

> "I know this sounds very callous, but remember the alternative. The callous acts have long since been committed by those who over the years have obstructed a birth rate solution or downgraded or ignored the entire problem. Now the time has come to pay the piper, and the same kind of obstructionists remain. If they succeed, we all go down the drain" (quoted in Neuhaus, 1971, p.166).

And though he softened this position in his subsequent global review of the relationship between population growth, resource availability and environmental disruption (Ehrlich and Ehrlich, 1972), he still feels that all of the major problems facing the world—starvation, malnutrition, disease, war, injustice, discrimination, etc.—could be alleviated by reduction in fertility, though he is less willing to suggest how this can be achieved.

Commoner, on the other hand, has always opposed coercion in any form as a method of limiting fertility, for he believes that the matter is largely cultural and political and hence beyond the ambit of demographers and other scientists. He has also long been troubled by what he sees as the misapplication of science and technology working against the interests of mankind, and by the deliberate obfuscation of adequate scientific information which prevents the interested layman from drawing his own conclusions (Commoner, 1966). His mission is to unravel the contradictory elements that make up the present environmental dilemma so as to provide the world with unpleasant but necessary political alternatives. He passionately believes that the informed human being is capable of taking appropriate and reasonable action and will not be stampeded into nonhumanitarian measures.

> "To resolve the environmental crisis, we shall need to forego, at last, the luxury of tolerating poverty, racial discrimination and war. In our unwitting march toward ecological suicide we have run out of options. Now that the bill for the environmental debt has been presented, our options have become reduced to two: either the rational, social organisation of the use and distribution of the earth's resources, or a new barbarism" (Commoner, 1972b, p.296).

'The new barbarism' is the so-called 'lifeboat ethics' developed first by Ehrlich and later propounded by Hardin (see chapter 1, pp.30–32).

As a result of this dispute, more sober-minded economists have ventured to clarify the relative roles of economic growth and population increase as variables influencing resource availability and environmental impact. Two of the most impressive efforts have been the Resources for the Future (RfF) study prepared for the President's Commission on Population and the American Future (Ridker, 1972b), and a UNESCO sponsored conference on Population, Resources, and the Environment held in Sweden (UNESCO, 1974). The RfF report used a model more simplified than the World models of *Limits*, for it was developed primarily to assess the effect of resource scarcity on the United States economy over the next fifty years. It concluded that there is no *urgent* problem of scarcity for any major industrialised nation [a view endorsed by the UNESCO study and by an even more recent Club of Rome report (Kaya and Suzuki, 1974)], *provided* that the new geopolitics of resource availability do not unduly interfere with market forces, and that sufficient political safeguards are established to ensure a reasonably reliable price mechanism (both highly debatable assumptions).

Both surveys emphasised the enormous influence of the price mechanism in improving extractive efficiencies, reducing demand, and stimulating materials recycling—all without seriously impairing economic well-being. For example, Fischman and Landsberg (1972, p.98) showed that up to 33% of potential United States metal demand could be saved by widespread recycling (though this amount varies from metal to metal—see table 2.2), while Ridker (1972b, p.23) concluded that projected materials demand to 2020 could be cut by 35% assuming a two-child family and the diversion of 1% of economic growth into increased leisure (table 2.3).

Table 2.2. The potential for metals recycling in the United States and its effect on world metal availability (based on Fischmann and Landsberg, 1972, p.98).

Metal	Current proportion recycled (%)	Feasible proportion recycled (%)	Potential resource saving to US (%)	Potential resource saving to world (%)
Iron	47·3	48·9	-	-
Copper	44·0	54·4	20	15
Lead	43·9	47·2	10	10
Aluminium	17·3	42·6	33	20
Zinc	16·5	34·6	20	40

Table 2.3. The effect of population and a different structure of economic activity on resource demands and residuals discharge in the United States (adapted from Ridker, 1972b, pp.45, 47).

Resource	Elasticity due to population (%)[a]	Elasticity due to economic mix (%)[a]	Residual	Elasticity due to population (%)[a]	Elasticity due to economic mix (%)[a]
Iron	0·56	0·85	Particulates	0·46	0·78
Aluminium	0·48	0·88	Hydrocarbons	0·29	0·59
Copper	0·56	0·97	Sulphur oxides	0·42	0·87
Phosphorus	0·74	0·92			
Nitrogen	0·46	0·93	Carbon monoxide	0·26	0·04
			Nitrogen oxides	0·29	0·31
			Biological oxygen demand	0·55	0·67
			Suspended solids	0·53	0·71
			Dissolved solids	0·56	0·69

[a] Percent change in resource requirements or residuals production associated with a one percent change in population and level of economic activity.

Both studies stressed the value of a resource-depletion tax and a residuals-generation charge as effective mechanisms to control environmental disruption while allowing economic growth to continue. The RfF analysis showed that the production of residuals could be curtailed even more dramatically if an effective residuals tax policy was implemented—up to 80% of anticipated levels both in high- and low-growth scenarios. However, the RfF authors were quick to point out that these reductions would not occur in large conurbations (where pollutant loads already exceed public health standards), nor do they relate to 'second generation' toxic residuals which are difficult to trace and to contain.

These studies [plus shorter descriptive reviews by Fisher (1971) and Ridker (1972a)] effectively destroy the Ehrlich thesis that population stabilisation *per se* will noticeably reduce resource demand and environmental degradation (see also Bahr *et al.*, 1972; Eilenstine and Cunningham, 1972; Choucri and Bennett, 1973; Cochrane, 1973; Kelley, 1974; Ridker, 1974; Sweezy and Owens, 1974). Much more effective influences would be changes in population distribution (to reduce the *concentrations* of environmental stress), variations in the amount and composition of economic consumption (a crucial set of factors), and more 'brutal' incentives to curtail disamenity and residuals generation through new legal and economic arrangements and better technology.

The optimism over resource availability in the medium term accords with the findings of the US President's Materials Policy Commission (1952) (the Paley Commission) which was equally confident that price incentives, fuelled by scarcity, would stimulate new technologies and encourage more efficient use. Though there are now many more misgivings about the ability of the modern 'market place' to determine prices, economists still point to the kind of evidence presented in figure 2.5 to illustrate that 'reserves' are not fixed amounts but highly variable quantities that relate to price, demand, technology, and entrepreneurial organisation. Thus they conclude that there is no reason why reserves should not continue to be 'found' as long as economic growth continues.

However, in the twenty years since the Paley Commission reported, the degree of resource dependence between the wealthy industrialised countries and many poor (but rich in resources) developing nations has caused a second 'blue ribbon' presidential commission (US National Commission on Materials Policy, 1973) to caution that resource availability will depend upon the willingness of the public to accept either the additional extractive and environmental costs of developing indigenous supplies or the national security and geopolitical risks of reliance on commodity imports. This is a difficult policy area because there are so many conflicting issues involved, but it seems likely that national governments will be tempted to relax environmental standards in face of economic slowdown (in the short run at least, though at the cost of much local political opposition—see chapter 1, pp.19–27). Simultaneously, efforts are now being made wherever possible to extend domestic production of key materials, even where current extraction costs exceed world prices. These could be politically explosive policy decisions for they undoubtedly will have conspicuous economic and environmental consequences. Bohi and Russell (1975) have tentatively estimated that the

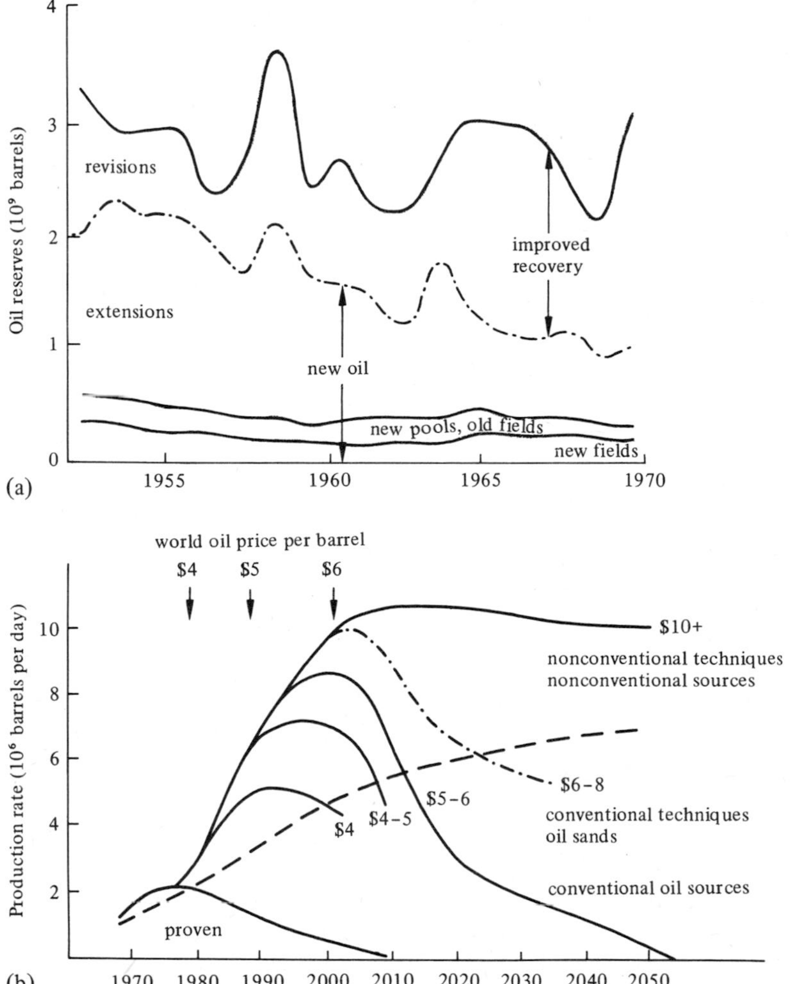

Figure 2.5. 'Reserves' of oil under various assumptions: (a) American estimates of oil supply reserves based on assumptions about extensions to existing fields, new finds, and improved recovery. It will be noted that additions to reserves are less than consumption, currently estimated to be 6×10^9 barrels annually. (Source: National Petroleum Council, 1971, p.35.) (b) Canadian estimates based on different oil prices (world and domestic) plus changing technology. These were produced before world oil prices rose to \$11·65 per barrel in January, 1974. (Source: Canada, Department of Energy Mines and Resources, 1973, p.102.)

United States could provide about 19 million barrels of indigenous liquid fuels per day (compared with 11 in 1973) at a cost of between $8 and $12 per barrel (1972 prices). With a powerful political as well as economic incentive to conserve oil demand, the authors claim that the United States could become self sufficient in oil by 1985, though much will depend upon various Government taxes and subsidies and the political response to increased domestic oil prices. However, for this policy to be worthwhile in economic terms, the world price of oil would have to remain above $10 (1972 prices) per barrel, an unlikely assumption even though the Ford Administration supports the notion of a 'floor price' for oil of $7.50 per barrel. Bohi and Russell (1975, p.10) conclude that the cost of self sufficiency in monetary terms alone could be between $34 and $66 billion per year—an "unacceptably costly target". A policy of commodity deals and improved storage facilities would be much cheaper, environmentally more healthy and generally more amicable. But energy costs will rise. Nordhaus (1974b) concludes that energy costs will rise in the US by 2·2% annually in real terms until 1985 and by 1·5% annually up to the year 2000, thus exerting some drag on the US economy from now on.

2.3.1 Resource conservation and economic growth

In sum, all these studies are relatively optimistic about resource adequacy, at least until the turn of the century and assuming no noticeable change in the distribution of world wealth or any unreasonable political interference. In fact many surveys do not even take into account much alteration in the pattern of growth of *per capita* resource demand. For example Kaya and Suzuki (1974, p.286) happily assume that by 1985 the world will have consumed an amount of energy equal to the 1970 *proven* world reserves of petroleum (crude oil and natural gas) and by 2000 a quantity equivalent to the entire *absolute* existing amount of petroleum. As do other optimistic economists, they assume that rising prices will stimulate new technologies of exploration and energy substitution that will allow energy-intensive economic growth to continue largely unhindered.

But need economic growth be so energy intensive? Are *per capita* GNP and *per capita* energy consumption causally connected? Darmstadter (1972a) believes that energy growth and economic growth are not necessarily linked, although current political thinking assumes that they are. Since 1966 the United States has begun to use more incremental units of energy to produce marginal additions to its wealth; in other words its energy inefficiency is increasing (figure 2.6). Darmstadter (1972b, pp.114–116) thinks that this is due partly to depressed energy prices (especially for gasoline) which encourage wasteful use and partly to diminishing returns in the technology of thermal generation efficiencies. Econometricians such as Chapman *et al.* (1972) feel that with proper pricing (including a reversal of the present block rate structure which favours high-energy consumers) energy demands could be substantially reduced with no diminution in economic health. They forecast that, by doubling the price of electricity, projected United States demand over the next twenty-five years could be cut by an amount greater than the present total electrical generating capacity of the nation (figure 2.7). Their findings are endorsed by Doctor and Anderson (1972) who show that California could reduce its electricity needs by more than its present consumption over the next twenty-five years by doubling prices and shifting to low-energy–high-value economic activities (such as insurance, research and development, small-scale high-value electronics) with no fall in anticipated *per capita* income levels. However, their proposals would affect employment and immigration as jobs would become scarcer and more specialised. The political implications of such a move could be profound.

Both these studies assume fairly dramatic (and somewhat optimistic) price elasticities of demand in electrical use for all sectors of the economy. In the case of Chapman *et al.* (1972), the estimated price elasticities are $-1 \cdot 3$, $-1 \cdot 5$, and $-1 \cdot 7$ for the residential, commercial, and industrial classes of use respectively. This means, for example, that an increase in electricity price of 10% would reduce residential consumption by about 13%, commercial use by about 15%, and industrial demand by about 17%. Baughman and Joskow (1975) confirm these conclusions in their analysis of the effect of fuel prices on reducing the potential purchase and existing

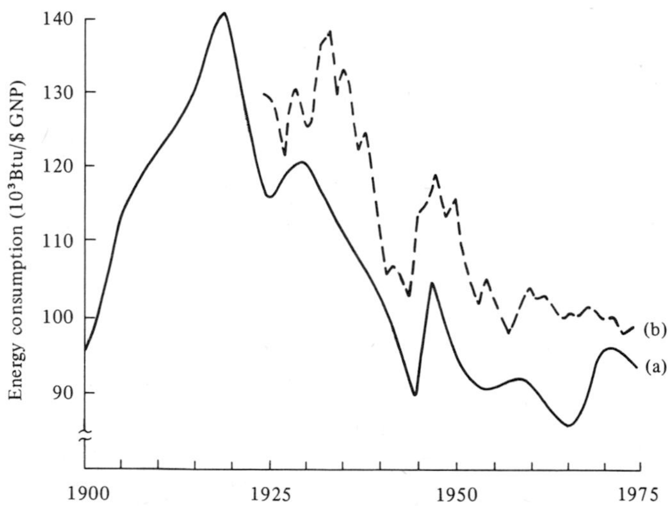

Figure 2.6. The cost of energy in relation to economic production. (a) US data. (Source: US Government Statistics.) (b) Canadian data. (Source: Canada, Department of Energy Mines and Resources, 1973, p.23.)

use of domestic electrical appliances. Given a 10% increase in electricity prices, for example, they estimate that electrical space heating could be cut by as much as 20% and electrical water heating by 17%.

The composition of economic activity is an all too easily forgotten element in influencing the pattern of resource consumption, though it is itself shaped by the structure of resource costs. For example, in areas with expensive energy the use of energy is much more efficient, and economic activities tend to be those that produce much economic value

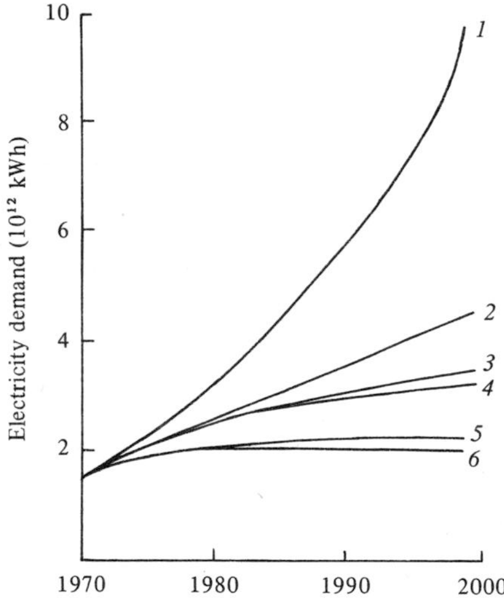

Figure 2.7. Electricity demand projections under various assumptions about price and population growth per annum: *1*, population growth 1·4%, GNP growth 4%, *per capita* income growth 2·9%, declining price 2·4% to 1980 and 1·2% thereafter; *2*, population, GNP and *per capita* income as for *1*, price constant; *3*, population, GNP, and *per capita* income as for *1*, prices rise ~2%; *4*, zero population growth by 2035, prices rise ~2%; *5*, population, GNP, and *per capita* income as for *1*, prices double by 2000; *6*, zero population growth by 2035, prices double by 2000. (Source: Chapman *et al.*, 1972, p.707.)

Table 2.4. Electricity price, electricity demand, and economic growth (adapted from Doctor and Anderson, 1972, p.97).

Region	Ratio of *per capita* personal income 1970/1950	Average cost of electricity in 1970 (¢/kWh)	Ratio of commercial and industrial electricity use to personal income	Ratio of electricity use in manufacturing (1966) to value added (kWh/$)
Massachusetts	2·67	2·028	0·59	0·93
Connecticut	2·59	1·739	0·65	0·80
California	2·39	1·349	0·90	1·14
Tennessee	3·10	0·732	2·85	5·53
Washington	2·39	0·510	2·41	5·36

for relatively low energy inputs, whereas in regions with inexpensive energy more energy-intensive industries (which do not necessarily produce more wealth) tend to congregate (table 2.4). Looked at in this light, the familiar regression line between *per capita* GNP and *per capita* energy use could easily be redrawn to indicate different energy efficiencies but similar national wealth (figure 2.8).

Figure 2.9 illustrates the relationship between energy cost and economic activity in another way. Whereas the United States has tended to use its electricity more efficiently as it has grown more prosperous, Canada, and especially British Columbia (where hydroelectric power is plentiful and remarkably cheap), has become wealthier despite very inefficient use of electricity. Until the present (and policies are now changing) British Columbians have enjoyed the 'luxury' of wasting cheap energy and consequently have not been encouraged to develop the kind of economic mix which creates additional wealth without raising energy demands. Goldberg (1973) concludes from all this that economic growth is normally associated with *more efficient* energy use, so that energy consumption and economic growth need not be linearly related (figure 2.10a). Malenbaum (1973) makes a similar deduction with respect to materials use: as a nation becomes more rich and changes its economic mix, so its commodity needs should diminish (figure 2.10b).

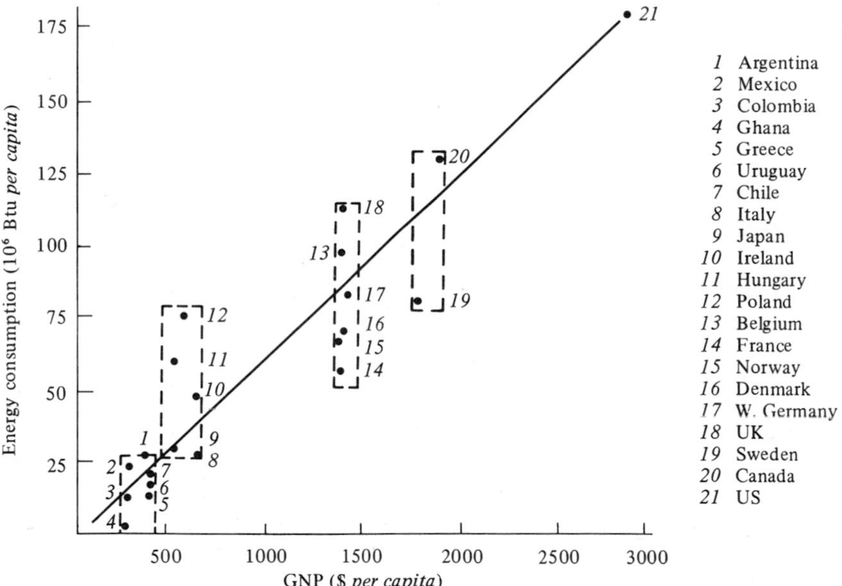

Figure 2.8. Energy consumption and national economic production. Two kinds of analysis of these data are possible. The conventional analysis assumes a regression line relating energy consumption to economic production. The less conventional analysis indicates that energy use may be linked more to price and the nature of economic activity than to GNP. (Source: UN Statistics.)

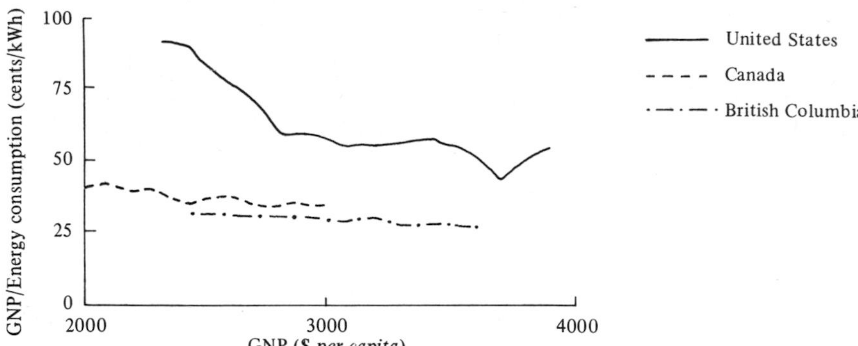

Figure 2.9. Energy consumption and economic growth: United States—increasing efficiency of energy use with growth; Canada—small improvement in efficiency of energy use with growth; British Columbia—no improvement in efficiency of energy use with growth. (Source: Goldberg, 1973, p.143.)

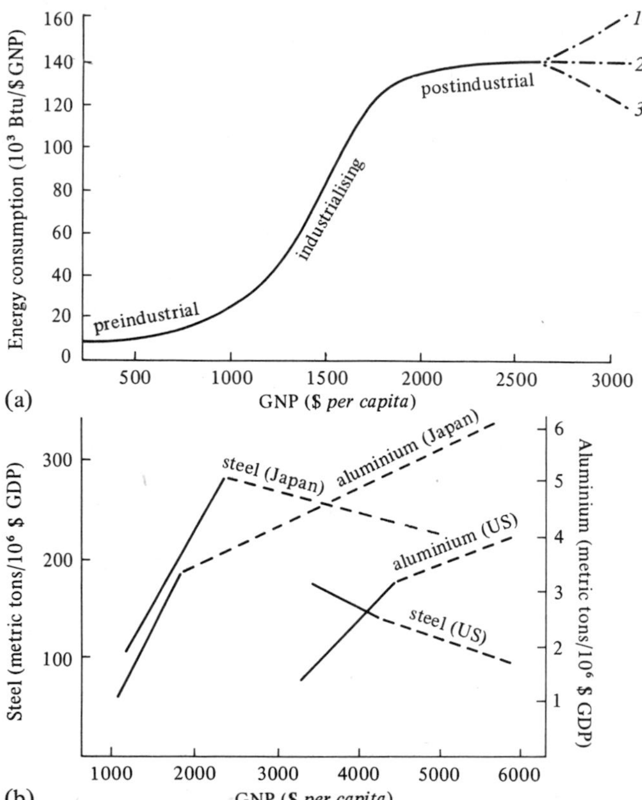

Figure 2.10. Energy and materials requirements and economic growth—a scenario: (a) Energy: alternative scenarios relate to *1*, declining efficiency of use and production; *2*, constant efficiency of use and production; *3*, increasing efficiency of use or production. (b) Materials: scenarios relate to efficiency of use and availability of substitutes. (Source: Malenbaum, 1973, pp.18-19.)

Two reports by the Ford Foundation Energy Policy Project (1974a, 1974b) claim that low or zero energy growth is quite compatible with continued economic growth. In a somewhat speculative fashion the Ford team indicate how energy projections can vary widely depending upon pricing, technology, and people's habits (figure 2.11). They even suggest that the United States could achieve a pattern of zero energy growth by the year 2000 with no reduction in national wealth or individual living standards, if a really massive effort is made toward energy conservation in all sectors of the economy, a switch from energy-intensive goods toward services (medicine, education), and the redesign of housing forms, the urban fabric, and transportation patterns to reduce energy wastage. But to achieve this would require a new philosophy, replacing the feeling that 'more is better' with that of 'enough is best'. It would also require a major departure from the widely held desire among most western peoples to own their own house, garden, and car. Despite this, it may be that the alternative of zero energy growth will be imposed upon postindustrial societies. In a revealing aside (1974b, p.94) the study team caution against putting too much hope in the technology of conservation (as opposed to making changes in economic mix, human aspirations, and consumption patterns), for:

> "... there are minimum amounts of energy required by the laws of physics to perform certain functions, such as materials processing ... . As this minimum is approached in any given process, further efficiency gains would become harder to achieve, and economic growth would have to slow down and ultimately cease if energy use is stable."

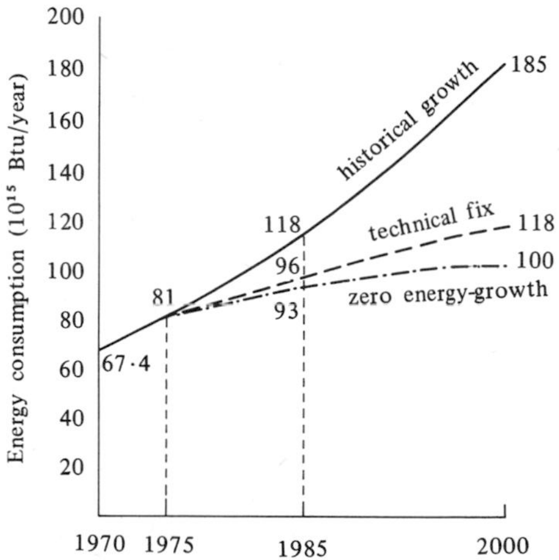

Figure 2.11. Energy consumption and alternative policy options. (Source: Ford Foundation Energy Policy Project, 1974a, p.40.)

The Ford Energy Project findings are undoubtedly controversial. There is a kind of ecocentric assumption that human habits *must* change because of energy limits. The Institute for Contemporary Studies (1975) deplore this view and argue that the free market should be granted much more freedom to find alternative energy sources and set prices accordingly. The group refuses to accept the idea that Americans must bow meekly to unsubstantiated doomsday conclusions and thus accept massive government intervention in the workings of their economy and the conduct of their affairs. Again we see how ideologies can influence seemingly respectable scientific analysis.

2.3.2 Energy accounting and energy availability

There is little doubt that, because western nations use energy very inefficiently, economic growth would not necessarily be seriously impeded by the imposition of tough energy conservation measures. The problem, as is so often the case, is more political and institutional than technological. Recently, for example, the chief energy adviser to the British Government admitted that many British firms had no proper energy accounting methods and so found it very difficult to adopt energy conservation practices; in fact no substantial energy savings in the industrial sector (which accounts for some 70% of total British oil demand) have been recorded since fuel prices tripled in late 1973.

A similar delay in political action and economic response has been observed with concern in the United States (Abelson, 1974a, 1974b; Sporn, 1974). It has taken longer than many thought for technologies, policies, and institutions geared to an abundance of cheap energy to recognise and respond to a new era of more expensive energy.

Because energy is seen as the limiting factor that determines the extent of economic activity, some scientists are attempting to model economic activities in terms of net energy budgets rather than more traditional monetary measures. The results are quite astounding. For example, in all western nations it is currently more costly (in energy terms) to produce food than to benefit by its consumption (figure 2.12) (Leach, 1975). In the United States the energy value of food is on average only one-tenth of the energy value of the inputs required to produce it [and only 2·5 times the fuel energy inputs alone (Pimentel *et al.*, 1973, p.448)]. This astonishing situation is largely attributable to the fact that nearly three-quarters of the United States food energy budget is consumed in off-farm distribution, storage, packaging, and retailing [including the gasoline consumption of purchasers driving to and from the supermarkets (Steinhart and Steinhart, 1974)]. By way of comparison, it has been estimated that cultures practising 'primitive' agriculture enjoy food energy efficiencies of unity or higher. These data indicate that, to feed the world on the basis of the United States style, intensive agriculture would require quite fantastic amounts of energy, so a shift to more ecologically harmonious, energy-conserving agricultural practices is quite mandatory (see also Revelle, 1974a; Allaby *et al.*, 1975). Nevertheless, in the short run assistance to the developing world in the form of energy intensive equipment and materials would have dramatic results for food production; here again is a case for *redistribution* rather than growth *per se*.

Energy budgeting is also in vogue in rather novel regional planning studies. A research team working for the US state of Oregon (Oregon, Special Projects Branch, 1973) has begun to prepare energy accounts for different state land-use plans as a guide to public policymaking. Likewise, a study group in Florida (L. Peterson, 1974) aims to calculate regional carrying capacities, again on the basis of energy accounting, as a guide to the estimation of state population-growth ceilings (see chapter 4, pp.163–167). In a similar vein, Chapman and Mortimer (1974), Price (1974), and Chapman (1975) have made pioneering attempts to calculate an energy budget for alternative means of energy generation. These studies tentatively conclude that a growth-orientated nuclear energy programme may not produce any net energy yields, since nearly all the power produced from any given nuclear plant will be consumed in preparing its fuel, maintaining its own operations, and preparing the next plant in line. Thus Price (1974, p.24) concludes that if Britain were to switch from fossil fuels to nuclear power in a hurry it might never be able to produce enough energy to do the job, even it if were to slow its rate of economic growth. Both Leach (1974) and a study commissioned by the Bechtel Corporation (1974) disagree with these findings, claiming that advanced breeder reactors should require no more than 2 to 5% of their energy output for

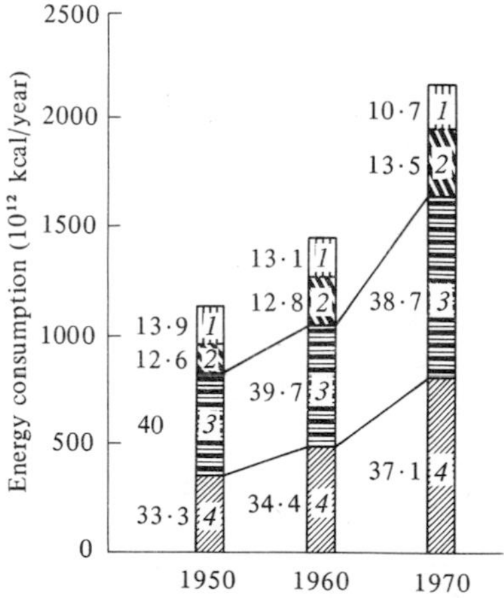

Figure 2.12. The energy budget of food production: *1*, fuel use in direct agricultural production (note decline in relative amount); *2*, rest of on-farm energy use (note decline in relative amount); *3*, energy use by processing industry; *4*, energy use by commercial outlets and purchasers. Figures are percentages of total energy consumption for each sector. [Adapted from Steinhart and Steinhart (1974), p.309.]

operation and maintenance. But the environmental energy specialists are not daunted by this claim, and the lively controversy should help to stimulate more sophisticated and much needed energy accounting studies over the next few years. Chapman (1975) concludes that, on the basis of energy budgeting, a programme of technologically intensive energy conservation would produce better results than the costly efforts to find new power sources; the low energy growth alternative carries with it too many politically and socially damaging consequences to be desirable. Brubaker (1975) endorses this view from the American perspective.

In the light of this kind of evidence, a number of economists are beginning to suggest that energy supplies (and hence ultimately resource availability) may be limited not so much by sheer physical shortages as by lack of capital. In other words, economic growth may simply not be able to pay its way in energy terms, so some form of economic steady state may be thrust upon the world by fiscal default. This is a vital issue that is most difficult to prove one way or the other because much of the evidence is secreted in the confidential memoranda of corporate accountants, who encourage their executive bosses to influence government tax policies by scaremongering while withholding much of the critical information. Nevertheless it is true that some large energy corporations (e.g. ARCO and their Rocky Mountain oil shale scheme) have abandoned capital-intensive energy projects on the grounds that even with rising real energy prices the estimated cash flows would not be profitable. Oil and gas companies surveying the North American arctic regions and the North Sea claim that only the more lucrative discoveries will prove financially rewarding, given the enormous technological uncertainties of exploration in these areas. For example, the cost of finding a new barrel of North Sea oil has risen from approximately £1200 to over £3000 in the past two years due to a combination of inflation, delays in the manufacture of exploration equipment, bad weather conditions, and a variety of unanticipated production problems (see Lovins, 1973). Pearse (1974a, p.216) and *The Economist* (1975, 1 March, p.70), however, state that much of this 'fiscal scare' is political hogwash, and with proper investment and timing plus a drive toward energy conservation these new ventures will in time prove amply rewarding. Small changes in rates of growth alter the timing of demand, which in turn influences investment security and profitability; so again it is the rate and mix of economic growth together with international resource trading agreements that appear to be the critical variables.

2.4 Population policies and environmental impact

Like economic growth, population growth is a relatively recent phenomenon in the course of human history, and, as figure 2.13 shows, population increases have undoubtedly reached alarming proportions over the past thirty years or so. Most developed countries are now experiencing the last stages of the so-called 'demographic transition' as death rates stabilise and birth rates drop to or below replacement level. Most demographers (Frejka, 1973a, 1973b; Westoff, 1974) now agree that all postindustrial nations together with most if not all communist countries, should have steady state populations within a generation or so (table 2.5). The current conventional wisdom associates declining birth rates with affluence, urbanism, and the social emancipation of women, though it is highly probable that fertility restraint has been forced upon many couples in affluent western nations by inflation, economic uncertainty, the loss of income should the mother not continue to work, and longer periods of formal educational training (see US Commission on Population Growth and the American Future, 1972, pp.196–198). So, for a variety of reasons North American and European women appear to want (and are having) fewer children than their mothers, and zero population growth

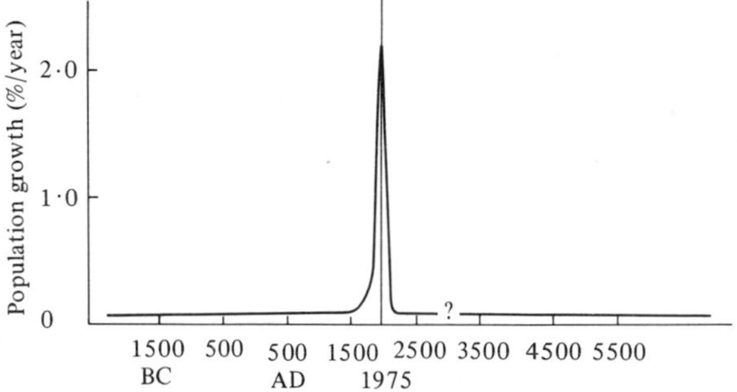

Figure 2.13. Population growth in the perspective of human history. This scenario assumes zero population growth by 2040, the most realistic of current UN projections. Population growth lasts for less than 1000 years.

Table 2.5. The timing of zero population growth. (Source: *UNESCO Courier,* number 27, May 1974, p.15.)

Region	Year when zero population growth should begin	Period of peak growth rate	Rate of natural increase during peak growth period (per 1000)	Period when population will reach largest absolute amount	Annual population increase (millions)
North America	2005	1955–1960	15·6	1980–1985	3·9
Europe	2000	1950–1955	8·8	1960–1965	4·0
Soviet Union	2015	1955–1960	17·6	1955–1960	3·6
Oceania	2020	1955–1960	16·9	1985–1990	0·6
East Asia	2005	1960–1965	17·5	1980–1985	17·3
South Asia	2025	1970–1975	28·1	2010–2015	46·6
Africa	2040	1985–1990	30·0	2020–2025	23·6
Latin America	2030	1975–1980	28·8	2005–2010	17·2

could be a very real possibility if the present trends away from pronatalist values continue, and if there is a widespread willingness to accept the demographic and economic implications of population stabilisation (see Ryder, 1973).

But as indigenous birthrates fall in these nations, the relative importance of immigration as a factor causing population growth rises. In Canada and the US about 50% and 20%, respectively, of annual population growth is now attributable to immigration (Ontario Conservation Council, 1973; Keely, 1974). And although many developed nations have already established immigrant quotas, some are actually considering further reductions (e.g. Australia, Canada, Scandinavia) primarily on environmental grounds and under pressure from environmentalist groups. The growing domestic political pressures to curtail immigration are partly due to the fact that about 80% of all immigrants tend to move into urban regions which are already congested, costly to service and maintain, and where the quality of life is deteriorating. But, equally, environmentalists are worried because immigrants, unlike babies, immediately make major demands on resources (for land, housing, schools, social services, recreation, and consumer goods) which, they feel, create greater collective environmental costs than the collective gains resulting from their contributions to the nation's wealth. Consequently, a number of developed nations are embarking on population–resources–environment inventories to assess the environmental impacts of various population policies. But no matter how 'objective' these national reviews try to be, it is difficult to avoid the conclusion that any reduction in immigration quotas will tend to discriminate in favour of those who meet national employment needs (low-paid dirty jobs, and highly-skilled high-income-generating managerial and professional occupations) and will reflect an element of chauvinistic nationalism.

The environmental consequences of population growth in the lesser developed nations, however, are even more difficult to assess because growth projections are so uncertain and patterns of development are so variable. Traditionally the chief weapon of population policies in these countries has been fertility control through family planning programmes, for most economists considered the Malthusian 'low level equilibrium trap' (where population gains simply absorbed any advances in productivity, drained off any potential for investment, and caused high dependency ratios) to be the major stumbling block to economic development. Assuming that population control was the key to economic takeoff, economists produced spectacular benefit–cost ratios to illustrate the value of a prevented birth (see Ohlin, 1967, pp.107–120; TEMPO, 1968; Enke, 1970). In fact the arguments appeared so persuasive that Ohlin (1967, p.120) concluded that "it is difficult to undertake *any* calculation of the economic gains that might be realised from population control which does not point to very spectacular benefits".

Yet despite quite substantial investment in family planning education and the dissemination of contraceptives, birth rates did not fall markedly in most countries during the late sixties and early seventies (see Notman, 1973). Consequently the modern Malthusianists like Ehrlich and Hardin peddled their desperate remedies of coercion and compulsory sterilisation. Some of the reasons for the continuation of high birth rates were undoubtedly cultural (difficulties in tramsitting reliable information, the constant battle against adverse rumour, the social stigmas of visiting health clinics, the lack of sufficient attention to the social role of the male). But many reasons were socioeconomic, since, for most rural families tilling tiny plots at the margin of subsistence, the extra child (particularly a boy) was a crucial addition to the labour force and a necessary investment in family security in a society that does not offer pensions or other old-age benefits (Neher, 1971).

So it became painfully clear that population policies could at most only be contributory elements to the much more fundamental issues of political reform, socioeconomic improvement, redistribution of resources, and protection of environmental quality throughout the world. Left-wing writers have long stressed that *poverty and underdevelopment* are created and sustained by colonial domination and imperialist multinational corporations, not by overpopulation and poor family planning (see Meek and Weissman, 1971; Neuhaus, 1971; Müller, 1973). Weissman (1970, p.30), for example, even accused the Rockefeller Foundation (a major donor of money for contraceptives) of promoting birth control to help puppet 'elites' retain power and maintain stable markets.

The recent UN World Population Conference held in Bucharest in August 1974 provided a ready forum for presenting such views, fanned by procommunist elements. For example, the report of an International Youth Conference stated that:

> "The primary causes of these conditions (poverty, hunger, unemployment, etc.) are the exploitative and repressive, social, economic and political structures, often the legacy of prolonged colonial repression, rather than overpopulation ... .
> It is essential, first of all, to carry out far-reaching socioeconomic changes, to liquidate the aftereffects of colonialism and neocolonialism, to combat the continuing and increasing dependence of developing countries on developed industrialised countries, to accelerate industrial and rural development and to promote social progress ..."

Despite the efforts of various pre-conference commissions to prepare a draft World Population Plan of Action, the final Plan was only grudgingly and tardily endorsed by member nations, after no less than 340 amendments (International Planned Parenthood Federation, 1974). The Plan is a rather vague document that had to straddle the divergent ideologies of Malthusian 'lifeboat ethics' and Marxist 'social justice', and a more moderate ecocentric view emphasising the quality and dignity of life within the context of ecological harmony and reordered global investment priorities. In the words of the Plan:

> "The Conference recommends that in planning development, especially the location of industry or business, and the distribution of social services and amenities, governments should give particular attention to the social and environmental costs and benefits involved, as well as equity and social justice, in the distribution of the benefits of development among all groups and regions."

The conference also acknowledged that traditional rights of free migration (both within and between nations) and the determination of family size might have to be restricted by environmental limitations. This crucial acknowledgement of the environmental implications of population growth was further recognised in the tentative agreement to initiate national population–resource–environment reviews, known as *Population Watch* studies (Johnson, 1974a, 1974b). Ideally the *Population Watch* reviews should draw up various scenarios of 'national futures' of the kind advocated by *Blueprint* and currently being modelled by various international organisations (Siebker and Kaya, 1974). Naturally these reviews will be very difficult to formulate and assemble but it is believed that the *Earthwatch* component of the UN's Environment Programme (Hardy, 1973) will, upon request, assist any nation proposing to embark on the *Population Watch* venture. Already the Netherlands and Norway have begun this task and Canada might soon follow, though it may be some time before less developed nations prepare these most important analyses. Nevertheless, the *Population Watch* proposal is a significant advance in coming to grips with the dilemma of harmonising economic growth, social improvement, and environmental protection in the context of resource availability and indigenous political and economic institutions.

3

Growth versus nongrowth—the search for solutions

3.1 The problem

The sciences of ecology and economics share a common Greek root *oikos*, which means household. Aristotle used the word *oeconomica* to describe "the arrangement of domestic activities most conducive to affectionate and harmonious relations within the family" (quoted in Adams, 1974a, p.280). Adams contends that the original (but now obsolete) role of economics was the management of the 'household'—a term that can be applied to dispersed human communities—where management meant careful husbandry of resources (especially effort) within a harmonious pattern of relationships among interacting parties. The 'obsolete' economics had much to do with *stability* by means of creative change, and *permanence* through compatible interaction with the ecosystem. While the 'household' should 'improve', it need not necessarily 'grow' in terms of the definition of growth provided in the previous chapter. Nowadays a swelling chorus from environmentalist economists is pleading for a return to this 'obsolete economics', for they sincerely believe that sustained economic growth as it is currently practiced is inimical to human well-being and incongruent with fundamental biophysical laws.

The growth-nongrowth debate has crackled vigorously since 1970, though Galbraith (1958) raised the question of artificially stimulated and unnecessary consumption much earlier, and Macinko (1965), noting that land is a finite commodity, urged planners to examine seriously the long-term implications of sustained growth a little before Mishan (1967, 1969, 1971b, 1971c, 1973a, 1973b, 1974a, 1974b) began his long series of discussions on the demerits of growth. The issue is now quite prominent in the economic literature (for comprehensive reviews see Johnston and Hardesty, 1971; Hodson, 1972; Maddox, 1972; Daly, 1973a; Olson, 1973; Weintraub *et al.*, 1973; Beckerman, 1974) so only a brief summary will be attempted here.

Let us begin by looking at the main criticisms of growth raised by the new breed of nongrowth economists.

3.1.1 The paradigm of growth

Daly (1973a) observes that, since the mid-nineteenth century at least, economists have simply accepted a paradigm of growth—most manifestly embodied in the infatuation with the monetary measure of Gross National Product (or its variant Gross Domestic Product) as an index of economic success or failure. Consequently they have built elaborate theories around the dangerously circular reasoning that growth is the solution for problems caused by growth. For example, efforts to overcome unemployment (such as capital investment) invariably increase productive capacity, which eventually outstrips demand to cause even more unemployment: so investment (i.e. the fuelling of growth) is at once a cure for and a cause of economic pathology (Daly, 1973a, p.5). Daly (1973b, p.151) coins the word 'growthmania' to describe the attitude in economic theory

> "... that begins with the theological assumption of infinite wants, and then with infinite hubris goes on to presume that the original sin of infinite wants has its redemption vouchsafed by the omnipotent saviour of technology, and that the first commandment is to produce more and more goods for more and more people, world without end. And that this is not only possible, but desirable."

Daly then introduces a second term, 'hypergrowthmania', to characterise the inclusion in growth calculations (through the GNP) of economic activities that only exist because of the malfunctioning of growth. Thus pollution control, garbage collection, and all the costs of keeping an ecologically unstable and delinquent society in order (police, fire services, social workers, bulletproof equipment) are all counted in GNP, so serving to maintain the illusion that growth is infinite. These, he claims, are all 'costs' of growth which are treated as benefits in this 'Alice in Wonderland accounting system'. When funeral expenses are counted as part of further growth, we have 'terminal hypergrowthmania'!

Mishan is equally acid in his attack on the complacency of growthmongers, whom he feels wallow in the emptiness of historical precedent and cling to the myth of progress with quite undeserved hubris. "The question I myself have been concerned with", he observes (Mishan, 1974a, p.119), "is *not* whether continued economic growth is able to make the already affluent citizens of the West [or the poor] better off [or happier] but whether *in fact* it is doing or is likely to do so over the foreseeable future". He frankly believes that growth decreases social satisfaction and that the paradigm is dangerous to the future of mankind, though he is unable to prove this contention conclusively.

It cannot be denied, however, that many economic institutions can only function in the expectation of growth. The antics of stock exchanges are a mystery to most people, but in reality stocks are little more than assumptions of growth on paper. Most North American cities pay their bills by means of bonds—credit notes granted by banks on the anticipation of continued urban affluence. New York City is all but bankrupt, since financial institutions are now quite unwilling to finance a city debt that has grown from $750 million to $6 billion in 3 years (*The Economist*, 1975, 5 April, pp.53–54). London is in similar grave financial difficulties for much the same reasons (*The Economist*, 1975, 24 May, pp.17–19). When confidence in growth declines, the sham of the growth paradigm is exposed.

Energy corporations indulge in enormous investments purely on the assumption that someone, someday, will buy their products. Thus demand projections have a curious habit of self-fulfilment (figures 3.1, 3.2), and control of consumption is resisted as a resource management alternative.

Following a massive cutback in the use of electricity (the result of a doubling of charges after the rise in world oil prices), many United States utility companies had to *raise* their rates still further to gather enough revenue to pay the debts arising from their heavy investment commitments (Skala, 1974). Yet the utilities were only obeying their legal mandates, for, as Daly (1973c, p.253) stresses, utilities have a responsibility to maintain their credit and attract capital. Laws, like economic theories, are promulgated on the paradigm of growth. Hodson (1972, p.38) is right when he concludes, "the great vested interest in growth makes sure, as best it can, that if the reality of growth is not present, the myth of it is kept alive".

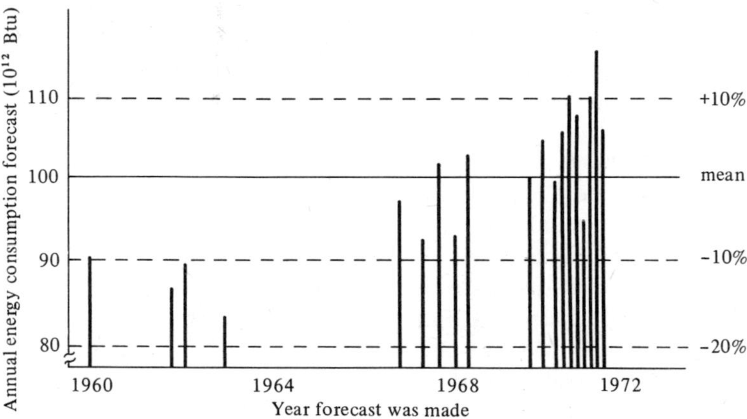

Figure 3.1. US energy demand projections to 200 estimated at various times. Note that the increase in consumption forecasts *grows* over time. (Source: US Government Statistics.)

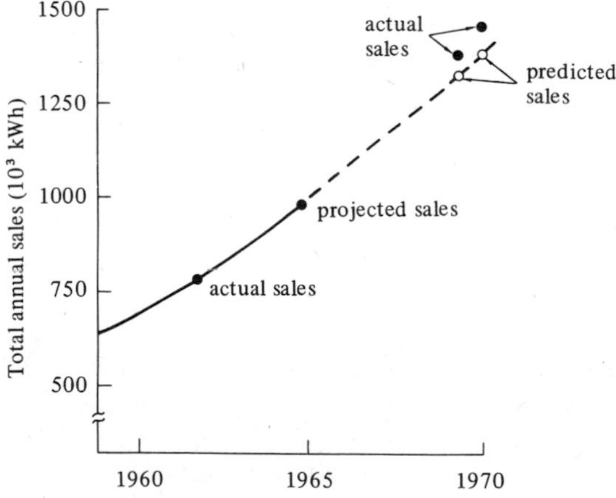

Figure 3.2. US electricity demand projections and consumption. The accuracy of the projections looks impressive; but utility corporation policies often encourage demand to meet predicted supply. (Source: Chapman *et al.*, 1972, p.705.)

E

As human understanding evolves, so paradigms change. In the social sciences, and especially in economics, revolution takes place when established orthodoxy clearly is inconsistent with obvious facts and when solutions based upon that orthodoxy expose its incompetence. The paradigm of growth is now under attack not just because of its chimerical extravagance but because it obfuscates more fundamental issues such as the control of the majority by an economic elite and the manipulation of public tastes. Opponents of the economic-growth cult also claim that it fails to distribute wealth more equitably, it encourages technocentric chauvinism, and it is unable to cope with pervasive disamenity and technological uncertainty. Growth can no longer offer the delusive escape valve of 'the easy way out'.

Daly and his like-minded colleagues wish to replace the growth paradigm with that of the 'steady state', a notion they believe has plenty of intellectual parallels in the physical and biological sciences. In fact, one argument used to justify the inevitability of the steady state is drawn from the first law of thermodynamics. How can man continue to produce utility when matter and energy can neither be created nor destroyed? Growth is only possible today because industrial man 'borrows' from a fixed stock of what Schumacher (1973, p.14) calls "natural capital"—fossil fuels, living nature, open space, peace, and solitude. Over 90% of the energy used today comes from a finite supply of available energy that has accumulated over aeons. As this energy is consumed, it is converted from an available commodity to the unusable forms of dissipated heat, waste matter, and useless gases. "In entropy terms", states Georgescu-Roegen (1973, p.42), "the cost of any biological or economic enterprise is always greater than the product ... [so] any such activity always results in a deficit." The production of any good or service, therefore, reduces the likelihood of increased and varied economic growth in the future, unless an abundant, low-entropy (i.e. readily available) energy source (such as sunlight, windpower, geothermal energy, or controlled nuclear fusion) is provided in such a manner that its net (earthly) energy yield is positive.

3.1.2 Relative versus absolute needs

Toward the end of one of his essays, Daly (1973a, pp.26–27) refers to a parable from *Isaiah* in which a man extravagantly burns the whole of a cedar tree even though he requires only half to cook his food and keep himself warm. "The rest of it, he makes into a god, his idol; and he falls down to it and worships it: he prays to it and says, 'Deliver me for thou art my god'!"

Even though the first part of the tree was burnt to provide necessary heat, the second part was consumed purely as self-indulgence. But where do absolute needs end and relative needs begin?

A major weakness of growth in the eyes of the nongrowth advocates is the diminishing marginal return of consumption. Most members of industrial societies already have far more goods than they require to satisfy their absolute needs, but far from turning to less materialistic values, they continue to consume because it has become an addictive means to other ends—idolatry, indulgence, status display, avarice, and power. The rich indulge in high consumption, observes Daly (1973a, p.25), because a large part of this is consumption of personal services rendered by the poor, which would not be available if everyone was rich. For Schumacher (1973, p.263) the Malthusian belief that conspicuous consumption by the rich encourages the poor to work harder is dangerous, counterproductive, and absurd: "the rich corrupt themselves by practising greed, and corrupt the rest of society by provoking envy". Mishan (1973a, p.74) disdainfully dismisses the "social worth of an additional transistor or other inane gadget" since he is sure that most kinds of consumer hardware and many hedonistic leisure-time activities create more social distress than they bestow private benefits. With Commoner (1972b) he feels that technology has given us more collective headaches without noticeably improving much of what we consume. Consumption vainly tries to ease the frustration that economic growth induces.

Implied in all this rhetoric is a certain intellectual arrogance which, no matter how well intentioned, reflects the values of a comfortable social minority. Mishan (1971b), for example, berates the introduction of the automobile as "the greatest single disaster to have befallen mankind" and despairs over television for eliminating a precision and clarity of expression, for debasing the English language, for amoralising self-judgement, and for displacing social bonds. He is convinced that a 'goodly proportion' of *per capita* GNP can be classified under such broad categories as "expendibles, usuries, regrettables, near garbage, and positively inimicals", the 'enjoyment' of which can only lead to more tension and widespread social distress. The products of growth, he therefore contends, do not improve 'well-being'. In view of these remarks it is little wonder that the political philosophies of John Stuart Mill are so popular, for many of the nongrowth school delight in his eloquent critique of 'dollar hunting' and of 'struggling to get on'.

The unspoken assumption is everywhere: materialism debases moral virtue and limits human understanding even though it may be the outcome of social injustice. "What do I miss as a human being if I have never heard of the Second Law of Thermodynamics?" asks Schumacher (1973, p.80). "The answer is: nothing. And what do I miss by not knowing Shakespeare? Unless I get my understanding from another source, I simply miss my life ... . Science cannot produce ideas by which we [can] live." To Hodson (1972, p.67) the 'true values' are "traditions, family relationships, security of home, natural surroundings and physical health"; the "reverence for growth, the envious strivings for more income, more consumption" have done much to undermine these precious virtues.

Similar sentiments are expressed at great length by Roszak (1973) and Taylor (1973), who are both convinced that all kinds of social and personal misery are directly attributable to an acquisitive society that has sadly misplaced its priorities.

There is some evidence to support these viewpoints, but the data are slim. Easterlin (1973) indicates that, despite their material affluence, many Americans feel now that they are 'worse off' than they were in 1957. A recent Gallup poll (Gallup, 1973) concluded that 21% of all Americans (18% whites and 44% nonwhites) were dissatisfied with the quality of their lives. Mishan (1971b, p.33) appeals to his memory:

> "The average *per capita* real income in America today is only about five times as high as it was in the Britain of 1950. But despite the rationing, my recollection is that life was far more comfortable and pleasant in the Britain of 1950 than it is in the America of today—especially in the larger cities."

The relative-needs argument provides meaty pickings for the progrowthers and socialists. Anthony Crosland (quoted in W. R. Johnson, 1973, p.165), currently the British Secretary of State for the Environment, puts it mildly:

> "The champions of the nogrowth society are often kindly and dedicated people. But they are affluent; and fundamentally, though not of course consciously, they want to kick the ladder down behind them. They are militant mainly about threats to rural peace and wildlife and well loved beauty spots; but little concerned with the far more desperate problem of the urban environment in which 80 per cent of our citizens live."

Beckerman (1974, pp.87–96) treats the relative-needs issue more harshly. Economists, he claims, are really interested in improving total social welfare and this means bettering the lot for "the average American secretary or Lancashire textile worker", not just in safeguarding the ephemeral values and jealously protected privileges of "the middle class, the middle-aged with enough time and money to go a little way off the beaten track but not quite rich enough to be protected from the masses on their yachts or private islands". H. G. Johnson (1975, p.327) is even more disdainful. "A good many alarmists," he says with confessed bias, "tend to reflect a conservative and aristocratic hankering after an earlier and simpler period of social organisation in which people knew and kept to their place, and upstarts could not become as affluent as oneself (or worse, destroy one's affluence) by making intelligent use of new resources and new technologies". As to the accusation that consumption simply escalates 'needs' so that people will never be 'satisfied', Beckerman (1974, p.92) attempts to demonstrate through a kind of null-hypothesis reasoning how futile this line of thinking can become:

> "... with both needs and satisfactions rising, but with the latter rising less than the former, one school of thought could say that welfare has risen on account of the rise in needs, another could say that it has fallen for the same reason, a third could say that welfare has fallen because the gap between needs and satisfaction has risen, and a fourth could say that welfare has risen because satisfactions have risen."

This is disagreeable hairsplitting but is precisely the kind of *reductio ad absurdum* that Coddington (1973) feels destroys much of Beckerman's progrowth views.

The 'relative needs' debate is very difficult to accept or to refute wholeheartedly. Undoubtedly there is some degree of class and income snobbery involved. The way in which people choose (or are persuaded or forced) to live and spend their incomes must be a matter for value judgement. Mishan (1973a, p.69) accepts this but questions whether their net welfare will improve as a result of their increasing expenditures, a judgement, as he puts it, "of fact, not ethics". Many growth advocates, on the other hand, are content to assume that as *per capita* wealth grows, a wider interest in public amenity will favour environmental protection, though H. G. Johnson (1975, p.330) admits that "it frequently takes considerable time to appreciate what is vulgar, dangerous or antisocial about the old ways, and what new ways will be more effective."

This matter is also terribly dependent on scale. Although there has always been something abhorrent about the flagrant extravagances of the rich, even if they did leave a magnificent architectural and cultural legacy, is this any worse than the continuing hesitancy on the part of wealthy nations today to assist the world's poor nations except in a time of catastrophe? The 'relative income' question can only be properly answered in the context of wider growth-nongrowth issues, particularly the misallocation of income and maldistributed environmental consequences of production and consumption—in short, environmental and social injustice.

3.1.3 Environment and social injustice

Critics of growth have long tried to show that growth exacerbates the unequal distribution of wealth. The rich not only get relatively richer, but also become better able to control growth and the institutions of growth to suit their purposes and maintain their hegemony over the poor. Though many economists concede that growth has improved the *real* living standards of the poor, they challenge the US President's Council of Economic Advisers' (1973) statement that the comparative position of the poor is far better than twenty years ago. Inevitably, the debate centres on the definition of 'poor', for, as economic tastes vary (partly due to growth and the expectations generated by growth), so relative aspirations change. W. R. Johnson (1973, p.171) feels that the official US definition of a 'poverty' income is half of what is really 'necessary' and a quarter of what is 'adequate'. He proceeds to show that relative income differentials have worsened since the early fifties (table 3.1), a point of view supported by Pirages and Ehrlich (1974, pp.270–274), and Smith and Franklin (1974). Brown (1972, pp.43–47) claims that growth, linked to adverse conditions of trade plus the protection of domestic industry, has also widened the gap between the rich nations and the poor (table 3.2). He also shows that income differentials are worsening within the poorer nations (table 3.3) as elites seek to protect their economic and political privileges.

The argument here is not that growth *per se* is bad, but that the abuse of legal and economic institutions based on the unfair allocation of power has meant that the outcome of growth is socially unjust. The 'establishment' that operates the organs of the economy and government constantly strives to secure its position, so growth becomes a major stock in trade to guarantee the stability of the system. For it is only through growth, it believes, that the poor can get better off without upsetting the political apple-cart. But many people feel that this philosophy is seriously counterproductive, since, as the fruits of progress are disproportionately shared, frustration leads to alienation and ultimately to violence. Adams (1972) concludes that the major reason for the very serious race riots in American cities during the mid-sixties was the blacks' perception of their

Table 3.1. Concentration of wealth in the United States. (Source: W. R. Johnson, 1973, p.177.)

Year	Wealth owned by top 0·5% of Americans as percentage of national wealth	Wealth owned by top 1% of Americans as percentage of national wealth
1922	29·8	31·6
1933	25·2	28·3
1939	28·0	30·6
1945	20·9	23·3
1949	20·9	23·3
1962	n.a.	31·0
1969	n.a.	28·0–34·0

Table 3.2. Income divergence between rich and poor nations. (Source: Brown, 1972, p.42.)

Year	Ratio between average incomes in industrialising societies and the rest of the world
1850	2:1
1950	10:1
1960	15:1
2000	30:1

relative deprivation, especially in terms of housing (figure 3.3). Seeing affluent white suburbs proliferate while promises of better housing in the ghettoes continually came to nothing was simply too much for thousands of victimised blacks who expressed their resentment in an almost carnival atmosphere of mass looting and destruction.

The serious difficulty presented by the argument that 'growth is the solution of all our ills' is the spiral of rising expectations, a matter of some concern for thoughtful moderates who recognise that fairer socioeconomic conditions must accompany environmental improvement, but who envisage the dangers of excessive egalitarianism. Nano (1974, p.118) puts this point well:

Table 3.3. Income differentials in poor countries. (Source: Brown, 1972, p.48.)

Country	Year	Ratio of income received by top 20% to bottom 20%
Argentina	1953	6·7
	1961	7·4
Ceylon	1953	10·3
	1963	11·6
Taiwan	1953	15·2
	1964	5·4
India	1952	6·1
	1960	5·2
Mexico	1950	9·8
	1963	17·0
Philippines	1957	12·2
	1965	15·8

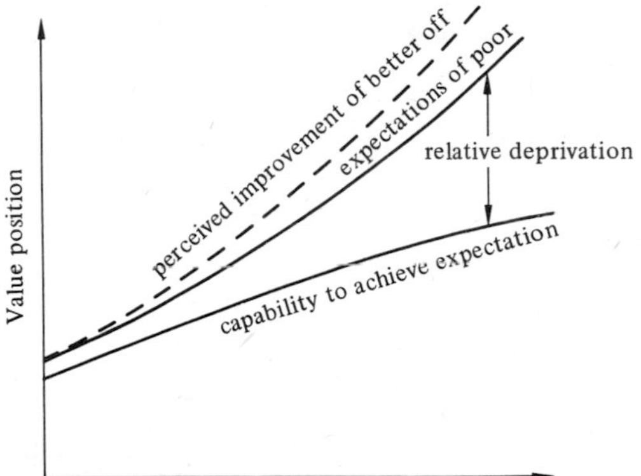

Figure 3.3. Rising expectations and social deprivation. Social deprivation is interpreted in relation to expectations and the perceived well-being of higher social classes. When expectations are persistently denied while the well-being of others appears to be steadily improving, social tension is bound to worsen.

"Since environmental resources are already overtaxed and there is nothing we can do about the existing number of people, and since population growth can at best be reduced only slowly, I believe there is a strong argument against propaganda for sharing ... why awaken or whip up new appetites or wants ... which cannot be satisfied? Revolutions of rising expectations should not be started before and unless the expectations can be satisfied, otherwise they make people more rather than less unhappy."

Coupled with the maldistribution of wealth created by the institutions of growth is the very serious misallocation of environmental quality. Since the rich can avoid the worst of the disamenities arising from growth, the poor and the politically weak have inevitably borne the brunt of pollution, squalor, and social decay. Or, as Neuhaus (1971, p.23) puts it, the rich exhibit 'the politics of choice', while the poor suffer the 'politics of necessity'. Nevertheless the rich do incur heavy 'avoidance' costs (in higher property values, double glazing, commuting expenses, landscaping, etc.) in seeking to escape disamenity, though these expenditures have never been fully calculated.

A survey by the US Environmental Protection Agency (EPA, 1971) and a recent Gallup poll (1973) confirm that the most serious environmental hardships are experienced by the inner-city poor, who complain about their plight but are unable to do much about it (tables 3.4 and 3.5). Environmental stress undoubtedly increases mortality and adds to the misery of an already doleful existence. Some three-fifths of the immobile

Table 3.4. Environmental hazards for the inner city poor. (Sources: Council on Environmental Quality, 1972, p.192; and US Environmental Protection Agency, 1971, p.19.)

Nuisance ($\mu g/m^3$)	Inner city		Suburb	Country
	average	peak		
Suspended particulates	102	260	40	21
Sulphur dioxide	65–80	372	60	40
Oxidants	125	n.a.	n.a.	n.a.
Lead	0·21	1·11	0·09	0·02
Nitrate ion	1·4	2·4	0·8	0·4
Sulphate ion	10·0	10·1	5·3	2·5

Symptom (% population affected)	Poor		Middle income		Upper income	
	white	nonwhite	white	nonwhite	white	nonwhite
Hypertension	23·5	35·5	11·1	19·7	11·8	26·6
Heart disease	16·6	29·7	6·0	17·2	7·9	26·0
Chronic illness	18·1	29·6	5·8	7·1	n.a.	n.a.

urban poor (about 16 million Americans according to the EPA estimate) are vulnerable to severe environmental health hazards; so the poor become sick and the sick become poor (see also Craig and Berlin, 1971; Zwerdling, 1973). They suffer three times the likelihood of heart disease, four times the likelihood of other chronic illness, and seventy times the likelihood of getting mugged, compared with affluent suburbanites.

Yet it is the comfortable beneficiaries of growth who are the main cause of many of these environmental ills for which they pay so little. For example, 60000 people are displaced annually in America to make way for the motorways along which the escapist suburbanites commute to work. The poor who are condemned to remain must suffer the associated visual blight, noise, and noxious fumes to say nothing of the depression of their property values. Zupan (1973) demonstrates how income and property values are inversely correlated with air pollution, implying that pollution is 'exported' to poverty areas whose inhabitants subsidise the environmental amenity and economic growth of the opulent (see also Freeman, 1972, pp.264–265).

Thus any 'social costs' are really 'class costs' because they are quite deliberately unfairly distributed among social classes (England and Bluestone, 1973, p.194). This state of affairs relates to the global community as much as (if not more so than) it does to sovereign populations. Allaby *et al.* (1975) comment that the affluent countries regularly 'export' famine to the poor nations since the rich can always afford to buy up scarce fertilisers and grain while the world's poor starve in almost silent protest. The existence of such noticeable disparities in environmental amenity displays most poignantly the failure of our institutions, which are so well adapted to 'progress' that they fail to come to grips with the wages of growth. Growth advocates believe that this is merely a matter for institutional reform (via reallocative devices such as taxes and legal rights to amenity), but they fail to recognise that such reform must be sanctioned by the people who gain most from the existing arrangements and who are therefore the most resistant to any change.

Table 3.5. How people view environmental quality (S = % satisfied, D = % dissatisfied). (Source: Gallup, 1973.)

	White		Nonwhite		Cities over one million		Towns under 2500	
	S	D	S	D	S	D	S	D
Quality of life	78	18	51	44	61	35	84	13
Quality of home	30	47	10	37	24	48	33	50
Noise conditions	15	79	30	59	25	66	5	90
Congestion conditions	13	83	41	49	28	65	3	84

3.1.4 The threat to mankind

Many advocates of growth admit that there are certain risks associated with modern technology that could endanger the future of the human race. H. G. Johnson (1975, p.331), for example, concludes that the real problems facing man will be

> "... the damage we may be doing to our oceans and our upper atmosphere by treating both as a costless medium for the transport of people and goods, and the oceans as an inexhaustible source of fish and crustaceans for human nourishment."

They acknowledge that man has the capacity irretrievably to degrade life-support systems and stress the need for proper studies of technology assessment to cope with this fact. They do not, however, feel that growth is a cause of this danger, simply that present institutions do not adequately come to grips with the wider implications of technological advance, though mechanisms exist to correct for this (see Roberts, 1973; Zeckhauser, 1973). In their view the issues are technological and managerial, not moral.

The antigrowth camp see this matter from quite a different angle. First, they believe that modern social and political institutions are *incapable* of proper consideration of such dangers, since no single organisation has the authority to undertake truly comprehensive long-term assessments of environmental impact. They charge that all effective institutions are locked into the paradigm of growth, and so respond mainly to the pressures of growth-orientated vested interests (Toffler, 1975). Some writers even assert that, because of their large size, many modern organisations (both public and private) lack any sense of formal direction; the 'crisis' in their view is a crisis of management. The issue is not simply a matter of growth, of course, but the familiar ecocentric–technocentric debate over control, complacency, and urgency. An orientation toward growth provides a favourable climate for these attributes, while a redirected philosophy of growth would replace these with the virtues of cooperation, humility, and permanence on a greatly decentralised scale of activity.

3.1.5 Growth and disamenity

One of the more prominent controversies in the growth–nongrowth debate centres around the relationship between economic growth and environmental disamenity (irrespective of the *distributional* issue discussed above). Basically the growth advocates believe that, because of economic progress, people are generally much better-off than they were, say, in Tudor or Dickensian times when sanitary conditions were appalling, disease was rampant, personal hygiene for the most part was nonexistent, and longevity was far less than today. In short, most people led lives of poverty and misery. By way of contrast, they argue, most modern industrialised peoples have broken clear of poverty and debilitating disease and can increasingly turn their attention to improving environmental amenities, as witnessed by (a) rising public interest in pollution control, and (b) declining pollution levels (see Beckerman, 1974, pp.60-79). The contrary view, equally devoid of systematic facts (partly, of course, because proper amenity accounting measures do not exist, but partly to suit the argument) acknowledges that some kinds of pollution have decreased, but claims that other more insidious environmental hazards (such as the release of toxic substances, alienation, social distress, 'industrial' stress diseases, etc.) have increased. Apart from the overall paucity of supporting data [and Coddington (1973, p.671) accuses Beckerman of manipulating what little there is], this dispute cannot easily be resolved because it is based on differing ideological premises about the function of growth and the ability of man to channel its positive features into social progress.

But one area where there is agreement on both sides is the inadequacy of GNP as an index of social welfare. (For reviews see Hodson, 1972, pp.50-72; Heller, 1972; McKean, 1973; Beckerman, 1974, pp.60-101.) GNP is a statistical measure of a nation's aggregate output of goods and services, including government services, capital goods, and increases in inventory. It is confined to a monetary accounting system which has limitations that Pigou (quoted in Beckerman, 1974, p.60) recognised over forty years ago:

> "The real objection is not that economic welfare (as measured by GNP) is a bad index of total welfare, but that an economic cause may affect noneconomic welfare in ways that cancel its effect on economic welfare."

Environmentalists assert that GNP fails as an adequate welfare accounting device on four counts.

(i) GNP does not deduct waste, deterioration, the replacement of capital, and the exhaustion of physical resources. This is part of Daly's 'growthmania' thesis, since present tax policies encourage the rapid write-off of capital equipment and count this as 'growth'. An index called the Net National Product does subtract depreciation, etc., but it is little used since data limitations make the nature of deductions rather controversial. Gross accounting, therefore, gives a very false picture of resource depletion, and of course completely ignores any physical deterioration in public goods such as roads and public buildings, though any costs of repairs or replacements would be included.

(ii) GNP does not recognise do-it-yourself maintenance. Although GNP will incorporate maintenance costs where someone is paid for his services, it does not, for example, recognise the efforts of unpaid labour towards the upkeep of property. Thus, if both husband and wife go out to work and hire a housekeeper to look after their property, both the goods and services they produce and the wages of the domestic help will count in GNP. But if either stays at home to maintain the house or grow vegetables, these labours will not be included in the national accounts.

Thus many features of an ecocentric self-sufficiency economy would not be recognised in GNP accounts.

(iii) GNP does not measure uncompensated externalities. Externalities are the costs and benefits created by individuals or firms in the process of conducting their affairs which impinge on society at large (or certainly third parties) for which neither the generators nor the recipients pay.

Where these externalities cause damages which cost money to remedy (cleanup of building facades, for example), or where costs are incurred to prevent damages from occurring in the first place (the construction of residuals control equipment), these costs are included in the GNP account. (This is part of Daly's growthmania thesis.) But where either amenities or disamenities are not paid for, then GNP ignores their occurrence. Thus social stress or family disruption 'caused' by a decaying postindustrial society (Taylor, 1973) would not appear in GNP balance sheets unless the delinquency created a need for additional police, prisons, and remand homes. The aggregate social costs of uncompensated environmental disamenity are probably very large and growing. The Council on Environmental Quality (1973a, pp.77–80) estimates these to be some \$80 per person in the United States for air pollution alone in 1967, rising to around \$120 per person by 1977 if pollution control is not improved. The cost of water pollution is more difficult to estimate. Kneese and Schultze (1975, p.78) estimate that it would cost \$61 billion to clean up municipal and industrial wastes by 80% over the decade 1971–1981. To clean these up entirely could cost as much as \$317 billion—only a third of what the Americans spent on the Vietnam war. The estimate for total environmental costs is simply incalculable.

(iv) GNP does measure 'regrettable necessities'. These are goods and services that society produces but which some people feel are of no positive value to social welfare. The prime candidate is military expenditure on manpower and hardware, though some people would also include such items as police, insurance, and fire services in this category. The problem here, as with other criticisms of GNP, is in attempting to make this index do something for which it was never designed and which it palpably cannot do, namely identify the 'goods and bads' of economic growth. As Okun (quoted in Beckerman, 1974, p.81) puts it:

> "To suggest that GNP could become *the* indication of social welfare is to imply that an appropriate price tag could be put on changes in all these social factors from one year to the next ... [and] is ... asking the national income statistician to play the role of a philosopher king, quantifying and evaluating all changes in the human scene."

Nevertheless economists have ventured to calculate a new kind of balance sheet that endeavours to take some of these social factors into account. Sametz (1968) estimated the additional benefits of leisure (a positive externality) on national accounts, and showed that these benefits represented a value equivalent to almost two thirds of conventional GNP. Nordhaus and Tobin (1972) attempted a more comprehensive account which they termed the Measure of Economic Welfare (MEW), which included additions for uncompensated benefits (such as leisure and nonmarketed services) and subtractions for uncompensated losses (including regrettable necessities, disamenity and other nonmarketed social costs). They compared MEW in the United States for 1929 and 1965, and, although their analysis was highly speculative, they tentatively concluded that the rate of increase of social costs is outpacing the rate of increase of social gains (figure 3.4). While Beckerman (1974, pp.85-86) is at pains to point out that these differential growth rates are affected by their proportional relationships to the original totals (the cost component being much smaller than the benefits component), he does recognise in a footnote (p.86) that "if these relative growth rates were to persist indefinitely, the former (i.e. the negative items) would eventually catch up with and overtake the latter (the favourable adjustments)".

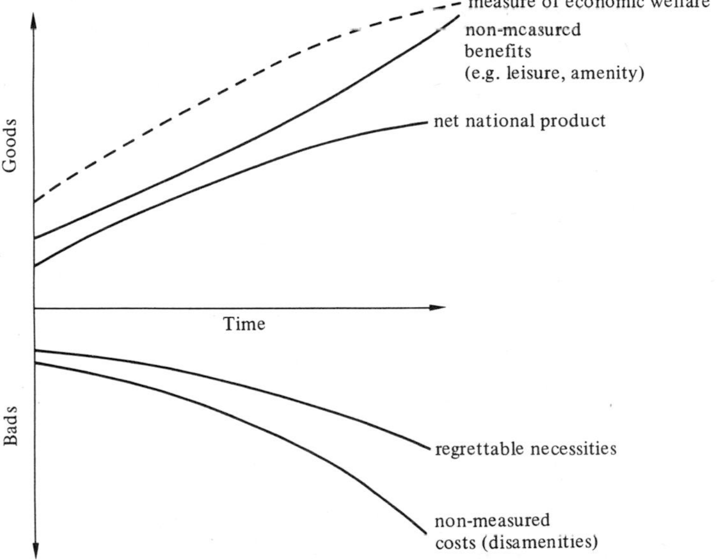

Figure 3.4. Shifts in net national product, nonmeasured costs and benefits, regrettable necessities and the measure of economic welfare—1929 to 1965. Unless nothing is done to combat it, the measure of economic welfare appears to decline in terms of diminishing annual increases. (Source: adapted from Nordhaus and Tobin, 1971; Beckerman, 1974, p.35.)

3.1.6 Some concluding observations

Obviously much more work needs to be done to unravel the tangled relationships between growth and its associated social and environmental repercussions. The reader will observe from the discussion presented above that much of the writing on this subject suffers from a serious deficiency of unequivocal supporting evidence and from liberal dosages of ideological blindness. Thus it becomes very difficult, if not impossible, to reach clear conclusions about the various issues raised. The central question remains to be answered: how can we redirect our creative energies to improve social well-being, given our cultural heritage of economic growth, material acquisition, and technocentric exploitation? Economic growth as it is currently pursued and organised probably still increases the economic welfare of the general majority at a personal level *in terms which these individuals find satisfying and acceptable.* Some (like Mishan) are prepared to make value judgements that the effects of this economic improvement are ultimately disagreeable and socially undesirable, but can we and indeed should we make such accusations? Undoubtedly, growth as we know it reduces the general happiness of the very rich and the very poor for quite different reasons and offends the sensibilities of many middle-class intellectuals. Being a member of this last group, I am inclined to sympathise with their view (particularly the feeling that our collective amenity is being eroded) but I remain aware of the dangers of making value judgements as to the benefits or otherwise of the pleasures of others. Nevertheless, I do agree with the anxieties expressed by Mishan (1974a, p.122)

> "Once we have reached the state of economic growth when the silence of the snow-covered hills is shattered by the whine of snowmobiles, when the quiet of country lanes can at any moment be broken by the roar of motor bikes, when the lake and sea shores are taken over by water-skiers and motor boats—which one of us can hope to get away from it all? Unmarred natural beauty, lakes, woodlands and quiet valleys, the restorative powers of the salt sea air, the stillness and serenity of mountain and wilderness—what has been left of this heritage? Goods that were once freely and abundantly available to our preindustrial forebears, and which are surely critical to our health and well-being, are already so scarce as to be virtually unattainable for ordinary men."

We are destroying a heritage that is quite irreplaceable and utterly central to our existence. I do believe it is possible to protect much of these values while still improving social well-being for everybody (and some suggestions are made in the next chapter), but I also recognise that some of our existing economic institutions will have to be changed to achieve this. In the section that follows, two kinds of alteration are postulated: the first tinkers with the existing economic structure, but is still politically implausible, while the second is more radical in that it sets specific ceilings on resource consumption and hence is even less politically acceptable.

3.2 The spaceship economy

An oft-quoted metaphor in the discussion on growth and nongrowth is the notion of a 'spaceship earth'. The concept was first launched in 1965 by the United States Ambassador to the United Nations, Adlai Stevenson, who, in a speech before the Economic and Social Council in Geneva, referred to the earth as a little spaceship on which mankind travels "dependent on its vulnerable supplies of air and soil". But the real message of the spaceship metaphor was driven home by the striking photographs taken by various astronauts of a life-filled, green and blue earth wrapped in spiralling white cloud, slowly revolving in a black and inert void. These photographs, far more than the academic Turner 'frontier' thesis, compelled people to realise the earth's utter finiteness and the crucial life-supporting role of our biosphere. The earth symbol soon became the ikon of environmentalists and the catchy slogan ('Only One Earth') of the UN Human Environment Conference (Ward and Dubos, 1972; Stone, 1973).

The spaceship idea was quickly seized upon by Boulding (1966) in his characterisation of a new 'environmental' economics, where pollution control and resource conservation could be woven into the fabric of economic growth. His recipe for a 'spaceship economy' (Boulding, 1966, pp.9–10) has since been accepted by many economists as the prescription for future economic policies:

> "In the spaceship economy, throughput is by no means a desideratum, and indeed is to be regarded as something to be minimized rather than maximized. The essential measure of the success of the economy is not production and consumption at all, but the nature, extent, quality and complexity of the total capital stock, including in this state of the human bodies and minds included in the system ... . The idea that both production and consumption are bad things rather than good things is very strange to economists, who have been obsessed with the income-flow concepts to the exclusion, almost, of capital-stock concepts."

Boulding compared this 'closed system' economics with the traditional open system economics of resource abundance, wasteful energy use, fast throughput, and the "reckless, exploitative, romantic and violent behaviour, which is characteristic of open societies". He called this the 'cowboy economy' which he recognised must end (figure 3.5).

Economists have subsequently leapt delightedly onto the spaceship bandwagon, beginning with a courageous attempt by three RfF analysts (Kneese, Ayres, and d'Arge, 1971) to develop a theoretical input–output model of a closed economic system based upon the time-honoured principles of general equilibrium theory. This was followed by more comprehensible attempts to portray residuals flows of the United States economy in a thermodynamic context (Kneese, 1971a; Victor, 1972;

Deininger, 1973; Enthoven and Freeman, 1973; Freeman *et al.*, 1973; Pratt, 1974). Some of these were used to find out what might happen in a nongrowth economy (Ayres and Kneese, 1971; Eilenstine and Cunningham, 1972; Sweezy and Owens, 1974), some to assess how major industries could clean up and still be profitable (Bower and Spofford, 1970; Russell, 1973; Spofford, 1973), and some to assess how residuals control policies would bear upon world economic growth and international trade (d'Arge, 1971, 1972; d'Arge and Kneese, 1972).

But before we discuss these spaceship economy models and their amendments, we should review some ideological criticisms of the spaceship metaphor. Some left-wing writers [for example Neuhaus (1971, p.80) and Enzensberger (1974, pp.16–17)] have berated the imagery as elitist and technocratic, a purely American invention that eschews the socialist's main contention—freedom for all mankind and the peaceful conduct of liberty. They feel that the RfF studies do nothing to reduce the political and economic control of the corporate–governmental elite; indeed, by 'tinkering at the margin', the residuals-balance approach perpetuates capitalistic dominance. (Ironically the corporate establishment is very suspicious of the residuals models since they close several of the favourable tax loopholes the companies would like to protect.) Some economists (e.g. Pearce, 1974; and Lecomber, 1974) have challenged the spaceship notion on the grounds that it is incompatible with ecological constraints. They contend that it tacitly assumes unending growth in a finite world, a view supported with incontrovertible thermodynamic evidence by Georgescu-Roegen (1973). White (1973, pp.63–64) is also disturbed by what he calls this 'ecologically terrifying' metaphor. "A spaceship is completely a human artifact", he comments, "designed to sustain human life and no other purpose ... . The spaceship mentality is the final sophistication of this disastrous man-centred view of the nature of things and the things of nature, and it has the present allurement of seeming to offer ecologic solutions without sacrifice of the old presuppositions."

Despite these justifiable criticisms, the spaceship metaphor is still a useful device by which to compare solutions proposed by both sides of the growth–nongrowth debate. Progrowth economists feel that pollution and other social disamenities are simply by-products of production, the

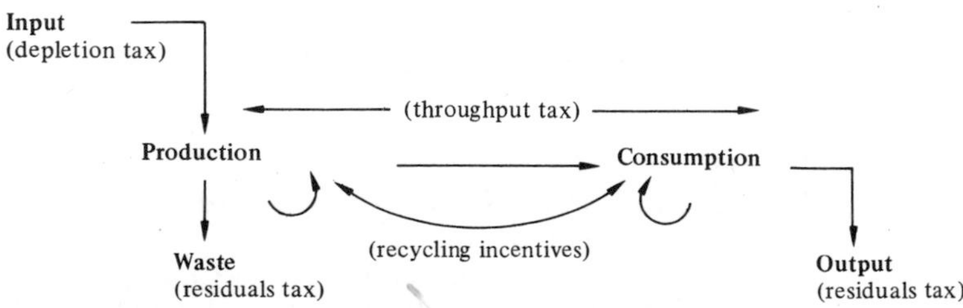

Figure 3.5. The Spaceship I economy.

outcomes of inappropriate allocative devices, and can be eliminated (or at least reduced to acceptable levels) by means of remedial taxes. As Roberts (1973, p.125) puts it: "the very best way to control pollution is to control pollution, not growth". He and others propose a Spaceship I model, in which taxes would be so designed as to encourage economic institutions to limit resource depletion, withhold residuals (or pay a charge which would be used to compensate losers and construct collective residuals removal schemes), encourage product durability (to slow up the rate of technological and product obsolescence and hence the rate of economic 'throughput'), and recycle and reuse 'waste' products (figure 3.5). Antigrowth economists, however, visualise a different spaceship, Spaceship II (figure 3.6). They see a *constant stock* of goods and people maintained at predetermined and politically acceptable levels by a politically controlled 'minimal' rate of maintenance throughput, by birth and death rates that are equal at the lowest feasible level, and by physical production and consumption rates that are also regulated by preset energy flows and rates of resource depletion (Daly, 1973b, p.152).

Though both models seek to encourage decentralised decisionmaking (or microvariability), so that firms or individuals are free (insofar as freedom is possible) to plan their own economies, the Spaceship II model envisages politically imposed ceilings on short run resource depletion and the production and consumption of goods (macrostability) imposed either by stiff taxes or by rationing. In Spaceship I growth would continue but its unpleasant side effects would be reduced and, wherever possible, competitive market forces would flourish. In Spaceship II (figure 3.6) growth would be limited by political fiat to accord with environmental constraints, and some of it would be compulsorily redirected into alternative goods and services, the redistribution of wealth and amenity, and the encouragement of low consumption; in other words, market

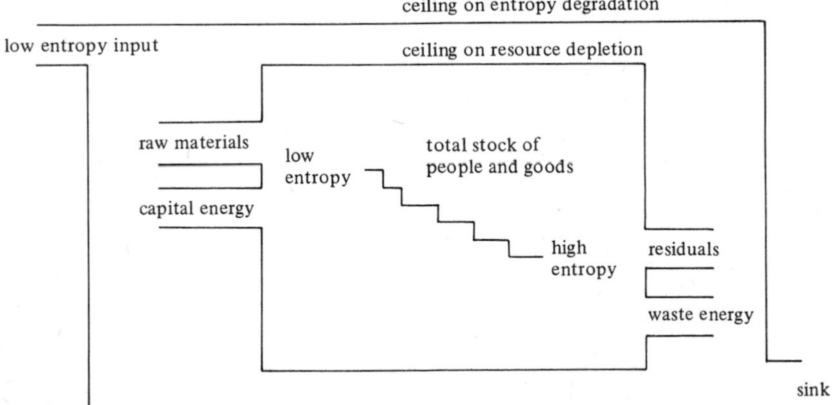

Figure 3.6. The Spaceship II economy.

forces would be combined with strict penalties. Though these models are based upon quite different premises they do agree on certain economic reforms, as discussed below. Where they disagree is on how these reforms should be implemented.

3.2.1 The resource depletion tax

Most academic economists now agree that the tax deductions available to firms exploiting finite reserves of natural resources should be abolished. At present, resource-depletion tax loopholes provide favourable tax reductions for depreciation schedules, depletion allowances, and other extraction cost write-offs. For example, oil companies based in the United States can deduct 22% of their gross (pretax) revenues, to an amount not exceeding 50% of net income for all costs of exploration and extraction. Not only does this 'depletion allowance' encourage very wasteful exploitation practices, but it provides a massive public subsidy to corporations and reduces the price of resource extraction to a level well below full social costs. In other words, the taxpayer is subsidising unnecessary depletion *and* unnecessary environmental damage. (For evidence see Green *et al.*, 1972, pp.278–283; Ridgeway, 1973, pp.4–11: for an alternative view, see Miller, 1975.) In addition to the lucrative depletion allowance, present US tax provisions (undoubtedly drafted with the 'advice' of the powerful oil lobby—see Weisberg, 1971, pp.132–145; Pirages and Ehrlich, 1974, pp.123–125) permit oil companies in the United States to claim a tax deduction on all royalties they pay for foreign oil, a figure that currently exceeds \$1 trillion (10^{12}) per year.

The effect of these two tax arrangements is to encourage vertically-integrated companies to inflate costs of oil extraction so as to write them off against taxable refining costs and revenues, and enjoy tax deductions on net foreign oil revenues. As a result oil corporations pay taxes at ludicrously low rates, sometimes less than 5% annually on net incomes exceeding \$30 billion (Green *et al.*, 1972, p.280). Though the depletion allowance was originally devised (in the US Income Tax Law of 1913) to assist only oil companies, it has since been extended to all economic activities which exploit natural resources. And while the depletion allowance for coal extraction is only 10%, it covers the cost not only of mining but also of 'preparing' and transporting coal (up to fifty miles). The concept of 'preparation' seems to have wide application since depletion allowance deductions are permissible against the costs of converting oil shale into oil (Ridgeway, 1973, p.24). It has been variously estimated that depletion allowances cost the United States taxpayer annually some \$1·3 billion for oil, \$1·45 billion for all minerals and \$40–\$50 million for coal. The politicoeconomic institutions developed during the period of 'cowboy' economics continue to encourage waste.

The resource extraction companies have long defended the depletion allowance on the grounds (a) that natural resources are crucial for the welfare of society, so scarcity must be discouraged, and (b) that since these resources are depletable, the actual act of consumption inevitably means a net loss to the company (and to the nation). Here is a fine example of Fife's (1971) contention that the wealthy can always exploit the commons up to the point of marginal profit and then take their investment elsewhere. Recognising that oil is a finite resource, all the big oil 'majors' have begun to expand horizontally into all forms of energy production, especially the coal, oil shale, and nuclear sectors (table 3.6). (See Ridgeway, 1973; Medwin, 1974; Tanzer, 1974.) A 'post-Watergate' US Congress now recognises the tremendous resource wastage (not to mention the tax loopholes) fostered by depletion allowances, and is currently preparing legislation to remove both the foreign royalty credits and depletion allowances so as to force companies to adopt more conservationist extraction policies. Yet at the same time the Ford administration remains anxious to subsidise domestic energy exploitation by relaxing price controls and proposing a guaranteed 'minimum floor price' for indigenous oil.

Both Spaceship models are in favour of much more punitive tax penalties for resource depletion. Spaceship I favours a new resource depletion tax which could be raised or lowered depending upon the relative 'scarcity' of the resource in question, though this kind of sliding scale is vulnerable to the manipulation of the estimates of reserves. Such a tax should discourage unnecessary depletion and promote more efficient extraction practices, thereby expanding the economic life of all resources. (For a comprehensive theoretical statement see Herfindahl and Kneese, 1974, pp.114–184). There are signs that the era of the depletion allowance is coming to an end. In March 1975, President Ford signed a tax bill which, amongst other things, stripped the big companies of their 22% oil depletion allowance, and reduced this to 15% for the small firms

Table 3.6. Horizontal integration of energy sectors by the major oil corporations. (Source: Netschert, 1972, p.73.)

Company	1969 assets ($ billion)	Gas	Oil shale	Coal	Uranium	Tar sands
Exxon	17·5	√	√	√	√	√
Texaco	9·3	√	√	√	√	0
Gulf	8·1	√	√	√	√	√
Mobil	7·1	√	√	0	√	0
Shell	4·3	√	√	√	√	√
Atlantic Richfield	4·2	√	√	√	√	√
Continental Oil	2·9	√	√	√	√	0
Sun Oil	2·5	√	√	√	√	√

over the next nine years. In addition tax credits for foreign oil royalty payments were reduced. This will add some $750 million in oil-related taxes by 1977.

A form of resource depletion tax was established by the socialist government of British Columbia (Canada) in 1973 through its Mineral Royalties Act. Under the terms of the Act mineral extracting companies pay a second royalty (a superroyalty), amounting to 50% on all revenues in excess of that guaranteeing a 20% return on investment. In a sense, the British Columbia government regard this as a form of 'social rent' on publicly owned mineral resources, for they wish to ensure that the British Columbia taxpayer benefits from high world market prices (a reflection of a boom in demand and/or a scarcity of supply) that would otherwise simply raise the profits of the mining industry through no actions of its own. The British Columbia government has proposed that another 'social rent' royalty be levied against the British Columbia forest industry (Pearce, 1974). In both cases it is difficult to forecast yet the longer-term effects of this legislation on resource depletion, and on corporate policy. Already there is evidence that some of the multinational companies engaged in resource extraction are investing in more profitable ventures elsewhere.

On the other hand, the Spaceship II model would impose short-run (say five year) ceilings on resource extraction (Daly, 1973b, pp.160–163) through a system of quotas. The legal rights to deplete each resource up to the amount specified in the quota would then be auctioned off by the government to firms and individuals who could resell or transfer these rights if they so wished. If growth persisted the quotas would be reduced, thus forcing up prices and encouraging even more conservation, especially in the resource-intensive sectors. Daly's ideas are drawn from Dales (1968, pp.77–100) who suggested that the government auction a fixed quota of 'pollution rights' (or 'amenity depletion rights') equal to the assimilative capacity of the receiving medium. The idea is to regulate the rate of depletion to predetermined levels so as to slow down the rate of resource throughput and curtail the increasingly unsustainable energy demands of extracting low-grade resources. Eventually, depletion quotas would be established at 'optimum' levels (presumably close to zero), so that a near-constant resource stock would largely be reused and recycled. The revenue from the depletion quota auctions would be used to encourage appropriate technologies and related investment for sustaining a steady state economy.

The two models diverge markedly on the role of price in determining resource availability. Spaceship I believes that prices (through unavoidable government intervention) can be adjusted so as to time the rate of resource extraction to socially optimal levels while still supporting economic growth. This view is held by a number of national governments who envisage some kind of participation in various resource extraction enterprises (to influence policy), but who prefer the use of taxes and price incentives over outright nationalisation (to encourage 'wise use'). This is also a politically expedient philosophy, since it is unlikely that the giant resource-extraction corporations would take kindly to the idea of depletion quotas, no matter how generous.

The Daly proposal, though ingenious, flies in the face of present-day political and economic realities. It would only be possible in a centralised socialist economy, and even then the mind boggles at the administrative complexities and the political infighting that it would induce. Nevertheless, some variant of the Daly scheme might occur if resource scarcities (whether 'real' or contrived by politically controlled pricing policies) become more severe or occur cyclically or unpredictably. The French government have already imposed a price 'ceiling' on oil imports each year (which means that if the price rises the amount of oil imported will fall); and both the British and American governments have formulated emergency rationing plans based on quotas to allocate oil to key sectors of the economy in the event of another international embargo.

It is possible that a form of pricing linked to quotas might be feasible both to limit demand and to redistribute income from resource 'wasters' to resource 'conservers'. One suggestion (proposed in a Congressional bill sponsored by Representative Ullman) is to raise the existing federal tax of 4¢ per gallon on motor fuel to 7¢, an act that should reduce gasoline consumption to the levels existing in 1973. If such a reduction did occur, no further tax would be needed, but for every 1% that consumption rose above that level, an additional 8¢ would be imposed. Progressive increase in this 'gasoline consumption' tax would continue up to 23¢ (which, with the original 7¢ would make the total tax 30¢ per gallon) if the increase in consumption over the 1973 level exceeded 3%. This kind of gasoline taxation is a potentially effective demand-reducing weapon in the United States where cars consume about 45% of all oil (compared to about 7% in Britain), and could reduce gasoline demand by as much as 10% (compared to less than 1% in Britain and France).

The Ullman bill proposes that part of this 'social dividend' revenue would be equally divided among all citizens over sixteen years of age irrespective of whether they owned a car or not. The gasoline consumption tax would thus be a means of penalising those who consumed resources excessively (presumably there would be safeguards for certain users who were dependent on the car) while 'rewarding' those who, for various reasons (not the least of which might be poverty), avoided consumption of this scarce resource. Part of the revenue would be diverted into more comfortable and accessible forms of public transport, and part into research and development of alternative sources of energy and locomotion (see Ayres and McKenna, 1972). A variation of the Ullman bill proposes that the tax be adjusted upwards or downwards as the 'reserves to production ratio' fell or rose. Hence part of the revenue could presumably be used to encourage further oil and gas extraction.

Though compatible with Spaceship II, the Ullman proposition was not acceptable to many vested interests, and, not surprisingly, it failed to gain the necessary Congressional support.

A related suggestion to the Ullman proposal, favoured by many economists is a 'white market' in resource ration coupons. The idea here is that all resource consumers (e.g. motorists, but it could apply to electricity or gas users equally well) are issued an equal number of coupons (the total number being fixed by a Daly type quota allowance). They would then be permitted to sell in recognised outlets any coupons superfluous to their requirements. Again the principle of transferring income from resource consumers to resource conservers would operate. Many economists prefer this idea to the more moderate proposal of a two-tier pricing system within a quota arrangement (as proposed by the UK National Economic Development Office, 1975), by which motorists would be granted some 12–16 gallons per month at a controlled price and unlimited supplies at considerably higher prices. All these proposals are more equitable (and more efficient to administer) than the traditional response of equal rationing which, unfortunately, appears to be the standard political reflex to any threatened scarcity.

3.2.2 The throughput tax

To reduce the rate of product obsolescence, Mills (quoted in Heller, 1973, p.24) proposed that the original producers or importers of resource commodities be charged a materials use fee, the level of which would be adjusted to reflect the social costs of the most environmentally harmful manner of disposal. To the extent that disposal was delayed, or less than maximally harmful, a portion of the fee would be refunded. Thus the tax, in part, would reflect the rate at which a product passes from usefulness to disuse and would provide an incentive to promote product durability. In the absence of such a tax, consumer advocates, like Ralph Nader in the United States and Michael Young in the United Kingdom, have long urged strict regulations against planned obsolescence through performance guarantees.

The throughput tax should provide a powerful incentive to encourage recycling. Again part of the problem here is the legacy of outdated, growth-orientated legislation which actively encourages practices wasteful of resources. For example, US interstate commerce regulations (the outcome of vested interest lobbying) penalise the use of recycled scrap by levying double the freight rates for all recycled metals compared with virgin ones (US National Commission on Materials Policy, 1973, chapter 4D) (see table 3.7). Another result of these discriminatory charges is the increase in the number of abandoned or disused automobiles (about one million are discarded each year in the United States), though the wider result has been to reduce the profitability of recycling (and hence the quantity of recycling). Likewise, solid waste generation (especially of plastics and paper products) is rising by staggering amounts (about 5% annually or doubling every fourteen years), and presenting a very real problem of disposal (see Marx, 1972).

The Council on Environmental Quality (1973a, p.202) is quite critical of this situation, for it believes that recycling is currently impeded primarily by adverse economic circumstances, rather than by inadequate technology. A variant of the throughput tax is the deposit on bottles and cans to encourage return and reuse. In an attempt to reduce litter and encourage recycling the Oregon legislature outlawed the 'pull-tab' beverage can and slapped a 5¢ deposit on all containers except beer bottles (for which the deposit is 2¢). The Council on Environmental Quality (1973a, p.204) reports that, although beverage sales are unchanged, litter has decreased by 81%, the manufacture of containers has fallen sharply, and beverage prices have actually dropped. But despite all the evidence in its favour, the throughput tax will not be politically popular. By way of a compromise, the US National Commission on Materials Policy (1973) recommends tax credits for recycling and materials reprocessing plants, and an equalisation of the discriminatory freight rates. Even incentives such as these could dramatically reduce resource depletion and lessen the problem of waste disposal, though they are still generally resisted by industry, which prefers to change its practices in its own time by regulation measured to suit its needs.

Table 3.7. US freight rates on recycled and virgin commodities. (Source: US National Commission on Materials Policy, 1973, pp.4D-18.)

Commodity	Ratio of revenue to fully allocated cost of service		'Profit' on service (%)	
	ICC[a]	DOT[b]	ICC[a]	DOT[b]
Iron ores	1·05	0·95	5	−5
Fluxing stone	0·81	0·78	−19	−22
Coke, screening, and breeze	0·94	0·89	−6	−11
Pulpwood and woodchips	0·72	0·70	−28	−30
Iron and steel scrap	1·33	1·22	33	22
Paper waste	1·06	0·99	6	−1

[a] Figures supplied by the Interstate Commerce Commission in 1966; [b] figures supplied by the Department of Transportation in 1969.
Shippers of scrap metal and paper waste pay freight rates far in excess of the real cost of service. Only in the case of iron ore (ICC 1966) do shippers of virgin commodities 'pay their way'. In part then, there is a subsidy by shippers of recycled goods paid to shippers of virgin materials.

3.2.3 The residuals tax

The concept of an effluent fee, proposed long ago by Kneese (see Kneese and Bower, 1968, pp.71–141) has subsequently been broadened into the idea of a residuals tax (see Freeman and Haveman, 1972a, 1972b; Freeman *et al.*, 1973). The switch to the use of 'residuals' was brought about by the recognition of thermodynamic realities, because usable materials are not actually consumed but converted into residuals (or high-entropy unusable products). Herfindahl and Kneese (1974, p.360) emphasise the significance of this new philosophy:

> "Almost all of standard economic theory is in reality concerned with services. Material objects are merely the vehicles which carry some of these services ... . Yet economists persist in referring to the 'final consumption' of goods as though material objects such as fuels, materials and finished goods somehow disappeared into the void—a practice that was comparatively harmless so long as air and water were almost literally 'free goods'."

There is in fact a *materials balance* of flows and services between the input of materials (energy, minerals, trees, etc.) and the output of unwanted residuals, the environment providing the necessary supplies and the vital assimilative capacities to maintain the equation. The RfF authors cited above prefer this 'new look' model because it permits the scrutiny of a variety of policy options (including changing the product mix and consumption rates), and shows clearly the interdependencies between material flows and residuals (such that single-purpose air *or* water *or* land pollution control policies are ineffective). It also helps to elucidate the relationship between population growth, resource consumption and pollution (discussed in chapter 2, pp.65–72) and provides a useful framework for creating new public agencies (with comprehensive control over all forms of pollution on a regional basis). The value of this approach is to demonstrate the environmental significance of a residuals tax while indicating that it is only one of many institutional devices that should be implemented.

The residuals tax has been investigated from a variety of theoretical angles and is generally regarded by both progrowth and steady state economists as a necessary tool for allocating resources fairly and more efficiently. (For general reviews see Randall, 1971; Auld, 1972; Norton and Parlour, 1972; Wenders, 1972; Dorfman and Dorfman, 1973; Edel, 1973, pp.85–110; D. N. Thompson, 1973; Beckerman, 1974, pp.136–179; Herfindahl and Kneese, 1974, pp.303–321; Mäler, 1974; for air pollution, see Montgomery, 1972; for water pollution, see Upton, 1971; Ferrar and Whinston, 1972.) On theoretical grounds the residuals tax is widely accepted as an optimising device that minimises net social costs and offers the discharger maximum freedom of choice under conditions of efficiency. And by the same theoretical criteria, the residuals tax is favourably compared with two alternative strategies: (a) a system of bribes or subsidies to polluters to withhold their effluents, or (b) the generally followed practice of regulations. The latter are determined either on a case-by-case basis for classes of effluent, according to ambient (water or air) receiving standards, or (as is usually the case) by means of some unspecified combination of both.

Although the voluminous literature on the subject dates back to the early sixties, it is only within the past two years that politicians have given any serious consideration to the idea of a residuals tax. In the United States, Krier and Montgomery (1973, p.101) report that the state of Vermont has enacted a programme to levy a fee on dischargers who do not comply with state water quality standards, an action that is being considered in a number of other states. Needless to say, the idea of a residuals tax is politically contentious. The United States government proposed a tax on the emission of sulphur dioxide (or on the use of sulphurous fuels) amounting to 10¢–15¢ per pound in excess of regional standards (Council on Environmental Quality, 1972, pp.115–116), but it died in committee. In 1971, Senator Proxmire introduced a scheme of 'national effluent charges' into the proposed Regional Water Quality Act (*Congressional Record. Senate*, 1971, S.16306–9), though again this has still to emerge as positive legislation. In the United Kingdom the Royal Commission on Environmental Pollution (Ashby, 1972b, pp.62–85) discussed and rejected the idea of effluent charges as being administratively cumbersome and unnecessarily punitive to small businesses. However, the Department of the Environment is supporting a modelling study of discharger response in the face of a residuals tax (Rowley *et al.*, 1975). In Canada the concept of an effluent charge is mentioned in the Canada Water Act (but not yet implemented). The British Columbia government is considering not only a residuals tax but an *additional* charge as 'social rent' for the use of clean air and water (figure 3.7). So it is relevant to review the advantages and disadvantages of the concept in the light of its political acceptability and administrative feasibility.

The theoretical arguments in favour of the residuals tax can be summarised as follows:

(i) It is economically efficient in the sense that it provides an incentive to polluters to reduce pollution up to the point where the costs to them of further pollution abatement would be greater than the additional social damages incurred (figure 3.8). In other words the tax is an optimising allocative scheme which forces polluters to bear the true social cost of contaminating common property resources. It is therefore a politically imposed extension of the price system, which prods the discharger to clean up to (politically) acceptable levels or pay a fee (fine) which is then deployed either to clean up the effluent for him or to compensate those who demonstrably suffer as a result of continued emissions.

(ii) It is also efficient in the sense that it tailors the nature and level of abatement to reflect the production function of the discharger and the assimilative capacity of the particular environment into which he is disposing his effluent. Because the regulatory approach generally sets *uniform* emission standards for similar classes of productive activity to cover wide regions, even nations, these can impose quite unnecessary costs on some firms and grant large subsidies to others, depending upon the characteristics of the production processes.

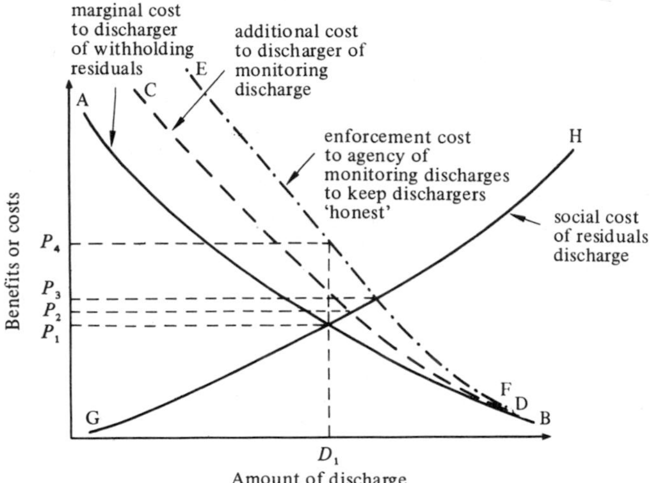

Figure 3.7. The residuals tax under various policy options: P_1, tax under marginal economic assumptions; P_2, tax plus costs of monitoring and reporting to discharger; P_3, tax plus monitoring costs plus enforcement costs by public agency; P_4, tax plus monitoring and enforcement costs plus additional 'penalty' to maintain residuals flow at politically acceptable levels.

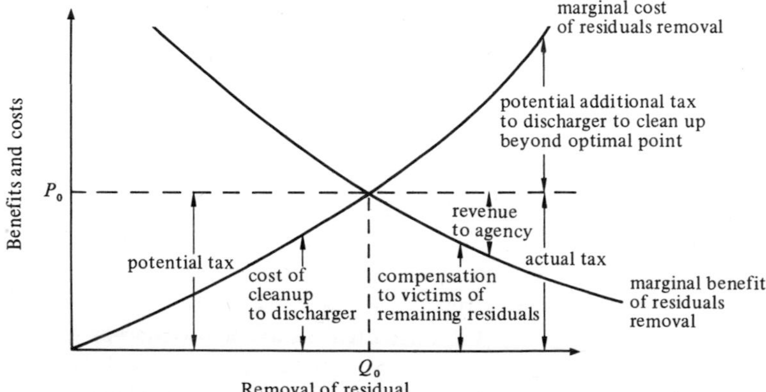

Figure 3.8. The economic theory of the residuals charge. P_0 is the optimal residuals tax, and Q_0 the optimal discharge of residuals.

Advocates of the residuals tax admit that variable regulations could be established to suit each discharger, but to do so would require very extensive, very costly information-gathering procedures (Dales, 1968, p.85). Dewees (1973) concludes that the quality of information generation and monitoring is critical to a residuals tax policy. Where effluent standards are in force, as the cost of measuring emissions and of prosecuting violators increases so the optimum amount of residuals increases. As Dewees puts it (p.29), "information costs drive a wedge between the marginal benefits and the costs of abatement". But for a residuals tax arrangement the optimal amount of pollution will be the same irrespective of information costs (to the point where the collection of information is so expensive that no control programme is warranted), since information costs only affect the accuracy which should be sought in determining emissions.

Krier and Montgomery (1973) believe that as the assimilative capacities of the environmental receiving media are reduced, the rising information costs of regulation will force governments to seek the more efficient alternative of the residuals tax. They claim that the residuals tax will give the same results as variable (tailored) emissions regulations at much lower administrative costs. This is a vital point, because it is on the grounds of 'transaction costs' rather than efficiency considerations *per se*, that the residuals tax is most favoured. Yet as we shall see this line of reasoning is the most readily challenged today. Even Krier and Montgomery (1973, pp.103–104) admit that the tax will not necessarily reduce pollution at least cost to each member of the regulated class (a point supported theoretically by Buchanan and Tullock, 1975), but they still contend that it should bring pollutant loads to socially acceptable levels at least social cost. However, if the tax is shown to be unfair *in individual cases*, political opposition from disadvantaged groups can be expected.

(iii) A refinement of the residuals tax proposal is to incorporate it legally within a system of property rights. Demsetz (1967) has put the case for the (private) payment of social costs by conferring upon those who would damage the commons the legal responsibilities of good conduct. In short, effluent discharge would be vested as a private right and attached to it would be specified social obligations. Demsetz feels that this is necessary to reduce the transaction costs incurred in bringing all polluters to heel. The pollution discharge rights idea of Dales (1968, pp.80–100) is one version of the property right proposal but is politically unacceptable, albeit appealing to admirers of Spaceship II.

Campbell *et al.* (1972) make a more practical suggestion when they propose a system of transferable discharge licences which could be linked in quantity and price to the assimilative capacity of the receiving medium. They criticise the present regulation procedures on the grounds that permits are fixed and not transferable, thereby making it very difficult for a firm to increase its production (and hence its waste load) without regular renegotiation or very costly investment. In addition, they claim that when new firms seek to enter areas where there are already high waste loads the regulation/permit system does not work efficiently, because permits are allocated by individual bargaining which rarely takes into account the existence of other polluting activities. In the view of Campbell *et al.*, since the essence of the licence system is scarcity, discharge licences can be apportioned and priced in such a way as to maximise social value. As the assimilative capacity is reached, prices can be adjusted to reduce the environmental pressure, while the licence still provides a basic guarantee of rights and tenure. In the case of discharging waste into bodies of water this licensing proposal enjoys the additional advantage that it can be tied in with existing water abstraction licences (though the authors suggest that these too should be priced to reflect marginal social costs).

In summary, the residuals tax is favoured because it substitutes the flexible incentive of the pricing mechanism for the cumbersome administrative machinery of the coercion implied by regulation and enforcement. It can be so designed as to reflect assimilative capacity (thereby making the most use of nature's powers of self-cleansing) while imposing relatively low transaction costs. Moreover, it can be levied to produce dramatic results without being seriously detrimental to economic growth or the distribution of political and economic power.

Tentative economic estimates made for the Council on Environmental Quality (1972, pp.302–304) indicate that an effective system of residuals taxes would slow the United States economy by 0·3% annually for the first four years following implementation, but only 0·1% after that, while the consumer price index and unemployment would rise by only 0·2% annually. The microeconomic impact on individual firms would be to raise costs 5–40% and prices 0–2% annually (the most affected activities being the manufacture of pulp and paper, and chemicals and metal refining) a cost far less severe than a 5% real increase in wages (table 3.8). European economists (OECD, 1972, pp.143–179; 1974) generally agree that a system of residuals charges would have a relatively minor effect on economic growth, employment, and price inflation, and that within five years any adverse effect would not be noticeable. They admit, however, that their findings are 'speculative'.

d'Arge and Kneese (1972) see some advantages of a residuals tax policy to the international community since the inflationary effects would depress United States and European exports, encouraging imports from and new investments in lesser developed nations. However, they stress that any disadvantageous effects on growth could be offset by domestic political pressures to subsidise export industry and reflate the economy, a response that smacks of Daly's growthmania thesis.

The whole question of residuals taxation cannot be isolated from political and economic realities. When some of these are taken into account the theoretical niceties of the idea crumble under the criticisms. Broadly speaking, criticism of the residuals tax falls into five areas: (1) environmental, (2) economic, (3) political, (4) administrative, and (5) legal.

Table 3.8. The economic impact of wastewater treatment (based on US Government data).

Industry	1967 value of shipments ($ million)	Annual treatment costs ($ million)	Treatment costs as % of shipments	5% increase in wages ($ million)	Treatment costs as % of 5% increase in wages
Food and kindred products	84062	260	0·3	506	51·3
Textiles	19733	80	0·4	218	36·7
Paper	20740	326	1·6	221	147·5
Chemicals	42470	421	1·0	325	129·5
Petroleum	22042	110	0·5	61	180·3
Rubber and plastics	12789	24	0·2	165	14·5
Primary metals	46550	396	0·9	492	80·4
Machinery (not electrical)	48357	42	0·1	708	5·9
Transportation equipment	68238	115	0·2	752	15·3

3.2.3.1 *The environmentalist critique*

Pearce (1974) thinks that a system of residuals charges would inevitably raise the waste load right to the margin of assimilative capacity, the very threshold of environmental tolerance (figure 3.9). This would occur even if the tax setters enjoyed the knowledge of buffering capacities (which he very much doubts), because some ecological costs cannot be observed or measured and economic accounting operates with the preferences of the current generation. Pearce feels that environmental economic policies must conform to the ecocentric principles of preserving reservoirs of biotic life, so that what most economists regard as social welfare optima should give way to eco-welfare optima, on the assumption that man must safeguard himself against the unknowable possibilities of ecosystem collapse. Pearce is not so much opposed to the residuals tax *per se* as to the technocentric assumptions that underlie it. He believes that any set of taxes would have to reflect political values that transcend the narrow, short-term, man-centred perspectives of economic analysis.

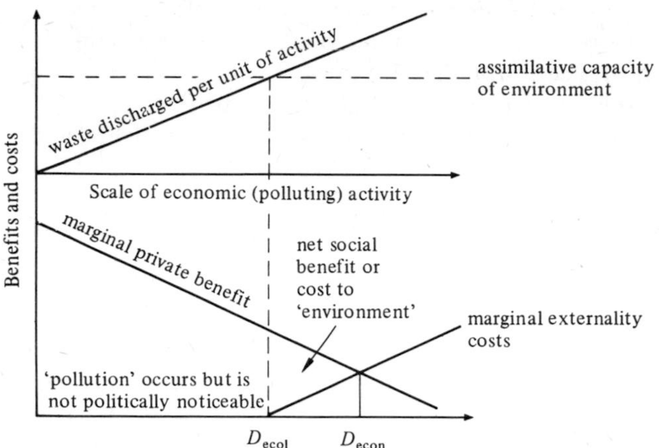

Figure 3.9. Ecological and economic criteria for setting a residuals charge. D_{ecol} and D_{econ} are the ecologically and economically optimal discharges of residuals respectively. (Source: Pearce, 1974, p.156.)

3.2.3.2 *The economic critique*

The disagreement here lies mainly in the realm of equity. Baumol (1972b) shows that any kind of crude private sector pricing adjustments are invariably regressive and the residuals tax is no exception. The poor have to pay proportionately more for all goods and services than the rich (figure 3.10). Yet the benefits of improved environmental amenity are likely to be valued more highly by the rich than by the poor. He concludes that only through the mechanism of income supplement or progressive taxation can this problem be overcome. The Council on

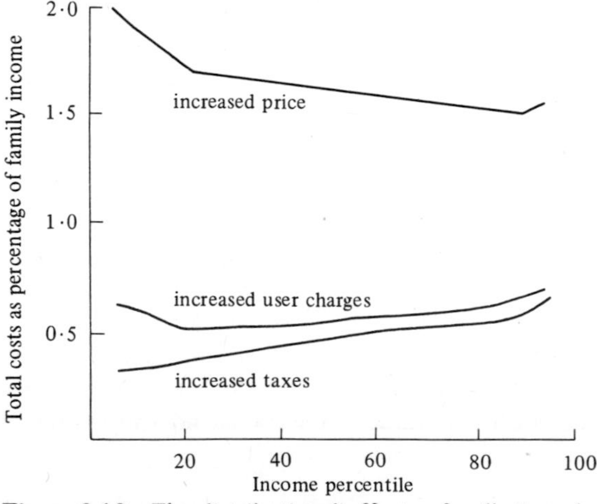

Figure 3.10. The distributional effects of pollution abatement. (Source: Council on Environmental Quality, 1973a, p.108.)

Environmental Quality (1973a, p.108), however, feels that though the net effect of a residuals tax will be regressive, it should be small in absolute terms and hence easily offset by adjustments in taxation. This view is hotly contested by England and Bluestone (1973, pp.194–195) who assert that lower-income families will suffer very real decreases in living standards after the implementation of a residuals tax. Burrows (1974, pp.281–282), on the other hand, thinks the distributional effects are uncertain irrespective of whether a system of taxes or of permits is adopted. He notes that uniform standards in other areas (such as health and safety regulations for employees) are set regardless of efficiency considerations, and that any policy instrument will induce inequitable results, given an uneven distribution of income and varied preferences.

A more serious criticism centres around the economic (and ecological) implications of the 'polluter must pay' principle. Because the tax idea is unashamedly geared to matters of efficiency and not equity, some feel that the imposition of a residuals tax would 'price out' the less economic enterprises through no fault of their own, thus serving to increase the concentration of economic activity. This aspect did not escape the notice of the British Royal Commission on Environmental Pollution (Ashby, 1972b, p.68) which concluded:

> "... it would not be in the public interest to allow a fixed resource (i.e. the assimilative capacity of a water body) to be allocated solely according to the ability to pay. It might lead to an imbalance between industrial and public needs, or to one kind of industry being put out of business by another because their waste effluents contained the same chargeable ingredient but their financial margins were entirely different. This suggests to us that acceptable pollution control could not be secured by charges alone, without taking political and social considerations into account."

A related objection is the somewhat naive assumption that firms will respond rationally and efficiently to the tax incentive to the point of minimising private costs and social damages (see Beckerman, 1974, p.161). Burrows (1974, pp.276–277) criticises the view (stated by economists such as Baumol and Oates, 1971, p.45) that pollution control can be 'finely tuned' to acceptable levels by adjusting the charge to encourage optimal response. Most firms lock themselves into expensive and 'lumpy' pollution control investment and thus cannot respond efficiently unless the price changes are very large (and then the response could well be very inefficient). 'Fine tuning' is an economic dream perhaps, but an accountant's nightmare. In any case, if inflation continues as a serious problem, the private sector may become less responsive to price changes. Dahmén (1971) comments that nationalised industries and public sector services (e.g. waste treatment authorities) are less sensitive to the dictates of economic efficiency than the competitive private sector, so in a socialised economy (or in an economy where the major polluters were nationalised industries) a system of negotiated standards would probably produce a more favourable response.

In an empirical investigation of paper mills and municipal treatment plants in Wisconsin, Dorcey (1973) finds that the familiar upward-sweeping average-cost curve of residuals abatement usually depicted in theoretical diagrams does not apply in real life. Average waste treatment cost functions appear to be remarkably insensitive to price over a wide range (figure 3.11), so a policy of uniform or zoned effluent charges would not necessarily produce the desired effect at least cost. A lot depends upon how individual dischargers will respond to the tax, but this becomes more of a political matter than an economic one. Galbraith (1973) believes that large corporations manipulate factor prices in such a way that they would not be hurt by a pollution charge, and many administrators feel that the charge would be absorbed through tax loopholes.

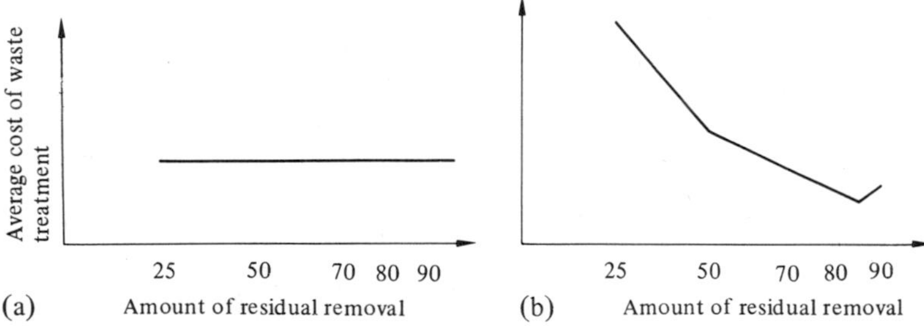

Figure 3.11. Residuals removal costs for (a) the pulp and paper industry and (b) municipal waste treatment. (Source: Dorcey, 1973, p.123.)

3.2.3.3 *The political critique*

Political scientists have long believed that pollution control is more a result of bargaining and concession trading between negotiating parties than simpleminded economic response (see Holden, 1966; Chevalier and Cartwright, 1967; Hagevick, 1970; Crenson, 1972). Despite his claim that "pollution ... is an economic problem which must be understood in economic terms," Ruff (1970, p.78) later admits that "economics has nothing to say about which efficient state is the best. That decision is a matter of personal and philosophical values, and ultimately must be decided by some political process".

Most of the economic literature simply dismisses the procedures for setting the critical standards. Kneese and Bower (1968, p.131) feel that "standards will be based on some, usually vague, consideration of damage costs vs. costs of quality improvement." Baumol and Oates (1971, p.48) admit that some combination of pricing and standards will be necessary for any residuals management scheme to be workable, but prefer that political intervention be avoided wherever possible because "methods of collective choice ... can at best be expected to provide only very rough approximations to optimal results". So they conclude that standards should only be used where market forces demonstrably fail but where some discharge could result in large social costs (e.g. small emissions of toxic pollutants with indeterminate long-term biological consequences).

Fox and Wible (1973) and Dorcey (1973), on the other hand, give much attention to the standard-setting and tax-negotiating aspects of a residuals charge policy. They conclude (a) that all relevant public interests are not included in the standard-setting process [in fact the public are legally excluded from regulatory decisionmaking in Canada (Lucas, 1969) and Britain (McLoughlin, 1973)], and (b) that in the absence of much critical information as to how polluters will react (both economically and politically) a pollution control agency will have to bargain with polluters over the correct tax to apply. Dorcey (1973) feels that the agencies must have reasonably reliable estimates of assimilative capacity, obtained through simulation studies and empirical investigations, in order to bargain effectively. If a polluter objects to a proposed charge, the onus should then be on him to show (a) why the estimate of the environmental impact of his discharge is unfair, and/or (b) that he could improve the quality of his discharge at no additional cost. A monitoring system of spot-check inspections and the equivalent of a discharge tax return would confirm the accuracy of his reply.

3.2.3.4 *The administrative critique*

A serious drawback of the residuals tax proposal is its lack of proof that administrative costs would be no more (and should be much less) than transactions costs for the standards–permits arrangement. Burrows (1974) investigates this matter thoroughly (but not empirically) and concludes that a system of variable standards tailored to particular classes of polluting enterprises would be administratively the most workable and least costly of all arrangements (though of course uniform standards offer the cheapest of all *administrative* costs). This is a difficult matter to prove because much of present day administrative cost is fixed, and the efficiency of many bureaucratic operations is a notoriously sensitive issue to investigate.

A general problem facing the residuals tax proposal is that it is not understood by administrators and dischargers. Because British local governments were not very experienced in setting discharge regulations (consents), for a long time they tended to use the Royal Commission 'guidelines' for domestic waste water quality (30 ppm suspended solids and 20 ppm BOD) irrespective of the degree of dilution offered by the receiving water. Many administrators consequently believe that if these standards are met, then 'pollution' does not occur (i.e. there are no measurable social costs), so an 'effluent charge' is quite unnecessary.

As firms and domestic ratepayers already pay for pollution control through a system of rates (taxes) and trade effluent charges (in the case of firms discharging into public sewers), some administrators and most polluters feel that the discharge is already 'paying' to clean up. Here is the view of one section of British industry on the matter of a residuals tax (Lines, 1974, p.106):

> "Responsible industry has come to regard effluent treatment cost as part of production costs ... . [The residuals tax] may seem to be a justifiable internalisation of the economics of effluent disposal, but it runs hard against the established principle that there should be an authority who decides (subject to negotiation, inquiry and appeal) what degree of pollution ... the environment ... can stand and sets limits on discharges accordingly ... . Setting limits to discharges under the present system of consents is highly scientific. It is related to real needs."

British industry might well be anxious about the possibility of a residuals charge. Even though the demand for water is lower than anticipated, the increasing need to reuse wastewater means that water abstraction and disposal charges could rise as high as £1 (1975 prices) per 1000 gallons. For some enterprises this could add up to £70000 onto their annual costs of production (Askew, 1975, p.7). At a time of high inflation and unemployment such an additional cost might well prove to be politically unacceptable.

3.2.3.5 *The legal critique*

Heath (1971) offers some useful observations on the residuals tax from the legal viewpoint. He observes that, whereas the original model for the idea, the Ruhr Genossenschaften (see Kneese and Bower, 1968, pp.237–262), simply involved a charge for a service (namely the collection and treatment of waste), it is legally quite a different matter to impose any additional charge that might produce a social benefit for which the polluter receives no compensation. This is a fundamental legal principle which will be discussed further in the next chapter, though it would appear that in the current political and social climate, the courts would favour such a charge without demanding that compensation be paid. If a charge is imposed, there are many legal definitions of a tax, some of which could, for example, provide convenient loopholes for *de facto* avoidance. (This is certainly a view held by many pollution control administrators.) Even if the proposed residuals tax survives that test, a polluter may still accuse the residuals management authority of 'arbitrary and capricious action' if it cannot show fairly how it arrived at the charge.

Sometimes existing legislation may inadvertently impede the full imposition of the residuals tax. For example, the UK Water Act (1973) requires that all water services (supply, sewerage, treatment, and disposal) be self-financing. This is a broadly-drafted provision which could be interpreted to mean that water service charges should meet (a) historic costs and current operating costs, or (b) provision (a) plus depreciation and replacement on current capital expenditure, or (c) provision (b) plus a contribution to future capital expansion (UK Jukes Committee, Vol.3, 1974, p.31). The accepted view is that of provision (b), which implies that any residuals charge could not be set statutorily to reflect marginal social costs. In addition, various British water management acts establish that charging for water services should be based on a principle of 'equity'. This is a subjective concept that is interpreted by the Jukes Committee (p.37) to mean either that charges relate simply to the costs imposed by the user on the system, or that consumers pay a similar charge in respect of a similar amount of water services, irrespective of efficiency considerations. Another provision, that of regional 'equalisation', also reduces the likelihood of imposing a 'pure' residuals charge. Equalisation is generally taken to mean the levy of a similar charge for all metered effluent (based on volume and quality) over a particular area irrespective of the costs borne by the water authority. Where the effluent is not metered (as in the case of domestic sewage) equalisation means the imposition of an equal poundage charge for sewerage services.

For the various reasons cited above a system of residuals taxes as visualised by many economists is unlikely to be adopted in practice. Nor should it be. Marginal-cost pricing is a remote reality at the best of times and even more implausible with respect to public goods. Any practical policy that may emerge from current political discussions about a residuals tax in the United States, Canada, or Britain will depend a lot on how the various affected interests interpret these criticisms raised in relation to their political requirements.

3.3 The steady state and social equity

A major imponderable facing the steady state idea is the political feasibility of redistributing wealth and social opportunity within a closed economic system (see Klein, 1972). Boulding (1973, p.95) expressed his disquiet as follows:

> "One reason why the progressive state is 'cheerful' is that social conflict is diminished by it. In the stationary state, there is no escape from the rigors of scarcity ... [and] investment in exploitation may pay better than in progress. Stationary states, therefore, are frequently mafia-type societies in which government is primarily an institution for redistributing income toward the more powerful and away from the weak. Therefore the problem of building political and constitutional defences against exploitation may emerge as the major political problem of the steady state."

Daly (1973b, pp.168–170) tackles this issue head-on by recommending maximum and minimum limits on wealth and income. He follows Mill's egalitarian philosophy that ownership of wealth is a guarantee against exploitation *only if everyone has a certain amount of it*; inequity of wealth inevitably leads to inequality (and abuse) of power. Daly therefore argues that the distribution of wealth should not be allowed to exceed a certain ratio of, say, twenty to one. There would be a guaranteed minimum income for all, and a ceiling to earnings beyond which the taxation would be 100%.

This proposal is supported by W. R. Johnson (1973) who believes that only a minute fraction of the population (albeit a politically powerful one) would really be affected by such a policy. He approves of a suggestion by Watts (*ibid*., p.181) for a 'credit income tax'. Under this scheme, everyone would initially pay a 'basic tax' of 33⅓% up to an annual income of $50000 (this would cover about 90% of the population). Those with incomes between $50000 and $100000 would pay 40% tax, and those earning over $100000 annually, 50% tax. Some of the revenue (it is not clear how much) would then be redistributed to everybody, regardless of income, depending on age and physical disabilities. The effect would be to shift median income toward the poorer 10% without losing any revenue for government programmes.

An even more utopian (and ludicrously impracticable) version of egalitarian income distribution is dreamed by W. A. Johnson (1973) who feels that everybody above the age of eighteen should be guaranteed $1000 annually to enable them to seek 'socially relevant' (but traditionally 'uneconomic') employment and 'ecologically harmonious' lifestyles; this scheme should be financed out of 'unnecessary' military expenditures. The whole idea would be to give some people a minimal incentive to strike out and explore new directions, to reduce their consumption habits, and hence slow down economic growth. Johnson does recognise that many would have to reorganise their psychological dependence on work, avoid the temptation of having children, and overcome their social reluctance to accept an annual free handout. W. R. Johnson (1973) is perhaps more realistic; he feels that redistributive mechanisms are acceptable neither to the rich, nor to the poor (because of the social stigma of aid), nor to the trade unions who fight hard to maintain economically trivial but socially crucial wage differentials.

Although large-scale income redistribution is not really very practicable at present, there are other, more sensible proposals which might produce a certain amount of reapportionment that would not only be socially equitable, but might help to lower overall resource consumption. Economists now recognise that declining block-pricing structures (whereby consumers pay less for increasing use) for public utilities are now quite unrealistic. The rationale behind this pricing structure has traditionally been that of economies of scale. But Cicchetti and Gillen (1973a) show that capital costs of large-scale power-producing plants are rising markedly owing to the greater safeguards required, partly because of rising maintenance requirements, and partly because of increased public opposition, especially to nuclear power plants (see also Lewis, 1972). They assert that long-term marginal costs are now *increasing*, making a mockery of growth-inducing declining-rate structures. Doctor and Anderson (1972) show that under present charging schemes domestic electricity consumers not only subsidise large power-demanding industrial users, but also that the low-income low-consumption individual pays an unfairly high proportion of his/her income on energy (figure 3.12). They believe that the pricing structure should be reversed; a certain minimum allotment of energy (say 200 kWh per month) could be donated free of charge without affecting total consumption, yet would provide substantial equity benefits. By charging higher prices for increasing amounts of use, the large consumers who enjoy the highest price elasticities would be given incentives to conserve. Individual household consumers of electricity who earn more than $20000 per year have price elasticities of about −1·2, compared with −0·7 for those with incomes of less than $2000 annually. The UK Jukes Committee (1974, p.35) propose a simple two-part tariff for all water services, where the first 'block' would be provided to meet essential needs at low cost, while the second 'block' would reflect (higher) marginal costs. Here is a more workable variation of the rationing scheme outlined by Daly (1973b) and discussed earlier. If the steady state idea is to have any meaning, as a matter of principle it should encourage people to consume less, preferably by providing a basic minimum standard of living and discouraging careless and excessive consumption. It deserves further attention.

The headache that policymakers face over restoring economic and environmental equity in developed nations is, however, trivial compared with the problems confronting politicians at a world level. As matters

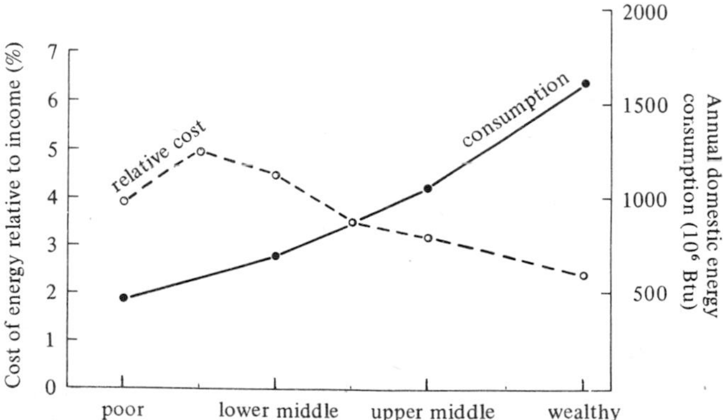

Figure 3.12. Energy consumption and cost relative to income. (Sources: Doctor and Anderson, 1972, p.114; Ford Energy Policy Project, 1974b, p.127.)

stand at present, pricing policies which reduce demand in western nations invariably lower world commodity prices. Unless the resource-rich nations can control supply and share revenue during periods of slump, they are extremely vulnerable to world-wide economic depression. Connelly and Perlman (1975) conclude that political forces, fired by deeply felt resentment of exploitation by western nations and large corporations, will spur many lesser-developed countries to band together to obtain an improved distribution of world wealth even if it means a continued economic slowdown in developed nations. Following the spectacular success of the OPEC cartel, other groups of commodity producing countries are similarly attempting to control world prices by limiting supply. Even though some of them have been promised financial assistance by certain OPEC members (Libya is to help the copper cartel and Venezuela is to aid

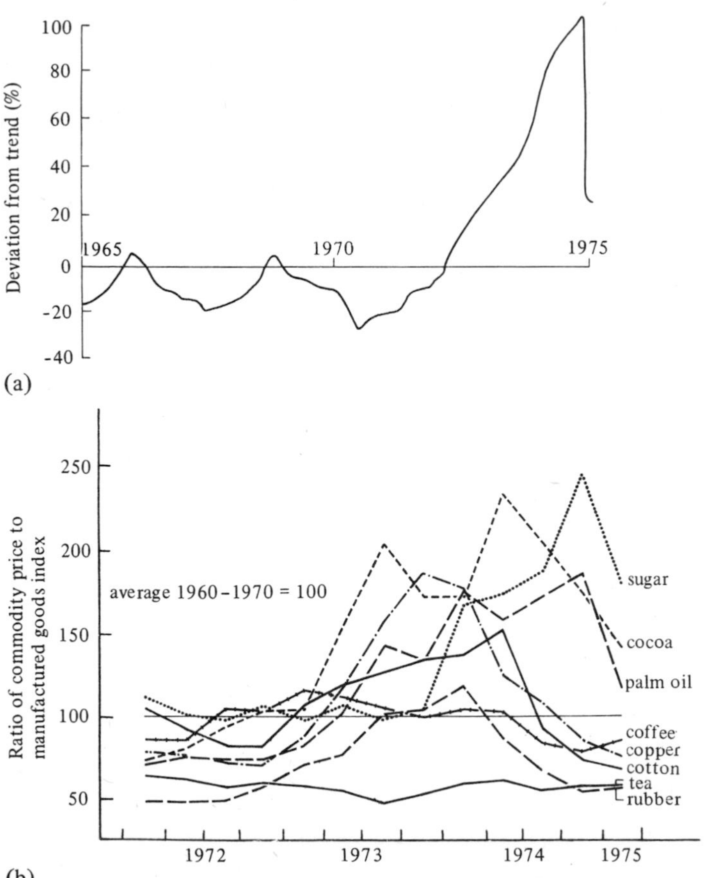

Figure 3.13. Boom and bust in the commodity markets: (a) fluctuations in price of industrial raw materials; (b) terms of trade (commodity price divided by manufactured goods index). (Source: *The Economist*, 14 June, 1975, p.49.)

the coffee cartel), economic realities show that cartels tend to collapse as high prices lessen demand, encourage the development of substitutes, and create costly and embarrassing gluts (Commodity Research Unit, 1975).

So several commodity producers are backing away from the cartel idea in favour of large-scale buffer stocks, jointly financed by producer and consumer nations, which should stabilise prices and ensure more reliable economic returns for producer nations. Figure 3.13 shows the tremendous price instability of raw materials that has occurred over the past three years of boom and bust. It is essential for political as well as economic stability that these peaks and troughs be levelled out. As it is now, the terms of trade for most countries that export raw materials are worsening because of inflationary rises in the import prices of the developed nations (Commonwealth Secretariat, 1975). Grondona (1975) argues in favour of the buffer-stock idea as a means of stabilising prices, though he recognises that complicated international agreements will have to be made to avoid the danger of price-fixing by the developed countries. The UN Commission on Trade and Development is also in favour of the buffer-stock solution (see *The Economist*, 15 March, 1975, pp.79–80), as, in principle, are the leaders of the Commonwealth countries and the European Economic Community, all of whom are anxious to guarantee supplies and stabilise prices, even if it means shifting the terms of trade to favour the developing countries. All this just might bring about a modicum of world wealth redistribution without destroying international political trust.

3.4 Some concluding comments

Whether the steady state notion is accepted or rejected, at the very least it casts doubts on the paradigm of growth and highlights the legacy of growth that is firmly embedded in most of our institutions. The whole concept of growth is so endemic that many shirk from contemplating any social arrangement where it is absent. Nevertheless, even the more optimistic economists (e.g. McKean, 1973; Olson *et al.*, 1973; Ridker, 1973) are somewhat fearful of the political and social consequences of continued rapid growth, especially the narrowing margin of precious time to make reasoned choice and necessary adjustments, the geopolitical dangers of resource dependency, and the unhappy prospect of increasing governmental intervention and regulation in all aspects of social affairs. Above all, they are worried about the possible loss of deeply cherished values such as peacefulness, solitude, a spiritual communion with nature, and the opportunity to make close friendships and conduct daily affairs on a friendly face-to-face basis—in short the values necessary for the love of the earth and the love of man. Though he knows he cannot prove it, Boulding (1973, pp.97–98) is afraid that man may have passed his peak in intellectual, scientific, and moral stature, so that we face the gravest of world problems ill-equipped with the essential tools. Maybe there is such a phenomenon as 'cultural entropy'; maybe the vital creative spark is becoming less constructively employed. If this indeed is the case, the spectre of the stationary state is all the more forbidding, and the agony of adjustment will be all the more painful.

What nobody can answer yet is whether the steady state can or will solve problems which stability itself will create (see Klein, 1972). Few have really come to grips with all the moral, social, economic, and political implications of an aging population that will require more expensive social attention and that will have fewer dependants; of a pattern of 'work' quite different from what we know today, where more time and effort will be devoted to social services and maintenance of social relationships and property; of the necessary redistribution of political influence which will obviously impinge upon industrial democracy, public participation, and environmental design; of the channeling of rising expectations into peaceful and creative individual and social enterprises which are compatible with biophysical limitations; and of the tolerance of cultural diversity and choice of living patterns which respect basic social rights. Above all, nobody has answered how nongrowth in the western nations will help the lesser developed nations, especially the resource-poor countries. However we decide to progress in the future, surely the emphasis must rest more with redistribution from the wealthy to the poor nations than has been the sad experience of the past. Well-meaning denial by the world's rich may make life even more intolerable for the poor.

4

Planning to guide growth and protect amenity

Public opinion polls have long reported that people prefer to live in communities slightly smaller than the ones in which they currently reside. Amongst the chief reasons cited are loss of 'friendliness', difficulty in moving about, a tendency to be in more and longer queues for everything from buying spirits to going to the dentist, and an increasing fear of crime and other manifestations of social violence. The smaller community, of course, does not necessarily avoid these problems; it simply appeals to the romantic nature of most urbanites as a 'better' place in which to live and rear a family. Policymakers have recognised this wish and have tried to move housing and jobs from the congested cities to new towns or regional growth centres and even to satellite villages surrounding growth poles. European regional planning appears to have been more successful in this regard than has been the case in North America (see Clawson and Hall, 1973), though more recently Hall (1975) and Eversley (1972, 1975a) have concluded that the European experience has not been very satisfactory from the viewpoint of social equity and environmental quality. In North America politicians and planners have tended to let market forces guide regional development, though in 1971 the Nixon administration announced a major shift in urban growth policy toward a goal of 'balanced growth' (i.e. decentralisation). Even so, some informed commentators (e.g. Wingo, 1972a; Alonso, 1973; Le Gates and Morgan, 1973) feel that under present policies this goal cannot be reached.

Why have efforts to decentralise failed to realise their objectives? Mainly because they have had to combat powerful forces which continue to encourage migration to large urban centres. Urban areas provide an attractive variety of job opportunities, professional and social services, and entertainment. They also harbour the important quaternary sectors of government, research and development, business management, and education. And, despite popular belief to the contrary, they contain fewer poor than their rural counterparts (table 4.1). In addition, agricultural policies have tended to push people off the land (presumably into the towns), while revenue sharing between national and local governments has long favoured the urban setting in which most politicians have their constituencies (see Wingo, 1972a, pp.4–5). Finally, national governments are well aware that the most cherished hope of almost every inhabitant of industrialised nations is an owner-occupied home on a reasonably sized plot of land, near but not actually within a largish urban mass, and postwar housing policies have tried to meet this need.

So it is not surprising that metropolitan areas are still very attractive to national and international migrants. In the United States, the President's Task Force on Land Use and Urban Growth (Reilly, 1973, p.84) predicts that by the year 2000 thirty-six million of the fifty-four million who will by then have been added to the American population (and of whom some fourteen million will be immigrants) will settle in the larger cities, creating a housing demand of 27000 new dwellings per week. Canadian estimates show similar trends; a federal government task force (Lithwick, 1970, p.154) forecasts that the nation's three largest cities (Montreal, Toronto, and Vancouver) will grow by more people in the next 25 years than have been added in the last 70, a formidable prospect for planners, treasurers, and citizens. The task force calculates that if their predictions are accurate, four million new housing units will be required, covering some 400 square miles in Toronto and 200 square miles in each of the other two cities. (See also MacNeill, 1971, pp.37–43.)

Migration is a way of life for North Americans. The average urban family moves at least seven times in its existence, and every year some twenty-one million Americans change residence. The long standing urban drift is accompanied by a new 'amenity migration' composed of two elements. One is the familiar centrifugal drift to the suburb, the small urban farm and the satellite community. Regions lying between 25 and 50 miles from major metropolitan complexes have taken the brunt of this migration, which is composed of the affluent middle class seeking cleaner air, peace and quiet, and good schools and other urban services for lower taxes. The modern status symbol is not the conspicuous consumption of material goods, which are so abundant as to be regarded as 'vulgar', but the private expropriation of environmental quality at a high price (see Santmire, 1973). Many communities within the urban penumbra have experienced a 50% increase in population in the past 10 years and could easily face another 50% increase over the next decade if nothing is done to stem the tide. The irony is that these communities are facing the kind of urban pressures which their residents moved there to avoid, so they are often in the vanguard of the nongrowth or guided-growth movement which has spread throughout suburban America since 1970.

Table 4.1. The geographical distribution of poor in the United States. (Source: Wingo, 1972a, p.12.)

	% Poor	Index of poverty (US = 100)[a]
Metropolitan areas	12·6	67
suburbs	6·7	33
Nonmetropolitan areas	32·0	150
rural farm	29·7	193
Urban areas	14·8	81
Rural areas	29·7	155

[a]
$$\text{Index of poverty} = \frac{\%\ \text{poor in sector}}{\%\ \text{nonpoor in sector}} \Bigg/ \frac{\%\ \text{poor in nation}}{\%\ \text{nonpoor in nation}} .$$

The other kind of amenity migration is the longer-distance spread of people to choice recreation areas and to sunshine regions. This exodus is composed of two groups: (a) retirees from the cold and grey northeast areas of the United States who seek to spend the rest of their days in the sun and warmth of the south and west, and (b) young and middle-aged people who want a vacation home for weekend and holiday use (Reilly, 1973, pp.263–293; Council on Environmental Quality, 1974, pp.21–27). The population of Florida has grown from four million in 1950 to seven million in 1970 and is projected to reach fourteen million by 2000 (Carter, 1973b). Over 4500 people migrate to Miami every month, so it is not surprising that the city has grown by over half a million in the last ten years. Similar explosive growth rates can be found in Texas, New Mexico, Arizona, Colorado, and the Pacific northwest.

But it is the 'second home' industry which is having the more devastating impact. Any amenity area within two hundred miles of a large city is vulnerable to considerable real-estate speculation. In many areas land values have risen by as much as 1000% in ten years, while the purchase prices of really choice sites (those with a view of or close to water) have escalated fiftyfold in the past decade. New England, the coastal areas of the south and west, and the mountain and desert states have taken the brunt of this weekly transhumance. In the United States in 1971 some 95 000 second homes were constructed (compared with annual figures of 20 000 in the 1940s and 75 000 in the 1960s) and this is projected to rise to 150000 annually before the decade is out (Reilly, 1973, p.265). The market potential is enormous, for at present only 5% of Americans (and 3% of Canadians) own second homes (compared with 50% of Swedes), and it is clear that ownership is now possible, and very much desired, among the moderately well-off. Residential lot sales vastly outnumber these building statistics. Cahn (1973a, p.4) estimates that in 1971 some 625 000 recreational lots (200 000 of which were in Florida) were subdivided by 10 000 developers. One desert subdivision in California covers 100000 acres, and over a million acres of Arizona have been plotted. Fraud is very common: many prospective purchasers are duped by a mixture of naive acquisitiveness and underhand sales promotion into buying worthless plots of land, site unseen, in totally unsuitable regions. But there is another element which Cahn (1973a, p.5) puts as follows:

> "... the lack of sales resistance by many people to this land-buying spree can be traced to the hoped-for fulfilment of dreams: the dream of the landless to own a piece of America; the dream of the citybound to get into the wide open spaces; the dream of the snowed-in northerner to have year-round sunshine living in Florida or the Southwest; and the dream of making it rich by investing in land."

Canadians are equally prone to acting on these dreams. Holling and Chambers (1973) describe an ingenious simulation model which showed that, regardless of what land-use control policies were adopted, the beautiful Gulf Islands off the coast of British Columbia would be lost in private acquisition (by Americans and other foreigners as well as Canadians) in a matter of a generation (figure 4.1). In fact the demand for amenity space is now so great among hemmed-in Vancouver residents that many are even investing in the adjacent US state of Washington where taxes are lower and land-use controls less exacting. This is ironic because the government of British Columbia has recently placed new restrictions on non-Canadian citizens buying up its public land! (Strict regulations on the purchase of land by non-Canadians, also in force in Saskatchewan and Newfoundland, are being considered by all other Canadian provinces, particularly in view of the ruling by the Supreme Court that protecting Canadian land from non-Canadian ownership is constitutional.)

If this new migration is not further controlled, almost all areas of scenic and ecological value will become denied to the public, while the cumulative environmental consequences could be catastrophic. Already some 70% of the Pacific coastline is in private hands, while probably a greater proportion of all lakeshores within five driving hours of major centres is likewise appropriated. Many waterfowl nesting and feeding sites have been drained, flood plains settled, and unstable slopes (and other hazardous areas) dug up and subdivided. The ecological impact is not confined to a few lost trees and muddy streams, for many key sites (the most famous of which is the Florida Everglades) are threatened with irreversible damage.

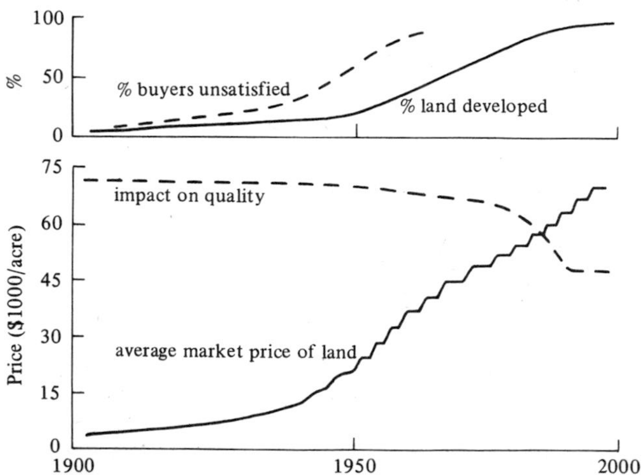

Figure 4.1. The Gulf Islands land-use simulation model. As private acquisition increases, recreational pressures on the remaining public lands create effects which exceed ecological tolerances. There is no substantial difference to these results when a land sales tax is simulated. Only strict zoning or a policy of guided growth will protect the remaining areas. (Source: Holling, 1971, p.5.)

The suddenness and scale of this quest for amenity has caught planners, community leaders, and environmental groups quite unawares, although since 1970 a number of interested groups have coalesced around the themes of limiting—or at least guiding—growth, and of protecting areas of critical ecological value. Motivations for involvement range from narrow-minded self-interest to a genuine concern over social harmony and environmental protection. Since these groups cannot actually stop growth (for sound legal and moral reasons), we shall call them proponents of guided growth, for they can alter the timing, structure, and pattern of growth in their communities. Guided-growth forces have appeared in large cities (e.g. Boulder, Toronto, Vancouver), in dozens of satellite towns, and in a few states (e.g. Florida and Oregon, and Colorado whose citizens rejected the proposed construction of the 1976 Winter Olympic Games facilities partly on financial and partly on antigrowth grounds). For the sake of clarity, let us distinguish three related policy areas that have emerged during the guided-growth debate, namely (a) attempts to restrict further migration into large cities, (b) efforts to limit the timing and amount of new development in small communities peripheral to large cities and in high-amenity areas, and (c) proposals to establish comprehensive regional land-use plans based on ecological principles.

4.1 Urban scale and environmental quality

North Americans are expressing increasing disquiet about the unpleasantness of big-city life as they are required to live it. The polls show that 45% as against 35% of the public feel that the quality of life in the American nation generally has deteriorated (US Senate Subcommittee on Intergovernmental Relations, 1973, p.61). Likewise Gallup (1973, p.2) found that 35% of Americans living in large metropolitan areas (and 44% of black Americans) were dissatisfied with the quality of their environments, compared with only 13% of inhabitants of small communities (with populations less than 2500). Only 13% of all persons interviewed (compared with 22% in 1966) would prefer to live in the city if given the opportunity to move to a nonurban area, and 80% of residents of cities in excess of half a million population would leave if possible. As Wingo (1973, p.4) emphasised, for most people 'the quality of life' means contentment with one's *immediate* environment—the house, the garden, local shopping facilities, neighbourly relationships, etc.—not so much the more general urban setting. These sobering statistics therefore indicate that most people see their neighbourhoods becoming less pleasurable communities in which to live.

The main contention of the political pressure groups who seek to curtail urban growth is that population growth creates disproportionately adverse environmental consequences in the forms of increasing public service costs, more expensive housing, congestion of roads and recreation areas, more noise, and air and water pollution (see Ehrlich and Holdern, 1971; P. A. Stone, 1972; Hoch, 1972b). While they recognise that legally it is impossible in any country to forbid the free movement of people from place to place, these pressure groups want moratoria on further downtown office building, public facilities, and new residential developments to keep out potential migrants through the 'politics of squeeze'. The Mayors of Vancouver and Toronto have publicly announced that they support regional plans to channel additional growth away from the urban core to satellite communities, while the city administrations of Toronto, Denver, and Minneapolis have actually begun to restrict further construction of office space downtown. The province of Alberta has moved to place a ceiling on all water supply, sewerage, and waste treatment costs in all major centres. In Britain, a recently formed group called 'Planners Against Growth' seeks to counter the current growth ideology of the Royal Town Planning Institute and prepare plans for different settlement patterns in the light of the acute resource shortages they believe Britain will have to face.

As a result of these moves, there will be increased pressure for office and housing space elsewhere, plus escalating land values in the stabilised urban areas. Unless there is fairly major reform of urban administrative or financial institutions, these nongrowth demands will inevitably worsen the plight of the metropolitan centres already burdened by debt, substandard housing, inadequate social services, and unemployment. Alonso (1973, pp.203–204), Morrison (1974, p.761), and Eversley (1972, 1975a) describe the likely result of conditions even now prevailing—a central city ghetto of the immobile and socially disadvantaged (the old, the black, and the unemployable) faced with deteriorating services and rising taxes, while businesses and the more affluent inhabitants flee to the attractive growth areas. Thus in a sense, central city nongrowth is already a fact, though it is not properly planned for.

4.1.1 The benefits of urban growth

Few economists favour environmentalist pressures to contain urban growth. Most experts (see for example Wingo, 1972a; P. A. Stone, 1972; Richardson, 1973) now agree that it is quite impossible to talk of an 'optimum city size' either in economic or in amenity terms, since the relevant data are either unavailable, noncomparable, or subject to so much value judgement as to be worthless. Richardson (1973) believes that the big city is vital to national economic prosperity and political reform, for only the city can provide sufficiently stimulating cultural and intellectual diversity to encourage innovation and constructive social change. Meier (1971) is convinced that modern environmentalism is the product not of rural minds but of urban-based ideals which have always tended to be more liberal and egalitarian.

Hoch (1972a) claims that, while urban areas are perhaps less desirable to live in than smaller communities, the discomforts of the city are mollified by higher average personal incomes. Even when wage rates are deflated to reflect the higher urban cost of living, there remain additional income compensations (table 4.2). But do these wage increments really offset the many disagreeable aspects of big-city living? Hoch simply demonstrates that personal gains are paid for (or subsidised) by losses in collective amenity.

Economics is urgently in need of a theory which takes into account the widespread nature of social disamenity. Figure 4.2 shows the kind of

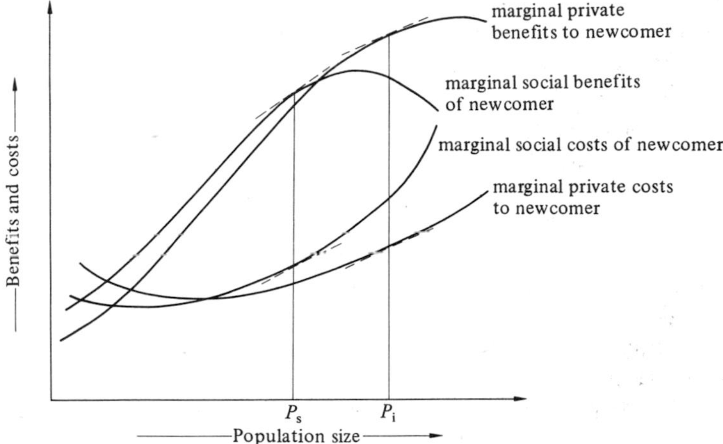

Figure 4.2. The benefits and costs of big city living as seen from two perspectives. P_s and P_i are the optimum populations from collective and from newcomer's viewpoints respectively.

Table 4.2. Deflated money income levels for standardised population. (Source: Hoch, 1972a, p.137.)

Locale, population (in thousands)	Assumed average population size (in thousands)	Deflated wage rate			
		north-east	north, central	south	west
Urban place					
<10	5	0·984	0·921	0·869	0·957
10–<100	50	0·979	0·975	0·928	0·990
SMSA					
<250	125	0·973	1·064	0·986	1·033
250–<500	375	0·953	1·045	1·028	1·003
500–<1000	750	0·970	1·111	1·042	1·039
1000+	2000	1·056	1·119	1·122	1·106
1000+ relative to (<10)		1·073	1·215	1·291	1·156

problem that such a theory must embrace if it is ever going to come to grips with the diseconomies of urban scale. The interaction of marginal costs and benefits depends upon the perspective of the observer. To the new urban immigrant the net private gain of entering the city is highly positive and remains so up to very large city sizes because he throws most of the additional costs of his entry onto the rest of the community. But the net benefit of an additional migrant is negative to the established resident of the large city, since he must suffer some of the additional social costs while gaining very little from the benefits that the immigrant provides. Hence the growing conflict between the immigrant and the established resident in most urban-growth disputes.

4.1.2 The diseconomies of urban growth

To what extent does urban scale result in diseconomies? P. A. Stone (1972), Hoch (1972b), and Berry and Horton (1974) review the statistical evidence in terms of costs of public services and agree that *per capita* costs begin to rise once communities surpass the 50000 mark (figure 4.3), though these curves are considerably influenced by density, urban morphology, and the age of the settlement (see also Howard and Kracht, 1972). There is ample reason to believe that, beyond a certain size, the costs of urban services, such as waste treatment, solid residuals collection, transportation, police and fire protection do rise disproportionately faster than the rate of population growth.

Many writers claim that the nonlinear relationship between city size and infrastructure costs is more a reflection of present inadequate institutional arrangements than simply the effect of scale (see Wingo, 1972b; Margolis, 1974). For example, nearly all urban services are financed out of property taxes, not user charges, so there is no incentive for consumers of such services to curtail excessive use. This criticism particularly applies to water supply and effluent disposal and to traffic congestion. The solution, these authors feel, is a more equitable system of tolls and taxes to increase efficiency of use by ensuring that user charges reflect marginal social costs. They concede that political factors perpetuate unnecessary inefficiencies and inhibit sensible technological innovation. For example, the rising costs of solid-waste disposal could be more than halved by the introduction of laboursaving collection mechanisms, the adoption of penalties and incentives to promote recycling, the operation of regional incinerators, and a willingness on the part of the public to sort their waste into specified categories (Spofford, 1973). But neither the trade unions (now highly paid) nor the public (who prefer not to think about waste) are anxious to cooperate, so waste removal costs continue to spiral and the environmental headaches of finding suitable solid-waste disposal sites worsen.

Feldman (1973) shows that the use of property tax as a source of revenue to finance urban services introduces another kind of inefficiency: because the dense, older centres are cheaper to service and maintain than the newer, more dispersed suburbs, a flat rate tax subsidises the suburbanite at the expense of the central city resident (see also Gabler, 1969; Wirt, 1971; Howard and Kracht, 1972). Even though the inner-city resident usually pays a lower property tax (though this is not always the case now that urban renewal is in vogue), he is invariablý paying proportionately more of his income on urban services than the suburbanite. Thus there is a double subsidy through a disproportionate rate structure

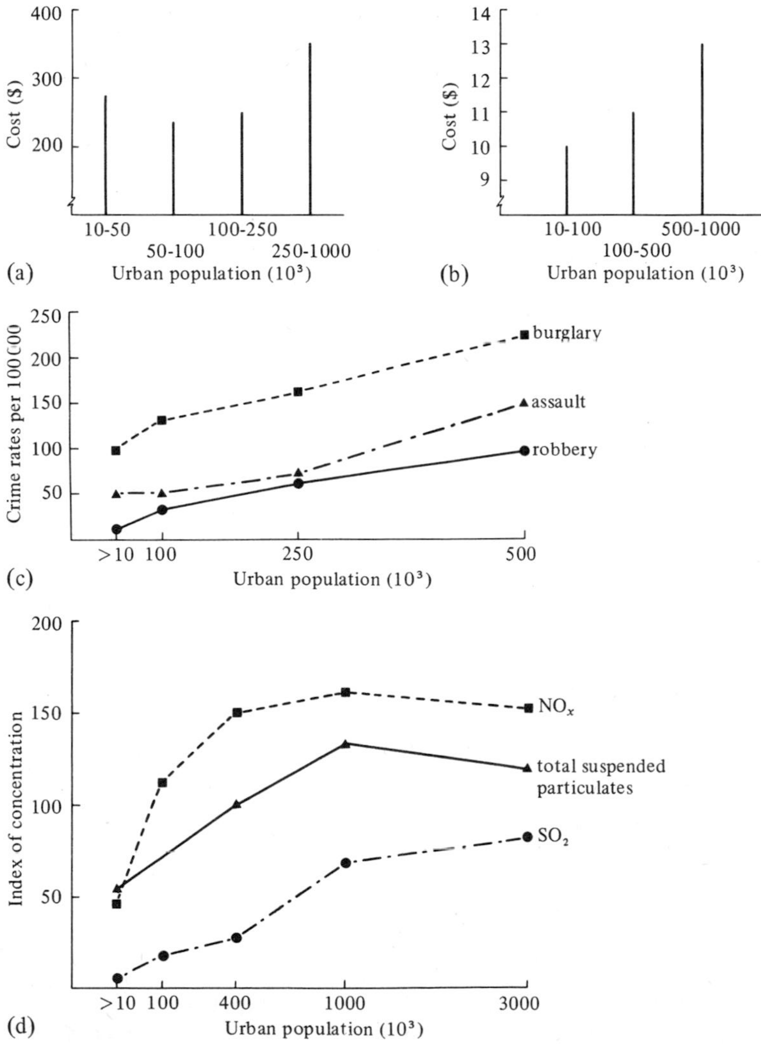

Figure 4.3. The diseconomies of urban scale: (a) average annual *per capita* costs for sewage treatment, (b) average collection costs per ton of waste disposal, (c) crime rates, (d) indices of air pollution. (Sources: Hoch, 1972b; Berry and Horton, 1974, p.85.)

and inequitable servicing costs. Again the need for reform in the financing of urban services is obvious. Some kind of urban income tax levied on a regional basis, or a commuter or payroll tax are now being considered as partial sources of urban revenue.

4.1.3 The disamenities of urban growth

While economists feel that, with political and institutional reform, growth need not necessarily produce diseconomies in infrastructure financing, it is much more difficult to assess the net effects of growth on urban disamenity. Again the problem here is that data are limited and one must resort to unsubstantiated value judgements. There is little doubt that pollution, noise, crime, congestion, and the like are statistically related to urban scale, but there is much dispute over the *causality* of this linkage and over the distributional (equity) effects of disamenity.

Taking cities as a whole, there is only patchy evidence that air and noise pollution increase with scale, or that mortality and morbidity are linked with population numbers (Hoch, 1972b, pp.248–254; Berry and Horton, 1974, pp.295–340; Crofton, 1974). While environmental stress is undoubtedly related to city size, the effect of such stress can only be evaluated in connection with social factors (such as the nature of the sufferer's occupation, the quality of his occupational environment, and his housing conditions, education, and family relationships) and personal habits (including diet, smoking patterns, and physical fitness). For example, Galle and his colleagues (1972) found no relationship between urban density (as conventionally measured) and social pathology (especially crime), but they did discover a correlation between social delinquency and the proximity of inhabitants (i.e. the relation between the number of people per room and the incidence of strained family relationships and antagonistic contacts with neighbours) and racial mix (see also Adams, 1972). In other words, it is the character of immediate personal and social environments that produces pathological stress, though undoubtedly the environments are shaped by urban size and social deprivation. Lave and Seskin (1970), Berry and Horton (1974), and Crofton (1974) all demonstrate clearly that air pollution is a far greater public-health danger when associated with adverse social conditions and health-endangering personal habits (especially smoking). Similarly, with respect to crime, Hoch (1972b, pp.271–272) finds no clear relationship to city size, but strong correlations with indices of social conditions (such as education, housing, social relationships, and unemployment).

Although it is difficult to prove that urban scale actually causes a deterioration in environmental quality, it is fair to conclude that under present inadequate political and economic institutions large cities tend to be more readily associated with the unfavourable social conditions that exacerbate the density and scale effects of disamenity. So user charges and tougher regulations will not eliminate the negative externalities of urban scale in the absence of quite fundamental social and political reform. This reform is all the more urgent if efforts to limit urban growth through the politics of squeeze are successful; otherwise the future for the central city resident is indeed bleak.

4.2 Policies to control urban growth

It is difficult to avoid the feeling that guided-growth proposals are made more to protect the amenities of existing residents than to shape regional development as a whole in a positive and constructive manner. The first American attempts to limit growth came from the 'amenity fringe' communities of the mountainous areas of the northeast and west, and the southern coast, though it soon spread to the wealthy satellite settlements near major urban centres. Residents in both types of impacted community have devised four major strategies to protect their amenities from the threat of further immigration (see Hughes, 1975; Rose, 1975b).

4.2.1 The growth moratorium

The postrevolution Articles of Confederation of the United States declare that "the people of each state shall have free ingress and regress to and from any other state, and shall enjoy therein all the privileges of trade and commerce ...". The basic rights of free movement have since been upheld by the United States Supreme Court on numerous occasions (see Reilly, 1973, pp.98-100). Canadian provinces (and municipalities which are legal dependants of the provinces) also cannot legally impede migration by any deliberate means. Yet a number of American communities have proposed outright ceilings on growth, arguing that it is in national, regional, and environmental interests to have growth curtailed. An even more extreme case was the attempt by the citizens of St. Petersburg, Florida, actually to force recent immigrants to leave: the bill failed only in second reading (Strong, 1975a, p.82). The most famous example is the 1972 decision by the citizens of Boca Raton, Florida, to limit the number of houses within the city limits to 40000, a move which would restrict the population to about 105000 (it is now around 40000), instead of a projected 200000 if growth were not restrained. Since then, a number of other Florida communities have passed building moratoria while they review their growth proposals, a tactic that has also been adopted by towns in other states (Council on Environmental Quality, 1973a, pp.220-221).

The growth moratorium is an excessive and unwieldy measure unlikely to withstand legal challenge. Apart from the obvious constitutional violation, these communities face a second legal hurdle, namely the right (or certainly the expectation) of landowners to increase the value of their land (i.e. develop their holdings) in accordance with reasonable safeguards to protect the public amenity. They claim that this right cannot be denied without due compensation. (This is known as the 'takings' issue and will be discussed in more detail below.) The recalcitrant communities counter these legal arguments with the defence that additional development will be socially detrimental and ecologically dangerous, so growth moratoria are perfectly legitimate protective regulations. In making their rulings the courts will have to strike the fine balance between what can reasonably be interpreted as 'legitimate community interest' and as 'unreasonable protectionism'.

4.2.2 The timing of community facilities

A thinly disguised variation of the growth moratorium is the phasing of community facilities (such as utility supplies and waste disposal) to correspond with a carefully-timed development plan. This simply replaces nongrowth with delayed growth or slowed growth, using the elementary mechanism of limiting urban services (which obviously control development) to carefully determined capacities. The notorious example of the 'development timing' ordinance is that of the community of Ramapo, New York, which has made all development subject to a phased capital improvement programme spanning an eighteen-year period (Franklin, 1973). Under the ordinance, residential subdivision is forbidden unless the developer is granted a permit, which in turn is dependent on the availability of basic services and urban amenities (sewers, drainage, parks, roads, and fire stations). Since the community will supply these services according to its phased capital improvement programme, development is effectively controlled, unless the developer himself is willing to construct the necessary infrastructure to community specifications. Ramapo legislators based this decision on the finding that rapid house building could not be supported by 'adequate social infrastructure' unless the local tax base was raised, and that hasty and improper servicing would probably lead to environmental degradation.

The development timing strategy is a clever avoidance of the constitutional dangers of the growth moratorium, because it appears to accommodate growth without seeming to be too discriminatory. The New York Court of Appeals upheld the Ramapo ordinance precisely on these grounds. "The ordinance", it said (quoted in Franklin, 1973, p.20), " is a growth device aimed at population stabilization", but it warned that there was something "inherently suspect" about schemes which could also be interpreted as discriminatory and exclusionary "in the hope of avoiding the very burden which growth must inevitably bring". Following the Ramapo success a large number of other wealthy suburban communities have passed development timing ordinances, for example Fairfax and Fauquier Counties in Virginia, and Montgomery County, Maryland (Council on Environmental Quality, 1973a, p.221). Miami has also adopted the device which is now becoming increasingly popular among metropolitan administrators.

The timing device exhibits all the problems of controlled-growth ordinances. Franklin (1973, pp.20–30) scrutinised it using three major evaluative criteria to test for discrimination, namely (a) whether it serves the people of the state or nation as a whole, (b) whether it denies housing opportunities to a racial minority, and (c) whether it limits freedom of movement and choice of residence. In the case of the Ramapo ordinance, he found it failed on all three counts, though most particularly on the second since it was apparent that the capital improvement programme was prepared in such a manner as to exclude all but the high-income house buyer. He remarks (p.26) that "it contemplates a continuation of expensive and exclusionary 'sprawl' which in all probability would have occurred—although somewhat faster—without the plan". In order to avoid the charge of *de facto* racial discrimination, a number of more progressive communities have proposed a phasing of development to include a specific (though usually inadequate) proportion of low- and middle-income housing before development permits are issues (see Stanford Environmental Law Society, 1973).

Two other features of phased development that deserve closer study are the degree of local control over regional development and the specific character of the final schemes. The Ramapo decision effectively directs state planning to conform to local ordinances and local directives. So there is no supervisory authority to decide whether the final scheme is the most efficient, or the most environmentally sound, or the most appropriate from a design viewpoint. In the absence of state or national intervention, development timing schemes, especially in the smaller communities, could well result in adverse social and environmental effects that pass unchecked in a broader context. Some kind of supervision by a 'larger entity' would seem desirable.

4.2.3 Large lot zoning

In the United States and Canada zoning by restricting minimum lot sizes is a time-honoured planning device to protect environmental quality and exclude any undesirable influences that might erode property values (see Babcock, 1969; Toll, 1969). Originally the zoning mechanism was used to ensure that incompatible uses in urban areas did not unduly and needlessly interfere with each other, but since 1945 it has become increasingly used in suburban and rural areas to safeguard particular vested interests (see Bosselman and Callies, 1971; Rose, 1973). Zoning as a growth control device emerged in the early 1970s and quickly proved to be highly successful, as its application has enjoyed a long and generally favourable legal history. The standard legal reference for minimum-lot-size zoning as a guided growth tool is the case of Sanborton, New Hampshire, which adopted a six-acre minimum-lot-size zoning ordinance in the remoter sections of the town and effectively stopped a developer from putting up 500 second homes for nearby urban residents. In the resulting lawsuit, the United States Court of Appeals upheld the ordinance as being a reasonable protection of the public welfare, in view of the adverse ecological effects that could otherwise have ensued. But the judge was fully aware of the potential manipulation of this device (quoted in Cahn, 1973b, p.17):

> "Where there is natural population growth, it has to go somewhere, unwelcome as it may be, and in that case we do not think it should be channelled by the happenstance of what town gets its veto in first."

Again some kind of balancing between legitimate community environmental aspirations and reasonable and equitable national (or regional) requirements must be found, for the crude use of the zoning mechanism cannot perform the task adequately. The province of Alberta is currently considering a province-wide industrial zoning plan which would prohibit 'dirty' industries from locating near urban areas. The scheme will be subject to extensive public hearings (Yurko, 1974).

4.2.4 The use of open space

A dramatic version of the large-lot zoning strategy to restrict growth is simply to buy up all remaining land and leave it as open space. This is a very popular strategy in wealthy communities which can afford the enormous capital costs and the loss of potential tax revenue, and has the additional advantage of providing additional recreational space. The Stanford Environmental Law Society (1973, pp.32–36) outlines a variety of quite legitimate devices for preserving open land:

(i) *Purchase through donation or voluntary transaction.* Some communities purchase 'development rights' from landowners as conservation easements or scenic easements. This is most effective if owners of critical ecological areas agree to such a plan, even though community purchase is often expensive. Donations can reduce the owner's property tax and may be tax deductable as a charitable donation. Communities need not purchase all 'development rights', only those they feel could be detrimental to their long-range plans (Council on Environmental Quality, 1974, pp.56–58). Not infrequently the landowner continues to manage his land in its present use.

(ii) *Land banking.* Communities may buy up extensive tracts of surrounding undeveloped land and resell these to developers in accordance with a guided growth plan (*ibid.*, pp.59–60). To avoid the danger of this practice encouraging speculation and increasing prices, many local governments purchase far in advance of need. In some European countries (especially Britain, Scandinavia, and the Netherlands) most or all development land is nationalised to curtail excessive property speculation. For example, the controversial UK Community Land Act (1975) enables local authorities to purchase land subject to development. In the United States and Canada interest in the land banking scheme is growing. The province of Alberta has introduced the 'restricted development area concept' which allows municipalities to freeze land for urban parks, and a

Land Purchase Fund Act which allows it to buy up land for future development (Yurko, 1974).

(iii) *Preferential assessment.* Preferential taxation is a method of lowering the tax burden on land such as farms, forests, wetlands, and historic sites which the community wishes to preserve, by assessing at less than its full market value. This is a popular idea among advocates of guided growth, for present tax policies unduly discriminate against owners of land with high amenity value, since normally much of it is assessed at *potential* value in use, not *actual* value in use (Council on Environmental Quality, 1974, pp.64–68). Though thirty-three US states have adopted the preferential assessment idea, it is not without its problems. There is always a danger that other land uses in the area will be unfairly taxed to maintain general community revenue. Also, speculators can purchase open land, keep it for long periods before development, and benefit from the lower tax rate. To avoid this, some states have contracted with landowners that they must withhold some or all of their property from development in perpetuity; alternatively they have prepared 'rollback' or 'deferred payment' clauses requiring the landowner to pay part or all of the tax arrears if he proposes to develop.

(iv) *Purchase of land for open space.* This is an expensive alternative because it requires that the community pay full compensation, but possibly get little revenue return from the undeveloped area. Nearby land values will escalate, however, so some gains may come from their increased tax returns. Generally, outright purchase of open space in perpetuity is more common in wealthy communities or in European countries where public open space is a scarcer commodity.

The open-space strategy is very popular in California where Marin County began the practice in 1965 by setting aside 200000 acres (of its 300000 acres) as an agricultural reserve at a cost of $200 per household annually over twenty years. One half of this land is dedicated to agriculture by virtue of special tax arrangements as discussed above. The other half is zoned into very large lots to restrict nonagricultural development. In both Santa Cruz and Monterey Counties up to half the remaining land has been reserved for twenty- to forty-acre-minimum lots.

The problems with the open-space strategy are how to justify the environmental value of protecting the land, avoid the 'takings' issue, and prove that the action is not arbitrary or discriminatory. To evade these legal challenges, the community of Palo Alto undertook cost–benefit analyses of leaving the remaining foothills area as open space compared with permitting various densities of development, and reached the conclusion that preservation of the open space would generate greater net benefits for the community. The planning consultants (Livingston and Blayney Associates, 1971) calculated that the discounted cost of servicing the additional development (including the extra classrooms, police and fire services, etc.) would be greater than the additional discounted revenues from property taxes and consumer spending. But it was the 'environmental' analysis that provided the clinching argument:

> "None of the alternatives studied would have any great social utility except those that include low–moderate income housing, and these would have significant disadvantages in other respects ... . Only those alternates with acre lots do not require major street widenings ... any of the development alternatives would do major ecological and visual damage to the area ... there would be potential slide problems and flood problems, particularly with development at 3 or 4 units per acre."

It should be stressed that the Palo Alto study is a pioneering one of its kind, and that it cannot be taken to imply that open-space purchase is always a better alternative. Clearly it will depend on the terrain, the proximity of other developments, the land-use mix of the existing settlement, and the anticipated service requirements of the proposed development. In fact, Livingston and Blayney Associates (1971, p.110) stress that in the free standing community, where revenue generation from property taxation is usually far more complicated and interdependent than in the Palo Alto example, it would be dangerous to accept without proper analysis the notion that the open-space alternative would be preferable to carefully planned development. Nevertheless, the Palo Alto study did survive the legal challenge of an uncompensated denial of private rights to develop and of an exclusionary complaint: on the former, the city felt that the foothills scheme was part of a region-wide comprehensive plan so the rezoning was justified in the public interest, while as to the latter the city stated that plenty of provision for low-income housing existed elsewhere in the community.

The Palo Alto case has encouraged environmental groups elsewhere to calculate the relative costs and benefits of additional housing. Paul (1970) reviewed several alternative proposals for the community of Half Moon Bay, California, and concluded that, even for the most desirable form of development, net losses to the community of \$50000 annually would be incurred after five years and of \$400000 after ten years (equivalent to an annual surcharge of \$85 on each existing homeowner). His cost–benefit analysis is summarised in table 4.3. The Stanford Environmental Law Society (1973) undertook a similar calculation for San Jose, and found that the city should substantially reduce its proposed development and reform its local tax system so as to channel the location and rate of growth more efficiently. A study in Denver estimated that every additional resident costs the community \$21 000 in servicing and capital expenditures, while a study in Florida showed that, if twenty single-family dwelling units were replaced by an apartment complex housing 270 families, the *extra* demand for community services would amount to:

12 acres for open space, 3 acres for service industry, 4 acres for retail stores, 11 classrooms, 400 cars, 120000 gallons of water daily, 100000 gallons of sewage daily, 2 firemen plus $8100 per year additional equipment, 12 teachers plus $12900 annually for additional facilities, 2 miles of improved streets, $39000 annually for health services, $4160 for recreation, and $69000 for other services (Cahn, 1973b, p.16; see also Systems Management Associates, 1972).

In conjunction with the Department of Housing and Urban Development and the Environmental Protection Agency, the Council on Environmental Quality (1974, pp.6–21) commissioned a study of the comparative costs of three kinds of residential patterns—unplanned sprawl, a combination of single and multiple family dwellings, and a compact, clustered development (Real Estate Research Corporation, 1974). From the summary presented in table 4.4 it will be seen that the traditional suburban sprawl (which caters to the 'American dream' of an owner-occupied single-family dwelling with a private garden) is far more expensive than the clustered alternative in every respect from land and servicing costs to energy consumption and environmental quality.

Yet the Council (pp.28–31) is fully aware that existing federal tax incentives encourage this wasteful pattern of subdivision. Tax deductions on mortgages favour home ownership over home rental, and depreciation allowances are higher for new construction than for rehabilitation. "The incentive is to build, depreciate, sell, and then build again. This creates an inducement to continue constructing new buildings where the land is

Table 4.3. Cost and benefits of alternative growth patterns. (Source: Council on Environmental Quality, 1974.)

	Low density, sprawl	Combination mix	High density, planned
Average acres per dwelling unit	0·6	0·4	0·27
Average acres open space around dwelling unit	0·0	0·2	0·33
Capital costs of community servicing ($ per dwelling unit)	49000	35000	30000
Operation and maintenance costs of community servicing ($ per dwelling unit)	2100	1900	1800
Air pollution emissions (pounds of residuals per dwelling unit)	235	180	140
Water pollution generation (pounds of residuals per dwelling unit)	1200	900	700
Energy demand (million Btu per dwelling unit)	410	310	220
Water demand (thousand gallons per dwelling unit)	120	90	75

cheap—the land cannot be depreciated—while allowing older buildings to decay" (p.29). Profits from buying and selling land are treated as capital gains and so are taxed at a lower rate than other sources of income, thus stimulating land speculation. And if the property is transferred to the owner's heirs before his death, then upon the owner's decease any subsequent land speculation is not even subject to capital gains tax. Finally, since in many states farmland, woodland, and open space are still assessed at full market value, it is a strong temptation for any owner to sell some of this land to developers to offset estate duties, unless preferential tax treatment can be obtained.

Canadian tax laws similarly favour sprawl over containment. The province of Alberta has recently removed the school foundation levy on its property taxes. This should help communities to raise sufficient revenue for residential and commercial land uses rather than having to rely on industry as was formerly the case (Yurko, 1974).

In the light of this evidence, many communities and states are looking very hard at methods of containing urban sprawl and ensuring that new residents bear more of the true cost of their settlement. The first matter will be discussed below; as to the second, the Florida State House Committee on Government Operations has recently passed a recommendation that all newcomers pay the marginal social services cost that they incur—a kind of real estate equivalent of the residuals tax—based on a statewide formula. They hope that such a charging scheme will encourage clustered decentralisation, since the levy will be much higher in the metropolitan regions and the areas of sprawl. In the face of legal challenge by developers the courts have upheld this proposal, as it aims to cover additional fiscal costs and thus is not unduly discriminatory. The guided-growth movement is certainly causing many people to think very hard about antiquated regional planning and financing institutions, but the most spectacular challenge has come from the legal front.

4.3 The taking issue

The Fifth Amendment to the US Constitution states that 'private property [shall not] be taken for public use without just compensation'. The critical word here is 'taken', for there are no clear guidelines as to what is meant by a 'taking'. The matter is easy when private property is physically expropriated, or relinquished for some public purpose such as the construction of a road or a transmission pylon. In such cases the authorities agree to compensate the owner up to the market value of his loss. But what if the 'loss' is not physical but aesthetic, or consists of a reduction in the options of use owing to a zoning regulation? Here there will be a diminution in value, but the owner still enjoys a certain freedom of use—should he still be compensated? This matter is not a boring legal wrangle but a crucial policy issue for environmental land-use planning; for the manner in which a 'taking' is interpreted will have critical implications for landscape amenity, controlled growth, and ecological protection. Nor is this matter confined to the United States, for it applies to all countries with an Anglo-American constitutional background. At present there are literally millions of dollars worth of court suits awaiting clarification as property owners are thwarted by environmental interests in developing their land to its maximum value.

Useful reviews of this interesting subject are provided by Bosselman *et al.* (1973) and by the Council on Environmental Quality (1973a, pp.121–153; 1974, pp.51–72). There are in fact no clear legal precedents with which to shape modern policy, only four rather vague 'theories' which tend to be contradictory, making the matter difficult for both jurists and planners.

(i) *The physical invasion theory* is the most clear-cut but the narrowest in practice. If a property owner's rights are physically expropriated, then compensation must be paid. But for most controlled-growth and environmental-planning issues private rights are diminished in part, not relinquished in full, so other legal principles must be found.

(ii) *The nuisance abatement theory* expresses the idea that when the diminution of value is incurred to protect the public from potential harm (for example from noxious pollutants, excessive noise, or demonstrably irreversible damage) then there should be no compensation. Put another way, a taking would only occur when specified private rights are denied for a purpose that is deemed useful to the public; it would not occur when the public is merely trying to protect its legitimate interests. Although laudable in principle, the nuisance abatement test could discriminate unfairly against activities that are deemed harmful only because public values change (for instance, when people living near airports become less noise tolerant) or because the nature of the use of the surrounding land alters (a classic problem in the controlled-growth dispute). This is a good example of how a perfectly reasonable legal precedent is inadequate in the face of modulating environmental values.

(iii) *The balancing test* aims at comparing the relative amounts of public benefit and private loss, though the problem here is one of self-contradiction. On the one hand, it can be argued that the greater the public gain and the more the private loss, the greater the cause for a 'taking'; but on the other hand to protect the demonstrable public interest might be all the more reason for regulating the use of the land. Since jurists love the principle of 'balancing the equities' this theory has provided most of the precedents for modern takings cases. The classic contribution is the opinion of Supreme Court Justice Holmes who ruled that in most instances any denial of private rights (even through regulation) for a public benefit should be regarded as a taking. In his own words:

> "The general rule at least is that while property may be regulated to a certain extent, if regulation goes too far it will be recognized as a taking" (quoted in Bosselman *et al.*, 1973, p.136).

The Holmes decision is now regarded as being 'conservative', 'wrong' or 'bedevilling' and a serious impediment to legal reform in the takings issue (see Bosselman *et al.*, 1973, pp.126–138). Holmes was excessively concerned over the denial of private rights by what he considered irresponsible use of police powers. But times and conditions have changed noticeably since his words were uttered (1922), and most liberal-minded lawyers feel that the Holmes dictum should be superseded by a more realistic balancing test, which after all is a useful exercise in any resource-management evaluation (see Bosselman *et al.*, 1973, pp.212–235).

(iv) *Diminution of value* is also a very popular test, for it focuses on the extent to which an existing or potential use (and profit-making enterprise) is restricted or diminished through regulation in the public interest. Unfortunately it does not state when 'unacceptable' reduction occurs, and recent court findings have reflected this uncertainty and lack of clear precedent. For example, a New Jersey court invalidated a zoning proposal aimed at making a certain area of meadowland into an ecologically projected swampland, as it believed that "the only practical use which can be made of the property [would be a] hunting or fishing preserve or a wildlife sanctuary, none of which could be considered productive" (quoted in Council on Environmental Quality, 1973a, p.134). The court concluded that a taking occurs when:

> "The ordinance so restricts the use that the land cannot practically be utilized for any reasonable purpose, or when the only permitted uses are those to which the property is not adapted or which are economically unfeasible" (*ibid.*, p.135).

On the other hand, a California court upheld a moratorium on landfilling in San Francisco Bay since the protective ordinances "were designed to preserve the existing character of the Bay while it determined how the Bay should be developed in the future" (*ibid.*, p.133).

The California ruling provides one clue to the resolution of the very troublesome taking issue. Where a comprehensive and democratically-devised regionwide environmental land-use plan is either in preparation or has been politically accepted, diminution of use in accord with such a plan should not be interpreted as a taking. Thus a Massachusetts court overruled an appeal by a plaintiff denied the opportunity to develop on a vulnerable flood plain on the grounds that though "it [was] clear that the petitioner [was] substantially restricted in the use of land, such restrictions must be balanced against the potential harm to community from overdevelopment of a flood plain area" (*ibid.*, p.135). Since the 'balancing' procedure must take into account profitmaking possibilities, clearly the regional environmental plan becomes a critical political document in determining the nature and shape of land use change.

The diminution-of-value test plays a most important role in the guided-growth aspects of land-use planning; hence the cautious compromise of adopting timing and zoning devices rather than outright limitation as guided-growth policy instruments, since these devices have a certain legal heritage. Nevertheless a New York court has stated the important principle that if a landowner could show that he was deprived of "any use of his property to which it was reasonably adapted", or if regulation "destroyed the greater part of the value of his property", his challenge could be upheld. Again the degree of environmental impact will probably become the crucial element. If a community can demonstrate beyond reasonable doubt that substantial environmental damage would occur as a result of a proposed development (or the contrary equivalent—if the developer cannot show that his design would *not* create an adverse environmental impact), then no consideration of taking need enter the judgement. For example, in the Sanborton case the court recognised the adverse ecological and social consequences of opening up the town to costly residential development, and concluded that at "this time of uncertainty as to the right balance between ecological and population pressures, we cannot help but feel that the town's ordinance, which severely restricts development, may properly stand for the present as a legitimate stop-gap measure" (quoted in Council on Environmental Quality, 1973a, p.139).

Further evidence of change in the interpretation of the taking issue can be found in recent court decisions that insist on adequate provisions for open space in new developments, either in the form of parks and other recreation areas or through special provisions for open space as part of the design itself. What in fact the courts are beginning to say is that land developers, irrespective of the purposes for which they are preparing their properties, must consider the public welfare implications of amenity, noise protection, open space, and aesthetic design as an integral part of their schemes, and not simply as reluctant afterthoughts. Far from diminishing the value of the final development, this legal requirement should enhance it, though admittedly at some extra cost to the developer.

It should be clear that this interesting transitional period in the interpretation of a 'taking' reveals vitally significant adjustments in ideology toward the role of private property, toward the nature of growth, and toward the notion of environmental landscape design. Private ownership will never be so sacrosanct again. The myth that a landowner can do what he pleases regardless of his neighbour's interests or the broader and longer-term public welfare is rapidly being eroded, even though there is still much resistance to its demise. Increasingly the courts are saying that certain social obligations must be respected when exercising the right to enjoy the use of private property. Although the rights to the making of profit as a result of use are not dead (and will never die), they are now noticeably tempered by a public recognition that the use of any piece of land or water must be compatible with environmental and social values. Bosselman *et al.* (1973, p.261) outline what appears to be a significant change in emphasis in the common law to reflect the new environmentalism:

> "The courts should 'presume' that any change in existing natural ecosystems is likely to have adverse consequences [that are] difficult to foresee. The proponent of [any] change should therefore be required to demonstrate, as well as possible, the nature and extent of any changes that will result. Such a presumption would build into common law a requirement that a prospective developer who wishes to challenge a governmental regulation prepare a statement similar to the environmental impact statements now required of public agencies under federal programs."

The 'quiet revolution' that Bosselman and Callies (1971) discovered is the growing extension of social authority over private ownership so that order and beauty are maintained and enhanced in the countryside and the town.

The attitude to growth is also changing, though again it is not so much a matter of growth versus no growth, as one of the scale and pattern of growth. Development is no longer viewed as an unmitigated blessing. The city fathers who for so long fought to attract new industry and jobs and who measured community pride in terms of shiny factories and rows of suburban houses are no longer being elected. More and more, they are being replaced by a new breed of environmental accountants who visualise growth in very different terms and who are proposing quite imaginative planning concepts to meet current demands for environmental design.

4.3.1 The taking issue in Britain

In Britain and Europe, where land-use conflicts and concern over the public-welfare aspects of landscape change are more pressing and more politically evident, much stricter regulations over the use of private property have been in force for some time. Under statutory guidelines for public consultation, British local authorities are required to produce structure plans (formerly development plans) which indicate the general nature and timing of the change of land use. In theory, therefore, the structure plan allows local authorities to guide any development to meet certain publicly acceptable requirements for which no compensation need be paid. Structure plans may include all kinds of provisions for open space and amenity, especially for particular buildings and landscapes which are generally regarded as worthy of protection. Compensation need be paid only when these plans clearly reduce land values to 'unreasonable' levels, or prohibit beneficial use to an 'unreasonable' extent. The British pattern is certainly much more restrictive than the North American one, though on balance it has certainly helped to protect the countryside and the townscape from the socially undesirable consequences of unrestrained private development. However, the system of planning consents does involve cumbersome and sometimes unnecessarily lengthy administrative procedures which are always vulnerable to capricious pressures and the discretionary but unpredictable conclusions of local planning officers.

The problem of delay in granting planning consents in Britain is a serious one, partly because the number of applications is so very large (though since the 1972 'boom' there has been some falling off in the annual rate), and partly because of the enormous costs in time and manpower of ensuring proper evaluation. If an application for development is turned down, or is objected to by neighbouring residents, resolution can take anywhere between nine months and eighteen months (Dobry, 1975, p.55). In a report to the Department of the Environment, Dobry (1975) noted that there were some 14000 appeals still undecided in December 1974. "A planning decision", he remarked (p.21) "which takes too long to reach is often, because of that, a bad decision whatever its content". To expedite matters he suggested a mechanism to streamline the consent procedure by dividing the planning applications into two categories: Category A would include all 'minor' schemes (such as extensions to existing buildings) which must be dealt with in forty-two days, and Category B for the larger schemes which require more attention and could take up to six months to be decided (Dobry, 1975). This proposal is viewed rather suspiciously by many environmentalists, who feel it could reduce the scope for nonstatutory consultation with amenity interests, widen the already considerable bureaucratic discretion, and dangerously streamline appeals procedures. In November 1975, the Environment Secretary issued a commentary on Dobry's proposals in which he rejected all the major suggestions on the grounds of budgetary restraint.

British planners are undeservedly fortunate in the matter of 'taking'. Bosselman *et al.* (1973, p.279) report that many of the smaller local authorities have served virtually no compulsory purchase orders (a legal mandate to pay compensation) over the past five years and that even the larger (urban) authorities admit that they rarely have to consider granting compensatory payments. However, the Land Compensation Act of 1973 has put an abrupt stop to this. The Act provides the monetary compensation be made to property owners who can demonstrate the possibility of 'injury' (either in terms of mental or physical health or of loss in property value) as a consequence of living close by a proposed noxious facility (such as a road or an airport) which is built for the public purpose. In effect, the Act explicitly recognises the nuisance abatement theory by giving compensation to those whose amenity is lowered as a result of some scheme which generates a public benefit. At present the Act only pertains to those immediately adjacent to *proposed* facilities and is effective only when these facilities are actually under construction or initially in operation. So it does not incorporate fully the monetary losses of preconstruction planning blight, nor does it in any way take into account the misfortunes of those countless people who have already suffered loss of amenity from similar previous schemes.

Local authorities have reacted rather nervously to the Act since it opens up a Pandora's box of implications. The Act deals only with damage to people, not to the land, and thus encourages planners to channel development into areas of low population density (or certainly low property value), which might be of considerable ecological or amenity value. If, as a result, noxious facilities are developed in areas of low property value, this practice could further distort the environmental injustices discussed in the previous chapter. The Act requires local authorities to devise money-based formulae for compensating loss of amenity, which for many cannot be subject to monetary calculation and as such is demeaning to them. In any case, the Act aims to base its compensatory payments largely on potential loss of property value, a criterion that is now widely discredited as bearing any reasonable relationship to the loss of amenity suffered. Though economists like to think that changes in property value provide a neat index of the degree of amenity or disamenity experienced, Pearce (1972) and Mishan (1974b) have effectively demonstrated that this is not the case (see chapter 5, pp.178–182).

The British experience gives some indication of the difficulties facing environmental planners as conflicts between the private and public interests grow. There is great danger that the whole takings process will become more bureaucratic and subject to rules and regulations that in no way take into account the true nature of individual losses or gains. As a result people may become resentful and obstructive, thereby delaying the procedures even more. There is no simple answer to this problem, though greater public consultation of more varied planning options should help, as will innovations in the design of developments to take into account public amenity requirements. These are discussed below.

4.4 Innovation in development design

The growing interest in ecological and amenity aspects of development has opened up avenues for quite imaginative schemes in development planning. Only broad concepts are described here; the reader is urged to go to the original sources for details.

4.4.1 The amenity compact

Zoning is now widely regarded as an excessively rigid instrument readily subject to arbitrary and discriminatory manipulation (Council on Environmental Quality, 1974, pp.51–54). Floor space ratios, open space provisions, and building heights, if fixed by inflexible formulae, often result in more poorly planned development than if no zoning ordinances existed at all. Several planners are beginning to suggest an 'amenity compact' whereby developers are granted reasonable amendments to zoning ordinances in return for providing certain public amenities, such as open space, a balcony, a playground, or even an underground transit stop as part of their schemes. Alternatively, the developer could be asked to contribute to a 'social amenity fund', the revenues from which would be used to provide a variety of public amenities (e.g. rest areas, walkways, bicycle paths). The amenity compact notion explicitly recognises that any development makes use of 'amenity rent', the social value of open space, aspect, fine views, etc., which belongs to the public as a kind of 'trust' (see chapter 8, pp.276–280). Any prospective developer should be required to compensate the public by ensuring, as far as possible, that in general amenity terms his scheme makes people no worse off. The notion implies that development of any kind is a privilege, not a right, and should recognise sensitively the social amenity values that are being disturbed. Community-minded developers also realise that an agreeable proposal will not only be politically more acceptable, but also should command higher prices and a better return.

An interesting example of the amenity compact is now statutorily possible in Canada under the amended Municipal Act of British Columbia (1972, Sections 702A, 702B, 703), under which local governments can enter into what are called 'land-use contracts' with developers who seek to amend existing zoning bylaws. Under the terms of a contract, when considering a development proposal (be it a single structure or a residential subdivision), the developer must pay due regard to (a) the efficiency and quality of the scheme, (b) the impact on present and future public costs, (c) the betterment of the environment, (d) the fulfilment of community goals, and (e) the provision of necessary public space. These sections provide local authorities with the opportunity to be very imaginative in negotiating with developers so as to protect the public amenity. In practice, however, local authority planners have not seized upon these provisions, and, with the exception of insisting upon a little more public open space in and around proposed schemes, they have tended to be rather conservative in their consultations.

A more enlightened version of the land-use contract is however being proposed in the Vancouver Downtown Plan, where developers may be asked to consult with citizens groups, planners, and other professionals before their proposals are finally approved. The design of any new development proposal would thus be integrated into a publicly acceptable downtown amenity design that aims to produce a pleasurable environment and appeals to the human scale (Vancouver Downtown Study, 1975).

Another version of the amenity compact idea could be incorporated into the design of clustered residential property where a central area of communal open space is provided as part of the scheme, available not only to residents but to the local community as well. An example of such a scheme is depicted in figure 4.4. The developer has designed his lots to mould into the contours of the land and has posted a performance bond

G

to guarantee that adequate sewage and drainage are supplied before construction begins. By opening up open space to nearby residents he hopes to gain acceptance of his proposal and hasten community integration. Another example, this time in the housing field (Marlin, 1974), is the use of 'performance' points to ensure that proposed residential development meets required social amenity standards. A developer must amass the necessary number of points (as outlined in table 4.4) before his development can proceed. This is an excellent example of inclusionary zoning—zoning through negotiation with citizens groups and resident clients which could foster community spirit and a wider interest in neighbourhood planning and amenity. It should also rid the housing landscape of the unpopular isolated towers surrounded by unused barren space which admittedly meet the mathematical requirements of floor space zoning regulations, but have no human appeal.

Table 4.4. Performance points for socially desirable housing design. (Source: Marlin, 1974, p.F1.)

Neighbourhood impact	
setback of street-fronting walls conform to existing plan	4·55
sunlit open space	3·60
street-fronting walls compatible in length with adjacent property	3·60
control of shadow on nearby buildings	3·05
street-fronting wall compatible in height with adjacent property	3·05
Apartment design	
size	3·75
amount of sunlight admitted to rooms	3·20
size of windows	3·20
protection of visual privacy	3·20
convenient parking and garage access	1·50
Recreation space	
type and size	8·50
provision for receiving winter sun	5·00
landscaping	2·75
covered parked cars	2·65
view of playing children from parked cars	2·65
trees	2·45
seating	1·00
Security and safety	
visual privacy between outdoor apartment space and lobby	3·90
visibility of street parking from building exit	2·25
short corridor lengths between elevator and apartment	1·85
visibility between apartment entrances	1·80

Each category adds up in total to 37 points (only selected examples are given here). Developers must provide designs to score 22 points or more before permission to build is granted.

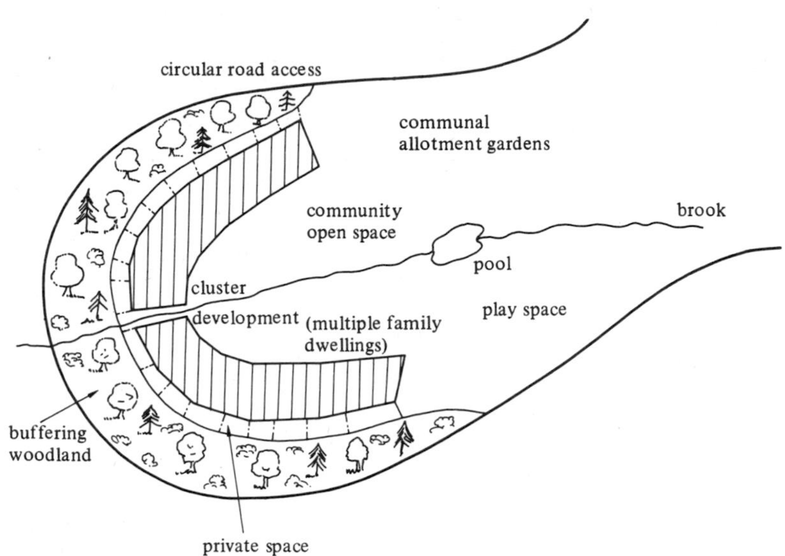

Figure 4.4. Clustered development and the provision of amenity.

4.4.2 Regional tax sharing

A major stumbling block in metropolitan regional planning in North America is the fact that revenue generation is left in the hands of many separate local governments. Any attempt to control growth or channel it from more to less congested areas is usually met with spirited resistance from the communities deprived of potential revenue or existing amenity. If guided growth is ever to be successful, some sort of tax-sharing arrangement between participating local governments will have to be instituted. As it is now recognised that further growth can result in a net cost to a community, areas which are faced with growth (according to a predetermined regional plan) should somehow be subsidised by the region at large, or blatant and inequitable exclusionary practices will worsen. For example, the Association of Bay Area Governments (1973) calculated that, in comparison with a continuation of the present pattern of growth, a policy of guided growth would save the whole community some \$1·5 billion between 1970 and 2000 even assuming the same ultimate regional population, since clustering would dramatically reduce the costs of buying up land and of providing extra utilities and transportation networks. Nevertheless, the costs of this pattern of development would obviously fall more heavily on some parts of the region than others. Winslow (1973) describes how a suburb of St. Louis deliberately zoned out cluster developments regardless of their aesthetic appeal, partly because they were not prepared to pay the extra costs of facilities and social services and partly because of racial discrimination. In fact Winslow stresses that guided growth in the absence of tax sharing can cause income distortions, since controlled growth may actually raise land values in the general area, thereby upsetting existing long-term development plans.

The metropolitan area of Minneapolis–St. Paul is attempting to overcome this kind of problem by instituting a tax-sharing policy in which only 60% of the real estate taxes paid by new businesses are passed on to the community in which they locate, the remainder being divided equally among all communities forming the region. This helps to rid regional planners of the political restrictions imposed by traditional local tax revenue arrangements, and encourages the whole region to share the gains and losses of growth. However, to be successful, the tax-sharing agreement requires a high degree of political vision, which, alas, is not commonly found.

4.4.3 Transferable development rights (TDR)

The idea of TDR stems from old royalty legislation for mineral prospecting, by which landholders were granted certain mineral rights depending upon how much of a mineral resource was found below their land. Extraction was based on these rights, which therefore acted as a kind of performance bond and conservation measure wrapped into one. The TDR are based on the fundamental principle (still not widely accepted in North America) that land is not so much a private commodity as a public resource. Land use regulations should thus be seen to work from the 'top down', the developer or landowner being granted certain rights out of the public amenity domain, not, as is usually the case, from the 'bottom up', whereby property holders claim illusory preexisting rights of private use (Costonis, 1973; Reilly, 1973, pp.140–143; Rose, 1975a).

Under a TDR scheme, each property owner would be granted a certain bundle of development rights in accordance with a community environmental plan which identifies the amount, nature, location, and timing of growth. (This would be a politically determined document which would obviously require extensive consultation with local interest groups before final adoption.) Developers would have to accumulate a specified number of TDR before they could construct their schemes: obviously ecologically sensitive areas would require a larger number of TDR while more 'tolerant' regions would need fewer. Thus growth could be patterned to conform to ecological conditions and the benefits of growth would be shared among the whole community. Farmers and other owners of valuable open space could sell their TDR at a suitable profit to permit development by others elsewhere; but having lost their TDR they would be required to keep their property as open space. The sale of the TDR would effectively annul any legal challenge of a taking. Lands purchased for schools, libraries, and other social services need not require TDR and so should be cheaper to purchase and develop.

The TDR are a form of Spaceship II quota zoning which recognises a limit to the exploitation of landscape amenity, a limit that must be fairly shared and carefully planned in both space and time. Growth is not stopped by those with selfish interests, but guided sensibly and shared fairly. But the TDR scheme is vulnerable precisely because it is environmental and egalitarian, and so requires a degree of cooperation and trust that is tragically rare in western cultures.

The only two test cases which have attempted to use the principle of the TDR failed before they could ever prove themselves. One was McHarg's (1969, pp.79–93) proposal to form a Real Estate Syndicate of all property owners in a Maryland valley. McHarg showed that by concentrating cluster development of housing and utility links on the ecologically tolerant valley sides, the precious valley floor, vulnerable to flooding and providing the major aquifers, could be left to fulfil its proper roles and provide recreational open space. The environmental plan would provide $7 million in excess revenue compared with a conventional plan of uncontrolled growth. If some of this revenue were granted to the valley landowners as compensation for their not developing their properties, by 1980 each would have received $3200 per acre from the syndicate. But every valley landowner knew that he might recoup a much higher profit (say $15 000 per acre) if, in the absence of the scheme, a developer happened to want his land. Obviously not everyone would be so fortunate, but while the possibility was there the valley property owners refused to join the syndicate. A similar combination of distrust and avarice befell the imaginative Brandywine scheme in Chester County, Pennsylvania (Thompson, 1969; Keene and Strong, 1970; Strong, 1975b) in spite of considerable efforts at public education and diplomacy throughout the design stage. Two popular slogans that emerged in the battle tell the story—"Land is manhood, the plan is castration"; "Stop the land grab—keep out 'Big Daddy' Government". Even though the federal and state governments favoured the plan, the local opposition was so severe that the proposal was scrapped.

4.4.4 The planned unit development (PUD)

Despite shifting positions on the question of compensation it is clear that imaginative environmental planning requires quite new resources of community leadership, trust, and consultation. A really worthwhile plan for guided growth should contain safeguards against both environmental and social injustices. Planned unit development or planned development districts incorporate the idea of transferable development rights with floating zones to guide development in orderly packages across whole communities. This avoids the administrative and political difficulties of rezoning or spot zoning in order to permit flexible community design within the philosophical context of the amenity compact described earlier. The PUD is therefore a communitywide amalgam of the techniques already outlined, to guide and time growth in accordance with environmental and community needs.

The city of Petaluma some forty miles north of San Francisco adopted this scheme in 1972 following an unexpectedly large population increase of 5000 people (20%) between 1969 and 1971. The city first adopted a long-range Environmental Design Plan into which it fitted the desired location, mix, and timing of residential development through a permit system (known as the Residential Development System, RDS, similar in concept to the New York housing performance scheme outlined in table 4.4) and a quota allocation arrangement. This required 100 units ± 10% to be constructed annually, planned unit cluster developments to be concentrated into one area, and 8–12% of the quota to be devoted to low and moderate income housing. Applications for development are considered by a Residential Development Board composed of politicians, planners, businessmen, and citizens (the latter having one third of the total vote). An RDS permit will only be accepted if the application scores at least 25 points in Category A and 50 points in Category B as outlined in table 4.5. Both the ratings and the actual values in any given instance are subject to public inquiry and appeal.

Though the Petaluma scheme is highly popular with its residents (a referendum found 80% approved of the plan), it nevertheless illustrates the political, social, and legal difficulties facing any form of guided growth, no matter how well-intentioned. In effect the city is reducing its growth rate by at least 50% of what would 'normally' occur. But a California

Table 4.5. The residential development points system for Petaluma, California. (Source: Stanford Environmental Law Society, 1973, p.113.)

	Quality of design (0–5)	Contribution to public welfare and amenity (0–10)
1 Site and architectural design: height, size, colour, location		
2 Site and architectural design: landscaping and screening		
3 Site and architectural design: traffic circulation, access and exit, safety and privacy		
4 Provision of public and/or private open space along Petaluma river or other creek		
5 Contributions and extension to foot or bicycle paths, trails, etc.		
6 Provision of needed public facilities—schoolrooms, links to traffic routes		
7 Extent to which development is orderly in relation to overall plan		
8 Provision of middle- and low-income units		

Schemes must score 25 on the 'quality of design' scale and 50 on the 'contribution to public welfare and amenity' scale before being granted permission to proceed.

court upheld a complaint by a development company and threw out the plan on the grounds that it was exclusionary and unconstitutional by denying free right of movement. Later, however, an appellate court reversed this ruling and the matter was referred to the Supreme Court which in March 1976 ruled not to hear the case, thus upholding the appellate court's decision. In the absence of statewide or national plans even the most sincere efforts to guide growth could be dangerously discriminatory, for they thwart normal patterns of migration which are mainly within and between cities. Alonso (1973, p.201) notes that, as a rule of thumb, it takes ten migratory moves in or out of a metropolis for a net gain or loss of one migrant.

4.5 The regional environmental plan

In 1971 two lawyers of the American Law Institute completed a report for the Council on Environmental Quality (Bosselman and Callies, 1971) in which they observed (p.3):

> "It has become increasingly apparent that the local zoning ordinance, virtually the sole means of land use control in the United States for over half a century, has proved woefully inadequate to control a host of problems of statewide significance, social problems as well as problems involving environmental pollution and destruction of our vital ecological systems, which threaten our very existence."

In their research they unearthed the beginnings of what they called 'a quiet revolution' in statewide ecological planning and land-use controls which have subsequently blossomed (see Finkler, 1972, 1973; Lamm and Davidson, 1972; Lamm, 1973; McAllister, 1973; Stanford Environmental Law Society, 1973; US Environmental Protection Agency, 1973b; Carter, 1973a, 1975; Kaiser and Reddings, 1974; Mannino, 1974). Many of these policies were hastily concocted under the pressure of undisciplined growth or the fear of irreversible environmental damage, so few can be said to be fair or equitable in all their implications. Partly to offset this, but partly also to assist states in disentangling the legal ramifications of such plans, the American Law Institute (ALI) has initiated a model land development code to serve as a prototype for comprehensive state environmental planning. A key aspect of the code is to leave most (about 90%) land-use questions to local authorities who are intensely jealous of the fiscal and political powers with which they shape their own communities. But the code does provide for statewide reviews of larger projects (especially developments with a regional impact such as airports, major subdivisions, and shopping centres, plus the protection of critical ecological areas). It is possible that the regional considerations which form a part of such assessments might supersede local interests, though this remains a very sensitive political issue (see Carter, 1973a; Little, 1974). Some states have adopted regionwide plans following the recommendations of the ALI code (e.g. Florida, Delaware, Washington, Oregon), while others have accepted variations of it. The main elements of the ALI code are as follows:

(i) *The requirement of environmental impact analyses for all schemes, public or private, significantly affecting the environment.* The idea of the environmental impact statement began with the US National Environmental Policy Act (1970; see chapter 8, p.282) and was quickly adopted by the states anxious to slow down their rates of development. In 1970 Vermont passed an Environmental Control Law (better known as Act 250) which required that "any proposed residential subdivision in excess of 10 acres, any commercial or industrial development of substantial size and any development above 2500 feet in elevation" be subject to an environmental impact review, and be evaluated by a statewide Environmental Board and seven District Commissions (mostly political appointments) in the context of a statewide plan (Bosselman and Callies, 1971, pp.54–108). The law was quite clearly aimed at second-home subdivisions, though all reasonably-sized developments are included. The California Environmental Quality Act of 1970 followed this pattern, as did subsequent acts in Colorado (1971), Hawaii (1971), Massachusetts (1972), New York (1972), Wisconsin (1972), and Montana (1973). Unfortunately, in the absence of planning aid the environmental impact requirement makes it difficult for small-scale developers to compete with better financed companies. In addition, these statements rarely include much of a review of the wider socioeconomic consequences of development. All too often they are the result of 'cookbook' studies using standard formulae and displaying little imagination or ingenuity. But the principle of an environmental review is sound; doubtless standards will improve with experience.

(ii) *The protection of 'critical environmental areas'.* Most state plans try to identify significant ecological areas (parks, seashores, wetlands, rivers, etc.) to be protected from most, if not all, kinds of development. The idea comes from McHarg's (1969) notion of 'areas of prohibition' which are ecologically unsuitable for development and too precious to be altered irreversibly. This concept is embodied in the Florida Environmental Land Use and Water Management Act of 1972 (see Carter, 1973b, 1975) which requires the legislature to recognise 'areas of critical state interest' (ACSI). The original intention was to protect some 25% of the Florida landscape under this provision, since much of the aquifer in the centre of the state is vital for the ecological survival of the southern region. However, politicking by the Florida Association of Homebuilders reduced the maximum designated area to only 5% of the state at any one time—an almost meaningless figure. Carter (1973b, pp.905–906) describes how local developers with political connections steadily reduced the areas specified as ACSI around the Big Cypress Swamp to a meaningless few acres. The opposition of local fruit growers, cattle ranchers, and real estate developers was simply too great.

The justification for, identification of, and designation of critical environmental areas pose challenging difficulties for many of the reasons already discussed in this chapter (taking, attitudes to land, local versus regional versus statewide authority, the nature of the consultation process, the distribution of political and economic influence). However, some states have set aside sizeable ecological and recreational areas. Examples include all the remaining publicly-owned Pacific coast (Washington, Oregon, and California have all issued development moratoria on the coastline), part of the Atlantic coast (in Florida, Delaware, and New Jersey), and a large section of the Adirondack Mountains. The Adirondack case is a fine example of environmental politics, for by tactics of cajoling and threatening the New York Department of Conservation produced a widely-acclaimed duo of Adirondack Master Plans (one for state owned lands and one for private lands) which zoned development in accordance with existing patterns of use and future environmental considerations (Vrooman, 1975). The scheme, outlined in table 4.6, is a good illustration of environmental planning, using a variety of incentives to embody modern ideas of guided growth.

Table 4.6. Land-use classification under the Adirondack Forest Preserve Master Plan. (Source: Adirondack Park Agency, 1973.)

Private lands zoning category	Density (buildings per square mile)	Lot size (front feet of shoreline)	Set back[a] (feet)	Buildings per linear mile
Industrial area	only adjacent to existing structures and zones of exploitation			
Hamlet	concentrated settlement		50	
Moderate-intensity use	500	100	50	53
Low-intensity use	200	200	75	26
Rural use	75	250	75	21
Resource management	15	300	125	18

[a] No more than 30% of trees in excess of 4 in diameter to be removed

State lands zoning category	Description	% of Park Area
Wilderness	untouched by man	45
Primitive	some buildings, only of wilderness character	4
Canoe	remote and unconfined rivers	
Wild forest	extensive recreational activity	51
Intensive use	campgrounds, launching areas, parking areas	
Wild, scenic, and recreational rivers	varying degrees of use, impoundment, access from 'wild' to 'recreational' category	
Travel corridors	intensive linear areas of development	

(iii) *'Developments of regional impact'* (DRI). Major development schemes such as harbours, airports, canals, industrial parks, and energy generating stations create costs and benefits that extend well beyond the immediate area in which they are situated. The ALI code aims to transfer much of the design and planning of such schemes to the state level since local authorities do not (or legally cannot) always take cognisance of the wider implications when limiting or rejecting proposals. The code also wants the states to regulate 'developments of regional benefit' (DRB) (usually proposals which are socially desirable but not necessarily wanted locally, such as low-income housing, regional waste-disposal systems, highways, etc.), again so that costs and benefits can be equitably shared.

Both are politically very contentious items. The Florida legislature all but killed the DRB idea and by a very narrow vote, though after adding a number of weakening amendments, it adopted the DRI proposal (including fragments of the DRB idea). The final policy does include a 'balancing' review of the social, political, and ecological factors of DRI on a case-by-case basis, though Carter (1973b, p.904) is worried that so much attention will be focused on the big cases that the small developments, whose cumulative effects will be substantial, could pass unscrutinised. He also notes (p.906) that the policy does not ask whether the DRI should be built at all (a serious omission in most planning studies), nor does it require that the DRI be located in accordance with a general state plan.

The Oregon Land Conservation and Development Act (1973) tries to resolve these difficulties by establishing both a Commission and a Citizens Involvement Advisory Committee (both of political appointees) to review (within a ninety-day period) and recommend whether certain activities of statewide significance should be permitted, and if so where they should be located. Little (1974) and McCall (1974) describe the political infighting that led up to the act, the evangelical state senator, the charismatic governor, the narrow-minded local interests, the currying of favour in the state legislature through day-long seminars, and the participation of vociferous citizens groups. In the end the Act left most of the decisionmaking authority at the county level, though it won in return a performance guarantee for all subdivisions (subject to independent review), a law limiting to two the number of representatives of the real estate profession on local planning commissions, the protection of agricultural reserves through special tax concessions, and compensation (subject to hearing and appeal) for those losing financially as a result of the DRI–DRB reviews.

(iv) *Alternative growth scenarios.* The Florida and Oregon stories illustrate the problems facing environmental planners who genuinely wish to combine social justice with environmental protection. Because power is unevenly distributed, the result is inevitably a politically distorted compromise, but at least it is a compromise which recognises certain basic environmental principles. In many ways the case histories of these two state efforts make more interesting reading than the utopian vision of the California Tomorrow Plan (Heller, 1971), prepared by California 2000, an organisation supporting guided growth. Nevertheless this document is valuable in that it indicates various growth options for the state and how they can be achieved (see figure 4.5).

It is perhaps the operational aspects of this proposal which are most interesting, because the authors pinpoint the weaknesses in present planning politics which must be overcome if guided environmental growth is ever to become a reality. One of these requirements is a substantial shift of power from central governments to regional commissions fed by a great variety of citizens consultative panels (whose members would be elected through new electoral procedures). This requirement also means policies aimed at improving the equality of distribution of social services and environmental quality through dispersal of job opportunities and the use of a state 'livability' fund. (This would be financed out of revenues gathered from amenity compacts, TDS, PUD, DRB, and the like if the community accepts the revolutionary notion of 'amenity rent'.) The plan also involves guided growth through zoning, open-space designation, the phased provision of services, and the Spaceship I type of incentives to reduce energy and materials demands and limit the emission of residuals.

Oregon used the same device of alternative growth scenarios as a means of alerting the public to the consequences of present growth trends in its study of the Willamette valley. Two 'futures' were prepared in detail, one assuming continuation of present policies and the other a pattern of guided growth. In the former, the study concluded that there would eventually be no open land or recreational areas of any size, and the cost of administrating the necessary local government would be enormous. As to the latter scenario, the study described clustered settlements and high speed transport links and well-integrated open space, but at a cost.

Problem	California I	California II
Obsolete governing institutions	continue fragmentation	regional decentralisation
Inaccessibility to citizen	increase centralisation	provide political strength
Maldistribution of welfare	more economic growth	public service jobs
Regressive tax structure	increase taxation	create farms, small industry
Inadequate finance	federal assistance	minimum working wage
Inadequate control of environmental disruption	more regulation	statewide ecological zoning plan protection of critical environmental areas
Population growth	incentives to disperse population	zero population growth policy
Scarcity of amenity resources	centralised regulation	regulations and incentives to guide growth
High consumptive patterns	use of 'corrective' prices	use of 'corrective' prices

Figure 4.5. Growth options for California. (Source: Heller, 1971, pp.110-111.)

"Individuals would have to sacrifice that dream of a single family house out in the country and the independence of the automobile to go everywhere" (McCall, 1974, p.8). The study, called 'Project Foresight', was converted into an exhibition as part of the successful public relations process leading up to the Land Conservation and Development Act. But whether people will pay the 'cost' when they are actually presented with the bill remains to be seen.

The idea of growth scenarios is now catching on elsewhere. It was used very effectively as part of a participatory regional planning exercise in central British Columbia (J. O'Riordan, 1976) to highlight the financial, social amenity, and ecological consequences of different patterns of growth, and, incidentally acted as a really valuable educational instrument in raising public awareness of the politics of planning (see chapter 7, pp.255–263). In Britain, the Structure Plan could be adapted to display alternative growth futures, though at present, unfortunately, statutory requirements tend to restrict the final plan to a single document. Nevertheless some imaginative long-range planners are embarking on this formidable task; proposals are currently being prepared in Berkshire and Hertfordshire.

The ALI code involves a revolution of political values that will not come easily or quickly. Carter (1973a) reports on the political infighting that has consistently blocked the proposed US Land Use Policy and Planning Assistance Bill, a piece of legislation that is based on the ALI principles and would require the completion of comprehensive state land-use plans as a condition of federal aid for regional development. At the time of writing (1975), this important bill remains in political stalemate. Whatever compromise is finally reached will reflect the balance of environmental and development forces likely to shape much of the American landscape over the next decade.

Alonso (1973) and Godwin and Shepard (1974) analyse the social-justice aspects of guided-growth plans more critically. All three are anxious to prove that in the current political climate the poor will always lose; for the battle is among power holders, development interests, middle class environmentalists, and liberal advocates for the poor, all of whom, they claim, are interested in maintaining the *status quo*. As Alonso (1973, p.197) observes:

> "This situation brings about strange alliances between, for instance, business groups and minority people, or ecologists and tax leagues. These same conflicts and contradictions are mirrored within many people, who traditional liberals, find themselves unable to reconcile their environmental interests with their concern for social equity."

They all conclude that regional growth plans should explicitly incorporate redistributive policies, including some sort of tax-sharing arrangement to compensate those who are disadvantaged by guided-growth programmes.

This of course means political organisation of the politically weak through what Godwin and Shepard (1974, p.26) term 'substantive measures' in place of the largely procedural features of most state plans today, and takes us into the realm of participatory planning and design (see chapter 7, pp.261–263).

4.6 Regional carrying-capacity studies

The culmination of the regional environmental plan is the carrying-capacity study (an idea drawn from range management), which tries to calculate just how many people the ecological systems of a given area can accommodate. The first planner to make use of the idea was McHarg (1969), though his methods were rather iconoclastic and arbitrary and certainly somewhat crude (see Gold, 1974). A more sophisticated version of McHarg's environmental design was devised by the ecologist Howard Odum (1971), a scientist who has devoted most of his life to the study of energy flow and utilisation in ecological systems. Odum was the first to apply the theory of energetics to human systems by means of computer analogue models based on cybernetic concepts. He quickly recognised (a) that all human settlements are enormously energy intensive (Manhattan requires 4000 kilocalories per square metre per day while a preindustrial settlement uses only 40), (b) they are maintained only because of massive energy 'borrowing', an arrangement that obviously cannot be indefinitely sustained, and, (c) as settlements grow they require more and more energy simply for maintenance. [L. Peterson (1974) estimates that the energy flow of a large American city rose from 400 kilocalories per square metre per day to 4000 between 1960 and 1970.]

These findings are based on two controversial principles drawn from ecological theory: (a) that organisms seek to maximise their efficiency of energy utilisation and (b) that there is a definable optimal use of environmental resources known as the carrying capacity. Ecologists do not agree on these two premises; some believe that ecological systems merely optimise energy flows at levels which in some respects can be quite wasteful and conclude that the carrying capacity is a highly variable figure depending upon the species studied and the flux of environmental conditions. For example, Gifford (1971, p.2) believes that Odum's work on ecological energetics is simply "a massive quantification of the obvious [that is] depressing in the extreme", though he applauds a "constructive alliance" with systems theorists to review the real needs of the human community.

Nevertheless, Odum (1971) has taken these two debatable assumptions and has devised a procedure for calculating the carrying capacities of regions through the energetics accounting device. The long-range goal of the regional plan is to obtain an annual or periodic output of energy equal to the amount that can be produced during the same period without permanently impairing long-term productivity, ecosystem integrity, or the quality of the land, air, and waters and their environmental values. An example of an energetics model for the state of Oregon is depicted in figure 4.6.

The real 'net cost' of an additional shopping centre or boat marina is the sum of all the energy needed to construct, maintain, and operate the facilities and resulting services, plus all the energy requirements of people travelling to and from such an activity node. On the assumption that everything can be costed in energy terms, then alternative scenarios for land use policies can be evaluated.

Energetics can be used to estimate the 'ceiling' population of an area on the assumption that it needs a certain minimum standard of living and activity mix. A pioneering effort at calculating the limiting population of the Pacific Northwest has been made by a study team working for the Pacific Northwest River Basins Commission (1973). The team first tried to assess the components that make up an essential minimum quality of existence based on various sociological and ecological best estimates. Their findings appear in table 4.7 and relate of course to the mythical 'average family'. The team then attempted to calculate the cost of achieving 1965 levels of air and water pollution (judged to be acceptable standards for today's public) given a 'feasible' level of residuals reduction (80% compared with 17% today) and a gross regional product (GRP) large enough to provide adequate economic comfort and control residuals (figure 4.7). An ingenious device was used to illustrate the energy and resource dependence of modern American affluence. This is the servant machine—the equivalent of one man's labour to produce part of his

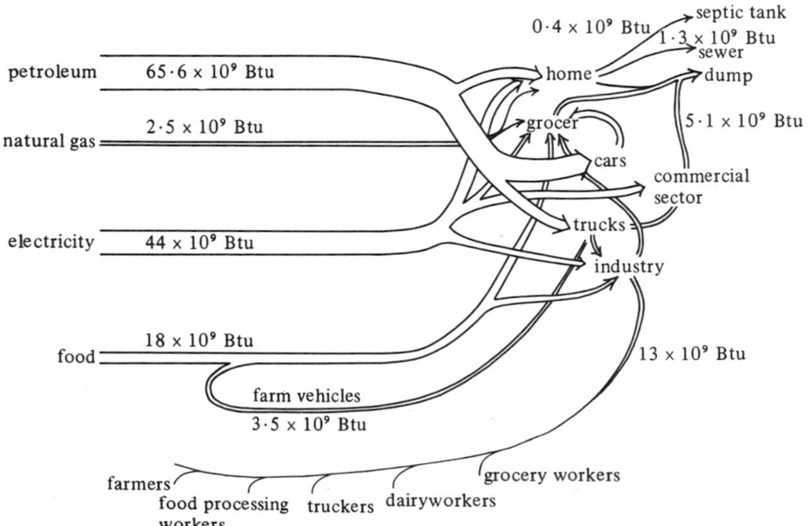

Figure 4.6. A simplified energetics model for food production and consumption—Oregon. (Source: Oregon, Special Projects Branch, 1973, p.13.)

Table 4.7. The minimal quality of life for an American. Figures used represent preliminary subjective estimates. (Source: Pacific Northwest River Basins Commission, 1973, p.93.)

Human needs		Means to satisfy needs (average annual *per capita* budget)															
		Food	Clothing	Housing	Transportation	Health	Education	Clean air	Clean water	Solid waste disposal	Quiet	Attractive surroundings	Recreation	Open space	Savings, misc.	Government (except 14 items)	Totals
1 Physiological	%	70	50	50	30	50	10	20	20	20	25	10	10	10			28
	$	672	225	600	210	160	38	30	32	22	40	13	40	32			2114
2 Security	%			15	15	20	30	10		10	10			20		65	21
	$			180	105	64	114	15		11	16			64		975	1544
3 Social	%	20	20	15	20	10	15	20	30	30	25	20	30	15	30	10	18
	$	192	90	180	140	32	57	30	48	33	40	26	120	48	168	150	1354
4 Ego	%	10	20	10	15	10	15	20	20	30	20	20	30	15	30	10	15
	$	96	90	120	105	32	57	30	32	33	32	26	120	48	168	150	1139
5 Self-fulfillment	%		10	10	20	10	30	30	30	10	20	30	30	40	40	15	18
	$		45	120	140	32	114	45	48	11	32	65	120	128	224	225	1349
6 Totals	%	100	100	100	100	100	100	100	100	100	100	100	100	100	100	100	100
	$	960	450	1200	700	320	380	150	160	110	160	130	400	320	560	1500	7500

annual requirements. The team assumes that one man can produce \$250 worth of goods and services unaided per year, so he is dependent upon (*per capita* GRP − \$250)/\$250 servant machines for his comfort. The average American requires 13 such 'machines' compared with 8·5 for a Swede, 8 for a Canadian, 5·6 for a West German, 2·8 for a Japanese, 2·3 for a Russian, and a mere fraction for an Indian. Even with a Spaceship I economy, the predictions are that 37 servant machines will be required for each individual in the study area by 2000 and that environmental tolerance limits dictate that the maximum tenable population for the region would be 9 million (assuming each would require \$9500 *per capita* income, 1965 dollars, from a GRP of \$85 billion). This compares with a 1972 population of 6·6 million and a GRP of \$23 billion, and a projected population of 12 million and a GRP of \$160 billion by 2020, assuming a continuation of present trends. Using estimates of recreation carrying capacity the study suggests that the maximum number of tourists should not exceed another 2 million annually.

Clearly this report is illustrative and exploratory, not didactic or alarmist. Nevertheless, by relating human aspirations for a minimum quality of life to indices of environmental tolerance, the study does

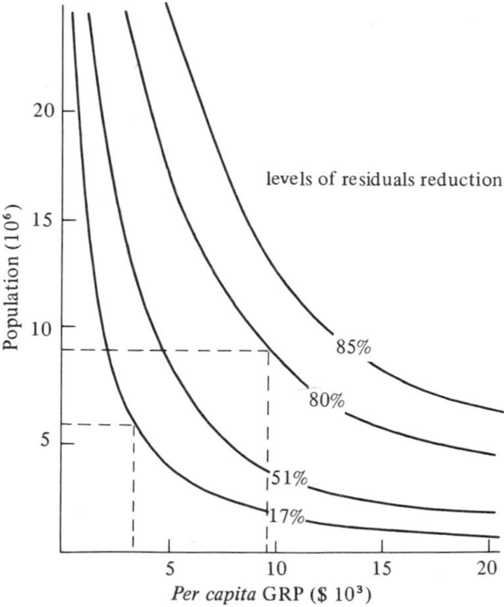

Figure 4.7. Population—resource 'ceilings' for the Pacific Northwest. Depending upon the level of residuals reduction and the politically acceptable 'benchmark' of living standards, the 'maximum' population for the state can be determined. With no improvement in residuals reduction, only a population of six million can be sustained at present living standards. With 80% reduction in residuals, nine million people can be 'accommodated'. (Source: Pacific Northwest River Basins Commission, 1973, p.58.)

highlight the critical interdependence between man's pleasure-seeking nature and his dependence on natural systems. Personal fulfilment cannot be found in an unstable ecological setting. The study obviously requires greater refinement (for instance in providing better measures of tolerance and disaggregating all data to the subregional level), but it provides a useful tool for political discussion about growth guidance. The Florida legislature has recently passed a law requiring that carrying-capacity studies of the kind described above be completed for a number of major areas in the state.

Westman and Gifford (1973) have proposed a scheme that would link the carrying-capacity idea to the Spaceship II model. They suggest that every individual and firm be granted a certain allocation of 'natural resource units' (NRUs), the total number of which would be fixed in relation to carrying capacity tolerances and the characteristics of use. All production and consumption would be determined through trading of NRUs according to a white-market pricing structure. The scheme is rather fanciful and fails to take into account the data limitations and dangers of political manipulation inherent in any rationing mechanism which is subject to bureaucratic discretion. But it should be reassessed rather than discarded, for in principle it faces up to the need to equate human aspirations with ecological limits and sociopolitical reform.

The *Population Watch* studies, the new breed of regional models now being prepared for the Club of Rome (Mesarovic and Pestel, 1975) and the refinement of *Blueprint* all coalesce around the theme of regional and national carrying capacities. There is no doubt that as these become more sophisticated they should be very powerful tools for national economic analysis and policy formulation, though a question mark must still hang over the political ramifications of their findings. Unless they are very sensitively prepared such studies could lead to an imposition of ceilings on growth and immigration that might cause much unnecessary suffering.

The measurement of environmental quality

It is only during the past fifteen years that economists have come to realise that the traditional microeconomic theory of Pareto optimality does not satisfactorily deal with the problem of externalities. The very term 'externality' indicates that economists have treated such events as incidental or peripheral to the production process. Early theories (e.g. Coase, 1960) assumed that such misallocative effects could easily be made good if the transacting parties would agree either to bribe or compensate one another according to the merits of the case. Fischer and Kerton (1973) and Fischer (1975), however, rightly suggest that the compensation theory is not satisfactory. Negative externalities (bads) are as technically integral to the economic production of goods and services as the products (goods) themselves (see also Kapp, 1970). A more relevant price–quantity relationship, therefore, should take the bads fully into account (figure 5.1), for optimal allocation of resources should reflect the *joint production* of goods and bads. Fischer and Kerton correctly emphasise that the extent of the production of bads is not properly known. This is partly because negative spillovers are difficult to measure and in any case are not completely 'perceived' by recipients (see chapter 6, pp.216–227), though it is also in the interests of those providing the goods and services to conceal the evidence or deliberately misinform the public and the relevant policymakers.

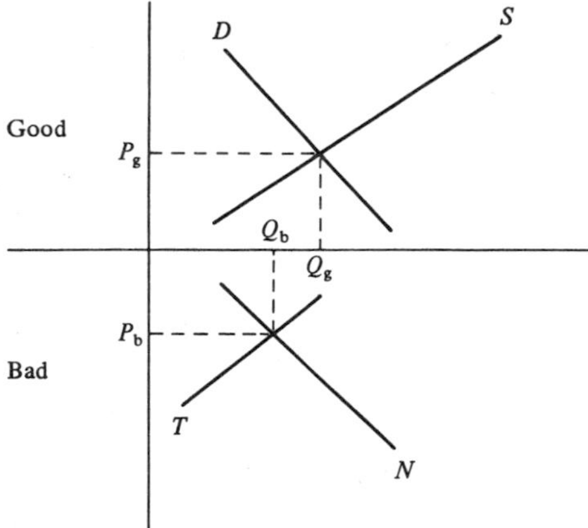

Figure 5.1. Goods, bads, and economic production: *D*—demand curve for good, *S*—supply curve for good, *N*—nuisance residual linked to production/consumption of good (not fully known), *T*—tolerance for nuisance (subject to political, social, psychological factors), Q_g—quantity of good supplied, Q_b—quantity of bads supplied, P_g—willingness to pay to consume good, P_b—willingness to pay to avoid bad. (Adapted from Fischer and Kenton, 1973.)

Economists and other social scientists are therefore intent on improving theory and methodology in order to measure the 'bads' and to discover how they are 'perceived' (see chapter 6, pp.216–227) and to assess how concealed and dubious information affects the policymaking process (see chapter 7, pp.230–241). I shall devote the rest of this chapter to the question of measuring the production of bads. (For good reviews, see Coomber and Biswas, 1973; Emmett, 1974.)

5.1 The principle of compensation variations

Coase's (1960) theorem of interparty compensation was based on the principle that property rights were necessary to determine liability and damage (see *Natural Resources Journal*, 1973b). The establishment of these rights was regarded by Coase as costless, as were negotiations which decided the direction and size of the compensatory payments. The only apparent issue to be resolved was how much and by whom the compensation was to be paid. But Coase's theorem only applies to a two-party case where property rights are well-defined. The real world does not often provide such simple examples, for multiparty transactions are involved, property rights and social obligations are not clearly defined, nor are assessments of gains and losses in utility which determine the size of compensation or bribe to be transacted.

Imagine, for example, two people in an enclosed space, one wishing to smoke, the other preferring a smokeless atmosphere. Standard microeconomic analysis would resolve this question on the grounds of what Mishan (1974b, p.61) calls 'compensation variations' (CV). If the nonsmoker is willing to pay, say 10 units for clean air, while the smoker is willing to accept say 8 units as compensation for the psychic suffering of abstinence, then the algebraic sum of the CV is $(+10-8)$ or $+2$. In this case if the nonsmoker pays the smoker, he is still better off, while the smoker is no worse off. This condition should satisfy the criteria for Pareto improvement of mutual welfare.

Before we discuss the question of who should compensate whom, it should be stressed that most calculations of compensation (or bribery) implicitly assume a model of rational economic man who can put a final and absolute price on anything and thus can pinpoint when his 'satisfaction' is maximised. In practice, this person does not exist. Faced with the opportunity of accepting payment for any sort of disamenity, the 'rational' individual will demand the largest possible sum he/she calculates can be extracted; for to part with any imagined rights to amenity most people will play for high stakes irrespective of what they might subjectively value the loss really to be worth. This is why compensation becomes such a politically manipulatory tool in modern day environmental politics.

But who is to compensate whom? At issue here is the lack of proper legal protection for amenity, a matter to which Mishan (1967, pp.36–42) has devoted much attention. Continuing with the two person smoking–nonsmoking example, the size and direction of the CV will depend on the individual's status in law. Should the law permit smoking then the nonsmoker must bribe the smoker who, knowing this situation, is likely to bid up his price on the grounds that his rights are being denied. If, however, the law only permits smoking on the basis of mutual consent, then the nonsmoker can extract a bribe from the smoker larger than he would be willing to pay the smoker not to smoke (again because he feels his rights are being infringed). In other words the direction and size of the compensation variation depends ultimately on the status of amenity rights, and, as we have noted in both chapters 3 and 4, amenity rights do not formally exist for most common property resources. By issuing consents for effluent discharge (following formal notification to 'interested' parties, or a public hearing), pollution control authorities grant dischargers legal rights to pollute, against which no third party has redress under the law unless he can show undue injury. Similarly, by granting a development permit, the planning authority offers certain rights to the new property owner against which *nonadjacent* property holders have no legal means of redress. (A central theme of the takings debate, discussed in chapter 4, is to grant nonadjacent third parties rights of appeal before the final plans are accepted.)

In the absence of any legally defensible amenity rights, individuals who cannot prove undue or special harm must suffer disamenity, however unintentionally created, without recourse to the law. Hence the arguments by Schelling (1971) and Mishan (1974b), that net social welfare is steadily deteriorating because of worsening communal negative externalities, which society would willingly pay to avoid but lacks the legal and political mechanisms by which to do so. Negative spillovers are, in effect, legally sanctioned and collectively subsidised, since any individual endeavouring to avoid these diseconomies is faced with very high transaction costs (defined as costs of avoidance, costs of legal redress, or costs of gathering the necessary political support) which can be expected far to outweigh his personal compensation variation (see Demsetz, 1967).

So present legal arrangements for determining the nature of property rights and the size and direction of compensation favour the powerful against the weak and development interests over ecocentrists. Mishan (1967, pp.36–42) and Goldie (1971) believe that the law should recognise citizens' amenity rights, so that those who experience disamenity of any kind would be legally entitled to compensation. "The guiding maxim I would offer" (Mishan, 1974b, p.80), later remarks, "is that it is more important to prevent avoidable suffering than to create further opportunities for self-indulgence. For this reason I favour the enactment of a charter of amenity rights of the citizen, inspired by the slogan 'No pollution without compensation'."

This proposal is quite compatible with both Spaceships I and II, since it would force all nuisance-generating activities to pay social costs or 'clean up', and implies that common property resources enjoy a social amenity 'rent' and can be 'used' only upon appropriate payment. This is quite revolutionary because it counteracts centuries of legal thinking which has been geared to encouraging economic growth and protecting private property. The amenity rights that exist today relate to private ownership not to the commons. For this reason it is unlikely that the Mishan suggestion will be accepted in full, though, as was made clear in the previous chapter, there have already been a number of changes in the law of property rights to improve environmental equity.

5.2 Reform of benefit–cost analysis

The growing interest in the measurement of externalities has caused a number of economists and other social scientists to reassess the benefit–cost accounting technique. In my previous book (O'Riordan, 1971a, pp.31–43) I considered some of the misgivings about this controversial evaluative device and suggested some areas for improvement. Since then benefit–cost accounting has waxed and waned in popularity, though variations of it (such as cost effectiveness and program budgeting) are still in common use (see Mishan, 1971d; Pearce, 1971; Wolfe, 1973). Nevertheless, many liberal economists agree with Schumacher (1973, pp.43–44) that benefit–cost analysis simply cannot do what it claims to do, namely take into account and balance all the distributional outcomes of any proposal, both in time (among present and future generations) and space (i.e. over people and places). Others, such as Adams (1972), feel that no matter how sophisticated and ingenious its computations, benefit–cost accounting can only lead to absurdly distorted conclusions, because the nature of the judgements that must be made defies 'technical' economic analysis. Limitations imposed by lack of data, inadequate predictive capabilities, or inability or unwillingness to calculate the full extent of distributional impacts restrict the validity of the technique. Even with thoughtful refinement, benefit–cost analysis can only at best be a guide to political choice, but some recent improvements are worth reviewing.

5.2.1 The inclusion of multiple goals

A serious criticism of the benefit–cost technique has been its single-minded devotion to the paradigm of efficiency by aiming to maximise net social benefit, usually defined in terms of net national economic welfare. This dangerously ignored many other legitimate political aspirations such as regional economic growth, income redistribution, and the protection of environmental quality. The theory of multiple objectives was tackled initially by M. Hill (1968) and developed by Major (1969) and Freeman (1969), but it is Hill who has put the idea into practice (Hill and Tzamir, 1972; Hill and Shechter, 1973). Recognising that multidimensional objective functions do not resolve intergoal conflicts, he produced a series of benefit–cost accounts (which he later aggregated) based on specific assumptions linked to goals which he weighted to reflect political priorities. He admits that these critical goal weightings should be determined along political lines and that they should change as political values modulate. This procedure has the advantage of incorporating political analysis into the benefit–cost account at an early stage (and indeed throughout evaluation) and encourages both politicians and the public explicitly to recognise the varying distributional outcomes of reaching different goals. Hence benefit–cost analysis can be used as part of participatory design. Hill's method could easily be incorporated into the alternative growth scenarios discussed in the previous chapter, for each scenario could be 'costed' and transformed into a regional development plan for public discussion. A typical example of the multiple objective function is depicted in figure 5.2.

The idea of using differing scenarios in benefit–cost accounts as part of participatory planning was first developed in the United States by the Corps of Engineers in their study of the Susquehanna Basin (Borton and Warner, 1971; Howe, 1971, pp.109–111). The Corps chose three major goal 'clusters'—national economic efficiency, regional development, and environmental quality—and devised three alternative plans and the corresponding benefit–cost accounts to suit (see table 5.1). The goal clusters were adopted by a coordinating committee and translated into plans by the engineers. The aim was to make the efficiency proposal the baseline 'least cost' alternative, and to compare the other two with it. [This comparative device was employed by Cicchetti (1972) in his partial equilibrium evaluation of the various alternatives for transporting Alaskan oil, although he admitted later (Cicchetti, 1973) that the effort was rather fruitless since political events dictated choice irrespective of economic calculations.]

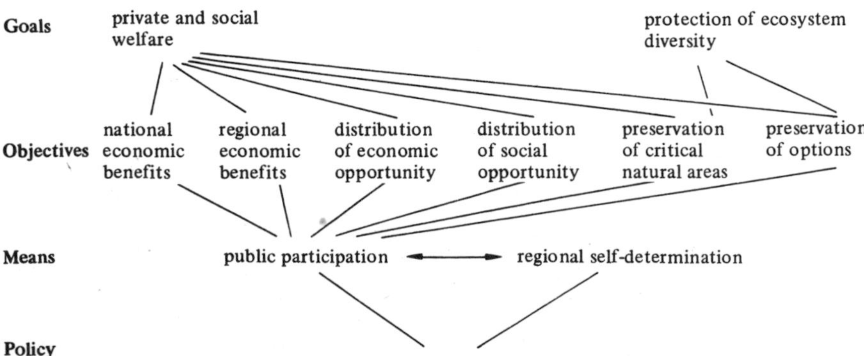

Figure 5.2. The multiple objective function in benefit cost appraisal. (Based on Hill and Shechter, 1973.)

The problem with the comparative approach is that it does not break clear from the efficiency criterion as the 'best' outcome, nor does it provide any accounting scope for compromise mixes of objectives which would presumably shape the final plan. The Corps have subsequently attempted to remedy these defects through public discussion of the goal clusters and of alternative designs for each goal mix, before any formal accounting is attempted (see Krouse, 1972; Shabman, 1972; Eigermann, 1974). In effect this means that the planning of resource management

Table 5.1. Multiple goal benefit-cost accounts for the Susquehanna river basin. (Source: Howe, 1971, p.112.)

Project type	Economic efficiency plan		Regional development plan		Environmental quality plan	
	number of projects	annual cost ($1000)	number of projects	annual cost ($1000)	number of projects	annual cost ($1000)
Reservoirs (major)	9	7805	14	16820	5	8040
Reservoirs (minor)	49	3900	94	5180	57	2635
Groundwater well fields	5	1465	3	565	7	2340
Diversion pipelines	1	2420	1	2420	1	2420
Diversion sewer lines	...	...	...	...	...	...
Advanced waste treatment	4	540	3	290	6	770
Mine drainage watersheds	2	610	3	5310	3	7260
Land treatment, 10^3 acres						
agricultural	995	2370	995	2370	995	2370
forest	735	775	735	775	735	775
pastureland	630	2210	630	2210	630	2210
reclamation	21	1055	21	1055	21	1055
Bank stabilization	...	...	...	...	...	...
Local flood protection	...	...	4	125	1	100
Floodplain management	moderate		low to moderate		moderate to intense	
Low (channel) dam use	...		moderate in one subbasin		moderate to substantial	
Small urban recreation	...	...	...	...	30	+
Total cost		22750		37120		29975

schemes is much more a political exercise than an econometric one. In British Columbia, the Okanagan Basin Study (J. O'Riordan, 1976) went even further in incorporating public opinion in the appraisal of multiple goals in the planning design, making benefit–cost analysis all the more a participatory tool.

These studies serve to underline the principle that any form of benefit–cost accounting should involve proper public evaluation and continuous political participation if it is ever to come to grips with the wide and long-term evaluation of externalities. In fact Coy *et al.* (1973) feel that democratic decisionmaking and 'social equality' should become explicit objectives of future benefit–cost accounting in addition to the three traditional goals already cited, though they feel that these should be revised to reflect new political attitudes about growth and environmental quality. The inclusion of these two new objectives would certainly help to clarify many of the distributional effects of resource projects which at present are not adequately covered.

5.2.2 Interest rate calculations

The choice of the appropriate discount rate with which to compare future costs and gains with alternative expenditures of present value funds has long been a bone of contention among economists. Howe (1971, pp.65–70) observes that economists fall into two groups over the matter of discount rates: (a) those who believe the rate should represent the pretax rate of return foregone on investments in the private sector when funds are transferred to public projects (i.e. it should reflect the opportunity cost of private capital with a range from 11 to 18%); and (b) those who think that the rate should reflect society's wish for 'leaving something for the future' rather than developing everything now (i.e. it should reflect society's time preference and a hedge against uncertainty with a range from 3 to 8%). Herfindahl and Kneese (1974, pp.204–221) provide an excellent theoretical discussion of these two views and conclude, not surprisingly (p.221), that "a simple average of the governmental bond rate (not exactly a precise concept in itself!) and the relevant private rate would be too low in view of the magnitude of private investment, but in the absence of a clearly better approach would be justifiable. At least", they add, "it has the virtue of simplicity."

Very small changes in the discount rate have a substantial effect on the benefit–cost account, especially if long term effects are valued highly (figure 5.3). Clearly the discount rate is a delicate political issue and one of great concern to environmentalists, who believe that traditional economic accounting does not, and cannot, properly incorporate potentially irreversible environmental damage. In practice, governments have permitted ludicrously low discount rates in relation to the private cost of capital, largely because powerful resource development lobbies favoured cheap resource exploitation at the 'cost' of environmental quality. Drew (1970) describes the political horse-trading that determines the allocation of US Corps of Engineers projects, while Berkman and Viscusi (1973, pp.83–89) show how the US Bureau of Reclamation deliberately encouraged the low discount rates even when they recognised that a higher rate would be appropriate. Even the US Water Resources Council (1971), in recommending a rise to 7% for the period 1972–1977, admitted that a rate of 10% would reflect more closely the true cost of borrowing capital. Economists (e.g. Haveman, 1970, p.70; Hanke, 1972b) are almost unanimous in urging governments to adopt the higher figure, but as yet to little avail.

Haveman (1965) brought attention to the fact that the use of a single interest rate cannot properly be justified since the economic characters of cost and benefit streams differ. With the adoption of multiple-objective functions, some economists now advocate the use of multiple discount rates to reflect different social time preference functions for each goal cluster. For example Marglin (1972, pp.18–20) feels that there should be a range of high discount rates for the regional growth objective (say 5 to 10%), medium rates for national economic development (2·5 to 7·5%) and low rates for environmental amenity (0 to 5%).

Krutilla (1967, 1971, 1973) and his RfF colleagues (Cicchetti and Freeman, 1971; Fisher and Krutilla, 1972; Fisher *et al.*, 1972; Krutilla and Cicchetti, 1972; K. Smith, 1974; Krutilla and Fisher, 1975) have devoted considerable time to developing a new theory of amenity evaluation based on the theoretical principles of option value and weighted discount rates. Their work centres on the proper economic evaluation of potentially irreversible environmental disruption, for instance the loss of a unique national asset or the destruction of a biotic habitat, such that alternative use of the resource in question is quite impossible. Option value is defined as a benefit accruing to an individual as a result of his retaining an option to consume the resource at some time in the future; in effect, it is a premium for risk avoidance, an additional willingness to pay in order to safeguard an environmental amenity from possibly irretrievable loss.

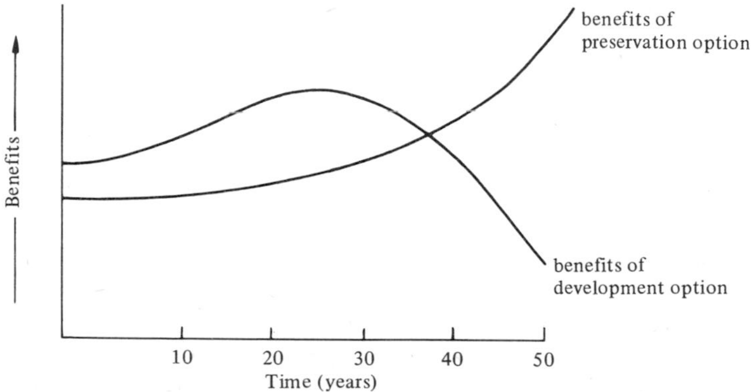

Figure 5.3. Time streams of benefits for the development and preservation option.

Krutilla and his coworkers assume that, given a choice between development and preservation, the public would be willing to pay a surcharge for the environmental service of the preservation option by lowering its discount rate and raising the discount rate for the development alternative. This conclusion is based on the fact that any technological option can be replaced by alternative technologies or will become obsolete owing to technological innovation. Both effects serve to shorten the time horizon of the benefits accruing to the 'development' alternative. [In the Hell's Canyon study, Krutilla (1971) estimated that the annual rate of technological progress would be 4 or 5%.] Because ecological amenity resources cannot be substituted and since they become scarcer as resource exploitation proceeds, Krutilla postulates that a materially affluent public will value environmental quality more highly in the future. In other words, because of economic growth and technological innovation, the marginal rate of substitution between the development and the amenity objectives will shift in favour of protecting amenity while the production possibility function between the two will expand in favour of the development alternative (figure 5.4). From this reasoning Krutilla concludes that the 'preservation' alternative should benefit from a 'negative surcharge' in the discount rate to reflect the longer time before its full benefits are realised.

The problems facing the Krutilla team are enormous. To begin with, it is very difficult to be sure of irreversibility. Even if the magnitude of certain effects can be postulated, so little is known of ecological systems, especially their 'threshold' levels and their 'resilience', that calculations of long-term damage have to be hedged. Then there are the equity questions. The amenity alternative inevitably values highly the demands of those whom Olson *et al.* (1973, pp.231–233) describe as 'ecofreaks' who are not content with anything less than ecological 'purity'. Despite the laudable

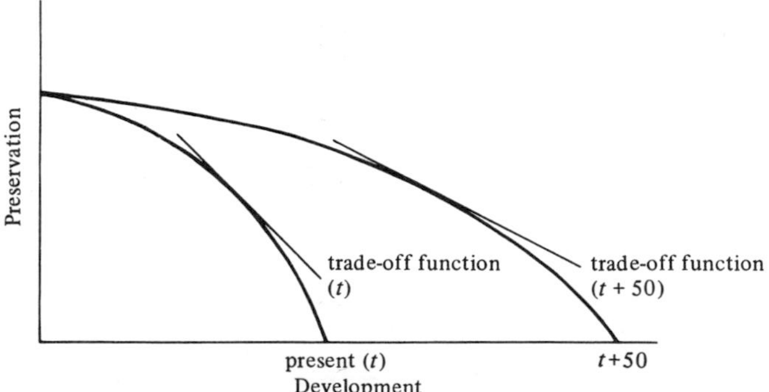

Figure 5.4. The production possibilities frontier for development versus preservation in a technologically innovative economy. Over time the willingness to protect irreplaceable environmental assets increases, as more and more produceable goods and services are required to 'pay' for the irreversible loss of unique areas and experiences.

intentions of the ecofreak, we must consider the cost that he may be imposing on the rest of society in achieving his objective. To choose the preservation option in one place may simply transfer disamenity elsewhere. For instance, in the Hell's Canyon example, the preservation alternative assumes that some other energy generating scheme will be constructed in place of the hydropower dams proposed for the Snake River. Krutilla (1971, pp.199–200) calculates the net benefits of the development alternative (the hydropower scheme) as being the difference in net cost between it and the cheapest power alternative. If this is a thermal plant, then in the absence of proper externality accounting, people suffering the additional disamenities from, say, a coal-burning plant, plus those who must live beside the ripped open landscape where the coal is mined, could be subsidising the option values of the environmental purists. Thus one man's psychic gain may be another's psychic loss. Who is to decide?

It is perhaps worth recording that Krutilla and his colleagues personally value wilderness very highly, so it is difficult for them to be entirely objective in their analyses. The use of the positive and negative surcharges to represent the 'annual weight of technological progress' and 'the social value of amenity', respectively, quickly load the benefit streams of the two alternatives in favour of the preservation option. While the principle of a discount variation is justified, Krutilla's figures assume a constant annual rate of technological innovation of 4% and a constant rise in society's valuation of recreational amenity also of 4% per year (in real terms) over the accounting period. A 1% variation in the latter changes the estimation of the benefits of the preservation option by between 39 and 49%. It is possible he could be erring as much on the preservation side of his calculus as the development proponents have overestimated their case in the past.

While Krutilla's bias is toward the natural wilderness, Krieger (1973) feels that uniqueness and irreproducibility are technocentric concepts that can be designed as much as imagined by man. Few visitors to the Niagara Falls realise that the Falls are artificially supported by careful injections of grout and that in any case the flow of the river is regulated. Without this costly intervention the limestone parapets would collapse naturally, resulting in a far less spectacular sight. Krieger's point is that artificial 'uniqueness' (such as Disneyland, Tivoli Gardens, and other carefully planned recreation sites) can be so designed as to attract large numbers of people, thereby lessening the pressure on the true natural assets. These latter can be protected more by careful environmental planning than by value-laden benefit–cost analyses.

But Krutilla's work serves a useful purpose in that it highlights the different time horizons of various development alternatives and focuses attention on the importance of indeterminacy in environmental accounting.

By urging caution and more scrutiny of what for too long have been interpreted as 'ephemeral' issues, his studies provide a valuable theoretical contribution to the ecocentric evaluation of resource management.

5.3 The evaluation of environmental quality

The measurement of qualitative and effective phenomena has always been a bit of a headache for social scientists. As will be discussed in chapter 6 (pp.216–227), individual and group evaluation of such things as beauty, fresh air, noise, fumes, and congestion cannot be precisely determined because people themselves are not very specific about their likes and dislikes. The best the researcher can achieve is a reasonably reliable and rationally consistent appraisal of environmental quality using a variety of 'neutral' indicators (or surrogate variables) which try to minimise any distortion resulting from the research design. But no device, no matter how carefully thought out, can overcome the inherently contradictory psychological and social processes which cause any assessment of environmental preferences to be trustworthy only within the narrow confines of the inquiry.

5.3.1 The use of property prices

Many economists and planners like to use changes and patterns of property value as useful surrogate measures of external amenity or disamenity, and point to obvious differences in property values in areas of high and low environmental quality to prove their case. While most of this work has been related to the dispersion of property prices due to disamenity effects, recreational economists have used the escalation of land values around new recreational sites (artificial lakes, national and state parks) to calculate part of the economic gains accruing from recreational land use decisions (see Schutjer and Hallberg, 1968; Epp, 1971; Tombaugh, 1971; Wennergren and Fullerton, 1972). For example, Beardsley (1972) reports that increases in land values at the perimeter of Cape Cod National Seashore account for over 70% of national economic benefits associated with the area. Similar work has been done for the Olympic National Park (Byers, 1970), and to justify expenditures on local parks, golf courses, and the preservation of open space. Studies in Elizabeth, New Jersey, and Oakland, California, showed that, compared with other property nearby, land adjacent to a new park more than doubled in value and held its price. The Oakland report concludes: "Not only do parks influence assessed valuations, they also have an effect on how residents perceive their neighbourhoods, and consequently a pride in the area is fostered by the presence of a park" (quoted in Council on Environmental Quality, 1974, p.69). It should be noted that incremental land value benefits are normally asymmetrically distributed to those who are already better off.

Looking at the other side of the coin, Hoch (1972b, pp.254–255) reviews a number of econometric studies which claim to measure the social harm of air pollution through the depression of property values.

Certainly there is plenty of evidence that property prices are negatively correlated with increases in pollutant indices. For instance, Ridker and Henning (1967) claimed that an additional 0·25 mg/100 cm^2 in the sulfation index would lower median house prices in metropolitan St. Louis by $250; Jaksch (1970) concluded that for every extra 20 tons of particulate matter per square mile per month, house values in Toledo, Oregon would drop in price by $580; and Anderson and Crocker (1971) estimated the elasticity of house prices with respect to air pollution in Washington, Kansas City, and St. Louis to be about −0·2. But these findings at best can only be crude estimates, since about three hundred air pollution monitoring stations are required to measure the spatial and temporal distribution of air pollution with any reliability, and most cities have fewer than ten. Then there are horrendous problems of statistical interpretation, particularly the problems of colinearity, since property prices reflect a bundle of multidimensional variables, such as accessibility, neighbourhood social characteristics, open space, greenery, the nature of the housing market (which in turn relates to employment opportunities and regional migration, to say nothing of the features of the actual building), only a few of which specifically relate to pollution. These kinds of complications have led the British to reassess their studies of the economic evaluation of air pollution, though the Americans have persevered. From table 5.2 it may be seen that about one-third of the estimated social costs of air pollution are attributable to depreciation in property values.

More work has been done on the effect on property values of noise, especially from motorways and airports (McLure, 1969; Flowerdew and Hammond, 1973; Starkie and Johnson, 1973, 1975; Troy, 1973; Whitbread and Bird, 1973; Walters, 1975). Figures 5.5 and 5.6 depict some of the calculations that are used to estimate who will be affected by new noise-generating schemes and to what extent. These are important diagrams because they form the basis for compensation paid to property owners immediately adjacent to such schemes, as for instance is now statutory policy under the British Land Compensation Act (see Flowerdew and Hammond, 1973). Diagrams such as these are also significant because of their ideological connotations. Many traditional economists expect

Table 5.2. The costs of air pollution in the United States. (Source: Council on Environmental Quality, 1973a, p.78.)

	1968 ($ billion)	1977 ($ billion)
Health	6·1	9·3
Residential property	5·2	8·0
Materials and vegetation	4·9	7·6
Total	16·2	24·9

that most people are willing to be 'bribed' to accept a certain degree of environmental nuisance. Walters (1975, p.126) criticises the British Treasury for holding back on a policy of openhanded compensation, since even large payments may still make the 'cheapest' alternative 'cheaper' than the next 'least expensive' alternative. Referring to the Third London

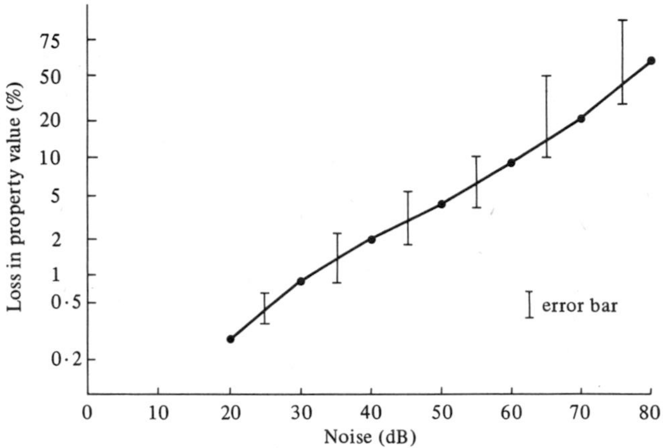

Figure 5.5. The effect of motorway noise on property values. Note the sharp discontinuity above 65 dB (A), the sound normally heard within 100 feet of a motorway of standard design. Road engineers aim to reduce the noise to 60-63 dB (A) to lower the cost of compensatory payments. (Adapted from Waller, 1974, p.100.)

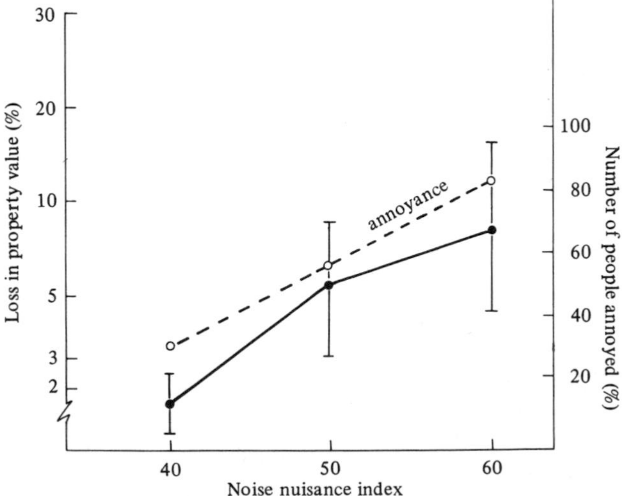

Figure 5.6. The effect of aircraft noise on property values. The bars represent ranges of property loss according to different locations. (Based on Waller, 1974, p.101.)

Airport issue, he comments:

> "... it is conceivable that compensation of the order of £25 million would have reduced the Cublington opposition to impotence if not enthusiastic support ... . The price system though apparently more expensive is in reality much cheaper than the politicial system."

Readers are urged to compare the account of the political activists' role in the Third London Airport dispute (Kimber and Richardson, 1974, pp.165–211).

It is precisely because property values are used so widely for the evaluation of noise and other disemenities that economists are anxious to demonstrate the conceptual inadequacies of this deceptively simple surrogate index. Mishan (1974b, pp.66–67) contends that the use of property prices is regressive since they only indicate the *relative* availability of amenity. The amount of compensation will depend upon the supply of amenity substitutes. The loss to a householder will be all the more serious if his home is in the last haven of real quiet, since any alternative site will be noisier. Though, other things being equal, the houses in the comparatively quieter areas will always command the higher price as noise becomes all-pervasive, house price differentials will remain the same even though the environment has deteriorated. Pearce (1972, pp.114–116) reformulates the traditional compensation model to incorporate an exponential increase in the value of absolute amenity as nuisance generally becomes more widespread. Basically this means placing an amenity premium on unaffected areas, though Pearce admits that this will distort compensatory payments in favour of the environmentally better-off.

Pearce (1972, pp.110–111) also claims that property values tell us nothing of the discomfort costs facing the individual who would like to move, but who is unable to do so because of occupational immobility or high transaction costs (including disruption of social ties) of migration. Noting that a Roskill Commission survey found that 8% of respondents declared that no compensatory payment would be sufficient to induce them to move, he adds:

> "The fundamental error lies in the unrecognised asymmetry between social costs which have associated monetary flows and those which do not. The decision to move house is based on the appraisal of *monetary* costs and benefits ... . Since noise annoyance costs tend to be almost entirely non-monetary ... it follows that the individual's *revealed* preference is highly likely in most cases to show up in favour of staying in the noisy area. His *actual* welfare position, however, has deteriorated."

Pearce also comments that property values underestimate disamenity effects, since prospective purchasers rarely have accurate information about all the nuisance elements of the location.

But the most damning criticism of the property price method is the built-in inequity of its calculation. Because more highly valued properties will lose more than less highly valued houses for the *same degree* of nuisance, the rich seem to suffer more (and hence tend to be compensated more) than the poor. This ignores the fact that the poor tend to be less mobile (even ghetto-bound) and hence must have a higher tolerance for disamenity in order to remain sane. In this connection, it is interesting to record Brodine's (1973, p.132) remarks that the individuals most susceptible to air pollution (i.e. the inner-city poor) are killed by a combination of personal illness and general environmental stress *at normal levels of air pollution*, so that their premature deaths are not recorded during serious air pollution episodes. The poor have to tolerate so many social and environmental indignities that they appear to respond only at much higher thresholds of disamenity than the relatively better-off. Neither house prices nor revealed preferences take these factors into account; if anything they tend to bias the evidence falsely in the opposite direction. In short, the unquestioned use of property prices as an index of amenity or disamenity, though widely used in environmental policymaking, tends to worsen the social inequities of environmental quality distribution to the benefit of those who already employ the politics of choice.

5.3.2 The annoyance index

Waller (1970, 1974) has been at pains to produce a neutral index of 'annoyance' to measure the relative impact of two or more incommensurable nuisance variables. He feels that techniques which try to measure willingness to pay fail largely because people find it impossible to estimate their welfare gains and losses in a hypothetical situation, and in any case are inclined to exaggerate their claims. It is so difficult for an individual to visualise the longer-term consequences of a bribe or a payment to improve his general amenity, even when the 'nuisance' is simulated either visually (Hopkinson, 1974) or aurally (e.g. by playing the recorded sound of motorway noise in a respondent's living room—see figure 5.7), for people tend instinctively to bias their judgements to their own advantage. So Waller adopted an annoyance scale, defined in terms of the percentage of people 'annoyed' at various levels of nuisance, to calculate expected social response to a number of disamenity effects. An aggregative function, he feels, has the advantage of levelling out individual variation, and can be used to calculate compensatory payments for single or multiple disamenity 'shocks'. At the same time it can help to indicate politically acceptable environmental quality performance standards for all kinds of nuisance generating facilities (figure 5.8).

The idea of aggregating annoyance indices into multivariate disamenity standards has been adopted by the Greater London Council (1974) in its efforts to quantify the public nuisance caused by traffic. The GLC is particularly interested in the likely public reaction to new transport schemes, and figure 5.9 gives some idea of the annoyance thresholds used for four disamenity variables associated with traffic, namely noise, pedestrian delay, carbon monoxide, and fumes. The GLC hoped to produce 'annoyance standards' which would form the basis of new traffic-scheme designs, but its various political subunits (the boroughs) do not

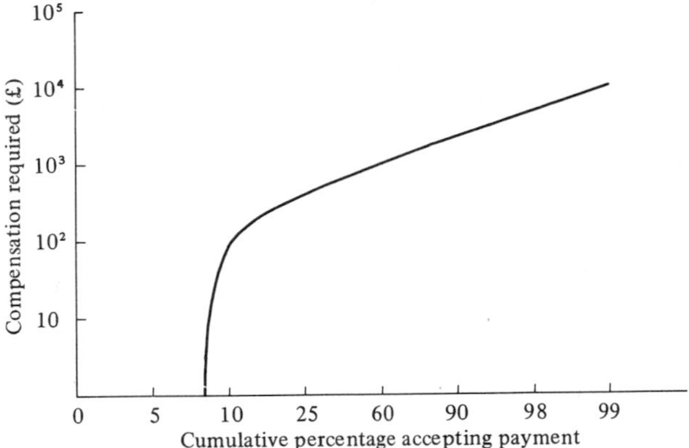

Figure 5.7. Willingness to be bribed to accept noise, given a 70 dB(A) median noise level indoors. The horizontal axis is based on a cumulative percent log scale. [Source: Waller (1974), p.96. Reprinted with permission from the Scottish Academic Press.]

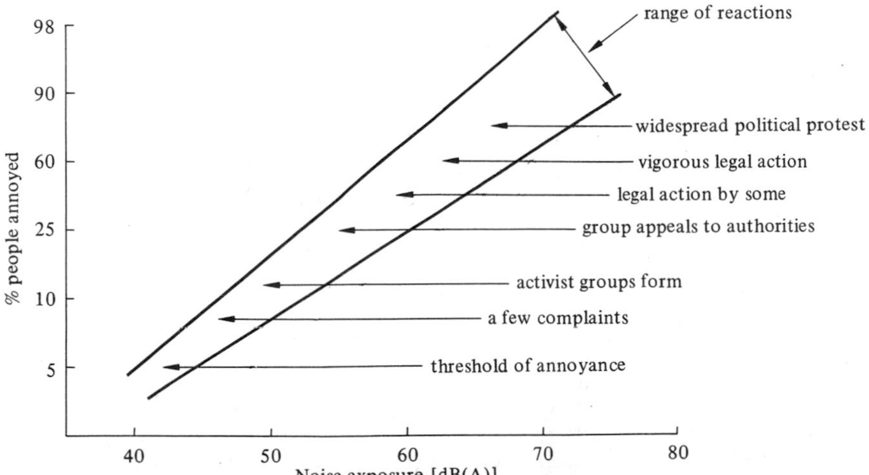

Figure 5.8. Community response to varying degrees of 'annoyance'. The vertical scale of annoyance is adjusted to accommodate a straight line response function. The function is largely descriptive, for there is a wide range of response depending upon particular circumstances. Note that the variation of response tends to increase with the level of annoyance. (Based on Berry, 1974, p.235.)

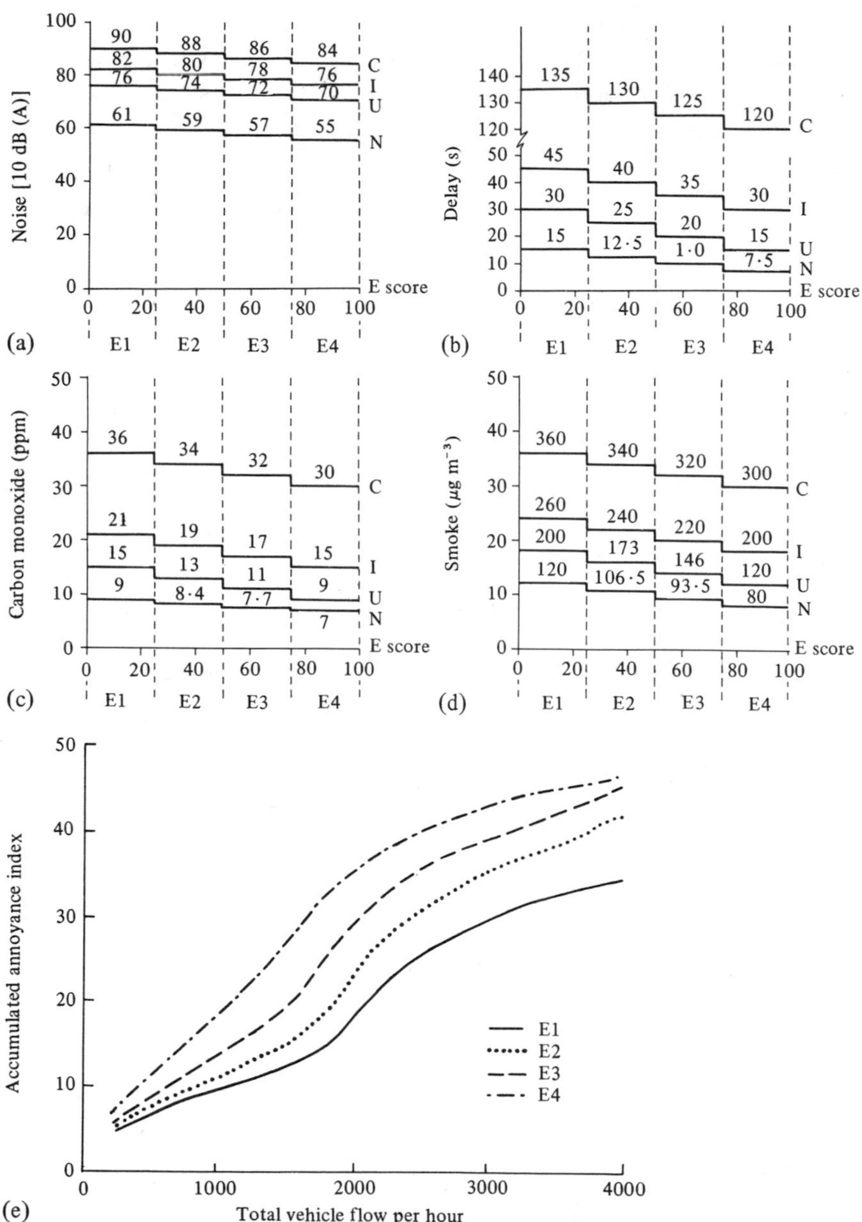

Figure 5.9. Aggregative index of traffic generated nuisance. The annoyance thresholds for four nuisance factors are estimated: (a) noise, (b) pedestrian delay, (c) carbon monoxide, (d) smoke, for each of four levels, C—severe; I—highly undesirable; U—undesirable, and N—noticeable. These are then aggregated into cumulative indices for four classes of road according to 'environmental vulnerability' on a scale of E1 to E4 (e). Environmental vulnerability relates to such factors as road width, associated land uses, and adjacent areas and buildings of amenity. (Source: Cassidy, 1976.)

agree over these threshold indices largely because of the variation in the socioeconomic characteristics of the populations and the existing distribution of noise from borough to borough. So no coordinated environmental quality plan for traffic management in the Greater London area has yet emerged.

The problem with the annoyance scale is that it is terribly difficult to calculate empirically with any reasonable reliability. Literally thousands of research tests would have to be conducted using various kinds of nuisance both singly and in combination in order to cover the required range of individuals and circumstances. A second difficulty is that 'annoyance' can only be interpreted in terms of direct sensory perception and prevailing cultural norms. Many environmental nuisances are not always perceived or widely recognised (for example toxic metals, chemical compounds, and certain gases) and so cannot be recorded. In addition, annoyance levels will change with time and conditions and probably do not fully reflect synergistic effects.

A third difficulty, and one common to all externality measuring techniques, is the propensity to aggregate *people* rather than deal with specific *individuals*. The annoyance index can only work if individual variation is diminished to a collective range of variance. So any policy decision or performance standard can ignore the possibly severe distress facing a particular individual. Not only do people vary enormously in their evaluation of nuisance but they tend to assess risk in terms of danger to *others* not to themselves (Starr, 1969). Burton *et al.* (1976) refer to a study of responses to a possible atomic bomb blast in Chicago. Though shoppers in the downtown loop estimated it would kill 97% of the city's residents, only 2% were prepared to admit that they, too, would die.

The ultimate 'nuisance' causes death; but how does one value one's life? The value of someone else's life is a matter of much actuarial interest, but it fails to include the pecuniary 'flavour' of self-assessment. Reviewing this aspect rather whimsically, Adams (1974b, p.623) observes that it is all a matter of scale and degree of risk: "If the planner can manage to spread the expected deaths over a population to reduce the individual risks to negligibility, no compensation will have to be paid at all." His point is that growing economic scale and bureaucratic centralisation are drawing the price of life downward. Because the likelihood of mortality from a particular hazard-generating activity for any given individual becomes increasingly improbable, almost any scheme is possible (and almost any normal level of pollution tolerable) even though policymakers know that some martyrs will definitely die unrecorded. Where do you place yourself in figure 5.10?

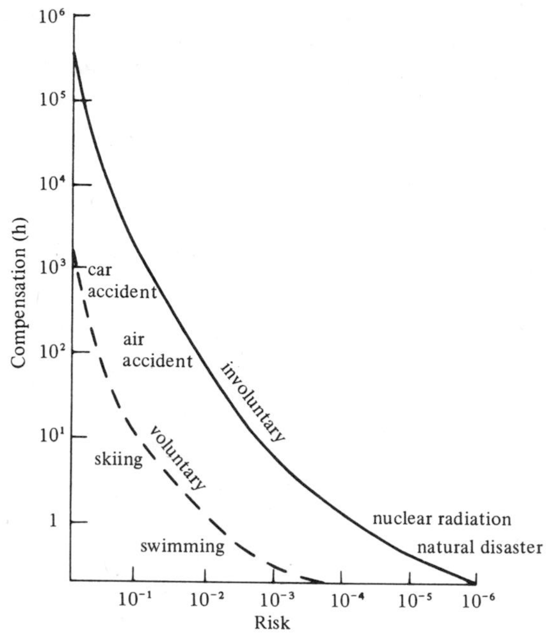

Figure 5.10. Risk and the valuation of one's life. The two curves differ depending on whether the risk is voluntarily or involuntarily undertaken (car and air accidents straddle the two). Generally, people accept voluntary risks more than involuntary ones. Starr (1969) believes the difference between the two curves could be as great as 10^3. (Based on Starr, 1969, p.1234; and Adams, 1974b, p.622.)

5.3.3 The priority evaluator

An ingenious method of soliciting the ranking of amenity preferences of individuals has been developed by a working group in Social and Community Planning Research under the direction of Hoinville (1971, 1975). Broadly speaking, Hoinville simulates a multidimensional trade-off matrix in which subjects allocate their amenity preferences under the constraint of limited 'amenity capital'. To begin with, each player is presented with a number of illustrated scales depicting progressively improving levels of environmental quality. Each set of pictures illustrates one particular environmental variable (noise, fumes, access to parks, etc.), and each illustration is priced (figure 5.11). The player is asked to identify his present situation on each scale, the points on which are summed to represent his existing amenity capital. Then he reallocates his capital to illustrate the situation he would most prefer. In so doing he is forced to make sacrifices, thereby choosing his amenities according to his own priorities. The prices on each amenity variable should approximate estimated community costs for achieving the relevant amenity standard, but this may be very difficult to calculate properly as there may be a variety of secondary and distributive costs involved. Nevertheless careful research should produce reasonably accurate figures, which, when linked into the matrix can show both players and planners the relative 'costs' of achieving incommensurable environmental amenities.

Hoinville calls this trade-off array a priority evaluator, for its primary function is to reveal the hierarchy of an individual's environmental preferences through the neutral medium of illustrated scales. The device can be converted into a game by transforming the prices to a number of pegs or dots which the player can attach to the images of his choice.

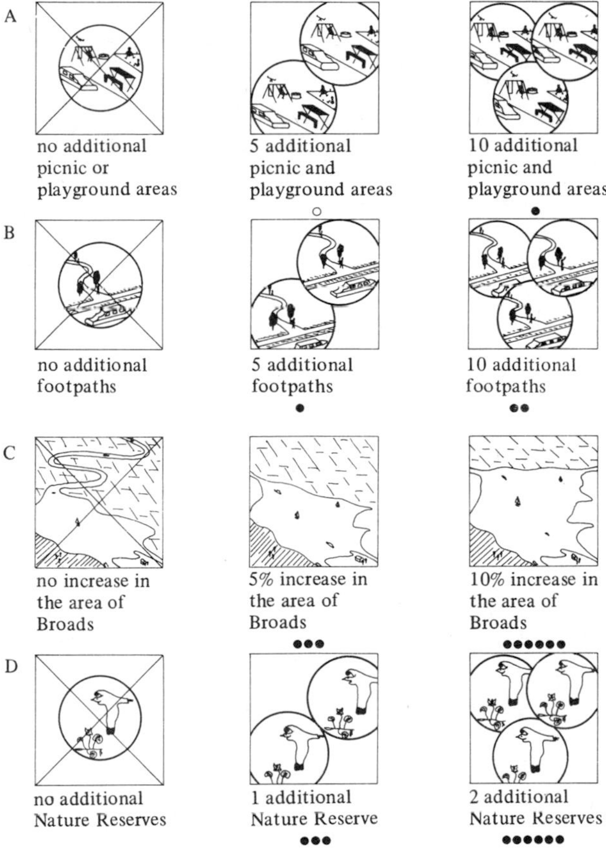

Figure 5.11. The priority evaluator. This is an example of the kind of planning choices that are available to improve the recreational carrying capacity of the Broadland region in England. To obtain an indication of how a sample of boat users would rank these options, each respondent is given a limited number of dots (the closed dots equalling £5000 and the open dots equalling £2500 in capital expenditure, maintenance, and operation over twenty years, or an additional 50p or £1 respectively per week on an average hire charge of £60) which he must allocate among the amenity choices provided. The total of dots attached to each picture represents the cost necessary to achieve the objective. (Printed by permission of Susan Southwell.)

Having experimented with the technique in a number of situations, Hoinville reports a reliable and consistent response from most participants. The device has great potential, for it can be used to compare how different socioeconomic groups in similar environmental circumstances allocate their preferences, or how particular individuals change their environmental priorities over time as they become more familiar with a new neighbourhood or as external conditions change. The technique can also be applied to activity groups, who would be expected to reveal some of their preferences through specific behavioural choices (for example, the type of recreational activity), to test the relationship between preference arrays and observed behaviour. The device has also great educational advantages, since it helps to make explicit the content and value of sacrifices that people instinctively make without the benefit of full multidimensional comparison. Thus they may be made more aware of what economists call their marginal rates of substitution among valued commodities. In a sense the evaluator is an illustrated version of Kelly's (1955) repertory grid test for measuring cognitive constructs, though it avoids much of the repetitive tedium of his technique.

Nevertheless the game, for all its potential, does have several limitations. First of all, it can only be used for individuals and cannot be aggregated to reveal community preferences. Second, it is really only effective if everyone evaluates his present situation similarly, otherwise the trade-offs become confused by the different starting points and amenity capital of each player. Third, the images are preselected and predefined pictorially, which may well restrict a player's preference array. Certainly the selection of the scales and the prices can influence the final results. Fourth, the device is a 'game' in the sense that no commitments are made and players are never faced with actually spending money and experiencing changes in their situation. Fifth, it only reveals valuable information about marginal trade-offs once the individual has achieved a reasonably balanced mix of desirable factors. 'Lumpy' investments to eliminate severe deprivations can distort the trade-off arrangement. Sixth, the game is limited by the player's experience and his understanding of the interactions among a wide range of incompatible variables. Intellectually, emotionally, and socially disadvantaged groups will experience a lot of difficulty with the game, and of course the really deprived groups in amenity terms will be virtually unable to play at all since they have very little amenity capital to allocate.

In sum, the priority evaluator offers a lot of promise for planners and educators in helping them to understand how individuals evaluate intangibles, but it still requires more refinement and careful testing in a variety of situations. One possibility would be to increase or decrease the available amenity capital to see how priorities change under tighter or slacker constraints. (In fact this might even be developed to simulate demand curves.) Another variation would be to ask the player to allocate his/her own amenity capital (i.e. play with the number of pegs or dots of his or her own choosing) but informing him/her that each unit of capital is worth so much of his/her total income. This is a version of the bidding technique in willingness-to-pay studies, where the respondent is offered a series of bribes or charges and requested to indicate how far he/she is prepared to go (see Davis and Knetsch, 1966), with the advantage that the player has more idea of what he/she is getting for his/her expenditures. Nevertheless the evaluator cannot be used beyond its fairly palpable limitations, and therefore should be employed in conjunction with a number of other useful techniques for soliciting community preferences. Simulation games such as the 'Aquarius' water management game (Kasperson and Howard, 1972), the community politics experiments of Swan (1970, 1971b), the participatory design techniques devised by Nicholson and Schreiner (1973) and the British *Bulletin of Environmental Education*, and the idea of problem-solving task-forces (Prince, 1970) are but some of many consciousness-raising mechanisms to assist political and educational awareness in a variety of environmental situations.

5.3.4 Recreational carrying capacity

A particular kind of disamenity measurement that has been the subject of intensive research over the past ten years is the psychological tolerance of recreationists to crowding and/or interactions with people with different recreational values. This work began with the pioneering study by Lucas (1964) who discovered that motorboaters and canoeists differed markedly in their definition of what constituted the 'wilderness', and that the canoeists sought sanctuary from the motorboaters whose activities they regarded as incompatible with their values. Lucas (1973) found generally that different categories of recreational user have different spatial as well as contextual perceptions of wilderness, and that they tend to zone themselves into separate areas so as to avoid contact with each other. This led to a quest for a sociometric index of wilderness purism that was first developed by Hendee *et al.* (1968), subsequently modified by Stankey (1973), and then further refined by Heberlein (1973b) who produced the unexceptional finding that wilderness enthusiasm or disinterest can be simply measured along a scale running from fascination with nature to fascination with the human artifact.

Despite the disagreement over the wilderness scale, the fact remains that recreationists display a marked intolerance when coming into contact with other recreationists following the same of different pursuits (see figure 5.12). Stankey and Lime (1973) review the voluminous literature on this subject, and Cicchetti and Smith (1973) and Menchik (1973) suggest possible mathematical models to compute the probability of interaction among different users to derive a reasonably accurate predictive index of congestion. The carrying-capacity studies demonstrate that recreational capacity is very much a function of management policy, for much of the frustration can be avoided by zoning access, restricting numbers through licensing or rationing, directing users to different areas, and generally guiding like-minded people toward each other (Hendee and Lucas, 1973; Lucas, 1973; Stankey *et al.*, 1974) (table 5.3). This may sound

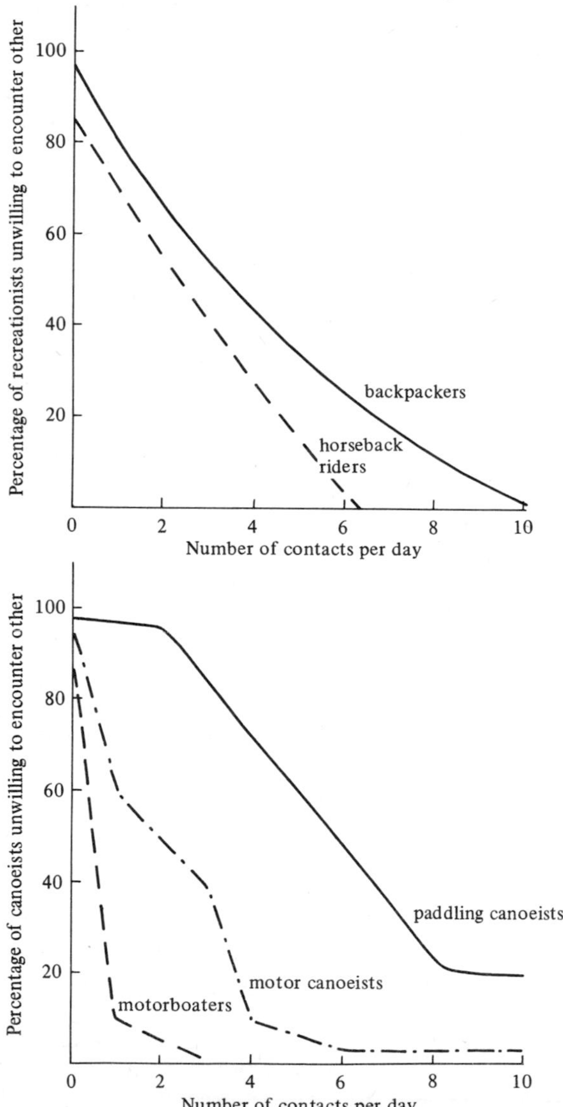

Figure 5.12. Tolerance for recreational interaction. Wilderness purists are more tolerant of other 'compatible' users (especially conoeists) and very intolerant indeed of 'incompatible' users (especially motorboaters). The infrequent encounter with a 'friendly' user often increases recreational satisfaction. (Source: Stankey, 1973, p.25.)

complicated, but in fact great gains in user satisfaction can be made at relatively little management cost—provided that both managers and users are made more fully aware of each other's points of view.

This communicative component in carrying-capacity assessment has been developed to an advanced level by means of a computerised information-retrieval system evolved by Clark and Stankey (1976) which records and codes all user comments made in the area in question and those made at public hearings or in local newspapers by politicians, etc., for subsequent assessment. This should help to overcome the noticeable gulf that divides manager from user in many areas of recreation policymaking, for example in wilderness use (Hendee *et al.*, 1968; Peterson, 1974a), forestry management (Hendee and Harris, 1970; Twight and Catton, 1975), and camping (Clark *et al.*, 1971), a gulf that can influence the sensitive management response that carrying-capacity studies show is so necessary.

Table 5.3. Visitor attitudes (percentage favouring adoption) to management options for improving recreational carrying capacity. (Source: Stankey, 1973.)

Managerial options	Boundary Waters Canoe Area $N = 206$	Bob Marshall $N = 120$	Bridger $N = 144$	High Unitas $N = 154$	Wilderness 'purists' $N = 248$
Portages to lakes presently inaccessible	73	-	-	-	74
Wilderness rangers	70	58	68	67	63
Wooden bridges across large rivers	-	67	65	62	57
More maps and pamphlets	60	52	60	55	54
Canoe rests	51	-	-	-	43
Signs indicating camping places	-	52	30	26	31
Simple pit toilets	63	43	22	25	28
More high quality trails	37	35	31	35	26
More campsites	46	22	16	15	17
Zoning recreational activities	13	20	19	21	-
Limiting party size	-	30	70	40	-
Rationing by reducing trail access	24	11	24	14	
Permits on arrival					28
Permits by lottery					18
Permits by reservation					43
Permits for designated camping					8
Entrance charge					23

Table 5.4. Recreational activity clusters. Note the relatively small number who participate in active pursuits. (Drawn from data supplied by Parks Canada.)

Canada		Quebec	
People consuming no recreational type	19·1%	as for national survey	17·9%
People who only drive for pleasure	15·3%	as for national survey	18·4%
Picnicking and driving for pleasure	13·2%	as for national survey	13·6%
Sight-seeing, picnicking, visiting parks, historic sites, driving for pleasure	11·5%	swimming, driving for pleasure	10·3%
Swimming, picknicking, driving for pleasure	16·9%	swimming, picknicking, driving for pleasure, walking	10·3%
Swimming, picnicking, visiting parks, sight-seeing, driving for pleasure	7·4%		
Sailing, climbing, walking-hiking, tennis, picnicking, sight-seeing, swimming, driving for pleasure, visits to parks	13·2%	swimming, photography, driving for pleasure, picnicking, walking, visiting parks	13·9%
Participated in all activities mentioned	3·4%	as diversified activities	6·2%

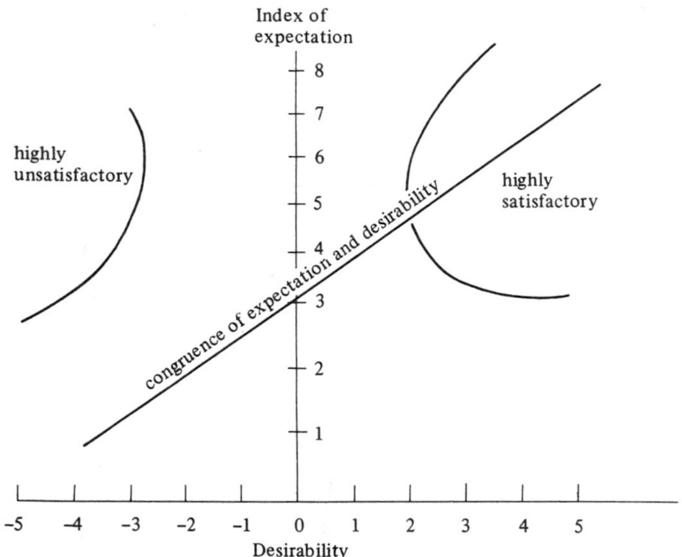

Figure 5.13. Evaluation of recreational experiences by perceived probability of occurrence. The diagonal line represents the congruity between the expectation of a recreational experience and its desirability. Departures from that line indicate a more or less satisfactory experience depending upon the relationship between probability and desirability. Naturally, recreation managers would like to maximise the probability of recreational experiences in the upper right hand area. (Based on Peterson, 1974b, p.184.)

Nevertheless much work still needs to be done to improve our understanding of carrying capacity. There is as yet little information about the cultural antecedents to recreational choice, why people choose certain activities and clusters of activities (table 5.4), what values they bring to them and how these values shape their expectations, and how these expectations are altered by the 'reality' of their actual participation. It is possible that tolerance to crowding and activity mix (and willingness to accept certain policy decisions) is closely associated with the complex relationship between expectation and reality, a linkage that remains tantalisingly hidden from our intelligence. Peterson (1974b) has made a useful contribution by asking users to relate the desirability or undesirability of large numbers of recreational experiences to their (the respondents') perceived probability of occurrence (figure 5.13). Thus he acquires some statistical index of the likely annoyances and unexpected frustrations, the frequent pleasures and the unanticipated delights. But he is still a long way from finding what 'mix' is truly satisfactory (if such an 'ideal' exists).

5.4 Environmental impact evaluation

The famous Section 102(2)(C) of the US National Environment Policy Act (NEPA) created environmental history by statutorily insisting that "every recommendation or report or proposal for legislation and other major Federal actions significantly affecting the quality of the human environment" must be accompanied by a detailed statement on

"(i) the environmental impact of the proposed action,
(ii) any adverse environmental effects which cannot be avoided should the proposal be implemented,
(iii) alternatives to the proposed action,
(iv) the relationship between local short-term uses of man's environment and the maintenance and enhancement of the long-term productivity, and
(v) any irreversible or irretrievable commitments of resources which would be involved in the proposed action should it be implemented."

The legal interpretation and political implications of '102' statements will be discussed at length in chapter 8 (pp.282–290); here we simply look at what form the environmental impact statement (EIS) has taken and its role in evaluating spillover effects in resource management. In principle, the legislation offers a free hand to environmentalists and developers to include and compare all conceivable outcomes (ecological, social, economic, psychological, and political) of any policy (including major technological innovations and military programmes) or specific proposal of reasonable scale undertaken by the federal government. Thus the perfect EIS should be the perfect environmental evaluation. Naturally, Section 102 quickly caught the excited attention of environmentalists the world over (and of course environmental consultants), who are now pressing for similar evaluation directives in other countries. The Council on Environmental Quality (1974, p.401) notes that twenty-one states and Puerto Rico have already passed legislation similar to NEPA and of these, thirteen states (and Puerto Rico) have adopted the EIS provisions. As outlined in chapter 4, some states now explicitly require comprehensive environmental evaluations for land-use plans of regional or even significant local importance.

In Canada the picture is more complicated, since the federal government has no constitutional authority to force environmental assessment reviews onto the provinces (Gibson, 1970; Thompson and Eddy, 1973). It has, however, issued guidelines for such reviews for some of its own projects (but not policy programmes) initiated by a federal department or agency, or funded by federal grants, or which may create environmental effects impinging on adjacent American peoples and territory (O'Riordan, 1976a). But these are not comprehensive statements, nor are they necessarily made public, as public hearings are only held at the discretion of the attorney general or national and provincial legislatures, and so tend to be influenced by political pressures. In addition, full reviews will only be authorised at the recommendation of an internal (Environment Canada) assessment panel who will review preliminary environment 'prediction statements' prepared by the initiating body. What information finally gets to a public hearing is, therefore, very much a matter for speculation. Under political pressure the Canadian government has embarked on two massive independent environmental assessments of the Arctic oil and gas pipeline proposals under its Territorial Lands Act (1970) and the Northern Inland Waters Act (1971), though Lucas (1976) contends that the results of these hearings will have little statutory authority and will not be binding on the developing agencies. Several provinces are currently reviewing the desirability of the impact statement and it is likely that Ontario and British Columbia will both adopt fairly tough versions as a result of effective political lobbying by environmentalist groups.

In Britain, the Department of the Environment set up a two-man task force to look into the possibility of extending the development review procedure, which already exists under various Town and Country Planning Acts, to include comprehensive environmental assessments. Their interim report (Catlow and Thirlwall, 1975) is cautiously in favour of enlarging the review procedure, but only for very large-scale proposals (a point much criticised by environmentalists who would like to see substantive reviews of governmental policy precede such environmental impact assessments), but the authors are aware of the cost implications of such a recommendation given Britain's current policy of economic restraint in the public sector. Nevertheless, the government is under pressure from two legal action groups, the Lawyers Ecology Group and the UK Committee for Environmental Information (1975) to adopt the '102' type of review. In mid-1975 the Department sponsored an important conference on the methodological techniques of environmental assessment which will probably form the background to new Departmental guidelines to local authorities (see also O'Riordan and Hey, 1976).

Up until now few impact statements have been true evaluations in the sense that all the wider- and longer-term repercussions of a proper spread of options (including doing nothing) are weighed and balanced. In fact two major criticisms of the 102 review are (a) that it is usually 'tacked on' to a predetermined decision rather than being built into resource evaluation procedures from the beginning, and (b) that it only reviews 'proximate alternatives' (e.g. other route alignments or power station sites) and does not consider major departures of policy (e.g. a move towards a Spaceship I or II type of economy to reduce the need for many proposals in the first place). In fact there is some dispute as to whether an agency can adopt a 'nonaction' alternative. Anderson (1973, p.218) states that the legislative background to Section 102(2)(C) (iii) indicates that options which should be considered include "alternative ways of accomplishing the objectives of the proposed action and the results of not accomplishing the proposed action". But environmental lawyers (e.g. Grad and Rockett, 1970; Sive, 1971) insist that the crucial question of whether or not to proceed is rarely discussed at a sufficiently early stage. They also claim that agencies hide behind their briefs to execute policy in order to avoid appearing 'inactive'.

Some US states have widened the scope of the environmental impact statement to include effects on (a) 'human life' (Michigan), (b) 'beneficial and adverse aspects' (Texas and Wisconsin), (c) 'related state and federal action' (Minnesota), (d) 'measures to mitigate the impact' (California, Maryland, Massachusetts, North Carolina, and Virginia), (e) 'the growth inducing impact' (California), and (f) wider economic ramifications. The Michigan order calls for "where appropriate, a discussion of the economic gains or losses, including the effect on employment, income levels, property taxes and the costs of alternatives to the proposed action" (Council on Environmental Quality, 1974, p.403). The California legislation (the California Environmental Quality Act, 1971) requires that EISs be prepared for private developments as well as all governmental proposals of significant scale, and that provisions should be made for broad public involvement. Other states have widely varying mandates for public participation ranging from 'notification' to full hearings (*ibid*., p.406).

But the Council on Environmental Quality, which is authorised to review all impact statements, is still concerned (1973a, p.213; 1974, pp.409–413) about the quality of many of the statements and has recently issued fresh guidelines about the preparation of such assessments (1973a, pp.416–439). Partly this is a problem of funds and trained manpower, not mendacity. The EPA along with a number of research institutes is currently preparing a variety of computer simulation models and data formats to assist local authorities in identifying environmental consequences (*ibid.*, p.410). Another review of methodology is provided by the Workshop on Impact Studies and the Environment of the United Nations SCOPE (Scientific Committee on Problems of the Environment) (Munn, 1975), which suggests that even more comprehensive and participatory procedures be adopted by all national and regional governments. It outlines the job of the environmental impact assessment as follows (Munn, 1975, p.34):

(i) Describe the proposed action (defined to include legislative proposals, policies, programmes, projects, and operational procedures) as well as alternatives;
(ii) predict the nature and magnitudes of the environmental effects (defined as a process set in motion or accelerated by man's actions);
(iii) identify the relevant human concerns;
(iv) list the impact indicators to be used (defined as measurable parameters of the magnitude of impact), for each define the magnitude, for the whole define the weights to be assigned as must be determined politically;
(v) relate (ii) to (iv) to determine the values of the impact indicators and the weighting of the total environmental impact (defined as the net change in man's health and well-being, including the well-being of the ecosystems on which man's survival depends, that results from an environmental effect and is related to the quality of the environment as it would exist with and without the same action);
(vi) make recommendations for one of the following
 acceptance of the project,
 remedial action,
 acceptance of one or more alternatives,
 rejection;
(vii) make recommendations for inspection procedures to be followed after action has been completed.

There are obviously enormous difficulties facing both those who must prepare and those who must judge impact assessments (for reviews see Leopold *et al.*, 1971; Ditton and Goodale, 1972; Webb, 1972; White, 1972; Fischer and Davis, 1973; Warner and Preston, 1973; Lyle and Von Wodtke, 1974; Morley, 1974b; Burchell and Listokin, 1975a; Munn, 1975). First of all there is the lack of an adequate data base pertaining to the existing state of the environment (both physical and human) from which to calculate impact (an example of the scope and level of information necessary is illustrated in figure 5.14). All too frequently agencies or their consultants are expected to produce an accurate picture of a regional ecology in a ludicrously short space of time (which can only lead to a wildly distorted interpretation), and then are asked to predict precisely what will happen if various project options are put into effect. Equally disquieting is the virtual vacuum of social and psychological information about public preferences and anticipated behaviour in the

ECOLOGY

Terrestrial species and populations
browsers and grazers (14)
crops (14)
natural vegetation (14)
pest species (14)
upland game birds (14)

Aquatic species and populations
commercial fisheries (14)
natural vegetation (14)
pest species (14)
sport fish (14)
waterfowl (14)

Terrestrial habitats and communities
food web index (12)
land use (12)
rare and endangered species (12)
species diversity (14)

Aquatic habitats and communities
food web index (12)
rare and endangered species (12)
river characteristics (12)
species diversity (14)

Ecosystems

AESTHETICS

Land
geologic surface material (6)
relief and topographic character (16)
width and alignment (10)

Air
odor and visual (3)
sounds (2)

Water
appearance of water (10)
land and water interface (16)
odor and floating material (6)
water surface area (10)
wooded and geologic shoreline (10)

Biota
animals—domestic (5)
animals—wild (5)
diversity of vegetation types (9)
variety within vegetation types (5)

Man-made objects
man-made objects (10)

Composition
composite effect (15)
unique composition (15)

PHYSICAL/CHEMICAL

Water quality
basin hydrologic loss (20)
biochemical oxygen demand (25)
dissolved oxygen (31)
fecal coliforms (18)
inorganic carbon (22)
inorganic nitrogen (25)
inorganic phosphate (28)
pesticides (16)
pH (18)
streamflow variation (28)
temperature (28)
total dissolved solids (25)
toxic substances (14)
turbidity (20)

Air quality
carbon monoxide (5)
hydrocarbons (5)
nitrogen oxides (10)
particulate matter (12)
photochemical oxidants (5)
sulfur oxides (10)
other (5)

Land pollution
land use (14)
soil erosion (14)

Noise pollution
noise (4)

HUMAN INTEREST/SOCIAL

Education/scientific
archeological (13)
ecological (13)
geological (11)
hydrological (11)

Historical
architecture and styles (11)
events (11)
persons (11)
religions and cultures (11)
"Western Frontier" (11)

Cultures
Indians (14)
other ethnic groups (7)
religious groups (7)

Mood/atmosphere
awe inspiration (11)
isolation/solitude (11)
mystery (4)
"oneness" with nature (11)

Life patterns
employment opportunities (13)
housing (13)
social interactions (11)

Figure 5.14. The scope of data requirements for environmental assessment. This is a kind of checklist devised by the Battelle environmental classification project. The numbers in brackets represent relative weights. (Source: Munn, 1975, p.65.)

event of a policy or a proposal being implemented. Usually all that can be done is a hasty public information campaign or a simple public opinion poll, both of which smack more of marketing research techniques than of sensitively handled consultative devices. In any case, this rarely gets round to outlining the differential impacts on various groups or reviewing major policy alternatives. Some systems ecologists (e.g. Odum, 1971; Watt, 1968, 1973; Walters, 1975) and regional scientists are preparing sophisticated simulation models to help planners evaluate the ecological consequences of different proposals, but the great danger here is that they may be all too readily believed, when at best they are presenting 'ball park' estimates based on a limited array of assumptions. The new breed of Club of Rome regional models and the proposed *Population Watch* scenarios face similar conceptual difficulties—even though they are in effect macroenvironmental impact statements. The fact is that ecological processes are not so well understood that outcomes can be forecast with confidence.

Then there is the very thorny question of weighting the findings. This clearly is a political issue, though there is some doubt whether even the most penetrating minds could satisfactorily evaluate a large matrix of interacting impacts, most of which are indeterminate and incommensurable. It is quite likely that national and local politicians view the idea of environmental assessment with much caution as they ponder the daunting prospect of 'balancing all the equities'. In addition, a comprehensive statement of the kind SCOPE would like to see might be a very sensitive political document, for it could reveal what the environmentalists press for but what politicians and many powerful interest groups wish to keep dormant, namely the maldistribution of environmental impact amongst the population at large. The American experience has demonstrated how '102' reviews energised environmental activist groups, liberal advocate planners, and many versions of environmental legal aid which some people might not like to see spread too far.

There is also the matter of training and procedure. Few agency personnel (and fewer decisionmakers) are trained to comprehend the complex trade-offs that must be made within and between impact statements. This requires coordination arrangements which are not readily found in large bureaucracies. Interagency and intradepartmental task forces are notorious for failing to reach a workable consensus, and for taking an inordinately long time to reach clear-cut policy decisions (see Downs, 1966). If the assessment is to come early in the proceedings, these very real administrative and group dynamics problems may well become insuperable without a major reform of bureaucratic mechanisms. How policy formulation institutions will respond to the unfamiliar multidisciplinary contextual and procedural demands of proper environmental reviews would make a fascinating study, for here all the problems of bureaucracy (secrecy, internal communications, the hierarchy of competence, responsiveness to nonroutine situations, consultation with interested parties) will be most thoroughly tested.

The environmental impact assessment is potentially the most exciting and challenging device for measuring and balancing incommensurables that has yet appeared. It focuses attention on all the techniques outlined earlier in this chapter, and raises several wider policy questions that have already been touched upon. For, to be truly effective, the impact evaluation must become part of the participatory design process, an evolutionary step that has major ramifications for administrative coordination, political choice, community involvement, and educational reform which will be analysed in the concluding chapters of this book.

Environmental cognition

Cognition is the all embracing process by which man separates himself from his environment, conceptualises it, and behaves within it according to his own inner logic. Man and nature are not, and cannot, be one and the same, for man is a thinking, feeling, and purpose-seeking organism to whom his surroundings are something 'apart'. Tuan (1974, p.14) characterises three cerebral levels of cognising environments: (a) *the reptilian brain* which drives man to pursue vital instinctive urges, including security, shelter, food, territory, and the formation of social hierarchies (for protection and order), (b) *the primitive (limbic) brain* which feeds all the drives of emotion, from aggression and selfishness to compassion and altruism, and (c) *the symbolic brain* which characterises and codifies the seemingly confusing mass of environmental information that man must deal with during the course of his life into meaningful patterns that help to rationalise his subsequent behaviour. Man in all his cultural forms symbolises natural phenomena so as to cope with his world and come to terms with it. [This theme is well developed by Tuan (1968, 1970, 1971, 1972, and 1974), especially in the last two citations.] "Man is egocentric", states Tuan (1971, p.4), "the world he organises is centred on himself." But he adds that man is also ethnocentric:

> "Worlds, whether those of individuals or of cultures are made up of the perceived elements in nature or external reality: they are distorted by human needs and desires; they are fantasies. It is a paradox that human beings can live in fantasy yet not only survive but prosper. Fantasy is more than gratuitous daydreaming: it is also man's effort to explain, to introduce order to life situations that so often seem baffling and contradictory."

Tuan is echoing the conclusions of Wright (1947) and Lowenthal (1961) who demonstrated that man, propelled by his yearnings, can imagine his environments to be quite different from what they 'actually' are, and so attempts to mould them to his likes either physically or psychologically. Dubos (1968, 1970) warns of the very real dangers if technological man continues in his efforts to design the 'perfect' environment free of stresses and trauma, since he believes that diversified environments are essential to bring out the unexpressed potential of man and to cater to his basic biological needs. He comments (1968, p.239):

> "One can take it for granted that latent potentialities have a better chance to become actualized when the social environment is sufficiently diversified to provide a variety of stimulating experiences, especially for the young ... . By contrast, if the surroundings and ways of life are highly stereotyped, the only components of man's nature that flourish are those adapted to the narrow range of prevailing conditions."

Tuan (1974) observes that the seemingly inchoate nature of his environment, its apparent contradictions and structured inconsistencies, compel man to segment and differentiate environmental stimuli into discrete and opposing entities. Life and death, earth and water, day and night, north and south all become associated with natural and human characteristics that shape behaviour and determine architectural design. Churches, temples, palaces, castles, town squares, and even the simplest peasant hut are shaped to reflect the symbolic significance of opposing environmental elements and the deeply felt need for order and meaning which typify most of man's artifacts.

Why has man been so eager to design his surroundings with so much symbolism? From his exhaustive review of the attitudes of civilised man toward nature, Glacken (1967) concludes that three contradictory beliefs have dominated: (a) a recognition that man's actions are to some extent determined by his physical surroundings, (b) a knowledge that man is capable of causing ecological damage, and (c) a feeling that the earth was designed for him to use so as to improve his mind as well as his economic and social conditions. To master nature was to upgrade the essence of man; as man progressed so the earth would be 'cultivated' to even greater perfection. Civilisation was therefore regarded as the application of purposive order by which a pliable earth was moulded to satisfy man's needs. This mastery over nature, if not by technology and artifact, then at least by conceptualisation and symbolism, was always a driving element of environmental construing.

Tuan (1974, p.248) concludes that the ideal environment embodies the inextricable linkage of two fundamental but opposing attributes, (a) the order, harmony, stability, and purpose of the cosmos, symbolised by man's works, and (b) the apparent disorder but essential nurture of the garden, symbolised by wild nature and window boxes, birdsong in the countryside, the autumn leaf colours, or the annual salmon spawning. Environmental construing is the endless search for the unattainable ideal; for in our struggle to achieve order and control we threaten the very basis of our existence, the other half of our model environment that we arrogantly assume will always be there.

The consequence is that all cultures, regardless of their technology, exhibit a duality of thought and action toward nature. "Philosophy, nature, poetry, gardens and orderly countryside are products of civilisation", observes Tuan (1968, p.184), "but so equally are the deforested mountains, the clogged streams, and, within the densely packed walled cities, the political intrigue". Granted, there is plenty of evidence that preindustrial cultures expressed a love, even a worship of the land and trees upon which they depended. This 'I–thou' philosophy has encouraged many a modern environmentalist to romanticise the rhetoric of 'primitive' cultures and the simple rustic existence of bygone days. But there are grounds for believing that most, if not all, of these peoples caused environmental disruption on fairly massive scales, possibly inadvertently, possibly deliberately. Guthrie (1971) postulates that all civilisations desire to control their own destinies. Tuan (1968) records that the ancient Chinese cut down or burned large areas of forest to destroy the habitats of unfriendly animals and people, to clear the land, to fertilise the soil, and to provide the fuel. But they thereby created pretty severe soil erosion. Despite their professed reverence for nature, Farb (1968) believes that the precolonial North American Indians were equally destructive, killing more buffalo than they required and burning wide areas of prairie.

There is much discussion over the idea of 'prehistoric overkill', the allegation that preneolithic hunting tribes destroyed far more animals than they appeared to require for food and hides. But the evidence is all very patchy and allows considerable latitude for speculation and prejudice. Certainly the conspicuous display of 'wealth' is common to most cultures who require a degree of social organisation for their survival, and wealth can take the form of an excessive accumulation of culturally prized objects, which in a hunting society might have been dead wild animals. "A culture's published ethos about its environment", observes Tuan (1970, p.244), "seldom covers more than a fraction of the total range of its attributes and practices pertaining to that environment. In the play of forces that govern the world, aesthetic and religious ideals rarely have a major role."

But all of this should not perhaps be regarded as mastery so much as 'coping', which includes coming to grips with social pressures as well as environmental ones. If this interpretation is correct, environmental disruption can be seen as the inadvertent outcome of imperfect collective institutions which fail to counteract the harmful side effects of man's inconsistent environmental behaviour. For man does demand incompatible wants from his surroundings. Kates (1969) recognises three separable objectives in environmental planning: (a) the protection of physical and mental health, (b) the enhancement of economic value, and (c) the preservation of sensory pleasure. The environment is to be all things to all men at all times; it is to be life supporting, useful, and yet beautiful. Man's mind and his institutions have frankly failed to achieve this trichotomy harmoniously, so we stumble along seeking, as Tuan (1974, p.284) described it, "an equilibrium that is not of this world".

The uneasy compromise which forms our environmental ideal is reflected in our confusion over what should be our proper behaviour toward our natural surroundings and fellow beings. This confusion in turn is evident in the controversies surrounding the historical roots to our environmental arrogance and the nature of the relationship between normative belief (or social ethos) and specific behaviour as manifest in individual activities. Let us look at each of these topics in turn.

6.1 The Judaeo-Christian debate

Part of man's seemingly infinite capacity to rationalise is his ability to fix blame, preferably on people or forces beyond his control. White (1967) provided such an avenue (though I doubt if he deliberately intended it this way) when he theorised that 'the Judaeo-Christian ethic' was the cause of western man's alienation from nature, his objectification of natural objects and processes, his anthropomorphism, and his quest for progress at all costs. "Christianity", he commented (p.1205), "is the most anthropocentric religion the world has seen ... . It has not only established a dualism of man and nature but has also insisted that it is God's will that man exploit nature for his proper ends." Christianity has been 'blamed' for providing the rhetorical justification for separating man from nature and decreeing that man could shape his own destiny. When this sentiment was combined with the marriage of science (aristocratic, speculative, and intellectual) and technology (artisan, empirical, action-orientated) that occurred during the agricultural and industrial revolutions, brain and brawn were linked to create our present day 'ecologic crisis'. Since man has now the technological capacity to destroy himself and this earth, but the intellectual capacity to save himself and protect the planet, it is in the moral realm of religion, which White defines as "beliefs about our nature and our destiny", that man must seek solutions (see also Fleischman, 1969).

White's thesis sparked off a lively debate over the role of Judaeo-Christian teaching in determining environmental cognition (see Elder, 1970; Fackre, 1971; Barbour, 1972; Steffenson *et al.*, 1973; Passmore, 1974). By far the most comprehensive statement is provided by Black (1970), who expounds the important anthropological thesis (p.27) that the purpose of myth (that is symbolic representations of our beginnings and our destiny—see also Eliade, 1968)—"is the elaboration of a model by which contradictions in the physical or intellectual environment may be avoided ... or 'mediated' by the accumulation of similar myths which operate together within the whole framework of society's beliefs, the effect of each constituent story being to reinforce the feeling of opacity which surrounds unpleasant or contradictory situations, real or imagined".

The myth in question is the famous text in *Genesis*, Chapter 1, verses 26-28:

> "And God said, let us make man in our image, after our likeness: and let him have dominion over the fish of the sea and over the fowl of the air, and over the cattle and over all the earth, and over every creeping thing that creepeth upon the earth. So God created man in his own image, in the image of God he created him: male and female created he them. And God blessed them and God said unto them, Be fruitful and multiply, and replenish the earth and subdue it: and have dominion over the fish of the sea, and over the fowl of the air and over every living thing that moveth upon the earth."

The contradictions that the myth shrouds fall into three parts. First, there is the duality between prophesy and command. Black (1970, p.35) believes that the two contentious statements about fertility and multiplication and about having dominion probably do not represent the earliest attitudes of man to his environment. They are more likely to be *post hoc* rationalisations, by a relatively advanced technological civilisation, of prophesies interpreted as commands that turned out as facts. This fits in with Glacken's idea of man's purposeful quest for an anthropocentrically designed earth where what *is* occurring is explained as what *was supposed* to happen. Second, there is the dichotomy between 'subdue' and 'replenish'. To subdue is to exert force and command complete control, an exhortation to continue the struggle against an inhospitable land. But, having 'won' the struggle, man's duty is to replenish, care, tend the land for his and the earth's mutual good.

The mediating check against potential disruption is *stewardship*, the middle path between destruction and ecological determinism. The stewardship idea is brilliantly analysed by Black (1970, pp.44–58), who remarks that in Biblical times the steward had the dual role of managing the estate for profit while also ensuring its long term viability. The desire to maximise short-term profit was tempered by the drive to ensure permanency of tenure. The steward was God's deputy or representative in a symbolic sense, the real *imago dei* who recognised God's omniscience and omnipotence but applied intelligence, reason and moral responsibility in his care of the sacred garden. The execution of stewardship was therefore the ultimate act of God's will on earth through his designated manager, man.

Equally central to the stewardship symbol was the notion of *property* which also mediated between the inherently disruptive tendencies of selfish acquisition and the restrictions imposed by social responsibility. Property was associated with three roles: (a) the display of status and wealth, (b) the recognition of social rights and obligations to other property owners and to posterity, and (c) concern for efficiency and the reduction of wasteful practices. These characteristics of property apply to publicly owned property in fiduciary right as much as to privately owned resources.

The third duality of the *Genesis* myth applies to the nature of the original relationship between man and other living creatures. The original text and various interpretations are all ambivalent as to the precise relationship between God, Man, and Nature. Black (1970, pp.40–41) illustrates two distinctly differing versions, one by Priestly, and the other in the Jahwist (earlier) edition (figures 6.1a, 6.1b). Priestly postulates that God first created the land, *then* the living things, and finally man who was to have control over this domain. The Jahwist interpretation has God creating man on a barren earth, *then* adding the garden for him to tend. In the latter case living things are companions of man, not objects for his use. Schaeffer (1970) accepts this latter hypothesis. God, he believes, is united with all things on earth through the whole act of creation. When the 'word was made God' all matter was embraced with divinity and equality of existence before God. The divergence of the two versions demonstrates the ancient uncertainty about the proper role of man on earth; possibly, too, it indicates the influence of social attitudes prevailing at the times these two significantly different interpretations were produced.

Black concludes that our ecological 'crisis' is not so much a product of Judaeo-Christian teaching as a fundamental uncertainty about the past and the future of man, a doubt that is rationalised in myth. The crucial mediating mechanisms of stewardship, social obligation, and a concern for posterity have become progressively weakened with the growing centralisation of social organisation, the rise of urbanism, the belief that economic improvement would eventually result in social happiness and the perfection of man's mind and institutions, and the egregious cant of utilitarianism which preached, in effect, that what was good for one man was good for all. Black is therefore not sanguine that those mediating forces can be restored in modern postindustrial cultures in the absence of widespread political and economic reform. Also he is unhappy with White's (1967) and Nasr's (1968) solutions for a new 'harmony with nature' ethic along the ecocentric lines of the life and work of St. Francis, since this would mean the "jettisoning of cherished western attitudes—particularly those stressing man's control of nature, on which the development of modern science has rested" (p.123). He argues instead for a restructuring of the western world view to interpret 'social good' not just in terms of the welfare of present generations, but also of *future* generations. "It seems to me", he concludes (p.123), "that almost the only course open to western man is based on a vision of mankind stretched out along the dimension of time ... . By redefining mankind in terms of the whole of humanity, dead, living, or as yet unborn, we may perhaps be able to assess what we do in terms of the good of mankind, regardless of the position of the individual along the time axis of the world." Thus we must bear the responsibility of projecting our ideals and standards of life into the continuum of history.

Black's analysis is a potent statement of the failure of our cultural institutions to cope with our environmental dilemma. Moncrief (1970) is

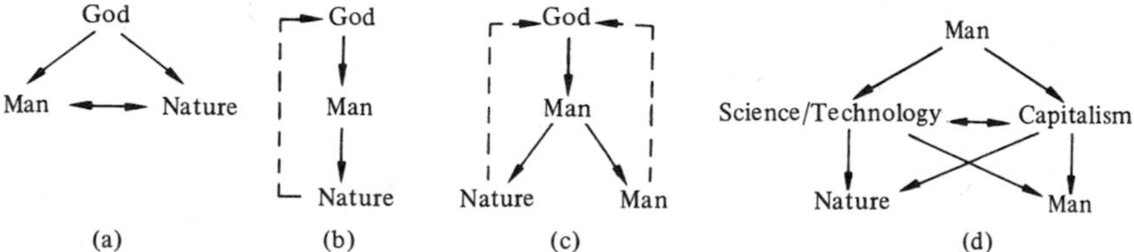

Figure 6.1. Interpretations of the relationship between God, Man, and Nature: (a) the Jahwist version; (b) the Priestlian version; (c) the Baconian version; (d) the Marxist version.

more critical of White's thesis, stating that the course of economic history in western nations has created (a) a lack of personal and moral direction about environmental responsibility, which is partly a product and partly the cause of our present inadequate management, (b) a collective inability to identify and resolve the resulting moral dilemma, and (c) an abiding Micawberish faith that something will inevitably bale us out, more often than not that 'something' being technology. He claims that many cultures, unless intellectually and numerically stable at low levels of energy flow, experience difficulties over managing the 'commons', irrespective of their religious beliefs, because evolutionary human progress inevitably leads to collective loss even though many people as individuals may appear to gain. Thus the failure of modern institutions is a product of cultural ethos, not of religious mythology, for without constant vigilance even the most benign institutions can introduce environmentally damaging effects that were never part of their original purpose. In answer to these criticisms, White (1973, p.62) modifies his views as follows:

> "... man–nature dualism is deep rooted in us ... until it is eradicated not only from our minds but also from our emotions we shall doubtless be unable to make fundamental changes in our attitudes and our actions affecting ecology. The religious problem is to find a viable equivalent to animism".

The second part of this chapter will review the structural psychological obstacles that must be overcome to eradicate this dualism.

Leiss (1972) offers a very penetrating analysis of the man–nature relationship from the vantage points of political philosophy and Marxist ideology. He interprets the Baconian view of 'domination over nature' (though he believes that Bacon was only voicing an established view among contemporary intellectuals) not so much as elitist dogma as an attack on outmoded scientific doctrines and a desire to use advances in science and technology to further social needs and eradicate political injustice. Thus Bacon regarded science in much the same way as Mill visualised economic growth, for Bacon was always aware of the need for ethical and religious restraint in the pursuit of truth and goodness (figure 6.1c). Scientific endeavour should always be tempered by respect for a grander teleological design. Leiss (p.189) quotes Bacon as saying, "Only let the human race recover that right over nature which belongs to it by divine bequest, and let power be given it; the exercise thereof will be governed by sound reason and true religion". Thus the strict Baconian view was much more prescient than commonly imagined; the fear of the misuse of man's prowess led Bacon to regard the main value of scientific advance as the freedom to develop his moral and ethical virtues, for therein lay the true challenge.

Leiss concludes that Bacon's fears were justified and that capitalist man abused his intellectual powers, not in the pursuit of peace and justice, but to produce conflict and inequity. Approvingly (p.195) he quotes C. S. Lewis: "Man's power over nature turns out to be a power exercised by some men over other men with nature as its instrument". So Leiss's view of the Man–Nature relationship can be depicted as in figure 6.1d. Domination of nature is not an object in itself but a reflection of social organisation and political philosophy; 'God' disappears from the scene. Precapitalistic societies, he remarks, were framed along the lines of feudal order, the allocation of work, familial patterns, and stability. Nature played an important symbolic role in sustaining the distribution of power and knowledge through the planned manipulation of ignorance, superstition, and false scientific dogma. The capitalist system, according to Marx and as interpreted by Leiss, alienates man from his work and his workplace and from his home and his family; and separates urbanised man generally from the humility, the pursuit of free inquiry, and above all the sense of wonder that only nature in its tangible essence can provide. Capitalism, Leiss contends, also creates conflict and division between workers, between worker and management, between urban man and rural man, and inevitably between man and nature. Mass production and mass behaviour feed an uncritical acceptance of irresponsible social mores, and a feeling of frustrated impotence induces a dislike of moral restraint and ethical inquiry. Here is Marx himself on the matter, in his economic and philosophical manuscripts of 1844 (Struik, 1973, p.114):

> "The object of labor is, therefore, the *objectification of man's species life* ... for he contemplates himself in a world that he has created. In tearing away from man the object of his production, therefore, estranged labor tears him from his species life, his real objectivity as a member of the species and transforms his advantage over animals into the disadvantage that his inorganic body, nature, is taken away from him."
>
> "Similarly, in degrading spontaneous, free activity to a means, estranged labor makes man's species life a means to his physical existence."

Bearing in mind that the majority in an industrialised society spend most of their lives either behind a machine or a desk in a largely secular and mostly impersonal atmosphere, Marx's words seem to have a profound truth for today's bitter labour disputes and sense of frustration. One also wonders whether the revisionist communism as practised in Eastern Europe and Russia is much different in this respect, for the critical schism of man from his community of fellows, including nature, is still evident, though perhaps not as freely expressed. Indeed so strong is the influence of both technology and the mode of production upon the lives of most people in capitalist and communist nations (with the possible exception of China), that figure 6.1d might even be amended by placing man below (i.e. subdominant to) these two central manipulating forces. Orleans and

Suttmeier (1970) suggest that this would not be the case in Communist China where the Mao ethic preaches frugality and the harnessing of technology to human needs. But some of the duality of rhetoric and fact seems still to be evident, for despite Mao's teachings, 'wastes' are not converted into productive 'treasures'.

Thus we return to the metaphor of nature as a symbol of political justice, and the infinite possibilities for the human race visualised by the romanticists of the last century and the political radicals of the present. If we accept Leiss's thesis that attitudes and behaviour toward nature are more the passive outcome of the evolution of social thought and governing institutions than an active component shaping these elements, then it is only possible to conceive of constructive change in environmental construing through "a new set of social institutions in which responsibility and authority are distributed widely among the citizenry and in which all individuals are encouraged to develop their critical faculties" (Leiss, 1972, p.197). Leo Marx (1970, p.951) agrees: only by overpowering the forces of domination—"the great business corporations, the military establishment, the universities, the scientific and technological elites, and the exhilarating expansionary ethos by which we all live"—can man be liberated to deal with the opportunities that nature offers. Then, and only then, will nature cease to be regarded as a source of power (and hence domination) and be seen for what it really is—the fount of human happiness. But in the struggle to reach this ideal, the inevitable contradictions must still be overcome. Leiss (1972, p.212) quotes Marcuse who summarises the matter rather well:

> "Pacification (of the struggle for existence) presupposes mastery of Nature ... . But there are two kinds of mastery: a repressive and a liberating one. The latter involves the reduction of misery, violence and cruelty ... . All joy and all happiness derive from an ability to transcend Nature—a transcendence on which the mastery of Nature is itself subordinated to liberation and pacification of existence".

6.2 Environmental words and environmental deeds

For over forty years social psychologists have been worrying themselves over the nature of the links (if indeed they exist) between verbal expressions of attitude and actual behaviour. (For good reviews see Deutscher, 1966; Kiesler *et al.*, 1969; Wicker, 1969; Thomas, 1971). For a long time the prevailing paradigm assumed a causal connection between words and deeds, first without any intervening variable, then with various latent and overt personal and situational factors mediating behavioural response, and later still with an added component for social obligation (figures 6.2a, 6.2b, 6.2c). Despite the cumbersome relationships in the later models, there remained a tacit acceptance among most workers of a model of rational man whose attitudes (in combination if not singly) did influence behaviour in some kind of ill-understood manner. de Fleur and Westie (1963, p.21) conclude:

> "The attitude is not the manifest responses themselves, or their probability but an intervening variable operating between stimulus and response and inferred from overt behaviour. This inner process is seen as giving both direction and consistency to the person's responses."

Campbell (1963) visualised attitudes as socially acquired behavioural dispositions, modified by experience, that guide behaviour over a specified range of situations. While acknowledging that behaviour partly determined experience, he concluded that attitudinal dispositions were the dominant force in guiding behaviour. So the prevailing belief held firm that, if attitudes are measured carefully, likely behavioural acts can be speculated upon with some degree of assurance. Despite all the field evidence to the contrary, this plausible but deceptively dangerous assumption still seems to be accepted by many policymakers and opinion pollsters.

The 'evidence' was derived largely from 'paper and pencil' tests conducted on psychology students under neatly controlled conditions, and based on the methodological paradigm that attitude influenced behaviour. But field research failed to substantiate these findings. Wicker (1969, p.25) reports that only about 10% of behavioural variance can be accounted for by attitudinal data. It was evident either that the models were imperfect or

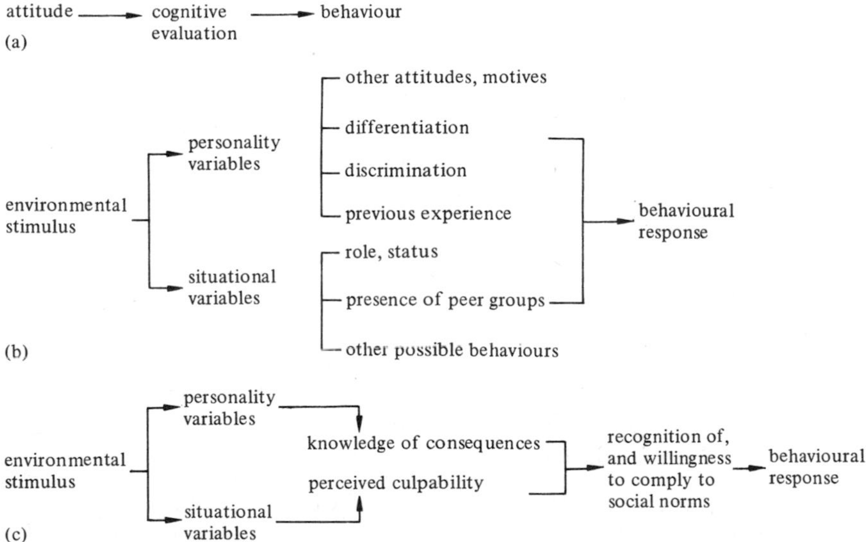

Figure 6.2. Interpretations of the relationship between attitudes and behaviour: (a) simple model of the attitude-behaviour relationship; (b) Wicker's (1969) version; (c) Wicker's version with contributions from Fishbein (1967) and Heberlein (1972).

that research methodologies were inadequate (Crespi, 1972). With regard to the latter point, Lauer (1971, p.248) comments that "the fault lies both in the failure to create research designs that reflect the complexity of the problem and in the tendency to reject the importance of the proximate causes of overt behaviour". As to the problem of the model, Wicker suggested a more comprehensive schema (figure 6.2b) in which he postulated that a number of very important 'latent process variables' had to be considered. These amending variables fell into two principal groups, the personality variables and the situational factors.

Items under the heading of 'personality variables' included other attitudes held by the individual—competing motives, the respondent's verbal and intellectual ability to conceptualise and describe his attitudes, and his feelings of personal efficacy (Wicker, 1969, pp.67–69). Of these, the matters of multiple cognitions and competing motives demand further scrutiny. The term 'cognition' will be used here to characterise discrete bundles of closely connected beliefs and feelings which relate to various facets of an object or situation, and which in sum constitute the mediating mechanism which Wicker regards as an attitude (see also Downs and Stea, 1974, pp.8–26).

It is helpful to visualise these cognitive 'bundles' as depicted in figure 6.3. At the 'core' of an attitude are dominant (or salient) cognitions, closely linked to a person's value system, which are held strongly and cherished. These will bear on a whole range of experiences of which the situation or object under observation is but one. Surrounding these dominant cognitions are more peripheral (or nonsalient) cognitions, less strongly connected to values, which may readily be exchanged for other equally peripheral cognitions. It is very probable that many of what can be called 'socially acceptable' cognitions fall into this latter category, cognitions that are elicited by public opinion polls and questionnaires or during conversation with social peers. Though most of the time they may in themselves have little bearing on behaviour, in certain circumstances they may be quite significant. Kiesler *et al.* (1969, p.35) sum up the methodological problems thus caused as follows:

> "Attitudinal measures frequently make broad and philosophical attitudes salient, whereas behavioural measures make specific and immediately personal attitudes salient. We can therefore expect a low correlation between attitude and behaviour in those cases where one set of subattitudes [cognitions] is salient in the testing situation, whereas another set [of cognitions] is salient in the behavioural situation."

There is always a danger, therefore, of picking up irrelevant cognitions and assuming that they will bear upon subsequent behaviour. This is probably the most difficult problem facing researchers in environmental cognition, for not only are the peripheral cognitions not terribly critical, but they may be inconsistent with other more relevant ones, because of the conflicting motives of the individual studied. Since many environmental objectives are superficially irreconcilable with other valued ends, the incompatibility of subattitudinal cognitions can add to the distortion between verbal statement and actual deed.

In this context it is worth commenting on the dangers inherent in such personality-testing devices as the 'environmental response inventory' (McKechnie, 1973). McKechnie's technique confronts the respondent with some 330 attitude statements, all of which he must answer spontaneously along a 'strongly agree–strongly disagree' scale. The results are factor-analysed into various environmentalist components. But the attitude battery is still preselected and the evaluation depends upon self-description of environmental likes and dislikes. When it is realised that there is a behavioural equivalent (figure 6.4) of the cognitive array portrayed in figure 6.3, it will be seen that even the fairly sophisticated response

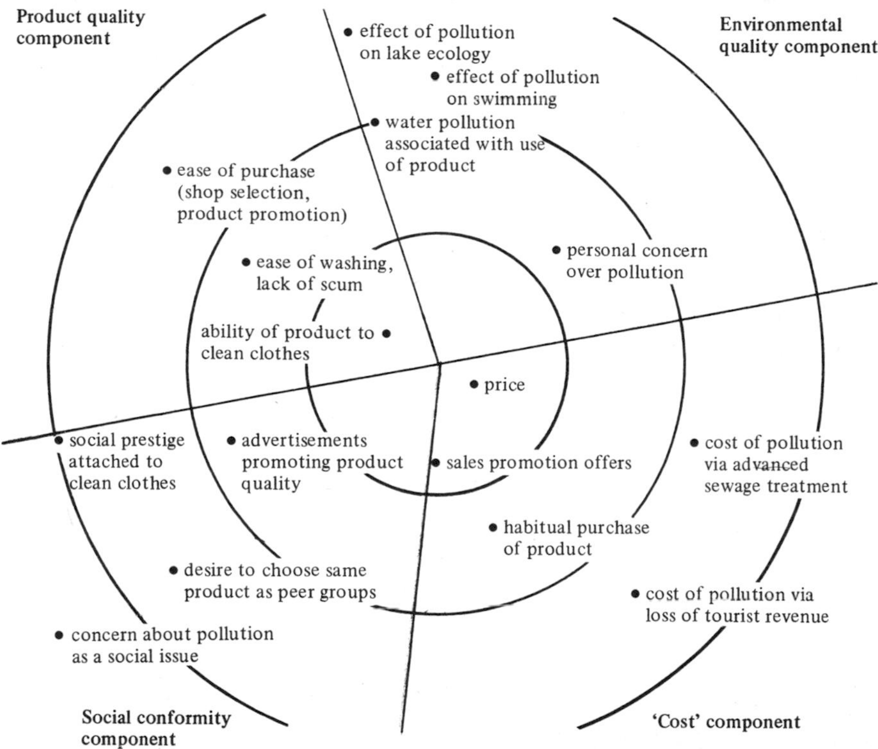

Figure 6.3. Salient and peripheral cognitions comprising an attitude. This is a highly schematic diagram of the kind of motives/attitudes that could relate to the act of purchasing a laundry detergent. More central cognitions will tend to influence behaviour more than the peripheral cognitions. The reader is invited to sketch similar cognitive maps for other environmental acts (such as littering), and possibly link the cognitions and assign weights to the relationships.

inventory cannot guarantee why, or in what way, people behave the way they do. For there are many possible behavioural options relevant to any given attitude (or cognitive cluster). Some of these behavioural choices will be known, some obscure, and some impossible to consider owing to financial, social, or political factors beyond the subject's control. So there need not be an inconsistency between reported attitude and observed behaviour, simply a failure or an inability on the part of the subject to consider other possible behaviour.

Wicker's (1969, pp.69–74) second set of latent process variables, the environmental or situational factors, helps to determine what alternative behaviours will be considered. Campbell (1963) believes that behaviour will be influenced by the *situational threshold*, where certain key forces cause a search for alternative behaviours. This idea is similar to the notion of 'behavioural thresholds' currently being investigated by the natural hazards research programme (Burton *et al.*, 1976)—those critical points of perceptual discontinuity where the hazard-prone may adopt a new kind of damage-avoidance behaviour. The presence of a peer group, especially if it happens to know how the subject feels about a given situation, certainly influences the situational threshold, as do the social communication networks which impinge upon the subject and the opportunities made available through public policy. We know very little about the environmental behaviour of people when they are utterly alone, whether

Figure 6.4. The variety of behavioural options. This figure is highly schematic, but it is designed to show that there are various positive and negative reasons underlying any behavioural act, and that social or political action will be dependent in part upon a sense of political efficacy.

the social sanctions which are so important in daily life still apply in solitude. Obviously this is a matter that each one of us can contemplate. Another situational variable of some importance in the study of environmental cognition is the occurrence of the unexpected event or situation which has never been previously experienced. How do people respond during periods of unanticipated environmental stress, such as a severe natural event or a dangerous pollution episode or an energy shortage? Here we cross situational thresholds where statements recorded beforehand may have little or no relevance.

A third set of mediating variables which have both personality and situational components is what Fishbein (1967, p.490) regards as 'social response influences', or 'perceived social sanctions', which cause the individual to comply with certain codes of conduct. These factors are more explicitly analysed by Heberlein (1972) and are depicted in figure 6.2c. Heberlein postulates that socially acceptable behaviour will be guided by three determinants. First, there are attitudes toward the behaviour itself, particularly the likely consequences of any action (or inaction) and the evaluation of these consequences. This is the *knowledge component* which is a function of experience, education, and the cognitive ability to visualise a mental model of cause and effect. Psychologists describe the facility to identify complex cognitive relationships as *differentiation* and the sharpness with which each differentiated element is visualised as *discrimination* (Schroder, 1971).

Second, there is the *culpability component*—the attribution of blame for one's actions and the identification of options that are less socially detrimental. In many 'commons' situations, for example, people voluntarily engage in antisocial behaviour because 'everyone else is doing it'. Some philosophers believe that the modern corporate and welfare state has taken away much of the sense of personal responsibility in work and play; people do things because they feel they 'have no choice'. In hazard response studies, Kirkby (1973) and Sims and Baumann (1974) found that adjustment to hazard was influenced by beliefs about fate. Those who felt they had little or no control over their lives tended to accept the threat of hazard (and were likely to suffer more), while those who thought they determined their own lives were more likely to adopt one or more behavioural adjustments. Culpability is evaluated by merging the pattern of cognitive differentiation and discrimination (figure 6.3) with the mental schema of alternative behaviour (figure 6.4). The skill of merging these two cognitive schemata, known as *integrative complexity*, is obviously a tremendously important facility in environmental cognition and an important objective in environmental education (chapter 9, pp.311–315), for there is reason to believe that early childhood experiences which promote a spirit of investigation and free inquiry improve proficiency in integrative complexity (Schroder, 1971).

The third constituent of the social response set is the *normative component* (also discussed by White, 1966, pp.108–109). This relates to beliefs about what one personally feels, beliefs about what society feels, and beliefs about what should be done in the communal interest. This judgement will be influenced by the social orientation of the individual, or, as Fishbein (1967, p.488) puts it, his "motivation to comply with the norm, that is his desire or lack of desire to do what he thinks he should do".

The forces which shape social obligation are most difficult to unravel. Certainly the social milieu (friends, peer group influences, the views of those who are respected, etc.), is crucial, but so too are institutional variables (for example the degree to which work, school or the home environments encourage a sense of responsibility or belonging). Here, certainly, is a critical research area, for we still know little of what these forces are and how they act singly or together. A model that is helpful here is the matrix prepared by Eckhardt and Hendershot (1967) to explain how individuals take into account what they perceive to be public opinion (figure 6.5). Superficially, the matrix is a simple variation of the twin themes of cognitive consistency and cognitive dissonance, the striving to complement belief and action (for a good review, see Kiesler *et al.*, 1969). The value of the model is its linkage of the desire for personal cognitive consistency with the need to conform to certain social norms expressed either by society at large or by 'significant others'. Environmental construing is as much a social process as it is a product of an individual's psychology.

In box A the individual is acting in a manner that is consonant with his own cognitive set and congruent with his interpretation of social norms. This is nonstressful behaviour which happily accounts for most of our everyday 'instinctive' cultural acts such as dressing and eating. In their pure form such acts should be socially constructive and personally satisfying. In box B, however, the behaviour is socially acceptable but personally undesirable; here would fit all the classic examples of socially

Relationship between behaviour and perceived social norms	Relationship between behaviour and personal values: Consonance	Dissonance
Congruent	A	B
Noncongruent	C	D

Figure 6.5. Individual and social sanctions on environmental behaviour. (Source: Eckhardt and Hendershot, 1967.)

obligatory conduct such as entertaining a disliked business associate or unwillingly denying oneself a third child. Because such an act is executed more for reasons of social conformity than personal preference, supportive public opinion is actively canvassed. In box C the conduct is socially unacceptable but personally desirable, for example the activities of 'freak' fringe groups or budding revolutionaries; here public opinion is deliberately avoided or is distorted to fit the norms of likeminded peers. This situation is often evident in environmental decisionmaking when politicians, about to make an environmentally unpopular decision, seek the support of those whom they regard as 'informed experts', and try to play down the opposition as being 'uninformed' or 'negativists' or 'romanticists' (see Pendakur, 1972). For example, when confronted by a group of citizens who embraced a whole array of socioeconomic backgrounds and who were protesting against the decision by Vancouver City Council to construct a freeway along the Vancouver waterfront, the prodevelopment Mayor characterised all his opposition as "Maoists, communists, pinkos, left-wingers and hamburgers" (defined as persons without university degrees), and called upon his council to rally in support of the freeway proposal (Guttstein, 1975, p.165). The advice of the specialised consultant (planner, engineer, sociologist, economist) may be boosted beyond the bounds of his professional competence (Sewell, 1971); but the expert will also seek support among his own kind if confronted by opposition groups claiming to have 'better' information. In this way debates over such controversial issues as the social dangers of nuclear power become almost unresolvable despite the factual data available (see Gillette, 1972c; Lewis, 1972; Union of Concerned Scientists, 1973).

Box D presents the most interesting situation, for here behaviour is both inconsistent with the individual's beliefs and incompatible with his perception of societal norms. How he will actually respond, though, will depend upon the centrality of the cognitive elements involved. At one extreme the person would be schizophrenic, totally divorcing his conduct from his beliefs. But where the cognitive elements are peripheral, box D represents most of our everyday 'antienvironmental' behaviour—driving cars and not maintaining the pollution control devices, trampling down bushes when the proper trail should be followed, consuming goods creating damage to the environment when more expensive or time consuming but environmentally 'sound' substitutes are available, or urinating in a bathing area even though a public toilet is available nearby. Sometimes this behaviour is rationalised by recourse to the knowledge and culpability components of the social response variables discussed above, sometimes because social sanctions may not be present.

But people as individuals cannot be entirely to blame for these dissonance-reducing rationalisations, for undoubtedly social and political factors have a role. It is appropriate to review this in the light of recent research findings on environmental cognition.

6.3 Environmental attitudes and environmental concern

Public opinion polls have recorded a variable public interest in environmental problems, reaching a peak during the period 1970–1972 (figure 6.6). In a survey of American polls, Munton and Brady (1970) and Erskine (1971) have shown that in the five years 1965–1970 the problem of reducing pollution rose from ninth of the ten most serious problems facing the United States to second (behind the state of the economy), and that the number of people expressing a willingness to contribute more of their incomes to clean up the environment rose from around 40% in 1967 to over 60% in 1970. These findings are supported by Trop and Roos (1971) and by Dillman and Christenson (1972) who conclude that a majority of Americans would like to see more governmental expenditures diverted into the cleanup of the environment even at the expense of other budgetary items. Canadian studies reveal similar findings (Burton and Auliciems, 1972; Auliciems *et al.*, 1972; Winham, 1972). Since then, however, public interest in environmental problems has waned, especially as inflation and unemployment tighten domestic budgets and raise the spectre of economic collapse. One can only conclude that polls largely reflect socially acceptable opinions that are influenced by media coverage and social communication. Furthermore, these findings cannot be compared methodologically since the objectives of the various surveys and the nature of the questions have differed. Many of the early studies were intended to be informational; the concept of 'pollution' was undifferentiated and only vaguely related to other social problems. Later studies were more systematic in their research objectives, correlating opinion on various facets of environmentalism with socioeconomic variables, other attitude and value indices, and personal experience.

Another reason why the results of opinion polls should be viewed with scepticism is that they rarely solicit deeply-held views or any expression of commitment. Most polls simply monitor weakly-held cognitions (usually

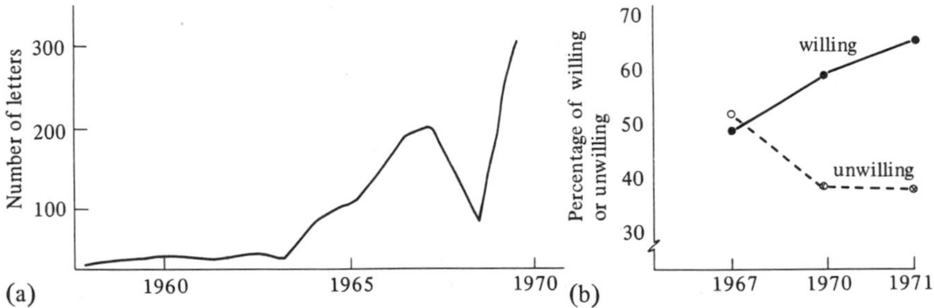

Figure 6.6. The variable history of public concern over the environmental crisis. (a) Number of letters to the *New York Times* regarding environmental pollution. (Source: Munton and Brady, 1970, p.5.) (b) Percentage willing or unwilling to pay $15 or more in additional taxes to finance a federal programme in air pollution abatement. (Source: Erskine, 1971, p.132.)

of a socially acceptable kind) concerning matters that most respondents have thought little about, but to which they must give spontaneous answers. Erickson and Luttberg (1973, p.17) assert that most Americans (about 83%) take very little interest in 'social questions' such as pollution, housing, and social and economic inequality, and demonstrate very little knowledge of the political alternatives being discussed. Converse (1964) found that shifts in public opinion over nonpersonal political issues can be explained as much by random factors and by research design (including the construction of the questionnaire and the nature of the interview) as by a genuine swing in public interest. He concluded that less than 20% of respondents held opinions that were meaningful to them even though two thirds, when pressed, offered a viewpoint.

From a policy perspective opinion polls purporting to tap environmental cognitions should be viewed with considerable caution, for their fickleness is no real indication of the public mood (Sprout, 1971; Downs, 1972). Nevertheless politicians are sometimes beguiled by an impressive array of statistics and may too readily adjudge the wrong top priorities (Etzioni, 1970). Some commentators have complained that the wave of environmental concern that swept the western world in the early 1970s served to divert public and political attention from the real social issues of injustice and deliberate discrimination.

In support of this contention they point to the not unexpected finding that people of high socioeconomic status appeared to be more knowledgeable and concerned about environmental issues than those in the lower income and status brackets (see Harry *et al.*, 1969; Marsh, 1969; Devall, 1970; David, 1971; Murch, 1971; O'Riordan, 1971b; Rogers, 1971; Constantine and Hauf, 1972; Dillman and Christenson, 1972; Tognacci *et al.*, 1972). These findings are unexceptional because they conform with the commonly held belief that as people's incomes rise and their social positions improve they will tend to hold more liberal opinions about a variety of social problems and to value environmental quality more highly. We can visualise a personal priorities hierarchy, similar to the national priorities hierarchy depicted in figure 1.1 and reminiscent of Maslow's (1954) hierarchy of human needs (figure 6.7). Those who enjoy comfortable personal circumstances (social mobility, an enjoyable well-paid job, a nice house, good education for their children) can afford to be bothered by 'cosmetic' disamenities such as air and water pollution or the damming of a distant valley, because these are the nuisances that cannot be readily avoided by the deployment of wealth or social status. Moreover, higher status groups feel that they can do something about such issues without any major change in their political power base, their income levels, or their daily existence. Therefore it is hardly surprising that the membership of environmental activist groups is largely drawn from middle income earners, whose motives for joining may be as much a reflection of social face-saving as of any personal interest (Harry *et al.*, 1969; Morrison, 1973).

By contrast, the poor and/or politically impotent cannot afford the luxury of worrying about environmental disamenity since their priorities rest with the necessities of life (i.e. food, jobs, housing, and education), and they face much higher transaction costs when attempting to improve environmental quality.

So the matter of environmental concern is closely allied to a sense of political efficacy. The lack of a decent life is both the major personal *and* social issue for the poor who feel powerless to change their situation. Why should they be willing to pay more to clean up the rivers on which only the rich will boat or fish? What perhaps really needs explaining is why the rich worry more about the cosmetic eradication of pollution than about the social injustices that are central to the environmental dilemma.

This is still an underresearched topic, though there is reason to believe that people generally prefer not to think about 'distasteful' subjects that are not regarded as personally relevant or about which they feel they can do little. In a study carried out among householders in Vancouver (Westwater Research, 1974) it was found that housewives had a remarkably accurate knowledge of the source and treatment of their water supply

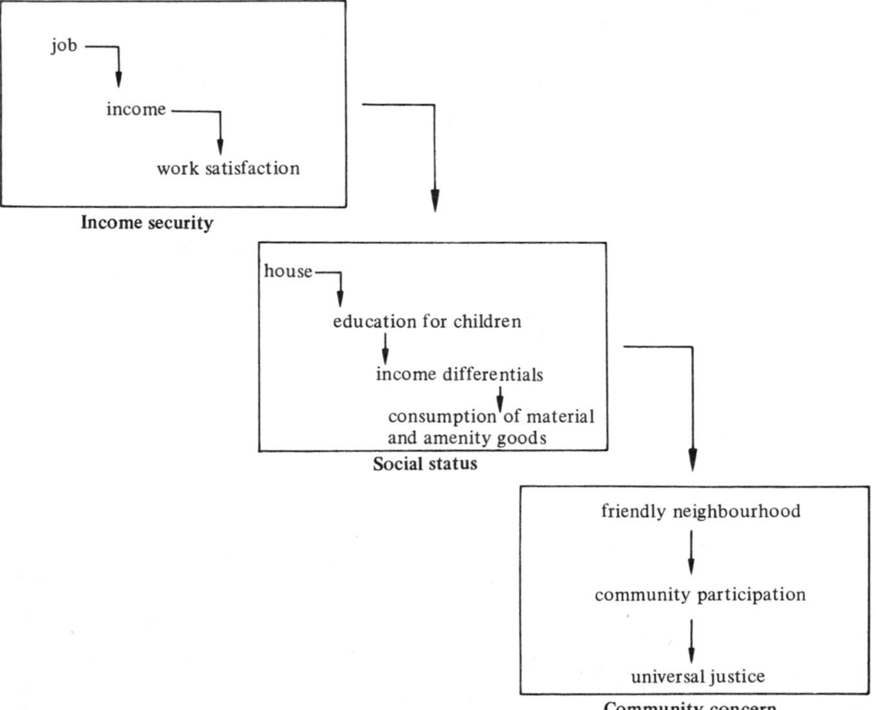

Figure 6.7. A hierarchy of personal priorities. Clearly, the rankings would differ from one individual to another.

(which was very important to them), but displayed a widespread ignorance about the sink and level of treatment of their domestic sewage. Water supply is a socially acceptable topic for conversation; sewage treatment, on the other hand, is rarely discussed over the garden fence or at the dinner table. It is probably not an accident that the two sources of household waste (the bathroom and the kitchen) are often particularly attractively decorated, so that when waste is discharged from the house it disappears as quickly from the mind. In a similar manner, commuters filter out disamenity areas from their minds on their way into town. The personal security of the interior of the automobile effectively isolates its occupant physically and mentally from his surroundings; it is not surprising that people are loathe to abandon their cars in favour of outdated and less comfortable public transport. Again, most people physically and psychologically brush aside any contact with those who are seen to be disadvantaged (such as spastics, racial minorities, beggars, and 'freaks'). So it is possible that the wealthy prefer not to relate social injustice to environmental stress, because it is a disturbing and potentially subversive connection which could be threatening to their privileged way of life.

A third major finding from environmental cognition studies is the sketchy and distorted information that most people have about the cause and content of environmental pollution (see for example David, 1971; Auliciems *et al.*, 1972; O'Riordan, 1972b; Wall, 1973). Uninformed people quite naturally blame 'someone or something else', seeking a scapegoat in simplistic symbolic cues such as visible residual discharges and diesel fumes from trucks and buses. Equally understandably they define environmental stress in terms of sensorily perceived phenomena, especially smoke, smog, smells, and noise. The silent, stealthy dangers (toxic gases, heavy metals, etc.) are not normally contemplated except by those who care to obtain the information. From a policy viewpoint there is a danger that political pressure tends to focus on the obvious manifestations of pollution, while lurking hazards remain in the political shadows (figure 6.8). From table 6.1 it will be noted that almost a third of Toronto residents reported health symptoms arising from gaseous pollutants that could never have reached the requisite concentrations to have caused those effects. Media coverage plus the images triggered off by a survey in which air pollution is frequently mentioned might well account for these somewhat inconsistent results. In addition, people become accustomed to pollutant loads, particularly if they vary little from place to place and from time to time, and many adopt rationalising responses (for example, stating that pollution is 'far worse' somewhere else, or denying that their neighbourhood is dirty even if they admit the town generally is polluted). These kinds of adaptation and acceptance are more noticeable amongst the poor and socially immobile and least found among the politically active and socially ambitious.

There is a strong temptation to conclude that a better educated and informed public would respond more 'accurately' to environmental pollution. But it is naive to assume that knowledge will necessarily heighten awareness, since information monitoring and retrieval are influenced by personal interest and commitment. Auliciems *et al.* (1972) found that the use of an air pollution index in southern Ontario failed to improve public interest or awareness of the pollutant load, and many people clearly did not understand what the index meant or what they should do when it reached episode threshold level. Heberlein (1972)

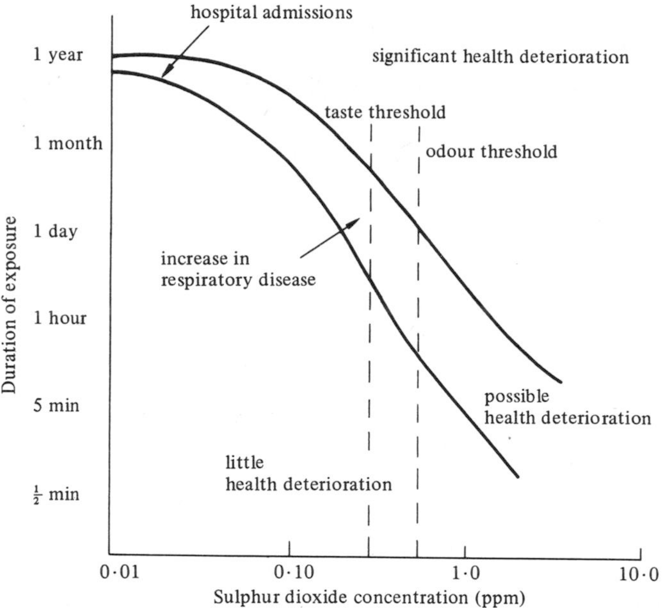

Figure 6.8. The environmental dangers of sulphur dioxide. It will be noted that sensory perceptual thresholds fall below the range of concentrations in which health dangers are reported. (Source: Berry and Horton, 1974, p.103.)

Table 6.1. Causes of air pollution as cognised by Toronto residents. (Source: Auliciems *et al.*, 1972, p.5.)

Order of presentation	Effect	Percentage identifying ill effects
1	particulate matter, dust	56·5
6	odour	54·5
3	discolouring of buildings, clothes, etc.	33·2
5	respiratory irritation	30·0
4	irritation of eyes	29·5
2	poor visibility or haze	21·5

reported that antilittering campaigns, just like antismoking campaigns, fail to stop the habitual offenders. Heberlein (1973a) is justifiably critical of what he calls the 'cognitive fix' (the information campaign), since, by aiming to change attitudes, it assumes (a) that man is a rational and consistent creature who will modify his motivations, on the basis of new information, from those of economic self-interest to altruism; (b) that by concentrating on one set of cognitions, other relevant cognitions will change; and (c) that the attitude shift will be sufficiently profound and long-lasting to influence behaviour. In the real world, people tend to direct information into selected channels on the basis of interest, previous experience, word of mouth communication, and degree of political consciousness. More often than not public information campaigns will reach only those who are already converted, while the less committed tend to 'switch off' because the information is directed at their peripheral cognitions which remain suppressed until triggered by some unusual event [such as a university researcher asking questions about pollution! (Mendelsohn, 1973)].

It would appear that monitoring public cognitions of environmental quality is a difficult exercise of dubious value. At best only a partial response from a complicated and inconsistent cognitive array will be tapped, and all too frequently those cognitions that are recorded will not be central to the prediction of pertinent behaviour. It is particularly unlikely that any useful data will be gleaned from hypothetical questions, since, for a researcher to ask people how they think—when they might respond to a condition they have not experienced and have rarely if ever given a thought to—is to do them and himself a disservice. It also ignores some well-documented evidence that untrained people discount low probabilities of future events virtually to zero unless the outcome is likely to be cataclysmic (Heberlein, 1973a). Kunreuther (1974) has demonstrated how people distort information about the likelihood of damage or danger to life caused by natural hazards (figure 6.9). Until the event has actually been experienced, there are numerous pathways which lead most people into not taking any anticipatory action. The immediate and tangible benefits of doing nothing beguile the uninitiated into a false sense of security.

A rather futile example of the hypothetical question is to ask people how much they would be willing to pay, or how much money they would be willing to see diverted from other items of public expenditure, so that pollution could be 'cleaned up'. (This kind of question is asked in almost all the studies cited in this section.) To begin with, the respondent cannot possibly know how much he will gain or lose by answering such a question. And even if a guess is attempted, it will probably be lower than the figure privately held to be appropriate, since most people prefer others to subsidise their pleasures. Thus it is not surprising that Burton and Auliciems (1972) found that, while 88% of Toronto citizens interviewed felt that the prevailing levels of air pollution were very or moderately unsatisfactory (the top rank in a list of ten community problems), 41% said they would not pay at all and only 30% would pay $40 or more to 'improve' the situation. Only 23% of a sample of New Westminster, B.C., residents contacted by Collins (1972) said they would pay $50 or more to see *all* pollution 'cleaned up', yet when the city council passed a bylaw levying $50 on all households and $28 on all apartments just to pay for primary sewage treatment, the only political reaction was with regard to the equity of the new payment. (Homeowners complained about the regressiveness of the tax and the fact that it bore no relation to waste generation.) Nevertheless, faced with an order to pay, and in the knowledge that everyone else was also going to pay, the public obeyed, proving that Collins' findings, gathered only three months before, bore little relationship to real-life response.

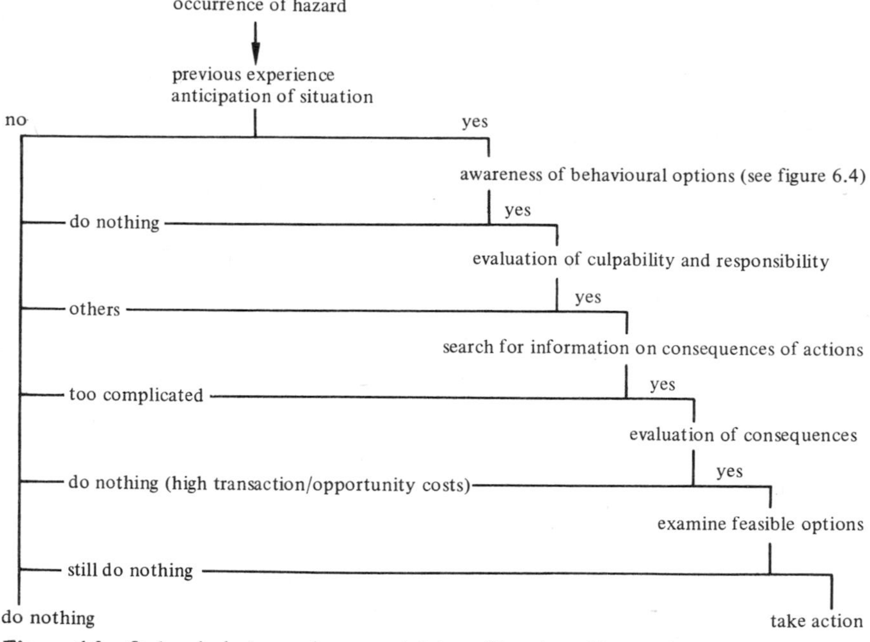

Figure 6.9. Ordered choice under uncertainty. (Based on Kunreuther, 1974, p.5a.)

6.4 The behaviour–cognition link

Bem (1970, pp.54–69) feels that the kind of models depicted in figure 6.2 have the directional pulse the wrong way round, and that with a change of behaviour a person will draw a new set of inferences about what he feels and believes. In fact, he will infer his own attitudes by observing his own behaviour (the self-perception theory). Taking this one stage further, Heberlein (1973a) contends that, as a general principle, people should be guided into alternative new behaviours through policies to restrict their present behaviours or change the social setting in which they act, whereupon they will seek consonant cognitions and thus become environmentally more 'aware'. He cites the example of barring certain kinds of boating from some lakes and then providing information to explain why. If this information can be phrased in such a way as to be consonant with the motivations of the users (and here is an important research area), the final result should be quite felicitous. Carefully thought-out behaviour 'control' may encourage people to seek more information about environmental problems and hence educate themselves (though this is a postulate that still requires verification). Clark and Hendee (1969) found that school students, given incentives to pick up campground litter in wilderness areas, came to believe in litter control and unashamedly admonished campers whom they caught littering. McCurdy (1970) reports that, following the introduction of a user fee in a National Wildlife Refuge, people who had initially opposed the idea of a charge became favourably disposed toward it, especially as they derived benefit from the improved facilities partially financed by the user fees.

But there are thresholds to behavioural alteration which, if passed, can be counterproductive. People did not join temperance societies following prohibition, nor will they vehemently support clean air if forced to maintain emission control devices on their cars. Wall (1973) did not find that people who had been obliged to change to smokeless fuels under the local government requirements of the UK Clean Air Act (1956) were any more concerned about air pollution than those who were still burning coal. Colombotos (1969) found that following the adoption of Medicare for the aged, many doctors who had previously held negative attitudes switched to favour the scheme. But they fiercely opposed Medicaid since this involved subsidised medical services to the poor and unemployed, who, many doctors felt, should 'get out and fend for themselves'.

Behavioural change will most likely alter attitudes when it conforms with other motivations. Bruvold (1973, pp.214–215) makes some useful suggestions in this regard. He finds that since only weak relations exist between any *one* attitude and a particular behaviour, and any *one* behaviour and a particular attitude, a policy to encourage environmentally compatible behaviour should aim at the relevant clusters of cognitions and behaviours (some positive and some negative) to make them all favourable to appropriate behaviour change. As an illustration he suggests that (pecuniary) incentives should be available to householders to overcome their reluctance to sort their solid wastes into easily recyclable categories. This, in combination with information about the hazards and costs of not so doing, plus facts about the environmental gains of proper solid waste management, might lead to the birth of a new waste removal programme.

Despite the limitations of behaviour-centred research, there is some value in studying people with environmentally responsive behaviour to see how their cognitive arrays and information sensors differ from those who persist in environmentally 'irresponsible' acts (O'Riordan, 1973). In an attack on attitude studies Schiff (1971, p.16) points out that research should be aimed not only at what people do (rather than what they think) but also at why they do it. Like Heberlein, she believes that "when one knows why a particular behaviour is preferred, one can attempt to change the behaviour by changing the advantages now seen accruing to it". This might be a good way to expose the fact that people are propelled by conflicting motivations (the product of incompatible values) which they attempt to reconcile by compartmentalising cognitions and actions.

Nevertheless, even when concentrating on only one aspect of observed behaviour, one cannot assume that connected behavioural actions will be consistent. Though environmental pressure groups are a dominant force in environmental politics, their members, like the rest of us, behave contrary to their beliefs. A wilderness researcher once told me that some of the worst ecological damage to the back country is caused by Sierra Club outings which consist of far too many people for such fragile terrain. Barnett (1971) found that members of Zero Population Growth Inc. showed a strong interest in family life, but were unable to commit themselves personally (by having fewer than two children) to the policy they advocated for society as a whole (since they believed America should reduce its population to 150 million). He concludes (p.764):

> "Particularly in view of the fact that this finding is from members of a population control organisation, it further supports the proposition that there is no intrinsic link between concern with population growth as a *general problem* and the *personal commitment* to limit the number of one's natural children to what is necessary for population stabilisation in one's lifetime."

The behaviour → attitude model is also unsatisfactory in that it assumes few, if any, impediments to behavioural choice. Those whose actions are restricted by social, economic, or political factors may well be forced to adopt consistent cognitive arrays against their better judgement (Svart, 1974). For example, McLean (1974) found that mothers living in a deprived urban area were deeply unhappy about the sordid physical environment that surrounded them, but had to accept it as their fate. So they valued highly the proximity of relatives and friendly neighbours, who provided a sense of social belonging. Many people who live in hazard-prone locations may be there not because they do not perceive the hazard, but because the hazardous places are cheap to buy or easy to squat on. Those who suffer lead pollution because they live beside motorways or factories may have no choice of alternative housing and so can be imprisoned to ill health. Yet, when asked about it, these same people play down the pollution hazard, because it may be psychologically and socially uncomfortable to do otherwise. It is therefore dangerous to isolate environmental cognition from the wider sociopolitical milieu in which people live.

Part of this milieu is the social fabric within which ideas and information spread. In 1965 Katz and Lazarsfield proved that many privately held cognitions (probably the vast majority of the nonexperienced cognitions) are in fact formed by communication through social networks of peers. Group-related attitudes appear to be formed by a relatively small number of 'opinion influentials', individuals who command the respect and attention of their more passive acquaintances who are members of their social groups. Katz and Lazarsfield (p.65) note that "the evidence strongly

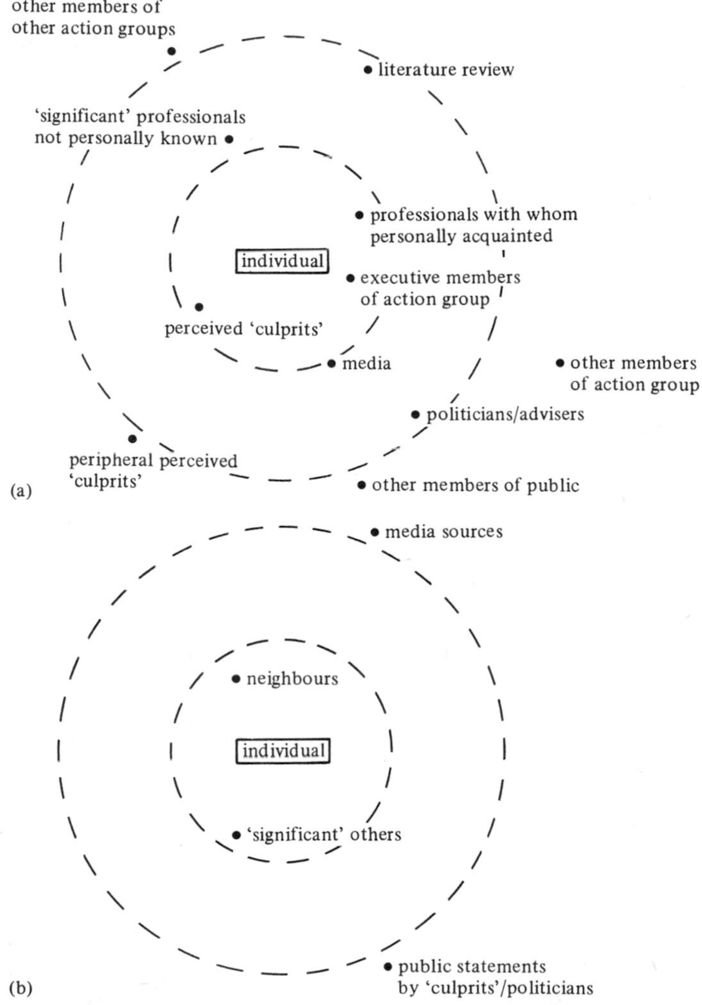

Figure 6.10. The flow of environmental information: (a) environmentally active individual; (b) environmentally inactive individual. (Based on Kirkby, 1973.)

suggests that opinions and attitudes often are maintained, sometimes generated, sometimes merely reinforced, in conjunction with others". It is therefore quite probable that casual conversation plays an important role in determining the form and extent of transmission of environmental information and in moulding public response. In some preliminary research Kirkby (1973) demonstrated that public cognitions about toxic air pollutants were influenced by the social milieu of the local community (figure 6.10), though certain critical pathways were sometimes obstructed for political, administrative or legal reasons. She contends that since the flow of information is so dependent on social networks, sampling procedures should explicitly take into account the social structure of the community. Egler (1969) postulated that public information about certain important pollutants was suppressed (possibly unintentionally) because the crucial data were circulated only among the professional and social networks of experts and bureaucrats. We shall see in the next chapter how social communication of environmental information can promote or retard effective public participation and improve or impede decisionmaking.

We still know very little about the interactions between information flows, experience, awareness, and concern in shaping cognitions and influencing individual behaviour and political action. It would seem unlikely that either the attitude → behaviour or the behaviour → attitude model is suitable, for neither properly takes into account the social and political forces that play such a major role in shaping cognitions and restricting behavioural options. Burton *et al.* (1975) have played with a third model of environmental cognition (figure 6.11) in which the individual 'negotiates' with environmental stimuli in a transactional framework. Here, man alters his environment to suit his requirements while he accepts the limitations created by the stimuli themselves and by social forces beyond his control. This model is as yet untested, but holds some promise since it recognises that in cognising and responding man learns to cope with his

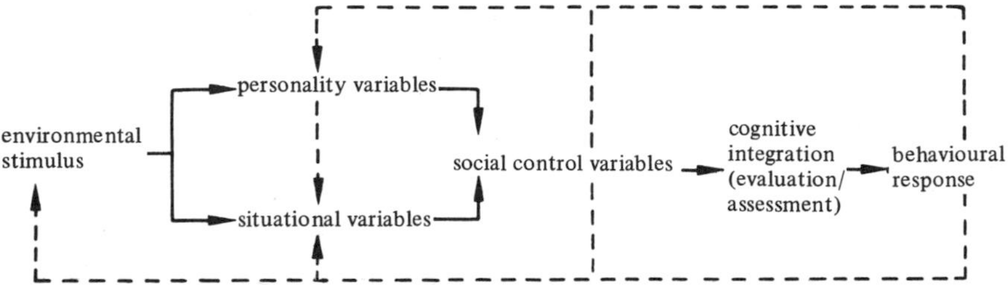

Figure 6.11. A transactional model of environmental cognition. The dashed lines represent 'negotiated' feedback/monitoring loops. The individual not only evaluates his *anticipated* behaviour (as in figure 6.2) but reviews his actions in the context of the original stimulus and the other process variables. Environmental behaviour thus becomes a *continuous learning process* of environmental adaptation, personal 'becoming', and social awareness.

surroundings and to change things a little to suit his requirements. This model bridges the mechanistic and rationalistic attitude–behaviour schema depicted in figure 6.2a (where there is no feedback) and the interactional arrangements of figure 6.2b and 6.2c (where there is feedback but it is narrowly defined), to place cognitive response in a real world framework of possibilities and impediments, hopes and fears, privilege and inequality. The transactional model of environmental cognition and behaviour, therefore, describes a process of individual 'becoming' and the recognition of political consciousness, while demonstrating that there are limits to man's alteration of his surroundings. It may be possible to visualise the integration of this idea into programmes for public participation and environmental education, areas that show great promise as a result of recent changes in decisionmaking procedures and the law.

7

The politics of environmentalism

Politics is more than the distribution and use of power—it is the socially acceptable process through which power is recognised, legitimate disagreements are arbitrated, and the public purpose (insofar as it is capable of definition) is executed. No one denies that the political mechanism is inegalitarian or that it favours the wants of a minority over the needs of a majority; but politics, for all its faults, is what we all live by, and, with various degrees of reluctance, we all accept. We accept it because we are all part of a 'political culture' (Almond and Verba, 1963) which establishes the norms and rules of procedure by which we are collectively governed.

Figure 7.1 schematically depicts the relationships that link the body politic, which includes the general public as it is divided into social groups, economic organisation and other sectional interests, and political lobbies and the like, and the elites—the elected or appointed community leaders, their senior administrators and special advisers, and other 'opinion influentials' such as interest group leaders. The policy environment so created is a transactional arrangement whereby the body politic senses its needs and makes demands, and provides the vital power base for the elites to decide on and act in the broad public interest.

This arrangement balances potentially divisive tensions. In granting power to the elites, the body politic must be constantly vigilant that their trust is not abused and that resulting policies reasonably reflect their sectional interests. From within their ranks, groups and individuals either appoint themselves or are elected to monitor political performance, and seek to ensure that their leaders (at whatever level) represent their views. For their part of the political bargain, the elites endeavour to 'accommodate' their policies to meet the perceived demands of their constituents, and employ a variety of 'legitimising' devices (such as elections, referenda, commissions of inquiry, and public hearings) to test political feeling and to permit them to intervene decisively and legitimately in the affairs of the

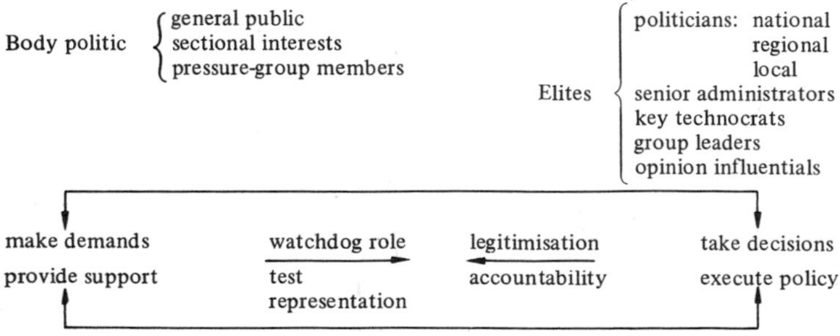

Figure 7.1. The political culture.

people at large. (For an excellent account of symbolism in politics, see Edelman, 1964.) This symbolic equipment also includes 'objective' evaluating devices such as structure plans, alternative growth scenarios, benefit–cost analyses, programme budgeting, and the various disamenity evaluation indices referred to in chapter 6. The function of these mechanisms is very important (though subject to manipulation), namely to justify to a watchful electorate that the distribution of gains and losses resulting from any likely decision is 'politically fair'.

The political culture which frames all policy evaluation and execution is a carefully orchestrated balance, not just between the power-sharing responsibilities of the body politic and their leaders, but between three other vital components of the political process, namely consensus and cleavage, political activism and passivity, and the separation of politicisation from socialisation (Almond and Verba, 1963, pp.337–375). Of these the consensus–cleavage tension is the most important, for it 'knits' together the fabric of the political culture. Consensus refers to a general agreement over the rules of the game, the roles of the participants, and the significance of the legitimising tools. It is achieved through what Dahl (1961, p.315) calls "a recurring process of interaction" between members of the political stratum and their nonpolitical clients. Political consensus is about means, not ends or substance.

Political cleavage is the disagreement among men of honestly differing persuasions about appropriate goals, tactics, and interpretations. It is precisely because these differences are potentially so disruptive that the policymaking process can only function if all those who participate agree to certain basic rules and recognise a degree of role specialisation. In short, politics is a healthy amalgam of trust and suspicion that permits the peaceful resolution of conflict. If the trust is not there, or if some people play by different rules, the stability of the whole hierarchy is threatened. This is why most, if not all, governments are genuinely concerned about illegal acts of political violence. Extremist environmental groups will not serve their cause by disrupting industrial activities, or sabotaging what they regard as environmentally damaging projects, or supporting acts of civil disobedience. These tactics are employed under the socially disintegrating rules of threat, violence, fear, and repression in order to obtain ends that are not legitimately defined. Consensus also transcends the failings of political personality. Even when misdemeanours occur in high places, the roles of political elites cannot be seriously discredited without creating unsettling doubt and insecurity. Individuals may default and be replaced, but, provided appropriate sanctions remain or are introduced, political authority should always remain.

Activity and passivity refer to levels of political participation. Almond and Verba (1963, p.357) believe that a passive majority is essential if active minorities are to be effective without being disruptive. But they hasten to add that passivity does not necessarily mean apathy, for they report that in many true democracies passivity is accompanied by a belief that, if or when political action is necessary, the influence of the passive majority will be felt. Thus the conviction that he could play an active civic role if need be keeps the passive citizen content, most of the time, to let the elites act authoritatively for him.

It is only for a tiny minority of truly active citizens (probably less than 0·1%) that these feelings merge with deeds (Milbrath, 1965; Burch, 1976). Despite all the rhetoric, mass citizen participation is not the political norm; in fact, efforts at mass mobilisation may lead to greater alienation, more frustration, increased cleavage, and in the end to very conservative decisions compared with a more efficient arrangement of political representation through pluralist interest groups. This point is developed by Wengert (1971a, 1976) who comments (1976):

> "There is reason to believe that in a nonhomogeneous community increased participation will highlight differences and increase conflict. The proper question is whether a condition for consensus already exists—in which case participation may further its realisation; but where a condition of diversity exists, participation can contribute little to conflict resolution and may even increase conflict by creating confrontations and inducing polarization."

He concludes that if social cleavage is endemic, increased political activism will have to be tempered by more authoritarian institutions which have the power to enforce unpopular decisions. This view is shared by Ophuls (1973) and Heilbroner (1974a, 1974b).

The balance between politicisation and socialisation is a third significant feature of the political culture. We noted in the previous chapter how cognitions and behaviour are shaped by a network of social communication and membership of symbolic identity groups. This network is based primarily on social relations, not political connections, since it is vital for political stability that cleavages are not superimposed along social lines. When this does occur, it can result in intractable civil strife transmitted from one generation to the next (as is currently the case in Northern Ireland).

7.1 The political culture of environmental politics

The political culture vis-à-vis environmental decisionmaking can be distinguished along four lines, (a) the relative degree of passivity/activity in the body politic, (b) the amount of legal, administrative, and political discretion granted to elites in the execution of policy, (c) the relative importance of bargaining and conciliation compared with consultation and compromise as mechanisms for conflict resolution, and (d) the role of the law in guaranteeing access to information, ensuring a proper airing of all relevant views, providing safeguards to citizens' rights and scrutinising political and administrative procedures. Since, by definition, the political culture will vary with the traditions, customs, institutions, and other cultural attributes of a political community, it will be useful to review these criteria in the context of three countries with which the author is familiar—the United States, Canada, and Great Britain.

7.1.1 Passivity-activity in the body politic

It is really not surprising that the impetus of the literature on political participation has so far come from America, for it is a nation that prides itself on its civic responsibility and political activism. This was observed by de Tocqueville back in the 1830s when he noted (1961, p.295):

> "Democracy does not confer the most skillful kind of government upon the people, but it produces that which the most skillful governments are frequently unable to awaken, namely an all-pervading and restless activity, a superabundant force, and an energy which is inseparable from it, and which may, under favourable circumstances, beget the most amazing benefits."

'Grass roots' activism is very much a part of the American political scene, fostered legally by the myriad of local government posts that must be filled by local ballot. Environmental action groups were spawned in America. To begin with there were the wilderness and wildlife lobbies such as the Sierra Club, the Wilderness Society, the Conservation Foundation, and the Izaak Walton League, all run by old-time conservationists who commanded the ear and the money of the politically powerful, but who were generally ineffectual in the face of economic self-interest (Kolko, 1963). Environmental organisations gradually recognised that to be effective they had to adopt the politically successful tactics of the resource development agencies. This led to a new breed of politicised environmental groups such as Friends of the Earth, the Environmental Defense Fund, the Environmental Policy Council, and Zero Population Growth Inc., some of which have opened up chapters in Britain (FOE, and ZPG as Population Stabilisation) and in Canada (FOE and the Sierra Club). This politicisation of environmental activism is a natural offshoot of the American political culture which has fully absorbed even the more radical of the new lobbies (see Morrison *et al.*, 1972).

Neither Britain nor Canada has the same political history of popular activism as the United States, though amenity organisations have been part of the British scene since the mid-19th century (Nicholson, 1970, pp.163–187; Allaby, 1971; Allison, 1975, pp.109–123; Lowe, 1975). It might even be argued that it is precisely because such organisations are so embedded in the political fabric (and because many of them are patronised by leading public figures) that activism in the sense of grass roots participation is less common. Britain is a nation where the invisible political power of influence through social and political connection is far more telling than the more dramatic placard-waving antics of politically ephemeral environmental groups. (For excellent case studies see Gregory, 1971; Kimber and Richardson, 1974; Rivers, 1974.)

British environmental managers tend to feel that the public is passive and will accept what is thought good for it. Lowenthal and Prince (1964, pp.325–329) suggest that most policymakers in England see themselves as custodians of the public interest and so are often quite oblivious to the gulf that divides them from 'grass root' feelings. The famous Skeffington Report (UK Committee on Public Participation in Planning, 1969) urged planners to consult with the public during and after the formulation of their proposals (but rarely before they became psychologically committed to certain assumptions and principles), and to *consider* techniques for informing the public. But, as Dennis (1972, p.222) remarks, "what is said about this ... is far exceeded in volume by ... recommendations for informing the public in order to ensure full understanding of the proposals and permit informed comment on them". He adds (p.223) that "what is conspicuously lacking in the Skeffington report is any sign that there might be other points of view which are equally entitled to ... authoritative airing when planning proposals are under discussion. 'What the public needs to know' is weighed down with complacency".

Styles (1971, p.165) correctly observes that "participation and the creation of a responsive elite is very much bound up with the organisation of government. Insofar as the proposals for local government reform do not help in the creation of a responsive and diffused elite [and he suggests they do not because neither the desire nor the necessary experience exists among top executives and policymakers in local government], then the planners' task in securing public response is going to be that much more difficult". The form and effectiveness of participation is thus very much bound up with the national political culture.

The Canadian experience lies somewhere between the two poles of participatory activism found in the United States and in Britain, but tends toward the American model. Environmental and political participation has been 'imported' into Canada from its southern neighbour both ideologically and physically through the immigration of American activists. A number of dedicated Canadian and American lawyers have been largely responsible for the mounting pressures on the federal and provincial governments to adopt legislation that would legally sanction public involvement (Morley, 1971, 1973, 1974a) though a number of equally dedicated conservationists have also been influential (Chant, 1970; Littlejohn and Pimlott, 1971; Allaby, 1971, pp.181–193; Brinkhurst and Chant, 1971).

7.1.2 The scope of discretion

Discretion is the freedom granted to policymakers and administrators to determine their own guidelines and judge the suitability of their actions. The scope of discretion afforded indicates how far society puts its faith in professional and administrative competence.

In Great Britain a traditional faith in administrative ability has resulted in the legal transfer of some authority to nonelected civil servants. This means that all kinds of regulatory policy making—the setting of ambient standards, determining consents for waste discharges, arriving at performance standards for road and building construction, deciding on what buildings or landscapes should be included in urban or rural conservation areas, etc.—are executed by selective consultation with particular interests, but with no requirement to inform the general public (Gregory, 1971, pp.1–35). Although the Skeffington Committee suggested forty ways of consulting with the public, it was left to the local authorities to decide what forms this participation should take.

Public access to all kinds of relevant facts in Britain is not an automatic right, since the publication of information is either controlled by statute or limited by ministerial discretion. For example, all data relevant to a proposed or actual effluent discharge are withheld from public scrutiny and even from those adjacent landowners who enjoy a special (riparian) interest in the discharge. McLoughlin (1973, p.360) notes that "a study of English pollution-control legislation generally shows that few safeguards for individuals have been incorporated, even where health and property may be materially affected". Under Section 32 of the Control of Pollution Act (1974) the statutory consents for all discharges are to be made public from April 1, 1976. However, this provision does not grant the public access to information about *actual discharges*, nor will it be possible to obtain data about discharges into trade sewers (Garner, 1975). In addition, Section 12 of the Rivers (Prevention of Pollution) Act (1961) is not repealed; this allows firms to plead with the responsible minister that no information relating to their waste discharges be disclosed, on the grounds of confidentiality (see Tinker, 1972).

In the past, control over information has been defended on the grounds of administrative competence; today it smacks of political secrecy. And all this is despite the idealism of the British statement on pollution for the Stockholm Conference (Ashby, 1972a, p.81) that the public must be "told the facts insofar as they are known", and they must be told the truth "even if [it] suggests unpalatable courses of action".

The Canadians have adopted British discretionary practice wholeheartedly. Jordan (1973, p.14) states that decisions about the scope and content of all kinds of environmental information that should be released rest with the minister in question (advised by his senior civil servants). He concludes:

> "There is no *positive* obligation on the Minister to make information (general or specific) available to the public. The decision by the Minister concerning approval or rejection of [any] proposal is made only on the basis of the actor and by the advocacy of the actor. The public has no *right* to participate in the process of decision making."

Lucas (1971, 1976) and Lucas and Moore (1973) expand upon this theme with respect to Canadian pollution control laws. These administrative statutes leave to the minister responsible or to the director of pollution control a veritable book of discretionary clauses; including the determination of whether the 'public interest' is involved when processing an application, and hence whether a public hearing should be convened, what information is 'relevant' at any public hearing, who is allowed to appear and make representations, and how much data about any proposed discharge should be made public. This state of affairs places considerable power in the hands of the politicians and their advisers, for control of knowledge is a powerful political weapon which weakens the effectiveness of citizen participation.

In the United States, administrative discretion is still widespread but legally tempered by two important pieces of legislation. The Freedom of Information Act (1966) is based on the important constitutional principle that all information is available to the public unless it can be shown to the satisfaction of the courts that full disclosure is either not in the public interest or potentially compromising to a firm or individual (privileged information). The National Environmental Policy Act, NEPA (1969) requires full disclosure of environmental impact for federal proposals and for policies significantly affecting the environment; again this is subject to judicial scrutiny. Nevertheless, in practice clever devices are employed to bypass these laws. Wade (1972) reports how firms and lobbies have successfully used the privilege clauses to avoid full disclosure and retain the administrative discretion upon which they rely, while Gillette (1972a, 1972b) and Baldwin (1973) show how NEPA is being manipulated to restrict the scope and detail of environmental reviews. Tactics include (a) not describing the exact nature of the proposal, (b) the use of pejorative phrases and biased data, (c) an emphasis on economic gains over environmental losses, (d) lack of proper citations to support factual evidence, (e) limited review of alternatives, especially the 'no action' option, (f) failure to review second- and third-order ramifications. Recent amendments to the Act have closed some, but not all, of these loopholes (Holden, 1975).

A healthy suspicion of administrative discretion has always existed in the United States, a suspicion led by the consumer advocate, Ralph Nader, who has investigated the dubious practices of environmental regulatory agencies in air pollution (Esposito, 1970), water pollution (Zwick and Benstock, 1971; Fallows, 1972), pesticides regulation (Wellford, 1971), timber management (Barney, 1972), irrigation and land reclamation (Berkman and Viscusi, 1973), and land speculation (Fellmeth, 1973). Nader's lead has been followed by a number of other excellent studies, including those by Drew (1970), A. E. Morgan (1971), Clusen (1973), and Heuvelmans (1974) on the Corps of Engineers; H. P. Green (1972a), Talbot (1972), Lewis (1972) and Young (1973) on energy regulation;

Guymer (1971), Seckler (1971), and Park *et al.* (1974) on water management; Ferguson and Bryson (1972) and Pendergraft (1972) on forestry management; Hagevick (1970), Schachter (1973), and Hagevick *et al.* (1974) on air quality management; Popkin (1967) and Haas *et al.* (1971) on weather management; Simms (1970) on soil conservation; Potter (1973) on oil spills; Hagenstein (1973) on the regulation of federal lands; and Babcock and Bosselman (1972), Linowes and Allensworth (1973), and Wolff (1973) on land regulation.

There is little doubt that publications such as these do affect policy and tighten the reins on administrative freedom. Esposito's brilliant analysis of malpractice in air pollution control, for instance, certainly spurred Senator Muskie's Air and Water Pollution Subcommittee of the Senate Committee on Interior and Insular Affairs to tighten up its proposed standards and increase government surveillance of air pollution control activities (as embodied in the 1970 Clean Air Act). The Nader reports also show how valuable it is to be able to penetrate environmental administration (something that is not so easily done in Britain and Canada).

7.1.3 Bargaining versus consultation

The standard North American model of environmental decisionmaking is based on bargaining and concession trading among political lobbies, all of whom have an interest in peaceful resolution of conflict. The implicit model is one of a polycentric power base in which disagreement and conflict centre around a decentralised network of countervailing political powers (see Braybrooke and Lindblom, 1963; Gore, 1964; Holden, 1966; Schoettle, 1972). In much of environmental policymaking, motives of self-interest are transmuted into what Allison (1975, p.21) defines as "publicly oriented wants—beliefs and principles about the 'social value' of certain courses of action". So it is not surprising that investigations of environmental issues make much of the tension between self-interest and the public good as symbolised by tussling political lobbies [see the Nader reports cited above, and Wengert (1955) for American examples; Chant (1970), Graham (1973), Lucas and Moore (1973) for Canadian studies; and Gregory (1971); Aldous (1972); Bugler (1972); Kennett (1973); Kimber and Richardson (1974); Rivers (1974) for British cases].

Wolpert and his coworkers (Mumphrey *et al.*, 1971; Mumphrey and Wolpert, 1973; Wolpert, 1976) explicitly incorporate bargaining as a means of conflict resolution in their quite sophisticated models of locational conflict. They assume that any proposal for an undesirable facility (a nuclear power station, sewage treatment plant, motorway, etc.) will generate hostility in the impacted neighbourhood. This will best be mollified by the provision of supplementary community benefits, which are really concessionary bribes. Failure to make these side payments could result in political stalemate that would add immeasurably to project costs. These bribes become a least-cost 'transaction payment' (part of total project costs), the nature of which will depend upon the political effectiveness of the opposition groups. If the threatened community has insufficient power to stop the proposal, then the side payments could be derisory.

The Wolpert model is an important contribution to environmental politics for it incorporates the threat of political opposition expressed as a threat of physical violence, the work of advocacy professionals, the clever manipulation of the law, or the more subtle pressures of political influence, within the traditional benefit–cost calculus. The ability of the opposition to use available political or legal institutions to halt development determines the nature of the bribe; the powerful will always win, the weak (in the absence of institutional reform) will progressively lose (figure 7.2). The Wolpert model envisages compensation in the form of additional community facilities, such as recreation centres or libraries, but it could just as easily include monetary payments as required under the British Land Compensation Act (1973). The trouble with the process (not the model) is that demands for compensation escalate, making it increasingly costly to site any noxious facilities except where few people reside and the environment 'doesn't matter', or where those who do live in the locality are politically weak (blacks, other racial minorities, and the poor). However, success in bargaining can be contagious. Wolpert (1976) notes that "the process is conditionally unstable because uncompensated spillover effects lead eventually to political recruitment and activation by those adversely affected".

It would be misleading, however, to assume that bargaining is the only means of conflict resolution in America. Bargaining is common when interest groups already exist in a particular political arena, or when they spontaneously form around a controversial proposal that causes anger or fear amongst the affected population. Although the highly controversial issues attract public attention and become the subjects of doctoral

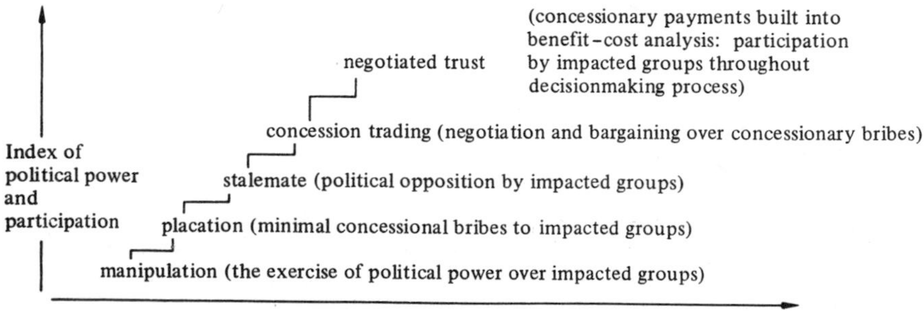

Figure 7.2. Political bargaining over the siting of obnoxious facilities. (After Wolpert, 1976.)

dissertations, most policy decisions (each with some degree of environmental impact) are made outside the public spotlight, where the 'decisional environment' is not so traumatic. Indeed the institutional setting may actually impede the kind of critical appraisal that bargaining often engenders. Sax (1970a, p.56) describes how such daily routine decisions may combine to produce a devastating effect on the environment.

> "The political and economic pressures which serve to tip the scale in favour of a specific project, though producing a seemingly rational result when considered in isolation, may serve cumulatively to produce exactly the opposite of the overall policy that the administrators want to achieve, that they are mandated to achieve by law and policy statements, and that they think they are achieving. The greatest [environmental] problems are often the outcome of the smallest-scale decisions, precisely because the ultimate, aggregate impacts of those decisions are so difficult to see and the pressures so difficult to cope with from the perspective of the insider."

The buffering mechanisms which protect the administrator are particularly well developed in environmental matters where problems are poorly defined, multiagency responsibilities are involved, no clearly defined public interest emerges and the information is sketchy and indeterminate. In such cases discussion between well-established interest groups, key advisers and policymakers is more likely to be the norm than is confrontationist negotiation.

British policymaking is based much more on consultative procedures than is the case in North America (see Tinker, 1972). This is partly a legacy of the paternalistic view of public administration and politics that was commonly held by the elite well into the twentieth century, and partly a reflection of the British temperament. Compromise via conciliation is an established British practice, now viewed with deep suspicion by environmentalists who dislike the 'closed club' atmosphere which discourages policymakers from being responsive to the public interest. Bugler (1972, p.11) quotes the Chief Inspector of Her Majesty's Alkali and Clean Air Inspectorate on the matter of coping with violators of emission consents:

> "We look on our job as educating industry, persuading it, cajoling it. We achieve far more this way. The Americans take a big stick and threaten 'solve your problem'. We say to industry 'Look, lads, we've got a problem'. In this way we've got industry well and truly tamed."

The cooperative approach is combined with flexible case-by-case evaluation to ensure that the most reasonable compromise is attained for each discharger.

The Inspectorate is noted for its patience and 'constructive' assistance. If a violating firm is unable or unwilling to clean up, the Inspectorate will contact its trade association in the hope that 'friendly persuasion' from fellow members will bring it to heel. Needless to say, if the fellow trade members are collectively slow in coming to terms with their pollution problems, either the trade effluent consents will reflect this political reality or prosecution involving a nominal fine will follow. British pollution control law specifies that so long as polluters make 'reasonable' efforts to control their waste emission, there will be no legal action. Recent American legislation, on the other hand, requires polluters to use the "best practicable" technology by 1977, and the "best available" technology by 1983 (de Nevers, 1973; Kneese and Schultze, 1975, pp.51-59).

Cooperation between regulators and the regulated is also the norm in the realm of water pollution control in Britain. In fact, a Ministry of Housing and Local Government circular (51/64) specifically stated that waste management was a matter for 'reasonable discussion'. More recently the Director of the Central Unit on Environmental Pollution at the Department of the Environment pointed out that "cooperation is the key to success" (*The Surveyor*, 21 March 1975, p.16).

But the result is widespread and flagrant violation of effluent consents. Roughly 60% of sewage treatment plants do not meet regulatory standards (UK Working Party on Sewage, 1970, p.23). Under the UK Water Act (1973) all sewage treatment works are now operated by regional water authorities, who are also responsible for regulating the waste flows. This example of judge, jury, and defendant all rolled into one is made all the more absurd when one realises that the water authorities aim to increase the pollutant loads passing through these (already overworked) treatment plants in order to have better control over industrial effluents. Yet the authorities are already burdened by debt, so to pay their crippling loan charges plus the capital and maintenance costs of upgrading these plants, trade effluent charges will either have to increase by 7% per year *in real terms* or the authorities will have to relax their standards (Gilliland, 1975, p.365). There is certainly some evidence that industry does not at present meet their statutory consents; a recent report by the Severn-Trent Water Authority (Tinker, 1975) found that 60% of industries replying to an official inquiry (40% of those contacted declined to respond) persistently exceeded their consents.

Yet prosecution is not relished, as it is costly, time consuming, and 'sets a bad tone'. The Clean Air Inspectorate has gone to the lengths of court proceedings only five times in the past fifty years (Bugler, 1972, p.12). The maximum fine was £100, and the large companies were never prosecuted. There were only 67 prosecutions for violations of river discharge consents in 1973 and in most cases the fines were derisory (McLoughlin, 1973). Indeed the penalty levied against a pollution control official for disclosing information about the nature of a discharge is far more severe than the fine for an offending polluter if he is caught! Consultation may preserve good relations and limit hostile political reaction to new policies on regulations, but it certainly does not guarantee that environmental quality is safeguarded.

An air of 'clubbiness' also pervades the established British amenity societies who would shudder at the whisper of the phrase 'political lobby'. In documenting the membership of the Council for Protection of Rural England (CPRE) (table 7.1), Allison (1975, pp.115–123) remarks on the high social status and prestige of the executive members who appeal to the "tasteful horror of educated public opinion" and who depend on "contacts and expertise ... to communicate evaluations and ideas through effective channels and have them taken seriously". He quotes the CPRE's Secretary as saying, "Fighting cases means publicity. Publicity means conflict and conflict can mean the loss of contacts and credibility." It is almost unthinkable that the CPRE (a major national amenity organisation) could envisage itself as part of the Wolpert model.

The Canadian picture is broadly similar to the British one, where 'closed door' consultations with special interest lobbies precede most federal government and provincial legislation relating to environmental matters. As was noted earlier, public access to these discussions in both Britain and Canada is, for the most part, legally barred. And, as in Britain, there is widespread violation of effluent discharge permits in Canada while legal prosecutions are generally discouraged (see Morley, 1972b, 1972c).

Table 7.1. Membership of British amenity societies. (Source: Allison, 1975, pp.120, 122.)

	Executive Committee of CPRE		Chairman and Secretaries of county branches of CPRE	
	N	%[a]	N	%[a]
In the House of Lords	7	7	6	14
Justice of the Peace or with civil honour	13	13	11	25
With relevant technical qualifications	13	13	8	18
With other academic qualifications	8	8	6	14
Of military rank	25	26	3	7
Males with none of the above	21	22	9	20
Females with none of the above	10	10	1	3

	Officers of the Conservation Society	
	N	%[a]
With titles	5	16
Doctors	5	16
Professors	10	31
With civil awards	7	22
None of these	5	16

[a] Percentages rounded off.

Concluding an extensive review of federal water quality legislation, Morley (1972a, pp.16–17) writes: "It is undoubtedly a valid assumption that there are a number of persons, including existing pulp and paper mills, who are presently discharging deleterious substances into waters frequented by fish contrary to the provisions of the Fisheries Act [1951]. Prosecutions for such violations are infrequent." While he has some evidence to support Morley's observation, Good (1971, p.286) finds that, in general, the federal agencies have been more assiduous in spotting violators and executing litigation than provincial authorities, where "the means of enforcement [are] often nonexistent and the performance, if any, has been inept".

To any student of environmental politics these are not surprising findings. In chapter 2 it was pointed out that environmental quality (especially of an amenity kind) has the lowest political priority. So as long as violators or would-be violators can show they are making 'reasonable efforts' to conform to the required quality protection standards (which they themselves help to determine), without threatening jobs or raising their costs to uncompetitive levels, they will be left alone. Moreover, it seems that the majority of the public accepts this arrangement. What keeps regulators and dischargers on their toes and undoubtedly reduces the worst environmental abuse are the political watchdog activities of self-appointed protection organisations and innovations in environmental law (discussed in the next chapter); without these our environments would be immeasurably worse off than they are today. Hence the great interest among students of environmental policies in the roles of citizen participation and of the law in shaping environmental decisions.

7.1.4 The role of environmental law

The influence of the law in modern environmental politics depends largely upon its constitutional role. While the great body of common law (handed down by judicial judgement through interpretation of precedent) is similar in Britain, Canada, and the United States (and indeed for all nations with an Anglo–Saxon heritage), the power of the courts in defining and sanctioning the common law and in reviewing statutory law will depend on the traditional relationship between the three great arbiters of political power—the legislature, the executive, and the judiciary (figure 7.3).

The American Constitution separates the powers of each of these three branches so that the courts can exert considerable influence in assessing the suitability of politically determined policy and the procedural correctness of all administrative activity. Although the courts are specifically apolitical in the sense that jurists are 'above' party allegiance, they obviously exert a political influence in scrutinising the operations of the other two branches of government and in defending civil rights. It is perhaps worthy of note that judicial litigation is based on adversary relationships and so is grounded in conflict. Perhaps this is one reason why American environmental politics is so bound up with the law (or vice versa).

In Britain, and to a lesser extent in Canada, a single major institution, namely Parliament, stands at the top of the hierarchy of power and is ultimately responsible for all delegation of power, including defining the duties of the courts. Lyon (1973, p.41) states that "the courts take no initiatives in important public issues such as those relating to the environment [and] are wary of intruding in areas of responsibility that they regard as belonging properly to the legislative or executive branch". Thus it would be misguided to look to the courts either in Britain or Canada for the kind of environmental policy innovations that have recently been experienced in the United States, for the courts in these countries are politically more subdued, and the judges and lawyers tend to be relatively more conservative in testing judicial authority (UK Committee for Environmental Information, 1975). In any case, legislative and executive competence in Britain and Canada are far more protected by constitution and by tradition than is the case in the United States. Despite the strenuous efforts by lawyers to upgrade the status of environmental law in these countries, it is futile to try and make courts of law perform functions they are neither designed for nor equipped to execute.

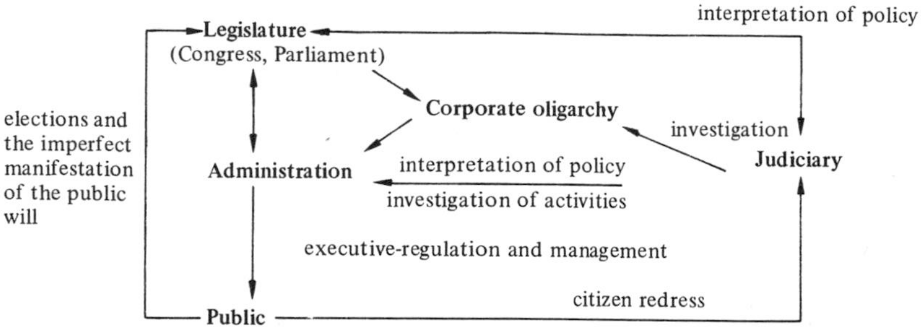

Figure 7.3. The political role of the courts.

7.2 Environmental policymaking

Policymaking has been defined by Schoettle (1972, p.149) as the "process of transformation which turns political inputs into political outputs". The nature of this process will relate in part to the norms and rules of a particular political culture, though it will also be influenced by complicated cognitive relationships arising from the values, aspirations, motivations, and beliefs of key actors and by the operational settings in which these people perform. It is therefore helpful to visualise the policymaking process as the interaction of three major variables: namely, the cognitive structures of key actors, the nature of the institutional environment, and the characteristics of the issues under investigation (figure 7.4). Not only do these variables interact but they change in complexion from day to day, place to place, and issue to issue. Add to this the obvious difficulties of identifying impotent personnel [many policymakers claim they simply do not know who makes what decisions or how (Brown, 1970)] and evaluating all these 'soft' data, and the problems facing the diligent researcher are clearly considerable.

Personality, opinion formation, and political behaviour interact through the meshing of three main components of the cognitive process—belief, evaluation, and social obligation—as they pertain to the actor's view of himself, of other actors, of the political setting, and of the various roles and rules encountered in the resolution of an issue. So there will be a matrix of cognitions about the credibility and political effectiveness of each information source.

This is an exceedingly important point in environmental politics. On referring to figure 6.3, we see that policymakers can brush aside what they regard as 'irrelevant opinion' in favour of 'supportive' viewpoints. Gregory (1971) shows how, time and again, environmental action groups successfully manipulate this aspect by asking an eminent 'figurehead' to endorse their cause. For example, in the battle over a proposed reservoir site in Upper Teesdale, the local action group recruited the support of eminent botanists (some of whom were not acquainted with the site) to stress the importance of protecting the relatively rare flora of the area. Despite their unfamiliarity with many of the larger issues at stake, the prestige and hence credibility of the scientists aroused public opinion. In the great Third London Airport dispute, the Poet Laureate, Sir John Betjeman, extolled with considerable political effect the merits of the countryside and old churches in two of the threatened areas. It is not surprising that environmentalist groups seek the most prominent

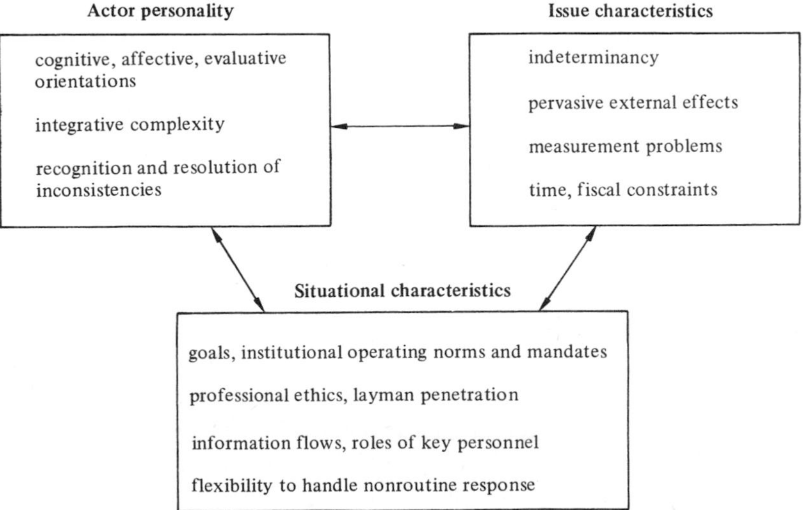

Figure 7.4. The policymaking process.

professionals around, regardless of their specific knowledge of the particular case under consideration, to add 'respectability' to their cause. Hence the great demand for professionals to assist environmental activists, a demand which presents something of a dilemma for academics who may not receive formal academic recognition for such time-consuming work, when they do gain prestige by working for the 'establishment' (Harvey, 1974). Consequently, one of the features of formal public inquiries is the effort made by opposing legal councils to destroy the testimonies of expert witnesses of the other side. Damage to credibility is sometimes a more successful tactic than damning the argument itself.

Differing cognitive orientations among participants in policymaking may lead to disagreement over what exactly constitutes the problem. With respect to environmental questions, ranging from the global 'crisis' to the protection of a 'unique' habitat, honest men and women may disagree violently over symptom and remedy, leaving the nonspecialist politician in some confusion. Speaking with the experience of a former Member of Parliament, Brooks (1974, p.40) admits that "the incapacity of lay politicians to understand the mysteries of science [and, we can add, of the social sciences] means that they can be duped by those who deliberately mystify them for their own game". In many a major environmental issue, key information withheld or abused by special interests (the oil lobby, the automobile lobby, etc.) can unduly influence the process of problem identification.

The ability to handle complex and probabilistic information and visualise the second- or third-order ramifications of various policy options is obviously an extremely valuable attribute for any decisionmaker. Yet it is an attribute that is difficult to evaluate in meaningful terms, so we can only speculate on how well individuals at various levels of government can actually cope. From the limited casework I have conducted (O'Riordan, 1972b), I concur with Brooks' observations that politicians often have to rely heavily on the advice of specialists [whom Brown (1970, p.146) vividly labels 'uncertainty absorbers'] to simplify information and reduce ambiguity to tolerable levels. So, inadvertently, and possibly without his full knowledge, the professional adviser can considerably influence the final decision (Sewell, 1974).

A related personality attribute is the ability to resolve inconsistency so as to take authoritative action. This can take various forms. The junior official, seeking to 'keep his nose clean' may uncover dubious practices or produce research findings that dispute accepted agency policy: should he report his evidence and, if so, to whom? Usually there are strict rules about revealing information, so what may be an act of conscience may in fact be illegal. Nader (1972) would like to see better statutory protection for what he regards as the "legal silencing of the bureaucratic serf". Gillette (1972c) documents such a case with respect to the as yet unresolved controversy over safeguards in nuclear power generation.

There may also be a dissonance between personal belief and social or institutional obligation of the kind facing a devout Catholic charged with administering a family-planning programme, or the wilderness hiker responsible for issuing mineral-prospecting permits for an unprotected part of the back country.

Mention has already been made of the forces shaping conformity of viewpoint and routinisation of procedures in most administrative organisations. This can result in great tensions when bureaucracies are confronted with unprecedented environmental issues and the demands of new pressure groups, for in such circumstances some of the rules may have to be changed. Gregory (1971, pp.7, 300–301) records that 'straightforward' cases of amenity planning are decided at the level of Senior or Chief Executive Officer. In the event of more 'difficult' decisions, senior civil servants' appraisals that undoubtedly influence the Minister's final and irrevocable decision are conditioned to some extent by their perception of the minister's 'amenity mindedness'. "Rightly or wrongly", he observes, "officials generally take the view that there is no point in making recommendations which they think it virtually certain that their political masters will not entertain." Frequently therefore, and especially so if senior officials have strong personalities, organisational policy comes to reflect the orientation of senior staff, whose views tend to be more conservative than those of their junior colleagues (Sewell, 1971, 1974).

Information flows are also distorted by organisational structure, a subject of great interest to students of environmental bureaucracies which are more and more becoming 'super agencies'. (The British Department of the Environment, for example, has nine Ministers, twenty-seven Permanent Secretaries and eighty Undersecretaries.) For here the notorious compartmentalisation of divisional responsibilities can inhibit the wise preparation of comprehensive policy reviews. This may result in what Brown (1970, p.142) calls "Gresham's Law of Planning" whereby simple routine jobs absorb all the time that should be spent on proper evaluation of policy, in the absence of which routinisation flourishes. Gillette (1971b) records how this malaise struck the US Environmental Protection Agency.

In the light of these remarks, it is not difficult to see what Brooks (1974) calls 'decision faking' becomes a more important pastime than decisionmaking, and how large organisations grow inherently more conservative both as to procedures and objectives. Braybrooke and Lindblom's (1963) notion of 'disjointed incrementalism' still remains the most accurate statement of organisational decisionmaking for students of environmental politics (see Ingram, 1973b). It is worth restating their findings as they serve to remind us that *radical* institutional reform, no matter how desirable, is not very likely:

(i) Choices are made at the margin of the *status quo*. Any tendency toward systems transformation is quickly blocked by countervailing pressures toward systems maintenance (Gore, 1964, p.113).

(ii) Only a limited array of options, none of which moves very far from established procedures, is considered, and only a limited range of consequences evaluated (Brown, 1970, pp.137–154).
(iii) The evaluative process is further distorted by discrepancies between agency objectives and agency performance which change the nature of the outcomes considered (Sax, 1970a, pp.52–107).
(iv) The problem itself is transformed in the process to 'fit' agency directives; problems are seen as stresses to be overcome rather than goals to be achieved (Levin, 1972).
(v) Analysis and evaluation occur sequentially, so policy is never what was predetermined but the unanticipated result of repeatedly narrowing choices. Thus decisions are often drifted into rather than preselected, as, slowly but surely, alternative courses of action are foreclosed (Castles *et al.*, 1971, pp.290–291).
(vi) Policymaking is dispersed throughout political institutions, impeding thoughtful comprehensive reviews of integrated 'megaproblems' (Downs, 1966; Schoettle, 1972).

Despite the attempts by researchers to prove otherwise, decisionmaking is rarely a conscious rational exercise where key actors can readily be identified and asked to explain how and why they evaluate information and make judgements. It is quite likely that organisations (and policymakers) sometimes become committed to decisions that have originated from little known individuals armed with biased interpretations of selected evidence. Students of environmental decisionmaking may find this disconcerting and frustrating, but the fact remains that without personal participation in a range of case studies the true flavour of policymaking cannot fully be appreciated. Postdecisional investigation by the outsider is readily susceptible to *post hoc* rationalisation by the participants which may be as much inadvertent as deliberate.

In spite of these empirical difficulties it is possible to sketch various decisional pathways that are common to environmental problems (figure 7.5). These are all based on the premise that most decisions take place in response to political stress initiated by pressure groups which are capable of mobilising political influence and/or significant public opinion. (Decision flows about top national priority issues such as national security and public health may well be activated by key individuals without recourse to public opinion, though even here some form of political lobby will almost certainly exist.) There appear to be four possible decisional paths (see O'Riordan, 1976b):

1. *Nondecisions*. Crenson (1972) applies to a case study of air pollution control politics the theory of nondecisionmaking first propounded by Bachrach and Baratz (1962). These two authors maintained that both pluralist and elitist models of decisionmaking fail to account for the exercise of power that "creates or reinforces social and political values and

institutional practices to limit the scope of the political process to public consideration of only those issues that are comparatively innocuous". Nondecisionmaking is really a misnomer, for it encompasses quite deliberate efforts by powerful groups to keep politically sensitive issues off the public agenda.

Environmental issues such as regulatory practices for pollution control are ideally suited to nondecisionmaking since no particular lobby is likely to gain more than any other if pollution is controlled, so only dedicated environmentalist groups are willing to invest resources in overcoming the high transaction costs (information costs, lobbying, etc.) of achieving tougher pollution control. Crenson (1972) found this to be the case in Chicago where efforts to upgrade polluting emissions were thwarted by a conspiracy of delaying tactics (failure to produce information, the setting up of boards of inquiry, deliberate efforts by power holders to obstruct investigation, lack of media concern) that amounted to what he called (p.184) "politically enforced neglect". Only evidence carefully documented by environmental groups, together with selective use of the law and of the media to activate public opinion, can do much to change such a state of affairs.

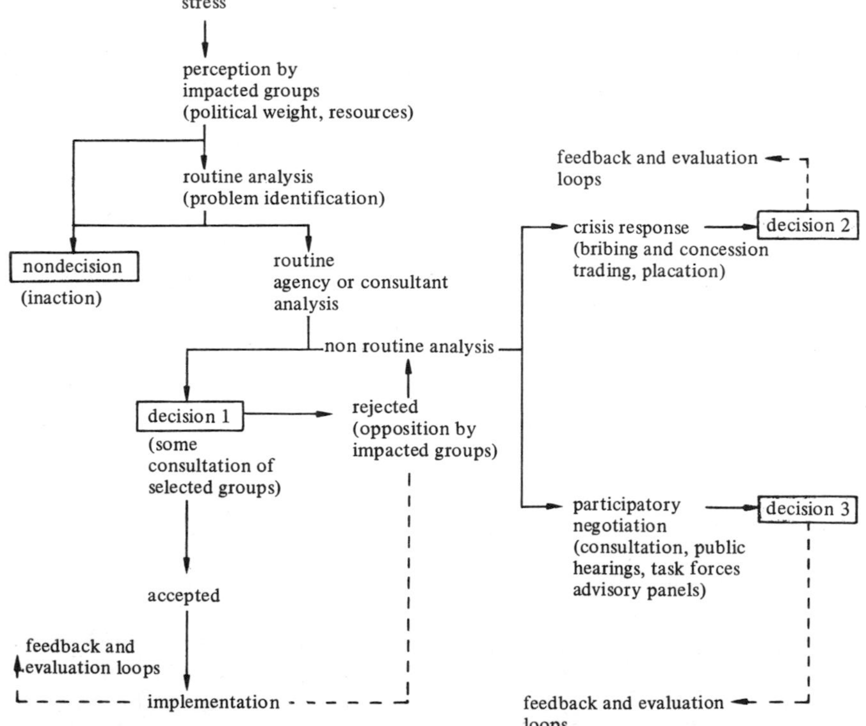

Figure 7.5. Decisional pathways in environmental policymaking.

Nondecisionmaking is probably more pervasive in environmental politics than is commonly realised. The Nader studies of United States regulatory agencies (cited earlier) all document the cozy relationships that are formed between the regulators and the regulated. It all begins to look like a fencing match where, despite the realistic looking parries, no damage is ever likely to be inflicted on either side. A lawyer in the air pollution control office of the Environmental Protection Agency once told me that the EPA had little power to force the automobile manufacturers' lobby to accept the agenda for reducing air pollution emissions as laid down in the 1970 Clean Air Act, since the lobby had all the technology, had bought out most of the leading automotive engineers, and could afford four lawyers for every one provided by the taxpayer (see Jacoby and Steinbruner, 1973; Ayres, 1975; Ditlow, 1975; O'Connor, 1975). Obviously, the lobby does not entirely control the rate of pollution control, but in the absence of really noticeable public support (or a countervailing government research organisation), it is the dominant force.

Straager (1970) supports the hypothesis of nondecisionmaking in a case study of how local government officials in Tucson, Arizona, waited until a water shortage problem became sufficiently serious to be salient to powerful interest groups, before placing it on the political agenda. His study is also of interest in emphasising that once environmental issues 'go public' the decisionmaking apparatus, the perceptions of decisionmakers, and the distribution of administrative responsibility, all change complexion, often in ways which policymakers cannot anticipate and prefer to avoid.

The Tucson experience is typical of the uncertainty facing administrators who grapple with open-ended environmental questions. Riedel (1972) reports on various nondecisionmaking delay tactics:
(i) restricting terms of reference to 'politically acceptable' investigations, or making the terms of reference deliberately vague;
(ii) manning investigative committees with 'safe' members (see Perl, 1971);
(iii) appointing a cross section of opinion that will never agree, or a narrow spectrum of opinion whose findings will be politically unacceptable.
Because all these devices make use of 'symbolic legitimacy' they often achieve their purpose, at least until citizens' organisations or other investigatory bodies effectively prove a case to the contrary.

2. *Routine decisions.* Nondecisionmaking tactics may backfire and force an issue onto the political agenda, though if the stress angers a 'politically significant public' it will immediately move into the administrative arena. Normally the agencies try to seek routine solutions which are compatible with their mandates. It is worth reemphasising that many agencies are not able to scan 'unusual' alternatives because they are statutorily obliged to perform clearly defined functions. British water supply authorities and electric utility companies in many countries have always claimed that their job is to meet demand, not to control it. In the United States it required a number of congressional enactments before flood plain planning became

an effective option in flood damage reduction policies. Routine decisions usually mean well-tried procedures carried out by people who are familiar with each other's duties and cognitions; there is little temptation to try anything too novel. Even 'nonroutine' procedures quickly become standardised in the absence of continued external stress.

3. *Nonroutine decisions.* Where a problem is unprecedented, enormously complicated, or where it requires cooperation with other individuals and organisations, innovative decisionmaking procedures must be employed. Environmental issues often demand nonroutine responses because they frequently involve threats to 'significant publics' not previously identified or consulted in routine analysis, but who carry enough political weight to cause trouble. Moreover, many environmental problems require consideration of untried solutions since they have not been encountered before, or because they induce much controversy among 'equally credible' professionals. Nonroutine decision paths invariably involve more extensive studies, including more comprehensive environmental impact assessment and longer public consultation, and frequently require direct political intervention. Two notable features of the nonroutine response are its commitment to precedent and its uncertainty of outcome. Any new policy sets a precedent that could lead to quite unexpected situations and might create new patterns of responsibility.

This is certainly true in the case of *crisis response* decisions where direct concessions are made to placate adversely-affected interests. Wolpert's findings mentioned earlier, together with the British experience following the enactment of the Land Compensation Act, demonstrate that compensatory bribes can induce subtle shifts in the power balance, lead to unrest among other disadvantaged groups, and may in the end result in greatly increased expenditures compared to the cost of the original facility. For example, the Greater London Council estimate that up to 75% of project costs can be attributed to compensation if both the actual payments and the administrative costs of assessment are included (personal communication from the chief environmental planner). It seems inevitable that growing demands for public participation, fuelled by precedent and policy changes such as environmental impact assessment, will only make matters more cumbersome and costly. In this connection, some writers (e.g. Aldous, 1972; Dennis, 1972; Sax, 1974) have suggested that some percentage (amounts range from 1–5%) of project costs be provided to fund impact assessment and public participation.

An alternative pathway currently being explored is *participatory negotiation*. Policymakers seek out community influentials who act as receivers and transmitters of interest group opinion and incorporate their sectional views throughout policy formulation. They participate in problem identification, goal setting, discussion of alternatives, and, hopefully, in the execution of the final decision. The objective is to translate community views into sound management plans, through an educative process in which policymakers and community leaders become aware of each other's requirements within the context of communal commitment. Ideally, decisions are reached by cooperative problemsolving, a device currently being tried by the Corps of Engineers (Eigermann, 1974) in a recently completed project in the Okanagan Valley, British Columbia (J. O'Riordan, 1976) and attempted in a much wider context in the Canadian 'Man and Resources' project (Chevalier *et al.*, 1974).

There are various possible formats for participatory negotiation. Heberlein (1976) suggests a series of community workshops where different policy options are advanced to monitor likely public response. The problem, however, is to make these credible when they can only be experimental. Clark and Stankey (1976) prefer a computerised public-opinion reference system, though this does not permit discussion. Another idea is the use of the Delphi technique (Linstone and Turoff, 1975) which aims to achieve a consensus of informed opinion through an iterative series of personal interrogations interspersed with interactive feedback. The idea is to reach harmonious conclusions while avoiding the face-to-face personality problems of the committee; its drawbacks lie mainly in the difficulties of accurate communication.

A variation of the committee is the problem-solving task force (J. Graham, 1973). Task groups could be composed of community leaders, professionals, and politicians, selected either on a regional or a functional basis, who are invited to suggest and assess various policy options with planners and resource managers. Self (1971) tends to favour a variation of the task-force idea, with a system of small, specialised functional councils, able to cope with matters of great technical complexity, advising a broadly elected government body. The Okanagan Basin Study (J. O'Riordan, 1976) made extensive use of citizen–professional task forces, which O'Riordan thinks should be formed early (before problems are diagnosed and goals identified), but left sufficiently flexible to permit a changing membership and a variety of discussion procedures. He feels that this device, coupled with an 'open door' policy and responsible media participation, should unearth the committed citizens who tend to become even more socially responsive as a result of participation, while avoiding the overexpenditure of manpower and resources involved in coaxing less-interested people to participate against their inclination.

The task-force device makes use of two fundamental characteristics of policymaking, namely that political communication takes place through social networks in which opinion influentials play important roles, and that social problems based on community conflict are best solved by what Thayer (1972, p.4) calls the "collegial, non-hierarchical, face-to-face, problem solving group, large enough to include the perspectives and expertise necessary to deal with the problem at hand, but small enough to assure each participant that his or her contribution is substantial, meaningful and indispensable to the process." Students of environmental politics are beginning to take a new look at the kind of problemsolving techniques proposed by Gordon (1961) and Prince (1970), especially as these methods are potentially revolutionary in terms of the distribution of power and the raising of civic consciousness (Kasperson and Breitbart, 1974, pp.49–53).

Task forces, workshops, etc., however, do not get round the difficulty of evaluating outcomes and making social choices. In a political democracy this is normally the prime function of the legislature. Haefele (1973) is anxious that this power be properly returned to the legislative arenas, which he feels have shrunk in recent years to mere "petty trading guilds" of interest groups and bureaucracies. While recognising the remorseless logic of Arrow's impossibility theorem (that social choices can never be allocated fairly or rationally), he proposes a regional form of government in which policy is formulated by generalist legislators whom he calls "general purpose representatives" (GPRs). The notion of the GPR involves a Madisonian view of political democracy, in which politicians are supposed to know and to resolve the widely differing views of both the powerful and the weak.

> "Such representatives would sit on all local and regional governmental bodies having jurisdiction over the district ... . The purpose of this building block approach would be twofold: (1) to give the representative control over the whole range of local issues so that he could use his vote in one assembly as a lever in another, thus providing an opportunity for registering intensity of preferences, and (2) to enable governments of varying territorial reach to be assembled (and ... disassembled) easily and conveniently with no damage to the basic political fabric of the area" (p.109).

The crux of Haefele's model is a vote-trading arena where community preferences are exchanged by the GPRs representing quite small subregions, though the total area for which they are collectively responsible encompasses all noticeable externalities. The GPRs would obviously become very powerful individuals whose activities would have to be scrutinised by watchful citizens, but who would provide the necessary political input for policy analysis by professionals (rather than have the bureaucrats assume the public interest, as Haefele implies is currently the case). Haefele (p.134) is unashamedly idealistic in all this:

> "If the GPR system has any merit, it is that it provides incentive for the elected official to know what his constituents want and do not want. It also provides the constituents with an appropriate focus to register their feelings. In an era when the words *participation* and *democracy* can be joined without any notion of redundancy arising the incentive and the focus may be worthwhile."

However, the Haefele proposal presupposes a degree of political communication and constituency interest in social questions that at present does not exist. Both Miller and Stokes (1963) and Luttberg (1971) have shown a wide gulf between the views of constituents about public issues and the understanding of these opinions by their political representatives. Almost invariably politicians are far more confident about the workability of the political system than the electorate, and, however obvious that observation may seem, it does indicate a breakdown of the political trust that is essential to Haefele's model and to the peaceful conduct of the political culture depicted in figure 7.1. Wandesforde-Smith (1974) remarks that Haefele avoids major constitutional and political questions by underestimating the reasons why the legislatures are relatively so weak when it comes to resolving today's environmental problems, and by ignoring the rigidities of the existing political framework.

Nevertheless, Haefele's ingenious suggestions should not be discarded out of hand, for he does face up to a most significant question in modern-day environmental politics, namely, given participation, impact reviews, and better articulated citizens' rights, who is to judge the relative merits of one case over another, and how? Some sort of regional government representation tied to specialist advisory councils and local citizens groups, along the lines advocated by Self (1971) and suggested in the Winnipeg model sketched in figure 7.6, might set us in the right direction.

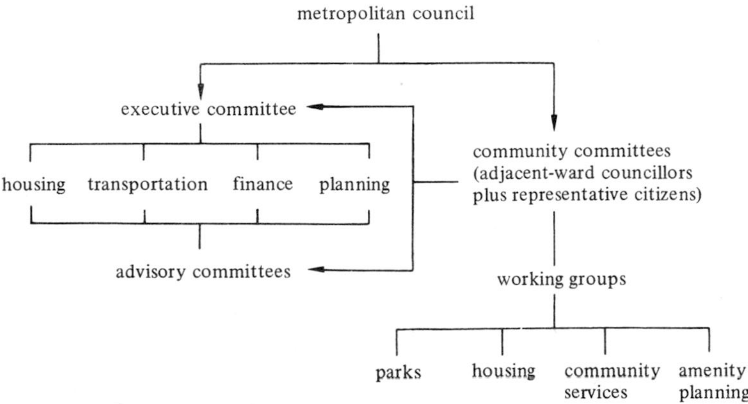

Figure 7.6. Community participation in the government of Metropolitan Winnipeg. The diagram simplifies the present situation in Winnipeg and is more illustrative than definitive. Nevertheless, the relationships between the executive political committee and the Metropolitan Ward Council (chaired by an elected mayor) and clusters of ward representatives and ward community councils is broadly accurate. The original plans envisaged that the ward community councils would be provided with limited budgets for on-the-spot community planning.

7.3 Environmental pressure groups

Polycentric models of political cultures all assume that political issues are exploited or suppressed through the activities of pressure groups, which are more or less politically effective according to their *resources* and *power* (Wooton, 1970). 'Resources' can be defined along three lines: (a) the level of organisation defined in terms of the relationships between the leadership and membership, and between sectional, regional, and national bodies; (b) the degree of expertise, as revealed by the credibility and exclusiveness of information available to the group; and (c) the ability to communicate information effectively both to the media and to target political and administrative personnel. 'Power' is the effective use of resources to influence decisions in desired directions, and obviously relates to the extent of bargaining strength or political prestige that an interest group can muster.

Any particular environmental issue will impinge upon the public in several different ways (figure 7.7). There will always be some who will simply not be aware of the problem, either because it does not appear to involve them or because it is low on their political agenda. Some people will resign themselves to the matter because they are political fatalists, or at least they like to use this as an excuse for doing nothing. Others will recognise the stress but resolve it by psychological adaptation or behavioural adjustment. A small group will seek to do something about it, either through traditional forms of political protest, such as letter writing, petition signing and the like, or by forming or joining a pressure group.

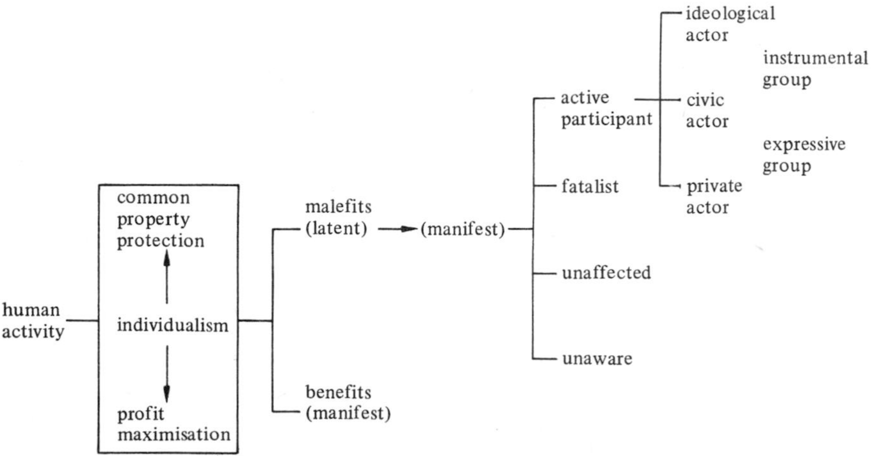

Figure 7.7. Public response to environmental issues. The numbers of people falling into any of the categories depicted will obviously vary enormously. Recently there has been a tendency for some citizens organisations to adopt both the instrumental and expressive group tactics in an attempt to change government policy through carefully planned campaigns in specific cases. (After O'Riordan, 1972a.)

We do not really know what makes certain issues controversial or how environmental pressure groups emerge out of the political culture. Just as the energy of a flowing river is normally dissipated harmlessly as heat, but can occasionally be channelled as a devastating flood, so it seems that political energy is normally diffused over a myriad of issues among a variety of interest groups. But every now and then this energy is focused into a force of considerable magnitude—as for instance with DDT, toxic metal residues in fish, nuclear safeguards, and supersonic transport. Obviously the media are very important in politicising environmental issues, but they reflect as much as influence public opinion, so some additional force must be at work.

This force is community activism in the form of a variety of environmental interest and pressure groups. These groups are cohesive because their membership shares values, agrees to means of pursuing their aims, and seeks to influence social choice in their favour through legitimate political action. Environmental activists can be distinguished according to their aims and strategies, though there is some overlap. *Private actors* are motivated primarily by personal and selfish reasons. Their participation is episodic and crisis orientated; they respond to a particular threat to their health or economic welfare, but pay little attention to the broader issues. They form *expressive* (or goal achieving) groups with the simple objective of removing the threat (even if it only means pushing it on to other people elsewhere). Their tactics are often quite ruthless and may include maximal use of the media, rallies, protest meetings, sit-ins, and the like. Usually private actors appear *after* a proposal is announced (i.e. after Decision I in figure 7.5), but before it is implemented. By virtue of the resources and power of their organisation they can be very effective because they are mobilised by a very real fear for their well-being. Most 'Save the ...' or 'Stop the ...' associations are of this kind, some of which may arise out of well-established social organisations such as ratepayers or parent–teacher associations.

Toward the other extreme are *ideological actors* who enter the political arena spurred by intellectual and moral motives, and visualise environmental problems in broad terms. They are less concerned with particular issues than with the whole pattern of human destiny, and consequently tend to be more interested in the abstract than the immediate. Ideological actors form *instrumental* (means orientated) groups that are interested in improving the process of decisionmaking as much as in changing the decisions themselves. So they fight to change the system and will often be found quietly, yet forcefully, pressing for much-needed institutional reform. Their tactics are more policy orientated than issue orientated, utilising the discrete but effective means of intellectual prowess and political influence. They know which people to contact, how to persuade them, how to use the media with repeated effect, and how to employ a variety of highly skilled professionals in preparing their evidence.

Somewhere between are the *civic actors* who are motivated by a more altruistic concern for the community as a whole even though their self-interest is also involved. Kasperson (1969) notes that such actors tend to be long-standing residents with a history of political concern and a knowledge of the local political process. The civic actor may be found in either the expressive or instrumental group, though as participatory strategies become more sophisticated he/she is more likely to be found in the latter, albeit the distinction between the two categories is now less clear.

Unless the environmental lobby is well-anchored within the political system, it is often quite difficult for leaders to maintain effective credibility, since the membership of the more politically ephemeral groups is seldom bound by lasting ties and all too readily leaves most matters of policy and finance to the executive. For example, Bartell and St. George (1974, p.41) found that over half the membership of the Sierra Club joined simply "to show general support of conservation without participation", and only 15% were prepared to become involved in political action. Not infrequently the leadership may abuse their positions, for example by using group sponsored publicity to run for political office or by employing certain tactics without formal membership support. Consequently many environmental groups wax and wane in size and activity, and at any time intragroup tensions may drain group energy, jeopardising its political power. [Bartell and St. George (1974) for example found a growing distrust of the political system among members of the Sierra Club and a willingness to support more militant tactics, but how far these views are widely diffused through the organisation is not known.] The main exceptions to these observations are (a) the issue-orientated expressive groups organised to protect a well-defined self-interest, where group cohesion is strong and the strategies of the leaders are demonstrably supported (by money and rallies, etc.), and (b) the national lobbies of well-established instrumental groups which are reasonably well-financed (though never wealthy), and well-organised (De Bell, 1970; Mitchell and Stallings, 1970; Clusen, 1973).

Because case studies vary tremendously and the political culture differs from one country to another, it is difficult to present more than general guidelines for environmental lobbying. Kimber and Richardson (1974, pp.215–225) provide some useful pointers which apply to most situations:
(i) *Advance intelligence.* Forewarned is forearmed: the more a group has access to policy determinations or decisions before these become legally, morally, or politically binding, the better its chances of success. There is nothing more stubborn than a local council or an evangelistic bureaucrat with its/his mind made up. This is where the environmental impact statement is helpful, as are judicious press leaks by sympathetic insiders. Obviously, friendly contacts in the 'right' places can be enormously useful. But obtaining advance warning is always difficult because governments, despite their public declarations to reduce secrecy, fully realise the dangers

of too much 'openness'. It is no wonder that journalists are befriended by environmentalist groups.

(ii) *Liaison with administrations.* Civil servants like to consult interest groups in advance of final decisions. Environmental groups have to gain sufficient public recognition to become regular 'ears' of governments. This can take a long time, for usually it means 'playing the game' so as to appear 'politically respectable'. This may pose a moral dilemma for those who believe that 'commando operations' to achieve immediate results are justifiable, even if they may jeopardise their group's political respectability. Sometimes environmental organisations resolve this dilemma by splitting into two—a respectable 'establishment' lobby and a legal/political action arm.

(iii) *Rational argument and expertise.* We have already noted the importance of prestigious figureheads, professional help, and sound (preferably original) data when environmental lobbies wish to confront the technical specialists. Environmental issues are usually so ambiguous that a case can very likely be undermined by a competent opposition. Maximum success will be achieved if an alternative proposal which is politically and administratively acceptable is suggested. On the other hand this may limit the value of proposals for institutional reform that many environmentalists believe are absolutely necessary.

(iv) *Relationships with legislators.* This is vital for waging tactical political battles against a well-organised opposition. Friendly contacts on key committees or boards nominating commissions of inquiry obviously help, and any government contact is useful in getting a feeling for the mood of the legislature and in acquiring advance information.

(v) *Relationships with mass media.* The media help to activate public interest and give the impression, at least, of aroused public opinion. The media also understand how to influence key people with good timing and judicious use of buzz words and images; they tend to be sympathetic to political 'underdogs' and 'the people versus big bureaucracy' battles.

(vi) *Sanctions.* Environmental lobbies must be prepared to invoke sanctions as a last resort. Certainly any evidence of committed support is desirable but still more effective is the credible threat of delay on procedural grounds. Almost any bureaucracy can make a procedural mistake. Some environmentalist groups employ lawyers to look for such errors, or for any evidence of 'arbitrary or capricious' action. These kinds of sanctions were invoked most effectively in the Trans Alaskan Pipeline issue (Cicchetti, 1973) and the Storm King case (Talbot, 1972), and are common in connection with housing and transportation decisions in urban areas (Pendakur, 1972; Sewell, 1972).

The influence of pressure groups in environmental politics is probably underestimated. Most informed commentators agree that these watchdog organisations play an essential role in mobilising political concern, raising citizen awareness of the inadequacies of the political and administrative system, and inducing changes in policymaking arrangements and the law to help alter the whole shape of the political culture and set vital precedents for future citizen participation.

7.4 The culture of participation

The matter of public participation in planning and resource allocation has received exhaustive attention from a number of perspectives, including rationale, strategy, political effectiveness, and problems of implementation. (For good reviews and literature citations see Reynolds, 1969; Carroll, 1971; Cook and Morgan, 1971; Starrs and Stewart, 1971; Aberbach and Walker, 1972; Clark, 1972; Cunningham, 1972; Hart, 1972; Pierce, 1972; Sewell and Burton, 1972; Strange, 1972; Thayer, 1972; Wilson, 1973; Nelson, 1974; Kasperson and Breitbart, 1974; Sewell and O'Riordan, 1976; Sewell and Coppock, 1976.)

What is less reported is the obvious fact that participation is an evolutionary process moulded by the political culture in which it develops. It can be seen from figure 7.8 that participation is essentially a means to social reform and political egalitarianism, a systems-transforming device that is regarded as revolutionary and subversive by many of the elite. The inevitable thrust of the participatory strategy is toward wider power sharing and the politicisation of citizen awareness into new democratic forms, particularly at the local level where the quality of the environment really is a matter of immediate interest and concern. It is not surprising therefore that participatory experiments, seen in this light, must constantly struggle against the suspicion and anxiety of power holders.

Of course, this need not be the case, for desirable participatory forms should *strengthen* the authority of a responsive elite. But their fear is understandable in view of the ready manipulation of genuine participatory efforts by politically radical groups who seek to seize power by illegal methods. So the evolution of participation seems to take the form of pulses of reform followed by periods of entrenchment. For example, the US Model Cities Program was originally designed to hand considerable decisionmaking power over to the inner-city poor. This laudable aim was thwarted because a few people abused the new powers, at the expense of the majority who initially were intellectually and educationally ill-equipped to handle the opportunities provided. Fears of a 'black take-over' of central city institutions were generated, fears that caused the Administration to delay implementation of the programme. Yet before revenue-sharing funds were allocated the courts insisted on 'adequate citizen representation' (Plager, 1971) so the whole scheme received a new breath of life.

From figure 7.8 it will be seen that the evolutionary path of participation is toward the right, that is toward greater power sharing and institutional reform, though naturally this will be more noticeable in planning and policymaking at the local level than on a global or national scale. This trend has been observed by Morrison *et al.* (1972) who report that since Earth Day (April 22, 1970) environmental organisations have shifted from a participation to a power orientation, though the authors also observe a change from a movement of consensus to one of conflict. These modulations in the culture of participation are occurring for four reasons. First, resource allocation in the face of widespread externalities and conflicting political interests requires the intervention of adversely affected groups. Second, because people are better educated, more informed, and more willing to participate in community affairs, they are more responsive to new participatory strategies. Third, many people enjoy a sufficiently high standard of living to be concerned about deteriorations in environmental quality which they find it increasingly hard to avoid.

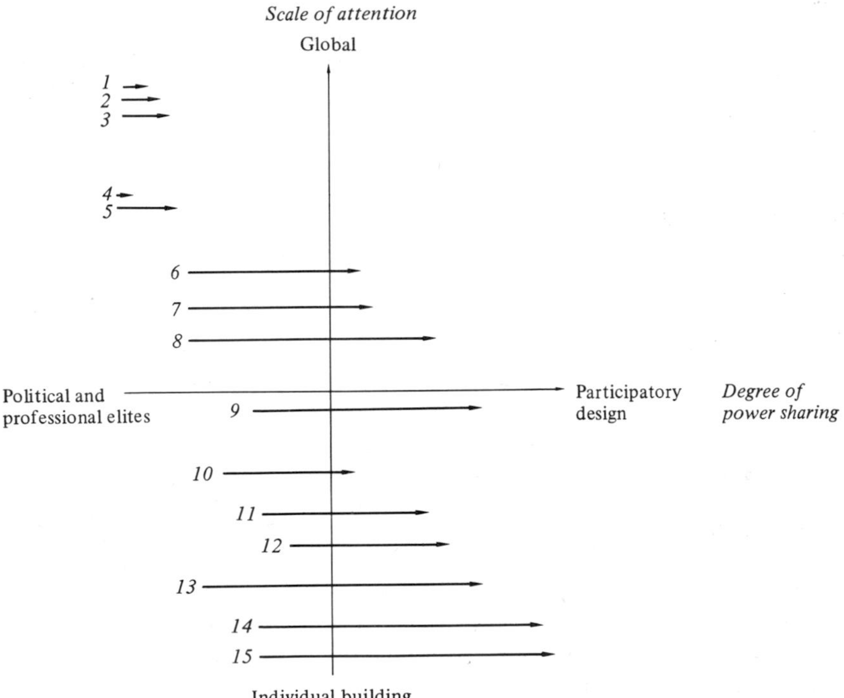

Figure 7.8. The evolution of participation in environmental policymaking. The arrows indicate the participatory shift for each of the examples illustrated over the past five years or so. The further to the right, the more participatory the policymaking and design experience. Obviously local proposals and activities hold the greatest potential for participatory design. The vertical axis represents scale: *1* Club of Rome studies, *2* UN Man and Biosphere studies, *3* UN Earthwatch, *4 Blueprint for Survival*, *5* UN Population Watch studies, *6* Canadian Man and Resources programme, *7* UK structure plan hearings, *8* Canadian and US Corps of Engineers river basin studies, *9* US state land use workshops (Florida, Oregon), *10* metropolitan goals projects, *11* urban downtown livability studies, *12* urban community housing programmes, *13* US model city programmes, *14* neighbourhood design projects, *15* cooperative housing schemes.

Fourth, the days of the paternalistic administrator, infallible expert, and trustee politician are over; people want to play a part in shaping their own surroundings.

Because the nature and scope of participation varies so much from country to country it is helpful to devise a checklist of criteria with which to review the likelihood and effectiveness of participatory activity. A suggested list is outlined below, but the reader may wish to make one of his/her own.

(i) The scope of citizens' environmental rights—amenity rights, rights to sue private developers, government agencies, and the like—in short the nature of legal standing (see chapter 8, pp.271-282).

(ii) The degree of access to information through statutory provision, environmental reviews, public hearings, community discussions, etc.

(iii) The use of participatory strategies such as ballots, referenda, hearings, opinion surveys, task force discussions, or local neighbourhood planning units, conducted either formally or informally. These techniques can be assessed in terms of the degree of interaction, the freedom to express views and the representativeness of the participants. They should also be reviewed in relation to the nature of the problem and the scale of its impact.

(iv) The use of the media in giving publicity to environmental issues. At all levels this can be effective, but especially so on the local scale. Community television is becoming recognised as an important medium for stimulating communication among those who are not normally active politically.

(v) The nature, content, scope, and political effectiveness of environmental impact assessments.

(vi) The nature, content, and scope of environmental education in the schools, colleges, and adult educational institutions. Environmental education can be especially effective if related to community issues, though its more general purpose is to improve people's awareness of their citizenship responsibilities, their political effectiveness (or lack of it), and their understanding of both social and biophysical environmental processes (chapter 9, pp.311-315).

7.4.1 Some dilemmas in participation

Participation, like democracy, is a slippery concept that appears to be socially desirable but is constantly endangered by malpractice. It is clear from figures 7.5 and 7.8 that participation can be used in a variety of ways to achieve a range of objectives. It is therefore worth considering some of the very real problems that are encountered (see T. O'Riordan, 1976c).

1. *From principles to practice.* Many participatory experiments are designed to cease at the point of decision rather than be carried through in modified forms as part of subsequent implementation. To ask citizens

to conceptualise notions, to review broad policy statements and to dream up future designs is useful and necessary but it involves no political commitment. No specific proposals need be discussed, and the power of execution remains with the administrative sector. Of course, in a democratic culture it is right and proper that decisions and power remain with elected leaders, but there is a very real need to devise valid forms of postdecisional participation to help with the execution and evaluation of a proposal as it evolves in practice.

2. *Representative versus participatory democracy.* In most western democracies politicians are elected as representatives of the public interest. Erickson and Luttberg (1973) note three forms of representation. First there is *trustee representation* in which the politician regards himself as a sort of altruistic citizen—a trustee of community affairs—who genuinely believes he is making some personal sacrifices for what he feels to be the public interest. The trustee representative is most likely to be found at the local government level (particularly in the small community), for here salaries are small, the prestige of office is relatively low, and few have the time or interest to be well-informed on all the relevant issues. In his investigation of what he calls 'citizen politicians', Prewett (1970) found that they are not generally sensitive to public opinion but are quite distressed by criticism from 'professional citizens' who, while carrying none of the responsibilities of public office, still get a lot of publicity over their allegations of political nonresponsiveness (see T. O'Riordan, 1972b).

Second, there are the *politico representatives* (usually found in metropolitan or regional government) who act partly as trustees and partly as delegates of their constituents, though for most environmental issues they act as trustees. Third, there are the *delegate representatives* (found mainly at the national level) who try to be responsive to their political constituencies by forging elaborate links with community leaders. Members of this group carry greater social prestige and regard electoral office more as an honour and a privilege than a public duty, so in their anxiety to get reelected they do respond to citizen initiatives. But, as noted earlier, there is still a wide gap between their voting behaviour and the views of scientifically sampled cross sections of public opinion. To what extent this is attributable to the difficulty of accurately assessing public opinion and how much to any real gulf in the perception of political priorities is not known.

If participation is seen as an attempt at power sharing, the problem is to retain democratic forms of power holding while ensuring adequate representation. Many politicians begin by being understandably dubious of participation, largely because they are not sure where it might lead. In the wrong hands, participation can all but halt executive action, anger the legitimate elite, exacerbate social divisions, and result in counter-productive and repressive social legislation. But in the right hands, participation can allay all these fears, encourage a spirit of genuine cooperation and a respectful recognition of roles. Thus successful participation is not simply a matter of tactics but very much one of personality and political ideology, attributes that can never be clearly defined.

3. *The representativeness of the participants.* The literature is replete with case studies that show that the politically active are normally from the middle to upper socioeconomic classes and regard themselves as politically competent (Almond and Verba, 1963, pp.244–265; Milbrath, 1965; Bartell and St. George, 1974). This is particularly so with ideological actors who feel politically effective when working as members of a group. Many sacrifice large amounts of time and effort, often for little demonstrable reward, motivated by a mixture of personal ideology, professional advancement, and public-spiritedness. However well-meaning, these people are not *representative* in the formal sense, for they are not elected and few canvass constituent support; indeed they may have very little idea as to who their supporters are. In the case of a number of local environmental groups their spokesmen are virtually self-appointed and make very little attempt to seek support from the membership. Some are successful because they master the art of making the right contacts, using the media, preparing and presenting briefs, and knowing how to be influential in committee; but many fail because they do not know how to use such ploys to advantage. Here again, education by experience can make all the difference.

For some environmental activists participation is a pathway to political success, since the publicity and political contacts make running for political office very enticing. The irony, of course, is that, once in power, the novice politician is tempted to thwart the process that put him there and which now threatens his political authority. At the other extreme, it is possible that activists who do become politicians try to make the political process achieve something for which it was not designed, namely the delegation of power on a mass basis. Someone ultimate has to be responsible for evaluating and weighing social choices, and this person must be accountable through formal electoral procedures.

4. *The job of participatory coordinator.* Most participatory programmes (especially of the 'negotiated trust' kind) require some kind of catalytic coordinator to ferret out opinion influentials and maintain liaison between citizen groups, professionals, and the politicians. This job requires a combination of talents that is rare: a knowledge of social processes and political theory, an understanding of planning principles, a familiarity with all kinds of technical information, a facility for explaining and clarifying detailed reports without excessive distortion, a sense of humour, an abiding interest in people as individuals, and a keen sense of occasion. Allied to these qualities must be a flexible readiness to tackle new approaches according to the situation. These are not ready-made attributes, but must be nurtured by experience, frustration, and achievement. The

danger is to become so committed to the job as to lose sight of the target, for there is always the attraction of wielding power for its own sake and thus succumbing to egomania. The coordinator must also bridge the gap between the demands of his citizen clients and his political clients in such a way as to build up and maintain a solid trust between all participants. The enormous potential of this position contrasted with the paucity of suitable applicants surely reflects the inadequacy of present educational policies.

7.4.2 The dilemmas confronted: participatory design

There is a great temptation to visualise participation as an adversary battle between citizen Davids and technocratic Goliaths. The 'we–they' dichotomy slips all too easily into rhetoric. John Graham (1973) talks of an 'authority crisis', a questioning of both the decisionmakers themselves and the traditional processes of making decisions. This is not participation, but confrontation, a game of power politics that may prove to be more unsettling than conciliatory. For participation really to have any meaning it must enter the realm of participatory design, whereby individuals as members of a community together imagine and plan their environments to fit their ideals. Here we are talking about group involvement in a continuing process of environmental education, in which people can pool their individual talents to shape collectively a better way of life for themselves.

This all sounds terribly idealistic, but the seeds have already been sown by adventurous planners, psychologists, architects, sociologists, and community leaders. The natural starting point is the neighbourhood where people have a joint interest in upgrading amenity and getting to know their fellows. Here local initiatives can produce fairly immediate results which encourage efforts at more ambitious schemes. *The Christian Science Monitor* (February 14–18, 1974) and the Council on Environmental Quality (1973a, pp.1–39) report on a number of imaginative and successful neighbourhood design schemes where public-spirited professionals assisted communities to renovate housing, plant trees and shrubs, and design play spaces and other communal meeting areas. Several cities are experimenting with a variety of participatory workshops to clarify metropolitan priorities (Toronto, Vancouver, New York, Philadelphia, Dallas), to revitalise the urban core (Toronto, Vancouver), to devise cooperative housing schemes, and to plan for amenity by renovating old buildings and protecting key environmental sites. Much of the success of these programmes can be measured in educational and psychological terms, for carefully and patiently planned schemes can create an exciting sense of vitality and community spirit in areas that were formerly grey and depressing. In addition, participatory design encourages people to think not just about physical layout and cosmetic appearance, but about the *process* of environmental interaction that can lead to a heightened group awareness of what they as a community can do. Here, surely, is the essence of the self ↔ community integration that is such a basic theme in environmentalism.

The actual design process takes as many different forms as there are community needs. However, there are some common elements. First, the process is not so much goal orientated as means orientated; it is an open-ended mechanism for unveiling latent talents and political awareness among people who, for various reasons, have consistently been discouraged from expressing their deeply felt needs either in words or images. Yet they reveal some of these needs through their behaviour. Children play in streets and disused construction sites that are not designed for play but meet their requirements of accessibility, parental scrutiny, group interaction, and excitement (Gold, 1972, 1973). People meet and talk in open squares or in pedestrian malls even though these areas may have been designed either for *looking at* or *moving through*, rather than for conversation and the simple everyday pleasure of observing others. Mothers avoid urban parks, even when well-planned, if they think they are unsafe or unsuitable for their children's play needs. [For good reviews see the annual proceedings of the Environmental Design and Research Association (EDRA), 1970 onwards; Craik, 1973; Nicholson and Schreiner, 1973; Downs and Stea, 1974; *Bulletin of Environmental Education*, various issues.] Encouraging people to articulate their environmental preferences through behaviour in workshops and other small-group arrangements is an avenue of great promise.

Second, the 'catalytic professionals' do not determine anything; they try to convert citizens' yearnings into the semblance of form through a continuing process of mutual education. The professional is merely a facilitator; the community becomes the planner. Ideally the planning coordinator should come from the community itself, for only community members fully empathise with the values of their fellows. The old idea of professional advocacy, by which specialists genuinely tried to help disadvantaged communities, is now in disrepute because it was so difficult for 'foreigners' to understand their clients' real needs (see Grabow and Heskin, 1973). Kasperson and Breitbart (1974, p.49) comment that "attempts to redress social and economic unbalances in society by assigning some people to the task of advocating *for* others are at best only ephemeral solutions to societal problems. Going *beyond* advocacy suggests that we cultivate a radical self-awareness and confidence in the minds of presently powerless citizens so that they may begin to advocate meaningfully for themselves".

This observation makes it plain that participatory design is as much a matter of political reform as it is the shaping of a better quality of life. A noble hope among those who believe in this process is that it will raise people's political consciousness from their personal problems to neighbourhood issues, to the community at large, and beyond. Starrs and

Stewart (1971, p.36) talk of embracing the traditional 'system-centred' understanding with a 'person-centred' viewpoint, a novel idea which may turn out to be "an exhilarating or a frightening experience". The overlapping of traditional information flows with community information networks should help to integrate basic processes of 'judging, acting, experimenting, experiencing, and becoming' which ideally should be indistinguishable. Liberal philosophers such as Platt (1966), Fromm (1968), Friere (1970), Goulet (1971, 1974), Weisskopf (1971, 1973), Ryan (1972), Kinkade (1973), and Illich (1974a) all talk of 'liberation' and 'becoming', the process of self-actualisation that breaks the shackles of political and occupational alienation. It is this alienation, they feel, that is the cause of the apathy, indifference, frustration, and discontent that have led to the present mess of a fragmented, conflict-ridden society and confrontationist politics which threaten the future of meaningful democracy. Participatory design, through workshops, task forces, community demonstration projects, embedded in the schools and encouraged by sensitive politicians, could be a vital step towards reshaping democracy. The current experiments need to be nurtured carefully for indeed they are very delicate plants.

Environmental law

The pulse of change in environmental law has come from the United States, where the judiciary enjoys the constitutional freedom to scrutinise the workings of both Congress and the executive agencies. Since the late sixties a number of environmental lawyers have capitalised on this independence to amend the statutory law and to revise a number of interpretations of the common law so that there are environmental quality safeguards for all citizens. Foremost among these men are Joseph Sax of the University of Michigan, David Sive of the Environmental Defense Fund, Malcolm Baldwin of the Conservation Foundation, and David Bosselman of the American Law Institute. Their counterparts in Canada are Alastair Lucas of the University of British Columbia, Greg Morley formerly at the University of Winnipeg, and David Estrin of the Canadian Environmental Law Foundation. In Britain the main proponents of environmental law reform are the journalists Jeremy Bugler (formerly of *The Observer*) and John Tinker (*New Scientist*) and the writers John Barr and Tony Aldous. All these individuals are fired by convictions that the law can help the citizen reassert his rights to a high-quality environment, that the freedom of action of the individual must be tempered by his obligation to others and to future generations, and that, with the help of professionals, the community is quite capable of determining its own environmental destiny. In addition they are disturbed by statutory secrecy in government and the constant inability of the citizen to air his views on matters in which he can show no special interest but where his well-being is vitally affected.

Environmental law is far more than petty courtroom haggling over damages to private property caused by pollution. It deals with the very essence of environmentalism, from the rights of the biosphere and the lithosphere to exist undisturbed to the rights of citizens to protect their health, welfare, and amenity; from guarantees of full disclosure of information from all public agencies to rights to be heard before tribunals either personally or through the offices of an advocate.

Why has environmental law become so tremendously important over the past five years? Largely because it is the only legitimate tool with which to prise open the political lid of secrecy and cast aside the bureaucratic shrouds of the 'insider perspective'. Environmental law is yet another environmental politicising device which transfers quite considerable political power to certain groups of people (a number that is growing steadily owing to the introduction of legal-aid schemes). The law is also politically effective because it demands more accountability from decisionmakers, and is changing the ground rules about environmental rights to favour those who are damaged rather than those who, by default, create disamenity spillovers.

But though the law is now very much a political weapon, it is itself altered by the changing political culture, for both the common law and statutory legislation reflect ambient social values. Throughout the industrial revolution and well into the present century, western nations were intent on creating wealth and exploiting environmental resources, whether they be clean air or water, undisturbed scenery, forests, or minerals. A belief in utilitarianism was matched by a love of private property, for private property conferred not only social status, but certain safeguards against environmental abuse. So, during the past hundred years, jurists and legislators have tended to favour use over preservation, private property rights over common property rights, and the generation of wealth and productivity over amenity, largely because society as a whole wanted it that way. The legal revolution of the 1970s is simply the outcome of the changing of social values toward environmental protection and more democratic policymaking, which have been described earlier in this book.

Given that the law is as much an instigator of reform as it is itself shaped by new political perspectives, what are its special advantages for environmental policymaking? Sax (1970a, pp.108–124) outlines these as follows:

(i) *Political impartiality.* Judges are widely respected for their political objectivity and integrity. They are not susceptible to political influence in the way that many politicians and senior administrators can scarcely avoid. They lack what Sax (p.109) calls the 'insider perspective', the myopia of institutional insularity.

(ii) *Professional decisionmakers.* Judges are trained to 'balance all the equities' no matter how apparently incommensurable these may be. But they can only do so within their strict interpretations of existing judicial precedent and statutory law. Judges are not politicians in that they cannot weigh normatively the relative merits of a case, nor can they take into account wider or more distant political implications. The precise determination of the 'public interest', as Haefele (1973) and others have pointed out, is the unique and proper role of the legislature.

(iii) *Private citizen initiatives.* One function of the courts is to redress the legitimate grievances of private citizens. Once a case has been made (and the money is available) any individual can have his complaint heard without fear of political meddling. Furthermore, the courts can require that responsible officials fully justify their actions before an impartial auditor. The citizen asserts rights which are entitled to enforcement; he is not a mere 'supplicant'. The Canadian lawyer, Alastair Lucas (1976) summarises the advantages of legal review for citizen participation in environmental policymaking:

(a) Affected persons likely to be unrepresented in environmental assessment and decisionmaking processes are provided with an opportunity to present their views.

(b) Members of the public may provide useful additional information to the decisionmaker, especially in terms of their own values.

(c) Accountability of political and administrative decisionmakers is likely to be reinforced if the process is open to public view. Openness puts pressure on administrators to follow *all* the required procedures in *all* cases.

(d) Public trust in the political and administrative process is enhanced since citizens know that their interests are either actually or potentially represented.

(e) Judicial review can open up public hearings to much more 'relevant' information than is usually the case. This includes evidence on basic policy issues (such as whether a proposal should be carried out), and on second- and third-order effects (including distributional questions), which are rarely aired in public.

However, there are drawbacks to the use of the law which undoubtedly limit its effective use. These are:

(i) *Legal process.* The role of the law is to safeguard rights and ensure that legislative mandates are being obeyed. If certain rights do not exist or are not constitutionally guaranteed then they cannot be protected. Sir Leslie Scarman (1974, pp.51–59), the distinguished British judge, has pointed out that there is no common law of environmental rights in the UK and that current statutory guidelines in the area of land use control do not adequately take the wider public interest into account. There is a legal lacuna here, about which in the absence of enactment by Parliament the British courts can do nothing.

The law is also very thorough. Legal technicalities may influence judicial decisions whatever the merits of the case. Thus clever lawyers (and usually those whose fees reflect their expertise) can be most successful in protecting their client's interests by careful manipulation of legal sematics especially where the law is weakly defined.

(ii) *Costs.* In Britain the losing party must pay all the costs (including damages where awarded) that accrue both to it and to the successful litigant. Environmental groups therefore face a high financial risk especially in untried cases. To overcome this serious difficulty the Lawyers Ecology Group may establish a cooperative fund financed from successful cases. (This procedure is used by the Anglers Cooperative Association in their battle against polluters—see section 8.1.5 below). In the United States, however, winning and losing litigants pay their own costs, irrespective of the outcome, so the financial risks to environmentalist plaintiffs are correspondingly smaller. But regardless of the allocation of costs, court cases are enormously expensive, especially where major interests are involved and important precedents may be set. Senior British advocates command fees in excess of £1000 per week and it is not unknown for some of the major American environmental battles to cost over $250000.

(iii) *Legal access.* The possibility of enormous expense associated with court cases deters many aggrieved parties from asserting their rights. True, there is legal aid, but in Britain at any rate this is only available for a limited number of circumstances and certainly environmentalist test cases would not qualify. The nature and availability of legal aid is obviously of some importance if the law is to achieve its true purpose—the protection of legitimate rights regardless of income or political influence.

8.1 The common law of environmental protection

The rules that govern environmental protection are broadly of two kinds. First, there are the statutory laws of the constitution, national and regional legislatures, and local governments. Second, there is the common law—the body of judicial interpretations that create the precedents upon which future cases are judged. Crudely speaking, the distinction between the two lies in the locus of authority: statutory law is written by politicians while common law is composed by judges, though modern rulings are much influenced by reference to statutory legislation (Reitze, 1971, p.799). Because common law is also based on precedent, it tends to be conservative in the face of novel situations. And because judicial rulings have in the past tended to favour environmental defilement over amenity, the common law is geared more towards protecting the rights of polluters and those favouring development over the rights of those canvassing for protection and preservation (Landau and Rheingold, 1971, p.27; Juergensmeyer, 1971a, 1971b). Traditionally there are four common law theories available to private individuals seeking redress against environmental damage in common law, namely, nuisance, trespass, negligence, and strict liability; and two major kinds of remedy, damages and injunction. With respect to water pollution, the common law of riparian rights can also be invoked.

8.1.1 Nuisance

The basic rule of the common law is *sic utere tuo et alienum non laudes*, which means 'use your own property in such a way as not to injure that of another'. This maxim recognises the mutual obligation of landowners to avoid excessive spillover effects, and limits any individual's rights of use of his own property to that point where he unreasonably prevents his neighbour from making productive use of his own property. It will immediately be seen that private nuisance remedies relate to private property ownership and reasonable rights of productive use (not to amenity *per se*). As Mishan (1974b) has demonstrated, the common law merely asserts Coase's (1960) theorem of compensation variations.

Under the nuisance theory an individual landowner can seek damages or an injunction against the person responsible for causing the damage if he can prove (a) that the damage is indisputably the result of the defendant's activities, (b) that he (the litigant) can show 'substantial' injury (damage peculiar to him and not shared by others), and (c) that his injury is 'unreasonable' (interferes with what the community defines as his lawful activities) (Eddy, 1971). It should be evident that the plaintiff's redress cannot be such that he places an unreasonable burden on the defendant's lawful interests—in other words total injunction may prove to be an excessive penalty.

The nuisance doctrine is of limited usefulness in environmental litigation for three reasons. First, it offers very restricting conditions of 'standing' (the right to judicial review—see below). Second, it is not helpful in cases where individuals 'come to the nuisance', i.e. where they purchase property near an existing activity (such as a factory or an airport) and then complain. Even though societal values about nuisance may change, courts may argue that when people purchase property they are assumed to be 'fully aware' of the surrounding situation. Third, nuisance may be avoided if the 'wrong' continues for a long period without complaint. Here a sort of 'prescriptive right' to continue the nuisance may exist, even though society's views as to what constitutes a disamenity may change. Finally, defendants have escaped nuisance prosecution by claiming that they are entitled to pursue their activities under statutory law. Juergensmeyer (1971b, p.219) quotes Viscount Dunedin:

> "When Parliament has authorised a certain thing to be made or done in a certain place, there can be no action for nuisance caused by the making or doing of that thing if the nuisance is the inevitable result of the making or doing so authorised."

In short, nuisance is a limited remedy applying to a very small number of controversial environmental issues. It provides no redress for the defilement of common property resources where the public interest at large is affected, nor does it really protect an individual's amenity interests unless he can show to a sympathetic court that amenity to him is of 'productive value'.

8.1.2 Trespass

Trespass occurs when there is a physical invasion of private property either by persons or polluting materials. It is defined as "any intrusion which invades a possessor's protected interest in exclusive possession, whether that intrusion is by visible or invisible pieces of matter or by energy which can be measured only by the mathematical language of the physicist" (Juergensmeyer, 1971b, p.221). Trespass differs from nuisance in that it is an invasion of the right to exclusive possession of the land—a direct interference—while nuisance is an invasion of the right to use and enjoy land—an indirect interference (Reitze, 1971, p.807). Thus trespass action can be used when there is evidence of the physical transmission of any substance (including smell and noise). Usually trespass litigation is tied in with nuisance and is therefore subject to the same limitations, though to be successful the litigant must normally prove that the damage was caused unintentionally (as opposed to carelessly).

8.1.3 Negligence

The concept of negligence is that of carelessness, a theory of liability that assumes a property owner (or public official) is totally responsible for *all* the consequences of his actions. In practice this means that the defendant has failed to take all due precautions, or failed to adhere to accepted standards of performance or rules of procedure. Under present United States air and water pollution control legislation, the negligence theory can be used against polluters who do not use the 'best practicable technology' (by 1977) or 'best available technology' (by 1983) (Kneese and Schultze, 1975, pp.58–68). In practice, the courts will have to balance the costs to the polluter of purchasing and using the necessary equipment against the costs to the community (including possible loss of jobs or exports) of seeking full compliance. Generally in negligence cases the burden of proof falls on the plaintiff to show undisputed connection between cause and effect and to produce clear evidence of carelessness—a difficult matter when there are really no clear judicial guidelines to pinpoint 'reasonable performance'.

8.1.4 Strict liability

The strict liability theory is invoked when certain activities endanger the public but are so unpredictable in occurrence or severity that there are no readily available safeguards. Even when the defendant is neither negligent nor capricious, he may yet be liable because he is still regarded as being socially responsible for his actions, no matter how apparently beneficial they may be both to him and to society generally. The spraying of toxic chemicals or the discharge of dangerous gases generally falls under the strict liability ruling, though it could well be extended to nuclear power generation (where extensive and expensive government insurance is now required) and even to the discharge of toxic wastes into water or air. The doctrine most frequently invoked in such cases is the ruling of *Rylands v. Fletcher* (quoted in Fraser, 1974, p.123):

> "A person, who for his own purposes brings onto his lands and collects or keeps there anything likely to do mischief if it escapes, must keep it in at his peril, and if he does not do so is *prima facie* answerable for all the damage which is the natural consequence of its escape."

Suits against automobile manufacturers have tended to fall into the category of *product liability* (Landau and Rheingold, 1971, pp.109–110), by which the manufacturer of a product is deemed liable for any injury resulting from the normal use of his product. The law is clear that he has a responsibility "to those whom he should expect to be endangered by its probable use", though, as is so often the case in environmental law, the problem of evidentiary proof is formidable—proof of the precise cause of the public danger and proof that the manufacturer has not taken all reasonable steps to prevent it. But if proof is available, the strict liability doctrine is applicable to the nuisance type of situation where the cause of the damage is regarded as unintentional, and where the injured person or thing is situated on public or private property. This widens the legal possibilities of bringing private action against a public nuisance.

8.1.5 Riparian rights

Riparian rights attach to property owners whose land or interests abut a watercourse (river or lake) in areas where the riparian doctrine is paramount as a means of determining water allocation (McLoughlin, 1972; Newsom and Sherratt, 1972, p.2). In theory riparian rights safeguard such people against any diminution of water quantity or quality, although in practice this rather strict doctrine is amended to permit reasonable use of water by neighbouring landowners. In other words the exercise of riparian rights is tempered by a duty to ensure that other legitimate users of the watercourse are not unduly harmed. In the words of a Massachusetts court (Juergensmeyer, 1971b, p.227), "each proprietor is entitled to use the stream in such reasonable manner, according to the usages and wants of the community, as will not be inconsistent with a like use by other proprietors above and below him". The courts are then arbiters of what is 'reasonable'.

Riparian rights can be invoked to protect water quality, a strategy that has been used with much success by private angling associations in England who, by virtue of their ownership of a river bank, enjoy riparian rights to water quality. Dales (1968, p.68–70) approvingly records the activities of the Anglers' Cooperative Association which has successfully investigated some 700 pollution cases in its pursuit of satisfactory water quality for game fish. However he cautions (p.70) that the workability of riparian rights in such cases depends upon "such apparently irrelevant factors as the English climate, English history and the particular social status enjoyed by the English nobility".

The use of the common law in environmental litigation is fraught with difficulties. First, the law is based on precedent and subsequent interpretations of that precedent. A single ruling by an authoritative but cautious judge can hold back legal reform for generations. At the opposite extreme a liberal ruling by a less cautious judge can lead to an almost unmanageable variety of later interpretations, some of which may be inconsistent or ambiguous. Second, since many environmental issues are unusual or possibly quite novel, recourse to precedent may prove to be undeniably restrictive, since every jurist is aware of the dangers of setting precedent for the reasons stated above. Third, because many common law precedents are confusing, clear rulings are virtually impossible. Accordingly, the party with the cleverest lawyer will often 'win' even though his case may be dubious, for 'reasonable doubt' is a powerful weapon in the legal arsenal.

Fourth, common law remedies, even if successfully pursued, do not always satisfy the plaintiff, since the courts may only decide in favour of damages rather than an injunction. This is a vital point for environmental policy since a ruling of damages implies that grievances can be righted simply by monetary compensation. Many litigants are far more interested either in total cessation of the nuisance (permanent injunction) or at least some kind of 'equivalent compensation' to make good their loss of amenity. To rely on damages as a remedy is to favour the more powerful, and to quantify the nonquantifiable; yet to use the injunction may impose undue hardships not only on the owner of the activity in dispute, but also on those who are dependent on that activity for their income or welfare. Here we come to the famous 'balancing of the equities' test where the pros and cons of different remedies are judged in a wider context. But is the context wide enough? Juergensmeyer (1971b, pp.232–233) correctly observes:

> "Where so many courts have gone wrong in the past is to balance only the interests of the parties before the courts ... . The proper use of the balancing concept, and the one which makes it a suitable theory for environmental litigation, is to balance (1) the damage to the defendant and the damage to society which would result from enjoining the activity which causes environmental harm, against (2) the damage to the plaintiff and the damage which society in general suffers from the environmentally harmful activity."

The courts are justifiably hesitant about using private litigation as a "purposeful mechanism to achieve direct public objectives greatly beyond the rights and interests before the court" (*Bloomer v. Atlantic Cement Company*, 1970). Environmental policymaking is a matter for governments, not courts. Even the foremost advocate of environmental law reform, Sax (1970a, p.115) is aware of the limitations of judicial redress:

> "Litigation ... provides an additional source of leverage in making environmental decisionmaking operate rationally, thoughtfully and with a sense of responsiveness to the entire range of citizen concerns. Courts alone cannot and will not do the job that is needed. But the courts can help to open the doors to a far more limber governmental process. The more leverage citizens have, the more responsive and responsible their officials and fellow citizens will be."

8.2 The rule of standing

A major drawback to common law litigation as a method of shaping environmental policy is its restricted definition of standing, or the right of a plaintiff to take his case before the courts. In practice, litigable rights only apply to an individual who has a proprietary interest and who can prove that damage to his property or his person is peculiar to himself and unreasonable. This means (a) if the individual has no particular ownership rights, and (b) if he cannot prove special injury which is worse for him than for others, then he may not be heard. This rather narrow interpretation of legal standing makes it difficult for environmentalists to deal with public nuisances where large numbers of people are equally aggrieved but none of whom has any private proprietary interest—to wit, negative spillovers damaging the commons. Normally in such situations only the attorney general has standing to act on behalf of the population at large. Naturally, as a politician, he is usually reluctant to prosecute unless the case is extremely clear-cut.

An example of the technical injustice created by the restrictive interpretation of standing occurred in 1970 when 350 fishermen in Placenta Bay, Newfoundland, were deprived of their livelihood after the discharge of toxic chemicals from a nearby phosphorus reduction plant destroyed the inshore fishery. The Supreme Court of Newfoundland (*Hickey v. Electric Reduction Co.*, 1970) ruled that the fishermen had no special proprietary rights to fish (i.e. the fish were regarded as common property resources), nor could any individual fisherman prove special discriminatory harm "particular, direct and substantial, over and above the injury ... inflicted upon the public in general". Here was a clear case of environmental mischief for which the fishermen could claim no compensation from the offending company. The compensation that was finally made was decided by political action, not judicial redress, and was paid by the Canadian taxpayer, not by the offending company.

Lucas and Moore (1973, pp.68–70) describe another inequity in the present law of standing. In 1965, having acquired land to build a copper extraction and concentration scheme in north Vancouver Island, the Utah Construction and Mining Company applied to the British Columbia Pollution Control Board for a permit to discharge nine million gallons of mill waste per day into a nearby inlet. Under provincial pollution control regulations the Director has discretionary powers to determine whether a hearing should be held and who is permitted to object. In this instance, once the permit had been applied for, it took him fourteen months to agree to hold the hearing, during which time the company invested considerable capital in its operations. Only four of 140 objectors were allowed to present their cases, but by that time it was politically impossible not to grant some sort of permit, since by delaying so long the provincial government had given *de facto* permission to the company to proceed.

A commercial fisherman who worked in the inlet in question applied to the court for *certiorari* quashing the permit, but, because he had not applied as a formal objector pursuing his cause 'in the public interest', the court ruled that he had no "qualifying private interest" (standing) and was therefore an "ineffective objector". Only those who own adjacent property or who already hold licences to discharge into the river or estuary in question are formally permitted to object and be heard; anyone else is acting in the public interest and has no legal standing unless so recognised by the Director. In this particular instance the court ruled that the plaintiff had not proceeded properly through the formal channels of objection. To quote the ruling (*Re Piatocka and Utah Construction and Mining Co.*, 1971):

> "If I were to hold that the Director was under a duty to consider the objection filed but not authorized by statute and to proceed judicially, in so doing I would render nugatory the clear intent of the statute to limit objections which must be considered to 'effective objections'."

In reviewing this case, Fraser (1974, p.121) comments wryly: "While we set up boards to protect the public interest, we have not accepted that a member of the public ought to have some say in protecting that interest."

A third example, equally frustrating to environmentalists, concerns the famous Mineral King decision (*Sierra Club v. Morton*, 1972) discussed by Sax (1973). Here the Sierra Club, acting as a body purporting to represent the public interest, sought to enjoin the granting of a road access permit to Walt Disney Enterprises Inc., who proposed to develop a large ski complex on National Forest land. Following a legal wrangle in the lower courts, the Supreme Court was asked to make a final ruling. It determined that the Sierra Club, as a *bona fide* public interest organisation, had no standing if its interest was simply to protect the area for the public at large (rather than for its members in particular), nor had any nonusing individual citizen any rights to sue. Judicial reviews, it said, must be confined to those who can demonstrate a 'direct stake' in the outcome, otherwise the judiciary would merely be the servants of those "who seek to do no more than vindicate their own value preferences through the judicial process"—i.e. those who seek to 'politicise' the courts. The Supreme Court did note, however, that it would authorise judicial review to the Sierra Club if it sought to sue on behalf of one or more of its members; it would also grant standing to any individual who could show that his particular aesthetic or recreational pleasures would be reduced ('injured in fact') by the decision to approve the access roadway. Moreover, the Court broke precedent by encouraging either or both of the plaintiffs to "assert the interests of the general public" as part of their testimony.

Nevertheless, Sax (1973) is critical of this important ruling since it restricts the rights of public interest organisations to vindicate the anxieties of the public at large (or potential anxieties of future generations) about possible ecological destruction. Nor, he claims, does it provide any opportunity for the citizen plaintiff to assert any legal rights over the protection of such areas, even though he may enjoy the 'option value' of knowing that such natural assets exist and can be visited at any time (a significant aspect of the benefits of preservation). As is so often the case, the matter is political. Environmental issues will "turn out to be litigable or not depending on the intensity of fear of retribution of the victims, or the persuasiveness of the organisation in obtaining user-victims as plaintiffs, or on the structure of the organisation as a membership organisation of users or not" (Sax, 1973, p.80). It is quite probable that judicial reviews will be contingent not so much on the real merits of the case, as on the nature of the 'interest' of the 'front man' put up by an environmental group to justify standing.

8.2.1 Standing under fire—some legal breakthroughs

The standing issue is crucial to environmentalists who believe strongly that citizens should be able to bypass poorly equipped political and economic institutions in order to protect environmental quality. They recognise that the law reflects prevailing political and social mores, and so are quite unashamedly testing innovative doctrines of standing to allow concerned individuals and organisations to vindicate their environmental interests. In their ceaseless efforts, they have unearthed a number of old doctrines and given birth to a few new theories which are described below.

8.2.1.1 *The class action*

In the usual class suit, the court must first determine whether a group of individuals has a common interest ('questions of law or fact common to a class'), whether the class action is better than other available means of litigation, and whether the person in whose name the suit is being brought will do a fair and adequate job of protecting the interest of the class (Adler, 1972). Class actions over environmental issues have not been favourably received by the courts, as each member of the class must still show a 'special interest' that is separable from the interests of the public at large. In other words, the class must *specifically* benefit from judicial redress, not *automatically* gain, as, for instance, they would do if successful litigation reduced air pollution. So class actions tend to be limited to groups who can show clear proprietary interest, such as fishermen, hunters, or native Indians who by lease, purchase, or treaty have rights to animals, land, etc. [For an excellent discussion of the usufructuary rights of Canadian Indians to the flora, fauna, and land upon which they depend for a livelihood, see Bird (1972).]

But in the Storm King Case (*Scenic Hudson Preservation Conference v. Federal Power Commission*, 1966) a federal court ruled that a class of interested citizens had the right to intervene in FPC hearings as an 'aggrieved party', even though it had no appreciable economic interests in the area. Those who showed 'special interest' by reason of their demonstrated concern over the preservation of scenic beauty, fish, wildlife, etc., had sufficient reason to be granted class standing. This, of course, was a major doctrinal breakthrough for United States environmental lobbies (Eddy, 1971, pp.206–211), for the event granted standing to a group who could prove that its aesthetic and psychic values, not their property interests, were at risk. Environmental lawyers like to distinguish between the 'special concern' test (as defined in the *Scenic Hudson* case) and the 'special use' test (used by the Supreme Court in the *Mineral King* case), though the matter remains judicially unclear.

In Canada and the United Kingdom the liberalisation of class action has not progressed nearly as far as it has in the United States, so class actions are still rarely used in environmental litigation. In fact, class actions are not generally available, as normally each property owner must prove his own damages (Elder, 1973, p.95). One problem is the considerable confusion surrounding precedents for determining the suitability of such actions, while the traditional conservatism of Canadian and British courts has not encouraged experimentation in this area.

8.2.1.2 *The qui tam initiative*

The ancient doctrine of sovereign immunity ('the king can do no wrong') has subsequently been tempered by statutes which provided judicial standing to informers whose evidence led to the successful prosecution and fining of a law violator, and for citizen-initiated legal action if the government failed to prosecute. This writ *qui tam* was resuscitated in 1970 by environmental groups who found it embodied in the 1899 US Rivers and Harbours Act (the 'Refuse Act'), which prescribes that no discharge into navigable waterways can be permitted until authorised by licence by the Corps of Engineers (US House Subcommittee on Conservation and Natural Resources, 1971; Boyd, 1972; Council on Environmental Quality, 1972, pp.119–123; Clusen, 1973, pp.77–78). In September 1970, $2000 was awarded under the Refuse Act to the Hudson River Fishermen's Association for supplying information about pollution of the Hudson River by the Penn Central Railroad, who were discharging pollutants without proper authorisation. In the following six months, some 130 similar convictions were won (table 8.1). These caused so much anxiety amongst industrial

Table 8.1. *Qui tam* initiatives and water pollution litigation. (Source: Council on Environmental Quality, 1972, p.121.)

	Fiscal years					
	1967	1968	1969	1970	1971	1972
Refuse Act						
criminal actions filed	56	41	46	129	191	81
convictions			42	59	127	130
civil actions filed				2	56	52
settlements					7	17
Federal Water Pollution Control Act						
new enforcement conferences	4	3	2	4	3	6
reconvening of conferences	5	6	8	8	9	7
180-day notices				10	9	82
municipalities				2	5	56
industry				8	4	26

and public sector polluters that they pressured for statutory clarification to curtail these newfound citizen's rights. Two important court rulings (*Kalur v. Resor*, 1971; and *US v. Pennsylvania Industrial Chemical Corporation*, 1972) effectively quashed the *qui tam* actions by concluding that no dischargers were liable until a proper federal permit programme was in effect, and that in any case environmental impact statements were required for all permit applications. Here is a case of potential counter productivity in environmental legislation, for the NEPA requirement could reduce the scope of citizen initiatives. Because *qui tam* writs *per se* have never been judicially upheld, it is difficult to evaluate how effective they could be in citizen scrutiny of agency performance.

8.2.1.3 *The public trust doctrine*

Sax (1970a, pp.158–174; 1970b) has persuasively argued that federal and regional governments have legal responsibilities to ensure that certain common property resources such as air, water, mountains, and lakes are held in trust for the free and unimpeded use of the general public. Dating from ancient Roman Law pertaining to natural objects, the theory of public trust rests on these related principles: (a) that certain resources, such as the air, waterways, or the seashore, are of such general significance that it would be unwise to transfer them entirely to private ownership, (b) that their benefits derive from a sort of 'natural amenity rent' that belongs to everybody, and (c) that in principle the duty of governments is to promote the interests of the general public rather than to redistribute goods from the public weal to sectional interests. Should the government not act to protect such resources as a trustee, a court action may be initiated by a citizen (Reitze, 1971, p.812).

Because the courts now recognise that some sort of balance must be struck between responsible private use of amenity resources and the protection of social well-being, they tend to rule that publicly owned resources cannot be appropriated by private interests without proper compensation. Moreover, the courts usually insist that the onus of proof should rest with the developer, not the public, to show that no overall injury will ensue as a consequence of a proposed action, and that specific benefits should be provided for the general public to compensate fully for any (amenity) losses that might be incurred. Sax (1970a, pp.167–169) records how the Wisconsin court has established a number of general guidelines to ensure that some sort of amenity compensation is made to the general public when common access resources are alienated from free public use. And Grad (1972, p.127) comments on the findings of the Massachusetts courts that public property already in use for one purpose (e.g. a park) cannot be converted for another public use (e.g. a housing estate) without proper legislative authorisation. However, the public trust doctrine has not really been tested to the full since there are no proper guidelines for the courts to determine how much of what 'trust' is really being destroyed in any particular case.

8.2.1.4 *Citizen environmental rights*
The logical extension of the public trust doctrine is a charter of citizen rights to a clean and healthy environment. This would enable the citizen to prosecute in the event of any injury to his well-being irrespective of whether or not his situation is unique. The legal background to this issue devolves from the interpretation of the Administrative Procedure Act (APA, 1967) in the United States, from the recommendations of the Ontario Royal Commission into Civil Rights (1968) in Canada, and the UK White Paper on Administrative Law (Cmnd. 4059, 1969).

The American legislation provides that:

> "A person suffering legal wrong because of agency action, or adversely affected or aggrieved by agency action within the meaning of a relevant statute, is entitled to judicial review thereof."

Prima facie this grants the individual citizen rights of redress (judicial review) for any governmental misdemeanour that is shown to be 'arbitrary, capricious and contrary to the law', but in practice interpretations have produced wildly inconsistent precedents. Because 'injury in fact' must be demonstrated, the APA provision restricts environmental rights, since it implies that a person's legal rights have been violated by *de facto* injury affecting his health or economic well-being.

To overcome this difficulty, Sax drew up a 'citizen's environmental charter' which was adopted by the State of Michigan in its Environmental Protection Act of 1970 (Sax, 1970a, pp.247–252; Sax and Connor, 1972). The Act seeks to recognise the public right to a decent environment as a legal right, to make it enforceable by permitting private citizens to sue as members of the public, and to formulate a clearer common law of environmental quality. This Act has stimulated similar proposals in other US states and even Congressional legislation (Crampton and Boyer, 1972, pp.419–425). All of these aim to allow a private citizen or class of persons the right to obtain declaratory or equitable relief from public or private violators, if he/she/they can show that the defendant's activities cause an adverse impact upon "the air, water, land or public trust of the United States". The Michigan Act states that where the plaintiff presents a reasonable case it is then up to the defendant to show that there was no feasible or prudent alternative to his/her activity, that it was consistent with the general requirements for protecting the public welfare, and that its social and economic benefits outweighed its social, economic, and environmental costs.

Sax (1974, pp.181–188) claims that the act works well and speedily (there averaged some two cases per month over the first thirty months) because most cases (about 80%) are settled out of court. One reason for the unusual speed of decision is the threat of preliminary injunctions on large, costly projects. Another feature of the Act is the extensive use made of it by public agencies threatened by community groups or individual litigants proposing legal action in the public interest to justify tougher action against violators of their regulations. This has particularly aided pollution enforcement agencies in their bargaining activities, a development that has been observed with great approval by citizens' groups elsewhere. In addition, the Act has helped public agencies to resolve politically sensitive resource issues, for private suits enable them to perform their proper, regulatory duties without embarrassing their relationship with particular clients. As a result, agencies have been able to get information into the community and so to politicise important resource issues in a manner which stirs up the public, alerts the legislature, and improves agency performance.

Crampton and Boyer (1972) and Grad (1972) are dubious about the merits of this kind of environmental rights reform, largely because they believe the executive agencies are constitutionally empowered to act, not simply to deliberate, that they have (or should have) access to all the best data available, and are the best (and only) judges of complicated technical evidence. Grad (1972, pp.129–130) fears that in their zeal for legal reform, environmental lawyers may reinstate the messy judicial meddling under substantive due process motions that could result in *more* not less administrative discretion. Sax (1974, pp.184–185) counters these arguments by commenting that properly drafted legislation need not impair constitutional responsibilities but should *improve* the performance of agencies, first by opening up their activities to citizen participation, and second by strengthening their political resolve to take proper action when it is required.

In any case, despite their constitutional remit, legislatures do not fully debate the substantive issues of resource management, nor do many politicians elected on the basis of their environmental views. In Britain, Friends of the Earth are currently attempting to force MPs to debate the nation's atomic energy programme, since the really crucial questions—whether to go nuclear at all and if so when, what kind of reactor to choose and why, what safeguards against radiation and other hazards should be provided in plant operation and fuel processing, transport, and disposal—have never formally been open to full political discussion.

The difference of viewpoint on this issue is fundamental to the role of environmental law and really hinges on political ideology. The cautious lawyers believe in the competence of the specialised agencies and in the ability of the legislature to provide unambiguous statutory guidelines. The reform group, on the other hand, doubt that agencies can see the full implications of their actions and are equally unhappy about the ability of our governing institutions to legislate clearly in the public interest.

Compare Crampton and Boyer (1972, p.414):

> "In contrast to the courts, agencies have a considerable advantage in their ability to use internal structuring and staffing policies in dealing with complex, multi-faceted problems. Agencies can subdivide technical problems into manageable subunits for staff analysis, retain outside consultants or create panels of independent experts, assign staff members to the task of advocating particular interests, undertake programs of testing or empirical research, and investigate various alternatives in a systematic fashion."

with Sax (1974, p.181):

> "... special knowledge in the highly trained mind produces its own limitations, and it may be argued that expertise sacrifices the insight of common sense to intensity of experience. It breeds an inability to accept new views from the very depths of its preoccupation with its own conclusions. Too often it fails to see round the subject: too often it lacks humility and breeds in its possessors an inability to see the obvious. There is also a class spirit about it, so that experts tend to neglect all evidence that does not come from their own ranks. Above all, where human problems are concerned, the expert fails to see that whatever judgements he makes which are not purely factual in nature bring with them a score of values which has no special validity about it."

and draw your own conclusions.

Sax's initiative has proved contagious. In the Canadian context, Fraser (1974) and Lucas (1976) believe that, even now, Canadian constitutional law actually guarantees environmental rights. They contend that individuals have always had the legal obligation not to abuse communal rights to common property resources (even when these resources were attached to their own land) because they used these on a trusteeship basis. Both Canadian and English lawyers quote the famous legal authority Blackstone in their advocacy of trusteeship rights:

> "There are some few things which, notwithstanding the general introduction and continuance of property, must still unavoidably remain in common ... such (among others) are the elements of light, air and water ... water is a moveable, wandering thing and must of necessity continue common by the law of nature; so that I can only have a temporary, transient, usufructuary property therein" (cited in Fraser, 1974, pp.117–118).

It seems inevitable that the whole principle of standing in relation to environmental issues will continue to change in favour of greater citizen rights. Lucas (1976) records a recent legal breakthrough in Canada, where a Manitoba court ruled that a citizen had standing in his attempt to stop the City of Winnipeg from sparying insecticide, even where there was no evidence of 'special and peculiar damage', since sections of the City of Winnipeg Act demonstrated an "express intention to involve citizen participation in municipal government". But the path to legal reform will not be smooth, because environmental issues inevitably involve wider questions. In the Winnipeg example the plaintiff still lost his case because he failed to prove that the social gains of not spraying the insecticide would outweigh the costs of providing an alternative to use of the chemical.

8.2.1.5 *Biotic rights*

Reference was made in chapter 1 to attempts by lawyers to bestow legal rights of existence on animate and inanimate objects along the lines advocated by Leopold (1949). The great judicial champion of this idea is Supreme Court Justice Douglas. In his dissenting opinion on the *Mineral King* case he stated:

> "Those who like it [Mineral King], fish it, hunt it, camp in it or frequent it merely to sit in solitude and wonderment are legitimate spokesmen for it, whether they may be a few or many. Those who have that intimate relation with the inanimate object about to be injured, polluted or otherwise despoiled are its legitimate spokesmen."

J. Stone (1972) has taken this theme to its logical absurdity by developing a guardianship theory whereby citizens could sue on behalf of natural objects. This is really an unnecessary extension of citizen rights, for if these were fully developed they would incorporate a private litigable interest to preserve wildlife and other natural objects.

8.2.1.6 *The fairness doctrine*

In 1971, Friends of the Earth successully appealed to the District of Columbia Court of Appeals against a Federal Communications Commission ruling that advertisers need not supply details of the environmental implications of the use of their products. The ruling was based on the fairness doctrine, which states that broadcasting companies have a duty to present a fair discussion of public issues by affording "reasonable opportunity for the presentation of conflicting views by appropriate spokesmen" (Wiggins, 1972, p.108). It is clear that, as a result of this case, the media will be obliged to counter all commercials for environmentally damaging goods with 'environmental advertisements' indicating the social costs of consuming such products. If these were mandatory, this could lead to much wider dissemination of information on environmental issues.

8.2.1.7 *The no-significant-degradation (*NSD*) issue*

A number of amendments to pollution control legislation in the United States (The Clean Air Act, 1970; The Water Pollution Control Act, 1972; The Noise Control Act, 1972) provide that citizens can prosecute their interests in the formulation of federal standards and can bring legal action directly against violators. In theory these amendments were designed to ameliorate the impact of the *qui tam* discussed earlier, and to provide support for federal and state agencies in their bargaining with polluters over the adoption of 'best available' and 'best practicable' technologies.

A number of environmental groups have taken the introductory preamble of the Clean Air Act ("to protect and enhance the quality of the Nation's air resources so as to promote the public health and welfare and the productive capacity of its population") to mean that states could insist on preserving air quality at levels significantly higher than that judged necessary simply to protect health and welfare (see Mihaly, 1972; Trumbull, 1972; Disselhorst, 1975). On a tied vote over a test case (*Sierra Club v. Ruckelshaus*, 1972), the Supreme Court effectively accepted the argument that areas of very high air quality (i.e. where ambient air quality is better than what is required by national air quality standards) could protect themselves from any 'significant degradation' either by insisting on most stringent levels of emission control or, possibly, by prohibiting certain kinds of development altogether. In March 1974 the Environmental Protection Agency recommended a change in the federal legislation to remove the NSD clause, since it "represents an unwarranted and unnecessary limitation on the range of choice of state and local governments in economic development and land use matters" (Council on Environmental Quality, 1974, p.131). However, it appears that states can still impose more stringent standards, and so determine for themselves what kind and rate of growth they would like with regard to the protection of air quality.

The NSD ruling has important policy implications. First, it provides a powerful lever for citizen environmental groups to have a say in determining the level of environmental quality over large areas of the nation. Second, it offers a legitimate strategy for states to develop guided growth programmes, a matter of great significance (see chapter 4, pp.157–163). Third, it can be used by air pollution control agencies to regulate emissions more effectively even in areas of high pollution. NSD was invoked by the Environmental Protection Agency in its attempts to reduce automobile traffic in American cities. During 1972 all major metropolitan areas filed emergency traffic control plans for operation when air quality reached certain minimal unacceptable levels. Adopted after formal public hearings these plans called for quite dramatic action, ranging from the banning of all downtown parking (in Boston), to restrictions on all automobiles except taxis (in Lower Manhattan), to gasoline rationing (in Los Angeles). To date none of these plans has been fully put to the test.

Fourth, the NSD clause could be used to upgrade existing emission control technologies. Environmental groups claim that the nondegradation clause should force polluters to develop new technologies or be forbidden either to continue operation or to locate in a certain area. And, if the emitting source expands production, it should *not* be allowed to increase its emissions (Disselhorst, 1975, p.767). Eventually the NSD clause could be used in the management of regionwide air quality based on meteorological and topographic airsheds.

Finally, the NSD issue is important since some environmentalists would like to apply it to the concept of an airshed 'carrying capacity', a Spaceship II idea which would determine the nature and extent of present and future air pollution emissions throughout the airshed. This could lead to the possibility of auctioning or issuing licences based on politically defined assimilative capacities as suggested by some proponents of the residuals tax. But all this assumes that NSD will survive further judicial challenge. Disselhorst (1975) believes it will not, as both political figures and Environmental Protection Agency administrators are at present seeking a compromise that would weaken the NSD provision. Already it has lost out to the 'energy crisis', for the use of high-sulphur fuels is now permitted in some areas.

The battle for citizen environmental rights is as much a political matter as it is a legal question, for it centres on well worn environmental themes—the degree of trust in the political process and administrative procedures, the ability of individuals to protect the general and long-term public welfare, the distribution of environmental justice, and the appropriate role of citizen participation. As political attitudes to these fundamental questions take on new complexions, the scope and definition of legal standing will evolve into new forms.

8.3 The National Environmental Policy Act

Perhaps the most important (and controversial) piece of environmental legislation ever promulgated is the U.S. National Environmental Policy Act (NEPA) signed into law on 1 January, 1970. There is little doubt that few, if any, Congressmen and even fewer resource managing agencies had any idea of its likely impact on environmental policymaking on that New Year's morning. In a paradoxical way, NEPA was well ahead of its time in terms of political and institutional preparedness, but almost too late in coming in terms of national recognition of environmental concern. It is worth noting from the legislative history of the Act (Council on Environmental Quality, 1972, pp.221-230; Anderson, 1973, pp.1-14) that it was modelled on the Employment Act of 1946. In directing Congress and the US Government to maintain a prosperous and stable national economy, this earlier piece of legislation made national economic growth a major and permanent national goal; it also established a three-man Council of Economic Advisers to report to the President and the nation about the state of the economy and the activities of both the legislative and executive branches in maintaining sound economic growth.

NEPA places environmental quality on the same priority footing as economic growth in its important preamble [Section 101(b)] that "it is the continuing responsibility of the Federal Government to use all practicable means, consistent with other essential considerations of national policy, to ...

(i) fulfil the responsibilities of each generation as trustee of the environment for succeeding generations;

(ii) assume for all Americans safe, healthful, productive, and aesthetically and culturally pleasing surroundings;

(iii) attain the widest range of beneficial uses of the environment without degradation, risk to health or safety, or any other undesirable or unintended consequences;

(iv) preserve important historic, cultural and natural aspects of our national heritage, and maintain, wherever possible, an environment which supports diversity, and variety of individual choice;

(v) achieve a balance between population and resource use which will permit high standards of living and a wide sharing of life's amenities; and

(vi) enhance the quality of renewable resources and approach the maximum attainable recycling of depletable resources."

In addition the Congress gave qualified recognition of citizen environmental rights and personal environmental obligations when it stated that "each person should enjoy a healthful environment" and that "each person has a responsibility to contribute to the preservation and enhancement of the environment". Anderson (1973, pp.5-6) notes that in the original language this amendment provided that "each person has a fundamental and unalienable right to a healthful environment"; but this was changed by subsequent political haggling to its present form, to avoid any legal support for the concept of citizen environmental rights.

The Section 101 provisions are reported in full because their noble rhetoric formally commits the American nation to a policy of environmental harmony. As part of this commitment the Act established a three-man Council on Environmental Quality to review annually the state of the nation's environment and assess critically the performance of Congress and government agencies in meeting these high-minded ideals. Actions, of course, speak louder than words, and it is a little saddening to record that the independence of the Council on Environmental Quality is somewhat stifled by political considerations. In 1973, for instance, its annual report was delayed owing to an argument over chapters on energy and materials recycling. Both were eventually omitted entirely, although a subdued energy statement was published separately (Council on Environmental Quality, 1973b). The Council has no veto power over any proposed actions which it feels may be detrimental to the environment, nor is it sufficiently staffed to undertake the necessary independent research to give it authority. In fact, most of its data and many of its reviews of impact statements are produced by the very agencies whose activities it is supposed to monitor. Sax's contention (1970a, p.92) that the Council appears to be more an arm of the administration than the independent advocate of the public interest still unfortunately appears to be true.

But perhaps too much is being expected of NEPA. It is after all a piece of administrative legislation designed to encourage (indeed compel) all federal executive agencies to take every possible environmental consideration into account when contemplating any kind of action, from policymaking through programme design to regulation; and wherever and whenever possible, to 'balance' these considerations with other, perhaps quite contradictory but equally legitimate mandates. It was thus primarily designed to open up procedural guidelines, not to reorder the nation's priorities.

There is still considerable controversy over how far NEPA should force agencies to alter their policies and practices in a substantial manner to take account of environmental quality. The evidence is growing (largely as a result of important court rulings—see Green, 1972b, and Anderson, 1973) that the act's substantive provisions should dominate, but it remains to be seen to what extent environmental considerations can hold sway when, say, military security, the economy, or jobs are at stake. Congress showed its own ambivalence on this matter in July 1973 when the Senate split 49–49 over whether to scrap the formal environmental impact review of the Transalaskan Pipeline. When its President (then former Vice-President Agnew) cast his vote in favour of abandoning the NEPA requirement, Congress in effect showed where its political priorities lay. In other areas of energy policymaking—the battle over conservation of demand versus the provision of more supply, whether to use pricing or rationing as a mechanism for controlling demand, whether to relax environmental quality standards to exploit domestic fuels—neither NEPA nor the Council on Environmental Quality has substantial influence. But it is probably fair to say that the existence of NEPA has certainly stopped a lurch to the environmental 'right' during a troublesome period of national reassessment about economic growth, resource availability, and international relations.

During the committee stages of NEPA, witnesses were well aware of the discrepancies between legislative rhetoric and political deeds. Anderson (1973, pp.6–8) describes the political bargaining that lay behind the famous 'action forcing' Section 102 with its statutory requirements for full environmental impact statements. The idea originated in testimony from Lynton Caldwell, a well-known and respected professor of government who has long advocated that environmental quality be both politically and administratively a major national goal (Caldwell, 1963, 1964, 1968, 1970a, 1971a, 1971b, 1972a, 1972b). In his testimony Caldwell suggested that the regulatory licensing procedures of various agencies should include "certain requirements with respect to environmental protection". Senator Henry Jackson, Chairman of the Senate Committee on Interior and Insular Affairs, seized upon this idea as being applicable to "all agencies that have responsibilities that affect the environment". The House spent some time juggling its version of the NEPA bill between two committees, trying to keep it from the one (the House Interior and Insular Affairs Committee) which, though nominally responsible by its terms of reference, was rather conservative in its interpretation of the proposed amendments.

The result of all this political manoeuvring was the famous Section 102, which is something of a compromise between Senator Jackson's belief that a requirement for a "detailed statement" of all environmental impacts be binding on all aspects of all agency activities, Senator Muskie's feeling that all regulatory activities relating to air and water pollution control be exempt from such statements, and Congressman Aspinal's contention that "nothing in this Act shall increase, decrease or change any responsibility of any federal official or agency", and that responsible officials should consult around and 'find' what environmental impacts might ensue from any proposed action. The final form of Section 102(2)(C) does require a "detailed statement", which agencies must comply with "to the fullest extent possible" for "all major federal action significantly affecting the quality of the human environment", such as "project proposals, proposals for new legislation, regulations, policy statements, or expansion or revision of ongoing programs". But the final wording of the Act was surprisingly vague about almost all of the key interpretative issues, indicating either that Congress expected the courts to "flesh out its skeletal statutory provisions" (Anderson, 1973, p.10), or that the chief actors in the NEPA drama were genuinely innocent of the ferocity of the tiger they were about to hold by the tail. This ambiguity of wording played a crucial role in the subsequent judicial interpretation of NEPA. It is interesting to note in this respect that in the United States Congressmen and Senators draft their own bills which consequently suffer in some cases from 'inartistic drafting'. In the UK and Canada, parliamentary legislation originates in the legal division of ministerial departments. Hence bills are carefully scrutinised for both their political and departmental implications before they reach the floor of the Commons.

Subsequent events have shown that both the courts and their executive agencies have responded to NEPA's uncertain legislative intent in an increasingly confident and comprehensive manner (Council on Environmental Quality, 1974, pp.352–381). But to begin with the agencies were understandably unsure of what was expected of them and, equally understandably, reluctant (and in many cases unable) to prepare the kind of review which the wording of the act intended but which would be impossible to achieve in full (White, 1972). This period of initial uncertainty ended when they were prodded into action by a number of now famous court rulings that have clarified much of NEPA's statutory intent.

8.3.1 Court rulings relating to NEPA

8.3.1.1 *Scope of the environmental impact statement (EIS)*

Within four months of NEPA's enactment, Judge Hart of the District of Columbia Court of Appeals ordered an injunction restraining the US

Secretary of the Interior from issuing a permit to allow the consortium of oil companies constructing the transalaskan oil pipeline to build a gravel access road across the public lands bordering their pipeway (*Wilderness Society v. Hickel,* 1970). Justice Hart ruled that an environmental impact statement was necessary before any regulatory decision could be made, and that this statement must be "full enough" to allow agency officials to make an "informed choice", though not so full as to be "unreasonably burdensome". This 'rule of reason' applied ostensibly to the range of alternatives to be considered, though the general discretionary language could be interpreted to hold for other circumstances.

How full is 'full'? In *Environmental Defense Fund v. Corps of Engineers* (1971), Judge Eisele pronounced:

> "At the very least NEPA is an environmental full disclosure law ... intended to make ... decision making more responsive and responsible. The 'detailed statement' required by S.102(2)(C) should, at a minimum, contain such information as will alert the President, the Council on Environmental Quality, the public and, indeed, the Congress to all known *possible* environmental consequences of proposed agency action."

This 'full disclosure' ruling is very important, for it supports the Congressional intent that "to make policy effective through action, a comprehensive system is required for the assembly and reporting of relevant knowledge and for placing ... for public discussion, the alternative courses of action that this knowledge suggests". Anderson (1973, p.207) concludes that the courts define a 'detailed' statement as one in which statements (a) are comprehensible by the layman and not pejoritatively prejudiced, (b) refer to the full range of knowledge available, and (c) discuss certain impacts which are typical of similar types of action.

Who should present the evidence for full disclosure? The courts are divided about this. In *Committee for Nuclear Responsibility v. Schlesinger* (1971) the Washington, DC Circuit Court noted that the statements need only include "responsible scientific opinion" and "hence there is room for discretion on the part of the officials preparing the statement" (though not for an assumption that their determination is conclusive). But in *Environmental Defense Fund v. Corps of Engineers* (1971) the court held that statements could include the contentious views of experts, concerned public or private citizens, or even ordinary lay citizens, so long as these views are 'responsible'. This latter ruling is preferable to environmentalists who feel that, because many resource-management matters involve equally valid but contradictory scientific evidence, wider views *should* be brought to bear on any decision.

8.3.1.2 *Substantive versus procedural requirements of NEPA*

Full disclosure as to 'possible' consequences may 'alert' policymakers but does not require them to alter their decisions. Can NEPA really 'force' agencies to abandon predetermined policies? This is an enormously controversial matter but one which should be considered in the limited context of NEPA's administrative orbit. In *Calvert Cliffs' Coordinating Committee v. AEC* (1971) Judge Wright expressed the view that:

> "The reviewing courts probably cannot reverse a substantive decision on its merits ... unless it be shown that the actual balance of costs and benefits that was struck was arbitrary or clearly gave insufficient weight to environmental values."

and in *Natural Resources Defense Council v. Morton* (1971) the court held:

> "The court [cannot] in any way substitute its judgement for that of the Executive agency involved unless the decision of the agency is found to be arbitrary, capricious, or an abuse of discretion, in which case the Court could require the agency to reconsider its decision."

However, environmentalists have taken heart at Judge Wright's expansive rulings in the *Calvert Cliffs'* case, rulings that are regarded as so important that they are outlined in some detail below (see Stribling, 1972; US Senate Committee on Interior and Insular Affairs, 1972):
(i) The Atomic Energy Commission is required to consider a 'detailed statement' when issuing licence applications for nuclear generating plants even if the parties at the hearings do not request such information. The EIS is to be an "essential component" of all agency decisionmaking.
(ii) The agency "must itself take the initiative of considering environmental values at every distinctive and comprehensive stage of the process beyond the staff's evaluation and recommendation". This is interpreted to mean that agencies must review the substantive evidence of the EIS and *balance* this evidence against all other nonenvironmental matters. [It should be stressed that NEPA does not *require* that 'nonenvironmental' questions (such as economic impact) be included in the EIS, though a number of agencies are voluntarily adding such information.] In the court's words, agencies must use a "systematic, interdisciplinary approach" and "identify and develop methods and procedures ... which will ensure that presently unquantified environmental amenities and values be given appropriate consideration in decisionmaking along with economic and technical considerations". This ruling in effect obliges the agencies, not the courts, to contemplate new procedures for balancing the pros and cons of all policies and programmes, and radically to reform their decisionmaking practices:

> "NEPA mandates a case by case balancing judgement on the part of federal agencies ... . The particular economic and technical benefits of planned action must be assessed and weighed against the environmental costs; alternatives must be considered which would affect the balance of values ... . The point of the individualized balancing analyses is to ensure ... that the optimally beneficial action is finally taken."

(iii) Each agency must be responsible for providing its own EIS and cannot merely rely on consultations with other interested agencies to obtain the necessary information. Data collection and analysis across a broad front is an integral part of the 'finely tuned' balancing process. But other agencies can publicly review and comment on a particular EIS.
(iv) The court quashed any likelihood of a 'grandfather clause' by stating that all NEPA requirements were enforceable from the beginning of 1970, so all relevant proposals not completed by the end of 1969 were subject to mandatory environmental review.

8.3.1.3 *NEPA and pollution control regulations*
The *Calvert Cliffs'* decision opened up the possibility that federal agencies could insist on environmental quality standards 'more strict' than those required by other statutes if, through the balancing process, they find that existing standards do not adequately protect the environment. However, this ruling is contentious, since Section 104 of NEPA states that it shall not "affect the specific statutory obligations of any federal agency to comply with criteria or standards of environmental quality". In any case the legislative intent is ambiguous, since NEPA was in force before the major environmental regulating agency, the Environmental Protection Agency, was created.

In enacting the 1972 Amendments to the Federal Water Pollution Control Act, Congress specifically exempted regulatory activities of the Environmental Protection Agency from environmental impact reviews, except for grants for new waste treatment works and permits for new sources of effluent. Courts have upheld this ruling for other regulatory actions on the grounds that the Environmental Protection Agency produces a 'functional equivalent' of an EIS when preparing its briefs. But, as an indication of the willingness of federal agencies to comply with NEPA, the Environmental Protection Agency has voluntarily decided to prepare EISs (subject of course to full public review) when determining national environmental quality standards and a variety of other regulatory guidelines. This should help to upgrade environmental standards to the point where the *Calvert Cliffs'* ruling may not have to apply.

8.3.2 NEPA in review
Perhaps understandably, the Council on Environmental Quality (1974, pp.371–410) is pleased with the first five years of NEPA. "NEPA is alive and well", it claims (p.413), "and has emerged as an integral and essential part of all Federal agencies' activities." As a result of over 250 litigations under NEPA, the Council feels that the orbit of the legislation is now very clear and agencies are more readily adopting the Council's guidelines for preparing EISs (*ibid.*, pp.506–522). Court rulings have widened considerably the definition of what proposals "significantly affect the environment" to cover projects that alter existing zoning regulations. And it was noted in chapter 5 (pp.193–199) that the scope of the modern EIS

includes analysis of second- and even third-order induced effects, such as economic impact, growth-inducing characteristics and compatibility with surrounding land uses, which in sum amount to *de facto* environmental benefit–cost analyses that could be linked to guided growth and regional carrying-capacity studies.

Anderson (1973) and Sax (1974) are not so sanguine about the achievements of NEPA. Both feel that the important provisions of Section 103, namely that all agencies should review and, where appropriate, amend their existing decisionmaking procedures to meet the full policy intent of NEPA (as outlined in Section 101) are not being adequately met. Sax (1974, p.175) claims that "it is uncommon to find cases in which agencies have done an environmental impact statement and then made a decision on the basis of the information acquired which shows the project should not go forward". He feels that only when citizens' groups are armed with the knowledge and the funds to evaluate fully the intricacies of the EIS will the agencies really change their ways, and work with informed and sophisticated citizens' organisations in a process of mutual education. In fact he believes that 1% of the capital costs of a proposal should be set aside to allow citizens' groups to undertake competent evaluations.

A small step in this direction was the ruling by the US Court of Appeals for the District of Columbia (*Wilderness Society v. Morton*, 1972) that environmentalist groups who successfully protected the public interest by acting as 'private attorneys general' were entitled to claim their legal fees from the losing defendant.

> "Where the law relies on private suits to effectuate Congressional policy in favor of broad public interests, attorney's fees are often necessary to ensure that private litigants will initiate such suits ... . Substantial benefits to the general public should not depend upon the financial status of the individual volunteering to serve as plaintiff or upon the charity of public-minded lawyers."

This decision gives a tremendous boost to public-interest lawyers who play such a vital role in environmental litigation, often at considerable financial sacrifice to themselves. Doubtless similar precedents will be anxiously sought by public-spirited environmental law organisations in Canada (The Canadian Enviromental Law Foundation) and Britain (The Lawyers Ecology Group). In this context it is interesting to report the recent entry in the New York Stock Exchange of the Public Equity Corporation, a stock company designed to make profits from lawsuits mounted against socially delinquent businesses. The Corporation will support class actions and other citizen-initiated litigations, sue in its own right and provide a research and legal aid service for citizen action groups. But to begin with, it may have to battle a number of suits contesting its own legality. It's future should provide fascinating analysis for those interested in the relationship between the law and the existing economic and political culture.

Anderson (1973, pp.268–274) remains sceptical of the substantive power of NEPA. For instance, he notes that agencies have not lost their statutory discretion about what to consider and how to proceed. In addition, agencies do not have to undertake a complete analysis of alternatives, merely to "study, develop and describe" those alternatives that will help responsible officials to identify problems. He further contends that the 'balancing' provision thrust upon the agencies in the *Calvert Cliffs'* ruling is so vague that any agency "will most likely resolve uncertainties in favour of the priorities set out in its original grant of authority", with the result that NEPA "may not actually achieve its ultimate purpose of changing the Congressionally recognized tendency of federal decisionmaking toward environmental neglect and destruction".

To make NEPA more effective Anderson favours the idea of overlapping 'tiers' of statements (1973, pp.290–292). An initial statement would be prepared for all major federal initiatives, including all legislation and new agency policies. This would cover all the pros and cons of differing alternatives and packages of alternatives, a process that would stimulate interagency consultation and imaginative political discussion. Subsequent statements would be provided for each iterative step in policy formulation, so that final project proposals need not contain the current laborious evaluations of philosophy and policy that are printed more for the record than for substantive review. Anderson's proposal explicitly recognises policy formation as a series of gradually narrowing choices, and encourages all participants to review the widest possible implications at the highest levels before irreversible political commitments are made. Above all it would help to achieve the real aim of NEPA, outlined in Sections 101 and 103, which is to incorporate fully the 'environmental perspective' in the conduct of human affairs.

NEPA is not simply a statute, it is an amazingly powerful educational tool for alerting all policymakers to the wider message of environmentalism. Already it has diverted traditional routine decisionmaking pathways into new avenues of interdisciplinary and multiagency patterns of assessment. Furthermore, it has stimulated a search for new methods of consultation among individuals and organisations that are beginning to revolutionise customary modes of decisionmaking.

But the search has only just begun. Anderson's suggestion of a wide ranging first tier policy review before specific proposals are advanced deserves thoughtful analysis. NEPA has stimulated an interest in preparatory investigation but this desperately needs to be improved at the strategic level where major policy choices must be made. In the UK for example numerous proposals have been advanced to reform existing parliamentary procedure so that Congress-style parliamentary committees, staffed by an adequate research secretariat, could review broad policy choices and the wider ramifications of specific pieces of legislation (figure 8.1). At present the mechanism is haphazard. The various standing committees are understaffed and overworked and few MPs have the time or the expertise to do an adequate job. The select committees rarely have time or broad enough terms of reference to cover all the areas they are asked to consider, and in any case their reports are often encumbered by partisan rhetoric. Even then many committee reports are not made available to backbench MPs who often vote with very little knowledge of the full facts. But the political stumbling blocks even to this limited degree of reform are formidable, while senior civil servants are also extremely wary of procedural change.

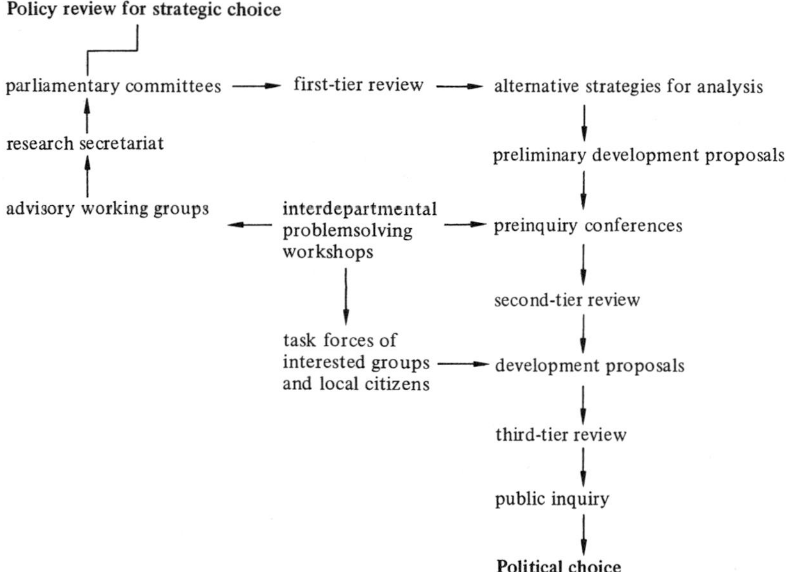

Figure 8.1. Environmental impact assessment via policy and project review. Environmental impact analysis becomes subsumed within a series of increasingly specific appraisals of policy, programme, and development proposals. Thus environmental assessment becomes not a special area for study, but part of a purposive review.

8.4 International environmental law

The measured success of NEPA, along with its equivalents in other US states and other countries, stands in sharp contrast to the tardy response of international law to environmental matters. In some ways this is not really surprising, in view of the fact that most international environmental issues (such as global pollution, exploitation of worldwide common property resources, total extinction or near extinction of certain species of flora and fauna, irreparable damage to unique landscapes and cultural monuments) are of recent vintage (or, to be more precise, have reached political agendas only in recent years). So students of international environmental law are confronted by a body of legal doctrine that was formulated during periods of relative resource abundance, when the generation of wealth was of far greater political importance than the generation of waste (Bourne, 1971; Brownlie, 1973; Utton, 1973). The more pessimistic almost despair of shaping this legacy of outmoded legal theory into an environmental mould, but there have been a number of promising developments in international law recently which offer some hope for reform. Nevertheless, declared intent and actual performance are far from being one and the same thing (Bleicher, 1972).

8.4.1 Territorial sovereignty and international liability

International law has long recognised the fundamental principle of mutual responsibility, to wit: "a State is, in spite of its territorial supremacy, not allowed to alter the natural conditions of its own territory to the disadvantage of the natural conditions of the territory of a neighbouring State" (Caldwell, 1973, p.190). In addition, treaties dating back to the turn of the century have endorsed the general principle that nations should cooperate to serve the mutual interests of their peoples. So the two much quoted Principles 21 and 22 of the UN Declaration on the Human Environment are little more than restatements of well-developed themes. These are:

> "... that states have ... the sovereign right to exploit their own resources pursuant to their own environmental policies, and the responsibility to ensure that activities within their jurisdiction or control do not cause damage to the environment of other states or of areas beyond the limits of national jurisdiction" (Principle 21).

and

> "... states shall cooperate to develop further the international law regarding liability and compensation for victims of pollution and other environmental damage caused by activities within their jurisdiction or control of such states to areas beyond their jurisdiction" (Principle 22).

It will be observed that Principle 21 is subject to all the failings of the liability doctrine (evidence of injury in fact, evidence of proof of damage, evidence of culpability), and still grants sovereign states the rights to determine their own environmental performance and regulatory practices. An example of the continuing tension between sovereign prerogatives and global responsibilities is shown in the UN General Assembly Resolution on Development and Environment (1972) which states:

> "... notwithstanding the general principles that might be agreed upon by the international community, criteria and minimal standards of preservation of the environment as a general rule will have to be defined at the national level and, in all cases, will have to reflect conditions and

> systems of values prevailing in each country, avoiding where necessary the use of norms valid in advanced countries, which may prove invalid and of unwarranted social cost for developing countries."

On a related matter, while the UN Stockholm Conference of 1972 did encourage all states to cooperate over information and provide advance warning of transnational pollution, this was only to happen where individual states considered it 'appropriate'. The original intent of the pre-conference draft resolution, namely, to adopt a kind of international NEPA, was quashed (see Teclaff, 1973, p.366). This draft resolution exhorted:

> "Relevant information must be supplied by States on activities or developments within their jurisdiction or under their control, whenever they believe, or have reason to believe, that such information is needed to avoid the risk of significant adverse effects on the environment in areas beyond ... national jurisdiction."

Although sovereignty remains a sensitive political matter, the notion of *absolute sovereignty* (as advocated in 1895 by US Attorney General Harmon in the dictum "the fundamental principle of international law is the absolute sovereignty of every nation as against all others, within its own territories") is now generally discredited in favour of a doctrine of limited territorial sovereignty or 'equitable utilisation' (Utton, 1973). This recognises the mutual rights of nations sharing a common resource by stating that their use must be 'reasonable', as judged by comparing and balancing the benefits to the utilising nation with the cost to all others. However, Bourne (1971, p.128) observes that the 'reasonable man' test does not assume liability except by special treaty or by "some element of fault, such as malice, recklessness or negligence". And even then, any damage (e.g. by pollution) has to be "of serious consequence and established by clear and convincing evidence".

The standard reference on international liability is the Trail Smelter Case adjudicated by a tribunal of the International Joint Commission, an arbitration body established in 1909 to deal with all kinds of transnational resource management problems between the United States and Canada (Bilder, 1972; O'Riordan, 1976a). In 1928 the Commission was asked to report on an incidence of damage to property in the State of Washington caused by pollution from an ore-refining smelter in Trail, British Columbia. In its final report, the tribunal established clearly the principle "that no state has the right to use or permit the use of its territory in such a manner as to cause injury ... to the territory of another or the property or persons therein."

Despite the apparent grandeur of the Trail Smelter ruling and the subsequent formal statement of equitable utilisation, the matter of international pollution control law is highly ambiguous and largely unenforceable. Though more legal clarity is called for, Utton (1973, p.300) is quite correct in pointing the finger of blame at the inadequacy of existing institutions rather than at poor legal drafting. "We may have escaped from the absolutism of the Harmon doctrine", he comments, "but we have not yet reached a [mature] stage of international management". The chief barrier is the reluctance of states to relinquish or to appear to relinquish their territorial sovereignty. Even the 1972 Great Lakes Agreement, signed between the United States and Canada to manage comprehensively the water quality of the Great Lakes (Bilder, 1972; O'Riordan, 1976a), and which granted the International Joint Commission new investigatory powers, accepted that "programs and other measures established to meet urgent problems would in no way affect the rights of each country to the use of its Great Lakes Waters".

Utton thinks that the only feasible solution to the sovereignty issue in the foreseeable future is the creation of flexible, open-ended arrangements based on a 'two tier' international system of (a) policymaking and coordination on the political side, and (b) information collection, analysis, and programme assessment "of unsurpassed credibility" on the scientific side. The power of international environmental commissions would lie in their objectivity and impeccable data assembly, but their authority could only be promoted through persuasion and reason. Utton quotes an informed source (p.305):

> "The power of ... knowledge to move governments stems from a grasp by policy makers of the full panoply of consequences that may flow from a failure to adjust national policy so as to take it into account; not simply consequences injurious to the environment; but political consequences both international and domestic, economic consequences, repercussions for a government's moral stature or prestige, and perhaps others."

Goldie (1973) believes that international scientific commissions should be responsible for preparing and publicising NEPA type environmental impact statements of the fullest kind, so as to force the principle of environmental protection upon the international community. [Under NEPA, the United States must prepare EISs for all federal initiatives in the international arena (Council on Environmental Quality, 1974, pp.399–400).] Political cooperatives representing sovereign states would do all the policymaking, but these assemblages should represent an appropriate resource area determined by "economic, ecologic and geographic considerations rather than the cartographic vagaries of historical accident". The river basin and inland sea are fairly obvious examples. With such organisations in existence, legal standing should be available to citizens and governments alike, and international adjudicatory tribunals should be set up to ensure that no defendant is outside the jurisdiction of the court. Caldwell (1973) and Teclaff (1973) believe that these tribunals, in all their deliberations, should be encouraged to consider the priceless heritage of the international environment, and should establish a clear principle of international brotherhood and environmental guardianship. In addition, they should protect vital global life-support systems and provide gene pools of selected plants and animals to safeguard genetic diversity.

These are still distant visions. At present it is still extraordinarily difficult to commit states to binding obligations in international environmental matters (Bleicher, 1972). The dismal failure of the International Whaling Commission to control two of its members (Russia and Japan) is a case in point (Council on Environmental Quality, 1974, pp.442–443). Nor are the Stockholm resolutions binding on UN members. The UN environmental programme is limited to four politically innocuous activities: (a) data acquisition and assessment, including the monitoring of environmental damage in areas of international jurisdiction, (b) quiet diplomacy to assist the settlement of disputes between member nations (usually out of court), (c) a variety of support services, such as providing technical cooperation to those who request it, education and training of officers, and public information, and (d) certain advisory management functions, such as advice on international agreements, indication of possible consequences of proposed international actions, and suggestions as to international environmental quality standards. It is primarily a reactive agency with very limited powers of independent investigation, though it could prove helpful in preparing evidence of international environmental damage and assisting political coordination among member nations (Hardy, 1973).

8.4.2 The law of the sea

The worldwide concern over the ecological consequences and shoreline property damage caused by the increasing likelihood of oil spills or of the inadvertent discharge of toxic substances has resulted in some interesting developments in the law of the sea. Again the problem centres on the enforceability of conventions and treaties which look most impressive on paper, for cooperating nation states have to rely more on the tenuous recognition of moral obligation than on the authority of judicial action to achieve results. For example, it took nearly thirty years before the draft convention of the Preliminary Conference on Oil Pollution of Navigable Waters (1926) was recognised by signatory states, and another twenty years before the Inter-Governmental Maritime Consultative Organisation (IMCO) signed its International Convention for the Prevention of Pollution from Ships (1954) (Teclaff, 1973, pp.368–376). But even this Convention, which bans the discharge of oily ballast from tankers in certain critical areas and controls the emission of toxic substances, still leaves a number of technical loopholes (for example, double bottomed boats are not mandatory) and unanswered legal questions. These questions include whether coastal states can promulgate environmental standards stricter than those accepted by the international community, and whether coastal states can prosecute if the oil which damages their coastlines is discharged in international waters. The answers are not clear, yet some 20% of all marine pollution comes from ships.

Some of these proposals raised in the IMCO Convention are being answered by unilateral action or through bilateral agreements which set interesting precedents. In 1970 Canada passed the Arctic Waters Pollution Prevention Act, which declared a 100 mile wide pollution free zone for all coastal waters north of the 60°N parallel (O'Riordan, 1976a). This Act in effect declared Canadian sovereignty over a zone 100 miles offshore (territorial sovereignty is conventionally restricted to 12 miles), thereby submitting all shipping in these waters to stiff Canadian regulations. There is a legal precedent for this kind of action: in 1948 President Truman declared that the United States was recognising a 250 mile economic interest over its coastal seabed. But the Canadian Prime Minister took the action primarily on environmental, not economic, grounds. "We do not doubt for a moment that the rest of the world would find us at fault and hold us liable", he said, "should we fail to ensure adequate protection of that environment from pollution or artificial deterioration" (*Hansard*, 1969, p.39). Later he commented that "Canada will not submit this legislation to the Hague Court [the International Court of Justice] so long as international law has not caught up with technological developments" (*Hansard*, 1972, p.4324). As a consequence of this legislation, Canada claims it can prosecute any ships found polluting its Arctic waters.

Other nations have broken the customary 12 mile territorial limit by unilateral declaration. Iceland proclaimed a zone of 50 miles when endeavouring to protect its vital fishery from British trawlers in 1972, and a number of third-world coastal states (e.g. Kenya, Senegal, Peru) have claimed territorial rights over 200 miles of offshore waters. More recently Iceland asserted its rights over a 200 mile zone by harassing British trawlers fishing for cod within these waters. There is little doubt that Iceland will win its case, probably in the March 1976 Law of the Sea Conference in New York, for two recent Law of the Sea Conferences (Caracas, 1974; Geneva, 1975) have approved in principle the idea of a 200 mile 'exclusive economic zone' over which coastal nations would have economic sovereignty to control—through regulations, permits, licence fees, and the like—the exploitation of fish, offshore petrochemicals, and seabed minerals. In fact this principle was recognised by all forty nations attending the 1950 Continental Shelf Convention which declared that coastal states had exclusive sovereign rights over exploration and exploitation of seabed resources for 3–200 miles, irrespective of technological ability (Christy, 1972). Rights of navigable passage (a key military issue) would remain unimpeded. In practice, however, coastal states will have to enter into complicated bilateral and multilateral treaties over the management of these exclusive economic zones, since much multinational economic activity already takes place here.

A more intractable issue is the control and management of resource exploitation in truly international waters—the open oceans. In 1967 the UN declared in its 'Maltese Resolution' that all the world's nations had a stake in the peaceful use of the seabed in the interests of mankind and in the protection of a common heritage. This 'common heritage' notion implies that all states have equal rights to international resources. As is now well-known, some areas of the deep ocean floor contain large deposits of minerals (especially manganese, copper, nickel, and cobalt) in the form of organic–inorganic nodules. Estimates of their worth range up to $6 billion, though these estimates will probably rise dramatically if world raw-material prices escalate and as the technology of extraction improves. Already the richer nations have begun to devise the means of scooping up and refining these metaliferous nodules; indeed a specially designed ship commissioned by the Howard Hughes organisation is actually already at work. Clearly, unless something is done soon, the technologically weaker states will lose out to the predatory prowess of the richer nations and corporations. The idea currently under serious consideration in the 1975 Law of the Sea Conference is the creation of an International Seabed Authority to license all developments, share out the seabed among different nations, encourage research and development for the poorer nations, and possibly even distribute some of the wealth. How this matter is to be resolved is critical, for it will signify the strength of the political and economic power of the lesser developed nations and thereby indicate the extent to which more equitable resource development will be possible.

8.4.3 Liability and insurance

As noted above there are at present no binding legal doctrines to compel those who commit international violations of environmental protection conventions to pay compensation. Goldie (1965, 1970, 1973) believes that the requirement of 'absolute liability' does have legal precedent and that the operators of any potentially damaging activities (oil tankers, offshore petrochemical wells, deep sea mining) should be legally liable for any injury caused by their operations. (Principle 21 of the UN Stockholm Conference supports this moral responsibility.) In practice, conventions or national legislations have recognised this *de facto* liability, spurred on by a number of spectacular oil spills off the British ('Torrey Canyon'), Canadian ('Arrow'), and American (Santa Barbara) coasts. For example, the International Convention on Civil Liability for Oil Pollution Damage (1969), the Tanker Owners Voluntary Agreement Concerning Liability for Oil Pollution (1970), and the Convention on the Establishment of an International Fund for Compensation of Oil Pollution Damage (1971), all recommended the adoption of a limited strict liability clause and suggested that insurance cover be found for claims of up to $30 million per ship (Teclaff, 1973, pp.370–372). The idea was to provide a fund to cover the costs of quantifiable damage so that immediate compensation would be available without awaiting due legal process. (In a sense this proposal was similar to the 'no fault' automobile plan.) However, the Civil Liability Convention was not signed by a sufficient number of participating states to have the force of law, and, while the Convention of the Fund does establish state responsibility for the ships involved, money will only be released when damages exceed $10 million and when the persons responsible are unable to pay.

Once again, a number of concerned nations have taken the matter into their own hands. The Canadian inquiry into the sinking of the supertanker 'Arrow' ('Arrow' Royal Commission, 1971, p.109) noted:

> "The difficulty of recovering damages which may very well be suffered in substantial amounts by private citizens and companies from oil spills on our coast makes it imperative that some better arrangement for their protection should be worked out in the future."

The result was the 1971 amendments to the Canadian Shipping Act which, amongst other things, established a Maritime Pollution Claims Fund that came into effect in February 1972. The Fund imposes a levy of 15 ¢ per ton on all oil carried into ports in the Maritime Provinces. The revenue (now about $20 million) will be used to meet the cleanup costs and the compensation costs (but not the costs of ecological damage) following any spill where specific liability cannot be proven. This is an innovative piece of legislation, for it bypasses the difficulty of ascertaining strict liability while placing the burden of compensation upon users, who must also meet stiff Canadian regulations over navigation and technical safeguards. An extension of this legislation being proposed to cover all shipping off the western Canadian coast is aimed specifically at tankers carrying Arctic oil to the States of Washington and California. However, this may be more difficult to implement since the tankers may never actually enter Canadian territorial waters. The Canadian precedent is probably a forerunner of a more general pattern of insurance protection, through user payments or government fees, covering various aspects of international resource development. For example, the British Government is now consulting with North Sea oil companies over a governmental insurance protection plan in the event of oil leakage from a well or pipeline.

8.4.4 Some concluding observations

The evolution of international law in environmental management provides fascinating study, for here the last bastions of territorial sovereignty, freedom of use of common heritage resources and economic exploitation vis-à-vis environmental protection, are being fully challenged by the serious events of the times—particularly resource scarcity, economic injustice and the threat of large scale ecocide. International arbitrating institutions, formerly quite inadequate to meet these pressing needs, are rapidly reassessing their functions and creating important precedents. Sometimes events have forced them into action (as for instance with the virtual extinction of some species of whales and certain wildlife habitats), but more often than not progress has been made by the dramatic actions of individual countries (and even specific individuals) which have induced an international response. As for the future, there is no doubt that the changing form of international law will increasingly become tied to the diplomatic intricacies of the geopolitics of resource availability and distribution, where new arrangements of world resources and power will meet their most important tests.

9

Can the centre hold?

"... things fall apart: the centre cannot hold;
mere anarchy is loosed upon the world,
the blood-dimmed tide is loosed, and everywhere
the ceremony of innocence is drowned;
the best lack all conviction, while the worst
are full of passionate intensity."

Yeats

The reader skimming through this book looking for clear and concise conclusions or a recipe for optimism or despair will be disappointed. The best I can offer is four observations:

1. Environmentalism challenges certain features of almost every aspect of the so-called western democratic (capitalist) culture—its motives, its aspirations, its institutions, its performance, and some of its achievements. It seeks a reformulation of national income accounts in favour of some kind of measure of economic and social well-being; it aims to substitute a love of humanity, companionship, a concern for posterity, and the joy of natural experiences for the persistent and widespread exploitation of people and the land, the desire for monetary reward, materialism, and striving for status; it hopes to alter institutional forms and procedures by replacing corporate hegemony, bureaucratic discretion, and routinisation with radical proposals for human-scale cooperative enterprise, and for consultation and participation; and it endeavours to encourage each one of us to recognise the ambiguities and inconsistencies of our beliefs and actions and to seek congruence. This reform will not come easily, for the legacy of 'nonenvironmental' institutional arrangements and psychological attitudes is long and well established.
2. Environmentalism does not offer a clear-cut alternative to our present discomforting existence; instead it points out a number of paradoxes and a struggle to find the middle way between equally tempting, but diverging, system states. The pathway out of our present predicament has never been charted and each step forward offers the choice of a number of alternative routes, all of which lead into unknown territory.
3. Environmentalism, then, is about conviction—conviction that a better mode of existence is possible, conviction that *homo sapiens* is capable of recognising his dilemmas and taking responsive action; conviction, above all, that a sense of collective happiness can infuse individual self-interest so that belief in the communal good will overcome a fear of personal sacrifice.
4. Environmentalism is a politicising and reformist movement, opening up our minds and our organisations to new ideas about fairness, sharing, permanence, and humility; encouraging us to contemplate and experiment

with new devices for evaluating and weighing the consequences of our beliefs and our actions, including new mechanisms for consultation, supervision, and arbitration; and enticing us with unprecedented possibilities in all fields of education.

Environmentalism as a vehicle for social reform is fuelled by two complementary anxieties. The first is an actual realisation that something must be done, because certain aspects of living are already intolerable. This is the realisation of scarcity—scarcity of certain wild species and landscapes, scarcity of low-cost (or at least low-environmental-cost) energy, food, and other raw materials; scarcity of public amenity and a growing scarcity of reasonably priced private amenity (up till now regarded as a way out). [See Wilson (1970) and Brubaker (1972) for useful collections of examples.] Secondly, there is a growing anxiety about the future—a pervasive uncertainty that has all but replaced the beguiling self-confidence which has characterised the ruling elite in western democracies ever since the industrial revolution. This widespread loss of faith in oneself, in others, and in the organs of government, is undoubtedly the more troublesome of the two anxieties, because without faith and a belief in the possibility of improvement for all mankind the centre cannot hold and civilisation as we know it will end. Falk (1972, pp.415-437) offers two contrasting pathways into the future to emphasise these dangers (figure 9.1): one leads to degenerative strife, the other to progressive egalitarianism and justice. He believes that the latter path will be followed—on the assumption that somehow our institutions will respond in time. Like other environmentalist philosophers he offers a simple binary choice: if man does not discover the routeway to utopia, destruction and misery must surely follow. Is this *really* the case? Can we and our collective institutions meet the challenge?

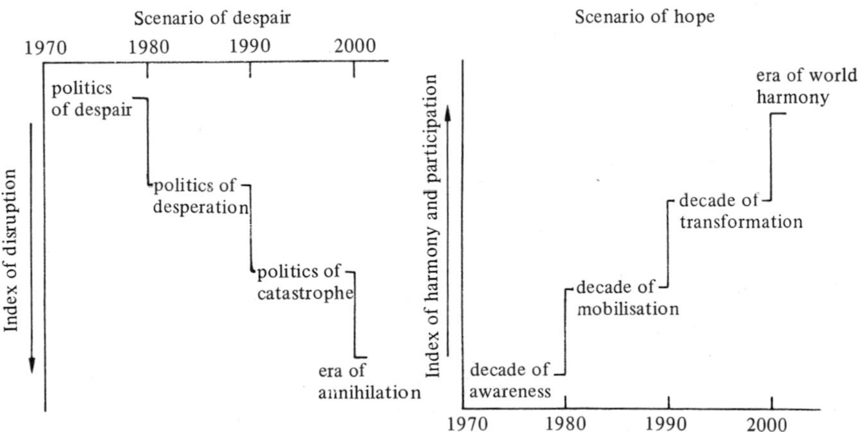

Figure 9.1. Alternative pathways to the future. (After Falk, 1971.)

9.1 Environmentalism and institutional reform

Lowi (1969) and Pirages and Ehrlich (1974, pp.128–138) sum up many of the doubts held by thoughtful people about the abilities of our present governing institutions to handle the environmental challenge. They conclude that the present system of liberal–pluralist politics cannot be sustained for the following reasons:

(i) Interest group politicking undermines principled and resolute policy-making in the interests of short-term expediency. 'Majoritarian' decisions tend to outweigh 'public interest' proposals because governments rarely lead, only follow (see Gans, 1973).

(ii) Political leaders rarely reach clear-cut decisions but prevaricate in the face of a welter of confusing and conflicting proposals. Almost inevitably a genuine calamity is required to produce strong action, though all too frequently crisis legislation is counterproductive to the resolution of the real problems at hand.

(iii) Legislative policies are constantly undermined by 'invisible' lobbying and sympathetic regulatory practices, so that the authority of the legislature is stealthily eroded.

(iv) The ruling oligarchies of government, corporations, and organised labour have no countervailing equivalents. Citizen participation will only be effective if it has resources, information, and a direct political lobby such as the courts and/or an ombudsman (Aldous, 1972, pp.264–283; Dennis, 1972, pp.220–236). The dominance of centralisation consistently weakens or kills spontaneous experimentation. For instance, present efforts in Britain to promote the small cooperative enterprise along lines advocated by Kropotkin and others are being thwarted by tax laws and other government policies that favour the large-scale (Ward, 1975).

(v) Pluralism is predicated upon compromise, but the fear of scarcity encourages confrontation and irresolution. In such circumstances only the powerful are satisfied, so the losers tend to search for undemocratic means of achieving their demands.

Pirages and Ehrlich proceed to countermand the six conventional wisdoms of democracy:

(a) The people do not rule. Government is largely controlled by centralised powerful interests whose primary concern is to guarantee the stability of their power base and to plan the conduct of human affairs to suit their terms of reference. This view is supported by most leftist writers (Bookchin, 1970; Weisberg, 1971; Hall, 1972; Tanzer, 1974) and by liberals such as Galbraith (1973), Taylor (1973), and Mumford (1974).

(b) Voters are neither concerned nor humane. They are alienated, frustrated, and confused, and are often forced to elect politicians from a group of candidates not of their choosing. Urbanisation, bureaucratic centralisation, mobility, and the dominance of technology, combined with the monotony and impersonalisation of most occupations, breed a

collective disinterest in the affairs of others, an almost inhuman lack of compassion for the weaker in distress.
(c) Political leaders do not serve the public, nor are they necessarily wise, nor do they really have command of the policy options with which they are confronted. Rarely do they consider that mankind might be *limiting* its options for the future, for few acknowledge any limits to their governing abilities or to their technological ingenuity (Ophuls, 1975). At least, this is the impression they seem to want to give.

Though Pirages and Ehrlich's conclusions suffer from exaggeration and partial truth, because they accord with many of our intuitive observations they serve to inflame our anxieties. We should take heed of Platt's (1969) and Toffler's (1975) advice, and turn more of our intellectual attention forward to investigating institutional performance and providing appropriate scientific information to cope with coalescing crises. But even if it is found that our institutions are failing, environmentalists are not united in their prescription for renaissance. Broadly speaking, there are four ideologically quite different proposals for institutional reform.

9.1.1 A new global order

Writers with an interest in the third world such as Falk (1971, pp.285–352), Brown (1972, pp.301–318), and Ward and Dubos (1972, pp.286–300) believe passionately in the amalgamation of national states into a new world order. Their proposals range from an extended version of the United Nations (Ward and Dubos), through some sort of global policy coordinating body (Brown), to world government (Falk). They all believe that global unity is the inevitable end state of human progress. "A unified global society must now be regarded not as a fiction or an ideal", writes Brown (1972, p.352), "but as the inevitable reality toward which we must move ... . Man has simply brought himself to the final step in the long progression extending throughout his existence as a species".

These writers all appear to believe that global order can be achieved by transferring the funds currently deployed as military expenditures to the institutions of peace and goodwill, through the recognition of mutual dependence between rich and poor nations, and the wise realisation that life-support systems can only be protected through a coercive common government. They point to the history of cooperative organisation that has characterised man's social evolution, and to the success of certain international agencies in promoting compassion and global awareness of man's predicament. But the tough issues of sovereignty and national self-determination remain unresolved. "[There] is [no] formal departure from sovereignty", admit Ward and Dubos (1972, p.293). "So locked are we within our tribal units, so possessive over national rights, so suspicious of any extension of international authority, that we may fail to sense the need for dedicated and committed action over the whole field of planetary necessities." All they can offer in the way of hope is the possibility that "a strict, literal definition of sovereignty gets blurred in practice, and the existence of continuous forums for debate and bargaining helps to instill the habit of cooperation into the affairs of reluctant governments".

These authors broadly share the views of Mesarovic and Pestel (1975, p.145) that global policymaking institutions must have the authority to execute carefully-considered long-term strategies (transcending national and short-term interests) by means of consultation and cooperation. And while they realise that all this may not be possible in view of the pessimistic findings of Pirages and Ehrlich (1974), in company with Dumont (1974) and Heilbroner (1974a), they assume that the imminence of a world ecological and economic crisis and the threat of social disorder will compel nationalist governments into a new world consciousness, a new ethic of resource conservation, a new morality of sharing, and a new concern for posterity. Had they been writing in 1975, I am sure they would point to the 'success' of the International Monetary Fund in 'recycling' (a gross misnomer) petrodollars throughout the industrialised world as a fine example of intergovernmental innovation during a period of crisis. But 'recycling' only delays the disaster and lengthens the fools' paradise, and in any case it has not noticeably helped the world's weaker nations (Cairncross and McRae, 1975). Even if the achievements of the IMF are acknowledged, will international monetary reform continue to progress in the absence of worldwide recession? And will the threat of long run economic slowdown spur other equally necessary international collaborative initiatives? With characteristic rhetorical flourish, Toffler (1975, p.3) states:

> "What we are seeing is the general crisis of industrialism ... a crisis that is simultaneously tearing up our energy base, our value systems, our communicative modes, our sense of space and time, our epistemology as well as our economy. What is happening ... is the breakdown of industrial civilization on the planet and the first fragmentary appearance of a wholly new and dramatically different social order. A superindustrial civilization that will be technological, but no longer industrial".

These gloomy predictions still assume that, when actually faced with calamity, mankind will respond forcefully and positively to safeguard civilisation. This may be the case when man is confronted with the very real possibility of annihilation from a clearly defined enemy who threatens everyone equally; then truly heroic efforts are made to protect existing liberties, as witnessed in the Second World War. But when the 'enemy' is at once ephemeral and all embracing (in the form of capitalism?), when the threat falls more heavily on the weak than on the strong, when even the strong begin to feel threatened, the response is far more difficult to forecast. Heilbroner (1974a) believes that the poorer nations will become so desperate for food and for the basic ingredients of economic development (especially as they realise how the rich nations can 'export' famine and resource scarcity by bidding higher prices during periods of shortage), that they will embark on 'wars of retribution'. He points to the recent explosion by India of a nuclear device, in clear contravention of the nuclear nonproliferation treaty, as a grim omen (see Wade, 1974).

Yet it is often dangerous and misleading to jump to pessimistic conclusions from a short-term view of selected events. When Italy was faced with its worst-ever economic crisis in late 1974, its politicians failed to achieve sufficient political unity to form a coalition government, and many citizens embarked upon a deliberate and systematic programme of civil disobedience that included a refusal to pay income tax, property taxes, and transit fares, and 'squatting' in government-subsidised housing. Here was the recipe for social disarray if ever there was one. Yet six months later, helped by foreign loans and worldwide slump in raw material prices, the Italians are no worse off than they were a year ago and have regained some of their political and economic stability. Perhaps this example is coloured by the special characteristics of the Italian political and social temperament, but it serves to show how a nation can fall very rapidly into a dangerous spiral of social degeneration when faith in its own government institutions collapses, yet how quickly this fall can be stopped by effective aid (assuming, of course, that 'effective aid' is always forthcoming). Since Italy, like Britain, still lives well beyond its real ability to pay, in the absence of some political willingness to reduce national wealth and share it more equitably, it is difficult to see how either nation can avoid a similar 'crisis of authority' in the near future.

9.1.2 Centralised authoritarianism

The possibility of widespread social disruption and civil disobedience in the event of an ecological–economic catastrophe has caused writers such as Toffler (1975) and Ophuls (1973, 1976) to consider new forms of centralised authoritarian control. Ophuls (1973, p.217) draws upon the political philosophy of Hobbes, who saw in man's struggle over the allocation of increasingly scarce resources a constant desire for power, and thus a perpetual state of war in which there "is no society, and, which is worst of all, a continual fear and danger of violent death; and the life of man solitary, poor, nasty, brutish and short". Ophuls (1973, p.225) agrees with Hobbes (and Hardin, 1974) that the only solution is some sort of centralised coercive state:

> "Individual conscience and the right kind of cultural attitudes are not by themselves sufficient to overcome the short-term calculations of utility that lead men to cause environmental degradation. Real altruism and genuine concern for posterity may not be entirely absent, but they are not present in sufficient quantities to avoid tragedy. Only a Hobbesian sovereign can deal with this situation effectively, and we are left then with the problem of determining the concrete shape of Leviathan".

Ophuls himself does not like this idea but regards it as a "tragic necessity" because the alternative is oblivion. His reasoning is similar to Hardin's 'lifeboat' theme, being based on a pessimistic view of man quite unable to manage the global commons through democratic means. So he advocates a Huxleyan *Brave New World* of mindless robots submitting to benign absolutism, whose behaviour is determined by status and setting. However, the crucial difference between the Ophulian 'New World' and the Huxleyan original is that in the former the creative essence of 'humanness' is obliterated, whereas Huxley's theme was the struggle to protect the precious independence and freedom of inquiry of man's spirit and draw attention to the dangers if these human commodities were to be lost.

The authoritarian scenario is appealing because it can relate both to right- and left-wing political systems, and there is some historical evidence to show that fascist and communistic dictatorships have been successful during times of widespread social change. Nevertheless it is repugnant to the basic ideologies of the principal western democracies, and assumes a submissiveness in the citizenry that is not revealed in thoughtful political inquiry (see Almond and Verba, 1963). Indeed the menace of such a possibility encourages the opposite response—a vigorous attention to new educational methods to train 'environmental citizens' (see below).

9.1.3 The authoritarian commune

Midway between the centralised authoritarian suggestions and the anarchic ecocentric proposals lies the notion of the authoritarian commune first advanced by Heilbroner (1974a). Again he is reluctant, indeed quite ambivalent, in advancing his recipe (1974b, p.12):

> "... my analysis leads me to place my hopes for the long term survival of man on his susceptibility to appeals to national identity and his willingness to accept authority. But my own beliefs incline me strongly in the opposite direction, detesting the claims of patriotism and mystical national unity, averse to hierarchies of sub- and super-ordination".

He advances the prospect of a blend of 'religious' orientation and 'military style discipline' such as might be found in a monastery and is probably best observed in modern China. The Chinese play down (but do not eliminate) the tendencies towards individualism and materialism by guaranteeing every citizen the basic minima of life—food, shelter, clothing, education, medical attention, and a job. The communal social system ensures that everyone is cared for either by an extended family or at least by friends. Economic organisation is built around collective labour and, wherever possible, regional self-sufficiency. The sharing and interchange of labour is an essential ingredient, as is collective and individual self-criticism. The 'cost' of all this is a certain denial of individual liberties and a prospect of personal economic improvement that is the same for everyone. As Robinson (1975, p.14) observes:

"The success of the Chinese economy in reducing the appeal of the money motive is connected with its success in economic development. When everyone has enough to eat today and hope of improvement tomorrow, when there is complete social security at the prevailing level of the standard of life and employment for all, then it is possible to appeal to the people to combat egoism and eschew privilege".

Many western observers look wistfully towards China as providing a workable model of the authoritarian commune, and, while the Chinese experience must be unique to the Chinese culture and temperament, doubtless much can be learned from this example that is pertinent to a world threatened by the double ogre of scarcity and injustice.

9.1.4 The anarchist solution

The classic ecocentric proposal is the self-reliant community modelled on anarchist lines (see chapter 1, pp.7–11). The idea of postindustrial tribalism is very appealing to liberal reformers who have a deep-seated faith in man's communal spirit and the dealienating advantages of the decentralised, self-governing community. Some, like Bookchin (1970), Weisberg (1971), Roszak (1973), and Taylor (1973) believe that man is capable of devising infinitely diverse cooperative forms, any one of which can lead to an exhilarating self-actualisation of the human spirit. Others like Theobald (1970, 1972), Edel (1973, pp.144–152), Roszak (1973), W. I. Thompson (1973), Illich (1974a, 1974b), and Pirages and Ehrlich (1974, pp.279–282) visualise some kind of nonhierarchical society that evolves out of sheer discontent with the present mess, first by 'opting out', then by conscious experimentation, and finally by formal government sanction. For Taylor (1973, p.51) the nonhierarchical commune is the only solution by which man can peacefully experience the necessary psyhological changes to face the future. These alterations include a shift from our predominantly 'patrist' mode (restrictive, authoritarian, conservative, backward-looking, unimaginative) to a more 'matrist' mode (permissive, egalitarian, democratic, optimistic, future-orientated, spontaneous) which will, in turn, promote the formation of the 'soft' ego of group consciousness and altruism (figure 9.2).

Value orientation	Range of relationships		
man → man	individualistic	*cooperative*	hierarchical
man → nature	dominant	*harmonious*	subservient
man → self	good	*redeeming*	evil
man → time	past orientation	*present orientation*	future orientation
man → purpose	doing	*becoming*	being
		Environmental mode	

Figure 9.2. Environmental value orientations.

9.2 Environmentalism and capitalism

It is quite impossible to predict in these uncertain times which one or combination of these prospects is in store for us. It seems to me that the central issue that has yet to be confronted is whether the capitalist mode of production and exploitation can be sustained in a world conscious of scarcity and the growing disparity of what might be called 'environmental privilege'. Currently we are witnessing an interesting shift in the pattern of power which would have fascinated Marx but might not entirely have pleased him. As I noted in earlier sections of this book, economic growth of the kind witnessed by the present generation has been made possible largely by the exploitation of underpriced resources, including much of the labour that was needed to convert these resources into highly priced goods. Within the last ten years or so both the owners of these resources and the mass of this labour have woken up to the fact that precisely because of their long exploitation and because there are no immediately available substitutes for the essential services that they provide they now have considerable power. Consequently both groups are now demanding what they regard as a fair price for their economic value. The trouble is that those who have long benefitted from the old economic order are unwilling to sacrifice either power or monetary wealth to this new elite. The short-run consequence of course is unilateral expropriation of resource wealth (e.g. OPEC of oil, Iceland of cod, and the budding commodity cartels of various raw materials), and the growing success of union militancy to achieve 'acceptable' working conditions and 'suitable' wages.

In a finite world this situation cannot be sustained. There simply is not the wealth in the existing economic system to allow for such a transfer of power and income without something or someone giving way. So what will happen? Here the great difficulties of prediction frustrate me. I can answer only by speculating on three possible consequences:

(i) If we are to continue with some variation of the labour theory of value, then it is possible that there will be a shift in the traditional pattern of exploitation away from the manipulation of the toiling masses toward the middle classes and the owners of production. In Britain for example it is no longer fashionable, nor indeed lucrative, to be the owner of a private industrial corporation (especially not a large one) whether as an individual or a shareholder, while in recent years the real income of the middle classes has fallen relative to that of skilled and militant labour. This pattern of power reversal is less evident (but still noticeable) in other industrialised countries (with the exception perhaps of Italy), where an enlargement of the middle class is taking place, with a concomitant shift in public values toward education, housing, and the environment.

But there is still a trend toward relieving the middle and upper income groups of some of their wealth and power. How far this will go depends upon the relative strengths of organised labour and the middle class, the willingness of the latter to adopt militant tactics, and the nature of political response. Already there are signs that an affluent but frightened meritocracy are electing rightist governments to protect their interests, but it is still not clear whether such governments will be able to pursue their electoral mandates. Given this general proposition of steady power reversal, the outcome can only be further interclass conflict and continued governmental intervention while many of the central objections of socialism fail to be achieved. Heilbroner (1976) tends to portray this general outcome in his description of the postindustrialised state where a curious amalgam of 'government owned' capitalism will force upon an unwilling public a degree of economic egalitarianism and environmental protection, though he remains uncertain of what all this will do to the individual spirit.

(ii) If, however, we are to replace the 'labour theory of value' with an 'environmental theory of value', then a different scenario emerges. This might be more appropriate for the resource rich, affluent industrialised countries such as those of North America and central and northern Europe. If all groups of labour are to continue to improve their financial well-being (and all current social surveys indicate that they wish to do this above all else), then the only 'exploitable' resources that can continue to suffer without fear of political backlash are the natural environment and the amenities of our social existence. Faced with the choice between a definite curtailment in real income and increased environmental stress, which will be the less unacceptable? In the absence of major institutional and political reform, the majority will opt for the latter course without any calculation of the likely consequences of such a decision. For instance the affluent middle income groups of North America and Europe are currently providing a spirited and remarkably successful opposition to the furtherance of nuclear power. Will their efforts be so widely supported when these people are confronted with an actual shortage of electric power? Or will they be prepared to make sacrifices in their accustomed ways of living to ensure that their neighbours are not unduly and unfairly affected? Assuming that there will be neither civil strife nor a rather unlikely revolution in consumption and pricing patterns, I can only visualise a period of continued environmental disruption (with associated economic and social consequences) at the expense of the aesthetic preferences of the sensitive minority. This is the 'business as usual' option which would entail an enormous commitment of resources, effort, and enterprise that would all but preclude the possibility of attending to quite radical alterations in technology and economic activity which might well be our only salvation. In both this and the previous scenario, the economically and politically deprived—the aged, the young, members of minority groups, and most of the developing world—will doubtless continue to suffer, and by their suffering subsidise the antics and the aspirations of the rest.

This scenario is what Du Boff (1974, pp.214–215) had in mind when he stated that economic growth (and environmental exploitation) appear to strengthen the very institutions and values that appear to be the cause of the present global dilemma:

> "Such growth, and its capital accumulation exigencies, create power positions that henceforth direct and guide the income generation process *and* the economic surplus that grows from it. Ruling classes and political elites, who possess action initiating power in the spheres of investment, pricing, technological innovation and the division of labour used in the production process and in private and public bureaucracies, cannot be expected at some later stage to relinquish control over the resulting 'growth dividend' ... . If these goals and privileges *are* the main causes of our social ills (including environmental decay), and if economic growth does fortify them then it is obvious that more growth is not the way to the better society."

(iii) If we are to abandon the two Marxist theories of value, there is a third, more hopeful, possibility and one which is essentially the message of this book, namely that we must individually and collectively seize the opportunities of the present situation to end the era of exploitation and enter a new age of humanitarian concern and cooperative endeavour with a driving desire to reestablish the old values of comfortable frugality and cheerful sharing. Certainly these are not the values of capitalism (nor, for that matter, of much of modern communism), nor will they appear if we continue to enlarge the organisation of government and the units of economic activity and fail to reform our present woefully inadequate educational preparation for such a new age. We undoubtedly have the knowledge and the ability to meet this challenge and to forge a new political order. Preferably this new order should be based upon some kind of amalgam of regional or 'community of interest' supranationalism with some elements of unified global policy in particular areas (food and population), together with increasingly determined attempts at local self-determination in the form of urban neighbourhood councils, village and parish communities, and various kinds of worker cooperatives. This apparently paradoxical mixture of organisational forms seems to me the only arrangement whereby man can manage the commons while also maintaining the individualism and diversity of ways of life that are essential to his 'becoming'. If this is to be successful, it must include guarantees for *everyone* of basic minima of existence (food, shelter, education, and medical attention), and the possibility of employment that is socially productive, personally rewarding, and carried on in pleasant surroundings. We already have the wealth and the technology to achieve all of this; we still lack the critical will of purpose to bring it about.

But whatever the form of our future governmental organisation, it will only be attained through struggle, hardship, and much misgiving.

Heilbroner (1974b, p.12) expresses it well:

> "There are periods in history in which it is not possible to reconcile the hopes of the moment and the needs of the future, when the luxury of a congruence between one's personal life and the collective direction of mankind cannot be established without doing violence to one's existence or to one's understanding. I believe that ours is such a time and that we must learn to live with its irreconcilable conflicts and contradictions."

9.3 Environmental education

If widespread calamity or social distress does not bring us to our senses first, imaginative forms of education may do so more pleasantly. Most of modern education is still tied to the classroom or laboratory, where the teachers dispense information and the pupils endeavour to assimilate it, despite research findings which show the inadequacies of this format. The hierarchical superiority of the quasi-omniscient lector is difficult to counter; when adventurous pupils rebel, all too often they are quickly repressed. The questioning, analytical mind, ever ready to develop new perspectives, seems more to be the product of happenstance in most of our educational establishments than the result of careful and well-planned training. How many educators consciously aim to open up an incipiently enquiring mind to the wide panorama of ideological alternatives? How many encourage their students to review major pieces of national, regional or local legislation and policymaking to the point where they can carry on an informed discussion with the responsible individuals concerned? How many genuinely try to raise the moral and ethical issues that underlie many of our present world problems? The answer is: "probably only a few, but certainly many more than five years ago; but give us better teaching conditions and more manageable class sizes and we could do a lot better". Education is at last waking up to the environmental challenge.

9.3.1 Universities and colleges

Looking at the higher education sector first, a number of colleges and universities have begun to develop curricula which break down traditional disciplinary barriers (see Steinhart and Chernack, 1969; Jones, 1971; Schoenfeld, 1971; Stapp, 1971; Swan, 1971b; Aldrich and Kormondy, 1972; OECD Centre for Educational Research and Innovation, 1973). Generally speaking, this has been most successful in new institutions where there is no legacy of separate academic departments or faculties which are responsible for determining research, tenure, and teaching requirements. The most promising curricula try to merge the sciences (earth sciences, life sciences, social sciences) with the moral and ethical questions raised by the humanities (especially philosophy, history, religion, and the philosophy of science). Ideally the students should gain an insight into the dominant social paradigms that shape our intellectual thought and influence the form and functioning of our institutions. For, without a fundamental grasp of the merits and failings of our own ideologies, it is difficult to build the launching pad from which to explore new intellectual territories.

What should the aims of new curricula be? Opinions differ, but there is broad agreement that the student should be trained to have:
(i) a comprehensive understanding of the interdependence of biophysical and social systems (the biosphere and the technosphere);
(ii) an ability to obtain factual information to help cement this understanding (the contextual component);
(iii) an ability to organise and analyse varied information to develop a higher awareness of system linkages (the methodological component);
(iv) a concern for the broader sociopolitical issues that impinge upon environmentalism;
(v) an ability to inform and consult with citizens and policymakers on the ramifications of certain courses of action (including doing nothing), and on how these people can play a more effective role in shaping the destiny of their own communities.

A suggested curriculum is sketched out in figure 9.3. It is often wise to avoid presenting much rigorous theory at too early a stage, since the incoming student may find the unadorned constructs rather indigestible. Inquiry comes from an interest that can be raised by first reviewing major resource/environmental issues on various scales, ranging from population and food to some local problem that has aroused the community interest. A multidisciplinary view of these problems can be gained by group teaching according to a carefully orchestrated plan. This not only alerts the students to the facts, but also encourages them to see the breadth of expertise required to comprehend and analyse environmental problems at any level. With the interest aroused, methodological

	Year of course			
	Year 1	Year 2	Year 3	Year 4
Feeder courses	Integrating themes	Methodology	Detailed assessments	Community case studies
biology	- ecosystem	data acquisition data analysis	detailed assessments of the relationship between population, resources and environment of quality for the nation, the region and the locality (including attempts at energy auditing and carrying capacity analysis)	identification of problems and policy issues
physics	- energy and entropy	integrated case studies, global, national, regional		
anthropology	- man and nature			consultation with relevant interests
sociology geography				analysis
politics economics	- governing institutions			assessment

Figure 9.3. A possible curriculum for environmental education.

techniques seen as applied to real life problems become much more palatable.

Students should then be prepared to tackle real world issues in multidisciplinary teams of, say, four to eight. Each team should have a mixed representation of disciplinary competence but would work as a group in identifying problems, choosing and analysing alternative courses of action, and suggesting the possible consequences of various options. Given cooperation from the local community, the group could report to local officials and members of the public as they proceed. Here is a chance for the university within a community to utilise its considerable talents in the public service. Some universities and colleges provide their students with an 'internship' experience in the local community, working part-time or even full-time in the civil service, private industry, or consulting firms. This has the advantages of combining a community service with real world experience, and of opening up avenues for future employment. Pirages and Ehrlich (1974, pp.195–200) suggest the idea of complementary sabbaticals whereby policymakers and advisers teach and learn within the university for periods of up to a year. Again this is a mutually satisfactory arrangement, for the visiting student has the opportunity to refresh his outlook and to lead seminars on the subjects of his particular expertise.

All these suggestions open up possibilities for forging new links between the university and the community—a currently deteriorating liaison that requires much attention. In addition, these proposals provide students with 'relevant' programmes of study combining self- and group-education with disciplinary rigour. But to be successful they require a large commitment of time and intellectual energy on the part of teachers and students alike, a sizeable financial investment (some of it could come from benefitting sectors in the community), and a shift from single-minded research to innovative participatory forms of education. As long as academic merit is judged on the basis of research first and teaching second (as is still the case in Britain, though less so in North America), only the more dedicated faculty may be tempted to experiment with new techniques.

Similar curricula could be developed for adult environmental education, though the time commitment necessary for case-study work may prove a bit of a problem. Some method of combining the advantages of the proposals outlined above within the time constraints imposed on extramural students is a desirable objective, for instilling a wider awareness amongst the general public is certainly to be encouraged. Well integrated 'crash courses' during vacations or periods of sabbatical leave, combined with multidisciplinary workshops devoted to discussion and analysis of ongoing case studies, could provide the bulk of the training.

9.3.2 Schools

The possibilities for expanding environmental education in the schools are enormous. The most pressing need is to promote an awareness of individual creative and intellectual potential, together with the experience of sharing and shouldering responsibility and understanding the values and aspirations of others. Pirages and Ehrlich (1974, pp.191–192) show how it is possible to educate children to cooperate rather than compete, to take an interest in the welfare of others, and to learn about the mutual obligation of caring for the global commons. Again the aim is to combine individual talent with a spirit of collective purpose. Schools could fulfil part of the data-gathering function for environmental-assessment reviews, collecting both biophysical information and socio-economic evidence. In some cases children may have access to the views of their parents where professional interviewers may not. This kind of effort could be directed both at 'base-line' data surveys and 'problem orientated' data analysis. The advantage of the latter approach is that pupils can become involved in the broader economic and politial aspects of real world problems, and in so doing become aware of their own political role, a learning process that, indisputably, should be part of modern education.

In view of the findings of psychologists (e.g. Schroder, 1971) that value systems and the ability to comprehend complex information are formed when the child is young, it would be rewarding to see environmental education incorporated right from the beginning of the school syllabus. An imaginative programme of study would range from exploring the child's 'inner space' to alerting his attention to global political questions. It would be preferable if part of the child's personal exploration took place in wild countryside, or at least in a nonurban setting, so that he could grow to understand the mightiness and grandeur of nature in the raw. For the wilderness is not merely an escape from today's problems; it provides an essential element of perspective, a time for the contemplation and self-analysis that precedes the discovery of what Schumacher (1973, pp.87–91) calls 'the centre'. There are literally millions of children today who have to date been deprived of the opportunity of ever attaining this 'point Omega', yet we have seen throughout this book that some deep sense of humility, moderation, and sharing is vital for the makeup of tomorrow's citizens.

In fact, environmental education is no more and no less than 'citizenship education', the development of personal commitment and social responsibility combined with a systems-centred holistic view of man in relation to nature (Ferkiss, 1974, describes ecological humanism in similar terms), tied to a fundamental faith in the institutions of man and his abilities. Citizenship also means political obligation: a readiness to participate in the shaping of the community (recognising that utopian blueprints must grow from what currently exists); an ability to assess, assimilate, and where necessary challenge public policy; and a willingness to serve in the interests of others. Citizenship is a vital moral, social, and political attribute that will be desperately needed and severely tested in the troublesome decades to come.

9.4 To environmental citizens

I cannot close without adding one more element to the citizenship theme. The story of environmentalism is the story of people, not of nature. Throughout the course of history, dedicated evangelistic individuals have sacrificed parts of their private lives to fight for causes that consumed their energies. Some of these people are household names now, but most are unsung heroes and heroines, teachers or housewives, local politicians or union members, wildlife enthusiasts or students. Collectively, this tiny minority have done more to change the face of environmentalism by their examples, exhortation, and persuasion than much of the writing in the bibliography that follows. Time and time again in my own experience of analysing environmental policymaking I have been impressed by the unexpected and immeasurable element of dedication shown by key individuals who clothe the skeletal decision flow diagrams with the attributes of humanity. They are people who 'stand apart' from their personal lives, their family commitments, their occupational requirements, and their immediate social obligations to demonstrate by their example what needs to be done and at what cost. It is to this anonymous brigade that I dedicate this book.

Abelson, P. H., 1971, "Changing attitudes towards environmental problems", *Science,* **172**, 517.

Abelson, P. H., 1974a, "No easy way out of the energy crisis", *Science,* **183**, 475.

Abelson, P. H., 1974b, "The deteriorating energy position", *Science,* **185**, 309.

Aberbach, J. D., Walker, J. L., 1972, "Citizen desires, policy outcomes and community control", *Urban Affairs Quarterly,* **8**, 55-76.

Adams, J. G. U., 1970, "Westminster: the fourth London airport?", *Area,* **2**, 1-9.

Adams, J. G. U., 1974a, "Obsolete economics", *Ecologist,* **4**, 280-289.

Adams, J. G. U., 1974b, "... and how much for your grandmother?", *Environment and Planning,* **6**, 619-626.

Adams, J. S., 1972, "The geography of riots and civil disorders in the 1960s", *Economic Geography,* **48**, 24-42.

Adams, J. S., Brauer, M., 1974, "Useful goal achievement measures: Zelder's suggestion indices", *Journal of the American Institute of Planners,* **40**, 430-438.

Adelman, M. A., 1974, "Politics, economics and world oil", *American Economic Review,* **64**, 58-67.

Adirondack Park Agency, 1973, *Adirondack Park Land Use and Development Plan* (Ray Brook, New York), two volumes.

Adler, C. A., 1975, *Ecological Fantasies: Death from Falling Watermelons* (Green Eagle Press, New York), 350 pp.

Adler, V. A., 1972, "The viability of class actions in environmental litigation", *Ecology Law Quarterly,* **2**, 533-570.

Adler-Karlsson, G., 1970, *Reclaiming the Canadian Economy* (Anansi, Toronto).

Agelasto, M. A., 1973, "Non growth and the poor; equity considerations in controlled growth policies", *Planning Comment,* **9**, 2-11.

Aldous, T., 1972, *Battle for the Environment* (Fontana Books, London), 283 pp.

Aldrich, J. L., Kormondy, E. J., 1972, *Environmental Education: Academia's Response* (Conservation Foundation, Washington, DC), 75 pp.

Allaby, M., 1971, *The Eco-Activists: Youth Fights for a Human Environment* (Charles Knight, London), 221 pp.

Allaby, M., Allen, F., 1974, *Robots Behind the Plow* (Rodale Press, Emmaus, Pa.), 175 pp.

Allaby, M., Blythe, C., Hines, C., Wardle, C., 1975, *Losing Ground* (Friends of the Earth, London) (2nd edition); *Ecologist,* **5**, 84-93.

Allison, L., 1975, *Environmental Planning: A Political and Philosophical Analysis* (Allen and Unwin, London), 130 pp.

Allsop, B., 1972, *Ecological Morality* (Muller, London).

Almond, G. M., Verba, S., 1963, *The Civic Culture* (Little Brown, Boston), 374 pp.

Alonso, W., 1971, "The economics of urban size", *Papers of the Regional Science Association,* **26**, 67-84.

Alonso, W., 1973, "Urban zero population growth", *Daedalus,* **102**, 191-206.

Amacher, R. C., Tollison, R. D., Willett, T. D., 1972, "The economics of fatal mistakes: fiscal mechanisms for preserving endangered species", *Public Policy,* **20**, 411-442.

Anderson, D., 1971, "Government and environment: a need for public participation", *University of British Columbia Law Review,* **6**, 111-114.

Anderson, F. R., 1973, *NEPA in the Courts: A Legal Analysis of the National Environmental Policy Act* (Johns Hopkins University Press, Baltimore), 315 pp.

Anderson, P. K., 1971, *Murder of the Ecosystem and Suicide of Man* (Brown, Dubuque, Iowa).

Anderson, R. J., Crocker, T. D., 1971, "Air pollution and residential property values", *Urban Studies,* **8**, 171-180.

Anderson, R. T., 1970, "Governmental responsibility for waste management in urban regions", *Natural Resources Journal,* **10**, 661-686.

Anderson, S. (Ed.), 1968, *Planning for Diversity and Choice* (MIT Press, Cambridge, Mass.), 340 pp.

Anderson, W. (Ed.), 1970, *Politics and Environment: A Reader in Ecological Crisis* (Goodyear, Pacific Palisades, Calif.), 362 pp.

Angeletti, E. M., 1973, "Transmorgrification: state and federal regulation of automotive air pollution", *Natural Resources Journal,* **13**, 448-479.

Angelopoulos, A., 1972, *The Third World and the Rich Countries: Prospects for the Year 2000* (Praeger, New York).

'Arrow' Royal Commission, 1971, Report of the Royal Commission on the Pollution of Canadian Waters by Oil, and Formal Investigation into the Grounding of the Steam Tanker 'Arrow' (Information Canada, Ottawa), 129 pp.

Artin, T., 1973, *Earth Talk: Independent Voices on the Environment* (Grossman, New York), 174 pp.

Ashby, E. (Chairman), 1972a, *Pollution: Nuisance or Nemesis?* (HMSO, London), 87 pp.

Ashby, E. (Chairman), 1972b, *Pollution in Some British Estuaries and Coastal Waters*, Third Report of The Royal Commission on Environmental Pollution (HMSO, London), 90 pp.

Askew, M. W., 1975, "Money down the drain?", *Environmental Pollution Management,* **5**, 7-9.

Association of Bay Area Governments, 1973, *Zoning and Growth* (Association of Bay Area Governments, San Francisco), 12 pp.

Attah, E. B., 1973, "Racial aspects of zero population growth", *Science,* **180**, 1143-1151.

Auerbach, C. A., 1972, "Pluralism and the administrative process", *Annals of the American Academy of Political and Social Science,* **400**, 1-14.

Auld, T. A. D., 1972, *Economic Thinking About Pollution Problems* (University of Toronto Press, Toronto), 184 pp.

Auliciems, A., Burton, I., Hewings, J., Schiff, M., Taylor, C., 1972, "The public use of scientific information on the quality of the environment: the case of Ontario's air pollution index" (Department of Geography, University of Toronto), 25 pp.

Ayres, R. E., 1975, "Enforcement of air pollution controls on stationary sources under the Clean Air Amendments of 1970", *Ecology Law Quarterly,* **4**, 441-478.

Ayres, R. U., Kneese, A. V., 1971, "Economic and ecological effects of a stationary economy", Reprint No. 99 (Resources of the Future, Washington), 12 pp.

Ayres, R. U., McKenna, R. V., 1972, *Alternatives to the Internal Combustion Engine* (Johns Hopkins University Press, Baltimore), 340 pp.

Babcock, R. F., 1969, *The Zoning Game: Municipal Practices and Policies* (University of Wisconsin Press, Madison), 202 pp.

Babcock, R. F., Bosselman, F. P., 1972, *Exclusionary Zoning: Land Use Regulation and Housing in the 1970s* (American Law Institute, Washington).

Bachmura, F. T., 1971, "The economics of vanishing species", *Natural Resources Journal,* **11**, 674-692.

Bachrach, P., 1973, *Power and Choice: Formulation of American Population Policy* (D. C. Heath, Lexington, Mass.), 150 pp.

Bachrach, P., Baratz, M. S., 1962, "Two faces of power", *American Political Science Review,* **56**, 947-952.

Bahr, H. M., Chadwick, B. A., Thomas, D. C., 1972, *Population, Resources and the Future* (Brigham Young University Press, Ogden, Utah).

Baldwin, M., 1973, "A review of Corps of Engineers practices under section 102 (2) (C) of the National Environmental Policy Act" (Conservation Foundation, Washington, DC).

Baldwin, M., Page, J. K. (Eds.), 1970, *Law and Environment* (Walker, New York), 570 pp.

Bangs, H. P., Jr., Mahler, S., 1970, "Users of local parks", *Journal of the American Institute of Planners,* **34**, 330-335.

Baran, P. A., Sweezy, P. M., 1968, *Monopoly Capital: An Essay on American Economic and Social Order* (Penguin Books, Harmondsworth), 377 pp.

Barber, W. J., 1967, *A History of Economic Thought* (Penguin Books, Harmondsworth), 259 pp.

Barbour, I. G. (Ed.), 1972, *Earth Might Be Fair: Reflections on Ethics, Religion and Ecology* (Prentice-Hall, Englewood Cliffs, NJ).

Barbour, I. G. (Ed.), 1973, *Western Man and Environmental Ethics* (Addison-Wesley, Reading, Mass.), 275 pp.

Barker, M. L., 1972, *The Structure and Content of Environmental Cognitions*, unpublished Doctoral Dissertation, Department of Geography, University of Toronto.

Barkley, P. W., Seckler, D. W., 1972, *Economic Growth and Environmental Decay: The Solution Becomes the Problem* (Harcourt, Brace and Jovanovich, New York), 192 pp.

Barnes, P., 1973, "The sharing of land and resources in America" (*The New Republic,* Washington), 60 pp.

Barnet, R. J., Müller, R., 1974, *The Earth Managers: The New World and the Global Corporations* (Simon and Schuster, New York).

Barnett, H. J., Morse, C., 1963, *Scarcity and Growth: The Economics of Natural Resource Availability* (Johns Hopkins University Press, Baltimore), 288 pp.

Barnett, L. D., 1971, "Education and religion as factors influencing attitudes towards population growth in the United States", *Social Biology,* **17**, 26-36.

Barney, D. R., 1972, *The Last Stand* (Centre for the Study of Responsive Law, Washington), 413 pp.

Bartell, T., St. George, A., 1974, "A trend analysis of environmentalists' organizational commitment, tactic advocacy and perceptions of government", *Journal of Voluntary Action Research,* **3**, 41-47.

Barton-Aschman Associates, 1970, *The Barrington, Illinois Area: A Cost Revenue Analysis of Land Use Alternatives* (Barrington Area Development Council, Barrington, Ill.).

Bates, D., 1972, *A Citizen's Guide to Air Pollution* (Queens University Press, Montreal), 136 pp.

Baughman, M., Joskow, P., 1975, "The effects of fuel prices on residential appliance choice in the U.S.", *Land Economics,* **51**, 41-49.

Baumol, W. J., 1972a, "On taxation and the control of externalities", *American Economic Review,* **52**, 307-322.

Baumol, W. J., 1972b, "Environmental protection and the distribution of incomes", in *Problems of Environmental Economics* (OECD, Paris), pp.67-76.

Baumol, W. J., Oates, W. E., 1971, "The use of standards and pricing for protection of the environment", *Swedish Journal of Economics,* **73**, 42-54.

Baumol, W. J., Oates, W. E., 1975, *The Theory of Environmental Policy: Externalities Public Outlays and the Quality of Life* (Prentice-Hall, Englewood Cliffs, NJ), 268 pp.

Beardsley, W. G., 1972, "The economic impact of recreational development: a synopsis", in *Outdoor Recreation Symposium,* Ed. W. Doolittle (Northeast Forest and Range Experimental Station, Upper Darby, Pa.), pp.28-33.

Beatty, R. G., 1973, *The DDT Myth: Triumph of the Amateurs* (John Day, New York), 188 pp.

Beazley, R. I., Holland, I. I., 1973, *Predicting the Success of Alternative Programs* (Southern Illinois University Press, Carbondale), 250 pp.

Bechtel Corporation, 1974, *Nuclear Energy Analysis* (Bechtel Corporation, New York).

Beckerman, W., 1973, "Economic growth and welfare", *Minerva,* **11**, 495-515.
Beckerman, W., 1974, *In Defence of Economic Growth* (Jonathan Cape, London), 257 pp.
Bell, D., 1973, *The Coming of the Post Industrial Society* (Basic Books, New York), 507 pp.
Bem, D., 1970, *Beliefs, Attitudes and Human Affairs* (Brooks Cole, Belmont, Calif.), 105 pp.
Benson, R. S., Wolman, H. (Eds), 1971, *Counter Budget: A Blueprint for Changing National Priorities* (Praeger, New York).
Berelson, B., 1973, *Population Policies in Developing Countries* (McGraw-Hill, Chicago).
Bergsten, C. F., 1973, "The threat from the Third World", *Foreign Policy,* **11**, 102-124.
Bergsten, C. F., 1974, "The threat is real", *Foreign Policy,* **14**, 84-90.
Berkman, R. L., Viscusi, W. K., 1973, *Damming the West: Ralph Nader's Study Group Report on the Bureau of Reclamation* (Grossman, New York), 266 pp.
Berland, T., 1970, *The Fight for Quiet* (Prentice-Hall, Englewood Cliffs, NJ), 294 pp.
Berman, M. B., Hammer, M. J., 1973, *The Impact of Electricity Price Increases on Income Groups: A Case Study of Los Angeles* (Rand Corporation, Santa Monica, Calif.), 40 pp.
Bernarde, M., 1973, *Our Precarious Habitat: An Integrated Approach Towards Understanding Man's Effect on His Environment* (Norton, New York, revised edition), 352 pp.
Berry, B. J. L., 1974, "Land use, urban form and environmental quality", Research Paper No.155, Department of Geography, University of Chicago, 440 pp.
Berry, B. J. L., Horton, F. E., 1974, *Urban Environmental Management: Planning for Pollution Control* (Prentice-Hall, Englewood Cliffs, NJ), 405 pp.
Berry, D., Staker, G., 1974, "The concept of justice in regional planning: justice as fairness", *Journal of the American Institute of Planners,* **40**, 414-421.
Bhagwati, J. N. (Ed.), 1973, *Economics and World Order* (Macmillan, New York).
Bilder, R. B., 1972, "Controlling Great Lakes pollution: a study in U.S.-Canadian environmental co-operation", *Michigan Law Review,* **70**, 469-556.
Bing, W., 1971, "The unforeseen wilderness", *Hudson Review,* **24**, 633-647.
Bird, M. J., 1972, "An analysis of federal interests affected by the proposed James Bay hydro development" (Environment Canada, Ottawa), 54 pp.
Black, J. N., 1970, *The Dominion of Man: The Search for Ecological Responsibility* (John Black, Edinburgh), 152 pp.
Blair, J. P., 1973, "A review of the filtering down theory", *Urban Affairs Quarterly,* **8**, 303-316.
Blair, R. D., 1974, "Problems of pollution standards: the Clean Air Act of 1970", *Land Economics,* **50**, 260-268.
Blake, J., 1971, "Reproductive motivation and population policy", *BioScience,* **21**, 215-224.
Blake, J., 1973, "The teenage birth control dilemma and public opinion", *Science,* **180**, 708-712.
Bleicher, S. A., 1972, "An overview of international environmental regulation", *Ecology Law Quarterly,* **2**, 1-90.
Blundy, D., Ryder, C., 1974, "Anti-pollution cash curbed: row grows over Britain's toxic dustbin", *The Sunday Times,* 1 December, p.7.
Bohi, D. R., Russell, M., 1975, *U.S. Energy Policy: Alternatives for Security* (Johns Hopkins University Press, Baltimore), 142 pp.
Bookchin, M., 1970, "Towards an ecological solution", in *Eco-Catastrophie* (Ramparts Press, Berkeley, Calif.), pp.42-53.
Bookchin, M., 1971, *Post-Scarcity Anarchism* (Ramparts Press, Berkeley, Calif.).

Boot, J. C. G., 1974, *Common Globe or Global Commons: Population Regulation and Income Distribution* (Dekker, New York), 160 pp.

Borgstrom, G., 1969, *Too Many: A Study of the Earth's Biological Limitations* (Macmillan, London), 368 pp.

Borgstrom, G., 1971, *The Hungry Planet: The Modern World at the Edge of Famine* (Collier, New York), 487 pp.

Borgstrom, G., 1973, *Focal Points: A Global Food Strategy* (Macmillan, New York).

Borsodi, R., 1933, 1972, *Flight from the City: An Experiment in Creative Living on the Land* (Harper Colophun, New York), 194 pp.

Borton, T. E., Warner, K. P., 1971, "Involving citizens in water resources planning; the communication-participation experiment in the Susquehanna River Basin", *Environment and Behavior,* **3**, 284-306.

Bosselman, F., Callies, D., 1971, *The Quiet Revolution in Land Use Control* (Government Printing Office, Washington), 327 pp.

Bosselman, F., Callies, D., Banta, J., 1973, *The Taking Issue: An Analysis of the Constitutional Limits of Land Use Control* (Government Printing Office, Washington), 329 pp.

Boulding, K. E., 1966, "The economics of the coming spaceship earth", in *Environmental Quality in a Growing Economy,* Ed. H. Jarrett (Johns Hopkins University Press, Baltimore), pp.3-14.

Boulding, K. E., 1972a, "The future of personal responsibility", *American Behavioral Scientist,* **15**, 329-359.

Boulding, K. E., 1972b, "New goals for society", in *Energy, Economic Growth and the Environment,* Ed. S. Schurr (Johns Hopkins University Press, Baltimore), pp.139-151.

Boulding, K. E., 1973, "The shadow of the stationary state", *Daedalus,* **102**, 89-102.

Boulding, K. E., 1974, "Ethics of growth", *Technology Review,* **10**, 10, 83.

Bourne, C. B., 1971, "International law and pollution of international rivers and lakes", *University of British Columbia Law Review,* **6**, 115-136.

Bower, B. T., Spofford, W. (Eds), 1970, "Symposium: Residuals and environmental quality management", *Natural Resources Journal,* **10**, 655-767.

Boyd, J., 1972, "Citizen enforcement of the Refuse Act: *Que Tam* flops; Mandamus next?", *Natural Resources Journal,* **12**, 298-305.

Boyd, R., 1973, "World dynamics: a note", *Science,* **177**, 516-519.

Boyle, R. H., Graves, J., Watkins, T. H., 1971, *The Water Hustlers* (Sierra Club Publications, San Francisco), 253 pp.

Braybrooke, D., Lindblom, C. E., 1963, *A Strategy for Decision* (Free Press, New York).

Brenner, M. J., 1974, *The Political Economy of America's Environmental Dilemma* (Saxon House, D. C. Heath, Farnborough, Hants.).

Brinkhurst, R. O., Chant, D. A., 1971, *This Good Good Earth: Our Fight for Survival* (Macmillan, Toronto), 166 pp.

Brodine, V., 1973, *Air Pollution* (Harcourt Brace Jovanovich, New York), 195 pp.

Broecker, W. S., 1969, "Man's oxygen reserves", *Science,* **168**, 1537-1539.

Brooks, D. B., 1973, "Some comments on the treatment of nonrenewable resources in *Limits to Growth*" (Department of Energy Mines and Resources, Ottawa), 13 pp.

Brooks, E., 1974, "Government decision-faking", *Transactions of the Institute of British Geographers,* **63**, 29-40.

Brooks, H., 1973a, "The technology of zero growth", *Daedalus,* **102**, 139-152.

Brooks, H. (Ed.), 1973b, "The social assessment of technology", *International Social Science Journal,* **3**, 247-387.

Brooks, P., 1971, *The Pursuit of Wilderness* (Houghton Mifflin, Boston).

Brooks, P., 1972, *The House of Life* (Houghton Mifflin, Boston), 340 pp.

Brown, H. S., 1954, *The Challenge of Man's Future* (Viking Press, New York), 290 pp.

Brown, L. R., 1972, *World Without Borders* (Random House, New York), 395 pp.
Brown, L. R., 1973, "Population and affluence: growing pressures on world food resources", *Population Bulletin,* **29**, 31 pp.
Brown, L. R., 1974a, *In the Human Interest: A Plan to Stabilize World Population* (McGraw-Hill, New York), 186 pp.
Brown, L. R., 1974b, *By Bread Alone* (Praeger, New York).
Brown, L. R., Finsterbusch, G. W., 1972, *Man and His Environment: Food* (Harper and Row, New York), 208 pp.
Brown, M. (Ed.), 1971, *The Social Responsibility of the Scientist* (Free Press, New York).
Brown, R. G. S., 1970, *The Administrative Process in Britain* (Methuen, London).
Brownlie, I., 1973, "A survey of international customary rules of environmental protection", *Natural Resources Journal,* **13**, 179-189.
Brubaker, S., 1972, *To Live on Earth: Man and His Environment in Perspective* (Mentor Books, New York), 239 pp.
Brubaker, S., 1975, *In Command of Tomorrow* (Johns Hopkins University Press, Baltimore), 178 pp.
Bruhn, J. G., 1972, "The ecological crisis and the work ethic", *International Journal of Environmental Studies,* **3**, 43-47.
Bruvold, W. H., 1972, "Consistency among attitudes, beliefs and behavior", *Journal of Social Psychology,* **86**, 127-134.
Bruvold, W. H., 1973, "Belief and behavior as determinants of environmental attitudes", *Environment and Behavior,* **5**, 202-218.
Bucaro, F., Wallechinsky, D., 1972, *Chico's Organic Gardening and Natural Living* (Lippencott Publishing Co., Philadelphia), 150 pp.
Buchanan, J. H., Tullock, G., 1975, "Polluters' profits and political response: direct controls versus taxes", *American Economic Review,* **65**, 139-147.
Bugler, J., 1972, *Polluting Britain: A Report* (Penguin Books, Harmondsworth), 176 pp.
Bunting, T., Gallant, V., 1971, "The environmental grab bag" (Department of Geography, University of Waterloo, Waterloo, Ontario), 23 pp.
Burch, W. R., Jr., 1970, "Fishes and loaves: some sociological observations on the environmental crisis", in *Man and His Environment: The Ecological Limits of Optimism,* Ed. F. Mergen (Yale University Press, New Haven), pp.30-53.
Burch, W. R., Jr., 1971, *Daydreams and Nightmares: A Sociological Essay on the American Environment* (Harper and Row, New York), 175 pp.
Burch, W. R., Jr., 1976, "Who participates—a sociological interpretation of national resource decisions", *Natural Resources Journal,* **16**, 41-54.
Burchell, R. W., Listokin, D., 1975a, *The Environmental Impact Handbook* (Center for Urban Policy Research, Rutgers University, New Brunswick, NJ), 231 pp.
Burchell, R. W., Listokin, D., 1975b, *Future Land Use: Energy, Environmental and Legal Constraints* (Center for Urban Policy Research, Rutgers University, New Brunswick, NJ), 364 pp.
Burrows, P., 1974, "Pricing versus regulation for environmental protection", in *Economic Policies and Social Goals: Aspects of Public Choice,* Ed. A. J. Culyer (Robertson, London), pp.273-283.
Burton, I., Auliciems, A., 1972, "Air pollution in Toronto", in *Perceptions and Attitudes in Resource Management,* Eds W. R. D. Sewell, I. Burton (Information Canada, Ottawa), pp.71-80.
Burton, I., Kates, R. W., Kirkby, A. V. T., 1975, "The cognitive reformation: geographical contributions to man-environment theory" (Department of Geography, Clark University, Worcester, Mass.), 26 pp.
Burton, I., White, G. F., Kates, R. W., 1976, *The Environment as Hazard* (Oxford University Press, New York).

Burton, T. L., 1972, *Natural Resource Policy in Canada: Issues and Perspectives* (McLelland and Stewart, Toronto), 168 pp.
Buttimer, A., 1974, *Values in Geography*, Resource Paper No.24 (A.A.G. Commission on College Geography, Washington), 58 pp.
Byers, W. M., 1970, *An Economic Impact Study of Olympic and Mt. Rainier National Parks, Washington* (National Park Service, Washington), 215 pp.
Cahn, R., 1973a, "Land in jeopardy" (The Christian Science Monitor, Boston), 32 pp.
Cahn, R., 1973b, "Where do we grow from here?" (The Christian Science Monitor, Boston), 31 pp.
Cairncross, F., McRae, H., 1975, *The Second Great Crash* (Methuen, London), 94 pp.
Calder, N. (Ed.), 1974, *Nature in the Round* (Viking Press, New York), 285 pp.
Caldwell, L. K., 1963, "Environment: a new focus for public policy", *Public Administration Review,* **23**, 132-139.
Caldwell, L. K., 1964, *Biopolitics: Science Ethics and Public Policy* (Yale University Press, New Haven, Conn.).
Caldwell, L. K., 1968, "Environmental policy: new directions in federal action", *Public Administration Review,* **28**, 301-348.
Caldwell, L. K., 1970a, "Authority and responsibility for environmental administration", *Annals of American Academy of Political and Social Science,* **389**, 107-115.
Caldwell, L. K., 1970b, "The ecosystem as a criterion for public land policy", *Natural Resources Journal,* **10**, 203-221.
Caldwell, L. K., 1971a, "Environmental policy in a hypertrophic society", *Natural Resources Journal,* **11**, 417-426.
Caldwell, L. K., 1971b, *Environment: A Challenge to Modern Society* (Anchor Books, New York), 294 pp.
Caldwell, L. K., 1972a, "Environmental quality as an administrative problem", *Annals of the American Academy of Political and Social Science,* **400**, 103-115.
Caldwell, L. K., 1972b, *In Defense of Earth* (Indiana University Press, Bloomington, Ind.), 292 pp.
Caldwell, L. K., 1973, "Concepts in development of international environmental policies", *Natural Resources Journal,* **13**, 190-202.
Caldwell, L. K., 1975, *Man and His Environment: Policy and Administration* (Harper and Row, New York), 164 pp.
Callahan, D., 1973, *The Tyranny of Survival* (Macmillan, New York).
Campbell, D. T., 1963, "Social attitudes and other acquired behavioral dispositions", in *Psychology: A Study of Science,* Ed. S. Koch (McGraw-Hill, New York), pp.94-172.
Campbell, R. S., Pearse, P. H., Scott, A., 1972, "Water allocation in British Columbia: economic assessment of public policy", *University of British Columbia Law Review,* **7**, 247-292.
Canada, Department of Energy, Mines and Resources, 1973, *An Energy Policy for Canada* (Information Canada, Ottawa), two volumes.
Canada-United States University Seminar, 1973, "A proposal for improving the management of the Great Lakes of the United States and Canada" (Cornell University Water Resources and Marine Sciences Center, Ithaca, New York), 76 pp.
Cantrill, A., Roll, C., 1971, *Hopes and Fears of American People* (Universe Books, New York).
Caponera, D. A., 1972, "Towards a new methodological approach in environmental law", *Natural Resources Journal,* **12**, 133-152.
Carroll, T. D., 1971, "Participatory technology", *Science,* **171**, 647-653.
Carter, L. J., 1973a, "Land use law (I): Congress on verge of modest beginning", *Science,* **182**, 691-697.

Carter, L. J., 1973b, "Land use law (II): Florida is a major testing ground", *Science,* **182**, 902-907.
Carter, L. J., 1973c, "Water projects: how to erase the pork barrel image", *Science,* **182**, 266-269.
Carter, L. J., 1973d, "Alaska pipeline: Congress deaf to environmentalists", *Science,* **181**, 326, 641-643.
Carter, L. J., 1974, "Law of the sea: fisheries plight poses dilemma for the United States", *Science,* **185**, 337-340.
Carter, L. J., 1975, *The Florida Experience* (Johns Hopkins University Press, Baltimore), 400 pp.
Cassidy, M., 1976, "Lessons to be learnt from case studies in London", in *Environmental Impact Assessment,* Eds T. O'Riordan, R. D. Hey (Saxon House, Farnborough, Hants.).
Castle, E. N., 1972, "Economics and the quality of life", *American Journal of Agricultural Economics,* **54**, 723-735.
Castles, F. G., Murray, D. J., Potter, D. C. (Eds), 1971, *Decisions, Organisations and Society* (Penguin Books, Harmondsworth), 407 pp.
Catlow, J., Thirlwall, C. G., 1975, "Environmental impact analysis study: draft interim report" (Department of the Environment, London), 45 pp.
Chan, K., Lager, K. F., 1974, *Growth Policy: Population, Environment and Beyond* (University of Michigan Press, Ann Arbor, Mich.).
Chant, D. A., 1970, *Pollution Probe* (New Press, Toronto), 203 pp.
Chapman, D., Tyrell, T., Mount, T., 1972, "Electricity demand growth and the energy crisis", *Science,* **178**, 703-708.
Chapman, P., 1975, *Fuels Paradise: Energy Options for Britain* (Penguin Books, Harmondsworth), 233 pp.
Chapman, P. F., Mortimer, N., 1974, "Energy inputs and outputs for nuclear power stations", Research Paper 005, Energy Research Group, The Open University, Milton Keynes.
Charles River Associates, 1972, "The effects of pollution control on the nonferrous metal industry, (a) aluminium, (b) lead, (c) zinc" (Council on Environmental Quality, Washington).
Chase, S., 1973, "The Club of Rome and its computer", *Bulletin of the Atomic Scientists,* **57**, 36-39.
Chernow, E., 1975, "Implementing the Clean Air Act in Los Angeles: the duty to achieve the impossible", *Ecology Law Quarterly,* **4**, 537-581.
Chevalier, M., Burns, T., Bailey, L., 1974, "Participatory planning in man-environment relations", Faculty of Environmental Studies, York University, Downsview, Ontario, 39 pp.
Chevalier, M., Cartwright, T. J., 1967, "Towards an action framework for the control of pollution", in *Pollution and Our Environment,* Paper D, 30-1, Canadian Council of Resource Ministers (Queens Printer, Ottawa), 52 pp.
Chevalier, M., Cartwright, T. J., 1971, "Public involvement in planning: the Delaware River case", in *Perception and Attitudes in Resource Management,* Eds W. R. D. Sewell, I. Burton (Information Canada, Ottawa), pp.111-120.
Choucri, N., Bennett, J. P., 1972, "Population, resources, technology; political implications of the environmental crisis", in *World Eco-Crisis,* Eds D. A. Kay, E. B. Skolnikoff (University of Wisconsin Press, Madison), pp.9-46.
Christy, F. T., 1972, "Fisheries management and the law of the sea", in *Economic Aspects of Fish Production* (OECD, Paris), pp.4-39.
Cicchetti, C. J., 1971, "Some economic issues in planning urban recreational facilities", *Land Economics,* **47**, 15-23.
Cicchetti, C. J., 1972, *Alaskan Oil: Alternative Routes and Markets* (Johns Hopkins University Press, Baltimore), 145 pp.

Cicchetti, C. J., 1973, "The wrong route", *Environment,* **15**, 4-12.
Cicchetti, C. J., Davis, R. K., Hanke, S. H., Haveman, R. H., 1973, "Evaluating federal water projects: a critique of proposed standards", *Science,* **181**, 723-727.
Cicchetti, C. J., Freeman, A. M. III, 1971, "Option demand and consumer surplus, further comments", *Quarterly Journal of Economics,* **85**, 522-539.
Cicchetti, C. J., Gillen, W. J., 1973a, "Electricity demand: economic incentives and environmental quality" (Environmental Defense Fund, Washington), 23 pp.
Cicchetti, C. J., Gillen, W. J., 1973b, "The mandatory oil import quota program: a consideration of economic efficiency and equity", *Natural Resources Journal,* **13**, 399-430.
Cicchetti, C. J., Seneca, J. J., Davidson, P., 1969, *The Demand and Supply of Outdoor Recreation* (New Jersey State University, New Brunswick), 301 pp.
Cicchetti, C. J., Smith, V. K., 1973, "Congestion, quality deterioration and optional uses: wilderness recreation in the Spanish Peaks Primitive Area", *Social Science Research,* **2**, 15-20.
Ciriacy-Wantrup, S. V., 1971, "The economics of environmental policy", *Land Economics,* **47**, 36-45.
Clark, C. W., 1973, "The economics of over-exploitation", *Science,* **181**, 630-634.
Clark, K., 1969, *Civilisation* (BBC Publications, London), 347 pp.
Clark, R. N., Hendee, J. C., 1969, "Littering behaviour in forest campgrounds" (Pacific Northwest Forest and Range Experiment Station, Seattle), 15 pp.
Clark, R. N., Hendee, J. C., Campbell, F. C., 1971, "Values, behavior and conflict in modern camping culture", *Journal of Leisure Research,* **3**, 143-159.
Clark, R. N., Stankey, G. H., 1976, "Analyzing public input to resource decisions: criteria, principles and case examples of the codinvolve system", *Natural Resources Journal,* **16**.
Clark, T. N. (Ed.), 1972, "Community power and decision making", *Current Sociology,* **20**, 133 pp.
Clarke, R., 1974, "Technology for alternative society and an alternative technology", *New Scientist,* **57**, 66-70.
Clawson, M., 1971, *Suburban Land Conversion in the United States: An Economic and Governmental Process* (Johns Hopkins University Press, Baltimore), 424 pp.
Clawson, M. (Ed.), 1973, *Modernizing Urban Land Policy* (Johns Hopkins University Press, Baltimore), 296 pp.
Clawson, M., Hall, P., 1973, *Planning and Urban Growth: An Anglo American Comparison* (Johns Hopkins University Press, Baltimore), 300 pp.
Clemens, W. C., Jr., 1973, "Ecology and international relations", *International Journal,* **28**, 1-27.
Clinton, R., Flash, W., Godwin, K. (Eds), 1972, *Political Science in Population Studies* (D. C. Heath, Lexington, Mass.).
Clusen, C. M., 1973, *Engineering a Victory for Our Environment: A Citizen's Guide to the U. S. Army Corps of Engineers* (Sierra Club, San Francisco), 80 pp.
Coale, A. S., 1970, "Man and his environment", *Science,* **170**, 132-136.
Coale, A. S., 1972, *The Growth and Structure of American Populations* (Princeton University Press, Princeton).
Coase, R. H., 1960, "The problem of social cost", *The Journal of Law and Economics,* **3**, 1-44.
Cobb, B., Cobb, H., 1973, *City People's Guide to Country Living* (Collier Books, New York), 186 pp.
Cobb, J. B., 1972, *Is it Too Late? A Theology of Ecology* (Bruce, New York).
Cochrane, S. H., 1973, "Population and development: A more general model", *Economic Development and Cultural Change,* **21**, 409-422.

Coddington, A., 1973, "Professor Beckerman in perspective", *Environment and Planning,* **5**, 667-672.
Cohen, R., 1972, *How to Make It on the Land: A Complete Guide to Survival in the Country* (Prentice-Hall, Englewood Cliffs, NJ), 218 pp.
Cole, H. S. D., Freeman, C., Jahoda, M., Pavitt, K. L. R., 1973, *Thinking About the Future: A Critique of the Limits to Growth* (Sussex University Press, Brighton), 216 pp., published in the United States as *Models of Doom* (Universe Books, New York).
Collins, M. P., 1972, *The Perception of Pollution by SPEC and by the Public in New Westminster,* unpublished M. A. Thesis, Department of Geography, Simon Fraser University, Burnaby, BC.
Colombotos, J., 1969, "Physicians and medicare: a before-after study of the effects of legislation on attitudes", *American Sociology Review,* **34**, 318-334.
Commodity Research Unit, 1975, *Problems and Prospects for Raw Materials* (Commodity Research Unit, London).
Commoner, B., 1966, *Science and Survival* (Viking Books, New York), 144 pp.
Commoner, B., 1972a, "The environmental cost of economic growth", in *Energy, Economic Growth and the Environment,* Ed. S. Schurr (Johns Hopkins University Press, Baltimore), pp.30-66.
Commoner, B., 1972b, *The Closing Circle: Man, Nature and Technology* (Knopf, New York), 300 pp.
Commoner, B., Corr, M., Stamler, P. J., 1971, "The causes of pollution", *Environment,* **13**, 2-10.
Commonwealth Secretariat, 1975, *Terms of Trade Policy for Primary Commodities* (Commonwealth Office, London).
Connelly, P., Perlman, R., 1975, *The Politics of Scarcity: Resource Conflicts in International Relations* (Oxford University Press, London), 162 pp.
Conner, J. A., Lochman, E. (Eds), 1972, *Economics and Decision Making for Environmental Quality* (University of Florida Press, Gainesville).
Connery, R. H., Gilmour, R. S., 1975, *The National Energy Problem* (Saxon House, D. C. Heath, Farnborough, Hants.).
Conservation Foundation, 1972, *National Parks for the Future* (Conservation Foundation, Washington), 278 pp.
Constantine, E., Hauf, K., 1972, "Environmental concern and Lake Tahoe: a study of elite perceptions, backgrounds and attitudes", *Environment and Behavior,* **4**, 209-242.
Constantine, L., Constantine, J., 1973, *Group Marriage* (Macmillan, New York).
Converse, P. E., 1964, "The nature of belief systems in mass publics", in *Ideology and Discontent,* Ed. D. Apter (Free Press, Glencoe, Ill.).
Cook, T. E., Morgan, P. M. (Eds), 1971, *Participatory Democracy* (Harper and Row, New York).
Cooley, R. A., Wandesforde-Smith, G., 1970, *Congress and the Environment* (University of Washington Press, Seattle), 127 pp.
Coomber, N. H., Biswas, A. K., 1973, *Evaluation of Environmental Intangibles* (Genera Press, Bronxville, NY), 74 pp.
Coppock, J. T., Sewell, W. R. D. (Eds), 1976, *Public Participation in Planning* (John Wiley, Chichester).
Costonis, J., 1973, "Development rights transfer: an exploratory essay", *Yale Law Journal,* **83** (November).
Council on Economic Priorities, 1972, *Paper Profits: Pollution in the Pulp and Paper Industry* (MIT Press, Cambridge, Mass.), 495 pp.
Council on Environmental Quality, 1970, *Environmental Quality: First Annual Report* (Government Printing Office, Washington), 326 pp.

Council on Environmental Quality, 1971, *Environmental Quality: Second Annual Report* (Government Printing Office, Washington), 326 pp.
Council on Environmental Quality, 1972, *Environmental Quality: Third Annual Report* (Government Printing Office, Washington), 436 pp.
Council on Environmental Quality, 1973a, *Environmental Quality: Fourth Annual Report* (Government Printing Office, Washington), 480 pp.
Council on Environmental Quality, 1973b, *Energy and the Environment: Electric Power* (Government Printing Office, Washington), 58 pp.
Council on Environmental Quality, 1974, *Environmental Quality: Fifth Annual Report* (Government Printing Office, Washington), 584 pp.
Cox, P. T., Grover, C. W., Siskin, B., 1971, "Effect of water resource investment on economic growth", *Water Resources Research,* **7**, 32-38.
Coy, J. G., Johnston, R. A., Richerson, P. J., 1973, "Critique of Water Resources Council's proposal principles and standards for planning water and related land resources", in *Environmental Quality and Water Development,* Ed. C. R. Goldman (Freeman, San Francisco), pp.478-494.
Craig, P. P., Berlin, E., 1971, "The air of poverty", *Environment,* **13**, 56-60.
Craik, K. H., 1972, "An ecological perspective on environmental decision making", *Human Ecology,* **1**, 69-80.
Craik, K. H., 1973, "Environmental psychology", *Annual Review of Psychology,* **24**, 403-422.
Crampton, R. C., Boyer, B. B., 1972, "Citizen suits in the environmental field: peril or promise?", *Ecology Law Quarterly,* **2**, 407-436.
Cranston, M., 1972, "Ethics and politics", *Encounter,* **38**, 16-26.
Creer, R. N., Gray, R. M., Trestow, M., 1970, "Differential response to air pollution as an environmental health problem", *Journal of Air Pollution Control Association,* **20**, 214-218.
Crenson, M. A., 1972, *The Un-Politics of Air Pollution* (Johns Hopkins University Press, Baltimore), 223 pp.
Crespi, I., 1972, "What kinds of attitude measures are predictive of behavior?", *Public Opinion Quarterly,* **35**, 327-334.
Crocker, T. D., 1971, "Externalities, property rights and transaction costs: an empirical study", *Journal of Law and Economics,* **14**, 451-464.
Crofton, E., 1974, "Urban environment and physical health", in *Environmental Quality,* Eds J. T. Coppock, C. B. Wilson (Scottish Academic Press, Edinburgh), pp.38-51.
Crosland, A., 1974, *Socialism Now* (Jonathan Cape, London), 255 pp.
Cross, N., Elliott, D., Roy, R., 1974, *Man Made Futures: Readings in Sociology, Technology and Design* (Hutchinson, London), 365 pp.
Crowe, B. L., 1969, "The tragedy of the commons revisited", *Science,* **166**, 1103-1107.
Cunningham, J. V., 1972, "Citizen participation in public affairs", *Public Administration Review,* **32**, 589-602.
Curtis, V. (Ed.), 1973, *Land Use and the Environment* (Environmental Protection Agency, Washington).
Dahl, R. H., 1961, *Who Governs?* (Yale University Press, New Haven, Conn.).
Dahl, R. H., Tufte, E., 1973, *Size and Democracy* (Oxford University Press, New York).
Dahmén, E., 1971, "Environmental control and economic systems", *The Swedish Journal of Economics,* **73**, 67-75.
Dales, J. H., 1968, *Pollution, Property and Prices* (University of Toronto Press, Toronto), 111 pp.
Daly, H. E., 1968, "On economics as a life science", *The Journal of Political Economy,* **76**, 392-406.

Daly, H. E., 1973a, "Introduction", in *Towards a Steady State Economy,* Ed. H. E. Daly (Freeman, San Francisco), pp.1-36.
Daly, H. E., 1973b, "The steady state economy: towards a political economy of biophysical equilibrium and moral growth", in *Towards a Steady State Economy,* Ed. H. E. Daly (Freeman, San Francisco), pp.149-174.
Daly, H. E., 1973c, "Electric power, employment and economic growth: a case study in growthmania", in *Towards a Steady State Economy*, Ed. H. E. Daly (Freeman, San Francisco), pp.252-282.
Daly, H. E., 1973d, "How to stabilize the economy", *The Ecologist,* **3**, 90-97.
Daly, H. E., 1974a, "The economics of the steady state", *American Economic Review,* **64**, 15-21.
Daly, H. E., 1974b, "Steady state economies vs. growthmania: a critique of the orthodox conceptions of growth wants, scarcity and efficiency", *Policy Science,* **1**, Summer.
d'Arge, R. C., 1971, "Essays on economic growth and environmental quality", *The Swedish Journal of Economics,* **73**, 25-41.
d'Arge, R. C., 1972, "Trade, environmental controls and the developing countries", *Problems of Environmental Economics* (OECD, Paris), pp.227-253.
d'Arge, R. C., Kneese, A. V., 1972, "Environmental quality and international trade", in *World Eco-Crisis: International Organizations in Response,* Eds D. A. Kay, E. B. Skolnikoff (University of Wisconsin Press, Madison), pp.255-303.
Darmstadter, J., 1972a, "Energy consumption: trends and patterns", in *Energy, Economic Growth and the Environment,* Ed. S. Schurr (Johns Hopkins University Press, Baltimore), pp.155-223.
Darmstadter, J., 1972b, "Energy", in *Population, Resources and the Environment,* Ed. R. Ridker (Government Printing Office, Washington), pp.103-149.
Dasmann, R. F., 1972, *Planet in Peril: Man and the Biosphere Today* (Penguin Books, Harmondsworth), 135 pp.
David, E. J. L., 1971, "Public perceptions of water quality", *Water Resources Research,* **7**, 453-457.
Davies, C. J. III, 1970, *The Politics of Pollution* (Pegasus Press, New York), 213 pp.
Davies, J. G., 1972, *The Evangelistic Bureaucrat: A Study of a Planning Exercise in Newcastle upon Tyne* (Tavistock Publications, London), 236 pp.
Davis, D., 1970, "The liberalized law of standing", *University of Chicago Law Review,* **37**, 450-469.
Davis, D. H., 1972, "Concensus or conflict: alternative strategies for the bureaucratic bargainer", *Public Choice,* **13**, 21-30.
Davis, R. K., Knetsch, J. L., 1966, "Comparisons of methods for recreation evaluation", in *Water Research,* Eds A. V. Kneese, S. C. Smith (Johns Hopkins University Press, Baltimore), pp.121-143.
Day, R. D., Koenig, E. F., 1975, "On some models of world cataclysm", *Land Economics,* **51**, 1-20.
De Bell, G. (Ed.), 1970, *The Voter's Guide to Environmental Politics* (Ballantine Books, New York), 310 pp.
de Fleur, M. L., Westie, F. R., 1963, "Attitude as a scientific concept", *Social Forces,* **42**, 17-31.
Deininger, R. A. (Ed.), 1973, *Models for Environmental Pollution Control* (Science Publishers, Ann Arbor, Mich.).
Demeny, P., 1974, "The populations of the underdeveloped countries", *Scientific American,* **231**, 148-159.
Demsetz, T., 1967, "Towards a theory of property rights", *American Economic Review,* **57**, 347-355.

Dennis, N., 1972, *Public Participation and Planners' Blight* (Faber and Faber, London), 337 pp.
Detwyler, T. R. (Ed.), 1971, *Man's Impact on Environment* (McGraw-Hill, New York), 709 pp.
Deutscher, I., 1966, "Words and deeds: social science and social policy", *Social Problems,* **13**, 235-254.
Devall, W. B., 1970, "Conservation: an upper middle class social movement: a replication", *Journal of Leisure Research,* **2**, 23-26.
Devine, D. J., 1972, *The Political Culture of the United States* (Little, Brown, Boston), 340 pp.
Dewees, D. N., 1973, "Costly information and the choice of policies for reducing externalities" (Department of Political Economy, University of Toronto), 31 pp.
Dick, D. T., 1974, *Pollution, Congestion and Nuisance: The Economics of Nonmarket Interdependence* (Saxon House, D. C. Heath, Farnborough, Hants.).
Dickerman, A. R., 1974, "A value orientated approach to water quality objectives", *Land Economics,* **50**, 398-403.
Dickson, D., 1974, *Alternative Technology* (Fontana-Collins, Glasgow).
Dillman, D. A., Christenson, J. A., 1972, "Public value for pollution control", in *Social Behavior, Natural Resources and the Environment,* Eds W. R. Burch, Jr., N. H. Cheek, Jr., L. Taylor (Harper and Row, New York), pp.214-236.
Disselhorst, T. M., 1975, "Sierra Club v. Ruckelshaus—on a clear day", *Ecology Law Quarterly,* **4**, 739-780.
Ditlow, C. M., 1975, "Federal regulation of motor vehicle emissions under the Clean Air Amendments of 1970", *Ecology Law Quarterly,* **4**, 495-522.
Ditton, R. B., Goodale, T. I., 1972, *Environmental Impact Analysis: Philosophy and Methods* (University of Wisconsin: Sea Grant Program, Madison), 163 pp.
Dobry, G., 1975, *Review of the Development Control System: Final Report* (HMSO, London), 235 pp.
Doctor, R. D., Anderson, K. P., 1972, *California's Electric Quandry: (3) Slowing the Growth Rate* (Rand Corporation, Santa Monica, Calif.), 141 pp.
Dolan, E. G., 1972, *TANSTAAFL: The Economic Strategy for Environmental Crisis* (Holt, Rinehart and Winston, New York), 115 pp.
Dorcey, A. H. J., 1973, "Effluent charges, information generation and bargaining behavior", *Natural Resources Journal,* **13**, 118-133.
Dorfman, R., Dorfman, D. (Eds), 1973, *Economics of the Environment: Selected Readings* (Norton, New York), 432 pp.
Douglas, W. O., 1972, *The Three Hundred Year War* (Random House, New York), 200 pp.
Downing, P. B., 1969, *The Economics of Urban Sewage Disposal* (Praeger, New York), 195 pp.
Downing, P. B., 1971, "Solving the air pollution problem: a social scientist's perspective", *Natural Resources Journal,* **11**, 693-713.
Downs, A., 1966, *Inside Bureaucracy* (Little Brown, Boston).
Downs, A., 1972, "Up and down with ecology—the issue attention cycle", *Public Interest,* **28**, 38-50.
Downs, R. M., Stea, D. (Eds), 1974, *Image and Environment* (Edward Arnold, London), 423 pp.
Drew, E. B., 1970, "Dam outrage: the story of the Army Engineers", *Atlantic Monthly,* April, 51-62.
Du Boff, R. B., 1974, "Economic ideology and the environment", in *Man and Environment, Ltd,* Eds H. G. T. Van Raay, A. E. Lugo (Rotterdam University Press, Rotterdam), pp.201-220.

Dubos, R., 1968, "Man and his environment: adaptations and interactions", in *The Fitness of Man's Environment*, Smithsman Annual II (Harper and Row, New York), pp.229-250.
Dubos, R., 1970, *Reason Awake: Science for Man* (Columbia University Press, New York), 273 pp.
Dumont, R., 1973, *The Hungry Future* (Praeger, New York).
Dumont, R., 1974, *Utopia or Else* (Deutsch, London), 171 pp.
Duverger, M., 1972, *Party Politics and Pressure Groups* (Nelson, New York), 168 pp.
Easterlin, R., 1973, "Does money buy happiness?", *The Public Interest*, **30**, 3-10.
Ebbin, C., Kasper, R., 1974, *Citizens' Groups and the Nuclear Power Controversy. Uses of Scientific and Technological Information* (MIT Press, Cambridge, Mass.), 307 pp.
Eckhardt, K. W., Hendershot, G., 1967, "Dissonance, congruance, and the perception of public opinion", *American Journal of Sociology*, **73**, 226-234.
The Ecologist, 1972, Rebuttals to *Blueprint*, **2** (4), 23-26; **2** (5), 27-30; **2** (7), 22-26; **2** (9), 23-26.
Eddy, H. R., 1971, "*Locus standi* and environmental control: a policy for comparison", *University of British Columbia Law Review*, **6**, 193-214.
Edel, M., 1973, *Economies and the Environment* (Prentice-Hall, Englewood Cliffs, NJ), 162 pp.
Edelman, M., 1964, *The Symbolic Use of Politics* (University of Illinois Press, Urbana).
Edwards, C. D., 1945, *A Cartel Policy for the United Nations* (Columbia University Press, New York), 116 pp.
Edwards, W. F., Langham, M., Headley, J. C., 1970, "Pesticide residues and environmental economics", *Natural Resources Journal*, **10**, 719-741.
Egler, F. E., 1969, "Pesticides-in our ecosystem", in *The Subversive Science: Essays Towards an Ecology of Man*, Eds P. Shepard, D. McKinley (Houghton Mifflin, Boston), pp.245-267.
Ehrenfeld, D. H., 1972, *Conserving Life on Earth* (Oxford University Press, New York), 337 pp.
Ehrlich, H. T., 1969, "Attitudes, behavior and the intervening variable", *American Sociologist*, **4**, 29-34.
Ehrlich, P. H., Holdern, J. R., 1971, "The impact of population growth", *Science*, **171**, 1212-1217.
Ehrlich, P. R., 1970, *The Population Bomb* (Ballantine Books, New York).
Ehrlich, P., 1974, *The End of Affluence* (Ballantine Books, New York), 307 pp.
Ehrlich, P. R., Ehrlich, A. H., 1972, *Population, Resources, Environment: Issues in Human Ecology* (Freeman, San Francisco), 509 pp.
Ehrlich, P. R., Harriman, R. L., 1971, *How to be a Survivor: A Plan to Save Spaceship Earth* (Ballantine Books, New York), 208 pp.
Eigermann, M., 1974, "The Merrimack River Basin Wastewater Study" (Corps of Engineers, Springfield, Va.).
Eilenstine, D., Cunningham, J. D., 1972, "Projected consumption patterns for a stationary population", *Population Studies*, **26**, 223-523.
Elder, J., 1970, *Crisis in Eden: A Religious Study of Man and Environment* (Abingdon Press, New York).
Elder, P. S., 1973, "The common law and the environment", in *Ask the People*, Ed. C. G. Morley (Agassiz Centre for Water Studies, University of Manitoba, Winnipeg), pp.89-97.
Eldridge, D., 1974, "Alternative possible looks at futures", *Futures*, **6**, 26-40.
Eliade, M., 1968, *Myth and Reality* (Harper Torchbooks, New York), 212 pp.

Elliott, C., 1973, "Fair chance for all: money and trade between equal partners" (UNCTAD/CESI, Geneva).
Emmett, B., 1974, "Evaluation of intangibles: state of the art" (National Science Council, Ottawa), 45 pp.
England, R., Bluestone, B., 1973, "Ecology and social conflict", in *Towards a Steady State Economy,* Ed. H. E. Daly (Freeman, San Francisco), pp.190-214.
English, A., 1975, "State implementation plans and air quality enforcement", *Ecology Law Quarterly,* **4**, 595-643.
Enke, S., 1970, "The economics of having children", *Policy Sciences,* **1**, 15-30.
Enke, S., 1971, *Calculating the Benefits of Slower Population Growth,* Tempo, General Electric Company (Center for Advanced Studies, Santa Barbara, Calif.), 92 pp.
Enthoven, A. C., Freeman, A. M. III. (Eds), 1973, *Pollution, Resources and the Environment* (Norton, New York), 306 pp.
Environmental Reporter Cases, 1972, *An Annual Compilation of Environmental Cases* (Bureau of National Affairs, Washington).
Enzensberger, H. M., 1974, "A critique of political ecology", *New Left Review,* **84**, 3-32.
Epp, D. J., 1971, "The effect of public land acquisition on outdoor recreation and on the real estate tax base", *Journal of Leisure Research,* **3**, 17-27.
Erickson, R. S., Luttberg, W. P., 1973, *American Public Opinion: Its Origins, Content and Impact* (John Wiley, New York), 332 pp.
Erskine, H., 1971, "The polls: pollution and its costs", *Public Opinion Quarterly,* **35**, 120-135.
Espinshade, T. J., 1972, "The price of children and the socio-economic theories of fertility", *Population Studies,* **24**, 207-222.
Esposito, J., 1970, *Vanishing Air* (Grossman, New York), 318 pp.
Estrin, D. A., Waigen, S., 1974, *Environment on Trial: A Citizen's Guide to Ontario Environmental Law* (Canadian Environmental Law Association, Toronto), 406 pp.
Etzioni, A., 1970, "The wrong top priority", *Science,* **168**, 921.
Eversley, D. E. C., 1972, "Rising costs and static incomes: some economic consequences of regional planning in London", *Urban Studies,* **9**, 347-368.
Eversley, D. E. C., 1975a, "Employment planning and income maintenance", *Town and Country Planning,* **43**, 206-209.
Eversley, D. E. C., 1975b, "Reform of local government finance: the limitations of a local income tax" (Centre for Environmental Studies, London), 40 pp.
Fabricant, N., Hallman, M., 1973, *Towards a Rational Power Policy* (George Braziller, New York), 292 pp.
Fackre, G., 1971, "Ecology and theology", *Religion in Life,* **40**, 210-224 (reprinted in Barbour, 1973, pp.117-131).
Fairbrother, N., 1972, *New Lives, New Landscapes* (Penguin Books, Harmondsworth), 370 pp.
Fairfield, R., 1973, *Communes, U.S.A.* (Penguin Books, Baltimore), 400 pp.
Falk, R. A., 1972, *This Endangered Planet: Prospects and Proposals for Human Survival* (Vintage Books, New York), 498 pp.
Fallows, J. M., 1972, *The Water Lords* (Grossman, New York), 285 pp.
Fanning, O., 1975, *Man and His Environment: Citizen Action* (Harper and Row, New York), 233 pp.
Farb, P., 1968, "Rise and fall of the Indian of the West", *Natural History,* **77**, 32-41.
Farvar, M. T., Milton, J. P. (Eds), 1972, *The Careless Technology: Ecology and International Development* (Natural History Press, New York), 1060 pp.

Feldman, S., 1973, "A note on the peak load pricing of urban water supply", Discussion Paper No. 1 (Department of Geography, Hebrew University of Jerusalem), 7 pp.
Feldman, S., Gonen, A., 1975, "The spatiotemporal pricing of some urban public services: urban ecology, equity and efficiency", *Environment and Planning A,* **7**, 315-326.
Fellmeth, R. C., 1973, *Politics of Land: Ralph Nader's Study Group on Land Use in California* (Grossman, New York), 730 pp.
Ferguson, A. B. Jr., Bryson, W. P., 1972, "Mineral king: a case study in Forest Service decision making", *Ecology Law Quarterly,* **2**, 493-532.
Ferkiss, V. C., 1970, *Technological Man: The Myth and Reality* (Mentor Books, New York), 270 pp.
Ferkiss, V. C., 1974, *The Future of Technological Civilization* (George Braziller, New York), 369 pp.
Ferrar, T. A., Whinston, A., 1972, "Taxation and water pollution control", *Natural Resources Journal,* **12**, 307-317.
Fife, D., 1971, "Killing the goose", *Environment,* **13**, 68-71.
Finkler, E., 1972, *Non Growth as a Planning Alternative* (American Society of Planning Officials, Chicago), 66 pp.
Finkler, E., 1973, *Non Growth: A Review of the Literature* (American Society of Planning Officials, Chicago), 18 pp.
Fischer, D. W., 1975, "Willingness to pay as a behavioural criterion for environmental decision making", *Journal of Environmental Management,* **3**, 29-41.
Fischer, D. W., Davis, G. S., 1973, "An approach to assessing environmental impacts", *Journal of Environmental Management,* **1**, 207-237.
Fischer, D. W., Kerton, R. R., 1973, "Toward a theory of environmental economics", Working Paper No.77 (Department of Economics, University of Waterloo, Waterloo, Ontario), 31 pp.
Fischman, L. L., Landsberg, H. H., 1972, "Adequacy of non fuel mineral and forest resources", in *Population, Resources and the Environment,* Ed. R. Ridker (Government Printing Office, Washington), pp.79-99.
Fishbein, M., 1967, "Attitude and the prediction of behavior", in *Readings in Attitude Theory and Measurement,* Ed. M. Fishbein (John Wiley, New York), pp.477-492.
Fisher, A. C., 1971, "Population and environmental quality", *Public Policy,* **19**, 19-36.
Fisher, A. C., Krutilla, J. V., 1972, "Determination of optimal capacity of resource based recreational facilities", *Natural Resources Journal,* **12**, 417-444.
Fisher, A. C., Krutilla, J. V., 1974, "Valuing long run ecological consequences and irreversibilities", Reprint No.117, Resources of the Future, Washington, 13 pp.
Fisher A. C., Krutilla, J. V., Cicchetti, C. J., 1972, "The economics of environmental preservation: a theoretical and empirical analysis", *American Economic Review,* **62**, 605-619.
Fisher, J. L., Ridker, R. G., 1973, "Population growth, resource availability and environmental quality", *American Economic Review,* **63**, 70-87.
Fleischman, P., 1969, "Conservation, the biological fallacy", *Landscape,* **18**, 23-27.
Flowerdew, A. D. J., Hammond, A., 1973, "City roads and the environment", *Regional Studies,* **7**, 123-136.
Ford Foundation Energy Policy Project, 1974a, *Exploring Energy Choices* (Ford Foundation, Washington), 81 pp.
Ford Foundation Energy Policy Project, 1974b, *A Time to Choose* (Ballinger, Cambridge, Mass.), 511 pp.
Forrester, J. W., 1969, *Urban Dynamics* (MIT Press, Cambridge, Mass.), 285 pp.
Forrester, J. W., 1970, *World Dynamics* (Wright-Allen Press, Boston).

Forrester, J. W., 1971, "Counterintuitive behavior of social systems", *Technology Review,* **83,** 52-68.

Foss, P. O. (Ed.), 1972, *Politics and Ecology* (Duxbury Press, Belmont, Calif.), 298 pp.

Foster, G. M., 1965, "Peasant society and the image of limited good", *American Anthropologist,* **67**, 293-315.

Fox, I. K., 1970, "The use of standards in achieving appropriate levels of tolerance", *Proceedings of the National Academy of Sciences USA,* **67**, 877-886.

Fox, I. K., Wible, L., 1973, "Information generation and communication to establish environmental quality objectives", *Natural Resources Journal,* **13,** 134-149.

Frank, A. G., 1972, *Capitalism and Underdevelopment in Latin America* (Penguin Books, Harmondsworth).

Frank, H. J., Wells, D. A., 1973, "United States oil imports: implications for the balance of payments", *Natural Resources Journal,* **13**, 431-447.

Franklin, H. M., 1973, "Controlling urban growth—but for whom?" (The Potomac Institute, Washington), 41 pp.

Fraser, D., 1971, *The People Problem* (Indiana University Press, Bloomington), 239 pp.

Fraser, J. A., 1974, "The role of the common law: its strengths and weaknesses in dealing with environmental problems", in *Canada's Environment: The Law on Trial,* Ed. C. G. Morley (Agassiz Centre for Water Studies, University of Manitoba, Winnipeg), pp.112-132.

Fraser-Darling, F., 1971, *Wilderness and Plenty* (Ballantine Books, New York), 112 pp.

Frederickson, J. J. (Ed.), 1972, "Curriculum essays on citizen politics, and administration in urban neighborhoods", *Public Administration Review,* **32**, 515-518.

Freeman, A. M., III, 1969, "Project design and evaluation with multiple objectives", in *The Analysis and Evaluation of Public Expenditures: The P.P.B. System,* Ed. R. Dorfman (US Congressional Joint Committee on Economics, Washington), pp.565-578.

Freeman, A. M., III, 1972, "The distribution of environmental quality", in *Environmental Quality Analysis,* Eds A. V. Kneese, B. T. Bower (Johns Hopkins University Press, Baltimore), pp.243-278.

Freeman, A. M., III, Haveman, R. H., 1970, "Benefit cost analysis and multiple objectives: current issues in water resources planning", *Water Resources Research,* **6,** 1533-1539.

Freeman, A. M., III, Haveman, R. H., 1971, "Water pollution control, river basin authorities and economic incentives: some current policy issues", *Public Policy,* **18,** 53-74.

Freeman, A. M., III, Haveman, R. H., 1972a, "Residuals charges for pollution control: a policy evaluation", *Science,* **177**, 322-329.

Freeman, A. M., III, Haveman, R. H., 1972b, "Clean rhetoric and dirty water", *The Public Interest,* **28**, 51-66.

Freeman, A. M., III, Haveman, R. H., Kneese, A. V., 1973, *The Economics of Environmental Policy* (John Wiley, New York), 184 pp.

Freeman, S. D., 1974, *Energy: The New Era* (Vintage Books, New York), 371 pp.

Frejka, T., 1973a, "The prospects for a stationary world population", *Scientific American,* **228**, 15-23.

Frejka, T., 1973b, *The Future of Population Growth: Alternative Paths to Equilibrium* (John Wiley, New York).

Frick, G. E., Ching, C. T. K., 1970, "Generation of local income from users of a rural public park", *Journal of Leisure Research,* **2**, 260-263.

Friedmann, J., 1973, "The public interest and community participation: towards a reconstruction of public philosophy", *Journal of the American Institute of Planners,* **39**, 2-7.

Friends of the Earth, 1972, *The Stockholm Conference* (Earth Island, London).

Friere, P., 1970, *The Pedagogy of the Oppressed* (Herder and Herder, New York), 776 pp.

Frisken, W. R., 1974, *The Atmospheric Environment* (Johns Hopkins University Press, Baltimore), 80 pp.

Fromm, E., 1968, *The Revolution of Hope: Towards a Humanized Technology* (Bantam Books, New York).

Fuchs, V. R., 1968, *The Service Economy* (Columbia University Press, New York).

Fuller, R. B., Walker, E. A., Killiam, T. R., Jr., 1970, *Approaching the Benign Environment* (Collier Books, London), 169 pp.

Gabler, L. R., 1969, "Economics and diseconomics of scale in urban public sectors", *Land Economics,* **45**, 425-434.

Gäfgen, G., 1974, "On the methodology and political economy of Galbraithian economics", *Kyklos,* **27**, 705-731.

Galbraith, J. K., 1958, "How much should a country consume?", in *Perspectives on Conservation: Essays on America's Natural Resources,* Ed. H. Jarrett (Johns Hopkins University Press, Baltimore), pp.89-99.

Galbraith, J. K., 1973, *Economics and the Public Purpose* (Houghton Mifflin, Boston), 324 pp.

Galle, O. R., Grove, W. R., McPherson, J. M., 1972, "Population density and pathology: what are the relations for man?", *Science,* **176**, 23-30.

Gallup, G., Jr., 1973, "What do Americans think about limiting growth?" (Public Opinion Research Center, Princeton, NJ), 23 pp.

Gans, H., 1972, "The positive functions of poverty", *American Journal of Sociology,* **78**, 275-289.

Gans, H., 1973, "Comment on Friedmann (1973)", *Journal of the American Institute of Planners,* **39**, 8-9.

Ganz, T., O'Brien, T., 1974, "New directions for our cities in the seventies", *Technology Review,* **86**, 10-19.

Garner, J., 1975, *Control of Pollution Act, 1974* (Butterworths, London), 157 pp.

Garton, W. A., 1972, "The state versus extraterritorial pollution—States' 'environmental rights' under federal common law", *Ecology Law Quarterly,* **2**, 313-332.

Garvey, G., 1972, *Energy, Ecology, Economy: A Framework for Environmental Policy* (Norton, New York), 232 pp.

Gentry, N. P., 1972, "Florida Oil Spill and Pollution Control Act: An intrusion into the federal maritime domain", *Natural Resources Journal,* **12**, 615-626.

Georgescu-Roegen, N., 1973, "The entropy law and the economic problem", in *Towards a Steady State Economy,* Ed. H. E. Daly (Freeman, San Francisco), pp.37-49.

Gibson, D., 1970, "Constitutional aspects of environmental management in Canada" (Information Canada, Ottawa), 33 pp.

Gifford, D., 1971, "Comment", *Bulletin, British Ecological Society,* **2**, 2.

Gillette, R., 1971a, "Population Act: proponents dismayed at funding levels", *Science,* **171**, 1221-1224.

Gillette, R., 1971b, "Environmental Protection Agency: chaos or 'administrative tension'?", *Science,* **173**, 703-707.

Gillette, R., 1972a, "National Environmental Policy Act: signs of backlash are evident", *Science,* **176**, 30-33.

Gillette, R., 1972b, "National Environmental Policy Act: how well is it working?", *Science,* **176**, 146-150.

Gillette, R., 1972c, "Nuclear reactor safety", *Science,* **176**, 492-498; **177**, 867-870, 970-975, 1080-1082; **178**, 482-484.

Gillette, R., 1972d, "*The Limits to Growth*: hard sell for a computer view of doomsday", *Science,* **175**, 1688-1692.

Gillette, R., 1975a, "EPA cites errors in AEC's reactor risk study", *Science,* **186**, 1008.
Gillette, R., 1975b, "William Anders: a new regulator enters a critical situation", *Science,* **187**, 1173-1175.
Gillette, R., 1975c, "Energy fusion: an energy option but weapons simulation is first", *Science,* **188**, 30-34.
Gillian, H., 1972, *For Better or For Worse, The Ecology of Urban America* (Chronicle Books, San Francisco), 188 pp.
Gilliland, E. J., 1975, "Charging for 'water' ", *Municipal and Public Services Journal,* **83**, 364-366.
Glacken, C. J., 1967, *Traces on the Rhodian Shore: Nature and Culture in Western Thought from Ancient Times to the End of the Eighteenth Century* (University of California Press, Berkeley, Calif.), 763 pp.
Godwin, R. K., Shepard, W. B., 1974, "State population policies: conflict and choice" (Battelle Memorial Foundation, Washington), 36 pp.
Goetham, L. Van, 1974, *The Fifth Horseman is Riding. A Celebration of the American Countryside and a Documentary of What We Are Doing to Destroy It* (Macmillan, New York), 150 pp.
Gold, A. J., 1974, "Design with nature: a critique", *Journal of the American Institute of Planners,* **40**, 284-286.
Gold, S. M., 1972, "Non use of urban parks", *Journal of the American Institute of Planners,* **38**, 369-378.
Gold, S. M., 1973, *Urban Recreation Planning* (Lea and Febiger, Philadelphia), 184 pp.
Goldberg, M., 1973, "Energy and economic growth: some costs, doubts and dangers", in *Energy and the Environment,* Eds I. Efford, B. M. Smith (University of British Columbia Press, Vancouver), pp.141-161.
Goldie, L. F. E., 1965, "Liability for damage and the progressive development of international law", *International and Comparative Law Quarterly,* **4**, 1189-1258.
Goldie, L. F. E., 1970, "International principles of responsibility for pollution", *Columbia Journal of Transnational Law,* **9**, 283-330.
Goldie, L. F. E., 1971, "Amenities rights—parallels to pollution taxes", *Natural Resources Journal,* **11**, 274-280.
Goldie, L. F. E., 1973, "International impact reports and the conservation of the ocean environment", *Natural Resources Journal,* **13**, 256-281.
Goldman, M., 1972, *The Spoils of Progress: Environmental Pollution and the Soviet Union* (MIT Press, Cambridge, Mass.).
Goldsmith, E. (Ed.), 1972a, *Can Britain Survive?* (Sphere Books, London), 290 pp.
Goldsmith, E., 1972b, "After the blueprint ... where?", in *Teach In for Survival,* Ed. M. Schwab (Robinson and Watkin Books, London), pp.55-63.
Goldsmith, E., 1974, "The caviar chimera", *The Ecologist,* **4**, 82-83.
Goldsmith, E., 1975, "Is science a religion?", *The Ecologist,* **5**, 50-62.
Goldsmith, E., Allen, R., Allaby, M., Davoll, J., Lawrence, S., 1972, "Blueprint for Survival", *The Ecologist,* **2**, 50 pp. (also Penguin Books, Harmondsworth; Houghton Mifflin, Boston).
Goldstein, J. H., 1969, *Competition for Wetlands in the Midwest: An Economic Analysis* (Johns Hopkins University Press, Baltimore), 120 pp.
Goldstein, J., 1970, *How to Manage Your Company Ecologically* (Rodale Press, Emmaus, Pa.).
Good, P., 1971, "Anti-pollution legislation and its enforcement: an empirical study", *University of British Columbia Law Review,* **6**, 271-286.
Goodey, B., 1971, *Perception of the Environment* (Centre for Urban and Regional Studies, University of Birmingham).
Goodman, P., Goodman, P., 1960, *Communitas* (Vintage Books, New York).
Goodman, R., 1972, *After the Planners* (Penguin Books, Harmondsworth), 261 pp.

Gordon, W., 1961, *Synectics* (Collier, New York).

Gore, W. J., 1964, *Administrative Decision Making: A Heuristic Model* (John Wiley, New York), 191 pp.

Gorfman, J. W., Tamplin, A. R., 1971, *Poisoned Power: The Case Against Nuclear Power Plants* (Rodale Press, Emmaus, Pa.), 368 pp.

Gould, N., 1974, "Peter Kropotkin: the anarchist prince", *The Ecologist,* **4**, 261-264.

Goulet, D., 1971, *The Cruel Choice: A New Concept in the Theory of Development* (Atheneum, New York).

Goulet, D., 1974, *The New Moral Order: Development Ethics and Liberation Theology* (Orbis Books, New York).

Grabow, S., Heskin, A., 1973, "Foundations for a radical concept of planning", *Journal of the American Institute of Planners,* **39**, 106-114.

Grad, F. P., 1972, "Review of Sax—*Defending the Environment: A Strategy for Citizen Action*", *Natural Resources Journal,* **12**, 125-131.

Grad, F. P., Rockett, L., 1970, "Environmental litigation: where the action is?", *Natural Resources Journal,* **10**, 742-762.

Graham, F., Jr., 1970, *Since Silent Spring* (Houghton Mifflin, Boston).

Graham, F., Jr., 1973, *Where the Place Called Morning Lies* (Viking Books, New York).

Graham, J., 1973, "Reflections on a planning failure", *Plan,* **3**, 51-75.

Grant, L. V., 1973, "Specialization as a strategy in legislative decision making", *American Journal of Political Science,* **17**, 123-147.

Greater London Council, 1974, "London's environment", First report of the Environmental and Pollution Control Group (County Hall, London), 19 pp.

Green, A. W., 1975, *Social Problems: Arena of Conflict* (McGraw-Hill, New York), 313 pp.

Green, H. P., 1972a, "Nuclear power licensing and regulation", *Annals of the American Academy of Political and Social Science,* **400**, 116-126.

Green, H. P., 1972b, *The National Environmental Policy Act and the Courts* (The Conservation Foundation, Washington), 31 pp.

Green, J. L., 1969, *Economic Ecology: Baselines for Urban Development* (University of Georgia Press, Athens).

Green, M. J., Moore, B. C., Jr., Wasserstein, B., 1972, *The Closed Enterprise System* (Bantam Books, New York), 476 pp.

Greer, S., 1973, "Toronto tries to put lid on growth", *The Vancouver Sun,* October 18, p.4.

Gregory, J. R., 1975, "Image of limited good, or expectation of reciprocity?", *Current Anthropology,* **16**, 73-92.

Gregory, R., 1971, *The Price of Amenity* (Macmillan, London), 301 pp.

Griffin, K., 1974, *The Political Economy of Agrarian Change* (Harvard University Press, Cambridge, Mass.).

Grondona, L. St. C., 1975, *Economic Stability is Attainable* (Hutchinson, London).

de Groot, I., Samuels, S., 1962, *People and Air Pollution: A Study of Attitudes in Buffalo, N. Y.* (New York State Department of Health, Air Pollution Control Board, Buffalo).

Gross, B. M. (Ed.), 1971, "Planning in an era of social revolution", *Public Administration Review,* **31**, 209-296.

Guthrie, D. A., 1971, "Primitive man's relationship to nature", *BioScience,* **21**, 721-723.

Guttstein, D., 1975, *Vancouver, Ltd.* (James Lorimer, Toronto), 192 pp.

Guymer, A., 1971, "Water supply for London, Ontario", in *Perception and Attitudes in Resource Management,* Eds W. R. D. Sewell, I. Burton (Information Canada, Ottawa), pp.61-63.

Haas, J. E., Boggs, K. E., Bonner, E. J., 1971, "Weather modification and the decision process", *Environment and Behavior,* **3**, 179-189.
Haefele, E. T., 1971, "A utility theory of representative government", *American Economic Review,* **61**, 351-367.
Haefele, E. T., 1973, *Representative Government and Environmental Management* (Johns Hopkins University Press, Baltimore), 188 pp.
Haefele, E. T. (Ed.), 1975, *The Governance of Common Property Resources* (Johns Hopkins University Press, Baltimore), 224 pp.
Hagenstein, P. R., 1972, "One third of the nation's land—evaluation of a policy recommendation", *Natural Resources Journal,* **12**, 56-75.
Hagenstein, P. R., 1973, "Changing an anachronism: Congress and the general law of 1872", *Natural Resources Journal,* **13**, 480-493.
Hagevik, G. H., 1970, *Decision Making and Air Pollution Control: A Review of Theory and Practice* (Praeger, New York), 217 pp.
Hagevik, G. H., Mandelker, D. R., Brail, R. K., 1974, *Air Quality Management and Land Use Planning: Legal, Administrative and Methodological Perspectives* (Praeger, New York), 332 pp.
Hagman, D. S., 1971, *Urban Planning and Land Development Law Control* (West, St. Paul, Minn.), 559 pp.
Hall, G., 1972, *Ecology: Can we Survive Under Capitalism?* (International Publishing, New York), 94 pp.
Hall, P., 1975, "Controlling the location of population and economic growth: experience of other countries with special reference to Great Britain" (Westwater Research Centre, Vancouver, BC), 30 pp.
Hamilton, L. D., 1972, "On radiation standards", *Bulletin of Atomic Scientists,* **56**, 30-33.
Hammond, A., Metz, W., Maugh, T., 1973, *Energy and the Future* (American Association for the Advancement of Science, Washington).
Hanke, S. H., 1972a, "Review of *Perspectives on Resource Management*", *Geographical Analysis,* **4**, 112-114.
Hanke, S. H. (Ed.), 1972b, *Benefits or Costs? An Assessment of the Water Resources Council's Proposed Principles and Standards* (Department of Geography and Environmental Engineering, Johns Hopkins University, Baltimore), 18 pp.
Hanks, J., Hanks, P., 1970, "An environmental Bill of Rights: the citizen suit and the National Environmental Policy Act", *Rutgers Law Review,* **24**, 230-269.
Hansen, N. M., 1970, *Rural Poverty and the Urban Crisis: A Strategy for National Development* (Indiana University Press, Bloomington).
Harberger, A. C., 1972, *Project Evaluation* (Macmillan, London), 323 pp.
Hardesty, J., Clement, N. C., Jencks, C. E., 1971, "Political economy and environmental destruction", *Review of Radical Political Economics,* **3**, 82-87.
Hardin, G., 1968, "The tragedy of the commons", *Science,* **162**, 1243-1248.
Hardin, G., 1972a, *Exploring New Ethics for Survival: The Voyage of the Spaceship Beagle* (Viking Books, New York), 264 pp.
Hardin, G., 1972b, "The survival of nations and civilisation", *Science,* **172**, 129.
Hardin, G., 1974, "The ethics of a lifeboat" (American Association for the Advancement of Science, Washington), 18 pp. Also in *BioScience,* **24**, October.
Hardy, M., 1971, "International control of marine pollution", *Natural Resources Journal,* **11**, 296-348.
Hardy, M., 1973, "The United Nations Environment Programme", *Natural Resources Journal,* **13**, 235-255.
Hare, J. K., 1970, "How should we treat environment?", *Science,* **167**, 352-355.
Harkin, D. A., 1974, "The decision for public and private ownership of resources", *Land Economics,* **50**, 144-150.

Harney, T. R., Disch, R. (Eds), 1971, *The Dying Generations: Perspectives on the Environmental Crisis* (Dell Books, New York), 423 pp.
Harrison, G., 1971, *Earthkeeping* (Houghton Mifflin, Boston).
Harry, J., Gale, R., Hendee, J., 1969, "Conservation: an upper middle class social movement", *Journal of Leisure Research,* **3**, 246-254.
Hart, D. K., 1972, "Theories of government related to decentralisation and citizen participation", *Public Administration Review,* **32**, 603-621.
Harvey, D., 1972, "Revolutionary and counter revolutionary theory in geography and the problem of ghetto formation", *Antipode,* **4**, 1-13.
Harvey, D., 1973, "A question of method for a matter of survival", paper presented at the Annual Meeting of the Association of American Geographers, Atlanta, Ga., 46 pp.
Harvey, D., 1974, "What kind of geography for what kind of public policy?", *Transactions of the Association of British Geographers,* **63**, 18-24.
Haveman, R. H., 1965, *Water Resource Investment and the Public Interest* (Vanderbilt University Press, Nashville, Tenn.), 199 pp.
Haveman, R. H., 1970, *The Economics of the Public Sector* (John Wiley, New York), 221 pp.
Havlick, I., 1970, "The construction of trust: an experiment in expanding democratic processes in water resources planning", *Water Spectrum,* **1**, 13-19.
Hawkes, N., 1972, "Human environment conference: search for a modus vivendi", *Science,* **175**, 736-738.
Hays, S. P., 1959, *Conservation and the Gospel of Efficiency* (Harvard University Press, Cambridge, Mass.), 277 pp.
Headley, J. C., 1972, "Agricultural productivity, technology and environmental quality", *American Journal of Agricultural Economics,* **54**, 749-763.
Heaney, J. P., Carter, B. J., Jr., Pyatt, E. E., 1971, "Costs for equivalent upstream reduction in waste water discharges", *Water Resources Research,* **7**, 458-462.
Heath, M. S., Jr., 1971, "Some legal questions relating to air quality management", in *Selecting Strategies for Air Quality Management,* Eds B. T. Bower, W. R. D. Sewell (Information Canada, Ottawa), pp.41-44.
Heberlein, T. A., 1972, "The land ethic realized: some social psychological explanations for changing environmental attitudes", *Journal of Social Issues,* **28**, 79-87.
Heberlein, T. A., 1973a, "The three fixes: technological, cognitive and structural" (Department of Renal Sociology, University of Wisconsin, Madison, Wis.), 23 pp.
Heberlein, T. A., 1973b, "Some psychological assumptions of user attitude surveys: the case of the wildernism scale", *Journal of Leisure Research,* **5**, 18-33.
Heberlein, T. A., 1976, "Some observations on alternative mechanisms for public involvement: the hearing, public opinion poll, the workshop and the experiment", *Natural Resources Journal,* **16**.
Hedgepeth, W., Stock, D., 1970, *The Alternative: Communal Life in North America* (Collier Books, London), 190 pp.
Heilbroner, R. L., 1972a, *In the Name of Profit* (Doubleday, Garden City, NY).
Heilbroner, R. L., 1972b, "Growth and survival", *Foreign Affairs,* **51**, 139-153.
Heilbroner, R. L., 1974a, *An Inquiry into the Human Prospect* (Harper and Row, New York), 148 pp.
Heilbroner, R. L., 1974b, "Learning to live with the future", *The Observer Review,* 29 December, p.13.
Heilbroner, R. L., 1976, *Business Civilization in Decline* (Marion Boyars, London).
Heilbroner, R. L., Allentuck, J., 1972, "Ecological 'balance' and the 'stationary state'", *Land Economics,* **48**, 205-211.

Helfrich, H. W., Jr., 1970, *The Environmental Crisis: Man's Struggle to Live With Himself* (Yale University Press, New Haven, Conn.), 187 pp.
Heller, A., 1971, *The California Tomorrow Plan* (Kaufmann, Los Altos, Calif.), 113 pp.
Heller, W. W., 1972, "Coming to terms with growth and the environment", in *Energy, Economic Growth and the Environment,* Ed. S. Schurr (Johns Hopkins Unversity Press, Baltimore), pp.3-29.
Hendee, J. C., Catton, W. R., Jr., Marlow, L. D., Brockman, C. F., 1968, "Wilderness users in the Pacific Northwest—their characteristics, values and management preferences", PNW-61, Pacific Northwest Forest and Range Experiment Station, Portland, Oregon, 92 pp.
Hendee, J. C., Gale, R. P., Catton, W. R., Jr., 1971, "A typology of outdoor recreation activity preferences", *Journal of Environmental Education,* **3**, 28-34.
Hendee, J. C., Harris, R. W., 1970, "Foresters' perception of wilderness user attitudes and preferences", *Journal of Forestry,* **68**, 759-762.
Hendee, J. C., Lucas, R. C., 1973, "Mandatory wilderness permits: a necessary management tool", *Journal of Forestry,* **71**, 206-207.
Hendee, J. C., Stankey, G. H., 1973, "Biocentricity in wilderness management", *BioScience,* **23**, 535-538.
Henning, D. H., 1971, "The ecology of the political administrative process for wilderness classification", *Natural Resources Journal,* **11**, 69-75.
Henshaw, R. S., 1971, *This Side of Yesterday: Extinction v. Utopia* (John Wiley, New York).
Herfindahl, O. C., Kneese, A. V., 1974, *Economic Theory of Natural Resources* (Charles Merrill, Columbus, Ohio), 415 pp.
Heuvelmans, M., 1974, *The River Killers* (Stackpole Press, Harrisburg, Pa.), 217 pp.
Hewitt, K., Burton, I., 1971, "The hazardousness of a place: a regional ecology of damaging events", Research Papers in Geography No.6, University of Toronto, 154 pp.
Hickel, W. J., 1971, *Who Owns America?* (Prentice-Hall, Englewood Cliffs, NJ), 328 pp.
Hill, A. M., 1973, *Making Things Do: Basic Things for Simple Living* (Sierra Club—Ballantine Books, New York), 147 pp.
Hill, D. M., 1970, *Participating in Local Affairs* (Penguin Books, Harmondsworth), 196 pp.
Hill, G., 1974, "Community growth controls", *New York Times,* July 28, 29, 30.
Hill, M., 1968, "A goals achievement matrix for evaluating alternative plans", *Journal of the American Institute of Planners,* **34**, 19-29.
Hill, M., Shechter, M., 1973, "Optimal goal achievement in the development of outdoor recreation facilities" (Centre for Urban and Regional Studies, Haifa), 16 pp.
Hill, M., Tzamir, Y., 1972, "Multidimensional evaluation of regional planning using multiple objectives", *Papers of the Regional Science Association,* **29**, 139-166.
Hines, L. G., 1973, *Environmental Issues: Population, Pollution and Economics* (Norton, New York), 352 pp.
Hirst, E., 1974, "Food related energy requirements", *Science,* **183**, 134-138.
Hite, J. C., Laurent, E. A., 1972, *Environmental Planning: An Economic Analysis* (Praeger, New York), 155 pp.
Hoch, I., 1972a, "Income and city size", *Urban Studies,* **9**, 299-328.
Hoch, I., 1972b, "Urban scale and environmental quality", in *Population, Resources and the Environment,* Ed. R. Ridker (Government Printing Office, Washington), pp.235-284.
Hodson, H. V., 1972, *The Diseconomics of Growth* (Ballantine Books, New York), 239 pp.

Hoggan, D. H., Mulder, J., Taylor, S. J., Oaks, D. E., Somers, B., 1974, *A Study of the Effectiveness of Water Resource Planning Groups* (Utah Water Research Laboratory, Logan), 339 pp.
Hoinville, G., 1971, "Evaluating community preferences", *Environment and Planning,* **3,** 33-50.
Hoinville, G., 1975, "Multidimensional trade offs: an appraisal of the priority evaluator approach", Social and Community Planning Research Working Paper, London, 84 pp.
Holden, C., 1971, "Public interest, new group seeks redefinition of scientists' role", *Science,* **173,** 131-132.
Holden, C., 1972, "Ehrlich versus Commoner: an environmental fallout", *Science,* **171,** 245-247.
Holden, C., 1973a, "Water commission: no more free rides for water users", *Science,* **180,** 165-168.
Holden, C., 1973b, "Energy: strategies loom but conservation lags", *Science,* **180,** 1155-1158.
Holden, C., 1973c, "Water projects: how to ease the pork barrel image", *Science,* **182,** 266-270.
Holden, C., 1975, "Congress strengthens Freedom of Information Act", *Science,* **187,** 242.
Holden, M., 1966, *Pollution Control as a Bargaining Process* (Cornell University Water Resources and Marine Sciences Center, Ithaca, New York), 53 pp.
Holdern, J., Herrera, P., 1972, *Energy—A Crisis in Power* (Sierra Club Books, San Francisco).
Hollander, S., 1973, *The Economics of Adam Smith* (University of Toronto Press, Toronto), 327 pp.
Holling, C. S., 1971, "GIRLS: Gulf Island Recreational Land Simulation" (School of Resource Ecology, University of British Columbia, Vancouver), 13 pp.
Holling, C. S., Chambers, A. S., 1973, "Resource science: the nurture of an infant", *BioScience,* **23,** 13-20.
Holling, C. S., Goldberg, M. A., 1971, "Ecology and planning", *Journal of the American Institute of Planners,* **37**, 221-230.
Hopkinson, R. G., 1974, "The evaluation of visual intrusion in transport situations", in *Environmental Quality,* Eds J. T. Coppock, C. B. Wilson (Scottish Academic Press, Edinburgh), pp.52-68.
Houston, D. B., 1971, "Ecosystems of national parks", *Science,* **172,** 648-652.
Howard, W. A., Kracht, J. B., 1972, "Bibliography: Optimum city size and municipal efficiency" (Council of Planning Librarians, Montecito, Ill.), 7 pp.
Howe, C. W., 1971, *Benefit Cost Analysis for Water System Planning* (American Geophysical Union, Washington), 139 pp.
Howe, C. W., Easter, K. W., 1971, *Interbasin Transfers of Water: Economic Issues and Impacts* (Johns Hopkins University Press, Baltimore), 212 pp.
Hudson, B. M., Sullivan, F., 1974, "Essay: limited growth: problems of full employment and the viciousness of easy solutions", *Socioeconomic Planning Sciences,* **8,** 113-122.
Hueckel, G., 1975, "A historical approach to future economic growth", *Science,* **187,** 925-931.
Hughes, J. W., 1975, *New Dimensions of Urban Planning Growth Controls* (Center for Urban Policy Research, Rutgers University, New Brunswick, N J), 246 pp.
Hutchison, B., 1972, "The storming of the world", *McLeans Magazine,* September 27-31, 48.
Huxley, J., 1964, *Essays of a Humanist* (Penguin Books, Harmondsworth), 283 pp.
Illich, I. L., 1974a, *Tools for Conviviality* (Harper and Row, New York).
Illich, I. L., 1974b, *Energy and Equity* (Harper and Row, New York).

Ingham, A., Simmons, P., 1975, "Natural resources and growing population", *The Review of Economic Studies,* **42**, 191-206.
Inglis, D. R., 1973, *Nuclear Energy: Its Physics and Its Social Challenge* (Addison-Wesley, Reading, Mass.).
Ingram, H. M., 1971, "Patterns of politics in water resources development", *Natural Resources Journal,* **11**, 102-118.
Ingram, H. M., 1973a, "The political economy of regional water institutions", *American Journal of Agricultural Economics,* **55**, 10-18.
Ingram, H. M., 1973b, "Information channels and environmental decision making", *Natural Resources Journal,* **13**, 150-169.
Institute for Contemporary Studies, 1975, *No Time to Confuse* (Institute for Contemporary Studies, San Francisco), 140 pp.
Institute of Society, Ethics and Life Sciences, 1972, *Ethics, Population and the American Tradition* (Hastings on Hudson, New York).
International Planned Parenthood Federation, 1974, "The U. N. Population Conference", *People,* **1**, 52 pp.
Jackson, H., 1974, "Four course menu in Rome", *The Guardian,* November 5, p.14.
Jackson, R., 1971, "Zero pollution: a trade off analysis", *Southern Economic Journal,* **38**, 97-100.
Jacoby, H. D., Steinbruner, J., 1973, "Federal policy on automotive emissions control" (Environmental Systems Program, Harvard University, Cambridge, Mass.).
Jacoby, N. H., 1970, "The environmental crisis", *The Center Magazine,* **3**, 37.
Jaksch, J., 1970, "Air pollution: its effect on residential property values in Toledo, Ohio", *Annals of Regional Science,* **6**, 43-52.
Jennings, B. H., Murphy, J. E. (Eds), 1973, *Interactions of Man and His Environment* (Plenum Press, New York), 150 pp.
Johnson, B., 1974a, "Population growth and environmental expectations", *International Social Science Journal,* **26**, 207-226.
Johnson, B., 1974b, "The recycling of Count Malthus", *The Ecologist,* **4**, 357-360.
Johnson, D. L., 1972, "Air pollution: public attitudes and public action", *American Behavioral Scientist,* **15**, 533-562.
Johnson, F., 1970, "Criminal law as a means to pollution control", Discussion Paper No.70-3, Department of Energy, Mines and Resources, Ottawa, 10 pp.
Johnson, H. G., 1970, "The economic approach to social questions", *Economica,* **35**, 1-21.
Johnson, H. G., 1971, "The Keynesian revolution and the monetarist counter revolution", *American Economic Review,* **61**, 1-14.
Johnson, H. G., 1973, "Economic growth and welfare", *Minerva,* **12**, 115-116.
Johnson, H. G., 1975, "Man and his environment", in *On Economics and Society* (University of Chicago Press, Chicago), pp.317-339.
Johnson, W. A., 1971, *Public Parks and Private Lands in England and Wales* (Johns Hopkins University Press, Baltimore).
Johnson, W. A., 1973, "The guaranteed income as an environmental measure", in *Towards a Steady State Economy,* Ed. H. E. Daly (Freeman, San Francisco), pp.175-189.
Johnson, W. R., 1973, "Should the poor buy no growth?", *Daedalus,* **102**, 165-190.
Johnston, D. M., 1973, "Marine pollution control: law science and politics", *International Journal,* **28**, 69-102.
Johnston, H. D., 1971, *No Deposit—No Return* (Addison-Wesley, Reading, Mass.).
Johnston, S., 1973, *The Population Problem* (John Wiley, New York), 218 pp.
Johnston, W. A., Hardesty, J. (Eds), 1971, *Economic Growth vs. the Environment* (Wadsworth, Belmont, Calif.), 201 pp.

Jones, C. O., 1972, "The limits of public support: air pollution agency development", *Public Administration Review,* **32**, 502-509.

Jones, P. H., 1971, *Proceedings: Environmental Studies—The Role of the University* (Institute of Environmental Sciences and Engineering, University of Toronto), 142 pp.

Jordan, F. J. E., 1973, "Environmental information and the public interest", in *Ask the People,* Ed. C. G. Morley (Agassiz Centre for Water Studies, University of Manitoba, Winnipeg), pp.10-15.

Juergensmeyer, J. C., 1971a, "A comparative view of legal aspects of pollution control", *Suffolk University Law Review,* **5**, 741-778.

Juergensmeyer, J. C., 1971b, "Common law remedies and protection of the environment", *University of British Columbia Law Review,* **6**, 215-236.

Juergensmeyer, J. C., Wadley, J. B., 1974, "The common lands concept: a 'commons' solution to a common environmental problem", *Natural Resources Journal,* **14**, 361-381.

Kaiser, E. J., Reddings, M. J., 1974, *Promoting Environmental Quality Through Urban Planning and Controls* (Environmental Protection Agency and Government Printing Office, Washington), 441 pp.

Kaje, R., 1973, "The Club of Rome", *Technological Forecasting and Social Change,* **5**, 331-334.

Kalter, R. J., 1969, *Criteria for Federal Evaluation of Resource Investments* (Cornell University Water and Marine Sciences Center, Ithaca, New York), 251 pp.

Kapp, K. W., 1970, "Environmental disruption and social costs: a challenge to economists", *Kyklos,* **23**, 833-840.

Kasperson, R. E., 1969, "Political behavior and the decision making process in the allocation of water resources between recreational and municipal use", *Natural Resources Journal,* **9**, 176-211.

Kasperson, R. E., Breitbart, M., 1974, *Participation, Decentralization and Advocacy Planning,* Resource Paper No.25, American Association of Geographers Commission on College Geography, Washington, 60 pp.

Kasperson, R. E., Howard, R., 1972, *The Aquarius Game* (Clark University, Worcester, Mass.).

Katers, D., 1973, *Cutting Loose: A Civilized Guide for Getting Out of the System* (Doubleday, New York), 198 pp.

Kates, R. W., 1969, "Comprehensive environmental planning", in *Regional Planning,* Ed. M. M. Hufschmidt (Praeger, New York), pp.67-87.

Kates, R. W., 1972, "Review of *Perspectives on Resource Management*", *Annals of the Association of American Geographers,* **62**, 519-520.

Kates, R. W., Haas, J. E., Amaral, D. J., Olson, R. A., Ramos, R., Olson, R., 1973, "Human impact of the Managua earthquake", *Science,* **182**, 981-990.

Katz, E., Lazarsfield, P. F., 1965, *Personal Influence: The Part Played by People in the Flow of Mass Communication* (Free Press, New York), 380 pp.

Kaufman, H., 1969, "Administrative decentralisation and political power", *Public Administration Review,* **29**, 3-12.

Kay, D. A., Skolnikoff, E. B. (Eds), 1972, *World Eco-Crisis: International Organizations in Response* (University of Wisconsin Press, Madison), 314 pp.

Kaya, Y., Suzuki, Y., 1974, "Global constraints and new vision for development", *Technological Forecasting and Social Change,* **6**, 277-298, 371-388.

Kaysen, C., 1972, "The computer that printed out WOLF", *Foreign Affairs,* **50**, 660-668.

Keely, C. B., 1974, "Immigration composition and population policy", *Science,* **185**, 587-593.

Keene, J. C., Strong, A. L., 1970, "The Brandywine plan", *Journal of the American Institute of Planners,* **36**, 50-59.

Kelley, A. C., 1974, "The role of population in models of economic growth", *American Economic Review,* **64**, 39-44.

Kelly, G. A., 1975, *The Psychology of Personal Constructs* (Norton, New York).

Kennan, G. F., 1970, "To prevent a world wasteland: a proposal", *Foreign Affairs,* **48**, 401-413.

Kennet, W., 1972, *Preservation* (Temple Smith, London).

Keynes, J. M., 1971, "Economic possibilities for our grandchildren", reprinted in *Economic Growth vs. the Environment,* Eds W. A. Johnson, J. Hardesty (Wadsworth, Belmont, Calif.), pp.189-193.

Kiesler, C. A., Collins, B. E., Miller, N., 1969, *Attitude Change: A Critical Analysis of Theoretical Approaches* (John Wiley, New York), 346 pp.

Kimber, R., Richardson, J. J. (Eds), 1974, *Campaigning for the Environment* (Routledge and Kegan Paul, London), 228 pp.

King-Hele, D., 1971, *The End of the Twentieth Century?* (Macmillan, Toronto), 206 pp.

Kinkade, K., 1973, *A Walden Two Experiment* (Morrow, New York), 271 pp.

Kirkby, A. V. T., 1973, "Some perspectives on environmental hazard research", discussion paper, Department of Geography, University of Toronto, 17 pp.

Klausner, S. Z., 1971, *On Man in His Environment: Social Scientific Foundations for Research and Policy* (Jossey Bass, San Francisco), 217 pp.

Klein, R., 1972, "Growth and its enemies", *Commentary,* **53**, 37-44.

Kneese, A. V. (Ed.), 1970, *Economics of Environmental Pollution in the U. S.* (Resources for the Future, Washington).

Kneese, A. V., 1971a, "Background for economic analysis of environmental pollution", *The Swedish Journal of Economics,* **73**, 1-24.

Kneese, A. V., 1971b, "Environmental pollution: economic policy", *American Economic Review,* **61**, 153-166.

Kneese, A. V., 1971c, "Strategies for environmental management", *Public Policy,* **19**, 37-52.

Kneese, A. V., Ayres, R. V., d'Arge, R. C., 1971, *Economics and the Environment: A Materials Balance Approach* (Johns Hopkins University Press, Baltimore), 119 pp.

Kneese, A. V., Bower, B. T., 1968, *Managing Water Quality: Economics, Technology, Institutions* (Johns Hopkins University Press, Baltimore), 318 pp.

Kneese, A. V., Bower, B. T. (Eds), 1971, *Environmental Quality Analysis: Theory and Method in the Social Sciences* (Johns Hopkins University Press, Baltimore), 395 pp.

Kneese, A. V., Rolfe, S. E., Harned, J. W. (Eds), 1971, *Managing the Environment: International Economic Co-operation for Pollution Control* (Praeger, New York).

Kneese, A. V., Schultze, C. L., 1975, *Pollution Prices and Public Policy* (Brookings Institute, Washington), 125 pp.

Knelman, F. H., 1973, "What happened at Stockholm", *International Journal,* **28**, 28-49.

Knetsch, J. L. (Ed.), 1969, *Federal Natural Resources Development: Basic Issues in Benefit and Cost Measurement* (Natural Resources Policy Center, George Washington University, Washington).

Knetsch, J. L., 1971, "Value comparisons in free flowing stream development", *Natural Resources Journal,* **11**, 624-635.

Knetsch, J. L., 1974, *Outdoor Recreation and Water Resources Planning* (American Geophysical Union, Washington), 118 pp.

Kodet, E. R., Angier, B., 1972, *Be Your Own Wilderness Doctor* (Pocket Books, New York), 173 pp.

Koelle, H. H., 1974, "An experimental study on the determination of a definition of the 'Quality of Life' ", *Regional Studies,* **8**, 1-10.
Koestner, E. J., McHugh, J. J., Kircher, R., 1973, *The Do It Yourself Environmental Handbook* (Little, Brown, Boston), 76 pp.
Kolko, G., 1963, *The Triumph of Conservatism* (Free Press, New York).
Kosobud, R. F., O'Neill, W. D., 1974, "A growth model with population endogenous", *American Economic Review,* **64**, 27-33.
Krasner, S. D., 1974, "Oil is the exception", *Foreign Policy,* **14**, 69-83.
Kravitz, S., 1973, "The dilemma of accountability", *Journal of Voluntary Action Research,* **2**, 36-47.
Krieger, M. H., 1973, "What's wrong with plastic trees?", *Science,* **179**, 446-455.
Krier, J. E., 1971, "Environmental watchdogs: some lessons from a study council", *Stanford Law Review,* **23**, 623-675.
Krier, J. E., Montgomery, W. D., 1973, "Resource allocation, information cost and the form of government intervention", *Natural Resources Journal,* **13**, 89-105.
Krouse, M. R., 1972, *Quality of Life and Income Redistribution Objectives for Water Resources Planning* (US Corps of Engineers, Washington), 55 pp.
Krutilla, J. V., 1967, "Conservation reconsidered", *American Economic Review,* **67**, 777-786.
Krutilla, J. V., 1971, "Evaluation of an aspect of environmental quality: Hells Canyon revisited", Resources for the Future Report No.93, Washington, 7 pp.
Krutilla, J. V. (Ed.), 1973, *Natural Environments: Theoretical and Applied Analyses* (Johns Hopkins University Press, Baltimore), 360 pp.
Krutilla, J. V., Cicchetti, C. J., 1972, "Evaluating benefits of environmental resources with special application to Hells Canyon", *Natural Resources Journal,* **12**, 1-29.
Krutilla, J. V., Fisher, A. C., 1975, *The Economics of Natural Environments: Studies in the Valuation of Community and Amenity Resources* (Johns Hopkins University Press, Baltimore), 283 pp.
Kubo, A. S., Rose, D. J., 1973, "Disposal of nuclear wastes", *Science,* **182**, 1205-1211.
Kunreuther, H., 1974, "Protection against natural hazards: a lexicographic approach" (Fels Institute for State and Local Government, University of Pennsylvania, Philadelphia), 25 pp.
Kwee, S. L., Mullendar, J. S. R. (Eds), 1972, *Growing Against Ourselves: The Energy Environment Tangle* (D. C. Heath, Lexington, Mass.), 268 pp.
Lakey, G., 1973, *Strategy for a Living Revolution* (Freeman, San Franciso).
Lakoff, S. A., 1971, "Knowledge, power and democratic theory", *Annals of American Academy of Political and Social Science,* **394**, 5-11.
Lamm, R. D., 1973, "Local growth: focus for a changing American value", *Equilibrium,* **1**, 4-8, 35-36.
Lamm, R. D., Davidson, A. G., 1972, "The legal control of population growth", *Denver Law Journal,* **49**, 1-35.
Land, G. T. L., 1974, *Grow or Die: The Unifying Principle of Transformation* (Dell/Delta, New York), 250 pp.
Landau, N. J., Rheingold, P. D., 1971, *The Environmental Law Handbook* (Ballantine Books, New York), 483 pp.
Landsberg, H. H., 1974a, "Low cost, abundant energy: Paradise lost?", *Resources for the Future Annual Report*, Washington, pp.27-49.
Landsberg, H. H., 1974b, "Assessing the materials threat", *Resources* (Resources for the Future, Washington), **47**, 1-4.
La Porte, L. F., 1972, *The Earth and Human Affairs* (Canfield Press, San Francisco), 175 pp.
Lauer, R. H., 1971, "The problems and values of attitude research", *Sociological Quarterly,* **12**, 247-252.

Lave, L. B., Seskin, E. P., 1970, "Air pollution and human health", *Science,* **169,** 723-733.
Laxer, J., 1971, *The Energy Poker Game* (New Press, Toronto), 69 pp.
Leach, G., 1974, "Nuclear energy balances in a world with ceilings" (International Institute for Environment and Development, London), 24 pp.
Leach G., 1975, *Energy and Food Production* (International Institute for Environment and Development, London), 151 pp.
Lecomber, R. J. C., 1974, "Growth, externalities and satisfaction—a reply to Beckerman", *International Journal of Social Economics,* **1**, 160-172.
Lecomber, R. J. C., 1975, *Economic Growth vs. the Environment* (Macmillan, London), 88 pp.
Lee, D. B., 1973, "Requiem for large scale models", *Journal of the American Institute of Planners,* **39**, 163-178.
Lee, K. N., 1973, "Options for environmental policy", *Science,* **182**, 911-912.
Le Gates, R. T., Morgan, M. T., 1973, "The perils of special revenue sharing for community development", *Journal of the American Institute of Planners,* **39,** 254-264.
Leiss, W., 1972, *The Domination of Nature* (George Braziller, New York), 231 pp.
Leith, C. K., 1970, *World Minerals and World Politics* (Kennikat Press, Port Washington, NY).
Le May, J., Harrison, E., 1974, *Environmental Land Use Problems: A Study of Northern New Jersey* (Dekker, New York), 296 pp.
Leone, R. C., 1972, "Public interest advocacy and the regulating process", *Annals, American Academy of Political and Social Science,* **400,** 46-58.
Leontief, W., 1970, "Environmental repercussions and the economic structure: an input-output approach", *Review of Economics and Statistics,* **52**, 262-271.
Leopold, A., 1949, *A Sand County Almanac* (Oxford University Press, New York), 269 pp.
Leopold, L. B., Clarke, F. E., Hanshaw, B. B., Balsley, J. R., 1971, *A Procedure for Evaluating Environmental Impact*, Circular 645, US Geological Survey, Washington, 16 pp.
Levi, D. R., Colyer, D., 1972, "Legal remedies for pollution abatement", *Science,* **175**, 1085-1087.
Levin, P. H., 1972, "On decisions and decision making", *Public Administration,* **50,** 19-44.
Lewis, R., 1972, *The Nuclear Power Rebellion* (Viking Books, New York), 231 pp.
Lieber, H., 1970, "Public administration and environmental quality", *Public Administration Review,* **30**, 277-286.
Lincoln, G. A., 1973, "Energy conservation", *Science,* **180**, 155-162.
Linder, S. B., 1970, *The Harried Leisure Class* (Columbia University Press, New York), 162 pp.
Line, L. (Ed.), 1973, *What We Can Save Now: An Audubon Primer for Defense* (Houghton Mifflin, Boston), 428 pp.
Lines, G., 1974, "Transition", *Chemistry and Industry,* 2 February, 101-107.
Linowes, R. R., Allensworth, D. T., 1973, *The Politics of Land Use: Planning, Zoning and the Private Developer* (Praeger, New York).
Linstone, H., Turoff, M. (Eds), 1975, *The Delphi Method: Techniques and Applications* (Addison-Wesley, Reading, Mass.).
Lithwick, N. H., 1970, *Urban Canada: Problems and Prospects* (Information Canada, Ottawa), 236 pp.
Little, C. E., 1974, *The New Oregon Trail: An Account of the Development and Passage of State Land Use Legislation in Oregon* (The Conservation Foundation, Washington), 37 pp.

Littlejohn, B. M., Pimlott, B. H., 1971, *Why Wilderness: A Report on Mismanagement in Lake Superior Provincial Park* (New Press, Toronto), 108 pp.
Livingston, J. A., 1972, *One Cosmic Instant* (Houghton Mifflin, Boston), 229 pp.
Livingston and Blayney Associates, 1971, *Foothills Environmental Design Study: Open Space Versus Development* (Palo Alto, Calif.), 190 pp.
Lockeretz, W., 1970, "Arrogance or clean air", *Science,* **168**, 651-652.
Loughlin, J. C., 1971, "A flood insurance model for sharing the costs of flood protection", *Water Resources Research,* **7**, 236-244.
Lovins, A. B., 1973, *World Energy Strategies* (Earth Island Resources, London), 131 pp.
Lowe, P. D., 1975, "The environmental lobby: a survey", *Built Environment Quarterly,* **1**, 73-76, 158-162, 235-238.
Lowenthal, D., 1961, "Geography, experience and imagination: towards a geographical epistemology", *Annals, Association of American Geographers,* **51**, 241-260.
Lowenthal, D. (Ed.), 1972, *Environmental Assessment: A Comparative Study of Four Cities* (American Geographical Society, New York), 68 pp.
Lowenthal, D., Prince, H., 1964, "The English landscape", *Geographical Review,* **54**, 325-329.
Lowi, T., 1969, *The End of Liberalism* (Norton, New York).
Lowry, D. T., 1973, "Demographic similarity: attitudinal similarity and attitude change", *Public Opinion Quarterly,* **37**, 192-208.
Lucas, A. R., 1969, "Water pollution control law in British Columbia", *University of British Columbia Law Review,* **4**, 56-86.
Lucas, A. R., 1971, "Legal techniques for pollution control: the role of the public", *University of British Columbia Law Review,* **6**, 167-191.
Lucas, A. R., 1976, "Legal foundations for public participation in environmental decision making", *Natural Resources Journal,* **16**, 73-102.
Lucas, A. R., Moore, P. A., 1973, " The Utah controversy: a case study of public participation in pollution control", *Natural Resources Journal,* **13**, 36-75.
Lucas, R. C., 1964, "Wilderness perception and use: the example of the Boundary Waters Canoe Area", *Natural Resources Journal,* **3**, 394-411.
Lucas, R. C., 1973, "Wilderness, a management framework", *Journal of Soil and Water Conservation,* **28**, 150-154.
Lui, B., 1975, "Quality of life; concept measure and results", *The American Journal of Economics and Sociology,* **36**, 1-13.
Lundber, F., 1969, *The Rich and the Super Rich* (Bantam Books, New York).
Luttberg, N. R., 1971, "The structure of public beliefs on state policies: a comparison with local and national findings", *Public Opinion Quarterly,* **37**, 104-116.
Lyle, J., Wodtke, M. Von, 1974, "Information system for environmental planning", *Journal of the American Institute of Planners,* **40**, 394-413.
Lyon, J. N., 1973, "Some general observations on the question of standing from the perspective of a constitutional lawyer", in *Ask the People,* Ed. C. G. Morley (Agassiz Centre for Water Studies, University of Manitoba, Winnipeg), pp.38-43.
Macinko, G., 1965, "Saturation: a problem evaded in planning land use", *Science,* **127**, 976.
Macinko, G., 1968, "Conservation trends and the future American environment", *The Biologist,* **50**, 1-19.
Macura, M., 1974, "Components of an international approach to population policy", *International Social Science Journal,* **2**, 1-12.
Maddox, J., 1972, *The Doomsday Syndrome* (McGraw-Hill, New York), 293 pp.
Maddox, J., 1975, *Beyond the Energy Crisis* (Hutchinson, London), 198 pp.
Major, D. C., 1969, "Benefit cost ratios for projects in multiple investment programs", *Water Resources Research,* **5**, 1174-1177.

Malenbaum, W., 1973, *United States Materials Requirements in the Year 2000* (National Commission on Materials Policy, Washington), 40 pp.
Mäler, K. V., 1974, *Environmental Economics: A Theoretical Enquiry* (Johns Hopkins University Press, Baltimore), 280 pp.
Malthus, R. T., 1969, "An essay on the principle of population", in *Population, Evolution and Birth Control,* Ed. G. Hardin (Freeman, San Francisco), pp.4-17.
Mannino, E. F. (Ed.), 1974, *State Land Use Programs: A Report to the Senate on Interior and Insular Affairs* (Government Printing Office, Washington), 95 pp.
Maplin Manifesto, 1973, *Ecologist,* **3**, 134-138.
Marglin, S., 1972, "Testimony to the Water Resources Council", in *Summary Analysis of the Public Response to the Proposed Principles and Standards,* Water Resources Council (Government Printing Office, Washington), 186 pp.
Margolis, J., 1974, "Fiscal issues in the reform of metropolitan governance", in *Reform as Reorganisation,* Ed. L. Wingo (Resources for the Future, Washington), pp.41-70.
Marlin, W., 1974, "Why people's values rank high in New York City", *The Christian Science Monitor,* June 17, p.F1.
Marris, R., Wood, A. (Eds), 1971, *The Corporate Economy* (Harvard University Press, Cambridge, Mass.).
Marsh, J., 1969, "A partial bibliography of perception and attitude studies of possible interest to geographers" (Department of Geography, University of Calgary), 22 pp.
Martin, A., 1975, *The Last Generation: The End of Survival?* (Fontana, London), 188 pp.
Marx, L., 1970, "American institutions and ecological ideals", *Science,* **170**, 945-952.
Marx, L., 1973, "Pastoral ideas and city troubles", in *Western Man and Environmental Ethics,* Ed. I. G. Barbour (Addison-Wesley, Reading, Mass.), pp.93-115.
Marx, W., 1972, *Man and His Environment: Waste* (Harper and Row, New York), 174 pp.
Marx, W., 1973, "Los Angeles and its mistress machine", *Bulletin of Atomic Scientists,* **57**, 5-7, 44-48.
Maslow, A. H., 1954, *Motivation and Personality* (Harper and Row, New York).
Mathur, V. K., Yamada, H., 1972, "An economic theory of pollution control", *Papers of the Regional Science Association,* **28**, 223-236.
Mattes, M. A., 1975, "The UN environment programme", *Environmental Policy and Law,* **1**, 53-70.
Mazur, A., Rosa, E., 1974, "Energy and life style", *Science,* **186**, 607-610.
McAllister, D. N., 1973, *Environment: A New Focus for Land Use Planning* (National Science Foundation, Washington).
McAvoy, P. (Ed.), 1970, *The Crisis of the Regulatory Commissions* (Norton, New York).
McCall, T., 1974, *The Oregon Land Use Story* (Local Government Relations Division, Salem), 18 pp.
McCallum, B., 1974, "Environmentally appropriate technology" (Advanced Concepts Centre, Environment Canada, Ottawa), 25 pp.
McCaull, J., Crossland, J., 1974, *Water Pollution* (Harcourt Brace Jovanovich, New York), 200 pp.
McConnell, G., 1965, "The conservation movement: past and present", in *Readings in Resource Management and Conservation,* Eds I. Burton, R. W. Kates (University of Chicago Press, Chicago), pp.189-201.
McConnell, G., 1971, "The environmental movement: ambiguities and meanings", *Natural Resources Journal,* **11**, 427-436.
McCurdy, J., 1970, "Recreationists' attitudes toward user fees: management implications", *Journal of Forestry Research,* **68**, 645-646.

McEvoy, J., III, 1972, "The American concern with environment", in *Social Behavior, Natural Resources and the Environment,* Eds W. R. Burch, Jr., N. H. Cheek, Jr., L. Taylor (Harper and Row, New York), pp.214-236.
McFarlane, L. J., 1973, "Letter to *The Ecologist*", *The Ecologist,* **3**, 39-40.
McGee, W J, 1909/10, "The conservation of natural resources", *Proceedings of the Mississippi Valley Historical Association,* **3**, 365-379.
McHarg, I. L., 1969, *Design with Nature* (Natural History Press, New York), 197 pp.
McKean, R. N., 1973, "Growth vs. no growth: an evaluation", *Daedalus,* **102**, 207-228.
McKechnie, G., 1973, "The environmental response inventory" (Institute of Personality Assessment, University of California, Berkeley).
McLean, V., 1974, "Environmental perceptions in a deprived area", in *Environmental Quality,* Eds J. T. Coppock, C. B. Wilson (Scottish Academic Press, Edinburgh), pp.178-189.
McLoughlin, J., 1972, *The Law Relating to Pollution* (Manchester University Press, Manchester).
McLoughlin, J., 1973, "Control of the pollution of inland waters", *Journal of Planning and Environmental Law,* **1**, 355-361.
McLure, P. T., 1969, "Indicators of the effect of jet noise on the value of real estate" (Rand Corporation, Santa Monica, Calif.), 37 pp.
MacNeill, J. W., 1971, *Environmental Management: A Report to the Privy Council on Environmental Management in Canada* (Information Canada, Ottawa), 190 pp.
McPhee, J., 1972, *Encounter with the Archdruid* (Sierra Club-Ballantine, New York), 215 pp.
Meade, J. E., 1964, *Efficiency, Equality and the Ownership of Property* (Allen and Unwin, London).
Meadows, D. H., Meadows, D. L., Randers, J., Behrens, W. W., III, 1972, *The Limits to Growth* (Universe Books, New York), 205 pp.
Meadows, D. H., Meadows, D. L., Randers, J., Behrens, W. W., III, 1973, "A response to Sussex", *Futures,* **5**, 135-152.
Meadows, D. L. (Ed.), 1973, *The Dynamics of Growth in a Finite World* (Wright-Allen Press, Cambridge, Mass.).
Meadows, D. L., Meadows, D. H. (Eds), 1973, *Towards Global Equilibrium: Collected Papers* (Wright-Allen Press, Cambridge, Mass.).
Medalia, N. Z., Finker, A. L., 1965, "Community perception of air quality: an opinion survey in Clarkston, Washington" (Department of Health Education and Welfare, Public Health Service Publication No.989-Ap-10, Washington).
Medwin, N., 1974, *The Energy Cartel: Who Runs the American Oil and Gas Industry?* (Vintage Books, New York), 204 pp.
Meek, R. L., Weissman, S. (Eds), 1971, *Marx, Engels and the Population Bomb* (Ramparts Press, Berkeley, Calif.), 215 pp.
Meier, R. C., 1971, "Insights into pollution", *Journal of Institute of American Planners,* **37**, 211-217.
Mellanby, K., 1975, *Can Britain Feed Itself?* (Merlin Press, London), 90 pp.
Menchik, M. D., 1973, "Optimal allocation of outdoor recreational use in the presence of ecological carrying capacity limitations and congestion effects", *Papers of the Regional Science Association,* **30**, 77-96.
Mendelsohn, H., 1973, "Some reasons why information campaigns can succeed", *Public Opinion Quarterly,* **37**, 50-62.
Mercer, D. C., 1970, "The geography of leisure", *Geography,* **55**, 261-273.
Mesarovic, M., Pestel, E., 1975, *Mankind at the Turning Point* (Hutchinson, London), 210 pp.

Michael, D. M., 1968, *The Unprepared Society: Planning for a Precarious Future* (Basic Books, New York), 132 pp.

Micklin, M., 1973, *Population and Environment: Current Issues in Human Ecology* (Dryden Press, Honsdale, Ill.), 480 pp.

Mihaly, M. B., 1972, "The Clear Air Act and the concept of non degradation, Sierra Club vs. Ruckelshaus", *Ecology Law Quarterly,* **2**, 801-836.

Mikdash, Z., 1974, "Collusion could work", *Foreign Policy,* **14**, 57-68.

Milbrath, L. W., 1965, *Political Participation* (Rand McNally, Chicago), 195 pp.

Mill, J. S., 1970, *Principles of Political Economy,* Ed. D. Winch (Penguin Books, Harmondsworth), 383 pp.

Miller, A. J., 1973, "Doomsday politics: prospects for international co-operation", *International Journal,* **28**, 121-133.

Miller, D. C., 1972, "The allocation of priorities to urban and environmental problems by powerful leaders and organizations", in *Social Behavior, Natural Resources and the Environment,* Eds W. R. Burch, Jr., N. H. Cheek, Jr., L. Taylor (Harper and Row, New York), pp.259-279.

Miller, E., 1975, "Percentage depletion and the level of domestic mineral production", *Natural Resources Journal,* **15**, 241-255.

Miller, G. T., Jr., 1975, *Living in the Environment: Concepts, Problems and Alternatives* (Wadsworth, Belmont, Calif.), 579 pp.

Miller, J., 1973, "Genetic erosion: crop plants threatened by government neglect", *Science,* **182**, 1231-1233.

Miller, W. E., Stokes, D. E., 1963, "Constituency influence in Congress", *American Political Science Review,* **57**, 45-56.

Mills, E. S., 1972, "Welfare aspects of national policy toward city sizes", *Urban Studies,* **9**, 117-124.

Mills, E. S., Davis, O., Kneese, A. V., 1974, *Economics of the Environment* (Resources for the Future, Washington).

Mishan, E. J., 1967, *The Costs of Economic Growth* (Penguin Books, Harmondsworth), 240 pp.

Mishan, E. J., 1969, *Technology and Growth: The Price We Pay* (Praeger, New York).

Mishan, E. J., 1971a, "The post war literature in externalities: an interpretative essay", *Journal of Economic Literature,* **9**, 1-28.

Mishan, E. J., 1971b, "On making the future safe for mankind", *Public Interest,* **24**, 33-61.

Mishan, E. J., 1971c, "Pangloss on pollution", *The Swedish Journal of Economics,* **73**, 113-121.

Mishan, E. J., 1971d, *Cost Benefit Analysis* (Allen and Unwin, London), 147 pp.

Mishan, E. J., 1973a, "Ills, bads and disamenities: the wages of growth", *Daedalus,* **102**, 63-88.

Mishan, E. J., 1973b, "To grow or not to grow", *Encounter,* **40**, 9-29.

Mishan, E. J., 1974a, "Economic growth and welfare", *Minerva,* **12**, 117-123.

Mishan, E. J., 1974b, "The economics of disamenity", *Natural Resources Journal,* **14**, 55-86.

Mitchell, B., 1970, "The institutional framework for water management in England and Wales", *Natural Resources Journal,* **10**, 566-589.

Mitchell, B., Draper, D., 1973, "Perspective on the nature and development of behavioural geography", *Geographical Viewpoint,* **2**, 353-373.

Mitchell, J. D., Stallings, C. L., 1970, *Ecotactics: The Sierra Club Handbook for Environment Activists* (Ballantine Books, New York), 288 pp.

Moncrief, L. W., 1970, "The cultural basis of our environmental crisis", *Science,* **170**, 508-512.

Montgomery, W. D., 1972, "Markets in licences and efficient pollution control programs", Social Science Working Paper number 9 (California Institute of Technology, Pasadena, Calif.), 38 pp.

Morgan, A. E., 1971, *Dams and Other Disasters* (Porter Sargent, Boston), 422 pp.

Morgan, F., 1970, *Pollution—Canada's Critical Challenge* (Ryerson Press, Toronto), 134 pp.

Morley, C. G. (Ed.), 1971, *The Last Bottle of Chianti and a Soft Boiled Egg. Proceedings of the Canadian Law and Environment Workshop No. 1* (Agassiz Centre for Water Studies, University of Manitoba, Winnipeg), 120 pp.

Morley, C. G., 1972a, "Legel developments in Canadian water management" (Environment Canada, Ottawa), 21 pp.

Morley, C. G., 1972b, "A co-operative approach to pollution problems in Canada" (Environment Canada, Ottawa), 22 pp.

Morley, C. G., 1972c, "Pollution as a crime: the Federal response" (Environment Canada, Ottawa), 26 pp.

Morley, C. G. (Ed.), 1973, *Ask the People: Proceedings of Canadian Law and Environment Workshop No. 2* (Agassiz Centre for Water Studies, University of Manitoba, Winnipeg), 145 pp.

Morley, C. G. (Ed.), 1974a, *Canada's Environment: The Law on Trial* (Agassiz Centre for Water Studies, University of Manitoba, Winnipeg), 219 pp.

Morley, C. G. (Ed.), 1974b, *Proceedings of the National Conference on Environmental Impact Assessment: Philosophy and Methodology* (Agassiz Centre for Water Studies, University of Manitoba, Winnipeg).

Morrison, D. E., 1973, "The environmental movement: conflict dynamics", *Journal of Voluntary Action Research,* **2**, 74-85.

Morrison, D. E., Hornback, K. E., Keith, W. K., 1972, "The environmental movement: some preliminary observations and predictions", in *Social Behavior, Natural Resources and the Environment,* Eds W. R. Burch, Jr., N. H. Cheek, Jr., L. Taylor (Harper and Row, New York), pp.259-279.

Morrison, P. A., 1974, "Urban growth and decline: San Jose and St. Louis in the 1960s", *Science,* **185**, 757-762.

Muir, J., 1971, "In wilderness is the preservation of the world", in *Americans and Environment,* Ed. J. Opie (D. C. Heath, Lexington, Mass.), pp.32-40.

Müller, R., 1973, "Poverty is the product", *Foreign Policy,* **13**, 71-102.

Müller, R., Morgenstein, R. D., 1974, "Multinational corporations and balancing payments impacts on LDCs: an econometric analysis of export pricing behavior", *Kyklos,* **27**, 304-331.

Muller, T., Dawson, G., 1972, *The Fiscal Impact of Residential and Commercial Development: A Case Study* (The Urban Institute, Washington), 140 pp.

Mumford, L., 1974, *Interpretations and Forecasts* (Harcourt Brace Jovanovich, New York).

Mumphrey, A. J., Seley, J. E., Wolpert, J., 1971, "A decision model for locating controversial facilities", *Journal of the American Institute of Planners,* **37**, 397-402.

Mumphrey, A. J., Wolpert, J., 1973, "Equity considerations and concessions in the siting of public facilities", *Economic Geography,* **49**, 109-121.

Munn, R. E. (Ed.), 1975, "Environmental impact assessment: principles and procedures", Report No.5 (SCOPE, Toronto), 165 pp.

Munton, D., Brady, L., 1970, *American Public Opinion and Environmental Pollution* (Behavioral Science Laboratory, Ohio State University, Columbus), 110 pp.

Murch, A. W., 1971, "Public concern for environmental pollution", *Public Opinion Quarterly,* **35**, 100-106.

Murdock, W. (Ed.), 1972, *Environment: Resources, Pollution and Society* (Sinauer, Stamford, Conn.).

Murdy, W. H., 1975, "Anthropocentrism: a modern version", *Science,* **187**, 1168-1172.
Murray, J. R., Minor, M. J., Bradburn, N. M., Cotterman, R. F., Frankel, M., Pisarski, A. E., 1974, "Evolution of public response to the energy crisis", *Science,* **184**, 257-263.
Mushkin, S. J. (Ed.), 1972, *Public Prices for Public Products* (The Urban Institute, Washington), 447 pp.
Myrdal, G., 1969, *Objectivity in Social Research* (Pantheon Books, New York), 111 pp.
Nader, R., 1972, "The scientist and his indentured professional societies", *Bulletin of the Atomic Scientists,* **56**, 43-46.
Nano, F. C., 1974, "Letter to *The Ecologist*", *The Ecologist,* **4**, 118.
NAS-NAE, 1972, *Urban Growth and Land Development: The Land Conversion Process,* Report of the Land Use Subcommittee of the Advisory Committee to HUD (National Academy of Sciences-National Academy of Engineering, Washington).
Nash, C. A., 1973, "Future generations and the social rate of discount", *Environment and Planning,* **5**, 611-617.
Nasr, S. H., 1968, *The Encounter of Man and Nature* (Allen and Unwin, London).
National Academy of Sciences, 1974, *Energy: Future Alternatives and Risks* (Ballinger, Cambridge, Mass.).
National Caucus of Labor Committees, 1972, *Blueprint for Extinction* (Cathedral Park Station, P. O. Box 295, New York), 20 pp.
National Petroleum Council, 1971, *U. S. Energy Outlook: An Initial Appraisal* (National Petroleum Council, Washington), two volumes.
Natural Resources Journal, 1972, "Symposium: the human environment: towards an international solution", *Natural Resources Journal,* **12**, 278 pp.
Natural Resources Journal, 1973a, "International law and environmental management: a symposium", *Natural Resources Journal,* **13**, 170 pp.
Natural Resources Journal, 1973b, "Coase theorem symposium", *Natural Resources Journal,* **13**, 557-715.
Nearing, H., Nearing, S., 1954, *Living the Good Life: How to Live Sanely and Simply in a Troubled World* (Schocken Books, New York), 400 pp.
Neher, P. A., 1971, "Peasants, procreation and pensions", *American Economic Review,* **51**, 380-390.
Nelson, R. F. W., 1974, "Running to catch up", *Canadian Public Administration,* **17**, 665-684.
Netschert, B. C., 1972, "The energy company: a monopoly trend in the energy markets", in *The Energy Crisis, Bulletin of the Atomic Scientists of Chicago,* pp.72-76.
Neuhaus, R., 1971, *In Defense of People: Ecology and the Seduction of Radicalism* (Macmillan, New York), 315 pp.
de Nevers, N., 1973, "Enforcing the Clean Air Act of 1970", *Scientific American,* **228**, 14-21.
Newman, D. K., Wahtel, D. D., 1975, *The American Energy Consumer* (Ballinger, Cambridge, Mass.).
Newsom, G., Sherratt, J. G., 1972, *Water Pollution* (John Sherratt, Altrincham, Cheshire), 322 pp.
Nicholson, M., 1970, *The Environmental Revolution: A Guide for the New Masters of the World* (Penguin Books, Harmondsworth), 416 pp.
Nicholson, M., 1973, *The Big Change: After The Environmental Revolution* (McGraw-Hill, New York).
Nicholson, S., Schreiner, B. K., 1973, *Community Participation in City Decision Making* (Open University Press, Milton Keynes), 72 pp.
Nordhaus, W. D., 1974a, "World dynamics: measurement without data", *Economic Journal,* **83**, 1156-1183.

Nordhaus, W. D., 1974b, "Resources as a constraint on growth", *American Economic Review,* **64**, 22-26.
Nordhaus, W. D., Tobin, J., 1972, "Is economic growth obsolete?", in *Fiftieth Anniversary Colloquium V,* National Bureau of Economic Research (Columbia University Press, New York).
Norton, G. A., Parlour, J. W., 1972, "The economic philosophy of pollution: a critique", *Environment and Planning,* **4**, 3-11.
Notman, D., 1973, *Population and Family Planning Programs: A Factbook* (Population Council, New York), 89 pp.
O'Connor, J. T., 1975, "The automobile controversy—federal control of vehicle emissions", *Ecology Law Quarterly,* **4**, 661-692.
O'Dell, P. R., 1973, *Oil and World Power: Background to the Oil Crisis* (Penguin Books, Harmondsworth), 236 pp.
Odum, H. E., 1971, *Environment, Power and Society* (John Wiley, New York), 307 pp.
OECD, 1972, *Expenditure Trends in OECD Countries* (OECD, Paris), 181 pp.
OECD, 1974, *Economic Implications of Pollution Control: A General Assessment* (OECD, Paris), 76 pp.
OECD, 1975, *Energy Demands to 1985* (OECD, Paris), two volumes.
OECD Centre for Educational Research and Innovation, 1973, *Environmental Education at the University Level* (OECD, Paris), 319 pp.
Ogle, R. A., 1972, "Institutional factors to encourage interagency co-operation in the management of natural resources", *Public Administration Review,* **32**, 17-23.
Ohlin, G., 1967, *Population Control and Economic Development* (OECD, Paris), 138 pp.
Okun, A. M., 1975, *Equality and Efficiency: The Big Trade Off* (Brookings Institution, Washington), 124 pp.
Olson, J., 1971, *Slaughter the Animals: Poison the Earth* (Simon and Schuster, New York), 286 pp.
Olson, M. C., 1971, "National income and the level of welfare", *American Statistical Association Bulletin,* **25**, 198-207.
Olson, M. (Ed.), 1973, "The no-growth society", *Daedalus,* **102**, 241 pp.; also *The No Growth Society* (Woburn Press, London), 337 pp.
Olson, M., Landsberg, H. H., Fisher, J. L., 1973, "Epilogue", *Daedalus,* **102**, 229-241.
Ontario Committee on Government Productivity, 1972, *Citizen Involvement* (Queen's Printer, Toronto), 42 pp.
Ontario Conservation Council, 1973, *A Population Policy for Canada?* (Ontario Conservation Council, Toronto), 59 pp.
Ophuls, W., 1973, "Leviathan or oblivion?", in *Towards a Steady State Economy,* Ed. H. E. Daly (Freeman, San Francisco), pp.215-230.
Ophuls, W., 1975, "Technological limits to growth revisited", *Alternatives,* **4**, 4-9.
Ophuls, W., 1976, *Ecology and the Politics of Scarcity.*
Opie, J. (Ed.), 1971, *Americans and Environment: The Controversy Over Ecology* (D. C. Heath, Lexington, Mass.), 203 pp.
Oppenheimer, J. C., Miller, L. A., 1970, "Environmental problems and legislative responses", *Annals of the American Academy of Political and Social Science,* **389**, 77-86.
Oregon, Special Projects Branch, 1973, "Energy and state government" (Office of the Governor, Salem), 53 pp.
O'Riordan, J., 1976, "The public involvement programme in the Okanagan Basin Study", *Natural Resources Journal,* **16**.
O'Riordan, T., 1970, "Geography and the new conservation", *Area,* **3**, 190-193.
O'Riordan, T., 1971a, *Perspectives on Resource Management* (Pion, London), 177 pp.
O'Riordan, T., 1971b, "Public opinion and environmental quality: a reappraisal", *Environment and Behavior,* **3**, 191-214.

O'Riordan, T., 1971c, "The third American conservation movement: new implications for public policy", *Journal of American Studies,* **5**, 155-171.
O'Riordan, T., 1972a, "Towards a strategy of public involvement", in *Perceptions and Attitudes in Resources Management,* Eds W. R. D. Sewell, I. Burton (Information Canada, Ottawa), pp.99-110.
O'Riordan, T., 1972b, "Decision making and environmental quality: an analysis of a water quality issue in the Okanagan Valley, British Columbia", in *Okanagan Water Decisions,* Ed. H. D. Foster (Department of Geography, University of Victoria, Victoria, BC), pp.1-111.
O'Riordan, T., 1973, "Some reflections on environmental attitudes and environmental behaviour", *Area,* **5**, 17-21.
O'Riordan, T., 1976a, "The role of environmental issues in Canadian-American policy making and administration", in *The American Environment: Perceptions and Policies,* Eds J. W. Watson, T. O'Riordan (John Wiley, Chichester), pp.277-328.
O'Riordan, T., 1976b, "Policy making and environmental management: some thoughts on processes and research issues", *Natural Resources Journal,* **16**, 55-72.
O'Riordan, T., 1976c, "Citizen participation in practice: some dilemmas and some possible solutions", in *Public Participation in Planning,* Eds J. T. Coppock, W. R. D. Sewell (John Wiley, Chichester).
O'Riordan, T., Hey, R. D. (Eds), 1976, *Environmental Impact Assessment* (Saxon House, D. C. Heath, Farnborough, Hants.).
Orleans, L. A., Suttmeier, R. P., 1970, "The Mao ethic and environmental quality", *Science,* **170**, 1173-1176.
Oser, J., 1973, *Must Men Starve?* (Allen Press, Oxford).
Ostrom, V., Ostrom, E., 1971, "Public choice: a different approach to the study of public administration", *Public Administration Review,* **31**, 203-206.
Outdoor Recreation Research Section, 1973, "A report on a search for structure in the patterns of participation of Canadians in outdoor recreation using cluster analysis work" (Parks Canada, Outdoor Recreation Research Section, Ottawa), 18 pp.
Owens, E., 1974, *Development Reconsidered* (D. C. Heath, Lexington, Mass.).
Pacific Northwest River Basins Commission, 1973, *Ecology and the Economy: A Concept for Balancing Long Range Goals* (Pacific Northwest River Basins Commission, Vancouver, Wash.), 118 pp.
Paddock, W., Paddock, E., 1973, "The browning of the green revolution", *The Progressive,* **37**, 29-32
Paddock, W., Paddock, P., 1967, *Famine, 1975* (Little Brown, Boston).
Papanek, V., 1973, *Design for the Real World* (Bantam Books, New York), 335 pp.
Park, J. R., Monks, J., Brown, C., 1974, *Decision Making in Water Resource Allocation* (D. C. Heath, Lexington, Mass.).
Parry, G., 1969, *Political Elites* (Allen and Unwin, London), 164 pp.
Passmore, J., 1974, *Man's Responsibility for Nature* (Duckworth, London), 213 pp.
Paul, J. T., 1970, "Do new residential developments pay their own way? A case study in Half Moon Bay, California" (Stanford Environmental Law Society, Stanford, California), 17 pp.
Pavitt, K. L. R., 1973, "Malthus and other economists", in *Thinking About the Future,* Eds H. S. D. Cole, C. Freeman, M. Jahoda, K. L. R. Pavitt (Sussex University Press, Brighton), pp.137-159.
Paxton, J. (Ed.), 1974, *The Statesman's Yearbook* (Macmillan, London).
Pearce, D. W., 1971, *Cost-Benefit Analysis* (Macmillan, London).
Pearce, D. W., 1972, "The economic evaluation of noise-generating and noise abatement projects", in *Problems of Environmental Economics* (OECD, Paris), pp.103-118.
Pearce, D. W., 1974, "Economic and ecological approaches to the optimal level of pollution", *International Journal of Social Economics,* **1**, 146-159.

Pearce, D. W. (Ed.), 1975, *Economics of Natural Resource Depletion* (Macmillan, Basingstoke), 220 pp.

Pearse, P. H. (Ed.), 1974a, *The McKenzie Pipeline: Arctic Gas and Canadian Energy Policy* (McClelland and Stewart, Toronto), 229 pp.

Pearse, P. H., 1974b, "Report of the task force on forestry royalties" (Department of Lands, Forests and Water Resources, Victoria, BC).

Pendakur, V. S., 1972, *Cities, Citizens and Freeways* (School of Community and Regional Planning, University of British Columbia, Vancouver), 170 pp.

Pendergraft, J., 1972, *Reforming Timber Management* (Stanford Environmental Law Society, Stanford, California), 107 pp.

Perl, M. L., 1971, "The scientific advisory system: some observations", *Science,* **173**, 1211-1215.

Perry, R. W., Cleveland, C. E., Gillespie, D. F., Lotz, R. E., 1975, "The organizational consequences of competing ideologies: conservationists and weekenders in the Sierra Club", *Annals of Regional Science,* **9**, 14-25.

Peterson, G. L., 1974a, "A comparison of the sentiments and perceptions of wilderness managers and canoeists in the Boundary Waters Canoe Area", *Journal of Leisure Research,* **6**, 194-206.

Peterson, G. L., 1974b, "Evaluating the quality of the wilderness environment: congruence between perception and aspiration", *Environment and Behavior,* **6**, 169-193.

Peterson, L., 1974, "Towards a general theory of planning design" (Department of Architecture, University of Florida, Gainesville).

Pierce, M. C., 1972, "Participation in decision making: a selected bibliography" (Council of Planning Librarians, Chicago), 15 pp.

Pimentel, D., Hurd, L. E., Bellotti, A. C., Forster, M. J., Oka, I. N., Sholes, O. D., Whitman, R. J., 1973, "Food production and the energy crisis", *Science,* **182**, 443-449.

Pinchot, G., 1910, *The Fight for Conservation* (Harcourt Brace, Garden City, NY).

Pirages, D. (Ed.), 1971, *Seeing Beyond: Personal, Social and Political Alternatives* (Addison-Wesley, Reading, Mass.).

Pirages, D. C., Ehrlich, P. R., 1974, *Ark II: Social Response to Environmental Imperatives* (Freeman, San Francisco), 338 pp.

Plager, S. J., 1971, "Policy, planning and the courts", *Journal of the American Institute of Planners,* **37**, 174-191.

Platt, J. R., 1966, *The Step to Man* (John Wiley, New York).

Platt, J. R., 1969, "What we must do", *Science,* **166**, 115-119.

Poleman, T. T., Freebairn, D. K. (Eds), 1973, *Food, Population and Employment: The Impact of the Green Revolution* (Praeger, New York).

Polunin, N. (Ed.), 1973, *The Environmental Future* (Barnes and Noble, New York), 660 pp.

Popkin, R., 1967, *The Environmental Science Services Administration* (Praeger, New York), 278 pp.

Porteous, J. D., 1971, "Design with people: the quality of the urban environment", *Environment and Behavior,* **3**, 155-178.

Potter, J., 1973, *Disaster by Oil: Oil Spills, Why They Happen and What They Can Do and How We Can End Them* (Macmillan, New York), 301 pp.

Potter, V. R., 1971, *Bioethics—Bridge to the Future* (Prentice-Hall, Englewood Cliffs, NJ), 199 pp.

Pratt, J. W. (Ed.), 1974, *Statistical and Mathematical Aspects of Pollution Problems* (Dekker, New York), 424 pp.

Prewett, K., 1970, *The Recruitment of Political Leaders: A Study of Citizen Politicians* (Bobbs-Merrill, Indianapolis).

Price, J., 1974, "Dynamic energy analysis and nuclear power" (Friends of the Earth, London), 30 pp.

Prince, G., 1970, *The Practice of Creativity* (Harper and Row, New York).

Ramsay, W., Anderson, C., 1972, *Managing the Environment: An Economic Primer* (Harper Torchbooks, New York), 273 pp.

Randall, A., 1971, "Market solutions to externality problems: theory and practice", *American Journal of Agricultural Economics,* **54**, 175-183.

Rankin, R. E., 1969, "Air pollution control and public apathy", *Journal of the Air Pollution Control Association,* **19**, 565-569.

Ray, M. E., 1974, *The Environmental Crisis and Corporate Debt Policy* (Saxon House, D. C. Heath, Farnborough, Hants.).

Real Estate Research Corporation, 1974, *The Costs of Sprawl: Environmental and Economic Costs of Alternative Residential Development Patterns at the Urban Fringe* (Government Printing Office, Washington), three volumes.

Reekie, F., 1975, *Background to Environmental Planning* (Edward Arnold, London), 135 pp.

Reich, C. A., 1970, *The Greening of America* (Random House, New York).

Reilly, W. K. (Ed.), 1973, *The Use of Land: A Citizens' Policy Guide to Urban Growth* (Thomas Crowell, New York), 308 pp.

Reiners, A., Smallwood, F. (Eds), 1970, *Undergraduate Education in Environmental Studies* (Public Affairs Centre, Dartmouth College, Hanover, N H).

Reitze, A. W., Jr., 1971, "Private remedies for environmental wrongs", *Suffolk University Law Review,* **5**, 779-819.

Resources for the Future, 1974, "An abundance of shortages", *Resources,* **45**, 11 pp.

Revelle, R., 1974a, "Food and population", *Scientific American,* **231**, 160-171.

Revelle, R., 1974b, "The ghost at the feast", *Science,* **186**, 500.

Reynolds, J. P., 1969, "Public participation in planning", *Town Planning Review,* **40**, 131-148.

Richardson, H. W., 1973, *The Economics of Urban Size* (Saxon House, D. C. Heath, Lexington, Mass.), 243 pp.

Ridgeway, J., 1971, *The Politics of Ecology* (Dutton, New York), 222 pp.

Ridgeway, J., 1973, *The Last Play: The Struggle to Monopolize the World's Energy Resources* (Mentor Books, New York), 361 pp.

Ridker, R. G., 1972a, "Population and pollution in the United States", *Science,* **176**, 1085-1090.

Ridker, R. G. (Ed.), 1972b, *Population, Resources and the Environment* (Government Printing Office, Washington), 377 pp.

Ridker, R. G., 1973, "To grow or not to grow: that's not the relevant question", *Science,* **182**, 1315-1318.

Ridker, R. G., 1974, "Resource and amenity implications of population changes", *American Economic Review,* **64**, 33-38.

Ridker, R. G., Henning, J. A., 1967, "The determinants of residential property values with special reference to air pollution", *Review of Economics and Statistics,* **49**, 246-257.

Riedel, J. A., 1972, "Citizen participation: myths and realities", *Public Administration Review,* **32**, 211-220.

Rienow, R., Rienow, L. T., 1970, *Man Against His Environment* (Ballantine Books, New York).

Rivers, P., 1974, *Politics by Pressure* (Harrap, London), 236 pp.

Roberts, M. J., 1971, "Organising water pollution control: the scope and structure of river basin authorities", *Public Policy,* **19**, 75-142.

Roberts, M. J., 1973, "On reforming economic growth", *Daedalus,* **102**, 119-138.

Roberts, R. E., 1971, *The New Communes: Living Together in America* (Prentice-Hall, Englewood Cliffs, NJ), 142 pp.
Robinson, G. S., 1973, "Evolution of the law of the seas—destruction of the pristine nature of basic oceanographic research", *Natural Resources Journal,* **13**, 504-510.
Robinson, J., 1964, *Economic Philosophy* (Pelican Books, Harmondsworth), 137 pp.
Robinson, J., 1975, *Economic Management in China* (Anglo-Chinese Educational Institute, London), 46 pp.
Rodale, R., 1973, *Sane Living in a Mad World. A Guide to the Organic Way of Life* (Signet Mentor, New York), 206 pp.
Rogers, W. H., Jr., 1971, "Ecology denied: the unmasking of a majority", *Washington Monthly,* **2**, 39-43.
Rose, J. G., 1973, "The courts and the balanced community: recent trends in New Jersey zoning law", *Journal of the American Institute of Planners,* **39**, 265-276.
Rose, J. G., 1975a, *The Transfer of Development Rights: A New Technique of Land Use Regulation* (Center for Urban Policy Research, Rutgers University, New Brunswick, NJ), 300 pp.
Rose, J. G., 1975b, *Legal Dimensions for Land Use Planning* (Center for Urban Policy Research, Rutgers University, New Brunswick, NJ), 330 pp.
Rosenbaum, W. A., 1973, *The Politics of Environmental Concern* (Praeger, New York).
Rosenberg, D., 1974, "James Bay update", *Alternatives,* **4**, 4-10.
Rosenfeld, S. S., 1974, "The politics of food", *Foreign Policy,* **14**, 17-29.
Roskill, J., 1971, *Final Report of the Royal Commission on the Third London Airport* (HMSO, London).
Ross, D. R., 1973, *A Public Citizen's Action Manual* (Grossman, New York), 237 pp.
Ross, D., Wolman, H., 1970, "Congress and pollution: the gentleman's agreement", *The Washington Monthly,* **2**, 13-20.
Ross, R., Staines, G. I., 1972, "The politics of analysing social problems", *Social Problems,* **20**, 18-40.
Roszak, T., 1969, *The Making of the Counterculture: Reflections on the Technocratic Society and Its Youthful Opposition* (Doubleday, Garden City, N Y), 303 pp.
Roszak, T., 1973, *Where the Wasteland Ends: Politics and Transcendence in Post-industrial Society,* second edition (Doubleday, Garden City, NY), 451 pp.
Rothenberg, J., 1970, "The economics of congestion and pollution: an integrated view", *American Economic Review,* **40**, 114-121.
Rothschild, V. H. III, 1971, "Comment: the standing problem", *Natural Resources Journal,* **11**, 391-394.
Rowley, C. K., Beavis, B., Elliott, D. J., 1975, "Studying industrial discharges to the River Tees", *Water,* April, 5-8.
Rudolf, A., Lucken, D., 1971, "The engineer and his work: a sociological perspective", *Science,* **172**, 1103-1108.
Ruff, L. E., 1970, "The economic common sense of pollution", *Public Interest,* **19**, 69-85.
Ruff, L. E., 1972, "Review of *Limits to Growth*", *Ecology Law Quarterly,* **2**, 879-886.
Runte, A., 1976, "Wealth, wilderness and wonderland", in *The American Environment: Perceptions and Policies,* Eds J. W. Watson, T. O'Riordan (John Wiley, Chichester), pp.47-62.
Russell, C. S., 1973, *Residuals Management in Industry: A Case Study of Petroleum Refining* (Johns Hopkins University Press, Baltimore), 210 pp.
Russell, C. S., Landsberg, H. H., 1971, "International environmental problems—a taxonomy", *Science,* **172**, 1307-1314.
Ryan, J. J., 1972, *The Humanization of Man* (Newman Press, New York), 224 pp.
Ryder, N. B., 1973, "Two cheers for ZPG", *Daedalus,* **102**, 45-62.

Salisbury, R., Heinz, J., 1970, "A theory of policy analysis and some preliminary applications", in *Policy Analysis in Political Science,* Ed. I. Sharkansky (Markham, San Francisco).

Sametz, A. W., 1968, "Production of goods and services: the measurement of economic growth", in *Indicators of Social Change: Concepts and Measurement,* Eds E. B. Sheldon, W. E. Moore (Russell Sage Foundation, New York).

Sanford, L. (Chairman), 1974, *Report of the National Park Policies Review Committee* (HMSO, London).

Santmire, H. P., 1973, "Historical dimensions of the American crisis", in *Western Man and Environmental Ethics,* Ed. I. G. Barbour (Addison-Wesley, Reading, Mass.), pp.66-92.

Sauer, R. (Ed.), 1971, *Voyages—Scenarios for the Ship Called Earth* (Ballantine Books, New York).

Sax, J., 1970a, *Defending the Environment: A Strategy for Citizen Action* (Knopf, New York), 252 pp.

Sax, J., 1970b, "The public trust doctrine in natural resource law", *Michigan Law Review,* **68**, 471-492.

Sax, J. L., 1971, "Takings, private property and public rights", *Yale Law Journal,* **81**, 149-171.

Sax, J., Connor, J., 1972, "Michigan's environmental Protection Act of 1970: a progress report", *Michigan Law Review,* **70**, 1003-1021.

Sax, J., 1973, "Standing to sue: a critical review of the Mineral King decision", *Natural Resources Journal,* **13**, 76-88.

Sax, J. L., 1974, "Environmental law—the U. S. experience", in *Canada's Environment: The Law on Trial,* Ed. C. G. Morley (Agassiz Centre for Water Studies, University of Manitoba, Winnipeg), pp.164-195.

Scarman, L., 1974, *English Law—the New Dimension* (Stevens, London), 88 pp.

Schachter, E. R., 1973, *Enforcing Air Pollution Controls: Case Study of New York City* (Praeger, New York).

Schaeffer, F. A., 1970, *Pollution and the Death of Man: The Christian View of Ecology* (Tyndale Press, Wheaton, Ill.), 93 pp.

Schelling, T. C., 1971, "On the ecology of micromotives", *The Public Interest,* **25**, 61-98.

Schiff, M., 1971, "Some considerations about attitude studies in resource management" (Department of Geography, Waterloo Lutheran University, Waterloo, Ontario), 21 pp.

Schoenfeld, C. (Ed.), 1971, *Outlines of Environmental Education* (Dember Educational Research Services, Madison, Wis.).

Schoenfeld, C. (Ed.), 1973, *Interpreting Environmental Issues* (Dember Educational Research Services, Madison, Wisconsin), 100 pp.

Schoettle, E. C. B., 1972, "The state of the art in policy studies", in *The Study of Policy Formation,* Eds R. A. Bauer, K. A. Gregen (Free Press, New York), pp.149-179.

Schroder, H. M., 1971, "Conceptual complexity and personality organization", in *Personality Theory and Information Processing,* Eds H. M. Schroder, P. Suedfeld (Ronald Press, New York), pp.240-273.

Schroeder, H. A., 1974, *The Poisons Around Us* (Indiana University Press, Bloomington), 135 pp.

Schumacher, E. F., 1973, *Small is Beautiful: Economics as if People Really Mattered* (Harper Torchbooks, New York), 290 pp.

Schuman, H., 1972, "Attitudes vs actions *versus* attitudes vs attitudes", *Public Opinion Quarterly,* **36**, 347-354.

Schusky, J., 1965, "Public awareness and concern with air pollution in the St. Louis metropolitan area" (Department of Health, Education and Welfare, Washington).
Schutjer, W. A., Hallberg, M. C., 1968, "Impact of water recreational development on rural property values", *American Journal of Agricultural Economics,* **50**, 572-583.
Schwab, M., 1972, "*A Blueprint for Survival* and the Aquarian revolution", in *Teach-In for Survival,* Ed. M. Schwab (Robinson and Watkins Books, London), pp.1-12.
Scott, D. L., 1974, *Pollution and the Electric Power Industry: Its Control and Costs* (Saxon House, D. C. Heath, Farnborough, Hants.).
Scott, N. R., 1974, "The psychology of wilderness", *Natural Resources Journal,* **14**, 231-238.
Seckler, D. W. (Ed.), 1971, *California Water: A Study in Resource Management* (University of California Press, Berkeley), 346 pp.
Self, P. D., 1971, "Elected representatives and management in local government—an alternative analysis", *Public Administration,* **49**, 269-278.
Sewell, J., 1972, *Up Against City Hall* (James Lewis and Samuel, Toronto), 179 pp.
Sewell, W. R. D., 1971, "Environmental perceptions and attitudes of engineers and public health officials", *Environment and Behavior,* **3**, 23-59.
Sewell, W. R. D., 1974, "The role of perceptions of professionals in environmental decision making", in *Environmental Quality,* Eds J. T. Coppock, C. B. Wilson (Scottish Academic Press, Edinburgh), pp.109-131.
Sewell, W. R. D., Burton, I. (Eds), 1972, *Perceptions and Attitudes in Resource Decision Making* (Information Canada, Ottawa).
Sewell, W. R. D., Coppock, J. T. (Eds), 1976, *Public Participation in Planning* (John Wiley, Chichester).
Sewell, W. R. D., O'Riordan, T. (Eds), 1976, "The culture of participation in environmental decision-making", *Natural Resources Journal,* **16**, 1-21.
Shabman, L. H., 1972, "Decision making in water resource investment and the potential for multi-objective planning", Technical Report No.42, Cornell University Water Resources and Marine Sciences Center, Ithaca, NY, 204 pp.
Shepard, J., Shepard, D., 1973, *Earth Watch: Notes on a Restless Planet* (Doubleday, Garden City, N Y).
Sickle, D. V., 1971, *The Ecological Citizen* (Harper and Row, New York).
Siebker, M., Kaya, T., 1974, "The Club of Rome report from Tokyo: toward a global vision of human problems", *Technological Forecasting and Social Change,* **6**, 231-260.
Sigel, R. A., Friesma, H. P., 1965, "Urban community leaders' knowledge of public opinion", *Western Political Quarterly,* **18**, 881-895.
Simmonds, W. H. C., 1974, "Bridging the chasm—the next step", *Technological Forecasting and Social Change,* **6**, 267-276.
Simmons, H. G., 1973, "Systems dynamics and technocracy", in *Thinking About the Future,* Eds H. S. D. Cole, C. Freeman, M. Jahoda, K. L. R. Pavitt (Sussex University Press, Brighton), pp.192-208.
Simmons, I. G., 1974, *The Ecology of Natural Resources* (Edward Arnold, London), 405 pp.
Simms, D. H., 1970, *The Soil Conservation Service* (Praeger, New York), 238 pp.
Simon, J. L., 1974, "The effects of income on fertility" (North Carolina Population Center, Chapel Hill, NC).
Simon, R. J., 1971, "Public attitudes towards population and pollution", *Public Opinion Quarterly,* **35**, 93-99.
Sims, J. H., Baumann, D. D., 1974, "The tornado threat: coping styles of the north and south", in *Human Behavior and the Environment: Interactions Between Man and His Physical World,* Eds J. H. Sims, D. D. Baumann (Maaroufa Press, Chicago), pp.108-125.

Singer, J. F., 1972, *Is There an Optimum Level of Population?* (McGraw-Hill, New York).

Sive, D., 1971, "Environmental policy and law", *Natural Resources Journal,* **11**, 467-478.

Skala, M., 1974, "Electric users may save watts, pay more", *Christian Science Monitor,* January 24, p.5.

Skinner, B. F., 1953, *Science and Human Behavior* (Macmillan, New York), 449 pp.

Skinner, B. F., 1971, *Beyond Freedom and Dignity* (Bantam Books, New York), 215 pp.

Slater, P., 1974, *Earthwalk* (Bantam Books, New York), 241 pp.

Slesser, M., 1972, *The Politics of Environment* (Allen and Unwin, London).

Smith, A., 1961, *The Wealth of Nations,* Ed. E. Cannan (Methuen, London).

Smith, C. L., Hogg, T. C., 1971, "Benefits and beneficiaries: contrasting economic and cultural distinctions", *Water Resources Research,* **7**, 254-263.

Smith, J. D., Franklin, S. D., 1974, "The concentration of personal wealth, 1922-1969", *American Economic Review,* **64**, 162-169.

Smith, K., 1974, *Technical Change, Relative Prices and Environmental Resources Evaluation* (Johns Hopkins University Press, Baltimore), 116 pp.

Smith, W. S., Schueneman, J. J., Zeidberg, L. D., 1964, "Public reaction to air pollution in Nashville, Tennessee", *Journal of the Air Pollution Control Association,* **14**, 445-448.

Solow, R. M., 1970, *Growth Theory: An Exposition* (Clarendon Press, Oxford), 109 pp.

Solow, R. M., 1974, "The economics of resources or the resources of economics", *American Economic Review,* **64**, 1-14.

Spofford, W. O., Jr., 1973, "Total environmental quality management models", in *Models for Environmental Pollution Control,* Ed. R. A. Deininger (Ann Arbor Science Publishers, Ann Arbor, Mich.).

Sporn, P., 1974, "Multiple failures of public and private institutions", *Science,* **184**, 284-286.

S P R Charter, 1962, *Man on Earth* (Grove Press, New York).

S P R Charter, 1972a, *The Choice and the Threat* (Ballantine Books, New York), 245 pp.

S P R Charter, 1972b, *The Planning Myth* (Applegate Press, San Francisco).

Sprout, H., 1971, "The environmental crisis in the context of American politics", in *The Politics of Ecosuicide,* Ed. L. L. Roos, Jr. (Holt, Rinehart and Winston, New York), pp.41-50.

Sprout, H., Sprout, M., 1971, *Towards a Politics of the Planet Earth* (Van Nostrand Reinhold, New York).

Stahl, D. E., 1973, "Cost repercussions of the no-growth movement", *Urban Land,* **32**, 17-20.

Stanford Environmental Law Society, 1973, *A Handbook for Controlling Local Growth* (Stanford University Law School, Stanford, California), 118 pp.

Stankey, G. H., 1971, "Wilderness carrying capacity and quality", *Naturalist,* **22**, 7-13.

Stankey, G. H., 1973, "Visitor perception of wilderness recreation carrying capacity", INT 142, Intermountain Forest and Range Experiment Station, Ogden, Utah, 61 pp.

Stankey, G. H., Lime, D. W., 1973, "Recreational carrying capacity: an annotated bibliography", INT-3, Intermountain Forest and Range Experiment Station, Ogden, Utah, 42 pp.

Stankey, G. H. Lucas, R. C., Lime, D. W., 1974, "Patterns of wilderness use as related to congestion and solitude", Intermountain Forest and Range Experiment Station, Missoula, Montana, 18 pp.

Stansbury, J., 1973, "An anatomy of suburban growth", *Equilibrium,* **1**, 9-11, 30-32, 34-35.

Stanyer, J., 1971, "Elected representatives and management in local government: a case of applied sociology and applied economics", *Public Administration,* **49**, 73-97.
Stapp, W. B., 1971, "An environmental education program (K-12), based on environmental encounters", *Environment and Behavior,* **3**, 263-283.
Starkie, D. N. M., Johnson, D. M., 1973, "Losses of residential amenity: an extended cost model", *Regional Studies,* **7**, 173-181.
Starkie, D. N. M., Johnson, D. M., 1975, *The Economic Value of Peace and Quiet* (Saxon House, D. C. Heath, Farnborough, Hants.).
Starr, C., 1969, "Social benefit versus technological risk", *Science,* **165**, 1232-1238.
Starr, R., Carlson, J., 1968, "Pollution and poverty: the strategy of cross commitment", *The Public Interest,* **10**, 104-132.
Starrs, C., Stewart, G., 1971, *Gone Today and Here Tomorrow: Issues Surrounding the Future of Citizen Involvement* (Committee on Government Productivity, Queen's Printer, Toronto), 71 pp.
Steadman, P., 1975, *Energy, Environment and Building* (Cambridge University Press, Cambridge).
Steffenson, D. I., Herrscher, W. J., Cook, R. S. (Eds), 1973, *Ethics for Environment: Three Religious Strategies* (University of Wisconsin Ecumenical Centre, Green Bay, Wis.).
Steinhart, C. E., Steinhart, J. S., 1974, *Energy: Sources, Use and Role in Human Affairs* (Duxbury Press, North Scituate, Mass.).
Steinhart, J. S., Chernak, S., 1969, "The universities and environmental quality: commitment to problem focussed education" (Office of Science and Technology, Government Printing Office, Washington), 72 pp.
Stent, G. S., 1975, "Limits to the scientific understanding of man", *Science,* **187**, 1052-1057.
Stephenson, T., 1973, "International structure of a voluntary political organization: a case study", *Journal of Voluntary Action Research,* **2**, 240-243.
Stillman, P. G., 1975, "The tragedy of the commons: a re-analysis", *Alternatives,* **4**, 12-15.
Stone, J., 1972, "Should trees have standing—toward legal rights for natural objects", *Southern Californian Law Review,* **45**, 450-488.
Stone, P. A., 1972, "The economics of the form and organisation of cities", *Urban Studies,* **9**, 329-346.
Stone, P. B., 1973, *Did We Save the Earth at Stockholm?: The People and Politics in the Conference on the Human Environment* (Earth Island, London), 203 pp.
Straager, J. A., 1970, "Public problems and non decision making—a study of the Tuscon water system", *Natural Resources Journal,* **10**, 545-556.
Strange, J. H., 1972, "The impact of citizen participation on public administration", *Public Administration Review,* **32**, 459-470.
Stribling, T., 1972, "National Environmental Policy Act interpreted as requiring strict procedural compliance of federal agencies", *Natural Resources Journal,* **12**, 116-124.
Strong, A. L., 1975a, "Regional land use planning: the conflict between national objectives and local autonomy", *Environmental Policy and Law,* **1**, 82-86.
Strong, A. L., 1975b, *Private Property and the Public Interest; The Brandywine Experience* (Johns Hopkins University Press, Baltimore).
Struik, D. J. (Ed.), 1973, *Karl Marx's Economic and Philosophic Manuscripts of 1844* (Lawrence and Wishart, London), 151 pp.
Styles, B. J., 1971, "Public participation—a reconsideration", *Journal of the Town Planning Institute,* **57**, 163-168.
Sullivan, A. L., Shaffer, M. L., 1975, "Biogeography of the megazoo", *Science,* **189**, 13-17.

Svart, L., 1974, "On the priority of behaviour in behavioural research: a dissenting view", *Area,* **6**, 301-305.
Swan, J. A., 1970, "Response to air pollution: a study of attitudes and coping strategies of high school youths", *Environment and Behavior,* **2**, 127-152.
Swan, J. A., 1971a, "Public response to air pollution", in *Psychology and the Environment,* Eds D. Carson, J. Wohwill (American Psychological Association, New York).
Swan, J. A., 1971b, "Environmental education: one approach to resolving the environmental crisis", *Environment and Behavior,* **3**, 223-229.
Swartz, S. H., 1970, "Moral decision making and behavior", in *Altruism and Helping Behavior,* Eds D. Macauley, H. Berkowitz (Academic Press, New York), pp.127-141.
Sweezy, A., Owens, A., 1974, "The impact of population growth on employment", *American Economic Review,* **64**, 45-50.
Symonds, R., Carder, M., 1973, *The United Nations and the Population Question* (Chatto and Windus, London), 236 pp.
Systems Management Associates, 1972, *The Tejon Lake Project: An Evaluation of Its Impact on Kern County Taxpayers* (Systems Management Associates, Bakersfield, California), 78 pp.
Talbot, A. R., 1972, *Power Along the Hudson: The Storm King Case* (Dutton, New York).
Tanzer, M., 1974, *The Energy Crisis: World Struggle for Power and Wealth* (Monthly Review Press, New York), 171 pp.
Tarter, D. E., 1969, "Attitude: the mental myth", *American Sociologist,* **5**, 273-275.
Taylor, G. R., 1973, *Rethink: Radical Proposals to Save a Disintegrating World* (Penguin Books, Harmondsworth), 358 pp.
Taylor, T. B., Humpstone, C. C., 1973, *The Restoration of the Earth* (Harper and Row, New York), 165 pp.
Teclaff, L. A., 1973, "The impact of environmental concern on the development of international law", *Natural Resources Journal,* **13**, 357-390.
Teich, A. H. (Ed.), 1972, *Technology and Man's Future* (Macmillan, Toronto), 274 pp.
Teilhard de Chardin, 1959, *The Phenomenon of Man* (Harper and Row, New York), 313 pp.
TEMPO, 1968, *Economic Benefits of Slowing Population Growth* (General Electric Center for Advanced Studies, Santa Barbara, Calif.), two volumes.
Terselle, S. (Ed.), 1971, *The Family Communes and Utopian Societies* (Harper, New York), 145 pp.
Thayer, F., 1972, *Participation and Liberal Democratic Government* (Queen's Printer, Toronto), 41 pp.
Theobald, R., 1970, *An Alternative Future for America II* (Swallow Press, Chicago).
Theobald, R., 1972, *Habit and Habitat* (Prentice-Hall, Englewood Cliffs, NJ).
Thomas, K. (Ed.), 1971, *Attitudes and Behaviour* (Penguin Books, Harmondsworth), 351 pp.
Thomas, W. A., 1972, *Indicators of Environmental Quality* (Plenum Press, New York), 275 pp.
Thompson, A. R., Eddy, H. R., 1973, "Jurisdictional problems of natural resource management in Canada", in *Essays on Aspects of Resource Policy,* Science Council of Canada (Information Canada, Ottawa), pp.67-95.
Thompson, D. N., 1973, *The Economics of Environmental Protection* (Winthrop Publishers, Cambridge, Mass.), 265 pp.
Thompson, P., 1969, "Brandywine Basin: defeat of an almost perfect plan", *Science,* **163**, 1180-1182.
Thompson, W. I., 1972, *At the Edge of History* (Harper, New York).
Thompson, W. I., 1973, *Passages Around the Earth: An Exploration of the New Planetary Culture* (Harper and Row, New York).

Thring, M. W., Crookes, R. J. (Eds), 1974, *Energy and Humanity* (Peter Peregrinus, Stevenage, Herts.), 196 pp.
Thurow, L., 1970, "Analysing the American income distribution", *American Economic Review,* **60**, 261-269.
Tinker, J., 1972, "Britain's environment—nanny knows best", *New Scientist,* 9 March, 530-534.
Tinker, J., 1975, "River pollution—the Midlands dirty dozen", *New Scientist,* 6 March, 551-554.
Tobin, J., Nordhaus, W., 1972, "Is economic growth obsolete?", in *National Bureau of Economic Research: Fiftieth Anniversary Colloquium* (Columbia University Press, New York), pp.1-81.
de Tocqueville, A., 1961, *Democracy in America,* translated by H. Reeve (Schocken Books, New York).
Toffler, A., 1975, *The Ecospasm Report* (McGraw-Hill, New York), 105 pp.
Tognacci, L. N., Weigel, R. H., Wideen, M. F., Vernon, D. A. T., 1972, "Environmental quality: how universal is public concern?", *Environment and Behavior,* **4**, 73-86.
Toll, S. E., 1969, *Zoned American* (Grossman, New York), 370 pp.
Tombaugh, L. W., 1971, "External benefits of natural environments", in *Outdoor Recreation Symposium,* Ed. W. Doolittle (Northeast Forest and Range Experimental Station, Upper Darby, Pa.), pp.73-77.
Townsend, J. (1786), 1969, "A dissertation on the poor laws", in *Population, Evolution and Birth Control,* Ed. G. Hardin (Freeman, San Francisco), pp.24-27.
Toynbee, A., 1972, "The religious background of the present environmental crisis", *International Journal of Environmental Studies,* **3**, 141-146.
Trop, C., Roos, L. L., Jr., 1971, "Public opinion and the environment", in *The Politics of Ecosuicide,* Ed. L. L. Roos, Jr. (Holt, Rinehart and Winston, New York), pp.52-63.
Troy, P. N., 1973, "Residents and their preferences: property prices and residential quality", *Regional Studies,* **7**, 183-192.
Trumbull, T. A., 1972, "Federal control of stationary air pollution", *Ecology Law Quarterly,* **2**, 283-312.
Tuan, Y. F., 1968, "Discrepancies between environmental attitudes and behaviour: examples form Europe and China", *Canadian Geographer,* **12**, 176-181.
Tuan, Y. F., 1970, "Our treatment of the environment in ideal and actuality", *American Scientist,* **58**, 244-249.
Tuan, Y. F., 1971, *Man and Nature,* Resource Paper No.10, Association of American Geographers, Washington, 49 pp.
Tuan, Y. F., 1972, "Structuralism, existentialism and environmental perception", *Environment and Behavior,* **6**, 319-331.
Tuan, Y. F., 1974, *Topophilia: A Study of Environmental Perception, Attitudes and Values* (Prentice-Hall, Englewood Cliffs, NJ), 248 pp.
Tucker, A., 1975, "Air of uncertainty", *The Guardian,* March 25, p.16.
Twight, B. W., Catton, W. R., Jr., 1975, "The politics of images: forest managers vs recreation publics", *Natural Resources Journal,* **15**, 297-306.
Tybout, R. A., Lof, G. O. G., 1970, "Solar house heating", *Natural Resources Journal,* **10**, 268-326.
UK, Central Policy Review Staff, 1974, *Energy Conservation* (HMSO, London).
UK, Committee for Environmental Conservation, 1975, *Proceedings of the Conference on Environmental Law* (Council for the Preservation of Rural England, London).
UK, Committee on Public Participation in Planning, 1969, *People and Planning* (HMSO, London), 71 pp.
UK, Jukes Committee, 1974, *The Water Services: Economic and Financial Policies* (HMSO, London), three reports.

UK, National Economic Development Office, 1974, *The Increased Cost of Energy—Implications for U.K. Industry* (HMSO, London).
UK, National Economic Development Office, 1975, *Energy Conservation in the United Kingdom* (HMSO, London).
UK, Working Party on Sewage, 1970, *Taken for Granted* (HMSO, London).
Ulph, O., 1973, "On the limits to growth", *Sierra Club Bulletin,* **58**, 10-22.
UN, Department of Economic and Social Affairs, 1972, *Urban Land Use Policies and Land Use Control Measures* (ST/ECA/167) (United Nations, Paris).
UNESCO, 1973, "Ecological effects of energy utilization in urban and industrial systems" (UNESCO, Paris).
UNESCO, 1974, *Population, Resources and the Environment* (UNESCO, Paris).
Union of Concerned Scientists, 1973, *The Nuclear Fuel Cycle: A Study of the Public Health, Environmental and National Security Effects of Nuclear Power* (PO Box 289, Cambridge, Mass.), 207 pp.
Upton, C., 1971, "Application of user charges to water quality management", *Water Resources Research,* **7**, 264-272.
US, Army Corps of Engineers, 1970, *The Susquehanna Community Participation Study* (I.W.R. Report No.70-6, US Corps of Engineers, Springfield, Va.).
US, Atomic Energy Commission, 1972, *Cost Benefit Analysis of the U.S. Breeder Reactor Program* (Government Printing Office, Washington), 1184 pp.
US, Commission on Population Growth and the American Future, 1972, *Population and the American Future* (New American Library, New York), 362 pp.
US, Environmental Protection Agency, 1971, *Our Urban Environment and Our Most Endangered People* (US Government Depository No.12854, Washington).
US, Environmental Protection Agency, 1973a, *Clean Air Proposals for the Los Angeles Area: Summary Report Under the 1970 Clean Air Act* (Government Printing Office, Washington).
US, Environmental Protection Agency, 1973b, *Working Papers on Alternative Futures and Environmental Quality* (Office of Research Development, Environmental Studies Division, Washington), 240 pp.
US, House Committee on Merchant Marine and Fisheries, 1971, *Administration of the National Environmental Policy Act* (Government Printing Office, Washington).
US, House of Representatives, Judiciary Committee, 1971, *Report of Anti-Trust Subcommittee on Diseconomies of Conglomerates* (Government Printing Office, Washington).
US, House Subcommittee on Conservation and Natural Resources, 1971, *Qui Tam Actions and the 1899 Refuse Act: Citizen's Lawsuits Against Polluters of the Nation's Waterways* (Government Printing Office, Washington).
US, National Commission on Materials Policy, 1973, *Material Needs and the Environment: Today and Tomorrow* (Government Printing Office, Washington), 230 pp.
US, President's Advisory Panel on Timber and the Environment, 1973, *Report of the President's Advisory Panel on Timber and the Environment* (Government Printing Office, Washington), 539 pp.
US, President's Council of Economic Advisers, 1973, *Economic Report of the President* (Government Printing Office, Washington), 280 pp.
US, President's Council of Economic Advisers, 1975, *Economic Report of the President* (Government Printing Office, Washington).
US, President's Materials Policy Commission, 1952, *Resources for Freedom* (Government Printing Office, Washington).
US, Public Land Law Review Commission, 1970, *One Third of the Nation's Land* (Government Printing Office, Washington), 342 pp.
US, Senate Committee on Interior and Insular Affairs, 1972, *Calvert Cliffs' Court Decision* (Government Printing Office, Washington), two volumes.

US, Senate Committee on Interior and Insular Affairs, 1973, *Congress and the Nation's Environment* (Government Printing Office, Washington), 1145 pp.

US, Senate Committee on Interior and Insular Affairs, 1974, *State Land Use Programs* (Government Printing Office, Washington), 95 pp.

US, Senate Subcommittee on Intergovernmental Relations, 1973, *Confidence and Concern: Citizens View American Government* (Government Printing Office, Washington), 342 pp.

US, Water Resources Council, 1971, *Proposed Principles and Standards for Planning Water and Related Land Resources* (Government Printing Office, Washington).

Utton, A. E., 1973, "International water quality law", *Natural Resources Journal,* **13**, 282-314.

Vacca, R., 1973, *The Coming Dark Age* (Rutgers University Press, New Brunswick, NJ).

Vancouver Downtown Study, 1975, *The Vancouver Downtown Plan* (City Planning Department, Vancouver, BC).

Van Tassel, A. J., 1975, *Our Environment: Outlook for the 1980s* (Saxon House, D. C. Heath, Farnborough, Hants.).

Verney, R. B. (Chairman), 1972, *Sinews for Survival: A Report on the Management of Natural Resources* (HMSO, London), 74 pp.

Victor, P. A., 1972, *Pollution: Economy and the Environment* (Allen and Unwin, London), 239 pp.

Vrooman, D. H., 1975, "Regional land use controls in the Adirondack Park", *The American Journal of Economics and Sociology,* **34**, 95-102.

Wade, N., 1971, "Decision on 2,4,5-T: leaked reports compel regulatory responsibility", *Science,* **173**, 610-615.

Wade, N., 1972, "Freedom of information: officials thwart public right to know", *Science,* **175**, 498-502.

Wade, N. H., 1973, "World food situation: pessimism comes back into vogue", *Science,* **181**, 634-638.

Wade, N., 1974, "Robert L. Heilbroner: portrait of a world without science", *Science,* **185**, 598-599.

Wagar, J. A., 1970, "Growth versus the quality of life", *Science,* **168**, 1179-1184.

Wagar, W. W., 1971, *Building the City of Man: Outlines for a World Civilization* (Grossman, New York), 180 pp.

Wall, G., 1973, "Public response to air pollution in south Yorkshire, England", *Environment and Behavior,* **5**, 219-248.

Wall, J. F., Dworsky, L. B., 1974, *Problems of Executive Reorganization* (Cornell University Water Resources and Marine Science Center, Ithaca, NY).

Waller, R. A., 1970, "Environmental quality, its measurement and control", *Regional Studies,* **4**, 177-191.

Waller, R. A., 1974, "The assessment of environmental standards", in *Environmental Quality,* Eds. J. T. Coppock, C. B. Wilson (Scottish Academic Press, Edinburgh), pp.90-108.

Walsh, J., 1974, "U.N. Conferences: topping any agenda is the question of development", *Science,* **185**, 1143-1144.

Walter, G. R., 1972, "Intertemporally optimum urban pollution", *Papers of the Regional Science Association,* **28**, 237-256.

Walters, A. A., 1975, *Noise and Prices* (Clarendon Press, Oxford), 147 pp.

Wandesforde-Smith, G., 1971, "The bureaucratic response to environmental politics", *Natural Resources Journal,* **11**, 479-488.

Wandesforde-Smith, G., 1974, "Review of Haefele (1973)", *Ecology Law Quarterly,* **4**, 415-423.

Wapner, S., Cohen, S., Kaplan, B. (Eds), 1975, *Experiencing Environments* (Plenum Press, New York).

Ward, B. (Ed.), 1973, *Who Speaks for Earth?* (Norton, New York), 167 pp.
Ward, B., Dubos, R., 1972, *Only One Earth* (Penguin Books, Harmondsworth), 299 pp.
Ward, C. (Ed.), 1974, *Peter Kropotkin: Fields, Factories and Workshops Tomorrow* (Allen and Unwin, London), 205 pp.
Ward, C., 1975, "Making jobs", *Town and Country Planning,* April, 201-203.
Warner, L. G., De Fleure, H. L., 1969, "Attitude as an interactional concept: social constraint and social distance as intervening variables between attitudes and action", *American Sociological Review,* **34**, 153-169.
Warner, M. L., Preston, E. H., 1973, *Review of Environmental Impact Assessment Methodologies* (Battelle Columbus Laboratory, Columbus, Ohio).
Watkins, G. C., 1970, "Prorationing and the economic efficiency of crude oil production: a comment", *Canadian Journal of Economics,* **3**, 511-515.
Watt, K. E. F., 1968, *Ecology and Resource Management: A Quantitative Approach* (McGraw-Hill, New York), 450 pp.
Watt, K. E. F., 1973, *Principles of Environmental Science* (McGraw-Hill, New York).
Watt, K. E. F., 1974, *The Titanic Effect: Planning for the Unthinkable* (Dutton, New York), 261 pp.
Waverman, L., 1970, "Fiscal instruments and pollution: an evaluation of Canadian legislation", *Canadian Tax Journal,* **18**, 505-508.
Webb, A., 1972, "Planning inquiries and amenity policy", *Policy and Politics,* **1**, 65-71.
Weinberg, A. M., 1970, "Technology and ecology: is there a need for confrontation?", *BioScience,* **23**, 41-45.
Weinberg, A. M., Hammond, R. P., 1970, "Limits to the use of energy", *American Scientist,* **58**, 412-418.
Weinstein, A. G., 1972, "Predicting behavior from attitudes", *Public Opinion Quarterly,* **36**, 355-360.
Weinstein, D., 1973, "Social science associations and the polity: advising, activism and apathy", *Journal of Voluntary Action Research,* **2**, 86-94.
Weintraub, A., Swartz, E., Aronson, J. R. (Eds), 1973, *The Economic Growth Controversy* (International Arts and Sciences Press, White Plains, NY).
Weisberg, B., 1971, *Beyond Repair: The Ecology of Capitalism* (Beacon Press, Boston), 184 pp.
Weisskopf, W., 1971, *Alteration and Economics* (Dutton, New York).
Weisskopf, W. A., 1973, "Economic growth versus existential balance", in *Toward a Steady State Economy,* Ed. H. E. Daly (Freeman, San Francisco), pp.240-251.
Weissman, S., 1970, "Why the population bomb is a Rockefeller baby", *Eco-Catastrophie* (Ramparts) (Canfield Press, San Francisco), pp.26-41.
Wellford, H., 1971, *Sowing the Wind: Pesticides, Meat and the Public Interest* (Center for the Study of Responsive Law, Washington).
Wenders, J. T., 1972, "Pollution control—uses of corrective taxes reconsidered", *Natural Resources Journal,* **12**, 76-82.
Wengert, N., 1955, *Natural Resources and the Political Struggle* (Doubleday, Garden City, NY), 71 pp.
Wengert, N., 1971a, "Public participation in water planning: a critique", *Water Resources Bulletin,* **7**, 26-32.
Wengert, N., 1971b, "Political and social accommodation: the political process and environmental preservation", *Natural Resources Journal,* **11**, 437-446.
Wengert, N., 1976, "Citizen participation: practice in search of a theory", *Natural Resources Journal,* **16**, 23-40.
Wennergren, E. B., Fullerton, H. H., 1972, "Estimating quality and location values of recreational resources", *Journal of Leisure Research,* **4**, 170-183.
Westlake, M., 1975, "The third world bids for a new economic order", *The Times,* February 13, p.19.

Westman, W. E., Gifford, R. M., 1973, "Environmental impact: controlling the overall level", *Science,* **181**, 819-824.
Westoff, C. F., 1974, "The populations of the developing countries", *Scientific American,* **231**, 108-121.
Weston, M., 1973, "The wrong kind of questions", *Toronto Star,* March 7, p.6.
Westwater Research, 1974, "Resident's survey of the Lower Fraser water quality" (Westwater Research Centre, University of British Columbia, Vancouver), 23 pp.
Whaley, R. S., 1970, "Multiple use decision making—where do we go from here?", *Natural Resources Journal,* **10**, 557-565.
Whitbread, M., Bird, H., 1973, "Rent, surplus and the evaluation of residential environments", *Regional Studies,* **7**, 193-223.
White, G. F., 1966, "The formation and role of public attitudes", in *Environmental Quality in a Growing Economy,* Ed. H. Jarrett (Johns Hopkins University Press, Baltimore), pp.105-127.
White, G. F., 1972, "Environmental impact statements", *The Professional Geographer,* **24**, 302-309.
White, L., Jr., 1967, "The historical roots of our ecologic crisis", *Science,* **155**, 1203-1207.
White, L., Jr., 1973, "Continuing the conversation", in *Western Man and Environmental Ethics,* Wd. I. G. Barbour (Addison-Wesley, Reading, Mass.), pp.55-64.
Whitman, W., 1955, *Leaves of Grass and Prose Works,* Ed. M. van Doren (Viking Books, New York).
Wicker, A. W., 1969, "Attitudes versus actions: the relationship of verbal and overt behavioral responses to attitude objects", *Journal of Social Issues,* **24**, 41-78.
Wiggins, B., 1972, "Applying the fairness doctrine to environmental issues—Friends of the Earth v. FCC", *Natural Resources Journal,* **12**, 108-115.
Willing, M. K., 1971, *Beyond Conception: Our Children's Children* (Gambit, Boston), 255 pp.
Wilson, C. (Ed.), 1970, *Man's Impact on the Global Environment: Assessments and Recommendations for Action* (MIT Press, Cambridge, Mass.), 306 pp.
Wilson, J. W., 1973, *People in the Way* (University of Toronto Press, Toronto), 200 pp.
Wingo, L., 1972a, "Issues in a national urban development strategy for the United States", *Urban Studies,* **9**, 3-28.
Wingo, L. (Ed.), 1972b, *Metropolitanization and Public Services* (Resources for the Future, Washington), 96 pp.
Wingo, L., 1973, "The quality of life: toward a microeconomic definition", *Urban Studies,* **10**, 3-18.
Winham, G., 1972, "Attitudes on pollution and growth in Hamilton, or 'there's an awful lot of talk these days about ecology' ", *Canadian Journal of Political Science,* **5**, 389-401.
Winn, D. J., 1973, "The psychology of smog", *The Nation,* March 5, 294-298.
Winslow, M., 1973, "Growth control and the poor", *Equilibrium,* **1**, 16-17.
Winter, J. A. (Ed.), 1971, *The Poor: A Culture of Poverty and Poverty of Culture* (Eerdmans Publishing Co., Grand Rapids, Mich.).
Wirt, J. G., 1971, *Optimization of Price and Quality in Service Systems* (Rand Corporation, Santa Monica, California), 184 pp.
Wise, D., 1973, *The Politics of Lying* (Random House, New York).
Wohwill, J. A., Carson, D. A. (Eds), 1972, *Environment and the Social Sciences: Perspectives and Applications* (American Psychological Association, New York).
Wolf, E. R., 1966, *Peasants* (Prentice-Hall, Englewood Cliffs, NJ).
Wolfe, J. N. (Ed.), 1973, *Cost Benefit and Cost Effectiveness: Studies and Analysis* (Allen and Unwin, London), 232 pp.
Wolfe, L. M., 1945, *Son of Wilderness: The Life of John Muir* (Knopf, New York).

Wolff, A., 1973, *Unreal Estate: The Lowdown on Land Hustling* (Sierra Club, San Francisco), 280 pp.
Wollman, N., Bonem, G. W., 1971, *The Outlook for Water, Quality, Quantity and National Growth* (Johns Hopkins University Press, Baltimore), 304 pp.
Wolozin, H., 1971, "Environmental control at the crossroads", *Journal of Economic Issues,* **5**, 26-41.
Wolpert, J., 1976, "Regressive siting of public facilities", *Natural Resources Journal,* **16**, 103-116.
Wood, D. F., 1970, "Wisconsin's statewide requirements for shoreland and floodplain zoning", *Natural Resources Journal,* **10**, 327-338.
Woodcock, G., 1974, "Anarchism and ecology", *The Ecologist,* **4**, 84-89.
Woods, B., 1972, *Ecosolutions: A Casebook for the Environmental Crisis* (Schenkman Publishing Co., Cambridge, Mass.).
Wooton, G., 1970, *Interest Groups* (Prentice-Hall, Englewood Cliffs, NJ).
World Development Movement, 1972, "End of an illusion: verdict on UNCTAD 3" (UK Standing Conference on the Second UN Development Decade, London).
Wright, T. K., 1947, "Terrae incognitae: the place of imagination in geography", *Annals, Association of American Geographers,* **37**, 1-15.
Young, E., Johnson, B., 1973, *The Law of the Sea*, Fabian Research Series, No.313, London.
Young, G., 1973, *Tourism: Blessing or Blight?* (Penguin Books, Harmondsworth).
Young, L. B., 1973, *Power Over People* (Oxford University Press, New York), 188 pp.
Yurko, W. J., 1974, "Population distribution and the quality of life" (Department of the Environment, Edmonton, Alberta), 15 pp.
Zeckhauser, R., 1973, "The risks of growth", *Daedalus,* **102**, 103-118.
Zentner, H. (Ed.), 1973, "Proceedings of interfaith Banff 'good life' conference on population, bio-medical technology and ethics" (Interfaith Community Action Committee, Calgary), 42 pp.
Zinhurst, C., 1970, *The Conservation Fraud* (Cowles, New York).
Zupan, J. M., 1973, *The Distribution of Air Quality in the New York Region* (Resources for the Future, Washington), 93 pp.
Zwerdling, D., 1973, "Poverty and pollution", *The Progressive,* **37**, 25-30.
Zwick, D., Benstock, Y., 1971, *Water Wasteland* (Grossman, New York), 482 pp.

Index